Elementary Differential Equations with Applications

second edition

Elementary Differential Equations with Applications

second edition

William R. Derrick
Stanley I. Grossman
University of Montana

⩕ **ADDISON-WESLEY PUBLISHING COMPANY**
Reading, Massachusetts ▪ Menlo Park, California
London ▪ Amsterdam ▪ Don Mills, Ontario ▪ Sydney

Sponsoring Editor: Stephen H. Quigley
Production Editor: Martha K. Morong
Designer: Vanessa Piñeiro
Illustrator: ANCO/Boston
Cover Design: Ann Scrimgeour Rose

Library of Congress Cataloging in Publication Data

Derrick, William R.
  Elementary differential equations with applications.

  Includes index.
  1. Differential equations. I. Grossman,
Stanley I., joint author. II. Title.
QA371.D43   1981   515′.35   80-22057
ISBN 0-201-03162-0

Preface

Since the time of Newton, differential equations have been of fundamental importance in the application of mathematics to the physical sciences. Lately, differential equations have gained increasing importance in the biological and social sciences. New information concerning the theory of differential equations and its application to all sciences appears at an increasing rate, leading to a continued interest in its study by students in all scientific disciplines.

Our goal in writing this book has been threefold:

1. To help the student grasp the nature and significance of differential and difference equations;

2. To provide the numerical tools necessary to solve problems not amenable to direct solution;

3. To provide a wealth of examples and problems in the biological and social sciences as well as in the physical sciences. (Applications are taken from chemistry, chemical engineering, air pollution, genetics, population dynamics, and gambling, as well as the more standard models of electrical circuits and mechanics.)

Generally, students enrolled in an elementary differential equations course are poorly prepared for a rigorous treatment of the subject. We have tried to alleviate this problem by isolating the material that requires greater sophistication than that normally acquired in the first year of calculus. The emphasis throughout is on making the text readable by frequent examples and by the inclusion of enough steps in the working of problems so that the student should experience no difficulty in following the calculations.

Readers familiar with the first edition of this book will note that the first eight chapters have been largely rewritten. Additions, deletions, and restructuring of material have been made to improve the clarity of the exposition. Four major changes are incorporated in this second edition:

1. An elementary (nonmatrix) treatment of linear systems of differential equations has been included in Chapter 3. This allows a natural and easy transition from linear higher-order equations to linear first-order systems.

2. Because of the importance of Laplace transform methods to engineering students, Chapter 6 has been reorganized and expanded. Emphasis has been placed on the techniques that are most useful to the practicing engineer and applied scientist.

3. Chapter 8 is now a self-contained treatment of matrix methods for solving linear systems of differential equations. Courses requiring linear algebra as a prerequisite should follow this development instead of the elementary treatment in Chapter 3.

4. All the material on difference equations is now contained in Chapter 4. The development, closely paralleling that of differential equations, may be omitted with no loss of continuity if time is a problem.

In addition, many new drill problems and practical applications have been included throughout the text. At the end of each chapter we have included a comprehensive set of review exercises that provide a summary of the problems considered in that chapter.

Although the range of topics covered in this book can best be determined from the table of contents, we offer here a brief overview of the organization. The first three chapters provide the core of any introductory course in differential equations: basic terminology, first-order equations, higher-order linear equations, and elementary linear systems. We have made an effort to avoid "cookbook" methods by showing how previous procedures lead to new techniques. The material on linear systems in Chapter 3 should be used in those courses where linear algebra is not a prerequisite. Chapter 4 consists of a treatment of difference equations that parallels the material on differential equations in the first three chapters. It can be omitted with no loss of continuity. Chapters 5, 6, and 7 are self-contained discussions of power series, Laplace transform, and numerical methods, respectively. They can be covered in any order and depth consistent with the goals of the course. A brief introduction to each method is contained in the first two sections of each chapter. These seven chapters constitute the "short-course" version of this text and are suitable for a three-hour, one-semester or a four-hour, one-quarter course. This text includes five additional chapters. Chapter 8 is a self-contained discussion of matrix methods for linear first-order systems. Courses requiring linear algebra as a prerequisite should use this material instead of the elementary procedures given in Chapter 3. Chapter 9 provides a fairly complete discussion of Lyapunov stability theory for differential equations. Chapter 10 contains the proofs of the basic existence–uniqueness theorems. The continuous dependence on initial conditions is also discussed. Chapters 11 and 12 provide an introductory treatment of boundary value problems, Fourier series, and partial differential equations. The basic concepts in Chapters 8–12 are developed in the first two or three sections of each chapter; the remaining sections are further extensions and applications of these ideas.

The independence of Chapters 4–12 and the early coverage of key concepts provide a wide variety of possible course curricula. At the University of Montana we teach two courses from this book:

a)   A four-hour, one-quarter introductory course consisting of the following material: Sections 1.1–1.3, 2.1–2.7, 3.1–3.12, 5.1, 5.2, 6.1, 6.2, and 7.1. The "short-course" version of this text is used in this course.

b)   A four-hour, two-quarter advanced undergraduate course covering the material in (a) as well as Sections 10.1, 10.2, 9.1–9.3, 8.1–8.6, 11.1–11.4, 11.7, and 12.1–12.3, plus selected topics at the instructor's discretion. This course uses this text.

Many other options are also possible depending on the background and interests of the students.

We are indebted to our colleagues, students, and the users of the first edition who have been kind enough to write us about their impressions and criticisms. We express particular appreciation to the following individuals, whose suggestions were most valuable in preparing this edition: Charles K. Cook (Tri-State University), Michael L. Engquist (Eastern Washington University), Dar-Veig Ho (Georgia Institute of Technology), Allan M. Krall (The Pennsylvania State University), James E. Mann, Jr. (University of Virginia), Harold S. Morton, Jr. (University of Virginia), Dean Phelps (Lock Haven State College), Merle D. Roach (University of Alabama at Huntsville), L. David Sabbagh (Bowling Green State University), David A. Sanchez (University of New Mexico), Thomas R. Savage (Saint Olaf College), J. D. Schurr (Michigan State University), Michael J. Sormani (College of Staten Island), and Katherine Yerion (Gonzaga University). Finally, we thank the editorial and production staff of Addison-Wesley for their assistance and encouragement.

Missoula, Montana   W. R. D.
November 1980   S. I. G.

Contents

1 INTRODUCTION

1.1	Differential equations	2
1.2	Classification of differential equations	9
1.3	Direction fields	12

2 FIRST-ORDER EQUATIONS

2.1	Direct methods	18
2.2	Substitution techniques	24
2.3	Linear equations	30
2.4	Exact equations	37
2.5	Simple electric circuits	42
2.6	Curves of pursuit	46
2.7	Compartmental analysis	51
	Review exercises	56

3 LINEAR DIFFERENTIAL EQUATIONS

3.1	Linearly independent solutions	60
3.2	Properties of solutions to the linear equation	65
3.3	Using one solution to find another	69
3.4	Homogeneous equations with constant coefficients: Real roots	72
3.5	Homogeneous equations with constant coefficients: Complex roots	76
3.6	Nonhomogeneous equations: The method of undetermined coefficients	80
3.7	Nonhomogeneous equations: Variation of constants	87
3.8	Vibratory motion	91

3.9	Electric circuits	100
3.10	The method of elimination for linear systems with constant coefficients	103
3.11	Linear systems: Theory	112
3.12	The solution of homogeneous linear systems with constant coefficients: The method of determinants	117
3.13	Electric circuits with several loops	125
3.14	A model based on the theory of epidemics	129
	Review exercises	134

4 DIFFERENCE EQUATIONS

4.1	Introduction	138
4.2	Linear first-order difference equations	143
4.3	An application of first-order difference equations	147
4.4	Properties of solutions to linear second-order equations	152
4.5	Using one solution to find another	156
4.6	Homogeneous equations with constant coefficients: The case of real roots	158
4.7	Homogeneous equations with constant coefficients: The complex case	161
4.8	Nonhomogeneous equations: Variation of constants	164
4.9	An application to games and quality control	168
	Review exercises	172

5 POWER SERIES SOLUTIONS OF DIFFERENTIAL EQUATIONS

5.1	Review of power series	176
5.2	The power series method: Examples	183
5.3	Ordinary and singular points	190
5.4	Bessel functions	206
5.5	Legendre polynomials	216
	Review exercises	223

6 LAPLACE TRANSFORMS

6.1	Introduction: Definition and basic properties of the Laplace transform	226
6.2	Solving initial value problems by Laplace transform methods	237
6.3	Step functions and impulse functions	251

6.4   Some differential equations with discontinuous forcing
      functions   260
6.5   The transform of convolution integrals   265
6.6   Laplace transform methods for systems   270
      Review exercises   276

7

NUMERICAL METHODS

7.1   First-order equations   280
7.2   An error analysis for Euler's method   287
7.3   Runge–Kutta formulas   291
7.4   Predictor-corrector formulas   294
7.5   The propagation of round-off error: An example of
      numerical instability   298
7.6   Systems and boundary value problems   301
      Review exercises   306

8

MATRICES AND SYSTEMS OF LINEAR
FIRST-ORDER EQUATIONS

8.1   Introduction   308
8.2   Fundamental sets and fundamental matrix solutions of a
      homogeneous system of differential equations   317
8.3   Eigenvalues and eigenvectors   329
8.4   The Cayley–Hamilton theorem   343
8.5   Fundamental matrix solutions in the constant-coefficients
      case   347
8.6   Nonhomogeneous systems   358
8.7   An application of nonhomogeneous systems: Forced
      oscillations   366
      Review exercises   370

9

NONLINEAR EQUATIONS AND STABILITY

9.1   Introduction   374
9.2   Critical points, stability, and phase portraits for linear
      systems   382
9.3   Stability of nonlinear systems   397
9.4   Lyapunov's method   407
      Review exercises   415

10 THE EXISTENCE AND UNIQUENESS OF SOLUTIONS

10.1	Successive approximations: A local existence-uniqueness theorem	420
10.2	Systems of linear differential equations	431

11 FOURIER SERIES AND BOUNDARY VALUE PROBLEMS

11.1	Introduction	440
11.2	Orthogonal sets of functions and Fourier series	447
11.3	Fourier series	458
11.4	Sturm–Liouville problems	468
11.5	Properties of Sturm–Liouville problems	473
11.6	The Sturm separation theorem and the zeros of Bessel functions	477
11.7	Nonhomogeneous boundary value problems	482
	Review exercises	488

12 PARTIAL DIFFERENTIAL EQUATIONS

12.1	Preliminaries	492
12.2	The vibrating string	497
12.3	Separation of variables	503
12.4	Two-dimensional heat flow and Laplace's theorem	512
12.5	Laplace transform methods for partial differential equations	526
	Review exercises	531

Appendix 1 Integral Tables	A–1
Appendix 2 Laplace Transforms	A–5
Appendix 3 Solving Differential Equations with a Programmable Calculator	A–9
Appendix 4 Determinants	A–13
Solutions to Odd-Numbered Exercises	S–1
Index	I–1

Introduction

1.1 DIFFERENTIAL EQUATIONS

Many of the basic laws of the physical sciences and, more recently, of the biological and social sciences are formulated in terms of mathematical relations involving certain known and unknown quantities and their derivatives. Such relations are called *differential* equations.

In Section 1.2, we will see how the various types of differential equations are classified. In the succeeding chapters we will discuss methods of solution or, when that is not possible, of obtaining information about the solutions (when they exist) of several classes of equations. In this section, we will show how some simple differential equations can arise.

Before citing any examples, however, we should emphasize that in the study of differential equations the most difficult problem is often to describe a real situation quantitatively. To do this, it is usually necessary to make simplifying assumptions that can be expressed in mathematical terms. Thus, for example, we initially describe the motion of a mass in space by assuming that (a) it is a point mass and (b) there is no friction or air resistance. These assumptions are not realistic, but the scientist can often glean valuable information from even highly idealized models that, once understood, can be modified to take other observable factors into account.

Example 1   A ball is dropped from the top of a building 44.1 meters high (1 meter = 3.28 feet). When will the ball hit the ground?

Assuming that the ball is a point mass and that there is no air resistance, the acceleration of the ball will be due entirely to the force of gravity. If we denote the height of the ball at any time t by $h(t)$, then $h'(t)$ is the velocity of the ball at time t, since velocity is the instantaneous rate of change of height with respect to time. Similarly, $h''(t)$ is the upward acceleration of the ball at time t, since acceleration is the rate of change of velocity with respect to time.

It has been found experimentally that the gravitational acceleration g is approximately 980 cm/sec^2, 980 centimeters per second per second ($= 32.2$ ft/sec^2) at the surface of the earth. Thus the acceleration of the ball is constant:

$$h''(t) = -980, \tag{1}$$

where the minus sign on the right-hand side of the equation indicates that the force of gravity acts downward. Integrating both sides of Eq. (1) with respect to t, we obtain

$$h'(t) = -980t + C_1, \tag{2}$$

where C_1 is a constant that we must determine. To find C_1, we set $t = 0$ in Eq. (2). Then $C_1 = h'(0) = 0$, since the initial velocity $h'(0)$ of the ball is zero as the ball is dropped from rest. Finally, integrating Eq. (2) once more with respect to t, we obtain

$$h(t) = -490t^2 + C_2. \tag{3}$$

The constant C_2 can also be determined by setting $t = 0$; $C_2 = h(0) = 4410$, the initial height (in centimeters). Since we wish to find the length of time it takes the ball to strike the ground, we set the left-hand side of Eq. (3) equal to zero and solve for t:

$$490t^2 = 4410 \quad \text{or} \quad t^2 = 9.$$

Thus $t = \pm 3$, and since $t = -3$ has no physical significance, the answer is $t = 3$ sec.

Example 2   *Newton's law of cooling* states that the rate of change of the temperature difference between an object and its surrounding medium is proportional to the temperature difference. Let $\Delta(t)$ denote this temperature difference at any time t. Since a rate of change is expressed mathematically by a derivative, we may translate Newton's law of cooling into the equation

$$\frac{d\Delta}{dt} = k\Delta, \tag{4}$$

where k is the constant of proportionality. Recalling from elementary calculus that $(ce^{kt})' = k(ce^{kt})$, we are led to a solution

$$\Delta(t) = \Delta_0 e^{kt} \tag{5}$$

of the differential equation (4), where Δ_0 is constant. To verify that Eq. (5) is a solution of Eq. (4), we simply substitute Eq. (5) into Eq. (4) and perform the indicated operations:

$$\frac{d}{dt}\Delta(t) = (\Delta_0 e^{kt})' = k\Delta_0 e^{kt} = k(\Delta_0 e^{kt}) = k\Delta(t).$$

If we set $t = 0$ in Eq. (5), we obtain

$$\Delta(0) = \Delta_0,$$

indicating that Δ_0 is the initial temperature difference between the object and its surrounding medium.

As a practical example, suppose that a pot of boiling water (100°C) is removed from the fire and allowed to cool at 20°C room temperature. Two minutes later, the temperature of the water in the pot is 80°C. What will be the temperature of the water five minutes after it has been removed from the fire?

Here the initial temperature difference is

$$\Delta(0) = 100° - 20° = 80°,$$

so that Eq. (5) becomes

$$\Delta(t) = 80e^{kt}. \tag{6}$$

When $t = 2$ minutes, the temperature difference is

$$\Delta(2) = 80° - 20° = 60°C,$$

so if we substitute $t = 2$ into Eq. (6), we obtain

$$60 = 80e^{2k},$$

or

$$e^{2k} = \tfrac{60}{80} = \tfrac{3}{4}.$$

Taking the natural logarithm of both sides of this equation, we get

$$2k = \ln \left(\tfrac{3}{4}\right),$$

or

$$k = \tfrac{1}{2} \ln \left(\tfrac{3}{4}\right).$$

Note that k is negative (≈ -0.1438) since the temperature difference must decrease as time increases.

Substituting this value of k into Eq. (6), we obtain

$$\Delta(t) = 80e^{(1/2)\ln(3/4)t} = 80\left(\tfrac{3}{4}\right)^{(1/2)t}, \tag{7}$$

since $e^{\ln x} = x$. Finally, to find the temperature of the water in the pot at $t = 5$ minutes, we first find the temperature difference by setting $t = 5$ in Eq. (7):

$$\Delta(5) = 80\left(\tfrac{3}{4}\right)^{5/2} \approx 38.9711.$$

Adding this difference to the room temperature of 20°C yields a temperature of approximately 58.9711°C for the water in the pot five minutes after it has been removed from the fire.

Example 3 Consider a bacteria population that is changing at a rate proportional to its size. If $P(t)$ represents the population at time t, then the equation of population growth is

$$\frac{dP}{dt} = \alpha P,$$

where α can be positive or negative depending on whether the population is growing or declining. As in the last example, a solution is given by

$$P(t) = P(0)e^{\alpha t},$$

where $P(0)$ is the initial population. If $\alpha > 0$, the population will *grow exponentially*, while if $\alpha < 0$, the population will *decline exponentially*. In the special case $\alpha = 0$, the population will remain constant at its equilibrium point $P(0)$.

To see how this equation can be used, suppose that a one-liter bottle of milk is tested for its bacterial content one day after it has been bottled, yielding a count of 500 organisms. One day later, the count is 8000 organisms. What was the bacterial count at the moment of bottling?

Here we know that $P(1) = 500$ and $P(2) = 8000$, so that

$$\frac{8000}{500} = \frac{P(2)}{P(1)} = \frac{P(0)e^{2\alpha}}{P(0)e^{\alpha}} = e^{\alpha}.$$

Taking the natural logarithm of the two ends of this equation, we obtain

$$\alpha = \ln \left(\tfrac{8000}{500}\right) = \ln (16).$$

Therefore,

$$P(t) = P(0)e^{(\ln 16)t} = P(0)(16)^{t}.$$

To find $P(0)$, we set $t = 1$ and use the fact that $P(1) = 500$ to get $16P(0) = 500$, or $P(0) = 31.25$. This represents the bacterial count at the moment of bottling.

Example 4　The growth rate per individual in a population is the difference between the average birth rate and the average death rate. Suppose that in a given population the average birth rate is a positive constant β, but the average death rate, due to the effects of crowding and increased competition for the available food, is proportional to the size of the population. Suppose that this constant of proportionality is $\delta > 0$. Since dP/dt is the growth rate of the population, the growth rate per individual of the population is

$$\frac{1}{P}\frac{dP}{dt}.$$

Then the differential equation that governs the growth of this population is

$$\frac{1}{P}\frac{dP}{dt} = \beta - \delta P.$$

Multiplying both sides of this equation by P, we have

$$\frac{dP}{dt} = P(\beta - \delta P), \tag{8}$$

which is called the *logistic equation*. The growth shown by this equation is called *logistic growth*. In Example 3 in Section 2.1 we shall find the solution

$$P(t) = \frac{\beta}{\delta + [\beta P(0)^{-1} - \delta]e^{-\beta t}} \tag{9}$$

for Eq. (8). Observe that as t gets larger, the term $e^{-\beta t}$ approaches zero since $\beta > 0$. Thus the population approaches a limiting value of β/δ

beyond which it cannot increase, since setting $P = \beta/\delta$ in Eq. (8) yields $dP/dt = 0$.

As a practical example, let us suppose that the world's resources will provide only enough food for six billion humans. The world's population was 1.6 billion in 1900 A.D. and 2.4 billion in 1950 A.D. Using the logistic equation, let us determine what the world's population will be in the year 2000 A.D.

Letting $t = 0$ in 1900 A.D. and dividing the numerator and denominator of the right-hand side of Eq. (9) by δ, we get

$$P(t) = \frac{\beta/\delta}{1 + \left(\dfrac{\beta}{\delta}\dfrac{1}{P(0)} - 1\right)e^{-\beta t}} = \frac{6{,}000{,}000{,}000}{1 + \left(\dfrac{6}{1.6} - 1\right)e^{-\beta t}}$$

$$= \frac{6{,}000{,}000{,}000}{1 + 2.75e^{-\beta t}}, \tag{10}$$

since the population cannot exceed the limiting value $\beta/\delta = 6{,}000{,}000{,}000$. Setting $t = 50$ in Eq. (10) and using $P(50) = 2{,}400{,}000{,}000$ (the population in the year 1950), we get

$$2{,}400{,}000{,}000 = \frac{6{,}000{,}000{,}000}{1 + 2.75e^{-50\beta}}$$

or

$$1 + 2.75e^{-50\beta} = \tfrac{6}{2.4} = 2.5.$$

Thus we find that

$$e^{-50\beta} = \frac{1.5}{2.75} = \frac{6}{11}$$

after multiplying numerator and denominator by 4. Taking the natural logarithm of both sides, we obtain

$$-50\beta = \ln\frac{6}{11}, \qquad \text{or} \quad \beta = \frac{-1}{50}\ln\frac{6}{11},$$

so that Eq. (10) can be rewritten as

$$P(t) = \frac{6{,}000{,}000{,}000}{1 + 2.75e^{(t/50)\ln(6/11)}} = \frac{6{,}000{,}000{,}000}{1 + 2.75\left(\dfrac{6}{11}\right)^{t/50}}.$$

To find the population in the year 2000 A.D., we set $t = 100$ (years after 1900 A.D.), obtaining

$$P(100) = \frac{6{,}000{,}000{,}000}{1 + 2.75\left(\dfrac{6}{11}\right)^2} = 3{,}300{,}000{,}000.$$

Example 5   Assume that an ecosystem contains a predator species that feeds exclusively on a prey species and that the prey population has an ample food supply at all times. Let $y(t)$ and $x(t)$ denote the populations of the predator and prey species, respectively. Since food is readily available, the birth rate of the prey species is very likely to be a constant independent of time. The death rate, however, will certainly depend on the number of predators.

On the other hand, the birth rate of the predator species will be affected by the uncertain food supply, whereas its death rate may well be constant. As in Example 4, we can write the growth rates per individual for the two species as

$$\frac{1}{x}\frac{dx}{dt} = a - by, \quad \frac{1}{y}\frac{dy}{dt} = \alpha x - \beta,$$

or

$$\frac{dx}{dt} = ax - bxy, \quad \frac{dy}{dt} = \alpha xy - \beta y, \tag{11}$$

where a, b, α, and β are positive constants of proportionality. Observe that neither equation can be solved independently of the other, which explains why these equations are called a *system* of differential equations.

Although there is no explicit solution for the predator–prey system (11) (that is, no one has succeeded in finding formulas for the dependent variables x and y in terms of the independent variable t), it is possible to obtain a relation between the two populations x and y. Thus, even if we cannot determine what the populations will be at a specific time, we will know what influence one population has on the other. Hence, we seek an expression for y in terms of x. Using the chain rule of calculus, we have

$$\frac{dy}{dt} = \frac{dy}{dx}\frac{dx}{dt}.$$

Replacing dy/dt and dx/dt by their values in Eq. (11), we have

$$\alpha xy - \beta y = \frac{dy}{dx} \cdot (ax - bxy),$$

or

$$\frac{dy}{dx} = \frac{\alpha xy - \beta y}{ax - bxy}. \tag{12}$$

In Exercise 28 in Section 2.1 we shall show that Eq. (12) has the solution

$$a \ln y - by = \alpha x - \beta \ln x + c, \tag{13}$$

which can be graphed when the parameters a, b, c, α, and β are known. A graph for a given set of parameters is shown in Fig. 1.

There remains the problem of interpreting the graph in Fig. 1. First, the constant c is determined by substituting the initial populations $x(0)$

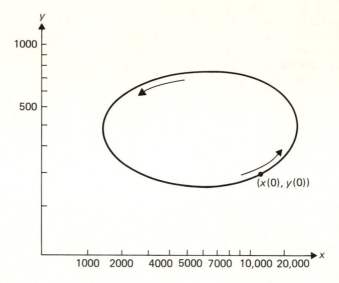

Figure 1

and $y(0)$ for x and y, respectively, into Eq. (13). Thus,

$$c = a \ln y(0) - by(0) - \alpha x(0) + \beta \ln x(0),$$

where a and α are the birth rates and b and β are the death rates of the prey and predator populations, respectively. The point $(x(0), y(0))$ is located somewhere on the closed curve that is shown in Fig. 1. As time increases, the point $(x(t), y(t))$ moves in a counterclockwise direction along the closed curve in Fig. 1. This situation illustrates the following cycle:

1. As the number of prey increases, the prey are easier to catch; this leads to an increase in the predator population, until

2. the number of predators is so large that they severely deplete the quantity of prey, causing

3. a large number of deaths by starvation in the predator population, and allowing

4. a reestablishment of the growth in the prey population.

EXERCISES 1.1

1. Solve the following differential equations by integrating both sides of the equation and evaluating y at the given x value.

a) $\dfrac{dy}{dx} = x + 3, \quad y(0) = 2$

b) $\dfrac{dy}{dx} = \dfrac{2x}{x^2 + 5}, \quad y(1) = 4$

c) $\dfrac{dy}{dx} = \tan^2 x, \quad y(0) = 1$

d) $\dfrac{d^2y}{dx^2} = x^2 - 9, \quad y(0) = 1, \quad y'(0) = 3$

e) $\dfrac{d^2y}{dx^2} = \sin x - \cos x,$

$\quad y(\pi/2) = 0, \quad y'(\pi/2) = 1$

2. A ball is thrown upward with an initial velocity v_0 m/sec from the top of a building h_0 m high. Find how high the ball travels and determine when it hits the ground for the following choices of v_0 and h_0; we neglect air resistance and let $g = -9.8$ m/sec^2.

    a) $v_0 = 49$ m/sec, $h_0 = 539$ m

    b) $v_0 = 14$ m/sec, $h_0 = 21$ m

    c) $v_0 = 21$ m/sec, $h_0 = 175$ m

    d) $v_0 = 7$ m/sec, $h_0 = 56$ m

    e) $v_0 = 7.7$ m/sec, $h_0 = 42$ m

3. An object is falling in a vacuum with constant acceleration g. Express its velocity as a function of its height.

4. The half-life of a radioactive substance is defined as the time required to decompose 50 percent of the substance. If $r(t)$ denotes the amount of the radioactive substance present after t years, $r(0) = r_0$, and the half-life is H years, what is a differential equation for $r(t)$ taking all side conditions into account?

5. A rocket is launched from an initial position (x_0, y_0) with an initial speed v_0 and with an angle θ $(0 \le \theta \le \pi/2)$. Find its horizontal and vertical coordinates $x(t)$ and $y(t)$ as functions of time. Assume that there is no air resistance, and that the force of gravity g is constant.

6. A bacteria population is known to double every three hours. If the population initially consists of 1000 bacteria, when will the population be 10,000?

In Exercises 7–10, use Newton's law of cooling to determine how long to bake a cake at the given oven temperature, assuming that it takes exactly 30 minutes to change 70°F dough into a 170°F cake in a 350°F oven.

7.   250°F   **8.**   400°F

9.   300°F   **10.**   200°F

In Exercises 11–14, assume that the population of the given country is growing at a rate proportional to the size of the population. Calculate each country's population in the year 2000 A.D. given the two census figures shown.

11. Australia: 1968 census = 12,100,000, 1973 census = 13,268,000

12. Colombia: 1968 census = 19,825,000, 1973 census = 23,210,000

13. Czechoslovakia: 1968 census = 14,362,000, 1973 census = 14,580,000

14. India: 1968 census = 523,893,000, 1973 census = 574,220,000

15. Assume India has resources that will provide only enough food for 750,000,000 humans. Using the information given in Exercise 14, find India's population in the year 2000 A.D.

1.2 CLASSIFICATION OF DIFFERENTIAL EQUATIONS

It should be apparent, if only from reading the examples in the previous section, that a great variety of types of differential equations can arise in the study of familiar phenomena. It is clearly necessary (and expedient) to study, independently, more restricted classes of these equations.

The most obvious classification is based on the nature of the derivative(s) in the equation. A differential equation involving only ordinary derivatives (derivatives of functions of one variable) is called an *ordinary differential equation*, whereas one containing partial derivatives is called a *partial differential equation*. We will postpone the further classification of partial differential equations until Chapter 12.

Since this section and the following two chapters are concerned with ordinary differential equations, we will drop the word ordinary and refer simply to differential equations. The *order* of a differential equation is defined to be the order of the highest derivative appearing in the equation.

Example 1   The following are examples of differential equations with indicated orders:

a) $\dfrac{dy}{dx} = ay$ (first order),

b) $x''(t) - 3x'(t) + x(t) = \cos t$ (second order),

c) $(y')^9 - 2\tan y = 6e^x$ (first order),

d) $(y^{iv})^{3/5} - 2y'' = \cos x$ (fourth order).

In Example 2 in Section 1.1, we obtained the differential equation (Eq. 4 in Section 1.1):

$$\frac{d\Delta}{dt} = k\Delta, \quad \Delta(0) = \Delta_0.$$

A solution was found to be

$$\Delta(t) = \Delta_0 e^{kt}.$$

This solution (which, as we shall see later, is the *only* solution) depends on the *initial* value of the unknown function $\Delta(t)$. Problems of this type are called *initial value problems*. In general, an initial value problem is a differential equation in which the values of the function and some of its derivatives at one point, called the *initial point*, are specified. Specifying the initial populations $x(0)$ and $y(0)$ in Example 5 in Section 1.1 yields an initial value problem for this system of differential equations.

We define a *solution* for an nth-order initial value problem as a function that is n times differentiable, satisfies the given differential equation, and satisfies the given initial conditions.

> In the chapter on "Existence and Uniqueness of Solutions" we will prove that in a large class of problems, *there is a unique solution to an nth-order differential equation if the value at a given point of the unknown function and all its derivatives up to the $(n-1)$st are specified.*

On the other hand, we may not know the population size of the prey species but may have adequate information concerning the population size of the predators at two points in time $y(0)$ and $y(a)$. These values and Eq. (11) in Section 1.1 constitute a boundary value problem. For a differential equation together with certain values of the function and its derivatives to qualify as a *boundary value problem*, it is necessary only that values be given for at least two different points.

The physical examples given in the previous section are such that in each case we know that a solution exists. However, there is an inherent danger in confusing physical reality with the mathematical model given by the differential equation we are using to represent the real problem. It may well be that our reasoning was faulty, in which case the equations obtained might bear no connection with reality. Then solutions to the equations need not exist. We should also note that not all differential equations have solutions. For example, the equation

$$\left(\frac{dy}{dx}\right)^2 + 3 = 0 \tag{1}$$

has no real-valued solutions, since dy/dx is imaginary. On the other hand, the equation

$$\left(\frac{dy}{dx}\right)^2 + y^2 = 0 \tag{2}$$

has zero as its only solution, whereas the equation

$$\frac{dy}{dx} + y = 0 \tag{3}$$

has an infinite set of solutions $y = ce^{-x}$ for any constant c.

EXERCISES 1.2

1. State the order of each of the following differential equations.

a) $y' + ay = \sin^2 x$

b) $\left(\frac{d^2x}{dt^2}\right)^3 - 3x\frac{dx}{dt} = 4\cos t$

c) $s'''(t) - s''(t) = 0$

d) $\frac{d^5y}{dx^5} = 0$

e) $y'' + y = 0$

f) $\left(\frac{dx}{dt}\right)^3 = x^5$

g) $x' - x^2 = 3x'''$

2. State whether each of the following differential equations is an initial value or a boundary value problem.

a) $y'' + \omega^2 y = 0, \quad y(0) = 0, \quad y(1) = 1$

b) $y'' + \omega^2 y = 0, \quad y(0) = 0, \quad y'(0) = 1$

c) $y'' + \omega^2 y = 0, \quad y(0) = 0, \quad y'(1) = 1$

d) $\left(\frac{dx}{dt}\right)^3 - 4x^2 = \sin t, \quad x(0) = 3$

e) $y''' + 3y'' - (y')^2 + e^y = \sin x,$
$\quad y(0) = 0, \quad y'(0) = 3, \quad y''(0) = 5$

f) $y''' + 3y'' - (y')^2 + e^y = \sin x,$
$\quad y(0) = y(1) = 0, \quad y'(0) = 2$

3. For each of the following differential equations, verify that the given function or functions are solutions.

a) $y'' + y = 0; \quad y_1 = 2\sin x, \quad y_2 = -5\cos x$

b) $y''' - y'' + y' - y = x; \quad y_1 = e^x - x - 1,$
$\quad y_2 = 3\cos x - x - 1,$
$\quad y_3 = \cos x + \sin x + e^x - x - 1$

c) $x^2 y'' - 2xy' + 2y = 0; \quad y_1 = x, \quad y_2 = x^2,$
$\quad y_3 = 2x - 3x^2$

d) $y'' - y = e^x; \quad y_1 = \frac{x}{2}e^x,$

$\quad y_2 = \left(4 + \frac{x}{2}\right)e^x + 3e^{-x}$

e) $y' = 2xy + 1;$ $y_1 = e^{x^2} + e^{x^2} \int_0^x e^{-s^2} ds$

f) $x^2 y'' + 5xy' + 4y = 0;$

$$y_1 = \frac{4 \ln x}{x^2}, \quad y_2 = \frac{-6}{x^2} \, (x > 0)$$

4. By "guessing" that there is a solution to the equation

$$y'' - 4y' + 5y = 0$$

of the form

$$y = e^{\alpha x} \cos bx,$$

find this solution. Can you "guess" a second solution?

5. By "guessing" that there is a solution to

$$y'' - 3y' - 4y = 0$$

of the form

$$y = e^{\alpha x}$$

for some constant a, find two solutions of the equation.

6. Given that $y_1(x)$ and $y_2(x)$ are two solutions of

the equation in Exercise 5, check to see that $y_3(x) = c_1 y_1(x) + c_2 y_2(x)$ is also a solution, where c_1 and c_2 are arbitrary constants, by substituting y_3 into the differential equation.

7. Determine $\varphi(x)$ so that the functions $\sin \ln x$ and $\cos \ln x (x > 0)$ are solutions of the differential equation

$$[\varphi(x)y']' + \frac{y}{x} = 0.$$

8. Show that $\sin(1/x)$ and $\cos(1/x)$ are solutions of the differential equation

$$\frac{d}{dx}\left(x^2 \frac{dy}{dx}\right) + \frac{y}{x^2} = 0.$$

9. Verify that $y_1 = \sinh x$ and $y_2 = \cosh x$ are solutions of the differential equation $y'' - y = 0$. [*Hint*: $\cosh x = \frac{1}{2}(e^x + e^{-x});$ $\sinh x = \frac{1}{2}(e^x - e^{-x})$.]

10. Suppose that $\varphi(x)$ is a solution of the initial value problem $y'' + yy' = x^3$, with $y(-1) = 1$, $y'(-1) = 2$. Find $\varphi''(-1)$ and $\varphi'''(-1)$.

11. Let $\varphi(x)$ be a solution to $y' = x^2 + y^2$ with $y(1) = 2$. Find $\varphi'(1)$, $\varphi''(1)$, and $\varphi'''(1)$.

1.3 DIRECTION FIELDS

A major portion of this book is taken up with the problem of solving differential equations. In part of Chapter 2 and all of Chapter 3, we will deal with linear differential equations. Linear differential equations are an important class of functions because it is often possible to obtain their solutions; that is, we can find solutions that can be expressed in terms of functions with which we are familiar. In parts of Chapter 2, we will discuss certain nonlinear differential equations for which solutions can be obtained. But these circumstances are the exception rather than the rule. A basic fact is that *most differential equations arising in applications cannot be solved.* That is, for most differential equations, it is impossible to express a solution in terms of elementary functions.

There are many ways to deal with this vexing problem. One is to look for numerical solutions. In other words, rather than look for a function $y(x)$ that solves the problem for every value of the independent variable x, we try to find an approximation to one or more values. This approach is discussed further in Chapter 7.

Another approach is to try to describe how solutions "behave." Typical questions that can be asked are:

1. Do solutions grow without bound as x increases?
2. Do solutions tend to zero?
3. Do solutions oscillate between certain values?

Much of the modern research on differential equations centers on finding answers to these questions. In this section, we describe one relatively simple way to obtain information about the solution to a differential equation.

Consider the first-order differential equation

$$y' = f(x, y). \tag{1}$$

Equation (1) contains a great deal of information. We shall prove in the chapter on "Existence and Uniqueness of Solutions" that under certain conditions Eq. (1) has a unique solution if we specify an initial condition. That is, there is a unique function $y(x)$ satisfying $y'(x) = f(x, y)$ and $y(x_0) = y_0$ for arbitrarily chosen numbers x_0 and y_0. The function $y(x)$ is a curve in the xy-plane. Even though we may not be able to find $y(x)$, we know the slope of y at every point on the curve. If the solution $y(x)$ passes through the point (x, y), then since $y' = f(x, y)$:

> The slope of the tangent line to the curve $y(x)$ at the point (x, y) is given by $f(x, y)$.

Thus, we know the direction of the solution curve $y(x)$ at any point in the xy-plane. The set of all these directions in the plane is called the *direction field* of the differential equation $y' = f(x, y)$. In many cases, we can use the direction field to sketch the solution to a differential equation without actually computing it.

Example 1   Consider the initial value problem

$$y' = 2xy, \quad y(0) = 1. \tag{2}$$

We have

$$y'(x) > 0, \quad \text{if} \quad xy > 0,$$

and

$$y'(x) < 0, \quad \text{if} \quad xy < 0.$$

Thus $y'(x) > 0$ in the first and third quadrants and $y'(x) < 0$ in the second and fourth quadrants. The direction field is sketched in Fig. 2. Note that since x and y are positive in the first quadrant, the slopes of the tangent

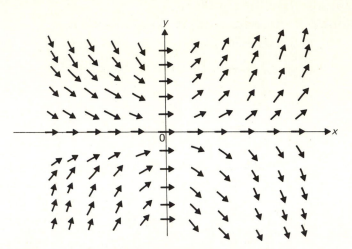

Figure 2

lines to any solution curve are positive, so that the solution curves increase and become steeper as x and y become larger. Along the axes, the solution is flat (has a horizontal tangent) because the derivative y' is zero. In the second quadrant, the slopes of the tangent lines are negative since $y' < 0$. Similar conditions apply in the third and fourth quadrants.

For the particular initial value problem we are considering in Eq. (2), we know that the solution curve must satisfy the initial condition $y(0) =$ 1. Thus, the solution curve must pass through the point $(0, 1)$. Since that point is on the y-axis, the curve is initially flat and moves into the first quadrant with increasing values of x. As x increases, the solution curve begins to rise as $y'(x) > 0$ in the first quadrant. Hence $y > 1$ for all values of $x > 0$. On the other hand, if we allow x to be negative, the solution curve extends into the second quadrant. Since the slope is negative in this quadrant, the solution curve is decreasing as the curve moves to the right. Because xy becomes larger in absolute value as we move away from the y-axis, the curve becomes steeper. Putting this all together, we obtain the sketch in Fig. 3.

We will show in Section 2.1 that the solution to Eq. (2) is

$$y(x) = e^{x^2}.$$

This function has the graph shown in Fig. 3.

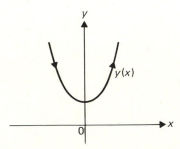

Figure 3

Example 2   Consider the differential equation

$$y'(x) = y(y + 1). \tag{3}$$

The following facts are evident:

$$y' > 0, \quad \text{if} \quad y < -1, \qquad\qquad y' = 0, \quad \text{if} \quad y = 0,$$
$$y' = 0, \quad \text{if} \quad y = -1, \qquad\qquad y' > 0, \quad \text{if} \quad y > 0.$$
$$y' < 0, \quad \text{if} \quad -1 < y < 0,$$

Since there is no x-term in the right-hand side of Eq. (3) the direction field depends only on the values of y. The direction field, together with eight possible solutions for eight different initial values $(0, y_0)$, is given in Fig. 4. Note that the curve $y(x) = 0$ is the unique solution for the initial value $(0, 0)$, and the curve $y(x) = -1$ is the unique solution passing through the initial value $(0, -1)$. Note, too, that if $y(0) > 0$, then $y(x)$ increases without bound as x increases. On the other hand, if $y(0) < 0$, then all solutions approach the line $y(x) = -1$. This is a substantial amount of information obtained with very little work. Using techniques that we will learn in Section 2.1, we find that the unique solution to

$$y' = y(y + 1), \quad y(0) = y_0$$

turns out to be

$$y(x) = \frac{y_0}{e^{-x} + y_0(e^{-x} - 1)}. \tag{4}$$

It is easy to verify that if $y_0 = 0$, then $y(x) = 0$ for every x, and if $y_0 = -1$, then $y(x) = -1$ for every x. For $y_0 > 0$, note that the denominator in Eq. (4) equals 1 when $x = 0$ but becomes negative as x increases, because e^{-x}

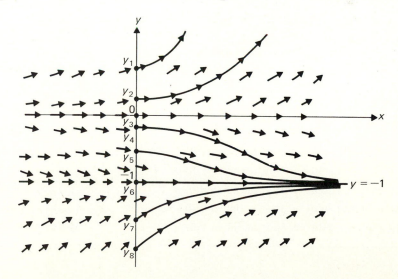

Figure 4

tends to zero. Thus, there is a value of x for which the denominator will vanish:

$$x = \ln\left[\frac{y_0 + 1}{y_0}\right].$$

Hence, the solution tends to infinity as x approaches $\ln[(y_0 + 1)/y_0]$. On the other hand, if $y_0 < 0$, the denominator in Eq. (4) remains positive and tends to $-y_0$ as x becomes arbitrarily large. Therefore, the solution curve approaches the line $y = -1$. This confirms the shape of our rough sketches in Fig. 4.

Of course, if we can solve the differential equation directly, we need not plot the direction field. Nevertheless, direction fields provide a quick and useful, if crude, tool for getting an idea of the shape of the solution. And if a solution is not readily obtainable, direction fields provide an important first step in analyzing the behavior of solutions.

EXERCISES 1.3

1. a) Plot the direction field for the differential equation
$$y' = y^{4/5}.$$
   b) Plot the solution that satisfies $y(0) = 2$.
   c) Plot the solution that satisfies $y(0) = -1$.

2. a) Plot the direction field for the equation $y' = y^{3/5}$.
   b) Plot the solution that satisfies $y(0) = 3$.
   c) Plot the solution that satisfies $y(0) = -2$.

3. a) Plot the direction field for the equation
$$y' = 2y(3 - y).$$
   b) Plot the solution that satisfies $y(0) = -1$.
   c) Plot the solution that satisfies $y(0) = 2$.
   d) Plot the solution that satisfies $y(0) = 4$.

4. a) Plot the direction field for the equation
$$y' = (y^2 - 4)(y - 4).$$
   b) Plot the solution that satisfies $y(0) = -3$.
   c) Plot the solution that satisfies $y(0) = -1$.
   d) Plot the solution that satisfies $y(0) = 1$.
   e) Plot the solution that satisfies $y(0) = 3$.
   f) Plot the solution that satisfies $y(0) = 5$.

5. a) Plot the direction field for the equation
$$y' = x^2 + y^2.$$
   b) Plot the solution that satisfies $y(1) = 2$.

6. a) Plot the direction field of the equation
$$y' = \frac{2xy}{1 + y^2}.$$
   b) Plot the solution that satisfies $y(1) = 1$.
   c) Plot the solution that satisfies $y(1) = -1$.

7. Plot the direction field of the equation
$$y' = \frac{4y - 5x}{y + x}.$$

8. a) Plot the direction field of the equation
$$y' = 1 + x + y.$$
   b) Plot the solution that satisfies $y(0) = 1$.

9. a) Plot the direction field of the equation
$$y' = e^{xy} - 1.$$
   b) Discuss the solution that passes through the origin.
   c) Compare the solution through $(0, 1)$ to that through $(0, -1)$.

First-Order Equations

Solving a first-order differential equation can be very difficult at times, since there is no general method that can be used for all cases. In this chapter we discuss a few of the most useful methods for solving first order equations. We shall discover in this and the subsequent chapters that our ability to solve linear differential equations is limited only by our capacity to perform integrations based on a well-developed general theory. On the other hand, as we shall also see, a multitude of methods are required to attack nonlinear equations and there is no guarantee that any of these techniques will succeed. For this reason, the procedures we discuss will appear to be merely a collection of tricks. They are based, however, on three underlying principles: substitution, separation of variables, and multiplication by a suitable function.

2.1 DIRECT METHODS

Consider the first-order differential equation

$$\frac{dy}{dx} = f(x, y). \tag{1}$$

If the function $f(x, y)$ does not involve the variable y, then the equation can be solved by integrating both sides with respect to x.

Example 1 Solve

$$\frac{dy}{dx} = x.$$

Integrating both sides of the equation with respect to x, we have

$$\int \frac{dy}{dx}\, dx = \int x\, dx.$$

Changing the variable of integration on the left-hand side, we obtain

$$y = \int dy = \int x\, dx = \frac{x^2}{2} + c.$$

Clearly this method will also work for higher-order equations of the form $y^{(n)} = f(x)$.

Almost as simple is the method of *separation of variables*, which may be used whenever the function $f(x, y)$ can be factored into a quotient

$$f(x, y) = \frac{g(x)}{h(y)},$$

where $g(x)$ and $h(y)$ are each functions of only *one* variable. Then Eq. (1) can be written in the form

$$h(y)\frac{dy}{dx} = g(x).$$

Integrating both sides of this equation with respect to x and changing variables on the left-hand side, we have

$$\int h(y)\, dy = \int h(y)\frac{dy}{dx}\, dx = \int g(x)\, dx + C.$$

Example 2   Solve the equation

$$\frac{dy}{dx} = 2xy.$$

We rewrite this equation as

$$\frac{1}{y}\, dy = 2x\, dx$$

so that we may automatically perform the change of variables. Integrating both sides yields

$$\ln y = x^2 + C,$$

and exponentiating both sides of the equation, we have

$$y = e^{x^2+C} = e^C e^{x^2} = C_1 e^{x^2}.$$

This is the *general solution* of the equation and involves an unspecified real constant C_1. Thus the differential equation $y' = 2xy$ has an infinite number of solutions, depending on the particular choice of C_1.

In Section 1.2 we mentioned the fundamental existence and uniqueness theorem for initial value problems. If we specify an initial condition in addition to the differential equation of Example 2 above, then the specified condition will completely determine the solution of the initial value problem. For example, if the initial condition is $y(1) = 2$, then substituting $x = 1$ into the general solution yields

$$2 = y(1) = C_1 e \quad \text{or} \quad C_1 = 2/e.$$

Thus the unique solution of the initial value problem

$$\frac{dy}{dx} = 2xy, \quad y(1) = 2,$$

is

$$y = 2e^{x^2-1}.$$

To obtain the unique solution of an initial value problem, it is necessary to specify as many initial conditions as the order of the equation. This fact will be proved in the chapter on "Existence and Uniqueness of Solutions."

Example 3   In Example 4 in Section 1.1 we derived the *logistic equation*

$$\frac{dP}{dt} = P(\beta - \delta P), \tag{2}$$

where β and δ were given constants. Separating the variables, we have

$$\frac{dP}{P(\beta - \delta P)} = dt. \tag{3}$$

Using partial fractions, it is easy to verify that

$$\frac{1}{P(\beta - \delta P)} = \frac{1}{\beta P} + \frac{\delta}{\beta(\beta - \delta P)}.$$

Substituting the right-hand side of this equation into Eq. (3) and integrating, we obtain

$$\frac{1}{\beta} \ln P - \frac{1}{\beta} \ln (\beta - \delta P) = t + C$$

or

$$\ln \left(\frac{P}{\beta - \delta P} \right)^{1/\beta} = t + C.$$

Exponentiating both sides of this equation and denoting the arbitrary constant e^C by C, we have

$$\frac{P}{\beta - \delta P} = Ce^{\beta t}. \tag{4}$$

[*Warning: We shall frequently make such changes of constant without further notice.*] Setting $t = 0$, we find that

$$\frac{P(0)}{\beta - \delta P(0)} = C, \tag{5}$$

and substituting this value of C into Eq. (4) yields

$$\frac{P(t)}{\beta - \delta P(t)} = \frac{P(0)}{\beta - \delta P(0)} e^{\beta t}.$$

Cross-multiplying and solving for $P(t)$, we obtain (after some algebra) the equation

$$P(t) = \frac{\beta}{\delta + [\beta P(0)^{-1} - \delta]e^{-\beta t}}, \tag{6}$$

which is the solution of the logistic equation (9) in Section 1.1.

The following two applications illustrate other practical uses of these methods.

Example 4   *Free fall.* According to Newton's second law of motion, the acceleration a of a body of mass m equals the total force F acting on it divided by the mass. Thus $F = ma$. If a body of mass m falls freely under the influence of gravity alone, then the weight (force) exerted is mg, where g is the acceleration due to gravity (which may be considered constant on the surface of the earth and approximately 32 feet per second per second). Let y be the distance of the body above the surface of the earth; then the upward acceleration of the body is d^2y/dt^2 and

$$m \frac{d^2y}{dt^2} = -mg, \tag{7}$$

where the negative sign indicates that gravity pulls downward. Canceling the m on both sides and integrating, we find that

$$\frac{dy}{dt} = -gt + v_0, \tag{8}$$

where v_0 is the velocity of the body at time $t = 0$. Integrating once more, we obtain

$$y = -\frac{gt^2}{2} + v_0 t + y_0, \tag{9}$$

where y_0 is the height of the body at time $t = 0$.

Retarded fall. If we assume in addition that air exerts a *resisting* force proportional to the velocity of the body, then Eq. (7) becomes

$$\frac{d^2y}{dt^2} = -g - c\frac{dy}{dt}, \quad c > 0. \tag{10}$$

(The minus sign indicates that the air resistance causes a deceleration.) Note that Eq. (10) does not contain any terms explicitly involving the dependent variable y. We can always reduce *any* second-order equation involving the independent variable and first and second derivatives of the dependent variable, such as Eq. (10), into a first-order equation by substituting $v = dy/dt$. Letting $v = dy/dt$, we have

$$\frac{dv}{dt} = -g - cv, \tag{11}$$

and separating variables yields

$$\int \frac{dv}{cv + g} = -\int dt,$$

so that

$$\frac{1}{c} \ln (cv + g) = -t + c_1,$$

which after exponentiation becomes

$$v = -\frac{g}{c} + c_2 e^{-ct}. \tag{12}$$

Since $c > 0$, $v \to -g/c$ as $t \to \infty$. This limiting value is called the *terminal velocity*. Observe by setting $t = 0$ in Eq. (12) that $c_2 = v_0 + g/c$, and if $v_0 = 0$, we obtain

$$v = \frac{g}{c} (e^{-ct} - 1).$$

To find the height y at any time t, we do an additional integration on Eq. (12).

EXERCISES 2.1

In Exercises 1 through 25, find the general solution explicitly, if possible. Otherwise find a relation that defines the solution implicitly. When an initial condition is given, find the particular solution that satisfies the condition.

1. $\dfrac{dy}{dx} = \dfrac{e^x}{2y}$

2. $xy' = 3y, \quad y(2) = 5$

3. $\dfrac{dy}{dx} = \dfrac{e^y x}{e^y + x^2 e^y}$

4. $\dfrac{dx}{dy} = x \cos y, \quad x\left(\dfrac{\pi}{2}\right) = 1$

5. $\dfrac{dz}{dr} = r^2(1 + z^2)$

6. $\dfrac{dy}{dx} + y = y(xe^{x^2} + 1), \quad y(0) = 1$

7. $\dfrac{dP}{dQ} = P(\cos Q + \sin Q)$

8. $\dfrac{dy}{dx} = y^2(1 + x^2), \quad y(0) = 1$

9. $\dfrac{ds}{dt} + 2s = st^2, \quad s(0) = 1$

10. $\dfrac{dy}{dx} = \sqrt{1 - y^2}$

11. $(1 + x)\dfrac{dy}{dx} = -3y, \quad y(6) = 7$

12. $\dfrac{dx}{dt} + (\cos t)e^x = 0$

13. $\cot x \dfrac{dy}{dx} + y + 3 = 0$

14. $\dfrac{dx}{dt} = x(1 - \sin t), \quad x(0) = 1$

15. $\dfrac{dy}{dx} + \sqrt{\dfrac{1 - y^2}{1 - x^2}} = 0$

16. $(\tan y)\dfrac{dy}{dx} + \tan x = 0, \quad y(0) = 0$

17. $x^2 \dfrac{dy}{dx} + y^2 = 0, \quad y(1) = 3$

18. $\dfrac{dy}{dx} = \dfrac{y^3 + 2y}{x^2 + 3x}, \quad y(1) = 1$

19. $e^x\left(\dfrac{dx}{dt} + 1\right) = 1, \quad x(0) = 1$

20. $\dfrac{ds}{dr} = \dfrac{s^2 + s - 2}{r^2 - 2r - 8}, \quad s(0) = 0$

21. $yy' = e^x$

22. $y' + y = y(xe^x + 1)$

23. $xy' = y(3 - x)$

24. $\dfrac{dy}{dx} = \dfrac{x^2 - xy - x + y}{xy - y^2}$

25. $\dfrac{dy}{dx} = \dfrac{x}{y} - \dfrac{x}{1 + y}, \quad y(0) = 1$

26. Consider a population $P(t)$ that is growing according to the equation $dP/dt = P(\alpha - \beta P)$ of logistic growth. Prove that the growth rate is at a maximum when the population is equal to half its equilibrium size.

27. The economist Vilfredo Pareto (1848–1923) discovered that the rate of decrease of the number of people y in a stable economy having an income of at least x dollars is directly proportional to the number of such people and inversely proportional to their income. Obtain an expression (Pareto's law) for y in terms of x.

28. Solve Eq. (12) in Section 1.1 by separating variables.

29. Bacteria are supplied as food to a protozoan population at a constant rate μ. It is observed that the bacteria are consumed at a rate that is proportional to the square of their numbers. The concentration $c(t)$ of the bacteria therefore satisfies the differential equation $dc/dt = \mu - \lambda c^2$, where λ is a positive constant.

   a) Determine $c(t)$ in terms of $c(0)$.

   b) What is the equilibrium concentration of the bacteria?

30. In some chemical reactions certain products catalyze their own formation. If $x(t)$ is the amount of such a product at time t, a possible model for the reaction is given by the differential equation $dx/dt = \alpha(\beta - x)$, where α and β are positive constants. According to this model, the reaction is completed when $x = \beta$, since this condition indicates that one of the chemicals has been depleted.

   a) Solve the equation in terms of the constants α, β, and $x(0)$.

   b) For $\alpha = 1$, $\beta = 200$, and $x(0) = 20$, draw a graph of $x(t)$ for $t > 0$.

*31. On a certain day it began to snow early in the morning and the snow continued to fall at a constant rate. The velocity at which a snowplow is able to clear a road is inversely proportional to the height of the accumulated snow. The snowplow started at 11 A.M. and had cleared four miles by 2 P.M. By 5 P.M. it had cleared another two miles. When did it start snowing?

*32. A large open cistern filled with water has the shape of a hemisphere with radius 25 ft. The bowl has a circular hole of radius 1 ft in the bottom. By Torricelli's law,† water will flow out of the hole with the same speed it would attain in falling freely from the level of the water to the hole. How long will it take for all the water to flow from the cistern?

*33. In Exercise 32, find the shape of the cistern that would ensure that the water level drops at a constant rate.‡

*34. The king and queen of Transylvania order coffee. The king adds a teaspoon of cool cream to the coffee at once but does not drink it immediately. The queen waits ten minutes and then adds the cream (at the same temperature). They then drink their coffee. Who drinks the hotter coffee? [*Hint*: Use Newton's law of cooling and assume that the temperature of the cream is less than the temperature of the air.]

Another equation that can be solved directly is *Clairaut's equation*:

$$y = xy' + f(y'). \tag{13}$$

We can differentiate both sides with respect to x to obtain

$$y' = y' + xy'' + f'(y')y'',$$

where the last term is a result of the chain rule. Canceling like terms, we get

$$[x + f'(y')]y'' = 0. \tag{14}$$

Since one of the factors must vanish, two different solutions arise:

i)　If $y'' = 0$, then $y' = c$, and substituting this value into Eq. (13) produces the *general solution*

$$y = cx + f(c), \tag{15}$$

which is a collection of straight lines.

---

† Evangelista Torricelli (1608–1647) was an Italian physicist.
‡ The ancient Egyptians (1380 B.C.) used water clocks based on this principle to tell time.

ii)   If $x + f'(y') = 0$, then $x = -f'(y')$, and Eq. (13) may be rewritten as

$$y = f(y') - y'f'(y').$$

Here x and y are both expressed in terms of functions of y', so that if we substitute $y' = t$, we will obtain the parametrized curve

$$x = -f'(t), \quad y = f(t) - tf'(t). \tag{16}$$

This curve is also a solution, called the *singular solution*, to Eq. (13). For example, the equation

$$y = xy' - e^{y'}$$

has the general solution $y = cx - e^c$ and the parametrized curve

$$x = e^t, \quad y = e^t(1 - t),$$

as a singular solution. Generally we can proceed no further, but in this case we can eliminate the parameter t by letting $t = \ln x$, so that the singular solution is given by

$$y = x(1 - \ln x), \quad x > 0.$$

In Exercises 35 through 39, find the general and singular solutions for each Clairaut equation.

35. $y = xy' + \ln y'$

36. $y = xy' + (y')^3$

37. $y = xy' - \sqrt{y'}$

38. $y = x\dfrac{dy}{dx} + \dfrac{1}{4}\left(\dfrac{dy}{dx}\right)^4$

39. $(y - xy')^2 - (y')^2 = 1$

2.2 SUBSTITUTION TECHNIQUES

In this section we present some special substitutions that may be used occasionally to solve a differential equation. Suppose that we are given a first-order differential equation of the form

$$\frac{dy}{dx} = F\left(\frac{y}{x}\right); \tag{1}$$

that is, the right-hand side of the equation can be written as a function of the variable y/x. It is then natural to try the substitution $z = y/x$. Since the function y depends on x, so does the function z. Differentiating $y = xz$ with respect to x, we have

$$\frac{dy}{dx} = z + x\frac{dz}{dx}. \tag{2}$$

Substituting $z = y/x$ and replacing the left-hand side of Eq. (1) by the right-hand side of Eq. (2), we obtain

$$z + x\frac{dz}{dx} = F(z).$$

The variables in this equation can be separated, since

$$x\frac{dz}{dx} = F(z) - z,$$

so that

$$\frac{dz}{F(z) - z} = \frac{dx}{x}.$$

A complete solution can now be obtained by integrating both sides of this equation and replacing each z by y/x. We illustrate this procedure in the next two examples.

Example 1   Solve the equation

$$\frac{dy}{dx} = \frac{x - y}{x + y}.$$

Dividing the numerator and denominator of the right-hand side of this equation by x yields

$$\frac{dy}{dx} = \frac{1 - (y/x)}{1 + (y/x)} = \frac{1 - z}{1 + z} = F(z).$$

Replacing the left-hand side by $z + x(dz/dx)$ and separating variables, we have (after some algebra)

$$\left(\frac{1 + z}{1 - 2z - z^2}\right) dz = \frac{dx}{x}.$$

After integrating, we obtain

$$\ln(1 - 2z - z^2) = -2\ln x + c = \ln(cx^{-2}),$$

so that exponentiating and replacing z by y/x leads to the implicit solution

$$1 - \frac{2y}{x} - \frac{y^2}{x^2} = \frac{c}{x^2}.$$

Finally, multiplying both sides by x^2 yields $x^2 - 2xy - y^2 = c$.

Example 2   Find the shape of a curved mirror such that light from a source at the origin will be reflected in a beam parallel to the x-axis.

By symmetry, the mirror has the shape of a surface of revolution obtained by revolving a curve about the x-axis. Let (x, y) be any point on the cross section in the xy-plane (see Fig. 1). The law of reflection states

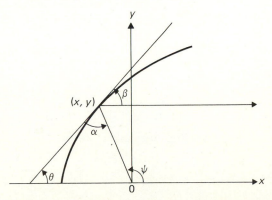

Figure 1

that the angle of incidence α must equal the angle of reflection β; thus $\alpha = \beta = \theta$. Since the interior angles of a triangle add up to 180°, we have $\psi = \alpha + \theta = 2\theta$. What is important about the angles θ and ψ is that

$$y' = \tan\theta \quad \text{and} \quad \frac{y}{x} = \tan\psi.$$

Using the trigonometric formula for the tangent of a double angle, we have

$$\frac{y}{x} = \tan\psi = \tan 2\theta = \frac{2\tan\theta}{1 - \tan^2\theta} = \frac{2y'}{1 - (y')^2}.$$

Solving for y', we obtain the quadratic equation

$$y(y')^2 + 2xy' - y = 0,$$

and by the quadratic formula we find that

$$y' = \frac{-x \pm \sqrt{x^2 + y^2}}{y}. \tag{3}$$

Since $y' > 0$, we need only consider the $+$ sign of the $\pm$ in Eq. (3), because $\sqrt{x^2 + y^2} > |x|$, yielding the differential equation

$$y' = \frac{-x + \sqrt{x^2 + y^2}}{y}. \tag{4}$$

Dividing the numerator and denominator of Eq. (4) by x, and remembering that $\sqrt{x^2 + y^2}/x = \sqrt{(x^2 + y^2)/x^2}$, we obtain

$$\frac{dy}{dx} = \frac{-1 + \sqrt{1 + (y/x)^2}}{y/x}. \tag{5}$$

Substituting $z = y/x$ into Eq. (5) and using Eq. (2), we get

$$z + x\frac{dz}{dx} = \frac{-1 + \sqrt{1 + z^2}}{z}$$

or, subtracting z from both sides and simplifying the right-hand side, we have

$$x\frac{dz}{dx} = \frac{\sqrt{1 + z^2} - (1 + z^2)}{z}.$$

Separating variables, we obtain

$$\frac{z\,dz}{\sqrt{1 + z^2}(1 - \sqrt{1 + z^2})} = \frac{dx}{x}. \tag{6}$$

To integrate the left-hand side of Eq. (6) we substitute

$$u = 1 - \sqrt{1 + z^2} \quad \text{and} \quad du = -\frac{z\, dz}{\sqrt{1 + z^2}},$$

obtaining

$$-\int \frac{du}{u} = \int \frac{dx}{x}$$

or

$$-\ln u = \ln x + c.$$

Exponentiating both sides, we get

$$\frac{1}{u} = cx$$

or, inverting both sides leads to

$$1 - \sqrt{1 + z^2} = -\frac{c}{x}.$$

Replacing z by y/x and simplifying, we have

$$1 + \frac{c}{x} = \sqrt{1 + \left(\frac{y}{x}\right)^2},$$

which may be squared to obtain

$$1 + \frac{2c}{x} + \frac{c^2}{x^2} = 1 + \frac{y^2}{x^2}. \tag{7}$$

Canceling the ones and multiplying both sides of Eq. (7) by x^2, we get

$$y^2 = 2cx + c^2,$$

which is the equation of the family of all parabolas with focus at the origin that are symmetric with respect to the x-axis.

Another useful technique applies to equations of the form

$$\frac{dy}{dx} = F(ax + by + c), \tag{8}$$

where a, b, and c are real constants. If the substitution $z = ax + by + c$ is made in Eq. (8), we will obtain

$$\frac{z' - a}{b} = F(z),$$

since $z' = a + by'$. This equation has separable variables.

Example 3   Solve

$$\frac{dy}{dx} = (x + y + 1)^2 - 2.$$

Letting $z = x + y + 1$, we have $z' = 1 + y'$ so that

$$z' - 1 = y' = (x + y + 1)^2 - 2$$
$$= z^2 - 2,$$

or

$$z' = z^2 - 1.$$

We now separate variables to obtain

$$\int \frac{dz}{z^2 - 1} = \int dx. \tag{9}$$

We can integrate the left-hand side of Eq. (9) by partial fractions since

$$\frac{1}{z^2 - 1} = \frac{1}{2}\left(\frac{1}{z - 1} - \frac{1}{z + 1}\right),$$

so that Eq. (9) yields

$$\tfrac{1}{2}[\ln(z - 1) - \ln(z + 1)] = x + c,$$

or

$$\ln\left(\frac{z - 1}{z + 1}\right) = 2x + c.$$

Exponentiating both sides, we obtain

$$\frac{z - 1}{z + 1} = ce^{2x},$$

or

$$(z - 1) = ce^{2x}(z + 1).$$

Gathering all terms involving z on one side and the remaining terms on the other, we get

$$z = \frac{1 + ce^{2x}}{1 - ce^{2x}}.$$

Finally, we replace z by $x + y + 1$, which yields

$$y = \frac{1 + ce^{2x}}{1 - ce^{2x}} - x - 1.$$

As these examples indicate we may make *any* substitution we want in trying to solve a differential equation. Of course, *there is no guarantee of success.* Moreover, there may be more than one substitution that will yield the answer, as illustrated in the following example.

Example 4   We reconsider Example 2, in which we were trying to find the shape of a curved mirror that will reflect light from a source at the origin in a beam parallel to the x-axis. Recall that the geometric considerations in Example 2 led to the differential equation [see Eq. (4)]

$$y' = \frac{-x + \sqrt{x^2 + y^2}}{y}. \tag{10}$$

Now, instead of proceeding as we did in Example 2, suppose we decide to substitute $z = x^2 + y^2$. Then,

$$\frac{dz}{dx} = 2x + 2y\frac{dy}{dx},$$

and replacing dy/dx by the right-hand side of Eq. (10), we have

$$\frac{dz}{dx} = 2x + 2y\left(\frac{-x + \sqrt{x^2 + y^2}}{y}\right)$$
$$= 2x - 2x + 2\sqrt{x^2 + y^2},$$

or

$$\frac{dz}{dx} = 2\sqrt{z}.$$

Separating variables gives us

$$\frac{dz}{2\sqrt{z}} = dx,$$

and integrating, we get

$$\sqrt{z} = x + c.$$

Replacing z by $x^2 + y^2$ and squaring both sides yields

$$x^2 + y^2 = x^2 + 2cx + c^2,$$

or

$$y^2 = 2cx + c^2.$$

Since c is arbitrary, we again have the same family of parabolas as before.

EXERCISES 2.2

Find the general solution in Exercises 1 through 10 by using the method given in Example 1. When an initial condition is given, find the particular solution that satisfies that condition.

1. $xy' - y = \sqrt{xy}$

2. $\dfrac{dx}{dt} = \dfrac{x}{t} + \cosh \dfrac{x}{t}$

3. $x\dfrac{dy}{dx} = xe^{y/x} + y, \quad y(1) = 0$

4. $2xyy' = x^2 + y^2, \quad y(-1) = 0$

5. $y' = \dfrac{y^2 + xy}{x^2}, \quad y(1) = 1$

6. $(x + v)\dfrac{dx}{dv} = x$

7. $\dfrac{dy}{dx} = \dfrac{2xy - y^2}{2xy - x^2}, \quad y(1) = 2$

8. $3xyy' + x^2 + y^2 = 0$

9. $xy' - y = \sqrt{x^2 + y^2}$

10. $\dfrac{dy}{dx} = \dfrac{x^2y + 2xy^2 - y^3}{2y^3 - xy^2 + x^3}$

Use the method given in Example 3 to solve Exercises 11 through 16.

11. $2y' = x^2 + 4xy + 4y^2 + 3$

12. $9y' + (x + y - 1)^2 = 0$

13. $(x + y)y' = 2x + 2y - 3$

14. $y' + 1 = \sqrt{x + y + 2}, \quad y(0) = 2$

15. $y' + \sin^2(x + y) = 0$

16. $y' = \dfrac{e^y}{e^x} - 1$

Find a substitution that provides a solution to each of Exercises 17 through 22.

17. $xy' + y = (xy)^3$

18. $xy' = \sqrt{1 - x^2y^2} - y$

19. $xy' = e^{xy} - y, \quad y(1) = 1$

20. $y' = y^2e^x - y$

21. $y' = (x + y)\ln(x + y) - 1$

22. $y' = y(\ln y + x^2 - 2x)$

23. Show, if $ad - bc \neq 0$, that there are constants h and k such that the substitution $x = u + h$ and $y = v + k$ converts the quotient

$$\frac{ax + by + m}{cx + dy + n}$$

into the quotient

$$\frac{au + bv}{cu + dv}.$$

Use Exercise 23 and the method given in Example 1 to find a solution for each of Exercises 24 through 29.

24. $\dfrac{dy}{dx} = \dfrac{x - y - 5}{x + y - 1}$

25. $y' = \dfrac{x + 2y + 2}{y - 2x}$

26. $y' = \dfrac{y - x - 1}{y + x}$

27. $\dfrac{dx}{dt} = \dfrac{x + 1}{x + t}$

28. $\dfrac{dy}{dx} = \dfrac{2x - 3y + 4}{4x + y - 6}$

29. $\dfrac{dy}{dx} = \dfrac{3x - y - 3}{x + y - 5}$

30. Solve the equation

$$\frac{dy}{dx} = \frac{1 - xy^2}{2x^2y}$$

by making the substitution $v = y/x^n$ for an appropriate value of n.

31. Use the method of Exercise 30 to solve

$$\frac{dx}{dt} = \frac{x - tx^2}{t + xt^2}.$$

2.3 LINEAR EQUATIONS

An nth-order differential equation is *linear* if it can be written in the form

$$\frac{d^ny}{dx^n} + a_{n-1}(x)\frac{d^{n-1}y}{dx^{n-1}} + \cdots + a_1(x)\frac{dy}{dx} + a_0(x)y = f(x).$$

Hence a first-order linear equation has the form

$$\frac{dy}{dx} + a(x)y = f(x),$$

while a second-order linear equation can be written as

$$\frac{d^2y}{dx^2} + a(x)\frac{dy}{dx} + b(x)y = f(x).$$

The notation indicates that $a(x)$, $b(x)$, $f(x)$, etc., are functions of x alone.

Before dealing with the general first-order linear equation

$$\frac{dy}{dx} + a(x)y = f(x), \tag{1}$$

we will illustrate some special cases. If $f(x) \equiv 0$ and $a(x) \equiv a$ is constant, then Eq. (1) becomes

$$\frac{dy}{dx} + ay = 0.$$

Separation of variables yields $dy/y = -a\,dx$. Upon integration we obtain $\ln y = -ax + c$, or

$$y = ce^{-ax}. \tag{2}$$

Equation (2) is the equation of *exponential decay* (if a is positive) or *exponential growth* (if a is negative), as shown in Examples 2 and 3 in Section 1.1 and illustrated in Fig. 2(a) and (b).

Figure 2

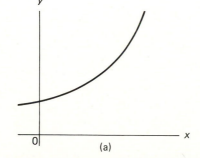

(a)

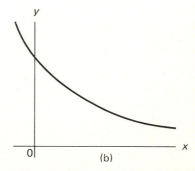

(b)

Example 1 Consider a population growing at a rate of 10 percent of the population size per unit time period and with an initial size of 1000 individuals. If $P(t)$ is the population at time t, then the growth equation is

$$\frac{dP}{dt} = 0.1P, \qquad P(0) = 1000.$$

Separating variables we obtain the general solution $P(t) = ce^{0.1t}$. Setting $t = 0$ yields the equation $1000 = P(0) = c$. Thus the solution to the problem is $P(t) = 1000e^{0.1t}$. For example, if each unit of time t is measured in weeks, the population after 10 weeks is $P(10) = 1000e \approx 2718$.

Let us now consider the more general example

$$\frac{dy}{dx} + ay = f(x). \tag{3}$$

It is now impossible to separate the variables. However, there is a simple method of solving Eq. (3) by multiplying both sides of the equation by an *integrating factor*. Since

$$\frac{d}{dx}(e^{ax}y) = e^{ax}\frac{dy}{dx} + e^{ax}ay = e^{ax}\left(\frac{dy}{dx} + ay\right),$$

we can multiply both sides of Eq. (3) by e^{ax} to obtain

$$\frac{d}{dx}(e^{ax}y) = e^{ax}\left(\frac{dy}{dx} + ay\right) = e^{ax}f(x). \tag{4}$$

Integrating both ends of Eq. (4), we obtain

$$e^{ax}y = \int e^{ax}f(x)\,dx + c,$$

or

$$y = e^{-ax}\left[\int f(x)e^{ax}\,dx + c\right].$$

Example 2   Consider the equation

$$\frac{dy}{dx} + 2y = x.$$

The integrating factor is e^{2x}, so that

$$(e^{2x}y)' = e^{2x}(y' + 2y) = xe^{2x},$$

or

$$e^{2x}y = \int xe^{2x}\,dx + c. \tag{5}$$

Integrating the right-hand side of Eq. (5) by parts, we have

$$e^{2x}y = \frac{xe^{2x}}{2} - \frac{1}{2}\int e^{2x}\,dx + c,$$

from which it follows that

$$y = e^{-2x}\left[\frac{xe^{2x}}{2} - \frac{e^{2x}}{4} + c\right]$$

or

$$y = \frac{x}{2} - \frac{1}{4} + ce^{-2x}.$$

We now return to the general linear first-order equation (1). Since differentiation and integration are inverse operations,

$$\frac{d}{dx}\int a(x)\,dx = a(x).$$

Then by the product rule,

$$\frac{d}{dx}(e^{\int a(x)\,dx}y) = e^{\int a(x)\,dx}\left[\frac{dy}{dx} + a(x)y\right],$$

so it is clear that $e^{\int a(x)\,dx}$ is a suitable integrating factor for Eq. (1). Multiplying both sides of Eq. (1) by this integrating factor, we find that

$$\frac{d}{dx}(e^{\int a(x)\,dx}y) = e^{\int a(x)\,dx}\left[\frac{dy}{dx} + a(x)y\right] = e^{\int a(x)\,dx}f(x),$$

and integrating both sides yields

$$e^{\int a(x)\,dx}y = \int f(x)e^{\int a(x)\,dx}\,dx + c,\tag{6}$$

which can be rewritten in the abbreviated form

$$y = e^{-\int a\,dx}\left[\int fe^{\int a\,dx}\,dx + c\right].\tag{7}$$

Equation (7) verifies the claim we made at the beginning of this chapter, since our ability to solve the first order equation (1) depends entirely on our capacity to perform the integrations in Eq. (7).

Example 3   Solve

$$\frac{dy}{dx} + \frac{2}{x}y = 5x^2.\tag{8}$$

We observe that Eq. (8) has the same form as Eq. (1) with $a(x) = 2/x$, and

$$\int a(x)\,dx = 2\int\frac{dx}{x} = 2\ln x = \ln x^2.$$

Multiplying both sides of the equation by $e^{\ln x^2} = x^2$ and integrating yields

$$x^2 y = \int 5x^2 \cdot x^2 \, dx + c = x^5 + c.$$

Thus $y = x^3 + cx^{-2}$ is the general solution of Eq. (8).

Example 4 Consider the equation $dy/dx = x^3 - 2xy$, where $y = 1$ when $x = 1$. Rewriting the equation as $dy/dx + 2xy = x^3$, we see that $a(x) = 2x$ and the integrating factor is $e^{\int a(x) dx} = e^{x^2}$. Thus multiplying both sides by e^{x^2} and integrating, we have

$$e^{x^2} y = \int x^3 e^{x^2} \, dx + c,$$

so that

$$y = e^{-x^2}\left[\int x^3 e^{x^2} \, dx + c\right].$$

We can integrate the integral by parts as follows:

$$\int x^3 e^{x^2} \, dx = \int x^2 (xe^{x^2}) \, dx = \frac{x^2 e^{x^2}}{2} - \int xe^{x^2} \, dx = e^{x^2}\left(\frac{x^2 - 1}{2}\right).$$

Thus replacing this term for the integral above, we have

$$y = e^{-x^2}\left[e^{x^2}\left(\frac{x^2 - 1}{2}\right) + c\right] = \frac{x^2 - 1}{2} + ce^{-x^2}.$$

Setting $x = 1$ yields

$$1 = y(1) = ce^{-1}.$$

Thus $c = e$ and the solution to the problem is

$$y = \tfrac{1}{2}(x^2 - 1) + e^{1-x^2}.$$

Example 5 *Intravenous feeding of glucose.* Infusion of glucose into the bloodstream is an important medical technique. To study this process, we define $G(t)$ to be the amount of glucose in the bloodstream of a patient at time t. Suppose that glucose is infused into the bloodstream at the constant rate of k grams per minute. At the same time the glucose is converted and removed from the bloodstream at a rate proportional to the amount of glucose present. Then the function $G(t)$ satisfies the first order differential equation

$$\frac{dG}{dt} = k - aG,$$

where a is a positive constant. In order to solve this equation, we write $dG/dt + aG = k$ and multiply both sides by the integrating factor e^{at}. The solution is $G(t) = ce^{-at} + k/a$. When $t = 0$, $c = G(0) - k/a$, so the solution can be written as

$$G(t) = \frac{k}{a} + \left[G(0) - \frac{k}{a} \right] e^{-at}.$$

As $t \to \infty$, the concentration of glucose approaches the equilibrium value k/a.

Certain nonlinear first-order equations can be reduced to linear equations by a suitable change of variables. The equation

$$\frac{dy}{dx} + a(x)y = f(x)y^n, \tag{9}$$

which is known as *Bernoulli's equation*, is of this type. Set $z = y^{1-n}$. Then $z' = (1 - n)y^{-n}y'$, so if we multiply both sides of Eq. (9) by $(1 - n)y^{-n}$, we obtain

$$(1 - n)y^{-n}y' + (1 - n)a(x)y^{1-n} = (1 - n)f(x)$$

or

$$\frac{dz}{dx} + (1 - n)a(x)z = (1 - n)f(x).$$

The equation is now linear and may be solved as before.

Example 6   Solve

$$\frac{dy}{dx} - \frac{y}{x} = -\frac{5}{2}x^2y^3. \tag{10}$$

Here $n = 3$, so we let $z = y^{-2}$, $z' = -2y^{-3}y'$, and multiply Eq. (10) by $-2y^{-3}$ to obtain

$$z' + \frac{2}{x}z = 5x^2,$$

which, we saw in Example 3, has the solution

$$y^{-2} = z = x^3 + cx^{-2}.$$

Thus

$$y = (x^3 + cx^{-2})^{-1/2}.$$

A similar procedure is used in the next problem.

Example 7 Solve

$$\frac{dy}{dx} + a(x)y = f(x)y \ln y. \tag{11}$$

We let $z = \ln y$. Then $z' = y'/y$, so that dividing Eq. (11) by y, we obtain the linear equation

$$\frac{dz}{dx} + a(x) = f(x)z.$$

EXERCISES 2.3

In Exercises 1 through 11, find the general solution for each equation. When an initial condition is given, find the particular solution that satisfies the condition.

1. $\dfrac{dx}{dt} = 3x$

2. $\dfrac{dy}{dx} + 22y = 0, \quad y(1) = 2$

3. $\dfrac{dx}{dt} = x + 1, \quad x(0) = 1$

4. $\dfrac{dy}{dx} + y = \sin x, \quad y(0) = 0$

5. $\dfrac{dx}{dy} - x \ln y = y^y$

6. $\dfrac{dy}{dx} + y = \dfrac{1}{1 + e^{2x}}$

7. $\dfrac{dy}{dx} - \dfrac{3}{x}y = x^3, \quad y(1) = 4$

8. $\dfrac{dx}{dt} + x \cot t = 2t \csc t$

9. $x' - 2x = t^2 e^{2t}$

10. $y' + \dfrac{2}{x}y = \dfrac{\cos x}{x^2}, \quad y(\pi) = 0$

11. $\dfrac{ds}{du} + s = ue^{-u} + 1$

12. Solve the equation

$$y - x\frac{dy}{dx} = \frac{dy}{dx}y^2e^y$$

by reversing the roles of x and y (that is, treat x as the dependent variable).

13. Use the method shown in Exercise 12 to solve

$$\frac{dy}{dx} = \frac{1}{e^{-y} - x}.$$

14. Find the solution of $dy/dx = 2(2x - y)$ that passes through the point $(0, -1)$.

15. Suppose that $T(t)$ is the temperature difference at time t between an object and its surrounding medium. By Newton's law of cooling, $dT/dt = -kT$, where $k > 0$. In terms of k, calculate the length of time it takes the temperature difference to decrease to

    a) one-half its original value;

    b) one-fourth its original value.

16. A chemical substance S is produced at the rate of r moles per minute in a chemical reaction. At the same time it is consumed at a rate of c moles per minute per mole of S. Let $S(t)$ be the number of moles of the chemical present at time t.

    a) Obtain the differential equation satisfied by $S(t)$.

    b) Determine $S(t)$ in terms of $S(0)$.

    c) Find the equilibrium amount of the chemical.

17. An infectious disease is introduced to a large population. The proportion of people who have been exposed to the disease increases with time. Suppose that $P(t)$ is the proportion of people who have been

exposed to the disease within t years of its introduction. If $P'(t) = [1 - P(t)]/3$ and $P(0) = 0$, after how many years will the proportion have increased to 90 percent?

In Exercises 18 through 23, find the general solution for each equation and a particular solution when an initial condition is given.

18. $\dfrac{dy}{dx} = -\dfrac{(6y^2 - x - 1)y}{2x}$

19. $y' = -y^3 x e^{-2x} + y$

20. $x\dfrac{dy}{dx} + y = x^4 y^3, \quad y(1) = 1$

21. $tx^2\dfrac{dx}{dt} + x^3 = t \cos t$

22. $\dfrac{dy}{dx} + \dfrac{3}{x} y = x^2 y^2, \quad y(1) = 2$

23. $xyy' - y^2 + x^2 = 0$

2.4 EXACT EQUATIONS

We shall now use partial derivatives to solve ordinary differential equations. Suppose that we take the total differential of the equation $g(x, y) = c$:

$$dg = \frac{\partial g}{\partial x} dx + \frac{\partial g}{\partial y} dy = 0. \tag{1}$$

For example, the equation $xy = c$ has the total differential $y\,dx + x\,dy = 0$, which may be rewritten as the differential equation $y' = -y/x$. Reversing the situation, suppose that we start with the differential equation

$$M(x, y)\,dx + N(x, y)\,dy = 0. \tag{2}$$

If we can find a function $g(x, y)$ such that

$$\frac{\partial g}{\partial x} = M \quad \text{and} \quad \frac{\partial g}{\partial y} = N,$$

then Eq. (2) becomes $dg = 0$, so that $g(x, y) = c$ is the general solution of Eq. (2). In this case $M\,dx + N\,dy$ is said to be an *exact differential*, and Eq. (2) is called an exact differential equation.

It is very easy to determine whether a differential equation is exact by using the *cross-derivative test*: *The equation $M(x, y)\,dx + N(x, y)\,dy = 0$ is exact if and only if*

$$\frac{\partial M}{\partial y} = \frac{\partial N}{\partial x}. \tag{3}$$

To verify the cross-derivative test, note that if $M\,dx + N\,dy = 0$ is exact, then $M = \partial g/\partial x$ and $N = \partial g/\partial y$ so that Eq. (3) becomes

$$\frac{\partial^2 g}{\partial y\,\partial x} = \frac{\partial^2 g}{\partial x\,\partial y}, \tag{4}$$

which is valid if both sides of the equation exist and are continuous. Thus, Eq. (3) must hold if the differential equation is exact. Conversely, we now assume that Eq. (3) holds and show how the function g is determined. Since g must satisfy $M = \partial g/\partial x$ and $N = \partial g/\partial y$, we integrate M with respect to x and N with respect to y:

$$g = \int \frac{\partial g}{\partial x}\, dx = \int M\, dx + h(y), \tag{5}$$

$$g = \int \frac{\partial g}{\partial y}\, dy = \int N\, dy + k(x). \tag{6}$$

The "constant of integration" $h(y)$ occurring in Eq. (5) is an arbitrary function of y since we must introduce the *most* general term that vanishes under *partial* differentiation with respect to x. Similarly, $k(x)$ is the most general term that vanishes under partial differentiation with respect to x. We must prove that *both* ways (5) and (6) of defining g yield the same function. Thus, we must show there is a function $h(y)$ in terms only of y and a function $k(x)$ in terms only of the variable x, such that

$$\int M\, dx + h(y) = \int N\, dy + k(x). \tag{7}$$

Rewriting Eq. (7) as

$$h(y) = \int N\, dy - \int M\, dx + k(x)$$

and differentiating both sides with respect to y, we have

$$h'(y) = N - \frac{\partial}{\partial y} \int M\, dx.$$

Using line integral results from calculus, if the region where $\partial M/\partial y = \partial N/\partial x$ is *simply connected* (has no "holes"), we can take the partial derivative inside the integral to get

$$h'(y) = N - \int \frac{\partial N}{\partial x}\, dx. \tag{8}$$

The right-hand side of Eq. (8) is a function of y alone because its partial derivative with respect to x vanishes. Hence, a function $h(y)$ in terms of y only does exist. A similar calculation guarantees the existence of $k(x)$, and the proof is complete.

Note that this proof contains a method for the computation of the general solution $g(x, y) = c$ of the exact differential equation: Adjust $h(y)$ and $k(x)$ in Eq. (7) so that both sides are equal. Then each side equals $g(x, y)$. The following example illustrates this method.

Example 1   Solve the equation

$$(1 - \sin x \tan y)\, dx + (\cos x \sec^2 y)\, dy = 0.$$

Letting $M(x, y) = 1 - \sin x \tan y$ and $N(x, y) = \cos x \sec^2 y$, we have

$$\frac{\partial M}{\partial y} = -\sin x \sec^2 y = \frac{\partial N}{\partial x},$$

so the equation is exact. If we integrate M with respect to x and N with respect to y, Eq. (7) becomes

$$\int (1 - \sin x \tan y)\, dx + h(y) = \int \cos x \sec^2 y\, dy + k(x),$$

or

$$x + \cos x \tan y + h(y) = \cos x \tan y + k(x).$$

Thus, setting $h(y) = 0$ and $k(x) = x$, we get the general solution

$$g(x, y) = x + \cos x \tan y = c.$$

It should be apparent that exact equations are comparatively rare, since the condition in Eq. (3) requires a precise balance of the functions M and N. For example,

$$(3x + 2y)\, dx + x\, dy = 0$$

is not exact. However, if we multiply the equation by x, then the new equation

$$(3x^2 + 2xy)\, dx + x^2\, dy = 0$$

is exact. The question we now must ask is: If

$$M(x, y)\, dx + N(x, y)\, dy = 0 \tag{9}$$

is not exact, under what conditions does an *integrating factor* $\mu(x, y)$ exist such that

$$\mu M\, dx + \mu N\, dy = 0$$

is exact? Surprisingly, the answer is, whenever Eq. (9) has a general solution $g(x, y) = c$. To see this, we solve Eq. (9) for dy/dx:

$$\frac{dy}{dx} = -\frac{M}{N} = -\frac{\partial g/\partial x}{\partial g/\partial y},$$

from which it follows that

$$\frac{\partial g/\partial x}{M} = \frac{\partial g/\partial y}{N}.$$

Denote either side of the equation above by $\mu(x, y)$. Then

$$\frac{\partial g}{\partial x} = \mu M, \quad \frac{\partial g}{\partial y} = \mu N, \tag{10}$$

and Eq. (9) has at least one integrating factor μ. However, finding integrating factors is in general very difficult. There is one procedure that is sometimes successful. Since Eq. (10) indicates that $\mu M\,dx + \mu N\,dy = 0$ is exact, by Eq. (3) we have

$$\mu\frac{\partial M}{\partial y} + M\frac{\partial \mu}{\partial y} = \frac{\partial}{\partial y}(\mu M) = \frac{\partial}{\partial x}(\mu N) = \mu\frac{\partial N}{\partial x} + N\frac{\partial \mu}{dx},$$

so that

$$\frac{1}{\mu}\left(N\frac{\partial \mu}{\partial x} - M\frac{\partial \mu}{\partial y}\right) = \frac{\partial M}{\partial y} - \frac{\partial N}{\partial x}. \tag{11}$$

In case the integrating factor μ depends only on x, Eq. (11) becomes

$$\frac{1}{\mu}\frac{d\mu}{dx} = \frac{\partial M/\partial y - \partial N/\partial x}{N} = k. \tag{12}$$

Since the left-hand side of this equation consists only of functions of x, k *must* also be a function of x. If this is indeed true, then μ can be found by separating the variables: $\mu(x) = e^{\int k(x)\,dx}$. A similar result holds if μ is a function of y alone, in which case

$$K = \frac{\partial M/\partial y - \partial N/\partial x}{-M}$$

is also a function of y. In this case, $\mu(y) = e^{\int K(y)\,dy}$ is the integrating factor.

Example 2 Solve the equation

$$(3x^2 - y^2)\,dy - 2xy\,dx = 0.$$

In this problem, $M = -2xy$ and $N = 3x^2 - y^2$, so that

$$\frac{\partial M}{\partial y} = -2x \quad \text{and} \quad \frac{\partial N}{\partial x} = 6x.$$

Then

$$K = \frac{\partial M/\partial y - \partial N/\partial x}{-M} = \frac{-4}{y},$$

so that

$$\mu = e^{-4\int y^{-1}\,dy} = e^{-4\ln y} = y^{-4}.$$

Multiplying the differential equations by y^{-4}, we obtain the exact equation

$$-\frac{2x}{y^3}\,dx + \left(\frac{3x^2 - y^2}{y^4}\right)\,dy = 0.$$

Integrating $M = -2x/y^3$ with respect to x and $N = (3x^2 - y^2)/y^4$ with respect to y, we get

$$-\int \frac{2x}{y^3}\, dx + h(y) = \int \frac{3x^2 - y^2}{y^4}\, dy + k(x),$$

or

$$-\frac{x^2}{y^3} + h(y) = -\frac{x^2}{y^3} + \frac{1}{y} + k(x).$$

Setting $k(x) = 0$ and $h(y) = 1/y$, we obtain the general solution

$$g(x, y) = \frac{1}{y} - \frac{x^2}{y^3} = c,$$

or

$$cy^3 - y^2 + x^2 = 0.$$

EXERCISES 2.4

In Exercises 1 through 11, verify that each given differential equation is exact and find the general solution. Find a particular solution when an initial condition is given.

1. $2xy\, dx + (x^2 + 1)\, dy = 0$

2. $[x \cos(x + y) + \sin(x + y)]\, dx$
   $\qquad\qquad + x \cos(x + y)\, dy = 0,$
   $y(1) = \pi/2 - 1$

3. $\left(4x^3 y^3 + \dfrac{1}{x}\right) dx + \left(3x^4 y^2 - \dfrac{1}{y}\right) dy = 0,$
   $x(e) = 1$

4. $\left[\dfrac{\ln(\ln y)}{x} + \dfrac{2}{3} xy^3\right] dx + \left[\dfrac{\ln x}{y \ln y} + x^2 y^2\right] dy = 0$

5. $(x - y \cos x)\, dx - \sin x\, dy = 0, \quad y(\pi/2) = 1$

6. $\cosh 2x \cosh 2y\, dx + \sinh 2x \sinh 2y\, dy = 0$

7. $(ye^{xy} + 4y^3)\, dx + (xe^{xy} + 12xy^2 - 2y)\, dy = 0,$
   $y(0) = 2$

8. $(3x^2 \ln x + x^2 - y)\, dx - x\, dy = 0, \quad y(1) = 5$

9. $(2xy + e^y)\, dx + (x^2 + xe^y)\, dy = 0$

10. $(x^2 + y^2)\, dx + 2xy\, dy = 0, \quad y(1) = 1$

11. $\left(\dfrac{1}{x} - \dfrac{y}{x^2 + y^2}\right) dx + \left(\dfrac{x}{x^2 + y^2} - \dfrac{1}{y}\right) dy = 0$

In Exercises 12 through 16, find the integrating factor for each differential equation and obtain the general solution.

12. $y\, dx + (y - x)\, dy = 0$

13. $(x^2 + y^2 + x)\, dx + y\, dy = 0$

14. $2y^2\, dx + (2x + 3xy)\, dy = 0$

15. $(x^2 + 2y)\, dx - x\, dy = 0$

16. $(x^2 + y^2)\, dx + (3xy)\, dy = 0$

17. Solve $xy\, dx + (x^2 + 2y^2 + 2)\, dy = 0$

18. Let $M = ya(xy)$ and $N = xb(xy)$. Show that $1/(xM - yN)$ is an integrating factor for

$$M\, dx + N\, dy = 0.$$

19. Use the result of Exercise 18 to solve the equation

$$2x^2 y^3\, dx + x^3 y^2\, dy = 0.$$

20. Solve $(x^2 + y^2 + 1)\, dx - (xy + y)\, dy = 0$ [*Hint*: Try an integrating factor of the form $\mu(x, y) = (x + 1)^n$.]

2.5 SIMPLE ELECTRIC CIRCUITS

In this section we shall consider simple electric circuits containing a resistor and an inductor or capacitor in series with a source of electromotive force (emf). Such circuits are shown in Fig. 3(a) and (b), and their action can be understood very easily without any special knowledge of electricity.

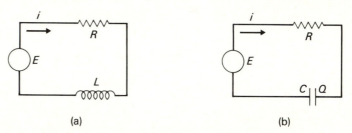

Figure 3   (a)   (b)

1. An electromotive force (emf) E (volts), usually a battery or generator, drives an electric charge Q (coulombs) and produces a current I (amperes). The current is defined as the rate of flow of the charge, and we can write

$$I = \frac{dQ}{dt}. \tag{1}$$

2. A resistor of resistance R (ohms) is a component of the circuit that opposes the current, dissipating the energy in the form of heat. It produces a drop in voltage given by *Ohm's law*:

$$E_R = RI. \tag{2}$$

3. An inductor of inductance L (henries) opposes any change in current by producing a voltage drop of

$$E_L = L\frac{dI}{dt}. \tag{3}$$

4. A capacitor of capacitance C (farads) stores charge. In so doing, it resists the flow of further charge, causing a drop in the voltage of

$$E_C = \frac{Q}{C}. \tag{4}$$

The quantities R, L, and C are usually constants associated with the particular component in the circuit; E may be a constant or a function of time. The fundamental principle guiding such circuits is given by *Kirchhoff's voltage law*:

> *The algebraic sum of all voltage drops around a closed circuit is zero.*

In the circuit of Fig. 3(a) the resistor and the inductor cause voltage drops of E_R and E_L, respectively. The emf, however, *provides* a voltage of E (that is, a voltage drop of $-E$). Thus Kirchhoff's voltage law yields

$$E_R + E_L - E = 0.$$

Transposing E to the other side of the equation and using Eqs. (2) and (3) to replace E_R and E_L, we have

$$L\frac{dI}{dt} + RI = E. \tag{5}$$

The following two examples illustrate the use of Eq. (5) in analyzing the circuit shown in Fig. 3(a).

Example 1　An inductance of 2 henries (h) and a resistance of 10 ohms (Ω) are connected in series with an emf of 100 volts (V). If the current is zero when $t = 0$, what is the current at the end of 0.1 second?

Since $L = 2$, $R = 10$, and $E = 100$, Eq. (5) and the initial current yield the initial value problem:

$$2\frac{dI}{dt} + 10I = 100, \quad I(0) = 0. \tag{6}$$

Dividing both sides of Eq. (6) by 2, we note that the resulting linear first-order equation has e^{5t} as an integrating factor, that is,

$$\frac{d}{dt}(e^{5t}I) = e^{5t}\left(\frac{dI}{dt} + 5I\right) = 50e^{5t}. \tag{7}$$

Integrating both ends of Eq. (7), we get

$$e^{5t}I(t) = 10e^{5t} + c,$$

or

$$I(t) = 10 + ce^{-5t}. \tag{8}$$

Setting $t = 0$ in Eq. (8) and using the initial condition $I(0) = 0$, we have

$$0 = I(0) = 10 + c,$$

which implies that $c = -10$. Substituting this value into Eq. (8), we obtain an equation for the current at all times t:

$$I(t) = 10(1 - e^{-5t}).$$

Thus, when $t = 0.1$, we have

$$I(0.1) = 10(1 - e^{-0.5}) = 3.93 \text{ amp.}$$

Example 2　Suppose that the emf $E = 100 \sin 60t$ volts but all other values remain the same as those given in Example 1. Then Eq. (5) yields

$$2\frac{dI}{dt} + 10I = 100 \sin 60t, \quad I(0) = 0. \tag{9}$$

Again dividing by 2 and multiplying both sides by the integrating factor e^{5t}, we have

$$\frac{d}{dt}(e^{5t}I) = e^{5t}\left(\frac{dI}{dt} + 5I\right) = 50e^{5t} \sin 60t. \tag{10}$$

Integrating both ends of Eq. (10) and using Formula 50 of Appendix 1, we obtain

$$I(t) = e^{-5t}\left[50 \int (\sin 60t)e^{5t}\, dt + c\right]$$

$$= e^{-5t}\left[50e^{5t}\left(\frac{5 \sin 60t - 60 \cos 60t}{3625}\right) + c\right]$$

$$= \frac{2 \sin 60t - 24 \cos 60t}{29} + ce^{-5t}.$$

Thus setting $t = 0$, we find that $c = 24/29$ and

$$I(0.1) = \frac{2 \sin 6 - 24 \cos 6}{29} + \frac{24}{29}e^{-0.5} = -0.31 \text{ amp.}$$

For the circuit in Fig. 3(b) we have $E_R + E_C - E = 0$, or

$$RI + \frac{Q}{C} = E.$$

Using the fact that $I = dQ/dt$, we obtain the linear first-order equation

$$R\frac{dQ}{dt} + \frac{Q}{C} = E. \tag{11}$$

The next example illustrates how to use Eq. (11).

Example 3   If a resistance of 2000 ohms and a capacitance of 5×10^{-6} farad (f) are connected in series with an emf of 100 volts, what is the current at $t = 0.1$ sec if $I(0) = 0.01$ ampere?

Setting $R = 2000$, $C = 5 \times 10^{-6}$, and $E = 100$ in Eq. (11), we have

$$2000\left(\frac{dQ}{dt} + 100Q\right) = 100,$$

or

$$\frac{dQ}{dt} + 100Q = \frac{1}{20}, \tag{12}$$

from which we can determine $Q(0)$ since

$$\tfrac{1}{20} = Q'(0) + 100Q(0) = I(0) + 100Q(0).$$

Thus,

$$Q(0) = \tfrac{1}{100}[\tfrac{1}{20} - I(0)] = 4 \times 10^{-4} \text{ coulombs.} \qquad \textbf{(13)}$$

Multiplying both sides of Eq. (12) by the integrating factor e^{100t}, we get

$$\frac{d}{dt}(e^{100t}Q) = \frac{e^{100t}}{20},$$

and integrating this equation yields

$$e^{100t}Q = \frac{e^{100t}}{2000} + c.$$

Dividing both sides by e^{100t} gives us

$$Q(t) = \tfrac{1}{2000} + ce^{-100t},$$

and setting $t = 0$, we find that $c = -10^{-4}$. Thus, the charge at all times t is

$$Q(t) = (5 - e^{-100t})/10^4,$$

and the current is

$$I(t) = Q'(t) = \tfrac{1}{100}e^{-100t}.$$

Thus $I(0.1) = 10^{-2}e^{-10} \approx 4.54 \times 10^{-7}$ amp.

EXERCISES 2.5

In Exercises 1 through 5, assume that the *RL* circuit shown in Fig. 3(a) has the given resistance, inductance, emf, and initial current. Find an expression for the current at all times t and calculate the current after one second.

1. $R = 10\,\Omega$, $L = 1\,h$, $E = 12\,V$, $I(0) = 0$ amp
2. $R = 8\,\Omega$, $L = 1\,h$, $E = 6\,V$, $I(0) = 1$ amp
3. $R = 50\,\Omega$, $L = 2\,h$, $E = 100\,V$, $I(0) = 0$ amp
4. $R = 10\,\Omega$, $L = 5\,h$, $E = 10\sin t\,V$, $I(0) = 1$ amp
5. $R = 10\,\Omega$, $L = 10\,h$, $E = e^t\,V$, $I(0) = 0$ amp

In Exercises 6 through 10, use the given resistance, capacitance, emf, and initial charge in the *RC* circuit shown in Fig. 3(b). Find an expression for the charge at all times t.

6. $R = 1\,\Omega$, $C = 1\,f$, $E = 12\,V$, $Q(0) = 0$ coulomb

7. $R = 10\,\Omega$, $C = 0.001\,f$, $E = 10\cos 60t\,V$, $Q(0) = 0$ coulomb
8. $R = 1\,\Omega$, $C = 0.01\,f$, $E = \sin 60t\,V$, $Q(0) = 0$ coulomb
9. $R = 100\,\Omega$, $C = 10^{-4}\,f$, $E = 100\,V$, $Q(0) = 1$ coulomb
10. $R = 200\,\Omega$, $C = 5 \times 10^{-5}\,f$, $E = 1000\,V$, $Q(0) = 1$ coulomb

11. Solve the problem in Example 3 with an emf of $100\sin 120\pi t$ volts.

12. An inductance of 1 henry and a resistance of 2 ohms are connected in series with a battery of $6e^{-0.0001t}$ volt. No current is flowing initially. When will the current measure 0.5 ampere?

13. A variable resistance $R = 1/(5 + t)$ ohms and a capacitance of 5×10^{-6} farad are connected in

series with an emf of 100 volts. If $Q(0) = 0$, what is the charge on the capacitor after one minute?

14. In the RC circuit [Fig. 3(b)] with constant voltage E, how long will it take the current to decrease to one-half its original value?

15. Suppose that the voltage in an RC circuit is $E(t) = E_0 \cos \omega t$, where $2\pi/\omega$ is the period of the cycle. Assuming that the initial charge is zero, what are the charge and current as functions of $R, C, \omega,$ and t?

16. Show that the current in Exercise 15 consists of two parts: a steady-state term that has a period of $2\pi/\omega$ and a transient term that tends to zero as t increases.

17. In Exercise 16 show that if R is small, then the transient term can be quite large for small values of t. (This is why fuses can blow when a switch is flipped.)

18. Find the steady-state current, given that a resistance of 2000 ohms and a capacitance of 3×10^{-6} farad are connected in series with an alternating emf of $120 \cos 2t$ volts.

19. Find an expression for the current of a series RL circuit, where $R = 100\,\Omega$, $L = 2\,\mathrm{h}$, $I(0) = 0$, and the emf voltage satisfies

$$E = \begin{cases} 6, & \text{for} \quad 0 \le t \le 10, \\ 7 - e^{10-t}, & \text{for} \quad t \ge 10. \end{cases}$$

20. Repeat Exercise 19 with $R = 100/(1 + t)$, all other values remaining the same.

2.6 CURVES OF PURSUIT†

Many interesting differential equations arise in studying the path of a pursuer in tracking prey. One of the earliest pursuit problems is stated below.

Example 1   A waterskier P located at the point $(a, 0)$ is being pulled by a motorboat Q located at the origin and traveling up the y-axis. Find the path of the waterskier if he or she heads directly toward the motorboat at all times. (This path is called a *tractrix*. See Fig. 4.)

Observe that the line PQ is tangent to the path that P will follow. Hence its slope is given by

$$\frac{dy}{dx} = -\frac{\sqrt{a^2 - x^2}}{x}, \tag{1}$$

since the length of PQ is a. Integrating both sides of Eq. (1) and using Formula 16 of Appendix 1, we have

$$y = -\int \frac{\sqrt{a^2 - x^2}}{x}\, dx + c$$
$$= a \ln\left(\frac{a + \sqrt{a^2 - x^2}}{x}\right) - \sqrt{a^2 - x^2} + c. \tag{2}$$

Since $y = 0$ when $x = a$, we see that $c = 0$ and thus the equation of the tractrix is

$$y = a \ln\left(\frac{a + \sqrt{a^2 - x^2}}{x}\right) - \sqrt{a^2 - x^2}.$$

† An interesting discussion of this topic is contained in A. Bernhart, "Curves of pursuit II," *Scripta Mathematica*, vol. 23 (1957), pp. 49–66.

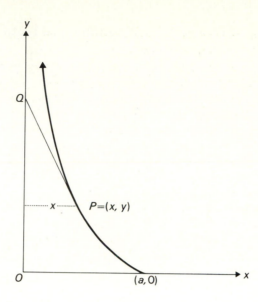

Figure 4

Example 2 Suppose that a hawk P at the point $(a, 0)$ spots a pigeon Q at the origin flying along the y-axis at a speed v. The hawk immediately flies toward the pigeon at a speed w. What will be the flight path of the hawk?

Let time $t = 0$ at the instant the hawk starts flying toward the pigeon. After t seconds the pigeon will be at the point $Q = (0, vt)$ and the hawk at $P = (x, y)$. Since the line PQ is again tangent to the path (see Fig. 4), we find that its slope is given by $y' = (y - vt)/x$, so that

$$xy' - y = -vt. \tag{3}$$

On the other hand, the length of the path traveled by the hawk can be computed by the formula for arc length of basic calculus

$$wt = \int ds = \int_x^a \sqrt{1 + (y')^2} \, dx. \tag{4}$$

Solving Eqs. (3) and (4) for t and equating them, we have

$$\frac{y - xy'}{v} = \frac{1}{w} \int_x^a \sqrt{1 + (y')^2} \, dx. \tag{5}$$

Differentiating both sides of Eq. (5) with respect to x yields

$$xy'' = \frac{v}{w} \sqrt{1 + (y')^2}. \tag{6}$$

Setting $p = y'$, we find that Eq. (6) becomes

$$xp' = \frac{v}{w} \sqrt{1 + p^2},$$

and we can separate the variables to obtain

$$\frac{dp}{\sqrt{1 + p^2}} = \frac{v}{w}\frac{dx}{x}.$$

Integrating both sides of this equation (see Formula 9 of Appendix 1), we have

$$\ln(p + \sqrt{1 + p^2}) = \frac{v}{w}\ln x - c.$$

Since $p = y' = 0$ when $x = a$ (the slope of the line PQ at $t = 0$ is zero), it follows that $c = (v/w)\ln a$. Exponentiating both sides of this equation yields

$$p + \sqrt{1 + p^2} = \left(\frac{x}{a}\right)^{v/w},$$

which, after some algebra, yields

$$\frac{dy}{dx} = p = \frac{1}{2}\left[\left(\frac{x}{a}\right)^{v/w} - \left(\frac{x}{a}\right)^{-v/w}\right]. \tag{7}$$

If we assume that the hawk flies faster than the pigeon ($w > v$), we may integrate Eq. (7) to obtain

$$y = \frac{a}{2}\left[\frac{(x/a)^{1+v/w}}{1 + v/w} - \frac{(x/a)^{1-v/w}}{1 - v/w} + c\right].$$

Since $y = 0$ when $x = a$, we have

$$c = -\frac{a}{2}\left[\frac{1}{1 + v/w} - \frac{1}{1 - v/w}\right] = \frac{avw}{w^2 - v^2}.$$

The hawk will catch the pigeon at $x = 0$ and $y = c = avw/(w^2 - v^2)$. The situation in which the hawk flies no faster than the pigeon ($w \leq v$) is discussed in Exercises 1 and 2.

Example 3   A destroyer is in a dense fog, which lifts for an instant, disclosing an enemy submarine on the surface four miles away. Suppose that the submarine dives immediately and proceeds at full speed in an unknown direction. What path should the destroyer select to be certain of passing directly over the submarine, if its velocity v is three times that of the submarine?

Suppose that the destroyer has traveled three miles toward the place where the submarine was spotted. Then the submarine lies on the circle of radius one mile centered at where it was when spotted (see Fig. 5), since its velocity is one-third that of the destroyer. Since the location of the submarine can be described easily in polar coordinates, we make use of polar coordinates and assume that $r = f(\theta)$ is the path the destroyer must

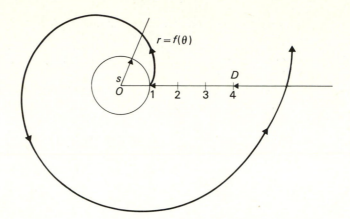

Figure 5

follow to be certain of passing over the submarine, regardless of the direction the latter chooses. Then the distance traveled by the submarine to the point where the paths will cross is $r - 1$, whereas that of the destroyer (which is three times longer) is given by the arc length formula in polar coordinates:

$$3(r - 1) = \int_0^\theta ds = \int_0^\theta \sqrt{(dr)^2 + (r\,d\theta)^2}$$

$$= \int_0^\theta \sqrt{(dr/d\theta)^2 + r^2}\,d\theta. \tag{8}$$

Differentiating both sides of Eq. (8) with respect to θ yields the differential equation

$$3r' = \sqrt{(r')^2 + r^2},$$

which simplifies to $8(r')^2 = r^2$. Taking the square roots of both sides and separating the variables, we have

$$\frac{dr}{r} = \frac{d\theta}{\sqrt{8}},$$

from which it follows that $\ln r = \theta/\sqrt{8} + c$, or

$$r = ce^{\theta/\sqrt{8}}. \tag{9}$$

Since $r = 1$ when $\theta = 0$, it follows that $c = 1$ and the path that the destroyer should follow is the spiral $r = e^{\theta/\sqrt{8}}$ after proceeding three miles toward where the submarine was spotted.

　　It should be noted that this path is not the only curve that the destroyer could follow. For example, suppose that the destroyer has gone six miles toward where the submarine was spotted (see Fig. 6). At this point, we can again follow a path $r = g(\theta)$. Since by now the submarine is two miles from the origin, the distance traveled by the submarine to

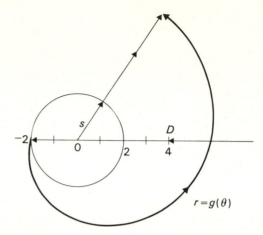

Figure 6

where the paths will cross is $r - 2$, whereas the destroyer must go a distance

$$3(r - 2) = \int_{-\pi}^{\theta} \sqrt{(dr/d\theta)^2 + r^2}\, d\theta. \tag{10}$$

Equation (10) again leads to the general solution (Eq. 9), but in this case $r = 2$ when $\theta = -\pi$, so that $c = 2e^{\pi/\sqrt{8}}$. Thus the spiral that the destroyer must follow is

$$r = 2e^{(\theta - \pi)/\sqrt{8}}.$$

Of course, the submarine captain can evade detection by not going at full speed or by following a curved trajectory.

EXERCISES 2.6

1. Suppose that $v = w$ in Example 2. Prove that

$$y = \frac{a}{2}\left\{\frac{1}{2}\left[\left(\frac{x}{a}\right)^2 - 1\right] - \ln\frac{x}{a}\right\},$$

so that the hawk will never catch the pigeon. Using Eqs. (4) and (7), show that the distance between the hawk and the pigeon is $(x^2 + a^2)/2a$ whenever the hawk is at the point (x, y) on the path. Thus the hawk will not come as close as $a/2$ to the pigeon.

2. Suppose that $v > w$ in Example 2. Show that

$$y = \frac{a}{2}\left[\frac{(x/a)^{1+v/w} - 1}{1 + v/w} + \frac{(a/x)^{v/w-1} - 1}{(v/w) - 1}\right],$$

so that the hawk will never catch the pigeon. Find the distance between the hawk and the pigeon in terms of the variable x.

3. Let the y-axis and the line $x = b$ be the banks of a river whose current has velocity v (in the negative y-direction). A man is at the origin, and his dog is at the point $(b, 0)$. When the man calls, the dog enters the river, swimming toward the man at a constant velocity $w(>v)$. What will be the path of the dog?

4. Where will the dog of Exercise 3 land if $w = v$?

5. Show that the dog of Exercise 3 will never land if $w < v$. Suppose that the man walks down river at the velocity v while calling his dog. Will the dog now be able to land?

6. In Example 3 suppose the destroyer proceeds to where the submarine was sighted, then turns 90° left and proceeds two miles before beginning the spiral search pattern. What is the equation of the path the destroyer should now follow?

7. Suppose the destroyer in Example 3 is only twice as fast as the submarine and the submarine is spotted when it is three miles away. Find a path that will guarantee the destroyer's passing over the submarine, assuming that both ships execute the same maneuvers as those given in the example.

8. Three snails at the corners of an equilateral triangle of side a begin to move with the same velocity, each toward the snail to its right. Centering the triangle at the origin with one vertex along the positive x-axis, find an equation for the slime path left by the snail that started on the x-axis.

9. Consider the same problem with four snails at the corners of the square $[0, a] \times [0, a]$. How far will the snails travel before they meet?

10. In Example 1 suppose that the waterskier is located at the point $(-a, 0)$ and the motorboat is traveling up the line $y = x$. What is the equation of the path of pursuit?

2.7 COMPARTMENTAL ANALYSIS

A complicated physical or biological process can often be divided into several distinct stages. The entire process can then be described by the interactions between the individual stages. Each such stage is called a *compartment* or pool, and the contents of each compartment are assumed to be well mixed. Material from one compartment is transferred to another and is immediately incorporated into the latter. Because of the name we have given to the stages, the entire process is called a *compartmental system.*† An *open* system is one in which there are inputs to or outputs from the system through one or more compartments. A system that is not open is said to be *closed*.

In this section we will investigate only the simplest such systems: the one-compartment system. Additional work on more complicated systems will be found in later chapters.

Figure 7 illustrates a one-compartment system consisting of a quantity $x(t)$ of material in the compartment, an input rate $i(t)$ at which material is being introduced to the system, and a *fractional transfer coefficient* k indicating the fraction of the material in the compartment that is being removed from the system per unit time. It is clear that the rate at which the quantity x is changing depends on the difference

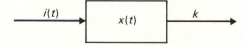

Figure 7

---

† This name is frequently used in mathematical biology. Engineers refer to such systems as *block diagrams*.

between the input and output at any time t, leading to the differential equation

$$\frac{dx}{dt} = i(t) - kx(t). \tag{1}$$

As we saw in Section 2.3, this linear equation has the solution

$$x(t) = e^{-kt}\left[\int i(t)e^{kt}\, dt + c\right]. \tag{2}$$

This simple model applies to many different problems, as we shall illustrate below.

Example 1   Strontium 90 (Sr^{90}) has a half-life of 25 years. If 10 grams of Sr^{90} are initially placed in a sealed container, how many grams will remain after 10 years?

Let $x(t)$ be the number of grams of Sr^{90} at time t (years). Since the number of atoms present is very large, the number decaying per unit time is directly proportional to the number present at that time. The constant of proportionality k is the fractional transfer coefficient. Since there is no input, the equation involved is

$$\frac{dx}{dt} = -kx(t). \tag{3}$$

Equation (3) has the solution $x(t) = x_0 e^{-kt}$, where $x_0 = 10$ grams. To find k, we set $t = 25$ to obtain

$$5 = 10e^{-25k},$$

from which we find, after taking logarithms, that $k = (\ln 2)/25$. Thus

$$x(10) = 10e^{-(10\ln 2)/25}$$
$$= 10(2)^{-2/5} \approx 7.579\, \mathrm{g}.$$

Example 2   Consider a tank holding 100 gallons of water in which are dissolved 50 pounds of salt. Suppose that 2 gallons of brine, each containing 1 pound of dissolved salt, run into the tank per minute, and the mixture, kept uniform by high-speed stirring, runs out of the tank at the rate of 2 gallons per minute. Find the amount of salt in the tank at any time t.

Let $x(t)$ be the number of pounds of salt at the end of t minutes. Since each gallon of brine that enters the compartment (tank) contains 1 pound of salt, we know that $i(t) = 2$. On the other hand, $k = \frac{2}{100}$ since 2 of the 100 gallons in the tank are being removed each minute. Thus Eq. (1) becomes

$$\frac{dx}{dt} = 2 - \frac{2}{100}x,$$

which has the solution

$$x(t) = e^{-t/50}\left[2\int e^{t/50}\,dt + c\right],$$

$$= 100 + ce^{-t/50}.$$

At $t = 0$ we have

$$50 = x(0) = 100 + c,$$

so that

$$x(t) = 100 - 50e^{-t/50}.$$

Observe that x increases and approaches the ratio of salt to water in the input stream as time increases.

The fractional transfer coefficient k may be a function of time, as we shall see in the following example.

Example 3 Suppose that, in Example 2, 3 gallons of brine, each containing 1 pound of salt, run into the tank each minute, and all other facts are the same. Now $i(t) = 3$, but since the quantity of brine in the tank increases with time, the fraction that is being transferred is $k = 2/(100 + t)$. The numerator of k is the number of gallons being removed, and $100 + t$ is the number of gallons in the tank at time t. The equation describing the system is

$$\frac{dx}{dt} = 3 - \frac{2x}{100 + t}. \tag{4}$$

Using Eq. (2), we see that Eq. (4) has the solution

$$x(t) = e^{-2\int dt/(100+t)}\left[3\int e^{2\int dt/(100+t)}\,dt + c\right]$$

$$= (100 + t) + c(100 + t)^{-2}.$$

Setting $t = 0$, we find that $c = -50(100)^2$, so that

$$x(t) = 100 + t - 50(1 + t/100)^{-2}.$$

After 100 minutes, we have

$$x(100) = 200 - 50/4 = 187.5\,\text{lb}$$

of salt in the tank.

The input function $i(t)$ may depend not only on time but also on the quantity present. Examples 3 and 4 in Section 1.1 are situations in which the input function depends on the quantity present, and in Example 4 of

Section 1.1 the fractional transfer coefficient $k = \delta P$ also depends on the quantity present.

Systems with periodic inputs and fractional transfer coefficients often occur in biological processes due to the diurnal period of activity. For example, ACTH (adrenocorticotropic hormone) secretion by the anterior pituitary follows a 24-hour cycle, which drives the secretion of adrenal steroids in such a way that the levels of these steroids in the blood plasma peaks near 8:00 A.M. and is at a minimum near 8:00 P.M.

Example 4   Let $k(t) = A + B \sin \omega t$, with $A > B$, in Eq. (1), which leads to the equation

$$\frac{dx}{dt} = i(t) - (A + B \sin \omega t)x. \tag{5}$$

Since

$$\int (A + B \sin \omega t)\, dt = At - \frac{B}{\omega} \cos \omega t + c,$$

we may use the integrating factor $e^{At+(B/\omega)(1-\cos \omega t)}$ on both sides of Eq. (5):

$$\frac{d}{dt}\left(e^{At+(B/\omega)(1-\cos \omega t)}x(t)\right) = e^{At+(B/\omega)(1-\cos \omega t)}[x' + (A + B \sin \omega t)x]$$

$$= e^{At+(B/\omega)(1-\cos \omega t)}i(t). \tag{6}$$

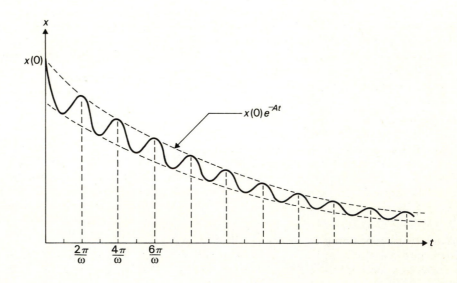

Figure 8

Integrating both sides of Eq. (6) from 0 to t, we have

$$e^{At+(B/\omega)(1-\cos\omega t)}x(t)\big|_0^t = \int_0^t i(t)e^{At+(B/\omega)(1-\cos\omega t)}\,dt,$$

or

$$x(t) = e^{-At-(B/\omega)(1-\cos\omega t)}\left[x(0) + \int_0^t i(t)e^{At+(B/\omega)(1-\cos\omega t)}\,dt\right]. \qquad (7)$$

Since $1 - \cos\omega t = 2\sin^2(\omega t/2)$, we can write Eq. (7) as

$$x(t) = e^{-At-2B\sin^2(\omega t/2)/\omega}\left[x(0) + \int_0^t i(t)e^{At+2B\sin^2(\omega t/2)/\omega}\,dt\right]. \qquad (8)$$

If $i(t) = 0$, then $x(t)$ behaves as shown in Fig. 8, where $x(0)e^{-At}$ is an upper bound, and the factor $e^{-2B\sin^2(\omega t/2)/\omega}$ oscillates between $e^{-2B/\omega}$ and 1.

EXERCISES 2.7

1. Carbon 14 (C^{14}) has a half-life of 5700 years and is uniformly distributed in the atmosphere in the form of carbon dioxide. Living plants absorb carbon dioxide and maintain a fixed ratio of C^{14} to the stable element C^{12}. At death, the disintegration of C^{14} changes this ratio. Compare the concentrations of C^{14} in two identical pieces of wood, one of them freshly cut, the other 2000 years old.

2. Radioactive iodine I^{131} is often used as a tracer in medicine. Suppose that a given dose Q_0 is injected into the bloodstream at time $t = 0$ and is evenly distributed in the entire bloodstream before any loss occurs. If the daily removal rate of the iodine by the kidney is k_1 percent, and k_2 percent by the thyroid gland, what percentage of the initial amount will still be in the blood after one day?

3. Suppose that an infected individual is introduced into a population of size N, all of whom are susceptible to the disease. If we assume that the rate of infection is proportional to the product of the numbers of infectives and susceptibles present, what will be the number of infections at any time t? Let k be the *specific infection rate*.

4. A tank initially contains 100 liters of fresh water. Brine containing 20 grams per liter of salt flows into the tank at the rate of 4 liters per minute, and the mixture, kept uniform by stirring,

runs out at the same rate. How long will it take for the quantity of salt in the tank to become 1 kilogram?

5. Given the same data as in Exercise 4, determine how long it will take for the quantity of salt in the tank to increase from 1 kilogram to $1\frac{1}{2}$ kilograms.

6. A tank contains 100 gallons of fresh water. Brine containing 2 pounds per gallon of salt runs into the tank at the rate of 4 gallons per minute, and the mixture, kept uniform by stirring, runs out at the rate of 2 gallons per minute. Find:

a) the amount of salt present when the tank has 120 gallons of brine;

b) the concentration of salt in the tank at the end of 20 minutes.

7. A tank contains 50 liters of water. Brine containing x grams per liter of salt enters the tank at the rate of 1.5 liters per minute. The mixture, thoroughly stirred, leaves the tank at the rate of 1 liter per minute. If the concentration is to be 20 grams per liter at the end of 20 minutes, what is the value of x?

8. A tank holds 500 gallons of brine. Brine containing 2 pounds per gallon of salt flows into the tank at the rate of 5 gallons per minute, and the mixture, kept uniform, flows out at the rate of 10 gallons per minute. If the maximum amount of salt is found in the tank at the end of 20 minutes, what was the initial salt content of the tank?

9. Phosphate excretion is at a minimum at 6:00 A.M. and rises to a peak at 6:00 P.M. If the rate of excretion is

$$\frac{1}{6} + \frac{1}{3}\cos\frac{\pi}{12}(t-6)$$

grams per hour at time t hours ($0 \le t \le 24$), the body contains 400 grams of phosphate, and the patient is only allowed to drink water, what is the amount of phosphate in the patient's body at all times t?

10. Suppose in Exercise 9 that the patient is allowed three meals during the day in such a way that the body takes in phosphate at a rate given by the formula

$$i(t) = \begin{cases} 1/3 \text{ g/hr}, & 8 \le t \le 16, \\ 0 \text{ g/hr}, & \text{otherwise.} \end{cases}$$

Obtain a formula for the amount of phosphate in the patient's body at all times t. When is it at a maximum?

11. Given a one-compartment system with k constant and $i(t) = A + B\sin\omega t$, $A > B$, find a solution of the system. How does it differ from that of the system in which the input is constant and the fractional transfer coefficient is periodic [see Eq. (8)]?

REVIEW EXERCISES FOR CHAPTER 2

Find the general solution to each of Exercises 1 through 30. When an initial condition is given, find the particular solution that satisfies the condition.

1. $x\dfrac{dy}{dx} = y^2$, $y(1) = 1$

2. $\dfrac{dy}{dx} = y\sqrt{1-x}$

3. $\dfrac{dy}{dx} = \dfrac{\sqrt{1-y^2}}{x}$

4. $x\dfrac{dy}{dx} = \tan y$, $y(1) = \dfrac{\pi}{2}$

5. $\dfrac{dy}{dx} + x = x(y^2 + 1)$

6. $xy' = y(1-2y)$, $y(1) = 2$

7. $yy' = \cos x$, $y(\pi) = 0$

8. $y' = xy(2-3y)$

9. $y = xy' + \dfrac{1}{y'}$

10. $y - xy' = \sqrt{1-(y')^2}$

11. $y' - xy = 0$, $y(1) = 1$

12. $xy' - y = x$, $y(1) = 1$

13. $y' - (\sin x)y = \sin x$

14. $y' - \dfrac{1}{x}y = e^x$

15. $(1 + x^2)y' + xy = \sqrt{1 + x^2}$

16. $y' - (\cos x)y = x^2$

17. $xy' - 2y = x^2$, $y(1) = 1$

18. $xy' + (1 - x)y = xe^x$, $y(1) = e$

19. $y' - xy = \begin{cases} 1, & x \le 0 \\ 0, & x > 0 \end{cases}$

20. $y' + xy = \begin{cases} x, & x \le 1 \\ 1, & x > 1 \end{cases}$

21. $y' = \dfrac{x - y}{x + 2y}$, $y(0) = 1$

22. $xy' = 2y + \sqrt{y^2 + x^2}$

23. $xy' = -y + \sqrt{xy + 1}$

24. $xy' = \sqrt{x^2y^2 - 1} - y$, $y(1) = 2$

25. $y' = y + xy^2$

26. $y' - xy = e^x y^3$

27. $(y - e^y \sec^2 x)\,dx + (x - e^y \tan x)\,dy = 0$

28. $(2x^2y^3 - y^2)\,dx + (x^3y^2 - x)\,dy = 0$

29. $\dfrac{dy}{dx} = \dfrac{3y^4 + 3x^2y^3 - x^4y}{xy^3 - 2x^5}$

30. $\dfrac{dy}{dx} + \dfrac{x + y\sqrt{x^2 + y^2}}{y + x\sqrt{x^2 + y^2}} = 0$

31. J. H. Lambert (1728–1777) observed that very thin transparent layers of matter absorb light in direct proportion to the thickness of the layer and the amount of light incident on that layer. Express Lambert's law as a differential equation and solve it.

32. The *law of mass action* states that the velocity of a chemical reaction (at constant temperature) is proportional to the product of the concentrations of the substances that are reacting. Consider the bimolecular reaction

$$Na + Cl \rightarrow NaCl,$$

where n moles per liter of sodium, Na, are combined with m moles per liter of chlorine, Cl, to produce salt. Let $x(t)$ be the number of moles per liter that have reacted after time t. Express the law of mass action as a differential equation, and solve it assuming $n \neq m$.

33. Repeat Exercise 32 assuming $n = m$.

34. A paper mill is located next to a river having a constant flow of $1000 \, \text{m}^3/\text{sec}$. that is situated at the only inlet to a lake having a volume of $10^9 \, \text{m}^3$. Assume that at time $t = 0$, the paper mill begins pumping pollutants into the river at the rate of $1 \, \text{m}^3/\text{sec}$, and the inflow and outflow of the lake are constant. How high a concentration of pollutant is there in the lake after 10 hr? after 100 hr? after one year?

35. Assume that the paper mill in Exercise 34 stops polluting the river at the end of one hour. Find an expression for the concentration of pollutant in the lake at all time t.

36. Assume the paper mill in Exercise 34 pollutes the river for one hour each day. Find an expression for the concentration of pollutant in the lake at all time t. What is the maximum concentration that the pollution will reach in the lake?

37. A $20' \times 12' \times 8'$ room contains 5 chain smokers who are playing poker. An exhaust fan is removing $10 \, \text{ft}^3/\text{min}$ of smoky air, which is replaced by pure air seeping in under the door. Each chain smoker is contributing $0.1 \, \text{ft}^3/\text{min}$ of smoke to the room. Find an expression for the concentration of smoke in the room at all time t, assuming the room contains no smoke at time $t = 0$.

38. A 6-ft chain weighing 10 lb per foot is placed on a frictionless table so that 1 ft of chain is hanging over the edge of the table. Find an equation describing the amount of chain still on the table for all time $t \geq 0$. (*Hint*: The mass of the chain that is falling changes with time.)

*39. A power cable, hanging from fixed towers, has a weight of w lb per foot.

   a) Let $y(x)$ be the position of the cable x ft horizontally away from a tower and T_H be the horizontal component of tension in the cable. Show that

$$y'(x + \Delta x) - y'(x) = \frac{w}{T_H} \Delta s,$$

   where Δs is the length of the cable over the horizontal interval of length Δx.

   b) Use part (a), the Pythagorean theorem, and limits to deduce the differential equation

$$y'' = \frac{w}{T_H} \sqrt{1 + (y')^2}.$$

   c) Solve the differential equation in part (b) to obtain an expression for $y'(x)$, assuming $y'(0) = 0$.

   d) If $y(0) = 0$, find $y(x)$.

40. A mountain climber starts from his base camp at 6:00 A.M. As he climbs, fatigue and oxygen deprivation take their toll so that the rate at which his elevation is increasing is inversely proportional to the elevation. At noon he is at an elevation of 19,000 ft, and at 2:00 P.M. he reaches the top of the mountain at 20,000 ft. How high was his base camp?

41. We have seen that the equation

$$y' + f(x)y = 0$$

has the general solution

$$y = ce^{-\int f(x)\,dx}.$$

This fact prompted J. L. Lagrange (1736–1813) to seek a solution of the equation

$$y' + f(x)y = g(x) \tag{1}$$

of the form

$$y = c(x)e^{-\int f(x)\,dx},$$

where $c = c(x)$ is a function of x.†

---

† This technique, called the method of *variation of constants*, can be extended to equations of higher order (see Section 3.7).

a) Show that $c'(x) = g(x)e^{\int f(x)\,dx}$.

b) Integrate part (a) to obtain the general solution to Eq. (1).

42. Use the method in Exercise 41 to solve the equation

$$y' + \frac{1}{x}y = e^x.$$

43. Consider the second-order linear equation

$$y'' + 5y' + 6y = 0. \qquad (2)$$

a) Let $z = y' + 2y$. Show that Eq. (2) reduces to

$$z' + 3z = 0. \qquad (3)$$

b) Solve Eq. (3), substitute z in the equation $y' + 2y = z$, and use the methods given in Section 2.3 to obtain the solution to Eq. (2).

44. Use the procedure outlined in Exercise 43 to find the general solution to

$$y'' + (a + b)y' + aby = 0,$$

where a and b are constants. (*Hint*: Let $z = y' + ay$.)

45. Use the method given in Exercise 43 to find the general solution to

$$y'' + 2ay' + a^2y = 0, \quad a \text{ constant}.$$

46. Suppose a constant capacitor is connected in series to an emf whose voltage is a sine wave. Show that the current is 90° out of phase with the voltage.

47. Repeat Exercise 46 with the capacitor replaced by an inductor. What can you say in this case?

Linear Differential Equations

3.1 LINEARLY INDEPENDENT SOLUTIONS

Although there is no procedure for explicitly solving arbitrary differential equations, systematic methods do exist for certain classes of differential equations. In this chapter we shall study a class of differential equations for which there are always unique solutions and present some methods for calculating them.

We recall that a differential equation is *linear* if it does not involve nonlinear functions (squares, exponentials, etc.) or products of the dependent variable and its derivatives. Thus $y'' + (x^3 \sin x)^5 y' + y = \cos x^3$ is linear, while $y'' + (y')^2 + y = 0$ is nonlinear. The most general second-order linear equation is

$$y''(x) + a(x)y'(x) + b(x)y(x) = f(x), \tag{1}$$

while the most general third-order linear equation is

$$y'''(x) + a(x)y''(x) + b(x)y'(x) + c(x)y(x) = f(x). \tag{2}$$

As we saw in Section 2.3, both Eqs. (1) and (2) are special cases of the general linear nth-order equation:

$$y^{(n)}(x) + a_{n-1}(x)y^{(n-1)}(x) + \cdots + a_1(x)y'(x) + a_0(x)y(x) = f(x).$$

In Section 2.3 we saw that when $a(x)$ and $f(x)$ are continuous, the linear first-order equation

$$y'(x) + a(x)y(x) = f(x)$$

has an infinite number of solutions given by Eq. (7) in Section 2.3. However, if one condition $y(x_0) = y_0$ is given, then, as we saw in Examples 4 and 5 in Section 2.3, the equation has a unique solution. We can restate this basic fact as follows.

If $a(x)$ and $f(x)$ are continuous, then the equation $y'(x) + a(x)y(x) = f(x)$ has one and only one solution that satisfies the initial condition $y(x_0) = y_0$.

This is a very nice result, for it tells us that every linear first-order equation with a given initial condition has a solution. We need only set about finding it. It turns out that this special property holds for linear differential equations of any order. The only difference is that in order to have a unique solution to a second-order equation, we must specify two initial conditions, for a third-order equation three conditions, and so on. One case of the following central theorem will be proved in the chapter on "Existence and Uniqueness of Solutions."

Theorem 1   Let $a_1(x)$, $a_2(x)$, ..., $a_n(x)$, and $f(x)$ be continuous functions on the interval $[x_0, x_1]$, and let $c_0, c_1, c_2, \ldots, c_{n-1}$ be n given constants. Then there exists a unique function $y(x)$ that satisfies the linear differential equation

$$y^{(n)} + a_1(x)y^{(n-1)} + a_2(x)y^{(n-2)} + \cdots + a_n(x)y = f(x)$$

on $[x_0, x_1]$ *and* the n initial conditions

$$y(x_0) = c_0, \quad y'(x_0) = c_1, \quad y''(x_0) = c_2, \ldots, y^{(n-1)}(x_0) = c_{n-1} \qquad \textbf{(3)}$$

Note   The conditions given in Eq. (3) all involve evaluations of the unknown function y and its derivatives at the *same* point x_0. Conditions at more than one point may also be given: For example, the condition $y(0) = 1$, $y(1) = 2$, are called *boundary conditions* and are much more difficult to handle. (Boundary conditions are discussed in Chapters 11 and 12.)

     If we apply Theorem 1 to the second-order equation (1), we have the following result.

If $a(x)$, $b(x)$, and $f(x)$ are continuous functions, then the equation

$$y''(x) + a(x)y'(x) + b(x)y(x) = f(x)$$

has a unique solution that satisfies the conditions

$$y(x_0) = y_0, \quad y'(x_0) = y_1,$$

for any real numbers x_0, y_0, and y_1.

     For simplicity we shall limit most of our discussion in this chapter to second-order linear equations (and associated systems). We emphasize, however, that *every* result we will prove can be extended to higher-order linear equations. Some of the exercises in this chapter will present these extensions.

     In some important applications, the continuity requirements for the functions $a(x)$, $b(x)$, and $f(x)$ in Eq. (1) do not hold. For example, in the case of the equation

$$(x - 1)y'' + x^2 y' + y = 0, \quad y(0) = 1, \quad y'(0) = 0,$$

the functions $a(x)$ and $b(x)$ are $x^2/(x - 1)$ and $1/(x - 1)$, respectively, which are discontinuous at $x = 1$. There are special techniques for handling some problems of this sort, which we will discuss in Chapter 5. In the remainder of this chapter we will assume, unless otherwise stated, that all functions in each equation are continuous for all real values of x.

     If the function $f(x)$ is identically zero, we say that Eq. (1) is *homogeneous*. Otherwise, it is *nonhomogeneous*. If the coefficient functions $a(x)$ and

$b(x)$ are constants, $a(x) \equiv a$ and $b(x) \equiv b$, then the equation is said to have *constant coefficients*. As we shall see, linear differential equations with constant coefficients are the easiest to solve.

Let y_1 and y_2 be any two functions. By a *linear combination* of y_1 and y_2, we mean a function $y(x)$ that can be written in the form

$$y(x) = c_1 y_1(x) + c_2 y_2(x)$$

for some constants c_1 and c_2. Two functions are *linearly independent* on an interval $[x_0, x_1]$ whenever the relation $c_1 y_1(x) + c_2 y_2(x) = 0$ for all x in $[x_0, x_1]$ implies that $c_1 = c_2 = 0$. Otherwise, they are *linearly dependent*. There is, however, an easier way to see that two functions y_1 and y_2 are linearly dependent. If $c_1 y_1(x) + c_2 y_2(x) = 0$ (where not both c_1 and c_2 are zero), we may suppose that $c_1 \neq 0$. Then, dividing the above expression by c_1, we obtain

$$y_1(x) + \frac{c_2}{c_1} y_2(x) = 0,$$

or

$$y_1(x) = -\frac{c_2}{c_1} y_2(x) = c y_2(x).$$

Therefore,

> Two functions are linearly dependent on the interval $[x_0, x_1]$ if and only if one of the functions is a constant multiple of the other.

The notions of linear combination and linear independence are central to the theory of linear homogeneous equations, as illustrated by the results that follow.

Theorem 2   Two linearly independent solutions of Eq. (1) can always be found.

Proof   The existence part of Theorem 1 guarantees that we can find a solution $y_1(x)$ to Eq. (1) satisfying

$$y_1(x_0) = 1 \quad \text{and} \quad y_1'(x_0) = 0. \tag{4}$$

Similarly, we can also find a solution $y_2(x)$ to Eq. (1) satisfying

$$y_2(x_0) = 0 \quad \text{and} \quad y_2'(x_0) = 1. \tag{5}$$

Consider the linear combination

$$c_1 y_1(x) + c_2 y_2(x) = 0. \tag{6}$$

Setting $x = x_0$, we obtain $c_1 = 0$. Differentiating Eq. (6), we have

$$c_1 y_1'(x) + c_2 y_2'(x) = 0,$$

and evaluating this equation at $x = x_0$ yields $c_2 = 0$. Hence, both constants c_1 and c_2 in Eq. (6) must be zero, which implies that the two solutions $y_1(x)$ and $y_2(x)$ of Eq. (1) are linearly independent. ∎

Even more can be said for the homogeneous equation

$$y'' + a(x)y' + b(x)y = 0. \tag{7}$$

Theorem 3   Let $y_1(x)$ and $y_2(x)$ be any two solutions of Eq. (7). Then any linear combination of them is also a solution of Eq. (7).

Proof   Let $y(x) = c_1 y_1(x) + c_2 y_2(x)$. Then

$$y'' + ay' + by = c_1 y_1'' + c_2 y_2'' + c_1 a y_1' + c_2 a y_2' + c_1 b y_1 + c_2 b y_2$$
$$= c_1(y_1'' + ay_1' + by_1) + c_2(y_2'' + ay_2' + by_2) = 0,$$

since y_1 and y_2 are solutions of the homogeneous equation (7). ∎

Combining Theorems 2 and 3, we have the following theorem.

Theorem 4   Let y be the unique solution of Eq. (7) that satisfies the initial conditions $y(x_0) = c_1$ and $y'(x_0) = c_2$. If y_1 and y_2 are the solutions of Eq. (7) that satisfy the initial conditions in Eqs. (4) and (5), respectively, then

$$y(x) = c_1 y_1(x) + c_2 y_2(x).$$

In other words, *any solution of Eq. (7) can be represented as a linear combination of these two special solutions.*

Proof   Let $Y(x) = c_1 y_1(x) + c_2 y_2(x)$. By Theorem 3, we have that $Y(x)$ is a solution to Eq. (1). Also,

$$Y(x_0) = c_1 y_1(x_0) + c_2 y_2(x_0) = c_1 \cdot 1 + c_2 \cdot 0 = c_1,$$

and

$$Y'(x_0) = c_1 y_1'(x_0) + c_2 y_2'(x_0) = c_1 \cdot 0 + c_2 \cdot 1 = c_2.$$

Thus $y(x)$ and $Y(x)$ both satisfy the same second-order equation and the same initial conditions. By the uniqueness guaranteed in Theorem 1, $Y(x) = y(x)$. ∎

In the next section we will prove that *any* pair of linearly independent solutions of Eq. (7) can be used to determine any other solution. What is remarkable about this fact is that *once we have found two linearly independent solutions y_1 and y_2 of Eq. (7), we have "essentially" found all* *the solutions of Eq.* (7). That is, the *general solution* of Eq. (7) is given by the linear combination

$$y(x) = c_1 y_1(x) + c_2 y_2(x),$$

where c_1 and c_2 are arbitrary constants.

EXERCISES 3.1

In Exercises 1 through 10, determine whether the given equation is linear or nonlinear. If it is linear, state whether it is homogeneous or nonhomogeneous with constant or variable coefficients.

1. $y'' + 2x^3 y' + y = 0$
2. $y'' + 2y' + y^2 = x$
3. $y'' + 3y' + yy' = 0$
4. $y'' + 3y' + 4y = 0$
5. $y'' + 3y' + 4y = \sin x$
6. $y'' + y(2 + 3y) = e^x$
7. $y'' + 4xy' + 2x^3 y = e^{2x}$
8. $y'' + \sin(xe^x)y' + 4xy = 0$
9. $3y'' + 16y' + 2y = 0$
10. $yy'y'' = 1$

The functions $y_1(x), y_2(x), \ldots, y_n(x)$ are *linearly independent* on an interval $[x_0, x_1]$

$$c_1 y_1(x) + c_2 y_2(x) + \cdots + c_n y_n(x) = 0,$$

for all x in $[x_0, x_1]$, implies that $c_1 = c_2 = \cdots = c_n = 0$. What is the maximum number of functions that can be linearly independent in each of the following exercises?

11. $y_0 = 1$, $y_1 = 1 + x$, $y_2 = x^2$,
    $y_3 = x(1 - x)$, $y_4 = x$
12. $y_0 = \sin^2 x$, $y_1 = 1$, $y_2 = \sin x \cos x$,
    $y_3 = \cos^2 x$, $y_4 = \sin 2x$
13. $y_0 = 1 + x$, $y_1 = 1 - x$, $y_2 = 1$,
    $y_3 = x^2$, $y_4 = 1 + x^2$
14. $y_0 = 2\cos^2 x - 1$, $y_1 = \cos^2 x - \sin^2 x$,
    $y_2 = 1 - 2\sin^2 x$, $y_3 = \cos 2x$

In Exercises 15 through 18, test each of the functions 1, x, x^2, and x^3 to see which functions satisfy the given differential equation. Then construct the *general solution* to the equation by writing a linear combination of the linearly independent solutions you have found.

15. $y'' = 0$
16. $y''' = 0$
17. $xy'' - y' = 0$
18. $x^2 y'' - 2xy' + 2y = 0$

19. Let $y_1(x)$ be a solution of the homogeneous equation

$$y'' + a(x)y' + b(x)y = 0$$

on the interval $\alpha \le x \le \beta$. Suppose that the curve y_1 is tangent to the x-axis at some point of this interval. Prove that y_1 must be identically zero.

20. Let $y_1(x)$ and $y_2(x)$ be two nonzero solutions of the homogeneous equation

$$y'' + a(x)y' + b(x)y = 0$$

on the interval $\alpha \le x \le \beta$. Suppose $y_1(x_0) = y_2(x_0) = 0$ for some point $\alpha \le x_0 \le \beta$. Show that y_2 is a constant multiple of y_1.

21. Show that the solutions y_1, y_2, and y_3 of the linear third-order differential equation

$$y''' + a_1(x)y'' + a_2(x)y' + a_3(x)y = 0$$

that satisfy the conditions

$$y_1(x_0) = 1, \quad y_1'(x_0) = 0, \quad y_1''(x_0) = 0,$$
$$y_2(x_0) = 0, \quad y_2'(x_0) = 1, \quad y_2''(x_0) = 0,$$

and

$$y_3(x_0) = 0, \quad y_3'(x_0) = 0, \quad y_3''(x_0) = 1,$$

respectively, are linearly independent.

22. Show that *any* solution of

$$y''' + a_1(x)y'' + a_2(x)y' + a_3(x)y = 0$$

can be expressed as a linear combination of the solutions y_1, y_2, y_3 given in Exercise 21. [*Hint:* If $y(x_0) = c_1, y'(x_0) = c_2$, and $y''(x_0) = c_3$, consider the linear combination $c_1 y_1 + c_2 y_2 + c_3 y_3$.]

3.2 PROPERTIES OF SOLUTIONS TO THE LINEAR EQUATION

In this section we will lay the theoretical groundwork for the remainder of the material in this chapter. Consider the homogeneous equation

$$y'' + a(x)y' + b(x)y = 0. \tag{1}$$

We shall assume throughout this section that $a(x)$ and $b(x)$ are continuous so that our basic existence–uniqueness theorem (Theorem 1 in Section 3.1) applies. The definitions and terminology we will introduce are applicable to higher-order equations as well as to the second-order equation (Eq. (1) above) in question. Higher-order equations are considered in Exercises 8 through 14.

Let y_1 and y_2 be two linearly independent solutions of Eq. (1). We will show that *any other solution of Eq. (1) can be written as a linear combination of y_1 and y_2*. This remarkable fact means that once we have found two linearly independent solutions of Eq. (1), we have "essentially" found *all* its solutions. However, before proving this claim, we introduce a new function that will be very useful in our calculations.

Let $y_1(x)$ and $y_2(x)$ be any two solutions to Eq. (1). The *Wronskian* of y_1 and y_2, $W(y_1, y_2)$, is defined as

$$W(y_1, y_2)(x) = y_1(x)y_2'(x) - y_1'(x)y_2(x). \tag{2}$$

Using the product rule of differentiation on Eq. (2), we see that

$$W'(y_1, y_2) = y_1y_2'' + y_1'y_2' - y_1'y_2' - y_1''y_2$$
$$= y_1y_2'' - y_1''y_2.$$

Since y_1 and y_2 are solutions of Eq. (1),

$$y_1'' + ay_1' + by_1 = 0 \qquad \text{and} \qquad y_2'' + ay_2' + by_2 = 0.$$

Multiplying the first of these equations by y_2 and the second by y_1 and subtracting, we obtain

$$y_1y_2'' - y_2y_1'' + a(y_1y_2' - y_2y_1') = 0,$$

which is just

$$W' + aW = 0. \tag{3}$$

By the methods given in Section 2.3, we see that the solution of Eq. (3) can be written as

$$W(y_1, y_2) = ce^{-\int a(x)\,dx} \tag{4}$$

for some arbitrary constant c. Equation (4) is known as *Abel's formula*.

Since an exponential is never zero, we see that $W(y_1, y_2)$ is either always zero (when $c = 0$) or never zero (when $c \neq 0$). The importance of this fact is given by the following lemma.

Lemma 1 The solutions $y_1(x)$ and $y_2(x)$ of Eq. (1) are linearly independent on $[x_0, x_1]$ if and only if $W(y_1, y_2) \neq 0$.

Proof We first show that if $W(y_1, y_2) = 0$, then y_1 and y_2 are linearly dependent. Let x_2 be a point in the interval $x_0 \leqslant x \leqslant x_1$. Consider the system of equations

$$c_1 y_1(x_2) + c_2 y_2(x_2) = 0,$$
$$c_1 y_1'(x_2) + c_2 y_2'(x_2) = 0. \tag{5}$$

The determinant of the system (5) is

$$y_1(x_2) y_2'(x_2) - y_2(x_2) y_1'(x_2) = W(y_1, y_2)(x_2) = 0.$$

Thus according to the theory of determinants (see Appendix 4), there exists a solution (c_1, c_2) for Eqs. (5) where c_1 and c_2 are not both equal to zero. Define $y(x) = c_1 y_1(x) + c_2 y_2(x)$. By Theorem 1 in Section 3.1, $y(x)$ is a solution of Eqs. (5). Then since c_1 and c_2 solve Eqs. (5),

$$y(x_2) = c_1 y_1(x_2) + c_2 y_2(x_2) = 0$$

and

$$y'(x_2) = c_1 y_1'(x_2) + c_2 y_2'(x_2) = 0.$$

Thus $y(x)$ solves the initial value problem

$$y'' + a(x)y' + b(x)y = 0, \quad y(x_2) = y'(x_2) = 0.$$

But this initial value problem also has the solution $y_3(x) \equiv 0$ for all values of x in $x_0 \leqslant x \leqslant x_1$. By Theorem 1 in Section 3.1 the solution of this initial value problem is unique so that necessarily $y(x) = y_3(x) = 0$. Thus

$$y(x) = c_1 y_1(x) + c_2 y_2(x) = 0,$$

for all values of x in $x_0 \leqslant x \leqslant x_1$, which proves that y_1 and y_2 are linearly dependent.

We now assume that $W(y_1, y_2) \neq 0$ in $[x_0, x_1]$ and shall prove that y_1 and y_2 are linearly independent. If y_1 and y_2 are not linearly independent, then there is a constant c such that $y_2 = cy_1$ or $y_1 = cy_2$. Assume that $y_2 = cy_1$. Then $y_2' = cy_1'$ and

$$W(y_1, y_2) = y_1 y_2' - y_1' y_2 = y_1(cy_1') - y_1'(cy_1) = 0.$$

But this contradicts the assumption that $W \neq 0$. Hence the solutions y_1 and y_2 must be independent. ∎

Example 1 Consider the equation $x'' + x = 0$. It is easy to verify that $x_1 = \cos t$ and $x_2 = \sin t$ are solutions. The Wronskian

$$W(x_1, x_2) = \cos t \cos t - \sin t(-\sin t) = \cos^2 t + \sin^2 t = 1,$$

so the solutions are linearly independent.

Using Lemma 1, we can prove the basic theorem mentioned above.

Theorem 2 Let $y_1(x)$ and $y_2(x)$ be two linearly independent solutions to Eq. (1) on the interval $[x_0, x_1]$ and let $y(x)$ be any other solution. Then $y(x)$ can be written as a linear combination of y_1 and y_2.

Proof Let $y(x_0) = a$ and $y'(x_0) = b$. Consider the linear system of equations in two unknowns c_1 and c_2:

$$y_1(x_0)c_1 + y_2(x_0)c_2 = a,$$
$$y_1'(x_0)c_1 + y_2'(x_0)c_2 = b. \tag{6}$$

As we saw earlier, the determinant of this system is $W(y_1, y_2)(x_0)$, which is nonzero since the solutions are linearly independent. Thus there is a unique solution (c_1, c_2) to Eqs. (6) and a solution $y^*(x) = c_1y_1(x) + c_2y_2(x)$ that satisfies the conditions $y^*(x_0) = a$ and $y^{*\prime}(x_0) = b$. Since every initial value problem has a unique solution (see Theorem 1 in Section 3.1), it must follow that $y(x) = y^*(x)$ on the interval $x_0 \leq x \leq x_1$, and so the proof is complete. ∎

In the above theorem, we showed that *every* solution can be written as a linear combination of linearly independent solutions. Therefore, we can talk about the general solution to Eq. (1). Let y_1 and y_2 be linearly independent solutions of Eq. (1). Then the *general solution* is given by

$$y(x) = c_1y_1(x) + c_2y_2(x),$$

where c_1 and c_2 are arbitrary constants.

We now turn briefly to the nonhomogeneous equation

$$y'' + a(x)y' + b(x)y = f(x). \tag{7}$$

Let y_p be any solution to Eq. (7). If we know the general solution to the homogeneous equation

$$y'' + a(x)y' + b(x)y = 0, \tag{8}$$

we can find all solutions to Eq. (7).

Theorem 3 Let $y_p(x)$ be a solution of Eq. (7) and let $y^*(x)$ be any other solution. Then $y^*(x) - y_p(x)$ is a solution of Eq. (8); that is,

$$y^*(x) = c_1y_1(x) + c_2y_2(x) + y_p(x)$$

for some constants c_1 and c_2, where y_1, y_2 are two linearly independent solutions of Eq. (8).

Proof   We have

$$(y^* - y_p)'' + a(y^* - y_p)' + b(y^* - y_p)$$
$$= (y^{*''} + ay^{*'} + by^*) - (y_p'' + ay_p' + by_p)$$
$$= f - f = 0. \blacksquare$$

Thus *in order to find all solutions to the nonhomogeneous problem, we need only find one solution to the nonhomogeneous problem and the general solution of the homogeneous problem.*

Example 2   It is easy to verify that $\frac{1}{2}te^t$ is a particular solution of $x'' - x = e^t$. Two linearly independent solutions of $x'' - x = 0$ are given by $x_1 = e^t$ and $x_2 = e^{-t}$. The general solution is therefore $x(t) = \frac{1}{2}te^t + c_1e^t + c_2e^{-t}$. Note that x_1 and x_2 are independent since $W(x_1, x_2) = e^t(-e^{-t}) - e^{-t}(e^t) = -2$.

In the next three sections we will present two methods for finding the general solution of the homogeneous problem. In Sections 3.6 and 3.7 techniques for obtaining the solution of the nonhomogeneous problem will be developed.

EXERCISES 3.2

1. a) Show that $y_1(x) = \sin x^2$ and $y_2(x) = \cos x^2$ are linearly independent solutions of

$$xy'' - y' + 4x^3y = 0.$$

  b) Calculate $W(y_1, y_2)$ and show that it is zero when $x = 0$. Does this result contradict Lemma 1? [*Hint*: In Lemma 1, as elsewhere in this section, it is assumed that $a(x)$ and $b(x)$ are continuous.]

2. Show that two solutions $y_1(x)$ and $y_2(x)$ to Eq. (1) are linearly dependent if and only if one is a constant multiple of the other.

3. Show that

$$y_1(x) = \sin x \quad \text{and} \quad y_2(x) = 4\sin x - 2\cos x$$

are linearly independent solutions of $y'' + y = 0$. Write the solution $y_3(x) = \cos x$ as a linear combination of y_1 and y_2.

4. Prove that $e^x \sin x$ and $e^x \cos x$ are linearly independent solutions of the equation

$$y'' - 2y' + 2y = 0.$$

a) Find a solution that satisfies the conditions $y(0) = 1$, $y'(0) = 4$.

b) Find another pair of linearly independent solutions.

5. Assume that some nonzero solution of

$$y'' + a(x)y' + b(x)y = 0, \quad y(0) = 0,$$

vanishes at some point x_1, where $x_1 > 0$. Prove that any other solution vanishes at $x = x_1$.

6. Define the function $s(x)$ to be the unique solution of the initial value problem

$$y'' + y = 0; \quad y(0) = 0, \quad y'(0) = 1,$$

and the function $c(x)$ as the solution of

$$y'' + y = 0; \quad y(0) = 1, \quad y'(0) = 0.$$

Without using trigonometry, prove that:

a) $\dfrac{ds}{dx} = c(x);$ b) $\dfrac{dc}{dx} = -s(x);$

c) $s^2 + c^2 = 1.$

7. a) Show that $y_1 = \sin \ln x^2$ and $y_2 = \cos \ln x^2$ are linearly independent solutions to

$$y'' + \frac{1}{x}y' + \frac{4}{x^2}y = 0 \quad (x > 0).$$

b) Calculate $W(y_1, y_2)$.

8. Consider the third-order equation

$$y''' + a(x)y'' + b(x)y' + c(x)y = 0,$$

where a, b, and c are continuous functions of x in some interval I. Prove that if $y_1(x)$, $y_2(x)$, and $y_3(x)$ are solutions to the equation, then so is any linear combination of them.

9. In Exercise 8 define the Wronskian $W(y_1, y_2, y_3)$ by the determinant

$$W(y_1, y_2, y_3)(x) = \begin{vmatrix} y_1 & y_2 & y_3 \\ y_1' & y_2' & y_3' \\ y_1'' & y_2'' & y_3'' \end{vmatrix}.$$

a) Show that W satisfies the differential equation

$$W'(x) = -a(x)W.$$

b) Prove that $W(y_1, y_2, y_3)(x)$ is either always zero or never zero.

10. a) Prove that the solutions $y_1(x)$, $y_2(x)$, $y_3(x)$ of the equation in Exercise 8 are linearly independent on $[x_0, x_1]$ if and only if $W(y_1, y_2, y_3) \neq 0$. (This is the analogue of Lemma 1 for third-order equations.)

b) Show that $\sin t$, $\cos t$, and e^t are linearly independent solutions of

$$y''' - y'' + y' - y = 0$$

on any interval (a, b) where $-\infty < a < b < \infty$.

11. Using the result of Exercise 10, find the unique solution to $y''' - y'' + y' - y = 0$ that satisfies the initial conditions $y(0) = 1$, $y'(0) = 0$, $y''(0) = 4$.

12. Show that if $y_1(x)$, $y_2(x)$, and $y_3(x)$ are three linearly independent solutions to the homogeneous equation of Exercise 8, then any other solution can be written as a linear combination of them.

13. Assume that $y_1(x)$ and $y_2(x)$ are two solutions to

$$y''' + a(x)y'' + b(x)y' + c(x)y = f(x).$$

Prove that $y_3(x) = y_1(x) - y_2(x)$ is a solution of the associated homogeneous equation.

*14. Generalize the results of Exercises 8, 9, 10(a), 12, and 13 for the nth-order linear equation

$$y^{(n)} + a_{n-1}(x)y^{(n-1)} + a_{n-2}(x)y^{(n-2)} + \cdots +$$
$$a_1(x)y' + a_0(x)y = f(x),$$

where the functions $a_i(x)$, $i = 0, 1, \ldots, n - 1$, are continuous on some interval I.

15. Let $y_1(x)$ be a solution of the equation

$$y'' + a(x)y' + b(x)y = f_1(x),$$

and let $y_2(x)$ be a solution of the equation

$$y'' + a(x)y' + b(x)y = f_2(x).$$

Show that $y_3(x) = y_1(x) + y_2(x)$ is a solution of the equation

$$y'' + a(x)y' + b(x)y = f_1(x) + f_2(x).$$

This important relation is called the *principle of superposition.*

3.3 USING ONE SOLUTION TO FIND ANOTHER

As we saw in Theorem 2 in Section 3.2, it is easy to write down the general solution of the homogeneous equation

$$y'' + a(x)y' + b(x)y = 0, \tag{1}$$

provided we know two linearly independent solutions y_1 and y_2 of Eq. (1). The general solution is then given by

$$y = c_1y_1 + c_2y_2,$$

where c_1 and c_2 are arbitrary constants. Unfortunately, there is no general procedure for determining y_1 and y_2. However, a standard procedure does exist for finding y_2 when y_1 is known. This method is of considerable importance, since it is often possible to find one solution by inspecting the equation or by trial and error.

We assume that y_1 is a nonzero solution of Eq. (1) and seek another solution y_2 such that y_1 and y_2 are linearly independent. If it can be found, then

$$\frac{y_2}{y_1} = v(x)$$

must be a nonconstant function of x, and $y_2 = vy_1$ must satisfy Eq. (1). Thus

$$(vy_1)'' + a(vy_1)' + b(vy_1) = 0$$

or, after differentiations and factoring,

$$v(y_1'' + ay_1' + by_1) + v'(2y_1' + ay_1) + v''y_1 = 0. \tag{2}$$

The first term in parentheses in Eq. (2) vanishes since y_1 is a solution of Eq. (1), so we obtain the equation

$$v''y_1 + v'(2y_1' + ay_1) = 0.$$

Dividing by $v'y_1$, we can rewrite this equation in the form

$$\frac{v''}{v'} = -2\frac{y_1'}{y_1} - a. \tag{3}$$

Setting $z = v'$ and integrating Eq. (3), we find that

$$\ln z = -2\ln y_1 - \int a(x)\,dx,$$

so that

$$v' = \frac{1}{y_1^2} e^{-\int a(x)\,dx}.$$

Since the exponential is never zero, v is nonconstant. To find v, we perform another integration and obtain

$$y_2 = vy_1 = y_1(x) \int \frac{e^{-\int a(x)\,dx}}{y_1^2(x)}\,dx. \tag{4}$$

We shall make frequent use of formula (4) in later chapters; the following examples are illustrations of how it can be used.

Example 1   Note that $y_1 = x$ is a solution of

$$x^2y'' - xy' + y = 0, \quad x > 0. \tag{5}$$

To find y_2, we rewrite Eq. (5) as

$$y'' - \left(\frac{1}{x}\right)y' + \left(\frac{1}{x^2}\right)y = 0.$$

Then $\int a(x)\, dx = -\ln x$, so that using formula (4), we have

$$y_2 = x\int \frac{x}{x^2}\, dx = x \ln x.$$

Thus the general solution of Eq. (5) is $y = c_1 x + c_2 x \ln x,\ x > 0$.

Example 2   Consider the *Legendre equation of order one*:

$$(1 - x^2)y'' - 2xy' + 2y = 0, \quad -1 < x < 1, \tag{6}$$

or

$$y'' - \frac{2x}{1 - x^2}\, y' + \frac{2y}{1 - x^2} = 0.$$

It is easy to verify that $y_1 = x$ is a solution. To find y_2, we note that $\int a(x)\, dx = \ln(1 - x^2)$, so that by Eq. (4)

$$y_2 = x\int \frac{e^{-\ln(1-x^2)}}{x^2}\, dx = x\int \frac{dx}{x^2(1 - x^2)}$$

$$= x\int \left(\frac{1}{x^2} + \frac{1}{1 - x^2}\right) dx = x\left[-\frac{1}{x} + \frac{1}{2}\ln\left(\frac{1 + x}{1 - x}\right)\right]$$

$$= \frac{x}{2}\ln\left(\frac{1 + x}{1 - x}\right) - 1.$$

Note that in this example y_2 is defined in $-1 < x < 1$ even though $v(0)$ is undefined.

EXERCISES 3.3

In each of Exercises 1 through 10 a second-order differential equation and one solution $y_1(x)$ are given. Verify that $y_1(x)$ is indeed a solution and find a second, linearly independent solution.

1. $y'' - 2y' + y = 0, \quad y_1(x) = e^x$

2. $y'' - 2xy' + 2y = 0, \quad y_1(x) = x$

3. $y'' - \left(\frac{2x}{1 - x^2}\right)y' + \left(\frac{6}{1 - x^2}\right)y = 0, \quad (|x| < 1)$

$$y_1(x) = \frac{3x^2 - 1}{2}$$

(This equation is called the *Legendre differential*

equation of order two.)

4. $y'' + \left(\frac{3}{x}\right)y' = 0, \quad y_1(x) = 1$

5. $x^2 y'' + xy' - 4y = 0, \quad y_1(x) = x^2$

[*Hint*: Divide by x^2 first.]

6. $x^2 y'' - 2xy' + (x^2 + 2)y = 0, \quad (x > 0),$
$y_1 = x \sin x$

7. $xy'' + (2x - 1)y' - 2y = 0, \quad (x > 0),\ y_1 = e^{-2x}$

8. $xy'' + (x - 1)y' + (3 - 12x)y = 0, \quad (x > 0),$
$y_1 = e^{3x}$

9. $xy'' - y' + 4x^3 y = 0, \quad (x > 0),\ y_1 = \sin(x^2)$

10. $x^{1/3}y'' + y' + \left(\dfrac{1}{4}x^{-1/3} - \dfrac{1}{6x} - 6x^{-5/3}\right)y = 0,$

$\quad y_1 = x^3 e^{-3x^{2/3}/4} \quad (x > 0)$

11. The *Bessel* differential equation is given by

$$x^2 y'' + xy' + (x^2 - p^2)y = 0.$$

For $p = \frac{1}{2}$, verify that $y_1(x) = (\sin x)/\sqrt{x}$ is a solution for $x > 0$. Find a second, linearly independent solution.

12. Letting $p = 0$ in the equation of Exercise 11, we obtain the *Bessel* differential equation of index zero that we will study in Chapter 5. One solution is the *Bessel function of order zero* denoted by $J_0(x)$. In terms of $J_0(x)$, find a second, linearly independent solution.

*13. Consider the third-order equation

$$y''' + a(x)y'' + b(x)y' + c(x)y = 0$$

and let $y_1(x)$ and $y_2(x)$ be two linearly independent

solutions. Define $y_3(x) = v(x)y_1(x)$ and assume that $y_3(x)$ is a solution to the equation.

   a) Find a second-order differential equation that is satisfied by v'.

   b) Show that $(y_2/y_1)'$ is a solution of this equation.

   c) Use the result of part (b) to find a second, linearly independent solution of the equation derived in part (a).

14. Consider the equation

$$y''' - \left(\frac{3}{x^2}\right)y' + \left(\frac{3}{x^3}\right)y = 0 \quad (x > 0).$$

   a) Show that $y_1(x) = x$ and $y_2(x) = x^3$ are two linearly independent solutions.

   b) Use the results of Exercise 13 to get a third, linearly independent solution.

3.4 HOMOGENEOUS EQUATIONS WITH CONSTANT COEFFICIENTS: REAL ROOTS

In this section we shall present a simple procedure for finding the general solution to the linear homogeneous equation with constant coefficients

$$y'' + ay' + by = 0. \tag{1}$$

We recall that for the comparable first-order equation $y' + ay = 0$ the general solution is $y(x) = ce^{-ax}$. It is then not implausible to "guess" that there may be a solution to Eq. (1) of the form $y(x) = e^{\lambda x}$ for some number λ (real or complex). Setting $y(x) = e^{\lambda x}$, we obtain $y' = \lambda e^{\lambda x}$ and $y'' = \lambda^2 e^{\lambda x}$ so that Eq. (1) yields

$$\lambda^2 e^{\lambda x} + a\lambda e^{\lambda x} + be^{\lambda x} = 0.$$

Since $e^{\lambda x} \neq 0$, we can divide this equation by $e^{\lambda x}$ to obtain

$$\boxed{\lambda^2 + a\lambda + b = 0,} \tag{2}$$

where a and b are real numbers. Equation (2) is called the *characteristic equation* of the differential equation (1). It is clear that if λ satisfies Eq. (2), then $y(x) = e^{\lambda x}$ is a solution to Eq. (1). As we saw in Section 3.2, we need only obtain two linearly independent solutions. Equation (2) has the roots

$$\lambda_1 = \frac{-a + \sqrt{a^2 - 4b}}{2} \quad \text{and} \quad \lambda_2 = \frac{-a - \sqrt{a^2 - 4b}}{2}. \tag{3}$$

There are three possibilities: $a^2 - 4b > 0$, $a^2 - 4b = 0$, $a^2 - 4b < 0$.

CASE 1   If $a^2 - 4b > 0$, then λ_1 and λ_2 are distinct real numbers (given by Eq. (3)) and $y_1(x) = e^{\lambda_1 x}$ and $y_2 = e^{\lambda_2 x}$ are distinct solutions.

These two solutions are linearly independent because

$$\frac{y_1}{y_2} = e^{(\lambda_1 - \lambda_2)x},$$

which is clearly not a constant when $\lambda_1 \neq \lambda_2$. Thus we have proved the following theorem.

Theorem 1   If $a^2 - 4b > 0$, then the general solution to Eq. (1) is given by

$$\boxed{y(x) = c_1 e^{\lambda_1 x} + c_2 e^{\lambda_2 x},}$$ **(4)**

where c_1 and c_2 are arbitrary constants and λ_1 and λ_2 are the real roots of Eq. (2).

Example 1   Consider the equation

$$y'' + 3y' - 10y = 0.$$

The characteristic equation is $\lambda^2 + 3\lambda - 10 = 0$, $a^2 - 4b = 49$, and the roots are $\lambda_1 = 2$ and $\lambda_2 = -5$ (the order in which the roots are taken is irrelevant). The general solution is

$$y(x) = c_1 e^{2x} + c_2 e^{-5x}.$$

If we specify the initial conditions $y(0) = 1$ and $y'(0) = 3$, for example, then differentiating and substituting $x = 0$ we obtain the simultaneous equations

$$c_1 + c_2 = 1,$$
$$2c_1 - 5c_2 = 3,$$

which have the unique solution $c_1 = \frac{8}{7}$ and $c_2 = -\frac{1}{7}$. The unique solution to the initial value problem is therefore

$$y(x) = \tfrac{1}{7}(8e^{2x} - e^{-5x}).$$

CASE 2   Suppose $a^2 - 4b = 0$. In this case Eq. (2) has the double root $\lambda_1 = \lambda_2 = -a/2$. Thus $y_1(x) = e^{-ax/2}$ is a solution of Eq. (1). To find the second solution y_2, we make use of Eq. (4) of Section 3.3 since one solution is known:

$$y_2 = y_1 \int \frac{e^{-ax}}{y_1^2}\, dx = e^{-ax/2} \int dx = xe^{-ax/2}.$$

Since $y_2/y_1 = x$, it follows that y_1 and y_2 are linearly independent. Hence we have the following result.

Theorem 2   If $a^2 - 4b = 0$, then the general solution to Eq. (1) is given by

$$y(x) = c_1 e^{-(a/2)x} + c_2 x e^{-(a/2)x},$$

where c_1 and c_2 are arbitrary constants.

Example 2   Consider the equation

$$y'' - 6y' + 9 = 0.$$

The characteristic equation is $\lambda^2 - 6\lambda + 9 = 0$, and $a^2 - 4b = 0$, yielding the unique double root $\lambda_1 = -a/2 = 3$. The general solution is

$$y(x) = c_1 e^{3x} + c_2 x e^{3x}.$$

If we use the initial conditions $y(0) = 1$, $y'(0) = 3$, we obtain the simultaneous equations

$$c_1 = 1,$$
$$3c_1 + c_2 = 3,$$

which yield the unique solution

$$y(x) = e^{3x}.$$

We will deal with the more complicated situation of complex roots $(a^2 - 4b < 0)$ in the next section.

EXERCISES 3.4

In Exercises 1 through 20, find the general solution of each equation. When initial conditions are specified, give the particular solution that satisfies them.

1. $y'' - 4y = 0$

2. $x'' + x' - 6x = 0$, $x(0) = 0$, $x'(0) = 5$

3. $y'' - 3y' + 2y = 0$

4. $y'' + 5y' + 6y = 0$, $y(0) = 1$, $y'(0) = 2$

5. $4x'' + 20x' + 25x = 0$, $x(0) = 1$, $x'(0) = 2$

6. $y'' + 6y' + 9y = 0$

7. $x'' - x' - 6x = 0$, $x(0) = -1$, $x'(0) = 1$

8. $y'' - 8y' + 16y = 0$, $y(0) = 2$, $y'(0) = -1$

9. $y'' - 5y' = 0$

10. $y'' + 17y' = 0$, $y(0) = 1$, $y'(0) = 0$

11. $y'' + 2\pi y' + \pi^2 y = 0$

12. $y'' - 13y' + 42y = 0$

13. $z'' + 2z' - 15z = 0$

14. $w'' + 8w' + 12w = 0$

15. $y'' - 8y' + 16y = 0$, $y(0) = 1$, $y'(0) = 6$

16. $y'' + 2y' + y = 0$, $y(1) = 2/e$, $y'(1) = -3/e$

17. $y'' - 2y = 0$

18. $y'' + 6y' + 5y = 0$

19. $y'' - 5y = 0$, $y(0) = 3$, $y'(0) = -\sqrt{5}$

20. $y'' - 2y' - 2y = 0$, $y(0) = 1$, $y'(0) = 1 + 3\sqrt{3}$

21. Consider the linear third-order homogeneous

equation with constant coefficients

$$y''' + ay'' + by' + cy = 0.$$

a) Show that $e^{\lambda x}$ is a solution if λ satisfies the characteristic equation

$$\lambda^3 + a\lambda^2 + b\lambda + c = 0.$$

b) Show that if the roots λ_1, λ_2, λ_3 of the characteristic equation are distinct, then $y_1 = e^{\lambda_1 x}$, $y_2 = e^{\lambda_2 x}$, and $y_3 = e^{\lambda_3 x}$ are linearly independent solutions of the equation (see Exercise 10 in Section 3.2). According to the result of Exercise 12 in Section 3.2, what is the general solution to the equation in this case?

c) Given that λ_1 is a double root, prove that $y_1(x) = e^{\lambda_1 x}$, $y_2(x) = xe^{\lambda_1 x}$, and $y_3(x) = e^{\lambda_2 x}$ are linearly independent solutions. What is the general solution?

d) Given that λ_1 is a triple root [that is, $\lambda^3 + a\lambda^2 + b\lambda + c = (\lambda - \lambda_1)^3$], show that $y_1(x) = e^{\lambda_1 x}$, $y_2(x) = xe^{\lambda_1 x}$, $y_3(x) = x^2 e^{\lambda_1 x}$ are linearly independent solutions. What is the general solution? (Note that the solution $x^2 e^{\lambda_1 x}$ can be derived from the solutions $e^{\lambda_1 x}$ and $xe^{\lambda_1 x}$ by using the technique outlined in Exercise 13 in Section 3.3.)

In Exercises 22 through 32, use the technique outlined in Exercise 13 to find the general solution for each of the given differential equations. Find a particular solution when indicated.

22. $y''' - y'' - y' + y = 0$

23. $y''' - 3y'' + 3y' - y = 0$, $y(0) = 1$, $y'(0) = 2$, $y''(0) = 3$

24. $x''' + 5x'' - x' - 5x = 0$

25. $y''' - 9y' = 0$, $y(0) = 3$, $y'(0) = 0$, $y''(0) = 18$

26. $y''' - 6y'' + 3y' + 10y = 0$

27. $y^{(4)} = 0$

28. $y^{(4)} - 9y'' = 0$

29. $y^{(4)} - 5y'' + 4y = 0$

30. $y^{(5)} - 2y''' + y' = 0$

31. $y^{(4)} - 4y'' = 0$, $y(0) = 1$, $y'(0) = 3$, $y''(0) = 0$, $y'''(0) = 16$

32. $y^{(4)} - 10y'' + 9y = 0$, $y(0) = 3$, $y'(0) = 9$, $y''(0) = 11$, $y'''(0) = 81$

Linear second-order differential equations may also be used in finding the solution to the *Riccati equation*:

$$y' + y^2 + a(x)y + b(x) = 0. \tag{5}$$

This nonlinear first-order equation frequently occurs in physical applications. To change Eq. (5) into a linear second-order equation, let $y = z'/z$. Then $y' = (z''/z) - (z'/z)^2$, so Eq. (5) becomes

$$\frac{z''}{z} - \left(\frac{z'}{z}\right)^2 + \left(\frac{z'}{z}\right)^2 + a(x)\left(\frac{z'}{z}\right) + b(x) = 0.$$

Multiplying by z, we obtain the linear second-order equation

$$z'' + a(x)z' + b(x)z = 0. \tag{6}$$

If the general solution to Eq. (6) can be found, the quotient $y = z'/z$ is the general solution to Eq. (5).

33. Suppose $z = c_1 z_1 + c_2 z_2$ is the general solution to Eq. (6). Explain why the quotient z'/z involves only one arbitrary constant. [*Hint*: Divide numerator and denominator by c_1.]

34. For arbitrary constants a, b, and c, find the substitution that changes the nonlinear equation

$$y' + ay^2 + by + c = 0$$

into a linear second-order equation with constant coefficients. What second-order equation is obtained?

Use the method above to find the general solution to the Riccati equations in Exercises 35 through 40. If an initial condition is specified, give the particular solution that satisfies that condition.

35. $y' + y^2 - 1 = 0$, $y(0) = -\frac{1}{3}$

36. $\dfrac{dx}{dt} + x^2 + 1 = 0$

37. $y' + y^2 - 2y + 1 = 0$

38. $y' + y^2 + 3y + 2 = 0$, $y(0) = 1$

39. $y' + y^2 - y - 2 = 0$

40. $y' + y^2 + 2y + 1 = 0$, $y(1) = 0$

3.5 HOMOGENEOUS EQUATIONS WITH CONSTANT COEFFICIENTS: COMPLEX ROOTS

Before dealing with the remaining case, let us briefly review some facts about complex numbers. A *complex number* z is any expression of the form $z = \alpha + i\beta$, where α and β are real and $i^2 = -1$. If $\beta = 0$, then z is a real number, whereas if $\alpha = 0$ and $\beta \neq 0$, then z is a *pure imaginary* number. Any complex number z can be represented as a vector in the xy-plane where α equals the x-coordinate and β equals the y-coordinate (see Fig. 1).

Figure 1

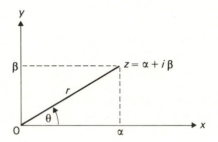

Any complex number $z = \alpha + i\beta$ can be described in terms of *polar coordinates*. Let r represent the distance from z to the origin and let θ represent the angle the vector z makes with the positive x-axis (see Fig. 1). Then it is evident that

$$r = \sqrt{\alpha^2 + \beta^2}, \quad \theta = \tan^{-1}\frac{\beta}{\alpha},$$

$$\alpha = r\cos\theta, \qquad \beta = r\sin\theta. \tag{1}$$

Using the last two relations above, we have

$$\boxed{z = r(\cos\theta + i\sin\theta).} \tag{2}$$

As can be proved by the ratio test, the following power series are convergent for all complex values of θ:

$$e^\theta = 1 + \theta + \frac{\theta^2}{2!} + \cdots + \frac{\theta^n}{n!} + \cdots = \sum_{n=0}^{\infty} \frac{\theta^n}{n!};$$

$$\cos\theta = 1 - \frac{\theta^2}{2!} + \frac{\theta^4}{4!} - \cdots = \sum_{n=0}^{\infty} (-1)^n \frac{\theta^{2n}}{(2n)!};$$

$$\sin\theta = \theta - \frac{\theta^3}{3!} + \frac{\theta^5}{5!} - \cdots = \sum_{n=0}^{\infty} (-1)^n \frac{\theta^{2n+1}}{(2n+1)!}.$$

Replacing θ by $i\theta$ in the power series e^θ and using the identity $i^2 = -1$, we have *Euler's formula*:

$$e^{i\theta} = 1 + i\theta - \frac{\theta^2}{2!} - \frac{i\theta^3}{3!} + \frac{\theta^4}{4!} + \frac{i\theta^5}{5!} - \frac{\theta^6}{6!} - \frac{i\theta^7}{7!} + \cdots$$

$$= \left(1 - \frac{\theta^2}{2!} + \frac{\theta^4}{4!} - \frac{\theta^6}{6!} + \cdots\right) + i\left(\theta - \frac{\theta^3}{3!} + \frac{\theta^5}{5!} - \frac{\theta^7}{7!} + \cdots\right)$$

$$= \cos\theta + i\sin\theta. \tag{3}$$

Thus any complex number $z = \alpha + i\beta$ can be represented in *polar form* by the expression

$$\boxed{z = re^{i\theta},} \tag{4}$$

where r and θ are as in Eqs. (1). Although Euler's formula was obtained by means of a power series, we shall make no further use of power series in this chapter.

Now we can return to our examination of the homogeneous equation with constant coefficients

$$y'' + ay' + by = 0 \tag{5}$$

where $a^2 - 4b < 0$.

CASE 3 Suppose $a^2 - 4b < 0$. The roots of the characteristic equation to Eq. (5) are

$$\lambda_1 = \alpha + i\beta, \quad \lambda_2 = \alpha - i\beta, \tag{6}$$

where $\alpha = -a/2$ and $\beta = \sqrt{4b - a^2}/2$. Thus $y_1 = e^{\lambda_1 x}$ and $y_2 = e^{\lambda_2 x}$ are solutions to Eq. (5). However, in this case it is useful to recall that any linear combination of solutions is also a solution (see Theorem 3 in Section 3.1), and instead consider the solutions

$$y_1^* = \frac{e^{\lambda_1 x} + e^{\lambda_2 x}}{2} \quad \text{and} \quad y_2^* = \frac{e^{\lambda_1 x} - e^{\lambda_2 x}}{2i}.$$

Since $\cos(-\theta) = \cos\theta$ and $\sin(-\theta) = -\sin\theta$, we can rewrite y_1^* as

$$y_1^* = \frac{e^{(\alpha+i\beta)x} + e^{(\alpha-i\beta)x}}{2} = \frac{e^{\alpha x}}{2}(e^{i\beta x} + e^{-i\beta x})$$

$$= \frac{e^{\alpha x}}{2}[\cos\beta x + i\sin\beta x + \cos(-\beta x) + i\sin(-\beta x)]$$

$$= e^{\alpha x}\cos\beta x.$$

Similarly, $y_2^* = e^{\alpha x} \sin \beta x$, and the linear independence of y_1^* and y_2^* follows easily since

$$\frac{y_1^*}{y_2^*} = \cot \beta x, \quad \beta \neq 0,$$

which is not a constant. Alternatively, it is easy to compute $W(y_1^*, y_2^*) = \beta e^{\alpha x} \neq 0$. Thus we have proved:

Theorem 1   If $a^2 - 4b < 0$, then the general solution to Eq. (5) is given by

$$\boxed{y(x) = e^{\alpha x}(c_1 \cos \beta x + c_2 \sin \beta x),} \qquad (7)$$

where c_1 and c_2 are arbitrary constants and

$$\alpha = -\frac{a}{2}, \quad \beta = \frac{\sqrt{4b - a^2}}{2}.$$

Example 1   Let $y'' + y = 0$. Then the characteristic equation is $\lambda^2 + 1 = 0$ with roots $\pm i$. We have $\alpha = 0$ and $\beta = 1$ so that the general solution is

$$y(x) = c_1 \cos x + c_2 \sin x. \qquad (8)$$

This is the equation of *harmonic motion.*

Example 2   Consider the equation $y'' + y' + y = 0$, $y(0) = 1$, $y'(0) = 3$. We have $\lambda^2 + \lambda + 1 = 0$ with roots $\lambda_1 = (-1 + i\sqrt{3})/2$ and $\lambda_2 = (-1 - i\sqrt{3})/2$. Then $\alpha = -\frac{1}{2}$ and $\beta = \sqrt{3}/2$, so that the general solution is

$$y(x) = e^{-x/2}\left(c_1 \cos \frac{\sqrt{3}}{2} x + c_2 \sin \frac{\sqrt{3}}{2} x\right).$$

To solve the initial value problem, we solve the simultaneous equations

$$c_1 = 1,$$
$$\frac{\sqrt{3}}{2} c_2 - \frac{1}{2} c_1 = 3.$$

Thus $c_1 = 1$, $c_2 = 7/\sqrt{3}$, and

$$y(x) = e^{-x/2}\left(\cos \frac{\sqrt{3}}{2} x + \frac{7}{\sqrt{3}} \sin \frac{\sqrt{3}}{2} x\right).$$

Example 3   Consider the equation

$$y^{iv} + 2y'' + y = 0. \qquad (9)$$

The characteristic equation is $\lambda^4 + 2\lambda^2 + 1 = (\lambda^2 + 1)^2 = 0$ with two double roots $\pm i$. As in Example 1, the roots $\pm i$ imply that $y_1 = \cos x$ and $y_2 = \sin x$ are solutions to Eq. (9). How can we find the other two linearly independent solutions of this fourth-order linear equation? We can try the method we used in Case 2 when we had a *real* double root. Multiplying y_1 and y_2 by x, we check to see whether $y_3 = x \cos x$ and $y_4 = x \sin x$ are solutions to Eq. (9):

$$y_3^{iv} + 2y_3'' + y_3 = (x \cos x + 4 \sin x) + 2(-x \cos x - 2 \sin x) + x \cos x$$
$$= 0,$$

and

$$y_4^{iv} + 2y_4'' + y_4 = (x \sin x - 4 \cos x) + 2(-x \sin x + 2 \cos x) + x \sin x$$
$$= 0.$$

Thus the general solution is

$$y = (c_1 + c_2 x) \cos x + (c_3 + c_4 x) \sin x.$$

Example 4 Consider the equation

$$y^{iv} - 8y''' + 42y'' - 104y' + 169y = 0.$$

The characteristic equation is $(\lambda^2 - 4\lambda + 13)^2 = 0$ with two double roots $2 \pm 3i$. The general solution is thus

$$y = e^{2x}[(c_1 + c_2 x) \cos 3x + (c_3 + c_4 x) \sin 3x].$$

EXERCISES 3.5

In Exercises 1 through 16, find the general solution of each equation. When initial conditions are specified, give the particular solution that satisfies them.

1. $y'' + 2y' + 2y = 0$

2. $8y'' + 4y' + y = 0$, $y(0) = 0$, $y'(0) = 1$

3. $x'' + x' + 7x = 0$

4. $y'' + y' + 2y = 0$

5. $\dfrac{d^2x}{d\theta^2} + 4x = 0$, $x\left(\dfrac{\pi}{4}\right) = 1$, $x'\left(\dfrac{\pi}{4}\right) = 3$

6. $y'' + y = 0$, $y(\pi) = 2$, $y'(\pi) = -1$

7. $y'' + \frac{1}{4}y = 0$, $y(\pi) = 1$, $y'(\pi) = -1$

8. $y'' + 6y' + 12y = 0$

9. $y'' + 2y' + 5y = 0$

10. $y'' + 2y' + 5y = 0$, $y(0) = 1$, $y'(0) = -3$

11. $y'' + 2y' + 2y = 0$, $y(\pi) = e^{-\pi}$, $y'(\pi) = -2e^{-\pi}$

12. $y'' + 2y' + 5y = 0$, $y(\pi) = e^{-\pi}$, $y'(\pi) = 3e^{-\pi}$

13. $y''' - y'' + y' - y = 0$

14. $y''' - 3y'' + 4y' - 2y = 0$, $y(0) = 1$, $y'(0) = 2$, $y''(0) = 3$

15. $y''' - 27y = 0$

16. $y^{(5)} + 2y''' + y' = 0$, $y(\pi/2) = 0$, $y'(\pi/2) = 1$, $y''(\pi/2) = 0$, $y'''(\pi/2) = -3$, $y^{(4)}(\pi/2) = 0$

The linear second-order equation

$$x^2y'' + axy' + by = 0, \qquad\qquad \textbf{(10)}$$

where a and b are constants, is known as the *Euler equation*. This variable-coefficient equation can be transformed into a constant-coefficient equation by making the substitution $x = e^t$. Then, using the chain rule, we have

$$\frac{dy}{dt} = \frac{dy}{dx} \cdot \frac{dx}{dt} = \frac{dy}{dx} \cdot e^t = x\frac{dy}{dx},$$

and

$$\frac{d^2y}{dt^2} = \frac{d}{dt}\left(\frac{dy}{dt}\right) = \frac{d}{dx}\left(\frac{dy}{dt}\right) \cdot \frac{dx}{dt}$$

$$= \frac{d}{dx}\left(x\frac{dy}{dx}\right) \cdot e^t = x\frac{d}{dx}\left(x\frac{dy}{dx}\right)$$

$$= x^2\frac{d^2y}{dx^2} + x\frac{dy}{dx}.$$

Substituting these identities in Eq. (10) yields

$$\frac{d^2y}{dt^2} + (a - 1)\frac{dy}{dt} + by = 0. \qquad \textbf{(11)}$$

Once the constant-coefficient linear equation (11) has been solved, the general solution to Eq. (10) can be obtained by replacing each t by $\ln|x|$ (remember, $x = e^t$). In Exercises 17 through 28, solve the given Euler equation using the method above. Find a particular solution when initial conditions are given.

17. $x^2y'' + xy' - y = 0$

18. $x^2y'' - 5xy' + 9y = 0$

19. $x^2y'' - xy' + 2y = 0$

20. $x^2y'' - 2y = 0, \quad y(1) = 3, \quad y'(1) = 1$

21. $4x^2y'' - 4xy' + 3y = 0, \quad y(1) = 0, \quad y'(1) = 1$

22. $x^2y'' + 3xy' + 2y = 0$

23. $x^2y'' - 3xy' + 3y = 0$

24. $x^2y'' + 5xy' + 4y = 0, \quad y(1) = 1, \quad y'(1) = 3$

25. $x^2y'' + 5xy' + 5y = 0$

26. $4x^2y'' - 8xy' + 8y = 0$

27. $x^2y'' + 2xy' - 12y = 0$

28. $x^2y'' + xy' + y = 0$

29. Show that the substitution $x = e^t$ can also be used to solve the third-order Euler equation

$$x^3y''' + x^2y'' - 2xy' + 2y = 0.$$

3.6 NONHOMOGENEOUS EQUATIONS: THE METHOD OF UNDETERMINED COEFFICIENTS

In this and the following section, we will present methods for finding a particular solution to the nonhomogeneous linear equation with constant coefficients

$$y'' + ay' + by = f(x). \qquad \textbf{(1)}$$

First, however, we shall prove a very useful result concerning nonhomogeneous equations called the *Principle of Superposition*:

Theorem 1   *Principle of Superposition.* Suppose the function $f(x)$ in Eq. (1) is a sum of two functions $f_1(x)$ and $f_2(x)$:

$$f(x) = f_1(x) + f_2(x).$$

If $y_1(x)$ is a solution of the equation

$$y'' + ay' + by = f_1(x) \qquad \textbf{(2)}$$

and $y_2(x)$ is a solution of the equation

$$y'' + ay' + by = f_2(x), \qquad \textbf{(3)}$$

then $y = y_1 + y_2$ is a solution of Eq. (1); that is, the solution of Eq. (1) is obtained by superimposing the solution of Eq. (3) on that of Eq. (2).

Proof   Substituting $y = y_1 + y_2$ in the left-hand side of Eq. (1), we have

$$y'' + ay' + by = (y_1'' + y_2'') + a(y_1' + y_2') + b(y_1 + y_2)$$
$$= (y_1'' + ay_1' + by_1) + (y_2'' + ay_2' + by_2)$$
$$= f_1 + f_2 = f,$$

since y_1 and y_2 are solutions of Eqs. (2) and (3), respectively. ∎

Briefly, the principle of superposition tells us that if we can split the function $f(x)$ into a sum of two (or more) simpler expressions $f_k(x)$, then we can restrict our attention to solving the nonhomogeneous equations

$$y'' + ay' + by = f_k(x), \quad k = 1, 2, \ldots, m, \tag{4}$$

because the solution to Eq. (1) is simply the sum of the solutions of these equations.

The method we shall present in this section *requires* that the function $f(x)$ in Eq. (1) be of *one* of the following three forms:

---

1. $P_n(x)$,

2. $P_n(x)e^{ax}$,   or

3. $e^{ax}[P_n(x) \cos bx + Q_n(x) \sin bx]$,

---

where $P_n(x)$ and $Q_n(x)$ are polynomials in x of degree n $(n \geqslant 0)$. The method we present below can also be used if $f(x)$ is a sum of functions $f_k(x)$ of these three forms, since by the Principle of Superposition we can solve each of the Eqs. (4) and add the solutions together. *However, if any term of $f(x)$ is not of one of these three forms, we cannot use the method of this section.*†

Note that the three forms involve a multitude of situations. The following three functions are all of one of these forms:

a) $2e^{3x}$ (the polynomial is the constant 2);

b) $e^{4x} \cos x$ (here $P_n(x) = 1$ and $Q_n(x) = 0$ are both polynomials of degree zero);

c) $x \cos x + \sin x$ (Here $a = 0$, $b = 1$, $P_n(x) = x + 0$,   and $Q_n(x) = 0 \cdot x + 1$).

The *method of undetermined coefficients* assumes that the solution to Eq. (1) is exactly of the same "form" as $f(x)$. The technique requires that we replace each dependent variable y in Eq. (1) with an expression of the same form as $f(x)$ having polynomial terms with *undetermined coefficients*. If we compare both sides of the resulting equation, it is then possible to "determine" the unknown coefficients. The method is best illustrated by a number of examples.

---

† Instead we must use the variation of constants method, which will be described in Section 3.7.

Example 1   Consider the equation

$$y'' - y = x^2. \tag{5}$$

Since $f(x) = x^2$ is a polynomial of degree two, we "guess" that Eq. (5) has a solution $y_p(x)$ that is a polynomial of degree two, that is,

$$y_p(x) = a + bx + cx^2.$$

After noting that $y_p'' = 2c$, we substitute $y_p(x)$ into Eq. (5) to obtain

$$2c - (a + bx + cx^2) = x^2.$$

Equating coefficients, we have

$$2c - a = 0, \quad -b = 0, \quad -c = 1,$$

which immediately yields $a = -2$, $b = 0$, $c = -1$, and the particular solution

$$y_p(x) = -2 - x^2.$$

This particular solution is easily verified by substitution into Eq. (5). Finally, since the general solution of the homogeneous equation $y'' - y = 0$ is given by

$$y = c_1 e^x + c_2 e^{-x},$$

the general solution of Eq. (5) is

$$y = c_1 e^x + c_2 e^{-x} - 2 - x^2.$$

Example 2   Let

$$y'' - 3y' + 2y = e^x \sin x. \tag{6}$$

Since $f(x)$ is of form 3 with $P_n(x) = 0$ and $Q_n(x) = 1$, we "guess" that there is a solution to Eq. (6) of the form

$$y_p(x) = ae^x \sin x + be^x \cos x.$$

Then

$$y_p'(x) = (a - b)e^x \sin x + (a + b)e^x \cos x$$

and

$$y_p''(x) = 2ae^x \cos x - 2be^x \sin x.$$

Substituting these expressions into Eq. (6) we have

$$e^x(2a \cos x - 2b \sin x) - 3e^x[(a - b)\sin x + (a + b)\cos x]$$
$$+ 2e^x(a \sin x + b \cos x) = e^x \sin x.$$

Dividing both sides by e^x and equating coefficients, we have

$$2a - 3(a + b) + 2b = 0,$$
$$-2b - 3(a - b) + 2a = 1,$$

which yield $a = -\frac{1}{2}$ and $b = \frac{1}{2}$ so that

$$y_p = \frac{e^x}{2}(\cos x - \sin x).$$

Again this result is easily verified by substitution. Finally, the general solution of Eq. (6) is

$$y = c_1 e^{2x} + c_2 e^x + \frac{e^x}{2}(\cos x - \sin x).$$

Example 3   Solve $y'' + y = xe^{2x}$.

Here $f(x)$ is of form 2, where $P_n(x)$ is a polynomial of degree one, so we try a solution of the form

$$y_p(x) = e^{2x}(a + bx).$$

Then

$$y_p'(x) = e^{2x}(2a + b + 2bx), \quad y_p''(x) = e^{2x}(4a + 4b + 4bx),$$

and substitution yields

$$e^{2x}(4a + 4b + 4bx) + e^{2x}(a + bx) = xe^{2x}.$$

Dividing both sides by e^{2x} and equating like powers of x, we obtain the equations

$$5a + 4b = 0, \quad 5b = 1.$$

Thus $a = -\frac{4}{25}$, $b = \frac{1}{5}$, and a particular solution is

$$y_p(x) = \frac{e^{2x}}{25}(5x - 4).$$

Therefore, the general solution of this example is

$$y(x) = c_1 \sin x + c_2 \cos x + \frac{e^{2x}}{25}(5x - 4).$$

We have observed that in using the method of undetermined coefficients, we "guess" that there is a solution y_p that has one of the three forms

$$P_n(x), \quad P_n(x)e^{ax}, \quad e^{ax}[P_n(x)\cos bx + Q_n(x)\sin bx].$$

Note that each of these forms is a sum of terms. Problems arise if one or more of these terms is a solution to the homogeneous equation

$$y'' + ay' + by = 0. \tag{7}$$

For example, for the equation

$$y'' - y = xe^x \qquad \textbf{(8)}$$

we try a solution of the form

$$y_p(x) = (a_0 + a_1 x)e^x. \qquad \textbf{(9)}$$

Note that the term $a_0 e^x$ is a solution to the homogeneous equation

$$y'' - y = 0.$$

If we substitute Eq. (9) into Eq. (8), we have

$$y_p' = (a_0 + a_1 + a_1 x)e^x, \qquad y_p'' = (a_0 + 2a_1 + a_1 x)e^x$$

and

$$y_p'' - y_p = 2a_1 e^x.$$

Clearly, no choice of the *constants* a_0 and a_1 will satisfy $2a_1 e^x = xe^x$.

When this situation occurs, the method of undetermined coefficients must be modified as follows:

> If any term of the "guessed" solution $y_p(x)$ is a solution of the homogeneous equation (7), multiply $y_p(x)$ by x repeatedly until no term of the product $x^k y_p(x)$ is a solution of Eq. (7). Then use the product $x^k y_p(x)$ to solve Eq. (1).

For example, multiplying the right side of Eq. (9) by x, we obtain our new guess

$$y_p = (a_0 x + a_1 x^2)e^x. \qquad \textbf{(10)}$$

Now no term of Eq. (10) is a solution to the homogeneous equation and we easily obtain the solution

$$y_p = \left(\frac{x^2 - x}{4}\right)e^x.$$

We will find the general solution to similar problems in Examples 4 and 5.

Example 4   Consider the equation

$$y'' - y = 2e^x.$$

Since the general solution of $y'' - y = 0$ is

$$y(x) = c_1 e^x + c_2 e^{-x},$$

we see that $f(x)$ is a solution to the homogeneous equation. We modify the method of undetermined coefficients. Multiplying $f(x) = 2e^x$ by x, we get

$2xe^x$, which is not a solution to the homogeneous equation $y'' - y = 0$. Thus, we consider a particular solution of the form

$$y_p = axe^x.$$

Then $y_p' = ae^x(x + 1)$, $y_p''(x) = ae^x(x + 2)$, and

$$y_p'' - y_p = ae^x(x + 2) - axe^x = 2ae^x = 2e^x.$$

Hence $a = 1$ and $y_p = xe^x$. Thus the general solution is

$$y(x) = c_1e^x + c_2e^{-x} + xe^x.$$

Example 5   Find the general solution of

$$y'' - 4y' + 4y = e^{2x}.$$

The homogeneous equation $y'' - 4y' + 4y = 0$ has the independent solutions e^{2x} and xe^{2x}. Thus, multiplying $f(x) = e^{2x}$ by x twice, we look for a particular solution of the form $y_p = ax^2e^{2x}$. Then

$$y_p' = ae^{2x}(2x^2 + 2x)$$

and

$$y_p'' = ae^{2x}(4x^2 + 8x + 2),$$

so that

$$y_p'' - 4y_p' + 4y_p = ae^{2x}(4x^2 + 8x + 2 - 8x^2 - 8x + 4x^2)$$
$$= 2ae^{2x} = e^{2x},$$

or $2a = 1$ and $a = \frac{1}{2}$. Thus $y_p = \frac{1}{2}x^2e^{2x}$ and the general solution is

$$y(x) = c_1e^{2x} + c_2xe^{2x} + \tfrac{1}{2}x^2e^{2x} = e^{2x}(c_1 + c_2x + \tfrac{1}{2}x^2).$$

Example 6   Consider the equation

$$y'' - y = x^2 + 2e^x.$$

Using the results of Examples 1 and 4 and the principle of superposition, we find immediately that a particular solution is given by

$$y_p(x) = -2 - x^2 + xe^x.$$

Let us now summarize the results of this section as follows: Consider the nonhomogeneous equation

$$y'' + ay' + by = f(x) \tag{11}$$

and the homogeneous equation

$$y'' + ay' + by = 0. \tag{12}$$

CASE 1   *No term in $f(x)$ is a solution of Eq.* (12). A particular solution of Eq. (11) will have the form $y_p(x)$ given by the table below:

$f(x)$	$y_p(x)$
$P_n(x)$	$a_0 + a_1x + a_2x^2 + \cdots + a_nx^n$
$P_n(x)e^{ax}$	$(a_0 + a_1x + a_2x^2 + \cdots + a_nx^n)e^{ax}$
$\left.\begin{array}{l}P_n(x)e^{ax}\sin bx \\ + \\ Q_n(x)e^{ax}\cos bx\end{array}\right\}$	$(a_0 + a_1x + a_2x^2 + \cdots + a_nx^n)e^{ax}\sin bx +$ $(c_0 + c_1x + c_2x^2 + \cdots + c_nx^n)e^{ax}\cos bx$

CASE 2   If any term of $f(x)$ is a solution of Eq. (12), then multiply the appropriate function $y_p(x)$ of Case 1 by x^k, where k is the smallest integer such that no term in $x^k y_p(x)$ is a solution of Eq. (12).

We note that the method of undetermined coefficients should be used only when $f(x)$ is in a "correct" form. The more general situation is dealt with in the next section.

EXERCISES 3.6

In Exercises 1 through 13, find the general solution of each given differential equation. If initial conditions are given, then find the particular solution that satisfies them.

1. $y'' + 4y = 3\sin x$

2. $y'' - y' - 6y = 20e^{-2x}$, $y(0) = 0$, $y'(0) = 6$

3. $y'' - 3y' + 2y = 6e^{3x}$

4. $y'' + y' = 3x^2$, $y(0) = 4$, $y'(0) = 0$

5. $y'' - 2y' + y = -4e^x$

6. $y'' - 4y' + 4y = 6xe^{2x}$, $y(0) = 0$, $y'(0) = 3$

7. $y'' - 7y' + 10y = 100x$, $y(0) = 0$, $y'(0) = 5$

8. $y'' + y = 1 + x + x^2$

9. $y'' + y' = x^3 - x^2$

10. $y'' + 4y = 16x\sin 2x$

11. $y'' - 4y' + 5y = 2e^{2x}\cos x$

12. $y'' - y' - 2y = x^2 + \cos x$

13. $y'' + 6y' + 9y = 10e^{-3x}$

Use the principle of superposition to find the general solution of each of the equations in Exercises 14 through 17.

14. $y'' + y = 1 + 2\sin x$

15. $y'' - 2y' - 3y = x - x^2 + e^x$

16. $y'' + 4y = 3\cos 2x - 7x^2$

17. $y'' + 4y' + 4y = xe^x + \sin x$

18. Show by the methods of this section that a particular solution of

$$y'' + 2ay' + b^2y = A\sin \omega x \quad (a, \omega > 0)$$

is given by

$$y = \frac{A\sin(\omega x - \alpha)}{\sqrt{(b^2 - \omega^2)^2 + 4\omega^2 a^2}},$$

where

$$\alpha = \tan^{-1}\frac{2a\omega}{(b^2 - \omega^2)}, \quad (0 < \alpha < \pi).$$

19. Let $f(x)$ be a polynomial of degree n. Show that there is always a solution that is a polynomial of degree n for $y'' + ay' + by = f(x)$, if $b \neq 0$.

20. Use the method indicated in Exercise 19 to find a particular solution of

$$y'' + 3y' + 2y = 9 + 2x - 2x^2.$$

3.7 NONHOMOGENEOUS EQUATIONS: VARIATION OF CONSTANTS†

In this section we shall consider a general procedure, due to J. L. Lagrange (1736–1813), for finding a particular solution of any nonhomogeneous linear equation

$$y'' + a(x)y' + b(x)y = f(x), \tag{1}$$

where the functions $a(x)$, $b(x)$, and $f(x)$ are continuous. To use this method it is necessary to know the general solution $c_1 y_1(x) + c_2 y_2(x)$ of the homogeneous equation

$$y'' + a(x)y' + b(x)y = 0. \tag{2}$$

If $a(x)$ and $b(x)$ are constants, then the general solution to Eq. (2) can always be obtained by the methods of Sections 3.4 and 3.5. If $a(x)$ and $b(x)$ are not both constants, it may be difficult to find this general solution; however, if one solution y_1 of Eq. (2) can be found, then the method of Section 3.3 will yield the general solution to Eq. (2).

Lagrange noticed that any particular solution y_p of Eq. (1) must have the property that y_p/y_1 and y_p/y_2 are not constants, suggesting that we look for a particular solution of Eq. (1) of the form

$$y(x) = c_1(x)y_1(x) + c_2(x)y_2(x). \tag{3}$$

This replacement of constants by variables gives the method its name. Differentiating Eq. (3), we obtain

$$y'(x) = c_1(x)y_1'(x) + c_2(x)y_2'(x) + c_1'(x)y_1(x) + c_2'(x)y_2(x).$$

To simplify this expression, it is convenient (see Exercise 20) to set

$$c_1'(x)y_1(x) + c_2'(x)y_2(x) = 0. \tag{4}$$

Then

$$y'(x) = c_1(x)y_1'(x) + c_2(x)y_2'(x).$$

Differentiating once again, we obtain

$$y''(x) = c_1(x)y_1''(x) + c_2(x)y_2''(x) + c_1'(x)y_1'(x) + c_2'(x)y_2'(x).$$

Substitution of the expressions for $y(x)$, $y'(x)$ and $y''(x)$ into Eq. (1) yields

$$y'' + a(x)y' + b(x)y = c_1(x)(y_1'' + ay_1' + by_1) + c_2(x)(y_2'' + ay_2' + by_2)$$
$$+ c_1'y_1' + c_2'y_2'$$
$$= f(x).$$

But y_1 and y_2 are solutions to the homogeneous equation so that the

---

† This procedure is also called the variation of parameters method, or Lagrange's method. (See also Review Exercise 41 in Chapter 2.)

equation above reduces to

$$c_1'y_1' + c_2'y_2' = f(x).$$ **(5)**

This gives a second equation relating $c_1'(x)$ and $c_2'(x)$, and we have the simultaneous equations

$$\begin{aligned} y_1c_1' + y_2c_2' &= 0, \\ y_1'c_1' + y_2'c_2' &= f(x). \end{aligned}$$ **(6)**

Before continuing with the discussion, we note that the problem has essentially been solved. Equations (6) uniquely determine c_1' and c_2', so that c_1 and c_2 can be obtained by integration when such an integration is possible.

To complete the derivation, we multiply the first of these equations by y_2', the second by y_2, and subtract to obtain $c_1'(x)$; c_2' can be determined in a similar manner. The solutions are thus:

$$\begin{aligned} c_1'(x) &= \frac{-f(x)y_2(x)}{y_1(x)y_2'(x) - y_1'(x)y_2(x)} = \frac{-f(x)y_2(x)}{W(y_1, y_2)(x)}, \\ c_2'(x) &= \frac{f(x)y_1(x)}{y_1(x)y_2'(x) - y_1'(x)y_2(x)} = \frac{f(x)y_1(x)}{W(y_1, y_2)(x)}. \end{aligned}$$

Note that the denominators here are not zero since they are both equal to $W(y_1, y_2)$, and y_1 and y_2 are linearly independent.

Finally, if we can integrate c_1' and c_2', we can substitute c_1 and c_2 into Eq. (3) to obtain a particular solution to the nonhomogeneous equation.

Example 1   Solve $y'' - y = e^x$ by the variation of constants method.

The solutions to the homogeneous equation are $y_1 = e^{-x}$ and $y_2 = e^x$. We obtain $W(y_1, y_2) = 2$, so that Eq. (7) becomes

$$c_1'(x) = \frac{-e^x e^x}{2} = \frac{-e^{2x}}{2}, \quad c_2'(x) = \frac{e^x e^{-x}}{2} = \frac{1}{2}.$$

Integrating these functions, we obtain $c_1(x) = -e^{2x}/4$ and $c_2(x) = x/2$. A particular solution is therefore

$$c_1(x)y_1(x) + c_2(x)y_2(x) = -\frac{e^x}{4} + \frac{x}{2}e^x,$$

and the general solution is

$$y(x) = c_1 e^x + c_2 e^{-x} + \frac{x}{2}e^x - \frac{e^x}{4} = c_1^* e^x + c_2^* e^{-x} + \frac{x}{2}e^x.$$

Example 2　　Determine the solution of

$$y'' + y = 2\cos x$$

that satisfies $y(0) = 5$ and $y'(0) = 2$.

　　　Here $y_1(x) = \cos x$, $y_2(x) = \sin x$, and $W(y_1, y_2) = 1$, so that $c_1' = -2\cos x \sin x$ and $c_2' = 2\cos^2 x$. Immediately we have $c_1(x) = \cos^2 x$ and $c_2(x) = x + \sin x \cos x$. Thus the general solution is

$$y = c_1 \cos x + c_2 \sin x + \cos^3 x + x \sin x + \sin^2 x \cos x$$

$$= c_1^* \cos x + c_2^* \sin x + x \sin x,$$

because

$$\cos^3 x + \sin^2 x \cos x = \cos x(\cos^2 x + \sin^2 x) = \cos x.$$

Since $5 = y(0) = c_1$ and $2 = y'(0) = c_2$, the required solution is

$$y(x) = (x + 2)\sin x + 5\cos x.$$

Example 3　　Solve $y'' + y = \tan x$.

　　　The solutions to the homogeneous equation are $y_1 = \cos x$ and $y_2 = \sin x$. Also $W(y_1, y_2) = 1$, so that Eqs. (7) become

$$c_1'(x) = -\tan x \sin x = -\frac{\sin^2 x}{\cos x} = \frac{\cos^2 x - 1}{\cos x} = \cos x - \sec x,$$

$$c_2'(x) = \tan x \cos x = \sin x.$$

Hence using the integrals 17, 22, and 33 in Appendix 1, we have

$$c_1(x) = \sin x - \ln|\sec x + \tan x|$$

and

$$c_2(x) = -\cos x.$$

Thus the particular solution is

$$y_p(x) = c_1(x)y_1(x) + c_2(x)y_2(x)$$

$$= \cos x \sin x - \cos x \ln|\sec x + \tan x| - \sin x \cos x$$

$$= -\cos x \ln|\sec x + \tan x|,$$

and the general solution is

$$y(x) = c_1 \cos x + c_2 \sin x - \cos x \ln|\sec x + \tan x|.$$

　　　Example 3 illustrates that there are instances in which we cannot apply the method of undetermined coefficients. (Try to "guess" a solution in this case.) As a rule, the method of undetermined coefficients is easier to use if the function $f(x)$ is in the right form. However, the method of variation of parameters is far more general, since it will yield a solution whenever the functions c_1' and c_2' have a known indefinite integral.

EXERCISES 3.7

In Exercises 1 through 10, find the general solution of each equation by the variation of constants method.

1. $y'' - y' = \sec^2 x - \tan x$

2. $y'' + y = \cot x$

3. $y'' + 4y = \sec 2x$

4. $y'' + 4y = \sec x \tan x$

5. $y'' - 2y' + y = \dfrac{e^x}{(1 - x)^2}$

6. $y'' - y = \sin^2 x$

7. $y'' - y = \dfrac{(2x - 1)e^x}{x^2}$

8. $y'' - 3y' - 4y = \dfrac{e^{4x}(5x - 2)}{x^3}$

9. $y'' - 4y' + 4y = \dfrac{e^{2x}}{(1 + x)}$

10. $y'' + 2y' + y = e^{-x} \ln |x|$

Using the method for solving Euler equations (see Eqs. 10 and 11 in Section 3.5), find the general solution of the nonhomogeneous Euler equations in Exercises 11 through 14 by the variation of constants method.

11. $x^2 y'' + 7xy' + 5y = x$

12. $x^2 y'' + 3xy' - 3y = 5x^2$

13. $x^2 y'' - 2y = \ln x, \quad (x > 0)$

14. $4x^2 y'' - 4xy' + 3y = \sin \ln (-x) \quad (x < 0)$

15. Find a particular solution of

$$y'' + \frac{1}{x} y' - \frac{y}{x^2} = \frac{1}{x^2 + x^3} \quad (x > 0),$$

given that two solutions of the associated homogeneous equations are $y_1 = x$ and $y_2 = 1/x$.

16. Find a particular solution of

$$y'' - \frac{2}{x} y' + \frac{2}{x^2} y = \frac{\ln |x|}{x} \quad (x > 0),$$

given the two homogeneous solutions $y_1 = x$ and $y_2 = x^2$.

17. Verify that

$$y = \frac{1}{\omega} \int_0^x f(t) \sin \omega(x - t) \, dt$$

is a particular solution of $y'' + \omega^2 y = f(x)$.

18. Consider the third-order equation

$$y''' + ay'' + by' + cy = f(x) \tag{8}$$

Let $y_1(x)$, $y_2(x)$, and $y_3(x)$ be three linearly independent solutions (see Exercises 8, 9, and 10 in Section 3.2). Assume that there is a solution of Eq. (8) of the form $y(x) = c_1(x)y_1(x) + c_2(x)y_2(x) + c_3(x)y_3(x)$.

a) Following the steps used in deriving the variation of constants procedure for second-order equations, derive a method for solving third-order equations.

b) Find a particular solution of the equation
$$y''' - 2y' - 4y = e^{-x} \tan x.$$

19. Use the method derived in Exercise 18 to find a particular solution of
$$y''' + 5y'' + 9y' + 5y = 2e^{-2x} \sec x.$$

*20. This exercise will show why there is no loss in generality in Eq. (4) by setting
$$c_1' y_1 + c_2' y_2 = 0.$$
Suppose instead that we let $c_1' y_1 + c_2' y_2 = z(x)$, with $z(x)$ an undetermined function of x.

a) Show that we then obtain the system
$$c_1' y_1 + c_2' y_2 = z,$$
$$c_1' y_1' + c_2' y_2' = f - z' - az.$$

b) Show that the system in part (a) has the solution
$$c_1' = \frac{-y_2 f}{W(y_1, y_2)} + \frac{(e^{\int a(x)\,dx} z y_2)'}{e^{\int a(x)\,dx} W(y_1, y_2)},$$
$$c_2' = \frac{y_1 f}{W(y_1, y_2)} - \frac{(e^{\int a(x)\,dx} z y_1)'}{e^{\int a(x)\,dx} W(y_1, y_2)}.$$

c) Integrate by parts to show that
$$\int \frac{(e^{\int a(x)\,dx} z y_i)'}{e^{\int a(x)\,dx} W(y_1, y_2)} \, dx = \frac{z y_i}{W(y_1, y_2)}, \quad i = 1, 2.$$

d) Conclude that the particular solution obtained by letting $c_1' y_1 + c_2' y_2 = z$ is identical to that obtained by assuming Eq. (4).

e) Letting t be a dummy variable of integration, show the particular solution can always be represented by the integral
$$y_p(x) = \int^x \frac{y_2(x)y_1(t) - y_1(x)y_2(t)}{W(y_1, y_2)(t)} f(t) \, dt.$$

3.8 VIBRATORY MOTION

Differential equations were first studied in attempts to describe the motion of particles. As a simple example, consider a mass m attached to a coiled spring of length l_0, the upper end of which is securely fastened (see Fig. 2).

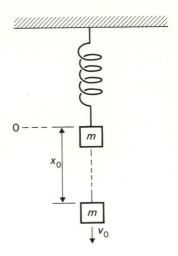

Figure 2

We have denoted by the number zero the equilibrium position of the mass on the spring, that is, the point where the mass remains at rest. Suppose that the mass is given an initial displacement x_0, and an initial velocity v_0. Can we describe the future movement of the mass? To do so, we make the following assumptions about the force† exerted by the spring on the mass:

1. It moves along a vertical line through the center of gravity of the mass (which is then treated as if it were a point mass), and its direction is always from the mass toward the point of equilibrium.

2. At any time t the magnitude of the force exerted on the mass is proportional to the difference between the length l of the spring and its equilibrium length l_0. The positive constant of proportionality k is called the *spring constant*, and the principle above is known as Hooke's law.

---

† The most common system of units are given in the table below.

Systems of units	Force	Length	Mass	Time
International (SI)	Newton (N)	Meter (m)	Kilogram (kg)	Second (s)
English	Pound (lb)	Foot (ft)	Slug	Second (s)

$1\,\text{N} = 1\,\text{kg-m/s}^2 = 0.22481\,\text{lb}$ $1\,\text{kg} = 0.06852\,\text{slug}$
$1\,\text{m} = 3.28084\,\text{ft}$ $1\,\text{lb} = 1\,\text{slug-ft/s}^2 = 4.4482\,\text{N}$

Newton's second law of motion states that the force F acting on this particle moving with varying velocity v is equal to the time rate of change of the momentum mv and, since the mass is constant,

$$F = \frac{d(mv)}{dt} = ma.$$

Equating the two forces and applying Hooke's law, we have

$$m \frac{d^2x}{dt^2} = -kx, \tag{1}$$

where $x(t)$ denotes the displacement from equilibrium of the spring and is positive when the spring is stretched. The negative sign in Eq. (1) is due to the fact that the force always acts toward the equilibrium position and therefore is in the negative direction when x is positive.

Note that we have assumed that all other forces acting on the spring (such as friction, air resistance, etc.) can be ignored. Equation (1) yields the initial value problem

$$\frac{d^2x}{dt^2} + \frac{k}{m} x = 0, \quad x(0) = x_0, \quad x'(0) = v_0. \tag{2}$$

To find the solution of Eq. (2), we note that the characteristic equation has the complex root $\pm i\omega_0$, where $\omega_0 = \sqrt{k/m}$, leading to the general solution

$$x(t) = c_1 \cos \omega_0 t + c_2 \sin \omega_0 t.$$

Using the initial conditions, we find that $c_1 = x_0$ and $c_2 = v_0/\omega_0$, so that the solution of Eq. (2) is given by

$$x(t) = x_0 \cos \omega_0 t + (v_0/\omega_0) \sin \omega_0 t. \tag{3}$$

Dividing both sides of Eq. (3) by $A = \sqrt{x_0^2 + (v_0/\omega_0)^2}$ and using the addition formula $\sin(\omega_0 t + \phi) = \sin \phi \cos \omega_0 t + \cos \phi \sin \omega_0 t$ with $\tan \phi = x_0 \omega_0 / v_0$, we can rewrite Eq. (3) as

$$x(t) = A \sin(\omega_0 t + \phi). \tag{4}$$

Because of Eq. (4), the motion of the mass is called *simple harmonic motion*.

From this equation it is clear that the mass oscillates between the extreme positions $\pm A$; A is called the *amplitude* of the motion. Since the sine term has period $2\pi/\omega_0$, this is the time required for each complete oscillation. The *natural frequency* f of the motion is the number of complete oscillations per unit time:[†]

$$f = \frac{\omega_0}{2\pi}. \tag{5}$$

---

† Cycles/sec = hertz (Hz)

Note that although the amplitude depends on the initial conditions, the frequency does not.

Example 1 Consider a spring fixed at its upper end and supporting a weight of 10 pounds at its lower end. Suppose the 10-pound weight stretches the spring by 6 inches. Find the equation of motion of the weight if it is drawn to a position 4 inches below its equilibrium position and released.

By Hooke's law, since a force of 10 lb stretches the spring by $\frac{1}{2}$ ft, $10 = k(\frac{1}{2})$ or $k = 20$ (lb/ft). We are given the initial values $x_0 = \frac{1}{3}$(ft) and $v_0 = 0$, so by Eq. (3) and the identity† $k/m = gk/w = 64 \, \text{s}^{-2}$, we obtain

$$x(t) = \tfrac{1}{3} \cos 8t \text{ ft.}$$

Thus the amplitude is $\frac{1}{3}$ ft ($= 4$ in.), and the frequency is $f = 4/\pi$ hertz.

Damped Vibrations

Throughout the above discussion we made the assumption that there were no external forces acting on the spring. This assumption, however, is not very realistic. To take care of such things as friction in the spring and air resistance, we now assume that there is a *damping* force (that tends to slow things down), which can be thought of as the resultant of all external forces (except gravity) acting on the spring. It is reasonable to assume that the magnitude of the damping force is proportional to the velocity of the particle (for example, the slower the movement, the smaller the air resistance). Therefore, to Eq. (1) we add the term $c(dx/dt)$, where c is the damping constant that depends on all external factors. This constant could be determined experimentally. The equation of motion then becomes

$$\frac{d^2x}{dt^2} = -\frac{k}{m}x - \frac{c}{m}\frac{dx}{dt}, \quad x(0) = x_0, \quad x'(0) = v_0. \tag{6}$$

[Of course, since c depends on external factors, it may very well not be a constant at all but may vary with time and position. In that case, c is really $c(t, x)$, and the equation becomes much harder to analyze than the constant coefficient case.]

To study Eq. (6), we first find the roots of the characteristic equation:

$$\frac{-c \pm \sqrt{c^2 - 4mk}}{2m}. \tag{7}$$

The nature of the general solution will depend on the discriminant $\sqrt{c^2 - 4mk}$. If $c^2 > 4mk$, then both roots will be negative since

---

† The identity $w = mg$ may be used to convert weight to mass. Keep in mind that pounds or Newtons are a unit of weight (force) whereas slugs or kilograms are units of mass. The gravitational constant $g = 9.80 \, \text{m/s}^2 = 32 \, \text{ft/s}^2$ (approximately).

$\sqrt{c^2 - 4mk} < c$. So in this case

$$x(t) = c_1 \exp\left(\frac{-c + \sqrt{c^2 - 4mk}}{2m}\, t\right) + c_2 \exp\left(\frac{-c - \sqrt{c^2 - 4mk}}{2m}\, t\right) \qquad (8)$$

will become small as t becomes large whatever the initial conditions may be. Similarly, in the event the discriminant vanishes, then

$$x(t) = e^{(-c/2m)t}(c_1 + c_2 t), \qquad (9)$$

and the solution has a similar behavior. For example, if $c = 5$ (lb-s/ft) in Example 1, then the discriminant vanishes since $4mk = 25$ and

$$x(t) = e^{-8t}(c_1 + c_2 t).$$

Applying the initial conditions yields

$$x(t) = \tfrac{1}{3} e^{-8t}(1 + 8t)\,\text{ft},$$

which has the graph shown in Fig. 3. We observe that the solution does not oscillate. This type of motion can take place in a viscous medium (such as oil or water).

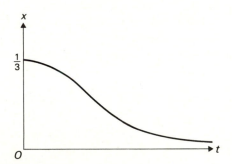

Figure 3

If $c^2 < 4mk$, then the general solution is

$$x(t) = e^{(-c/2m)t}\left(c_1 \cos\frac{\sqrt{4mk - c^2}}{2m}\, t + c_2 \sin\frac{\sqrt{4mk - c^2}}{2m}\, t\right), \qquad (10)$$

which shows an oscillation with frequency

$$f = \frac{\sqrt{4mk - c^2}}{4\pi m}.$$

The factor $e^{(-c/2m)t}$ is called the *damping factor*. Letting $c = 4$ (lb-s/ft) in Example 1 leads to the general solution

$$x(t) = e^{-32t/5}(c_1 \cos\tfrac{24}{5}t + c_2 \sin\tfrac{24}{5}t)\,\text{ft}.$$

Using the initial values, we find that $c_1 = \tfrac{1}{3}$, $c_2 = \tfrac{4}{9}$, and the motion is illustrated in Fig. 4.

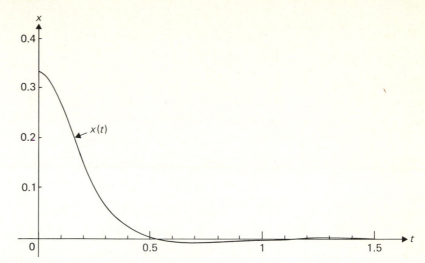

Figure 4

Forced Vibrations

The motion of the mass considered in the two cases above is determined by the inherent forces of the spring-weight system and the natural forces acting on the system. Accordingly, the vibrations are called *free* or *natural* vibrations. We will now assume that the mass is also subject to an external periodic force $F_0 \sin \omega t$, due to the motion of the object to which the upper end of the spring is attached (see Fig. 5). In this case the mass will undergo *forced vibrations*.

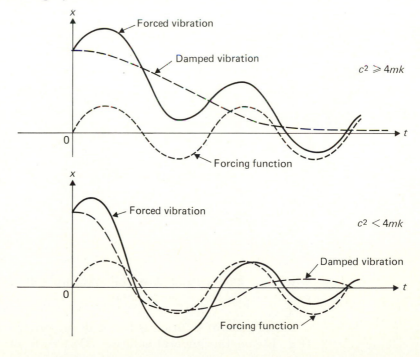

Figure 5

Equation (6) may be replaced by the nonhomogeneous second-order differential equation

$$m \frac{d^2x}{dt^2} = -kx - c\frac{dx}{dt} + F_0 \sin \omega t,$$

which we write in the form

$$\frac{d^2x}{dt^2} + \frac{c}{m}\frac{dx}{dt} + \frac{k}{m}x = \frac{F_0}{m}\sin \omega t. \tag{11}$$

By the method of undetermined coefficients, we know that $x(t)$ has a particular solution of the form

$$x_p(t) = b_1 \cos \omega t + b_2 \sin \omega t. \tag{12}$$

Substituting this function into Eq. (11) yields the simultaneous equations

$$(\omega_0^2 - \omega^2)b_1 + \frac{c\omega}{m}b_2 = 0,$$

$$-\frac{c\omega}{m}b_1 + (\omega_0^2 - \omega^2)b_2 = \frac{F_0}{m}, \tag{13}$$

where $\omega_0 = \sqrt{k/m}$, from which we obtain

$$b_1 = \frac{-F_0 c\omega}{m^2(\omega_0^2 - \omega^2)^2 + (c\omega)^2},$$

$$b_2 = \frac{F_0 m(\omega_0^2 - \omega^2)}{m^2(\omega_0^2 - \omega^2)^2 + (c\omega)^2}.$$

Using the same method we used to obtain Eq. (4), we have

$$x_p = A \sin (\omega t + \phi), \tag{14}$$

where

$$A = \frac{F_0/k}{\sqrt{\left[1 - \left(\dfrac{\omega}{\omega_0}\right)^2\right]^2 + \left(2\dfrac{c}{c_0}\dfrac{\omega}{\omega_0}\right)^2}},$$

and

$$\tan \phi = \frac{2\dfrac{c}{c_0}\dfrac{\omega}{\omega_0}}{\left(\dfrac{\omega}{\omega_0}\right)^2 - 1},$$

with $c_0 = 2m\omega_0$. Here A is the amplitude of the motion, ϕ is the *phase angle*, c/c_0 is the *damping ratio*, and ω/ω_0 is the *frequency ratio* of the motion.

The general solution is found by superimposing the periodic function (Eq. 14) on the general solution (Eqs. 8, 9, or 10) of the homogeneous equation. Since the solution of the homogeneous equation damps out as t increases, the general solution will be very close to Eq. (14) for large values of t. Figure 5 illustrates two typical situations.

It is interesting to see what occurs if the damping constant c vanishes. There are two cases.

CASE 1   If $\omega^2 \neq \omega_0^2$, we superimpose the periodic function (Eq. 14) on the general solution of the homogeneous equation $x'' + \omega_0^2 x = 0$, obtaining

$$x(t) = c_1 \cos \omega_0 t + c_2 \sin \omega_0 t + \frac{F_0/k}{1 - (\omega/\omega_0)^2} \sin \omega t. \tag{15}$$

Using the initial conditions, we find that

$$c_1 = x_0 \quad \text{and} \quad c_2 = \frac{v_0}{\omega_0} - \frac{(F_0/k)(\omega/\omega_0)}{1 - (\omega/\omega_0)^2}$$

so that

$$x(t) = A \sin(\omega_0 t + \phi) + \frac{F_0/k}{1 - (\omega/\omega_0)^2} \sin \omega t,$$

where

$$A = \sqrt{c_1^2 + c_2^2} \quad \text{and} \quad \tan \phi = c_1/c_2.$$

Hence the motion in this case is simply the sum of two sinusoidal curves as illustrated in Fig. 6.

Figure 6

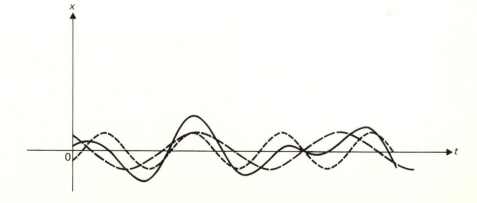

CASE 2   If $\omega^2 = \omega_0^2$, we must seek a particular solution of the form

$$x_p(t) = b_1 t \cos \omega t + b_2 t \sin \omega t, \tag{16}$$

since Eq. (12) is a solution of the homogeneous equation (2). (See Form 3 in our discussion of undetermined coefficients in Section 3.6.) Substituting

Eq. (16) into Eq. (2), we get

$$b_1 = \frac{-F_0}{2m\omega} \quad \text{and} \quad b_2 = 0,$$

so the general solution has the form

$$x(t) = c_1 \cos \omega t + c_2 \sin \omega t - \frac{F_0}{2m\omega} t \cos \omega t. \qquad \textbf{(17)}$$

Note that as t increases the vibrations caused by the last term in Eq. (17) will increase *without bound*. The external force is said to be in *resonance* with the vibrating mass. It is evident that the displacement will become so large that the elastic limit of the spring will be exceeded, leading to fracture or to a permanent distortion in the spring.

Suppose that c is positive but very close to zero while $\omega^2 = \omega_0^2$. Note that Eq. (13) will yield $b_1 = -F_0/c\omega$ and $b_2 = 0$ when substituted in Eq. (12). Superimposing $x_p(t) = -(F_0/c\omega) \cos \omega t$ on Eq. (10) and letting $c_0 = 2m\omega_0$, we obtain

$$x(t) = e^{(-c/c_0)\omega_0 t}\left(c_1 \cos \omega_0 \sqrt{1 - \left(\frac{c}{c_0}\right)^2} t + c_2 \sin \omega_0 \sqrt{1 - \left(\frac{c}{c_0}\right)^2} t\right) - \frac{F_0}{c\omega} \cos \omega t.$$

$$\textbf{(18)}$$

Since c/c_0 is very small, for small values of t we see that Eq. (18) can be approximated as

$$x(t) \approx c_1 \cos \omega t + c_2 \sin \omega t - \frac{F_0}{2m\omega}\left(\frac{2m}{c}\right) \cos \omega t,$$

which bears a marked resemblance to Eq. (17) *when Eq. (17) is evaluated at large values of t* (since $2m/c$ is large). Thus, the *damped* spring problem approaches resonance. This phenomenon is extremely important in engineering since resonance may produce undesirable effects such as metal fatigue and structural fracture, as well as desirable objectives such as sound and light amplification.

EXERCISES 3.8

In Exercises 1 through 6, determine the equation of motion of a mass m attached to a coiled spring with spring constant k initially displaced a distance x_0 from equilibrium and released with velocity v_0 subject to:

a) no damping or external forces,

b) a damping constant c, but no external force,

c) an external force $F_0 \sin \omega t$, but no damping,

d) both a damping constant and external force $F_0 \sin \omega t$.

1. $m = 10$ kg, $k = 1000$ N/m, $x_0 = 1$ m, $v_0 = 0$, $c = 200$ N/(m/s), $F_0 = 1$ N, $\omega = 10$ rad/s

2. $m = 10\,\text{kg}$, $k = 10\,\text{N/m}$, $x_0 = 0$, $v_0 = 1\,\text{m/s}$, $c = 20\,\text{N/(m/s)}$, $F_0 = 1\,\text{N}$, $\omega = 1\,\text{rad/s}$

3. $m = 10\,\text{kg}$, $k = 10\,\text{N/m}$, $x_0 = 3\,\text{m}$, $v_0 = 4\,\text{m/s}$, $c = 10\sqrt{5}\,\text{N/(m/s)}$, $F_0 = 1\,\text{N}$, $\omega = 1\,\text{rad/s}$

4. $m = 1\,\text{kg}$, $k = 16\,\text{N/m}$, $x_0 = 4\,\text{m}$, $v_0 = 0$, $c = 10\,\text{N/(m/s)}$, $F_0 = 4\,\text{N}$, $\omega = 4\,\text{rad/s}$

5. $m = 1\,\text{kg}$, $k = 25\,\text{N/m}$, $x_0 = 0\,\text{m}$, $v_0 = 3\,\text{m/s}$, $c = 8\,\text{N/(m/s)}$, $F_0 = 1\,\text{N}$, $\omega = 3\,\text{rad/s}$

6. $m = 9\,\text{kg}$, $k = 1\,\text{N/m}$, $x_0 = 4\,\text{m}$, $v_0 = 1\,\text{m/s}$, $c = 10\,\text{N/(m/s)}$, $F_0 = 2\,\text{N}$, $\omega = \frac{1}{3}\,\text{rad/s}$

7. One end of a rubber band is fixed at a point A. A 1-kg mass, attached to the other end, stretches the rubber band vertically to the point B in such a way that the length AB is 16 cm greater than the natural length of the band. If the mass is further drawn to a position 8 cm below B and released, what will be its velocity (if we neglect resistance) as it passes the position B?

8. If in Exercise 7 the mass is released at a position 8 cm above B, what will be its velocity as it passes 1 cm above B?

9. A cylindrical block of wood of radius and height 1 ft and weighing 12.48 lb floats with its axis vertical in water (62.4 lb per ft³). If it is depressed so that the surface of the water is tangent to the block, and is then released, what will be its period of vibration and equation of motion? Neglect resistance. (*Hint:* The upward force on the block is equal to the weight of the water displaced by the block.)

10. A cubical block of wood, 1 ft on a side, is depressed so that its upper face lies along the surface of the water, and is then released. The period of vibration is found to be 1 s. Neglecting resistance, what is the weight of the block of wood?

11. A 10-g mass suspended from a spring vibrates freely, the resistance being numerically equal to half the velocity (in m/s) at any instant. If the period of the motion is 8 s, what is the spring constant (in kg/s²)?

12. A weight w (lb) is suspended from a spring whose constant is 10 lb/ft. The motion of the weight is subject to a resistance (lb) numerically equal to half the velocity (ft/s). If the motion is to have a 1-s period, what are the possible values of w?

13. A 1-g mass is hanging at rest on a spring that is stretched 25 cm by the weight. The upper end of the spring is given the periodic force $0.01 \sin 2t$ N and air resistance has a magnitude 0.0216 (g/s) times the velocity in meters per second. Find the equation of motion of the mass.

14. An ideal pendulum consists of a weightless rod of length l attached at one end to a frictionless hinge and supporting a body of mass m at the other end. Suppose the pendulum is displaced an angle θ_0 and released (see Fig. 7). The tangential acceleration of the ideal pendulum is $l\theta''$, and must be proportional, by Newton's second law of motion, to the tangential component of gravitational force.

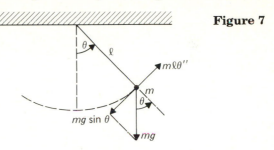

Figure 7

a) Neglecting air resistance, show that the ideal pendulum satisfies the nonlinear initial value problem

$$l\frac{d^2\theta}{dt^2} = -g\sin\theta, \quad \theta(0) = \theta_0, \quad \theta'(0) = 0. \tag{19}$$

b) Assuming θ_0 is small, explain why Eq. (19) may be approximated by the linear initial value problem

$$\frac{d^2\theta}{dt^2} + \frac{g}{l}\theta = 0, \quad \theta(0) = \theta_0, \quad \theta'(0) = 0. \tag{20}$$

c) Solve Eq. (20) assuming that the rod is 6 inches long and that the initial displacement $\theta_0 = 0.5$ radian. What is the frequency of the pendulum?

15. A grandfather clock has a pendulum that is one meter long. The clock ticks each time the pendulum reaches the rightmost extent of its swing. Neglecting friction and air resistance, and assuming that the motion is small, determine how many times the clock ticks in one minute.

3.9 ELECTRIC CIRCUITS

We shall make use of the concepts developed in Section 2.5 and the methods of this chapter to study a simple electric circuit containing a resistor, an inductor, and a capacitor in series with an electromotive force (Fig. 8). Suppose that R, L, C, and E are constants. Applying Kirchhoff's law, we obtain

$$L\frac{dI}{dt} + RI + \frac{Q}{C} = E. \tag{1}$$

Since $dQ/dt = I$, we differentiate Eq. (1) to get the second-order homogeneous differential equation

$$L\frac{d^2I}{dt^2} + R\frac{dI}{dt} + \frac{I}{C} = 0. \tag{2}$$

To solve this equation, we note that the characteristic equation

$$\lambda^2 + \frac{R}{L}\lambda + \frac{1}{CL} = 0$$

has the following roots:

$$\lambda_1 = \frac{-R + \sqrt{R^2 - 4L/C}}{2L}, \quad \lambda_2 = \frac{-R - \sqrt{R^2 - 4L/C}}{2L},$$

or, rewriting the radical in dimensionless units,† we have

$$\lambda_1 = \frac{R}{2L}\left(-1 + \sqrt{1 - \frac{4L}{CR^2}}\right), \quad \lambda_2 = \frac{R}{2L}\left(-1 - \sqrt{1 - \frac{4L}{CR^2}}\right). \tag{3}$$

Equation (2) may now be solved using the methods of Sections 3.4 and 3.5.

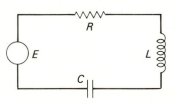

Figure 8

Example 1   Let $L = 1$ henry (h), $R = 100$ ohms (Ω), $C = 10^{-4}$ farads (f), and $E = 1000$ volts (V) in the circuit shown in Fig. 8. Suppose that no charge is present and no current is flowing at time $t = 0$ when E is applied. By Eq. (3) we see that the characteristic equation has the roots $\lambda_1 = -50 + 50\sqrt{3}i$

---

†   1 henry = 1 volt-s/amp; 1 farad = 1 coul/volt; 1 ohm = 1 volt/amp; 1 coul = 1 amp-s.

and $\lambda_2 = -50 - 50\sqrt{3}i$. Thus

$$I(t) = e^{-50t}(c_1 \cos 50\sqrt{3}t + c_2 \sin 50\sqrt{3}t).$$

Applying the initial condition $I(0) = 0$, we have $c_1 = 0$. Hence

$$I(t) = c_2 e^{-50t} \sin 50\sqrt{3}t.$$

To establish the value of c_2, we must make use of Eq. (1) and the initial condition $Q(0) = 0$. Since

$$Q(t) = C\left(E - L\frac{dI}{dt} - RI\right)$$

$$= \frac{1}{10} - \frac{c_2}{200}e^{-50t}(\sin 50\sqrt{3}t + \sqrt{3}\cos 50\sqrt{3}t),$$

it follows that for $t = 0$, $c_2 = 20/\sqrt{3}$. Thus

$$Q(t) = \frac{1}{10} - \frac{1}{10\sqrt{3}}e^{-50t}(\sin 50\sqrt{3}t + \sqrt{3}\cos 50\sqrt{3}t)$$

and

$$I(t) = \frac{20}{\sqrt{3}}e^{-50t}\sin 50\sqrt{3}t.$$

From these equations we observe that the current will rapidly damp out and that the charge will rapidly approach its steady-state value of $\frac{1}{10}$ coulomb (coul).

Example 2 Let the inductance, resistance, and capacitance in Example 1 remain the same, but suppose $E = 962 \sin 60t$. By Eq. (1) we have

$$\frac{dI}{dt} + 100I + 10^4 Q = 962 \sin 60t, \tag{4}$$

and converting Eq. (4) so that all expressions are in terms of $Q(t)$, we obtain

$$\frac{d^2Q}{dt^2} + 100\frac{dQ}{dt} + 10^4 Q = 962 \sin 60t. \tag{5}$$

It is evident that Eq. (5) has a particular solution of the form

$$Q_p(t) = A_1 \sin 60t + A_2 \cos 60t. \tag{6}$$

To determine the values A_1 and A_2, we substitute Eq. (6) into Eq. (4), obtaining the simultaneous equations

$$6400A_1 - 6000A_2 = 962,$$
$$6000A_1 + 6400A_2 = 0.$$

Thus $A_1 = \frac{1}{125}$, $A_2 = -\frac{3}{400}$, and since the general solution of the homogeneous equation is the same as that of Eq. (2), the general solution of Eq. (1) is

$$Q(t) = e^{-50t}(c_1 \cos 50\sqrt{3}t + c_2 \sin 50\sqrt{3}t) + \tfrac{1}{125}\sin 60t - \tfrac{3}{400}\cos 60t. \quad (7)$$

Differentiating Eq. (7), we obtain

$$I(t) = 50e^{-50t}[(\sqrt{3}c_2 - c_1)\cos 50\sqrt{3}t - (c_2 + \sqrt{3}c_1)\sin 50\sqrt{3}t]$$
$$+ \tfrac{12}{25}\cos 60t + \tfrac{9}{20}\sin 60t.$$

Setting $t = 0$ and using the initial conditions, we obtain the simultaneous equations

$$c_1 = \tfrac{3}{400},$$
$$50(\sqrt{3}c_2 - c_1) = -\tfrac{12}{25}.$$

Therefore, $c_1 = \frac{3}{400}$ and $c_2 = -7\sqrt{3}/10{,}000$, so that

$$Q(t) = \frac{e^{-50t}}{10{,}000}(75\cos 50\sqrt{3}t - 7\sqrt{3}\sin 50\sqrt{3}t) + \frac{80\sin 60t - 75\cos 60t}{10{,}000},$$
$$I(t) = \frac{-e^{-50t}}{100}(48\cos 50\sqrt{3}t + 34\sqrt{3}\sin 50\sqrt{3}t) + \frac{48\cos 60t + 45\sin 60t}{100}.$$

EXERCISES 3.9

1. In Example 1, let $L = 10$ h, $R = 250\,\Omega$, $C = 10^{-3}$ f, and $E = 900$ V. With the same assumptions, calculate the current and charge for all values of $t \geq 0$.

2. In Exercise 1, suppose instead that $E = 50\cos 30t$. Find $Q(t)$ for $t \geq 0$.

In Exercises 3 through 6, find the steady-state current in the *RLC* circuit of Fig. 8 where:

3. $L = 5$ henrys, $R = 10$ ohms, $C = 0.1$ farad, $E = 25\sin t$ volts.

4. $L = 10$ henrys, $R = 40$ ohms, $C = 0.025$ farad, $E = 100\cos 5t$ volts.

5. $L = 1$ henry, $R = 7$ ohms, $C = 0.1$ farad, $E = 100\sin 10t$ volts.

6. $L = 2.5$ henrys, $R = 10$ ohms, $C = 0.08$ farad, $E = 100\cos 5t$ volts.

Find the transient current in the *RLC* circuit of Fig. 8 for Exercises 7 through 12.

7. Exercise 3.

8. Exercise 4.

9. Exercise 5.

10. Exercise 6.

11. $L = 20$ henrys, $R = 40$ ohms, $C = 10^{-3}$ farad, $E = 500\sin t$ volts.

12. $L = 24$ henrys, $R = 48$ ohms, $C = 0.375$ farad, $E = 900\cos 2t$ volts.

13. Given that $L = 1$ h, $R = 1200\,\Omega$, $C = 10^{-6}$ f, $I(0) = Q(0) = 0$, and $E = 100\sin 600t$ volts, determine the transient current and the steady-state current.

14. Find the ratio of the current flowing in the circuit of Exercise 13 to that which would be flowing if there were no resistance, at $t = 0.001$ s.

15. Consider the system governed by Eq. (1) for the case where the resistance is zero and $E = E_0 \sin \omega t$. Show that the solution consists of two parts, a general solution with frequency $1/\sqrt{LC}$ and a particular solution with frequency ω. The frequency $1/\sqrt{LC}$ is called the *natural* frequency of the circuit. Note that if $\omega = 1/\sqrt{LC}$, then the particular solution disappears.

16. To allow for different variations of the voltage, let us assume in Eq. (1) that $E = E_0 e^{it}$ ($= E_0 \cos t + iE_0 \sin t$). Assume also, as in Exercise 15, that $R = 0$. Finally, for simplicity assume that $E_0 = L = C = 1$. Then $1 = \omega = 1/\sqrt{LC}$.

a) Show that Eq. (2) becomes

$$\frac{d^2 I}{dt^2} + I = e^{it}.$$

b) Determine λ such that $I(t) = \lambda t e^{it}$ is a solution.

c) Calculate the general solution and show

that the magnitude of the current increases without bound as t increases. This phenomenon will produce resonance.

17. Let an inductance of L henries, a resistance of R ohms, and a capacitance of C farads be connected in series with an emf of $E_0 \sin \omega t$ volts. Suppose $Q(0) = I(0) = 0$, and $4L > R^2 C$.

a) Find the expressions for $Q(t)$ and $I(t)$.

b) What value of ω will produce resonance?

18. Solve Exercise 17 for $4L = R^2 C$.

19. Solve Exercise 17 for $4L < R^2 C$.

3.10 THE METHOD OF ELIMINATION FOR LINEAR SYSTEMS WITH CONSTANT COEFFICIENTS

In the preceding sections we discussed the problem of finding the solution to a single linear differential equation. In the rest of this chapter we will discuss an elementary method for solving a system of simultaneous first-order linear differential equations by converting the system into a single higher-order linear differential equation that may then be solved by the methods we have already seen. Systems of simultaneous differential equations arise in problems involving more than one unknown function, each of which is a function of a single independent variable (which often is time). For the sake of consistency throughout the remaining sections of this chapter, we will denote the independent variable by t and the dependent variables by $x(t)$ and $y(t)$ or by the subscripted letters $x_1(t), x_2(t), \ldots, x_n(t)$.

Although some familiarity with the elementary properties of determinants (see Appendix 4) will be useful, no use of matrix methods in solving systems of simultaneous linear differential equations will be made in this chapter. A complete discussion of matrix methods for solving systems of linear differential equations can be found in Chapter 8. In this section we shall give some examples of how simple systems arise and shall describe an elementary procedure for finding their solution.

Example 1 Suppose that a chemical solution flows from one container, at a rate proportional to its volume, into a second container. It flows out from the second container at a constant rate. Let $x(t)$ and $y(t)$ denote the volumes of solution in the first and second containers, respectively, at time t. (The containers may be, for example, cells, in which case we are describing a diffusion process across a cell wall.) To establish the necessary equations, we note that the change in volume equals the difference between input and output in each container. The change in volume is the derivative of volume with respect to time. Since no chemical is flowing into the first container, the change in its volume equals the output:

$$\frac{dx}{dt} = -c_1 x,$$

where c_1 is a positive constant of proportionality. The amount of solution $c_1 x$ flowing out of the first container is the input of the second container. Let c_2 be the constant output of the second container. Then the change in volume in the second container equals the difference between its input and output:

$$\frac{dy}{dt} = c_1 x - c_2.$$

Thus we can describe the flow of solution by means of two differential equations. Since more than one differential equation is involved, we say that we have obtained a *system of differential equations*:

$$\frac{dx}{dt} = -c_1 x,$$
$$\frac{dy}{dt} = c_1 x - c_2, \tag{1}$$

where c_1 and c_2 are positive constants. By a solution of the system (1) we shall mean a pair of functions $x(t)$, $y(t)$ that simultaneously satisfy the two equations in (1). It is easy to solve this system by solving the two equations successively (this is not usually possible). If we denote the initial volumes in the two containers by $x(0)$ and $y(0)$, respectively, we see that the first equation has the solution

$$x(t) = x(0)e^{-c_1 t}. \tag{2}$$

Substituting Eq. (2) into the second equation of (1), we obtain the equation

$$\frac{dy}{dt} = c_1 x(0)e^{-c_1 t} - c_2,$$

which, upon integration, yields the solution

$$y(t) = y(0) + x(0)(1 - e^{-c_1 t}) - c_2 t. \tag{3}$$

Equations (2) and (3) together constitute the unique solution of system (1) which satisfies the given initial conditions.

Example 2   Let tank X contain 100 gallons of brine in which 100 pounds of salt is dissolved and tank Y contain 100 gallons of water. Suppose water flows into tank X at the rate of 2 gallons per minute, and the mixture flows from tank X into tank Y at 3 gallons per minute. From Y one gallon is pumped

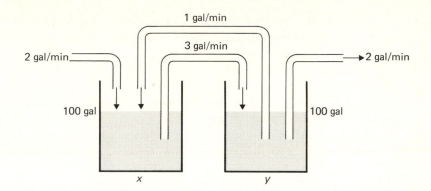

Figure 9

back to X (establishing *feedback*) while 2 gallons are flushed away. We wish to find the amount of salt in both tanks at all time t. (See Fig. 9.)

If we let $x(t)$ and $y(t)$ represent the number of pounds of salt in tanks X and Y at time t, and note that the change in weight equals the difference between input and output, we can again derive a system of linear first-order equations. Tanks X and Y initially contain $x(0) = 100$ and $y(0) = 0$ pounds of salt, respectively, at time $t = 0$. The quantities $x/100$ and $y/100$ are, respectively, the amounts of salt contained in each gallon of water taken from tanks X and Y at time t. Three gallons are being removed from tank X and added to tank Y, while only one of the three gallons removed from tank Y is put in tank X. Thus we have the system

$$\frac{dx}{dt} = -3\frac{x}{100} + \frac{y}{100}, \quad x(0) = 100$$

$$\frac{dy}{dt} = 3\frac{x}{100} - 3\frac{y}{100}, \quad y(0) = 0. \tag{4}$$

Since both equations in the system (4) involve *both* dependent variables, we cannot immediately solve for one of the variables, as we did in Example 1. Instead, we will use the operation of differentiation to eliminate one of the dependent variables. Suppose we begin by solving the second equation for $x(t)$ in terms of the dependent variable y and its derivative:

$$x = y + \frac{100}{3}\frac{dy}{dt}. \tag{5}$$

Differentiating Eq. (5) and equating the left-hand side to the right-hand side of the first equation in the system (4), we have

$$\frac{-3x}{100} + \frac{y}{100} = \frac{dx}{dt} = \frac{dy}{dt} + \frac{100}{3}\frac{d^2y}{dt^2}. \tag{6}$$

Replacing the x-term on the left-hand side of Eq. (6) with Eq. (5) produces the second-order linear equation

$$\frac{100}{3} \frac{d^2y}{dt^2} + 2\frac{dy}{dt} + \frac{2y}{100} = 0. \tag{7}$$

The initial conditions for Eq. (7) are obtained directly from the system (4), since $y(0) = 0$ and

$$y'(0) = 3\frac{x(0)}{100} - 3\frac{y(0)}{100} = 3. \tag{8}$$

Multiplying both sides of Eq. (7) by $\frac{3}{100}$, we have the initial value problem

$$y'' + \frac{6}{100}y' + \frac{6}{(100)^2}y = 0, \quad y(0) = 0, \quad y'(0) = 3. \tag{9}$$

The characteristic equation for (9) has the roots

$$\lambda_1 = \frac{-3 + \sqrt{3}}{100}, \quad \lambda_2 = \frac{-3 - \sqrt{3}}{100}$$

so that the general solution is

$$y(t) = c_1 e^{[(-3+\sqrt{3})t]/100} + c_2 e^{[(-3-\sqrt{3})t]/100}.$$

Using the initial conditions we obtain the simultaneous equations

$$c_1 + c_2 = 0,$$

$$\frac{-3 + \sqrt{3}}{100}c_1 - \frac{3 + \sqrt{3}}{100}c_2 = 3.$$

These have the unique solution $c_1 = -c_2 = 50\sqrt{3}$. Hence

$$y(t) = 50\sqrt{3}[e^{[(-3+\sqrt{3})t]/100} - e^{[(-3-\sqrt{3})t]/100}]$$

and substituting this function into the right-hand side of Eq. (5) we obtain

$$x(t) = 50[e^{[(-3+\sqrt{3})t]/100} + e^{[(-3-\sqrt{3})t]/100}].$$

Note that, as is evident from the problem, the amounts of salt in the two tanks approach zero, as time tends to infinity.

The technique we have used in solving Example 2 is called the *method of elimination*, since all but one dependent variable is eliminated by repeated differentiation. The method is quite elementary but requires many calculations. In Section 3.12 we will introduce a direct way of obtaining the solution without doing the elimination procedure. Nevertheless, because of its simplicity, elimination can be a very useful tool.

Example 3 Consider the system

$$x' = x + y, \qquad x(0) = 1,$$
$$y' = -3x - y, \quad y(0) = 0. \tag{10}$$

Differentiating the first equation and substituting the second equation for y', we have

$$x'' = x' + (-3x - y). \tag{11}$$

Solving the first equation of the system (10) for y and substituting that expression in Eq. (11), we obtain

$$x'' + 2x = 0.$$

Thus

$$x(t) = c_1 \cos \sqrt{2}t + c_2 \sin \sqrt{2}t.$$

Then, according to the first equation of the system (10),

$$y = x' - x = -\sqrt{2}c_1 \sin \sqrt{2}t + \sqrt{2}c_2 \cos \sqrt{2}t - c_1 \cos \sqrt{2}t - c_2 \sin \sqrt{2}t$$
$$= (c_2\sqrt{2} - c_1) \cos \sqrt{2}t - (\sqrt{2}c_1 + c_2) \sin \sqrt{2}t.$$

Using the initial conditions, we find that

$$x(0) = c_1 = 1, \quad y(0) = c_2\sqrt{2} - c_1 = 0, \quad \text{or} \quad c_2 = 1/\sqrt{2}.$$

Therefore, the unique solution of the system (10) is given by the pair of functions

$$x(t) = \cos \sqrt{2}t + \frac{1}{\sqrt{2}} \sin \sqrt{2}t,$$

$$y(t) = -\left(\sqrt{2} + \frac{1}{\sqrt{2}}\right) \sin \sqrt{2}t = -\frac{3}{\sqrt{2}} \sin \sqrt{2}t.$$

Example 4 Consider the system

$$x' = 2x + y + t,$$
$$y' = x + 2y + t^2. \tag{12}$$

Proceeding as before, we obtain

$$x'' = 2x' + y' + 1 = 2x' + (x + 2y + t^2) + 1$$
$$= 2x' + x + (2x' - 4x - 2t) + t^2 + 1$$

or

$$x'' - 4x' + 3x = t^2 - 2t + 1 = (t - 1)^2. \tag{13}$$

The solution to the homogeneous part of Eq. (13) is $x(t) = c_1e^t + c_2e^{3t}$. A particular solution of Eq. (13) is easily found to be $\frac{1}{3}t^2 + \frac{2}{9}t + \frac{11}{27}$, so the general solution of Eq. (13) is

$$x(t) = c_1 e^t + c_2 e^{3t} + \tfrac{1}{3}t^2 + \tfrac{2}{9}t + \tfrac{11}{27}.$$

As before, since $y = x' - 2x - t$, we obtain

$$y(t) = c_1 e^t + 3c_2 e^{3t} + \tfrac{2}{3}t + \tfrac{2}{9} - 2c_1 e^t - 2c_2 e^{3t} - \tfrac{2}{3}t^2 - \tfrac{4}{9}t - \tfrac{22}{27} - t$$

or

$$y(t) = -c_1 e^t + c_2 e^{3t} - \tfrac{2}{3}t^2 - \tfrac{7}{9}t - \tfrac{16}{27}.$$

The method illustrated in the last three examples can easily be generalized to apply to linear systems with three or more equations. *A linear system of n first-order equations usually reduces to an nth-order linear differential equation*, because it generally requires one differentiation to eliminate each variable $x_2, \ldots, x_n$ from the system.

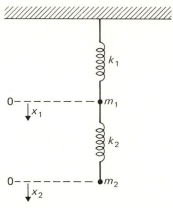

Figure 10

Example 5   As a fifth example, we consider the mass-spring system of Fig. 10, which is a direct generalization of the system described in Section 3.8. In this example we have two masses suspended by springs in series with spring constants k_1 and k_2 (see Section 3.8). If the vertical displacements from equilibrium of the two masses are denoted by $x_1(t)$ and $x_2(t)$, respectively, then using assumptions (a) and (b) (Hooke's law) of Section 3.8, we find that the net forces acting on the two masses are given by

$$F_1 = -k_1 x_1 + k_2(x_2 - x_1),$$
$$F_2 = -k_2(x_2 - x_1).$$

Here the positive direction is downward. Note that the first spring is compressed when $x_1 < 0$ and the second spring is compressed when $x_1 > x_2$. The equations of motion are

$$m_1 \frac{d^2 x_1}{dt^2} = -k_1 x_1 + k_2(x_2 - x_1) = -(k_1 + k_2)x_1 + k_2 x_2,$$

$$m_2 \frac{d^2 x_2}{dt^2} = -k_2(x_2 - x_1) = k_1 x_1 - k_2 x_2,$$

(14)

which comprise a system of two second-order linear differential equations with constant coefficients.

We will now show that linear differential equations (and systems) of *any* order can be converted, by the introduction of new variables, into a system of first-order differential equations. This concept is very important since it means that the study of first-order linear systems provides a unified theory for all linear differential equations and systems. From a practical point of view it means, for example, that once we know how to solve first-order linear systems, with constant coefficients, we will be able to solve any constant-coefficient linear differential equation or system.

To rewrite system (14) as a first-order system, we define the new variables $x_3 = x_1'$ and $x_4 = x_2'$. Then $x_3' = x_1''$, $x_4' = x_2''$ and (14) can be expressed as the system of four first-order equations

$$
\begin{aligned}
x_1' &= x_3, \\
x_2' &= x_4, \\
x_3' &= -\left(\frac{k_1 + k_2}{m_1}\right)x_1 + \left(\frac{k_2}{m_1}\right)x_2, \\
x_4' &= \left(\frac{k_2}{m_2}\right)x_1 - \left(\frac{k_2}{m_2}\right)x_2.
\end{aligned}
\tag{15}
$$

If we wish, we can now use the method of elimination to reduce system (15) to a single fourth-order linear differential equation that can be solved by the techniques shown in Sections 3.1–3.7. (See Exercise 27.)

Theorem 1 The linear nth-order differential equation

$$
x^{(n)} + a_1(t)x^{(n-1)} + a_2(t)x^{(n-2)} + \cdots + a_{n-1}(t)x' + a_n(t)x = f(t) \tag{16}
$$

can be rewritten as a system of n first-order linear equations.

Proof Define $x_1 = x$, $x_2 = x'$, $x_3 = x''$, ..., $x_n = x^{(n-1)}$. Then we have

$$
\begin{aligned}
x_1' &= x_2, \\
x_2' &= x_3, \\
&\;\;\vdots \\
x_{n-1}' &= x_n, \\
x_n' &= -a_n x_1 - a_{n-1}x_2 - \cdots - a_1 x_n + f. \;\blacksquare
\end{aligned}
\tag{17}
$$

In some cases, Theorem 1 can be generalized to nonlinear differential equations. (See Exercise 28.)

Suppose that n initial conditions are specified for the nth-order equation (16):

$$
x(t_0) = c_1, \quad x'(t_0) = c_2, \ldots, x^{(n-1)}(t_0) = c_n.
$$

These initial conditions can be immediately transformed into an initial condition for system (17):

$$x_1(t_0) = c_1, \quad x_2(t_0) = c_2, \ldots, x_n(t_0) = c_n.$$

Example 6   Consider the initial value problem

$$t^3 x''' + 4t^2 x'' - 8tx' + 8x = 0, \quad x(2) = 3, \quad x'(2) = -6, \quad x''(2) = 14.$$

Defining $x_1 = x, x_2 = x', x_3 = x''$, we obtain the system

$$x_1' = x_2,$$
$$x_2' = x_3,$$
$$x_3' = \frac{-8}{t^3} x_1 + \frac{8}{t^2} x_2 - \frac{4}{t} x_3,$$

with the initial condition $x_1(2) = 3, x_2(2) = -6, x_3(2) = 14$.

EXERCISES 3.10

In Exercises 1 through 9, find the general solution of each given system of equations. When initial conditions are given, find the unique solution.

1. $x' = x + 2y,$
   $y' = 3x + 2y$

2. $x' = x + 2y + t - 1, \quad x(0) = 0$
   $y' = 3x + 2y - 5t - 2, \quad y(0) = 4$

3. $x' = -4x - y,$
   $y' = x - 2y$

4. $x' = x + y, \quad x(0) = 1,$
   $y' = y, \quad y(0) = 0$

5. $x' = 8x - y,$
   $y' = 4x + 12y$

6. $x' = 2x + y + 3e^{2t},$
   $y' = -4x + 2y + te^{2t}$

7. $x' = 3x + 3y + t,$
   $y' = -x - y + 1$

8. $x' = 4x + y, \quad x(\pi/4) = 0,$
   $y' = -8x + 8y, \quad y(\pi/4) = 1$

9. $x' = 12x - 17y,$
   $y' = 4x - 4y$

10. By elimination, find a solution to the following nonlinear system:

$$x' = x + \sin x \cos x + 2y,$$
$$y' = (x + \sin x \cos x + 2y) \sin^2 x + x$$

In Exercises 11 through 17, transform each given equation into a system of first-order equations.

11. $x'' + 2x' + 3x = 0$

12. $x'' - 6tx' + 3t^3 x = \cos t$

13. $x''' - x'' + (x')^2 - x^3 = t$

14. $x^{iv} - \cos x(t) = t$

15. $x''' + xx'' - x'x^4 = \sin t$

16. $xx'x''x''' = t^5$

17. $x''' - 3x'' + 4x' - x = 0$

18. A mass m moves in xyz-space according to the following equations of motion:

$$mx'' = f(t, x, y, z),$$
$$my'' = g(t, x, y, z),$$
$$mz'' = h(t, x, y, z).$$

Transform these equations into a system of six first-order equations.

19. Consider the uncoupled system

$$x_1' = x_1, \quad x_2' = x_2.$$

a) What is the general solution of this system?

b) Show that there is no second-order equation equivalent to this system. (*Hint:* Show that any second-order equation has solutions that are not solutions of this system.) This shows that first-order systems are more general than higher-order equations in the sense that any of the latter can be written as a first-order system, but not vice versa.

Use the method of elimination to solve the systems in Exercises 20 and 21.

20. $x_1' = x_1,$
$x_2' = 2x_1 + x_2 - 2x_3,$
$x_3' = 3x_1 + 2x_2 + x_3$

21. $x_1' = x_1 + x_2 + x_3,$
$x_2' = 2x_1 + x_2 - x_3,$
$x_3' = -8x_1 - 5x_2 - 3x_3$

22. In Example 2, when does tank Y contain a maximum amount of salt? How much salt is in tank Y at that time?

23. Suppose in Example 2 that the rate of flow from tank Y to tank X is two gallons per minute (instead of one) and all other facts are unchanged. Find the equations for the amount of salt in each tank at all times t.

24. Tank X contains 500 gal of brine in which 500 lb of salt are dissolved. Tank Y contains 500 gal of water. Water flows into tank X at the rate of 30 gal/min, and the mixture flows into Y at the rate of 40 gal/min. From Y the solution is pumped back into X at the rate of 10 gal/min and into a third tank at the rate of 30 gal/min. Find the maximum amount of salt in Y. When does this concentration occur?

25. Suppose in Exercise 24 that tank X contains 1000 gal of brine. Solve the problem, given that all other conditions are unchanged.

26. Consider the mass-spring system illustrated in Fig. 11. Here three masses are suspended in series by three springs with spring constants k_1, k_2, and k_3, respectively. Formulate a system of second-order differential equations that describes this system.

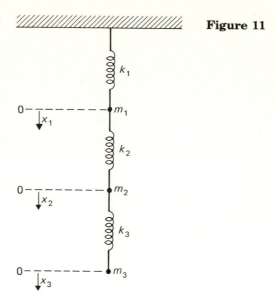

Figure 11

27. Find a single fourth-order linear differential equation in terms of the dependent variable x_1 for the system (14). Find a solution to the system if $m_1 = 1\,\text{kg}$, $m_2 = 2\,\text{kg}$, $k_1 = k_2 = 4\,\text{N/m}$.

28. Show that the differential equation

$$x^{(n)} = g(t, x, x', \ldots, x^{(n-1)})$$

can be transformed into a system of n first-order equations.

29. In a study concerning the distribution of radioactive potassium K^{42} between red blood cells and the plasma of the human blood, C. W. Sheppard and W. R. Martin [*J. Gen. Physiol*, **33**: 703–722 (1950)] added K^{42} to freshly drawn blood. They discovered that although the total amount of potassium (stable and radioactive) in the red cells and in the plasma remained practically constant during the experiment, the radioactivity was gradually transmitted from the plasma to the red cells. Thus the behavior of the radioactivity is that of a linear closed two-compartment system. If the fractional transfer coefficient from the plasma to the cells is $k_{12} = 30.1$ percent per hour, while $k_{21} = 1.7$ percent per hour, and the initial radioactivity was 800 counts per minute in the plasma and 25 counts per minute in the red cells, what is the number of counts per minute in the red cells after 300 minutes?

30. The presence of temperature inversions and low wind speeds will often trap air pollutants in a mountain valley for an extended period of time. Gaseous sulfur compounds are often a significant air pollution problem, and their study is complicated by their rapid oxidation. Hydrogen sulfide, H_2S, oxidizes into sulfur dioxide, SO_2, which in turn oxidizes into a sulphate. The following model has been proposed† for determining the concentrations $x(t)$ and $y(t)$ of H_2S and SO_2, respectively, in

a fixed airshed. Let

$$\frac{dx}{dt} = -\alpha x + \gamma, \qquad \frac{dy}{dt} = \alpha x - \beta y + \delta,$$

where the constants α and β are the conversion rates of H_2S into SO_2 and SO_2 into sulphate, respectively, and γ and δ are the production rates of H_2S and SO_2, respectively. Solve the equations sequentially and estimate the concentration levels that could be reached under a prolonged air pollution episode.

3.11 LINEAR SYSTEMS: THEORY

In this section we will consider the linear system of two-first-order equations

$$\begin{aligned} x' &= a_{11}(t)x + a_{12}(t)y + f_1, \\ y' &= a_{21}(t)x + a_{22}(t)y + f_2, \end{aligned} \tag{1}$$

and the associated homogeneous system (i.e., $f_1 = f_2 = 0$)

$$\begin{aligned} x' &= a_{11}(t)x + a_{12}(t)y, \\ y' &= a_{21}(t)x + a_{22}(t)y. \end{aligned} \tag{2}$$

The point of view here will emphasize the similarities between such systems and the linear second-order equations discussed in Section 3.2. That there is a parallel between the two theories should not be surprising, since we have already shown in Section 3.10 that any linear second-order equation can always be transformed into a system of the form of Eq. (1).

By a *solution* of system (1) [or (2)] we will mean a *pair* of functions $\{x(t), y(t)\}$ that possess first derivatives and that satisfy the given equations. This is a formal statement of what we have been assuming all along. The following theorem will be proved in the chapter on "Existence and Uniqueness of Solutions."

Theorem 1   If the functions $a_{11}(t)$, $a_{12}(t)$, $a_{21}(t)$, $a_{22}(t)$, $f_1(t)$, and $f_2(t)$ are continuous, then given any numbers t_0, x_0, and y_0, there exists exactly one solution $\{x(t), y(t)\}$ of system (1) that satisfies $x(t_0) = x_0$ and $y(t_0) = y_0$.

---

† R. L. Bohac, "A Mathematical Model for the Conversion of Sulphur Compounds in the Missoula Valley Airshed," *Proceedings of the Montana Academy of Science* (1974).

The pair of functions $\{x_3(t), y_3(t)\}$ is a *linear combination* of the pairs $\{x_1(t), y_1(t)\}$ and $\{x_2(t), y_2(t)\}$ if there exist constants c_1 and c_2 such that the following two equations hold:

$$x_3(t) = c_1x_1(t) + c_2x_2(t),$$
$$y_3(t) = c_1y_1(t) + c_2y_2(t). \tag{3}$$

The next theorem is the systems analogue of Theorem 3 in Section 3.1. Its easy proof is left as an exercise.

Theorem 2   If $\{x_1(t), y_1(t)\}$ and $\{x_2(t), y_2(t)\}$ are solutions of the homogeneous system (2), then any linear combination of them is also a solution of the system (2).

Example 1   Consider the system

$$x' = -x + 6y,$$
$$y' = x - 2y. \tag{4}$$

It is easy to verify that $\{-2e^{-4t}, e^{-4t}\}$ and $\{3e^t, e^t\}$ are solutions of Eqs. (4). Hence, by Theorem 2, the pair $\{-2c_1e^{-4t} + 3c_2e^t, c_1e^{-4t} + c_2e^t\}$ is a solution of Eqs. (4) for any constants c_1 and c_2.

We define two pairs of functions $\{x_1(t), y_1(t)\}$ and $\{x_2(t), y_2(t)\}$ to be *linearly independent* if whenever the equations

$$c_1x_1(t) + c_2x_2(t) = 0,$$
$$c_1y_1(t) + c_2y_2(t) = 0, \tag{5}$$

hold for all values of t, then $c_1 = c_2 = 0$. In Example 1, the two given pairs of solutions are linearly independent since $c_1e^{-4t} + c_2e^t$ vanishes for all t only when $c_1 = c_2 = 0$.

Given two solutions $\{x_1(t), y_1(t)\}$ and $\{x_2(t), y_2(t)\}$, we define the *Wronskian* of the two solutions by the following determinant:

$$W(t) = \begin{vmatrix} x_1(t) & x_2(t) \\ y_1(t) & y_2(t) \end{vmatrix} = x_1(t)y_2(t) - x_2(t)y_1(t). \tag{6}$$

We can then prove the next theorem.

Theorem 3   If $W(t) \neq 0$ for every t, then Eqs. (3) is the *general solution* of the homogeneous system (2) in the sense that given any solution $\{x^*, y^*\}$ of system (2), there exist constants c_1 and c_2 such that

$$x^* = c_1x_1 + c_2x_2,$$
$$y^* = c_1y_1 + c_2y_2. \tag{7}$$

Proof   Let t_0 be given and consider the linear system of two equations in the unknown quantities c_1 and c_2:

$$c_1 x_1(t_0) + c_2 x_2(t_0) = x^*(t_0),$$
$$c_1 y_1(t_0) + c_2 y_2(t_0) = y^*(t_0). \tag{8}$$

The determinant of this system is $W(t_0)$, which is nonzero by assumption. Thus there is a unique pair of constants $\{c_1, c_2\}$ satisfying Eqs. (8). By Theorem 2,

$$\{c_1 x_1(t) + c_2 x_2(t), \; c_1 y_1(t) + c_2 y_2(t)\}$$

is a solution of Eqs. (2). But by Eqs. (8), this solution satisfies the same initial conditions at t_0 as the solution $\{x^*(t), y^*(t)\}$. By the uniqueness part of Theorem 1, these solutions must be identical for all t. ∎

Example 2   In Example 1 the Wronskian $W(t)$ is

$$W(t) = \begin{vmatrix} -2e^{-4t} & e^{-4t} \\ 3e^t & e^t \end{vmatrix} = -2e^{-3t} - 3e^{-3t} = -5e^{-3t} \neq 0.$$

Hence we need look no further for the general solution of system (4).

In view of the condition required in Theorem 3 that the Wronskian $W(t)$ never vanish, we shall consider the properties of the Wronskian more carefully. Let $\{x_1, y_1\}$ and $\{x_2, y_2\}$ be two solutions of the homogeneous system (2). Since $W(t) = x_1 y_2 - x_2 y_1$, we have

$$W'(t) = x_1 y_2' + x_1' y_2 - x_2 y_1' - x_2' y_1$$
$$= x_1(a_{21} x_2 + a_{22} y_2) + y_2(a_{11} x_1 + a_{12} y_1) - x_2(a_{21} x_1 + a_{22} y_1)$$
$$- y_1(a_{11} x_2 + a_{12} y_1).$$

Multiplying these expressions through and canceling like terms, we obtain

$$W' = a_{11} x_1 y_2 + a_{22} x_1 y_2 - a_{11} x_2 y_1 - a_{22} x_2 y_1$$
$$= (a_{11} + a_{22})(x_1 y_2 - x_2 y_1) = (a_{11} + a_{22}) W.$$

Thus

$$W(t) = W(t_0) \exp\left[\int_{t_0}^{t} [a_{11}(u) + a_{22}(u)] \, du \right]. \tag{9}$$

We have shown the following theorem to be true.

Theorem 4   Let $\{x_1, y_1\}$ and $\{x_2, y_2\}$ be two solutions of the homogeneous system (2). Then the Wronskian $W(t)$ is either always zero or never zero in any interval (since $\exp x \neq 0$ for any x).

We are now ready to state the theorem that links linear independence with a nonvanishing Wronskian (see Lemma 1 in Section 3.2).

Theorem 5   Two solutions $\{x_1(t), y_1(t)\}$ and $\{x_2(t), y_2(t)\}$ are linearly independent if and only if $W(t) \neq 0$.

Proof   Let the solutions be linearly independent and suppose $W(t) = 0$. Then $x_1 y_2 = x_2 y_1$ or $x_1/x_2 = y_1/y_2 = c$ for some constant c. Then $x_1 = cx_2$ and $y_1 = cy_2$, so that the solutions are dependent, which is a contradiction. Hence $W(t) \neq 0$. Conversely, let $W(t) \neq 0$. If the solutions were dependent, then there would exist constants c_1 and c_2, not both zero, such that

$$c_1 x_1 + c_2 x_2 = 0,$$
$$c_1 y_1 + c_2 y_2 = 0.$$

Assuming that $c_1 \neq 0$, we then have $x_1 = cx_2$, $y_1 = cy_2$, where $c = -c_2/c_1$. But then

$$W(t) = x_1 y_2 - x_2 y_1 = cx_2 y_2 - cx_2 y_2 = 0,$$

which is again a contradiction. Therefore the solutions are linearly independent. ∎

We may summarize the contents of the previous four theorems in the following statement. *Let $\{x_1, y_1\}$ and $\{x_2, y_2\}$ be solutions of the homogeneous linear system*

$$x' = a_{11}x + a_{12}y,$$
$$y' = a_{21}x + a_{22}y. \tag{10}$$

Then $\{c_1 x_1 + c_2 x_2, c_1 y_1 + c_2 y_2\}$ will be the general solution of the system (10) *provided that* $W(t) \neq 0$; *that is, provided the solutions $\{x_1, y_1\}$ and $\{x_2, y_2\}$ are linearly independent.*

Finally, let us consider the nonhomogeneous system (1). The following theorem is the direct analogue of Theorem 3 in Section 3.2. Its proof, easily patterned after that of Theorem 3, is left as an exercise.

Theorem 6   Let $\{x^*, y^*\}$ be the general solution of the system (1), and let $\{x_p, y_p\}$ be any solution of (1). Then $\{x^* - x_p, y^* - y_p\}$ is the general solution of the homogeneous equation (10). In other words, the general solution of the system (1) can be written as the sum of the general solution of the homogeneous system (10) and any particular solution of the nonhomogeneous system (1).

Example 3   Consider the system

$$x' = 3x + 3y + t,$$
$$y' = -x - y + 1. \tag{11}$$

We could solve this system by the methods given in the previous section. Here we note first that $\{1, -1\}$ and $\{-3e^{2t}, e^{2t}\}$ are solutions to the homogeneous system

$$x' = 3x + 3y,$$
$$y' = -x - y.$$

A particular solution to the system (11) is $\{-\frac{1}{4}(t^2 + 9t + 3), \frac{1}{4}(t^2 + 7t)\}$. The general solution to (11) is, therefore,

$$\{x(t), y(t)\} = \{c_1 - 3c_2e^{2t} - \tfrac{1}{4}(t^2 + 9t + 3), -c_1 + c_2e^{2t} + \tfrac{1}{4}(t^2 + 7t)\}.$$

We close this section by noting that the theorems in this section can easily be generalized to apply to systems of three or more equations.

EXERCISES 3.11

1. a) Show that

$$\{e^{-3t}, -e^{-3t}\} \quad \text{and} \quad \{(1-t)e^{-3t}, te^{-3t}\}$$

are solutions to

$$x' = -4x - y,$$
$$y' = x - 2y.$$

b) Calculate the Wronskian and verify that the solutions are linearly independent.

c) Write the general solution to the system.

2. a) Show that $\{e^{2t} \cos 2t, -2e^{2t} \sin 2t\}$ and $\{e^{2t} \sin 2t, 2e^{2t} \cos 2t\}$ are solutions of the system

$$x' = 2x + y,$$
$$y' = -4x + 2y.$$

b) Calculate the Wronskian of these solutions and show that they are linearly independent.

c) Show that $\{\frac{1}{4}te^{2t}, -\frac{11}{4}e^{2t}\}$ is a solution of the nonhomogeneous system

$$x' = 2x + y + 3e^{2t},$$
$$y' = -4x + 2y + te^{2t}.$$

d) Combining (a) and (c), write the general solution of the nonhomogeneous equation in (c).

3. a) Show that

$$\{\sin t^2, 2t \cos t^2\} \quad \text{and} \quad \{\cos t^2, -2t \sin t^2\}$$

are solutions of the system

$$x' = y,$$
$$y' = -4t^2x + \frac{1}{t}y.$$

b) Show that the solutions are linearly independent.

c) Show that $W(0) = 0$.

d) Explain the apparent contradiction of Theorem 5.

4. a) Show that $\{\sin \ln t^2, (2/t) \cos \ln t^2\}$ and $\{\cos \ln t^2, -(2/t) \sin \ln t^2\}$ are linearly independent solutions of the system

$$x' = y,$$
$$y' = -\frac{4}{t^2}x - \frac{1}{t}y.$$

b) Calculate the Wronskian $W(t)$.

5. Prove Theorem 2.

6. Prove Theorem 6.

3.12 THE SOLUTION OF HOMOGENEOUS LINEAR SYSTEMS WITH CONSTANT COEFFICIENTS: THE METHOD OF DETERMINANTS

As we saw in Section 3.10, the method of elimination can be used to solve systems of linear equations with constant coefficients. Since the algebraic manipulations required can get cumbersome, we shall develop in this section a more efficient method of obtaining the solution of homogeneous systems. Nonhomogeneous systems are discussed in Exercises 9 through 14. Consider the homogeneous system

$$\begin{aligned} x' &= a_{11}x + a_{12}y, \\ y' &= a_{21}x + a_{22}y, \end{aligned} \tag{1}$$

where the a_{ij} are constants. Our main tool for solving second-order linear homogeneous equations with constant coefficients involved obtaining a characteristic equation by "guessing" that the solution had the form $y = e^{\lambda x}$.

Parallel to the method of Section 3.4, we guess that there is a solution to the system (1) of the form $\{\alpha e^{\lambda t}, \beta e^{\lambda t}\}$, where α, β, and λ are constants yet to be determined. Substituting $x(t) = \alpha e^{\lambda t}$ and $y(t) = \beta e^{\lambda t}$ into Eqs. (1), we obtain

$$\begin{aligned} x' &= \alpha\lambda e^{\lambda t} = a_{11}\alpha e^{\lambda t} + a_{12}\beta e^{\lambda t}, \\ y' &= \beta\lambda e^{\lambda t} = a_{21}\alpha e^{\lambda t} + a_{22}\beta e^{\lambda t}. \end{aligned}$$

After dividing by $e^{\lambda t}$, we obtain the linear system

$$\begin{aligned} (a_{11} - \lambda)\alpha + a_{12}\beta &= 0, \\ a_{21}\alpha + (a_{22} - \lambda)\beta &= 0. \end{aligned} \tag{2}$$

We would like to find values for λ such that the system of Eqs. (2) has a solution $\{\alpha, \beta\}$ where α and β are not both zero. According to the theory of determinants (see Appendix 4), such a solution will occur whenever the determinant of the system

$$\begin{aligned} D &= \begin{vmatrix} a_{11} - \lambda & a_{12} \\ a_{21} & a_{22} - \lambda \end{vmatrix} \\ &= (a_{11} - \lambda)(a_{22} - \lambda) - a_{21}a_{12} \end{aligned} \tag{3}$$

equals zero. Solving the equation $D = 0$, we obtain the quadratic equation

$$\lambda^2 - (a_{11} + a_{22})\lambda + (a_{11}a_{22} - a_{21}a_{12}) = 0. \tag{4}$$

We define this to be the *characteristic equation* of the system (1). That we are using the same term again is no accident, as we shall now demonstrate. Suppose we differentiate the first equation in the system (1) and eliminate the function $y(t)$:

$$x'' = a_{11}x' + a_{12}(a_{21}x + a_{22}y).$$

Then

$$x'' - a_{11}x' - a_{12}a_{21}x = a_{22}a_{12}y = a_{22}(x' - a_{11}x),$$

and gathering like terms, we obtain the homogeneous equation

$$x'' - (a_{11} + a_{22})x' + (a_{11}a_{22} - a_{12}a_{21})x = 0. \tag{5}$$

The characteristic equation for Eq. (5) is exactly the same as Eq. (4). Hence the algebraic steps needed to obtain Eq. (5) can be avoided by setting the determinant $D = 0$.

As in Sections 3.4 and 3.5, there are three cases to consider depending on whether the two roots λ_1 and λ_2 of the characteristic equation are real and distinct, real and equal, or complex conjugates. We will deal with the three cases separately.

CASE 1   *Distinct real roots.* If λ_1 and λ_2 are distinct real numbers, then corresponding to λ_1 and λ_2 we have the solution pairs to the system (1) $\{\alpha_1 e^{\lambda_1 t}, \beta_1 e^{\lambda_1 t}\}$ and $\{\alpha_2 e^{\lambda_2 t}, \beta_2 e^{\lambda_2 t}\}$, respectively. To find the constants α_1 and β_1 (not both zero), replace λ in the system of equations (2) by the value λ_1. The procedure is repeated for α_2, β_2, and λ_2. We note that these constants are not unique. In fact, for each number λ_1 or λ_2, there are an infinite number of pairs $\{\alpha, \beta\}$ that satisfy the system (2). To see this, we observe that if $\{\alpha, \beta\}$ is a solution pair, then so is $\{c\alpha, c\beta\}$ for any real number c. Finally, the solution pairs given above are linearly independent, since, if not, there exists a constant c such that $\alpha_2 e^{\lambda_2 t} = c\alpha_1 e^{\lambda_1 t}$ and $\beta_2 e^{\lambda_2 t} = c\beta_1 e^{\lambda_1 t}$, which is clearly impossible because $\lambda_1 \neq \lambda_2$. We therefore have proved:

Theorem 1   If λ_1 and λ_2 are distinct real roots of Eq. (4), then two linearly independent solutions of the system (1) are given by $\{\alpha_1 e^{\lambda_1 t}, \beta_1 e^{\lambda_1 t}\}$ and $\{\alpha_2 e^{\lambda_2 t}, \beta_2 e^{\lambda_2 t}\}$, where the pairs $\{\alpha_1, \beta_1\}$ and $\{\alpha_2, \beta_2\}$ are solutions of the system (2), with $\lambda = \lambda_1$ and $\lambda = \lambda_2$, respectively.

Example 1   Consider the system (see Examples 1 and 2 in Section 3.11)

$$x' = -x + 6y,$$
$$y' = x - 2y.$$

Here $a_{11} = -1$, $\alpha_{12} = 6$, $a_{21} = 1$, $a_{22} = -2$, and Eq. (3) becomes

$$D = \begin{vmatrix} -1 - \lambda & 6 \\ 1 & -2 - \lambda \end{vmatrix} = (\lambda + 2)(\lambda + 1) - 6 = \lambda^2 + 3\lambda - 4 = 0,$$

which has the roots $\lambda_1 = -4$, $\lambda_2 = 1$. For $\lambda_1 = -4$ the system of equations (2) yields

$$3\alpha_1 + 6\beta_1 = 0,$$
$$\alpha_1 + 2\beta_1 = 0.$$

Noting that the first equation is a multiple of the second, we see that $\alpha_1 = -2\beta_1$, so that $\{-2, 1\}$ is a solution. Hence a first solution pair is $\{-2e^{-4t}, e^{-4t}\}$. Similarly, with $\lambda_2 = 1$, we obtain the equations

$$-2\alpha_2 + 6\beta_2 = 0,$$
$$\alpha_2 - 3\beta_2 = 0,$$

which has a solution $\alpha_2 = 3$, $\beta_2 = 1$. Thus a second linearly independent solution is given by the pair $\{3e^t, e^t\}$. By Theorem 3 in Section 3.11, the general solution is given by the pair

$$\{x(t), y(t)\} = \{-2c_1e^{-4t} + 3c_2e^t, c_1e^{-4t} + c_2e^t\}.$$

CASE 2   *Two equal roots.* When $\lambda_1 = \lambda_2$, one obvious solution pair is $\{\alpha_1e^{\lambda_1 t}, \beta_1e^{\lambda_1 t}\}$. The other solution $\{\alpha_2e^{\lambda_2 t}, \beta_2e^{\lambda_2 t}\}$ given by Theorem 1 is not linearly independent unless $a_{11} = a_{22}$ and $a_{12} = a_{21} = 0$. In the latter case we have the uncoupled system of equations

$$x' = a_{11}x, \quad y' = a_{22}y,$$

with the linearly independent solution pairs $\{\alpha_1e^{\lambda_1 t}, 0\}$ and $\{0, \beta_2e^{\lambda_1 t}\}$, $\lambda_1 = \lambda_2 = a_{11} = a_{22}$. (The equations are said to be uncoupled because each involves only one dependent variable.) On the basis of our results in Section 3.4, we would expect that a second linearly independent solution has the form $\{\alpha_2te^{\lambda_1 t}, \beta_2te^{\lambda_1 t}\}$. This, however, *does not turn out to be the case*. Rather, the second linearly independent solution has the form

$$\{x(t), y(t)\} = \{(\alpha_2 + \alpha_3t)e^{\lambda_1 t}, (\beta_2 + \beta_3t)e^{\lambda_1 t}\}. \tag{6}$$

To calculate the constants α_2, α_3, β_2, and β_3, it is necessary to substitute back into the original system (1). This is best shown by an example.

Example 2   Consider the system

$$x' = -4x - y,$$
$$y' = x - 2y. \tag{7}$$

Equation (3) is

$$D = \begin{vmatrix} -4 - \lambda & -1 \\ 1 & -2 - \lambda \end{vmatrix} = (\lambda + 4)(\lambda + 2) + 1 = \lambda^2 + 6\lambda + 9 = 0,$$

which has the double root $\lambda_1 = \lambda_2 = -3$. From the system (2), with $\lambda = -3$, we find that

$$-\alpha_1 - \beta_1 = 0,$$
$$\alpha_1 + \beta_1 = 0.$$

A nontrivial solution is $\alpha_1 = 1$, $\beta_1 = -1$, yielding the solution pair $\{e^{-3t}, -e^{-3t}\}$.

If we try to find a solution of the form $\{\alpha_2 t e^{-3t}, \beta_2 t e^{-3t}\}$ we immediately run into trouble, since the derivatives on the left-hand side of the system (7) produce terms of the form ce^{-3t} not present on the right-hand side of (7). This explains why we must seek a solution of the form

$$\{(\alpha_2 + \alpha_3 t)e^{-3t}, (\beta_2 + \beta_3 t)e^{-3t}\}. \tag{8}$$

Substituting the pair (8) into the system (7), we obtain

$$e^{-3t}(\alpha_3 - 3\alpha_2 - 3\alpha_3 t) = -4(\alpha_2 + \alpha_3 t)e^{-3t} - (\beta_2 + \beta_3 t)e^{-3t}$$
$$e^{-3t}(\beta_3 - 3\beta_2 - 3\beta_3 t) = (\alpha_2 + \alpha_3 t)e^{-3t} - 2(\beta_2 + \beta_3 t)e^{-3t}.$$

Equating constant terms and multiples of t and dividing by e^{-3t}, we obtain the linearly dependent system of equations

$$\alpha_3 - 3\alpha_2 = -4\alpha_2 - \beta_2,$$
$$-3\alpha_3 = -4\alpha_3 - \beta_3,$$
$$\beta_3 - 3\beta_2 = \alpha_2 - 2\beta_2,$$
$$-3\beta_3 = \alpha_3 - 2\beta_3.$$

One solution is $\alpha_2 = 1$, $\beta_2 = -2$, $\alpha_3 = 1$, $\beta_3 = -1$. Thus a second solution of the system (7) is $\{(1 + t)e^{-3t}, (-2 - t)e^{-3t}\}$. It is easy to verify that the solution pairs above are linearly independent, since $|W(t)| = 1$.

We summarize these results by stating the following theorem.

Theorem 2 Let Eq. (4) have two equal real roots $\lambda_1 = \lambda_2$. Then there exist constants α_1, α_2, α_3, β_1, β_2, and β_3 such that two linearly independent solutions of the system (1) are given by

$$\{x_1(t), y_1(t)\} = \{\alpha_1 e^{\lambda_1 t}, \beta_1 e^{\lambda_1 t}\},$$
$$\{x_2(t), y_2(t)\} = \{(\alpha_2 + \alpha_3 t)e^{\lambda_1 t}, (\beta_2 + \beta_3 t)e^{\lambda_1 t}\}. \tag{9}$$

The constants α_1 and β_1 are found as a nontrivial solution of the homogeneous system of Eqs. (2), while the other constants are found by substituting the second equation of (9) back into the system (1).

Remark In the substitution process, we always obtain a homogeneous system of four equations in the four unknowns α_2, β_2, α_3, and β_3. That this system has nontrivial solutions follows from the fact that the determinant of the system is zero. The proof is left as Exercise 8.

CASE 3 *Complex conjugate roots.* Let $\lambda_1 = a + ib$ and $\lambda_2 = a - ib$, where a and b are real and $b \neq 0$. Then the solution pairs $\{\alpha_1 e^{(a+ib)t}, \beta_1 e^{(a+ib)t}\}$ and $\{\alpha_2 e^{(a-ib)t}, \beta_2 e^{(a-ib)t}\}$ are linearly independent. However, the constants α_1, β_1, α_2, and β_2, obtained from the system (2) are complex numbers. To obtain real solution pairs we must proceed as follows. Let $\alpha_1 = A_1 + iA_2$, $\beta_1 = B_1 + iB_2$ and apply Euler's formula, $e^{i\theta} = \cos\theta + i\sin\theta$, to the first complex solution pair, obtaining

$$x(t) = (A_1 + iA_2)e^{at}(\cos bt + i\sin bt),$$
$$y(t) = (B_1 + iB_2)e^{at}(\cos bt + i\sin bt). \tag{10}$$

Multiplying and remembering that $i^2 = -1$, we obtain the equations

$$x(t) = e^{at}[(A_1\cos bt - A_2\sin bt) + i(A_1\sin bt + A_2\cos bt)],$$
$$y(t) = e^{at}[(B_1\cos bt - B_2\sin bt) + i(B_1\sin bt + B_2\cos bt)].$$

Now, since the coefficients of the system (1) are *real*, the only way $\{x, y\}$ can be a solution pair is for all the real terms and, similarly, the imaginary terms to cancel out. Thus the real parts of x and y must form a solution pair of the system (1), as must the imaginary parts:

$$\{x_1(t), y_1(t)\} = \{e^{at}(A_1\cos bt - A_2\sin bt), e^{at}(B_1\cos bt - B_2\sin bt)\},$$
$$\{x_2(t), y_2(t)\} = \{e^{at}(A_1\sin bt + A_2\cos bt), e^{at}(B_1\sin bt + B_2\cos bt)\}. \tag{11}$$

The Wronskian of the solution pairs (11) is easily computed:

$$W(t) = e^{2at}(A_1B_2 - A_2B_1).$$

We want to show that the pairs (11) are linearly independent. Suppose otherwise. Then $W(t) = 0$, which means that $A_1B_2 = A_2B_1$. This implies that $B_2\alpha_1 = A_2\beta_1$ (according to the definition of α_1 and β_1). Now, neither α_1 nor β_1 vanishes, since if either were zero, so would be the other, and the solution pair (10) would be trivial. Also A_2 can't vanish, since if it did, so would B_2, and the first equation of the system (2) would prevent λ_1 from being complex. Multiplying the first equation of the system (2) by A_2, using the identity $B_2\alpha_1 = A_2\beta_1$, and dividing by α_1, we have

$$(a_{11} - \lambda_1)A_2 + a_{12}B_2 = 0.$$

But then λ_1 again is not complex. Therefore, it is impossible that $W(t)$ could vanish, and we have proved the following theorem.

Theorem 3 If Eq. (4) has the complex roots $\lambda_1 = a + ib$ and $\lambda_2 = a - ib$, then two linearly independent solution pairs of the system (1) are given by the system (11).

Example 3   Consider the system

$$x' = 4x + y,$$
$$y' = -8x + 8y,$$ **(12)**

with

$$D = \begin{vmatrix} 4 - \lambda & 1 \\ -8 & 8 - \lambda \end{vmatrix} = \lambda^2 - 12\lambda + 40 = 0.$$

The roots of the characteristic equation are $\lambda_1 = 6 + 2i$ and $\lambda_2 = 6 - 2i$, so that Theorem 3 yields the linearly independent solution pairs

$$\{x_1(t), y_1(t)\} = \{e^{6t}(A_1 \cos 2t - A_2 \sin 2t), e^{6t}(B_1 \cos 2t - B_2 \sin 2t)\},$$
$$\{x_2(t), y_2(t)\} = \{e^{6t}(A_1 \sin 2t + A_2 \cos 2t), e^{6t}(B_1 \sin 2t + B_2 \cos 2t)\}.$$

Substituting the first equation into the system (12) yields, after a great deal of algebra, the system of equations

$$(2A_1 - 2A_2 - B_1) \cos 2t - (2A_1 + 2A_2 - B_2) \sin 2t = 0,$$
$$(8A_1 - 2B_1 - 2B_2) \cos 2t - (8A_2 + 2B_1 - 2B_2) \sin 2t = 0.$$

Since t is arbitrary and the functions $\sin 2t$ and $\cos 2t$ are linearly independent, the terms in parentheses must all vanish. A choice of values that will accomplish this goal is $A_1 = 1$, $A_2 = \frac{1}{2}$, $B_1 = 1$, and $B_2 = 3$. Thus two linearly independent solution pairs to the system (12) are $\{e^{6t}(\cos 2t - \frac{1}{2} \sin 2t), \quad e^{6t}(\cos 2t - 3 \sin 2t)\}$ and $\{e^{6t}(\sin 2t + \frac{1}{2} \cos 2t), e^{6t}(\sin 2t + 3 \cos 2t)\}$. The general solution of the system (12) is a linear combination of these two pairs.

Example 4   Most biological systems are controlled by the production of enzymes or hormones that stimulate or inhibit the secretion of some compound. For example, the pancreatic hormone glucagon stimulates the release of glucose from the liver to the plasma. A rise in blood glucose inhibits the secretion of glucagon but causes an increase in the production of the hormone insulin. Insulin, in turn, aids in the removal of glucose from the blood and in its conversion to glycogen in the muscle tissue. Let G and I be the deviations of plasma glucose and plasma insulin from the normal (fasting) level, respectively. We then have the system

$$\frac{dG}{dt} = -k_{11}G - k_{12}I,$$
$$\frac{dI}{dt} = k_{21}G - k_{22}I,$$ **(13)**

where the positive constants k_{ij} are model parameters, some of which may be determined experimentally. It is known that the system (13) exhibits a strongly damped oscillatory behavior, since direct injection of glucose into the blood will produce a fall of blood glucose to a level below fasting in about one and a half hours followed by a rise slightly above the fasting level in about three hours. Hence, the characteristic equation of the system (13),

$$D = \begin{vmatrix} -k_{11} - \lambda & -k_{12} \\ k_{21} & -k_{22} - \lambda \end{vmatrix} = (k_{11} + \lambda)(k_{22} + \lambda) + k_{12}k_{21}$$

$$= \lambda^2 + (k_{11} + k_{22})\lambda + (k_{11}k_{22} + k_{12}k_{21}) = 0,$$

must have complex conjugate roots $-a \pm ib$, with $a = (k_{11} + k_{22})/2$ and $b = \sqrt{k_{12}k_{21} - (k_{11} - k_{22})^2/4}$, since only complex roots can lead to oscillatory behavior. By Theorem 3, we have the solution pairs

$$\{G_1, I_1\} = \{e^{-at}(A_1\cos bt - A_2 \sin bt), e^{-at}(B_1 \cos bt - B_2 \sin bt)\},$$
$$\{G_2, I_2\} = \{e^{-at}(A_1 \sin bt + A_2 \cos bt), e^{-at}(B_1 \sin bt + B_2 \cos bt)\}. \tag{14}$$

Since the period of the oscillation is approximately three hours, we may set $b = 2\pi/3$ and measure time in hours. Substituting the first equation of the system (14) into Eqs. (13) we obtain the equations

$$(-aA_1 - bA_2 + k_{11}A_1 + k_{12}B_1) \cos bt$$
$$+ (aA_2 - bA_1 - k_{11}A_2 - k_{12}B_2) \sin bt = 0,$$
$$(-aB_1 - bB_2 - k_{21}A_1 + k_{22}B_1) \cos bt$$
$$+ (aB_2 - bB_1 + k_{21}A_2 - k_{22}B_2) \sin bt = 0.$$

These equations must hold for all t. Thus all the terms in parentheses must vanish. A choice of values for which this occurs is $A_1 = 1$, $A_2 = 0$, $B_1 = (k_{22} - k_{11})/2k_{12}$, and $B_2 = -b/k_{12}$. Then the general solution of the system (13) is given by the pair $\{G(t), I(t)\}$ with

$$G(t) = e^{-at}[c_1 \cos bt + c_2 \sin bt],$$

$$I(t) = e^{-at}\left[\frac{k_{22} - k_{11}}{2k_{12}}(c_1 \cos bt + c_2 \sin bt) + \frac{b}{k_{12}}(c_1 \sin bt - c_2 \cos bt)\right].$$

Assume now that the glucose injection was administered at a time when plasma insulin and glucose were at fasting levels and that the glucose was diffused completely in the blood before the insulin level began to increase ($t = 0$). Then $G(0) = G_0$ equals the ratio of the volume of glucose administered to blood volume, and $I(0) = 0$. Since $G(t)$ is at a maximum when $t = 0$, it follows that $c_1 = G_0$ and $c_2 = 0$. Hence

$$G(t) = G_0 e^{-at} \cos bt. \tag{15}$$

But

$$0 = I(0) = \frac{k_{22} - k_{11}}{2k_{12}} G_0,$$

so that $k_{11} = k_{22}$, $b = \sqrt{k_{12}k_{21}} = 2\pi/3$, and

$$I(t) = G_0 \frac{b}{k_{12}} e^{-at} \sin bt.$$

If the minimum level $G(\frac{3}{2})$ (<0) is known, then by Eq. (15),

$$e^{3a/2} = |G(\tfrac{3}{2})|/G_0,$$

so that

$$k_{11} = a = \frac{2}{3} \ln \frac{|G(\tfrac{3}{2})|}{G_0}.$$

If we determine the plasma insulin at any given time $t_0 > 0$, we can then evaluate the parameters k_{12} and k_{21}.

EXERCISES 3.12

In Exercises 1 through 7, use the method of determinants to find two linearly independent solutions for each given system.

1. $x' = 4x - 3y$,
$y' = 5x - 4y$

2. $x' = 7x + 6y$,
$y' = 2x + 6y$

3. $x' = -x + y$,
$y' = -5x + 3y$

4. $x' = x + y$,
$y' = -x + 3y$

5. $x' = -4x - y$,
$y' = x - 2y$

6. $x' = 4x - 2y$,
$y' = 5x + 2y$

7. $x' = 4x - 3y$,
$y' = 8x - 6y$

8. Substituting the second solution pair (9) into the system (1), obtain the homogeneous system of linear equations

$$
\begin{aligned}
(\lambda - a_{11})\alpha_2 + \alpha_3 - a_{12}\beta_2 &= 0, \\
(\lambda - a_{11})\alpha_3 - a_{12}\beta_3 &= 0, \\
-a_{21}\alpha_2 + (\lambda - a_{22})\beta_2 + \beta_3 &= 0, \\
-a_{21}\alpha_3 + (\lambda - a_{22})\beta_3 &= 0.
\end{aligned}
\tag{16}
$$

a) Show that since $\lambda_1 = \lambda_2 = (a_{11} + a_{22})/2$, the second and fourth equations of the system (16) are identical.

b) Prove that if two equations of a linear system are multiples of each other, then the determinant of the system is zero.

c) Conclude from parts (a) and (b) that the determinant of the system (16) is zero, and from this that (16) has nontrivial solutions.

9. Consider the nonhomogeneous equations

$$
\begin{aligned}
x' &= a_{11}x + a_{12}y + f_1, \\
y' &= a_{21}x + a_{22}y + f_2.
\end{aligned}
\tag{17}
$$

Let $\{x_1, y_1\}$ and $\{x_2, y_2\}$ be two linearly independent solution pairs of the homogeneous system (1). Show that

$$
\begin{aligned}
x_p(t) &= v_1(t)x_1(t) + v_2(t)x_2(t), \\
y_p(t) &= v_1(t)y_1(t) + v_2(t)y_2(t),
\end{aligned}
$$

is a particular solution of the system (17) if v_1 and v_2 satisfy the equations

$$
\begin{aligned}
v_1'x_1 + v_2'x_2 &= f_1, \\
v_1'y_1 + v_2'y_2 &= f_2.
\end{aligned}
$$

This process for finding a particular solution of the nonhomogeneous system (16) is called the *variation of constants method for systems*. Note the close parallel between this method and the method given in Section 3.7.

In Exercises 10 through 14, use the variation of constants method to find a particular solution for each given nonhomogeneous system.

10. $x' = 2x + y + 3e^{2t}$,
$y' = -4x + 2y + te^{2t}$

11. $x' = 3x + 3y + t$,
$y' = -x - y + 1$

12. $x' = -2x + y$,
$y' = -3x + 2y + 2 \sin t$

13. $x' = -x + y + \cos t,$
$\quad y' = -5x + 3y$

14. $x' = 3x - 2y + t,$
$\quad y' = 2x - 2y + 3e^t$

15. In an experiment of cholesterol turnover in humans, radioactive cholesterol $-4 - C^{14}$ was injected intravenously and the total plasma cholesterol and radioactivity were measured. It was discovered that the turnover of cholesterol behaves like a two compartment system.† The compartment consisting of the organs and blood has a rapid turnover, while the turnover in the other compart-ment is much slower. Assume that the body intakes and excretes all cholesterol through the first compartment. Let $x(t)$ and $y(t)$ denote the deviations from normal cholesterol levels in each compartment. Suppose that the daily fractional transfer coefficient from compartment x is 0.134, of which 0.036 is the input to compartment y, and that the transfer coefficient from compartment y is 0.02.

a) Describe the problem discussed above as a system of homogeneous linear differential equations.

b) Obtain the general solution of the system.

3.13 ELECTRIC CIRCUITS WITH SEVERAL LOOPS

We shall make use of the concepts developed in Sections 2.5 and 3.9 to study electrical networks with two or more coupled closed circuits. The two fundamental principles governing such networks are the two laws of Kirchhoff:

> **1.** The algebraic sum of all voltage drops around any closed circuit is zero.
>
> **2.** The algebraic sum of the currents flowing into any junction in the network is zero.

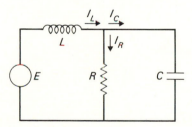

Figure 12

Consider the circuit in Fig. 12. There are two loops. By Kirchhoff's voltage law, we obtain

$$L\frac{dI_L}{dt} + RI_R = E, \tag{1}$$

$$\frac{Q_C}{C} - RI_R = 0. \tag{2}$$

---

† D. S. Goodman and R. P. Noble, "Turnover of Plasma Cholesterol in Man," *J. Clin. Invest.* **47**: 231–241 (1968).

Since $I = dQ/dt$, the second equation may be rewritten as

$$\frac{I_C}{C} - R\frac{dI_R}{dt} = 0. \tag{3}$$

By Kirchhoff's current law, we have

$$I_L = I_C + I_R, \tag{4}$$

which, if substituted into Eq. (3), yields, together with Eq. (1), the nonhomogeneous system of linear first-order differential equations

$$\frac{dI_L}{dt} = -\frac{R}{L}I_R + \frac{E}{L},$$

$$\frac{dI_R}{dt} = \frac{I_L}{RC} - \frac{I_R}{RC}. \tag{5}$$

The characteristic equation of this system is

$$D = \begin{vmatrix} -\lambda & -R/L \\ 1/RC & -\lambda - 1/RC \end{vmatrix} = \lambda(\lambda + 1/RC) + 1/LC$$

$$= \lambda^2 + \lambda/RC + 1/LC = 0. \tag{6}$$

The roots of Eq. (6) are $(-L \pm \sqrt{L^2 - 4R^2LC})/2RLC$.

If $L > 4R^2C$, the roots are different negative numbers λ_1, λ_2 (because $\sqrt{L^2 - 4R^2LC} < \sqrt{L^2} = L$) and we obtain the solution pairs

$$\{I_{L1}, I_{R1}\} = \{\alpha_1 e^{\lambda_1 t}, \beta_1 e^{\lambda_1 t}\},$$

$$\{I_{L2}, I_{R2}\} = \{\alpha_2 e^{\lambda_2 t}, \beta_2 e^{\lambda_2 t}\},$$

of the homogeneous system

$$\frac{dI_L}{dt} = -\frac{R}{L}I_R,$$

$$\frac{dI_R}{dt} = \frac{I_L}{RC} - \frac{I_R}{RC}. \tag{7}$$

The coefficients α_j and β_j satisfy Eqs. (2) in Section 3.12 so that the first equation becomes

$$-\lambda_j\alpha_j - (R/L)\beta_j = 0, \quad j = 1, 2 \tag{8}$$

which implies that $\alpha_j = -R\beta_j/L\lambda_j$. Hence the general solution of the homogeneous system (7) is given by

$$\{R(k_1 e^{\lambda_1 t} + k_2 e^{\lambda_2 t}), -L(k_1\lambda_1 e^{\lambda_1 t} + k_2\lambda_2 e^{\lambda_2 t})\}.$$

To find the general solution of the system (5), we must obtain a particular solution of Eqs. (5). Suppose E is constant. Then the pair $\{E/R, E/R\}$ is easily seen to be a particular solution of the system (5). Thus the general solution of the nonhomogeneous system (5) is

$$\{I_L, I_R\} = \{R(k_1 e^{\lambda_1 t} + k_2 e^{\lambda_2 t}) + E/R, \ -L(k_1\lambda_1 e^{\lambda_1 t} + k_2\lambda_2 e^{\lambda_2 t}) + E/R\}.$$

From this equation it is clear that as time increases, both currents I_L and I_R tend to E/R since λ_1 and $\lambda_2 < 0$, and hence I_C tends to zero, by Eq. (4).

If $L = 4R^2C$, we have a double root $\lambda_1 = -1/2RC$. By Theorem 2 in Section 3.12, the homogeneous equation has the solution pairs

$$\{I_{L1}, I_{R1}\} = \{\alpha_1 e^{\lambda_1 t}, \beta_1 e^{\lambda_1 t}\},$$
$$\{I_{L2}, I_{R2}\} = \{(\alpha_2 t + \alpha_3)e^{\lambda_1 t}, (\beta_2 t + \beta_3)e^{\lambda_1 t}\}.$$

The coefficients α_1, β_1 satisfy Eq. (8), so $\alpha_1 = \beta_1/2$. To obtain the other four coefficients α_2, α_3, β_2, and β_3, we must substitute $\{I_{L2}, I_{R2}\}$ into the system (7). After some algebra we obtain $\alpha_2 = \beta_2/2$, $\beta_2 + \lambda_1(2\alpha_3 - \beta_3) = 0$. The selection $\alpha_2 = \frac{1}{2}$, $\alpha_3 = 2RC$, $\beta_2 = 1$, $\beta_3 = 2RC$ satisfies these two equations, so that the system (5) has the general solution

$$\{I_L, I_R\} = \left\{\frac{1}{2} e^{\lambda_1 t}[k_1 + k_2(t + 4RC)] + \frac{E}{R}, \ e^{\lambda_1 t}[k_1 + k_2(t + 2RC)] + \frac{E}{R}\right\}.$$

As time increases, again I_L and I_R tend to E/R while I_C tends to 0.

Finally, if $L < 4R^2C$, λ_1 and λ_2 are complex conjugates and the solution pairs of the homogeneous system (7) are

$$\{I_{L1}, I_{R1}\} = \{e^{at}(A_1 \cos bt - A_2 \sin bt), \ e^{at}(B_1 \cos bt - B_2 \sin bt)\},$$
$$\{I_{L2}, I_{R2}\} = \{e^{at}(A_1 \sin bt + A_2 \cos bt), \ e^{at}(B_1 \sin bt + B_2 \cos bt)\},$$

where $a = -1/2RC < 0$, and $b = \sqrt{4R^2LC - L^2}/2RLC$. By Eq. (4) these equations yield damped oscillations with I_L and I_R tending to E/R and I_C tending to zero as t tends to infinity.

Example 1   Suppose $R = 100$ ohms, $L = 1$ henry, $C = 10^{-4}$ farads, and $E = 100$ volts. Clearly $L < 4R^2C$, so the roots of the characteristic equation, $a \pm ib$, are complex conjugates. Here

$$a = -\frac{1}{2RC} = -50, \quad b = \frac{\sqrt{4R^2LC - L^2}}{2RLC} = 50\sqrt{3},$$

.and the two independent solution pairs of the homogeneous equation (7) are

$$\{I_{L1}, I_{R1}\}$$

$$= \{e^{-50t}(A_1 \cos 50\sqrt{3}t - A_2 \sin 50\sqrt{3}t), \ e^{-50t}(B_1 \cos 50\sqrt{3}t - B_2 \sin 50\sqrt{3}t)\},$$

$$\{I_{L2}, I_{R2}\}$$

$$= \{e^{-50t}(A_1 \sin 50\sqrt{3}t + A_2 \cos 50\sqrt{3}t), \ e^{-50t}(B_1 \sin 50\sqrt{3}t + B_2 \cos 50\sqrt{3}t)\}.$$

Substituting these equations into the system (7) yields the homogeneous system of equations

$$
\begin{aligned}
-50A_1 - 50\sqrt{3}A_2 + 100B_1 \qquad\qquad &= 0, \\
-50\sqrt{3}A_1 + 50A_2 \qquad\qquad - 100B_2 &= 0, \\
-100A_1 \qquad\qquad + 50B_1 - 50\sqrt{3}B_2 &= 0, \\
100A_2 - 50\sqrt{3}B_1 - 50B_2 &= 0.
\end{aligned}
\tag{9}
$$

A selection of values satisfying the system (9) is provided by setting $A_1 = 2$, $A_2 = 0$, $B_1 = 1$, and $B_2 = -\sqrt{3}$. Thus the general solution has the form

$$
\begin{aligned}
\{I_L, I_R\} = \{&2e^{-50t}(k_1 \cos 50\sqrt{3}t + k_2 \sin 50\sqrt{3}t) + 1, \\
&e^{-50t}[(k_1 - \sqrt{3}k_2) \cos 50\sqrt{3}t + (k_2 + \sqrt{3}k_1) \sin 50\sqrt{3}t] + 1\}.
\end{aligned}
$$

In this example we have used the fact that $E/R = 1$.

EXERCISES 3.13

1. Let $R = 100$ ohms, $L = 4$ henries, $C = 10^{-4}$ farads and $E = 100$ volts in the network of Fig. 12. Suppose the currents I_R and I_L are both zero at time $t = 0$. Find the currents when $t = 0.001$ second.

2. Let $L = 1$ henry in Exercise 1 and suppose all the other facts are unchanged. Find the currents when $t = 0.001$ second and 0.1 second.

3. Let $L = 8$ henries in Exercise 1 and suppose all the other facts are unchanged. Find the currents when $t = 0.001$ second and 0.1 second.

4. Suppose $E = 100e^{-1000t}$ volts and all the other values are unchanged in Exercise 1. Do:

a) Exercise 1.

b) Exercise 2.

c) Exercise 3.

5. Repeat Exercise 4 for $E = 100 \sin 60\pi t$.

6. Find the current at time t in each loop of the network in Fig. 13 given that $E = 100$ volts, $R = 10$ ohms, and $L = 10$ henries.

7. Repeat Exercise 6 for $E = 10 \sin t$.

8. Consider the air-core transformer network shown in Fig. 14 with $E = 10 \cos t$, $R = 1$, $L = 2$, and mutual inductance $L_* = -1$ (which depends on the relative modes of winding of the two coils involved). Treating the mutual inductance as an inductance for each circuit, find the two circuit currents at all times t assuming they are zero at $t = 0$.

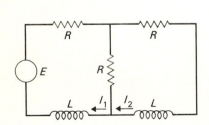
Figure 13

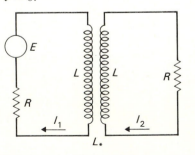
Figure 14

3.14 A MODEL BASED ON THE THEORY OF EPIDEMICS

In 1957, N. T. J. Bailey published a book† on the mathematical theory of epidemics, in which he described a number of models that had been used in studying the transmission of disease. In this section we shall consider a particularly elementary case of one of these models and illustrate the implications that can be drawn from its solution.

We assume that a population of fixed size N can be separated into three distinct classes:

1. $S(t)$ denotes the number of individuals in the population at time t who are *susceptible* to a given contagious disease.

2. $I(t)$ is the number of individuals at time t in the population who are *infective*, that is, they have the disease and are contagious.

3. $R(t)$ denotes the number of individuals at time t who have *recovered* from the disease and are now immune to further infection.

Because of the letters that are used in describing each class of individuals, this model is usually called an SIR epidemic. Note that this classification yields the equation

$$S(t) + I(t) + R(t) = N. \tag{1}$$

We now assume that the spread of the disease is governed by the following rules:

---

1. The rate of change of the susceptible population is proportional to the size of the susceptible population when the number of infectives exceeds a given cutoff value; and

2. The rate at which infectives recover from the disease is proportional to the size of the infective population.

These rules are simplistic, but do bear some connection with reality. In the first, we assume that when the number of infectives $I(t)$ exceeds the cutoff value I_*, they are able to infect susceptible individuals in the population. This takes into account the fact that often infectives are quarantined or kept apart from the susceptible population. Note that the first rule can be written as a differential equation:

$$\frac{dS}{dt} = \begin{cases} -\alpha S, & \text{if} \quad I(t) > I_*, \\ 0, & \text{if} \quad I(t) \le I_*. \end{cases} \tag{2}$$

---

† N. T. J. Bailey, *The Mathematical Theory of Epidemics.* New York: Harper (1957).

Since each susceptible who catches the disease becomes infected, the rate of change of the infective population is the difference between the newly infected individuals and those who are recovering from the disease. Thus

$$\frac{dI}{dt} = \begin{cases} \alpha S - \beta I, & \text{if } I(t) > I_*, \\ -\beta I, & \text{if } I(t) \le I_*. \end{cases} \tag{3}$$

The constants of proportionality α and β are called the *infection rate* and *recovery rate*, respectively. Finally, the rate of change of the recovered individuals is precisely

$$\frac{dR}{dt} = \beta I. \tag{4}$$

To determine the solution uniquely we need initial conditions. For simplicity, let's assume that no individuals in the population are immune to the disease, that is, $R(0) = 0$, and that initially $I(0)$ individuals are infective (perhaps they all went to a convention together). Further, we assume that the infection and recovery rates are equal, hence $\alpha = \beta$ (the case in which they are unequal will be considered in the exercises). We then have two cases:

CASE 1 If $I(0) \le I_*$, no further individuals will be infected since $dS/dt = 0$, implying that

$$S(t) = S(0) = N - I(0),$$

for all t, by Eq. (1) since $R(0) = 0$. This represents the situation in which a very few infective convention delegates are immediately quarantined.

Figure 15

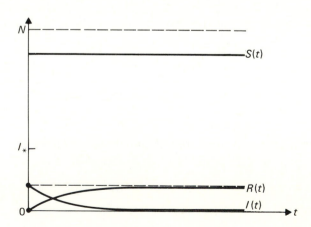

Then, from Eq. (3) and since $\alpha = \beta$, we have

$$\frac{dI}{dt} = -\alpha I,$$

so that

$$I(t) = I(0)e^{-\alpha t}$$

and

$$R(t) = N - S(t) - I(t)$$

$$= I(0)(1 - e^{-\alpha t}).$$

The graphs of the three populations are shown in Fig. 15 and indicate that the disease ran its course without causing any further infections.

CASE 2   If $I(0) > I_*$, there must be an interval $0 \leq t < T$ on which $I(t) > I_*$, since I must be continuous. For all t in $[0, T)$ the disease will spread to the susceptible population. Thus, from Eq. (2),

$$S(t) = S(0)e^{-\alpha t}, \quad \text{for} \quad 0 \leq t < T. \tag{5}$$

Substituting this function into Eq. (3), we have

$$\frac{dI}{dt} + \alpha I = \alpha S(0)e^{-\alpha t}. \tag{6}$$

Multiplying both sides of Eq. (6) by the integrating factor $e^{\alpha t}$, we obtain

$$\frac{d}{dt}(Ie^{\alpha t}) = \alpha S(0),$$

so that

$$Ie^{\alpha t} = \alpha S(0)t + C,$$

and the general solution to Eq. (6) is

$$I(t) = ce^{-\alpha t} + \alpha S(0)te^{-\alpha t}. \tag{7}$$

Setting $t = 0$, we see that $c = I(0)$ so Eq. (7) becomes

$$I(t) = [I(0) + \alpha S(0)t]e^{-\alpha t}, \quad \text{for} \quad 0 \leq t < T. \tag{8}$$

Two times are of particular importance:

1. What is the value of T?

2. When will the number of infectives be at a maximum?

The first question is important since at time T *no further susceptibles* *become infective*, that is, the epidemic has run its course. We know that at $t = T$, the right-hand side of Eq. (8) will equal I_*, or

$$I_* = [I(0) + \alpha S(0)T]e^{-\alpha T}. \tag{9}$$

But $S(T) = \lim_{t \to \infty} S(t) = S(\infty)$ is the susceptible population that escapes infection and

$$S(\infty) = S(T) = S(0)e^{-\alpha T},$$

so that

$$T = \frac{1}{\alpha} \ln \frac{S(0)}{S(\infty)}. \tag{10}$$

Thus, if we can find an expression for $S(\infty)$, we can use Eq. (10) to predict the end of the epidemic. Substituting Eq. (10) for T in Eq. (9), we get

$$I_* = \left[I(0) + S(0) \ln \frac{S(0)}{S(\infty)} \right] \frac{S(\infty)}{S(0)}$$

or

$$\frac{I_*}{S(\infty)} = \frac{I(0)}{S(0)} + \ln \frac{S(0)}{S(\infty)},$$

from which we obtain the expression

$$\frac{I_*}{S(\infty)} + \ln S(\infty) = \frac{I(0)}{S(0)} + \ln S(0). \tag{11}$$

Since I_* and all the terms on the right-hand side of Eq. (11) are known, we can use this equation to determine $S(\infty)$. The quantity $N - S(\infty)$ is called the *size* of the epidemic, since it consists of all the individuals who contracted the disease.

To answer the second question, we maximize $I(t)$ in Eq. (8). Setting

$$I'(t) = [\alpha S(0) - \alpha I(0) - \alpha^2 S(0)t]e^{-\alpha t} = 0,$$

we obtain the time at which I attains its maximum value:

$$t_{\max} = \frac{1}{\alpha} \left(1 - \frac{I(0)}{S(0)} \right).$$

Hence, substituting $t_{\max}$ into Eq. (8), we obtain

$$I_{\max} = S(0)e^{-[1-I(0)/S(0)]} = S(t_{\max}), \tag{12}$$

which indicates that at time $t_{\max}$ there are just as many susceptibles as infectives.

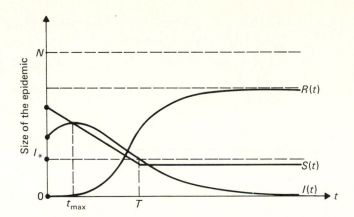

Figure 16

When $t > T$, no further susceptibles become infected, so the number of infectives is given by

$$I(t) = I_* e^{-\alpha(t-T)}.$$

Figure 16 shows the graphs of the three populations.

If you are interested in learning more about epidemic models, you should consult the following:

1. Paul Waltman, *Deterministic Threshold Models in the Theory of Epidemics*. Lecture Notes in Biomathematics, Vol. 1. New York: Springer-Verlag (1974).

2. Klaus Dietz, "Epidemics and Rumours: A Survey," *J. Roy. Stat. Soc. Ser. A.*, **130**: 505–528 (1967).

EXERCISES 3.14

1. Prove that $S(\infty) < I_*$, by showing that $S(t) < I(t)$ on the interval $t_{\max} \leqslant t \leqslant T$. What can you conclude about $S(\infty)$ if you allow I_* to decrease to zero?

2. Show that $t_{\max} < 1/\alpha$.

3. Show that $I(1/\alpha) = 1/e$ and $S(1/\alpha) = S(0)/e$, and conclude that $I_{\max} > 1/e$.

4. Show that the curve $I = I(t)$ has an inflection point at $t = t_{\max} + 1/\alpha$.

5. Prove that

$$T = \frac{1}{\alpha}\left(\frac{I_*}{S(\infty)} - \frac{I(0)}{S(0)}\right),$$

and conclude that

$$T = t_{\max} + \frac{1}{\alpha}\left(\frac{I_*}{S(\infty)} - 1\right).$$

What happens if I_* decreases to zero?

In Exercises 6 through 10, assume that $\alpha > \beta$ and $I(0) > I_*$.

6. Show that for $0 \leqslant t < T$,

$$I(t) = I(0)e^{-\beta t} + \frac{\alpha S(0)}{\alpha - \beta}(e^{-\beta t} - e^{-\alpha t}).$$

7. Use Exercise 6 to show that

$$t_{max} = \frac{1}{\alpha - \beta} \ln \left[\left(\frac{\alpha S(0)}{\beta} \right) \left(\frac{\alpha}{\alpha - \beta I(0)} \right) \right]$$

and

$$I_{max} = \frac{\alpha}{\beta} S(t_{max}).$$

8. Show that $I = I(t)$ has an inflection point at

$$t = t_{max} + \frac{1}{\alpha - \beta} \ln \left(\frac{\alpha}{\beta} \right).$$

9. Prove that

$$I_{max} > \left(\frac{\beta}{\alpha} \right)^{\beta/(\alpha-\beta)}.$$

10. Show that

$$S(\infty) = \left[\left(\frac{1}{S(0)} \right)^{\beta/\alpha} \left(\frac{\alpha - \beta I(0)}{\alpha} \right) - I_* \left(\frac{\alpha - \beta}{\alpha} \right) \right]^{\alpha/(\alpha-\beta)}.$$

For Exercises 11 through 15, we change the first rule governing the spread of the disease (see p. 129) to the following:

1′. The rate of change of the susceptible population is jointly proportional to the product of the number of susceptibles and infectives.

11. Show that you obtain the nonlinear system

$$S' = -\alpha IS,$$
$$I' = \alpha IS - \beta I,$$
$$R' = \beta I.$$

Show that the infection dies out if $S(t) < \beta/\alpha$. This is called the *threshold phenomenon*.

12. Prove that

$$I(t) = N + \frac{\beta}{\alpha} \ln \frac{S(t)}{S(0)} - S(t).$$

(*Hint:* Consider dI/dS.)

13. Prove that

$$I_{max} = 1 + \frac{\beta}{\alpha} \left[\ln \left(\frac{\beta}{\alpha S(0)} \right) - 1 \right]$$

$$\geq 1 - \frac{\beta}{\alpha} \left[1 + \ln \left(\frac{\alpha}{\beta} \right) \right] > 0.$$

14. Show that $S(\infty)$ satisfies the identity

$$S(\infty) + \frac{\beta}{\alpha} \ln \frac{1}{S(\infty)} = N + \frac{\beta}{\alpha} \ln \frac{1}{S(0)}.$$

15. Prove that $S(\infty) \geq S(0)e^{-\alpha N/\beta} > 0$. (*Hint:* Consider dS/dR.)

REVIEW EXERCISES FOR CHAPTER 3

In Exercises 1 through 5, a second-order differential equation and one solution $y_1(x)$ are given. Verify that $y_1(x)$ is indeed a solution and find a second linearly independent solution.

1. $y'' + 4y = 0;$ $y_1(x) = \sin 2x$

2. $y'' - 6y' + 9y = 0;$ $y_1(x) = e^{3x}$

3. $x^2 y'' + xy' - 4y = 0;$ $y_1(x) = x^2$

4. $y'' + \frac{1}{x} y' + \left(1 - \frac{1}{4x^2} \right) y = 0;$ $y_1(x) = x^{-1/2} \sin x.$

5. $(1 - x^2)y'' - 2xy' + 2y = 0;$ $y_1(x) = x$

In Exercises 6 through 22, find the general solution to the given equation. If initial conditions are given, find the particular solution that satisfies them.

6. $y'' - 9y' + 20y = 0$

7. $y'' - 9y' + 20y = 0;$ $y(0) = 3,$ $y'(0) = 2$

8. $y'' - 3y' + 4y = 0$

9. $y'' - 3y' + 4y = 0;$ $y(0) = 0,$ $y'(0) = 1$

10. $y'' = 0$

11. $4y'' + 4y' + y = 0$

12. $y'' - 11y = 0$

13. $y'' - 2y' + 7y = 0$

14. $y'' - y' - 2y = \sin 2x$

15. $y''' - 6y'' + 11y' - 6y = 0$

16. $y'' - 2y' + y = xe^x$

17. $y'' - 2y' + y = x^2 - 1;$　$y(0) = 2,$　$y'(0) = 1$

18. $y'' + y = \sec x,$　$0 < x < \dfrac{\pi}{2}$

19. $y'' - 2y' + y = \dfrac{2e^x}{x^3}$

20. $y'' + 4y' + 4y = e^{-2x}/x^2;$　$x > 0$

21. $x^2 y'' + 5xy' + 4y = 0;$　$x > 0$

22. $x^2 y'' - 2xy' + 3y = 0;$　$x > 0$

In Exercises 23 through 25, transform the equation into a first-order system.

23. $x''' - 6x'' + 2x' - 5x = 0$

24. $x'' - 3x' + 4t^2 x = \sin t$

25. $xx'' + x'x''' = \ln t$

In Exercises 26 through 30, find the general solution for each system.

26. $x' = x + y,$
　　$y' = 9x + y$

27. $x' = x + 2y,$
　　$y' = 4x + 3y$

28. $x' = 4x - y,$
　　$y' = x + 2y$

29. $x' = 3x + 2y,$
　　$y' = -5x + y$

30. $x' = x - 4y,$
　　$y' = x + y$

31. Find the general solution to

$$x' = -x \qquad\;\; - 3e^{-2t},$$
$$y' = -2x - y - 6e^{-2t}.$$

32. Find the unique solution to

$$x' = -4x - 6y + 9e^{-3t};\quad x(0) = -9,$$
$$y' = \;\;\;\; x + \;\; y - 5e^{-3t};\quad y(0) = \;\;\;\; 4.$$

Difference Equations

4.1 INTRODUCTION

Difference equations are the discrete analogs of differential equations. Differential equations arise in physical and biological systems where we are interested in studying the instantaneous rate of change (derivative) of one variable with respect to another. Thus we may be interested in the velocity at a given instant of a particle moving in a trajectory or the rate of growth at a particular moment of a bacteria population. On the other hand, there are many systems where it is of prime interest to study changes (differences) in the systems, rather than rates of change.

Although the theory of differential equations has been with us for a long time, it is only recently that difference equations have received the kind of attention they deserve. This recent attention is due, in large part, to the advent of the computer with which many types of equations (including ordinary and partial differential equations) can be solved numerically by making use of difference equation formulations. In a sense this is an ironic development, since many differential equations are obtained by starting with difference equations and, by taking a limit, deriving an approximating differential equation. (Most population growth models are of this type.) This used to be the procedure because until recently the differential equations were easier to solve. Unfortunately, differential equations that arose originally from difference equations are sometimes approximated by new difference equations, often very different from the original ones. In Chapter 7 we will study numerical methods and illustrate the process by which a differential equation can be approximated by a difference equation. In this chapter we show how difference equations can arise and indicate how a wide variety of them can be solved.

Example 1   A patient in a hospital is suddenly switched to oxygen. Let V be the volume of gas contained in the lungs after inspiration, and V_D the amount present at the end of expiration (commonly called the *dead space*). Assuming uniform and complete mixing of the gases in the lungs, what is the concentration of nitrogen in the lungs at the end of the nth inspiration?

The amount of nitrogen in the lungs at the end of the nth inspiration must equal the amount in the dead space at the end of the $(n-1)$st expiration. If x_n is the concentration of nitrogen in the lungs at the end of the nth inspiration, then

$$Vx_n = V_D x_{n-1}. \tag{1}$$

Subtracting Vx_{n-1} from both sides of Eq. (1), we have

$$V(x_n - x_{n-1}) = (V_D - V)x_{n-1}. \tag{2}$$

The difference $x_n - x_{n-1}$ is the discrete analog of a derivative, since it measures the change in concentration of nitrogen in the lungs. Thus Eq. (2) is a discrete version of a first-order differential equation.

If we can find an expression (in n) for the concentrations x_n that satisfies Eq. (1) for all values of $n = 1, 2, 3, \ldots$, then we say we have a solution for the difference equation (1). It is easy to solve Eq. (1) since

$$x_n = \frac{V_D}{V} x_{n-1} = \left(\frac{V_D}{V}\right)^2 x_{n-2} = \cdots = \left(\frac{V_D}{V}\right)^n x_0,$$

where x_0 is the concentration of nitrogen in the air.

Example 2   A fish population grows in such a way that the growth in any year is twice the growth in the preceding year. To analyze this situation, we let P_n denote the population of the fish after n years. The growth during the period between the nth year and the $(n + 1)$st year is $P_{n+1} - P_n$. The equation governing population growth is therefore

$$P_{n+1} - P_n = 2(P_n - P_{n-1}),$$

which can be rewritten as

$$P_{n+1} = 3P_n - 2P_{n-1}. \tag{3}$$

If we specify the initial population P_0 and the population after one year, P_1, then Eq. (3) becomes an *initial value problem* that clearly has a unique solution. For example, if $P_0 = 50$ and $P_1 = 70$, then $P_2 = 3P_1 - 2P_0 = 110$, $P_3 = 3P_2 - 2P_1 = 190$, $P_4 = 3P_3 - 2P_2$, and so on. Of course, this method of obtaining P_n is cumbersome, but it does illustrate the fact that initial value difference problems are *usually* solvable by successive iteration.

Before citing further examples, we can formally define a *difference equation* as an equation that relates the values of x_n for different values of n. If N_1 and N_2 are, respectively, the largest and smallest values of n that occur in the equation, then the *order* of the difference equation is $N_1 - N_2$.

Equation (3) is a difference equation of order $(n + 1) - (n - 1) = 2$, whereas Eq. (1) is of the first order.

Example 3   Suppose that transverse forces $F_1, \ldots, F_n$ are applied to a string at n points spaced equally h units apart on the x-axis (see Fig. 1). To analyze this situation, we assume that between any two successive points at which forces are applied, the tension is constant (of course, this constant may vary with the interval). We also assume that the weight of the string is negligible. If y_k denotes the deflection of the string in the y- (transverse) direction, and if θ_k denotes the angle between the direction of tension and the positive x-axis, then we have (see Fig. 1)

$$\tan \theta_k = \frac{y_{k+1} - y_k}{h}$$

or

$$y_{k+1} - y_k = h \tan \theta_k. \tag{4}$$

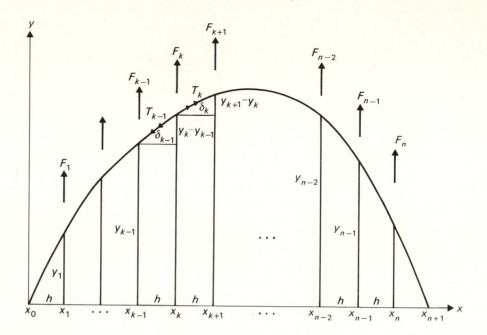

Figure 1

Note that between any two successive points, since the tension is constant, the direction of the tension vector is constant. If we assume that the string is stationary ($y' = 0$), then the resultant of all the forces at the point (x_k, y_k) must be zero. The component of T_k in the y-direction is $T_k \sin \theta_k$, and the component of $-T_{k-1}$ in that direction is $-T_{k-1} \sin \theta_{k-1}$. Adding the applied force F_k at that point, we obtain

$$T_k \sin \theta_k - T_{k-1} \sin \theta_{k-1} + F_k = 0. \tag{5}$$

Similarly, in the x-direction we obtain

$$T_k \cos \theta_k - T_{k-1} \cos \theta_{k-1} = 0. \tag{6}$$

Equation (6) indicates that the x-component of the tension does not vary, so we denote $T_k \cos \theta_k$ by T^*, a constant. Substituting this into Eq. (5), we obtain

$$T^* \frac{\sin \theta_k}{\cos \theta_k} - T^* \frac{\sin \theta_{k-1}}{\cos \theta_{k-1}} + F_k = 0$$

or

$$T^*(\tan \theta_k - \tan \theta_{k-1}) + F_k = 0. \tag{7}$$

Combining Eqs. (4) and (7), we obtain the second-order difference equation

$$\frac{T^*}{h}[(y_{k+1} - y_k) - (y_k - y_{k-1})] + F_k = 0$$

or

$$y_{k+1} - 2y_k + y_{k-1} + \frac{h}{T^*} F_k = 0. \tag{8}$$

However, unlike the previous example, it is clearly inappropriate to specify initial values for y_0 and y_1. Rather, we have the obvious boundary conditions

$$y_0 = 0, \quad y_{n+1} = 0. \tag{9}$$

Equations (8) and (9) together form a second-order *boundary value problem*. This problem so far has not been completely formulated since T^* is not known. However, if y_1 and the initial tension T_0 are known, then $\tan \theta_0 = y_1/h$, and we find that

$$T^* = T_0 \cos \theta_0 = \frac{T_0}{\sqrt{1 + (y_1/h)^2}}.$$

In this chapter we shall devote our attention to *linear* difference equations, that is, equations of the form

$$y_{n+k} + a_n y_{n+k-1} + \cdots + b_n y_{n+1} + c_n y_n = f_n, \tag{10}$$

consisting only of sums of the unknown terms $y_{n+k}, y_{n+k-1}, \ldots, y_n$. In particular, we shall study the first-order linear difference equation

$$y_{n+1} + a_n y_n = f_n \tag{11}$$

and the second-order difference equation

$$y_{n+2} + a_n y_{n+1} + b_n y_n = f_n. \tag{12}$$

Note that if a_n and f_n are known for every integer $n \geq 0$ and y_0 is given, then by Eq. (11)

$$y_1 = -a_0 y_0 + f_0,$$
$$y_2 = -a_1 y_1 + f_1, \ldots,$$

and successive iteration will determine all the values y_n. A similar result holds for Eq. (12) if a_n, b_n, and f_n are known and the two initial values y_0 and y_1 are specified. Thus, for linear difference equations we have the following existence–uniqueness theorem.

Theorem 1   Suppose the sequences $a_n, \ldots, b_n, c_n, f_n$ are defined for every integer $n \geq 0$, and the values $y_0, y_1, \ldots, y_{k-1}$ are specified. Then there is a unique sequence of value y_n that is the solution to the linear kth-order difference equation

$$y_{n+k} + a_n y_{n+k-1} + \cdots + b_n y_{n+1} + c_n y_n = f_n.$$

In analogy to the terminology of Chapter 3, Eq. (10) is said to be *homogeneous* if $f_n = 0$ for every n. Otherwise, it is said to be *nonhomogeneous*. If a_n and b_n are constants independent of n, then Eq. (10) is said to have *constant coefficients*.

Although Theorem 1 guarantees a unique solution to the linear initial value problem, we shall seek in the next few sections methods for obtaining the general solution to Eq. (10) in a way that does not involve continued iteration. In the process we will discover important links between the solutions of linear difference equations and those of comparable linear differential equations.

EXERCISES 4.1

In Exercises 1 through 10, determine whether each given difference equation is nonlinear or linear; if the latter, state whether the equation is homogeneous or nonhomogeneous, with constant or variable coefficients.

1. $y_{n+2} - n + y_n = 0$

2. $y_{n+2} - n^2 + y_n^2 = 0$

3. $y_{n+2} - y_{n+1}y_n = \sin n$

4. $6y_{n+2} - (n + 1)^2 y_{n+1} + e^{n^2} y_n = \sqrt{6n}$

5. $y_{n+1} - 3y_{n+4} + y_n = 0$

6. $y_{n+2} - \sqrt{y_n} = \sqrt{n}$

7. $y_{n+2}y_n = 3$

8. $2y_{n+2} - 5y_{n+1} + 17y_n = n^{7/2}$

9. $\sqrt{y_{n+2} + y_{n+1}} - y_n = n$

10. $y_{n+2} - \sqrt{y_{n+1}} - y_n = 3$

11. Use graphs to illustrate the discrete growth processes, from the initial time $n = 0$, given by the following formulas. Does x_n approach a limiting (or equilibrium) value as n approaches infinity?

a) $x_n = 100 + 100(2)^{-n}$

b) $x_n = 100 + 100\left(\dfrac{1}{1 + n^2}\right)$

c) $x_n = 100 + 5n^2$

d) $x_n = \sqrt{9 + n}$

12. Verify that $x_n = n^2 + n$ is a solution of the difference equation $x_{n+1} - x_n = 2(n + 1)$ and that $y_n = n^2 + n + c$ is also a solution for any constant c.

13. Verify that, for any constant k, $x_n = k2^{n(n+1)/2}$ is a solution of the difference equation $x_n = 2^n x_{n-1}$.

14. The growth of a bacteria culture in a nutrient medium is observed every two hours, and every time it is found that the bacteria population is thirty percent larger than at the previous measurement.

a) Describe this growth process by means of a difference equation for P_n, the population after n hours.

b) What is the order of the difference equation?

c) Given that the initial population is 1000, determine P_2 and P_4.

15. The per capita production of garbage in the United States is estimated to be approximately five pounds per day and is increasing at the rate of four percent per year. Let g_n be the average daily production of garbage per capita n years from now.

a) Describe the growth of garbage production by means of a difference equation.

b) Determine g_2 and g_4.

16. By "guessing" that there are solutions to $y_{n+2} - 3y_{n+1} - 4y_n = 0$ of the form $y_n = \lambda^n$ for some constant λ, find two solutions of the equation.

17. Given that y_n and z_n are solutions of the difference equation

$$y_{n+2} + a_n y_{n+1} + b_n y_n = 0,$$

where a_n and b_n are functions of n, show that for any two constants c_1 and c_2, $w_n = c_1 y_n + c_2 z_n$ is also a solution.

18. Show that for any two constants c_1 and c_2,
$$y_n = \tfrac{1}{14}(n - \tfrac{9}{14})^2 + c_1 + c_2(-6)^n$$
is a solution to the difference equation
$$y_{n+2} + 5y_{n+1} - 6y_n = n.$$

19. Verify that $y_n = n2^{n-1}$ is a solution of the difference equation
$$y_{n+2} - 3y_{n+1} + 2y_n = 2^n.$$

20. Verify that $x_n = 2^n$ and $y_n = n2^n$ are solutions to the difference equation
$$y_{n+2} - 4y_{n+1} + 4y_n = 0.$$

21. Verify that for any constants c_1 and c_2,
$$z_n = c_1 2^n + c_2 n 2^n + \frac{n^2}{8} 2^n$$
is a solution of the difference equation
$$x_{n+2} - 4x_{n+1} + 4x_n = 2^n.$$

22. Verify that $x_n = c_1 \sin(2n\pi/3) + c_2 \cos(2n\pi/3)$ is a solution of the difference equation
$$y_{n+2} + y_{n+1} + y_n = 0,$$
for any two constants c_1 and c_2. Find a solution that satisfies the initial conditions $y_0 = 1$ and $y_1 = 2$.

23. The gamma function is defined by
$$\Gamma(n) = \int_0^\infty e^{-t} t^{n-1}\, dt.$$
Show that it satisfies the difference equation $\Gamma(n) = (n-1)\Gamma(n-1)$, and prove that $\Gamma(n) = (n-1)!$, where n is a positive integer.

24. Let
$$I_k(x) = \int_0^\pi \frac{\cos kt - \cos kx}{\cos t - \cos x}\, dt.$$
Show that I_k satisfies the difference equation
$$I_{k+1}(x) - 2I_k(x)\cos x + I_{k-1}(x) = 0.$$

25. Show that if the two first values of a solution y_n of the homogeneous linear equation
$$y_{n+2} + a_n y_{n+1} + b_n y_n = 0$$
are zero, then $y_n = 0$ for all n.

26. Suppose that x_n and y_n are solutions of the homogeneous linear equation
$$y_{n+2} + a_n y_{n+1} + b_n y_n = 0,$$
and $x_k = y_k = 0$ for some integer k. Show that there is a constant c such that $y_n = cx_n$ for all $n \geq k$.

4.2 LINEAR FIRST-ORDER DIFFERENCE EQUATIONS

Before dealing with the general first-order linear equation
$$y_{n+1} - a_n y_n = f_n, \tag{1}$$
it is useful to consider the special case
$$y_{n+1} - ay_n = 0, \tag{2}$$
where a is constant. We can rewrite Eq. (2) as
$$y_{n+1} = ay_n$$
and iterating successively we have
$$y_{n+1} = ay_n = a(ay_{n-1}) = \cdots = a^{n+1}y_0, \tag{3}$$
which is the general solution of Eq. (2). If we compare Eq. (3) with the general solution $y = y(0)e^{ax}$ of the first-order linear differential equation
$$y' - ay = 0,$$
it is easy to see that y_0 corresponds to $y(0)$ and the product a^{n+1} corresponds to e^{ax}. Since exponential functions were of fundamental importance

in solving linear differential equations (see Sections 2.3, 3.4, and 3.5), it is not unreasonable to hope that products may be useful in solving linear difference equations.

Next, we examine what happens if the equation is nonhomogeneous by considering

$$y_{n+1} - ay_n = f_n, \tag{4}$$

with a constant, for known values of the sequence f_n. Using successive iterations, we have

$$y_1 = ay_0 + f_0,$$
$$y_2 = ay_1 + f_1 = a^2 y_0 + f_1 + af_0,$$
$$\vdots$$
$$y_{n+1} = a^{n+1} y_0 + \sum_{k=0}^{n} a^{n-k} f_k. \tag{5}$$

Comparing Eq. (5) to the solution $y = e^{ax}[c + \int f(x)e^{-ax}\,dx]$ of

$$y' - ay = f(x),$$

we again see that a^{n+1} corresponds to e^{ax}, and

$$\sum_{k=0}^{n} a^{n-k} f_k = a^{n+1} \sum_{k=0}^{n} a^{-(k+1)} f_k$$

corresponds to $e^{ax} \int f(x)e^{-ax}\,dx$.

Example 1 An amoeba population has an initial size of 1000. It is observed that on the average one out of every ten amoebas reproduces by cell division every hour. Approximately how many amoebas will there be after 20 hours?

We let y_n be the number of amoebas present after n hours. Then the population growth over the next hour is given by

$$y_{n+1} - y_n = \tfrac{1}{10}y_n,$$

which implies that $y_{n+1} = (1.1)y_n$. The general solution given by Eq. (3) is

$$y_{n+1} = (1.1)^{n+1} y_0, \quad y_0 = 1000.$$

Thus $y_{20} = (1.1)^{20}(1000) \approx 6727$.

Example 2 Suppose in the previous example that a leak from another container is introducing 30 additional amoebas into the population every hour. How many will there be after 20 hours?

The equation becomes

$$y_{n+1} - y_n = \tfrac{1}{10}y_n + 30,$$

or $y_{n+1} = (1.1)y_n + 30$, which by Eq. (5) has the solution

$$y_{n+1} = (1.1)^{n+1}(1000) + \sum_{k=0}^{n} (1.1)^{n-k}(30).$$

The sum of the first $n + 1$ terms of a geometrical progression satisfies the identity $1 + a + a^2 + \cdots + a^n = (a^{n+1} - 1)/(a - 1)$, so that the solution of Example 2 is given by

$$y_{n+1} = 1000(1.1)^{n+1} + 30\left(\frac{(1.1)^{n+1} - 1}{1.1 - 1}\right),$$

and $y_{20} \approx 8445$.

Finally, we look at the general first-order linear equation

$$y_{n+1} - a_n y_n = f_n. \tag{6}$$

Proceeding inductively, we obtain

$$y_1 = a_0 y_0 + f_0, \quad y_2 = a_1 y_1 + f_1 = a_1 a_0 y_0 + a_1 f_0 + f_1, \ldots,$$

and, in general

$$\begin{aligned} y_{n+1} &= (a_n a_{n-1} \cdots a_1 a_0) y_0 + (a_n \cdots a_1) f_0 + (a_n \cdots a_2) f_1 + \cdots \\ &\quad + a_n f_{n-1} + f_n \\ &= \left(\prod_{k=0}^{n} a_k\right) y_0 + \sum_{k=0}^{n} \left(\prod_{j=k+1}^{n} a_j\right) f_k, \end{aligned} \tag{7}$$

where we define the "empty" product by

$$\prod_{j=n+1}^{n} a_j = 1.$$

Comparing Eq. (7) to the solution

$$y = e^{\int a(x)\,dx}\left[c + \int f(x) e^{-\int a(x)\,dx}\,dx\right]$$

of the linear differential equation $y' - a(x)y = f(x)$, it is apparent that the product $\prod_{k=0}^{n} a_k$ corresponds to the exponential $e^{\int a(x)\,dx}$.

Example 3   Solve the difference equation $y_{n+1} = (n + 1)y_n$.

Here $a_n = n + 1$ and $f_n = 0$. Using Eq. (7) or proceeding inductively, we find that

$$y_{n+1} = \left(\prod_{k=0}^{n} (k + 1)\right) y_0 = (n + 1)! y_0.$$

It is possible to solve some nonlinear difference equations that are similar to Bernoulli's equation. The equation

$$y_{n+1} = \frac{a_n y_n}{1 - f_n y_n},$$

can be written in the form

$$y_{n+1} = a_n y_n + f_n y_n y_{n+1}. \tag{8}$$

This is comparable to Bernoulli's equation [Eq. (9) of Section 2.3]. Proceeding in a similar manner, we try the substitution

$$z_n = \frac{1}{y_n}. \tag{9}$$

After dividing both sides of Eq. (8) by $y_n y_{n+1}$, we obtain

$$z_n = a_n z_{n+1} + f_n,$$

or

$$z_{n+1} = \frac{z_n - f_n}{a_n}.$$

Using the methods of this section, we find that

$$z_{n+1} = \left(\prod_{k=0}^{n} a_k^{-1} \right) z_0 - \sum_{k=0}^{n} \left(\prod_{j=k+1}^{n} a_j^{-1} \right) \frac{f_k}{a_k}. \tag{10}$$

Substitution of Eq. (9) into Eq. (10) then yields the solution

$$y_{n+1}^{-1} = \left(\prod_{k=0}^{n} a_k^{-1} \right) y_0^{-1} - \sum_{k=0}^{n} \left(\prod_{j=k}^{n} a_j^{-1} \right) f_k.$$

Similarly, we have the nonlinear *Riccati* (difference) *equation*

$$y_n y_{n-1} + a_n y_n + b_n y_{n-1} = c_n. \tag{11}$$

To find the resemblance to the Riccati differential equation [Eq. (4) of Section 3.4], we rewrite Eq. (11) in the form

$$(y_n - y_{n-1}) + y_n y_{n+1} + [(a_n - 1)y_n + (b_n + 1)y_{n-1}] - c_n = 0.$$

In order to obtain a linear equation, we substitute

$$y_n = \frac{x_n}{x_{n+1}} - b_n,$$

into Eq. (11). After simplification Eq. (11) becomes

$$(a_n b_n + c_n)x_{n+1} - (a_n - b_{n-1})x_n - x_{n-1} = 0,$$

which is a second-order linear equation. Methods for solving such equations when a_n, b_n, and c_n are constants will be presented in Section 4.6.

EXERCISES 4.2

In Exercises 1 through 9, find the general solution of each difference equation and a particular solution when an initial condition is specified.

1. $y_{n+1} - y_n = 2^{-n}$

2. $y_{n+1} = \dfrac{n+5}{n+3} y_n$

3. $y_{n+1} - 3y_n = 3y_{n+1} - y_n$

4. $2y_{n+1} = y_n, \quad y_0 = 1$

5. $(n+1)y_{n+1} = (n+2)y_n, \quad y_0 = 1$

6. $y_{n+1} = ny_n$

7. $y_{n+1} - 5y_n = 2, \quad y_0 = 2$

8. $y_{n+1} - ny_n = n!, \quad y_0 = 5$

9. $y_{n+1} - e^{-2n}y_n = e^{-n^2}$

10. Radium transmutes at a rate of one percent every twenty-five years. Consider a sample of r_0 grams of radium. If r_n is the amount of radium remaining in the sample after $25n$ years, obtain a difference equation for r_n and find its solution. How much radium will be left after one hundred years?

11. A fair coin is marked 1 on one side and 2 on the other side. The coin is tossed repeatedly and a cumulative score of the outcomes is recorded. Define P_n to be the probability that at some time the cumulative score will take on the value n. Prove that $P_n = 1 - \frac{1}{2}P_{n-1}$. Assuming that $P_0 = 1$, derive the formula for P_n.

12. In constructing a mathematical model of a population, it is assumed that the probability P_n that a couple produces exactly n offspring satisfies the equation $P_n = 0.7P_{n-1}$. Find P_n in terms of P_0 and determine P_0 from the fact that

$$P_0 + P_1 + P_2 + \cdots = 1.$$

13. An alternative model to Exercise 12 is given by $P_n = (1/n)P_{n-1}$. For this model, find P_n in terms of P_0 and prove that $P_0 = 1/e$.

14. Let x_k denote the number of permutations of n objects taken k at a time. For every permutation of k objects, we can get a total of $n - k$ permutations of $k + 1$ objects by taking one of the remaining $n - k$ objects and placing it at the end. Thus $x_{k+1} = (n - k)x_k$. Prove that the number of permutations of n objects taken k at a time is $n!/(n - k)!$.

15. If in Exercise 14 we let x_n denote the number of combinations of the n objects (order does not count), then every permutation of $k + 1$ objects occurs (in different orders) $k + 1$ times. Thus

$$x_{k+1} = \frac{n - k}{k + 1} x_n.$$

Prove that the number of combinations of n objects taken k at a time is

$$\frac{n!}{(n - k)!k!} \equiv \binom{n}{k}.$$

The expression on the right-hand side is called the *binomial coefficient*.

16. Reduce the equation $y_n(1 + ay_{n-1}) = 1$ to a linear second-order equation by making an appropriate substitution.

17. Reduce each of the following nonlinear Riccati equations to linear second-order equations by making an appropriate substitution.

  a) $y_{n+1}y_n + 2y_{n+1} + 4y_n = n$

  b) $y_{n+1}y_n - 3^n y_{n+1} + (3^{n+1} - 2)y_n$
  $$+ 3^n(3^{n+1} - 2) = 0$$

18. Solve the equation $y_{n+1} = 2y_n^2 - 1$ by means of the substitution $y_n = \cos x_n$.

19. The *Clairaut difference equation* is of the form

$$y_n = n(y_{n+1} - y_n) + f(y_{n+1} - y_n).$$

Note that the *first difference* $y_{n+1} - y_n$ (denoted by Δy_n) plays the role of the derivative in differential equations. For the equation $y_n = n\Delta y_n + (\Delta y_n)^2$, first take the first differences of both sides and then make the substitution $\Delta y_n = x_n$. Show that:

  a) the resulting equation can be written in the form

   $$(x_{n+1} - x_n)(x_{n+1} + x_n + n + 1) = 0;$$

  b) the condition $x_{n+1} - x_n = 0$ yields the *general solution* $y_n = nc + c^2$, c arbitrary;

  c) the condition $x_{n+1} + x_n + n + 1 = 0$ implies that $y_{n+1} = -x_n x_{n+1}$, and thus we get the *singular solution*

   $$y_n = \left[\sqrt{y_0} + \frac{1 - (-1)^n}{4}\right] - \left(\frac{n}{2}\right)^2.$$

4.3 AN APPLICATION OF FIRST-ORDER DIFFERENCE EQUATIONS: NEWTON'S METHOD

An important problem in mathematics is finding the roots of a given equation

$$F(x) = 0. \tag{1}$$

Using Taylor's theorem centered at the value x_n, we can express this function in the form

$$0 = F(x) = F(x_n) + F'(x_n)(x - x_n) + \frac{F''(x_n)}{2!}(x - x_n)^2 + \cdots. \qquad (2)$$

Omitting all but the first two terms on the right-hand side of Eq. (2) and solving for x yields the equation

$$x = x_n - \frac{F(x_n)}{F'(x_n)}.$$

If we call this new value x_{n+1}, we obtain the first-order difference equation

$$x_{n+1} = x_n - \frac{F(x_n)}{F'(x_n)}, \qquad (3)$$

known as *Newton's formula*. The value x_{n+1} is an approximation to some root of Eq. (1). Of course, since we have ignored all but the first two terms of Taylor's series to obtain this value, it is very unlikely that x_{n+1} is actually a root of (1). However, if the value x_n is close to a root x, then the quantity $x - x_n$ is near zero, so that the effect of the terms involving higher powers of $x - x_n$, in Taylor's series, may be negligible.

Rewriting Eq. (3) as

$$F'(x_n) = \frac{F(x_n)}{x_n - x_{n+1}},$$

we obtain a graphic interpretation of the procedure (see Fig. 2). Since the derivative $F'(x_n)$ is the slope of the tangent to the curve $y = F(x)$ at $x = x_n$ and this slope is $\tan \alpha$, the tangent line intersects the x-axis at x_{n+1}.

Figure 2

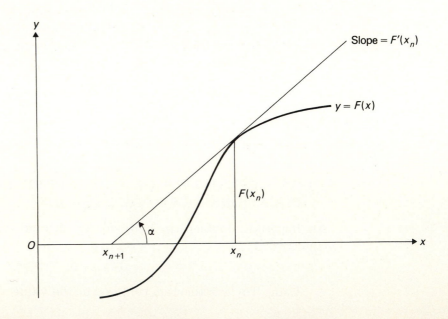

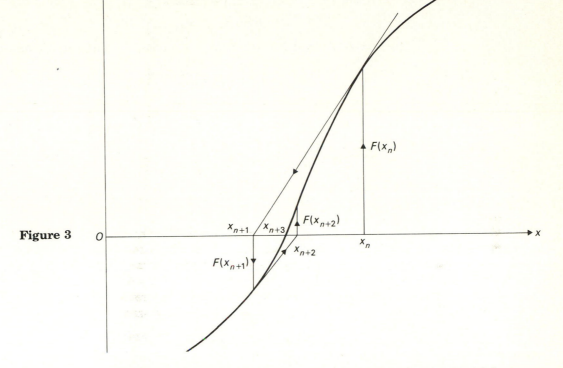

Figure 3

The procedure for finding a root consists of making an initial guess x_0 and repeatedly applying Eq. (3) to generate a sequence $\{x_n\}$ that we hope converges to a solution of Eq. (1). (See Fig. 3.) Conditions that guarantee the method will work are given in the following theorem.

Theorem 1   Suppose that on some interval $a \leqslant x \leqslant b$, $F(x)$ is defined, twice continuously differentiable, and that:

    i) $F(a)$ and $F(b)$ have different signs;

    ii) $F'(x) \neq 0$ for every x in $a \leqslant x \leqslant b$;

    iii) $F''(x)$ does not change sign on $a \leqslant x \leqslant b$;

    iv) if $F'(a) \leqslant F'(b)$, then $|F(a)/F'(a)| \leqslant b - a$; if $F'(b) \leqslant F'(a)$, then $|F(b)/F'(b)| \leqslant b - a$.

Then Newton's method converges to the *unique* solution x^* of $F(x) = 0$ for any initial choice x_0 in the interval $a \leqslant x \leqslant b$.

The proof of this theorem will not be given here, but the reader can find one in the footnoted reference below.†

This method can be applied to a variety of practical problems.

---

† Peter Henrici, *Elements of Numerical Analysis*. New York: Wiley (1964), p. 79.

Example 1   Let $r > 1$ and let us formulate an algorithm for calculating the square root of r. Let

$$F(x) = x^2 - r, \quad x > 0.$$

Then $F'(x) = 2x$ and Newton's method yields the difference equation

$$x_{n+1} = x_n - \frac{(x_n^2 - r)}{2x_n}$$

or

$$x_{n+1} = \frac{1}{2}\left(x_n + \frac{r}{x_n}\right). \tag{4}$$

It is easy to use formula (4) on a pocket calculator. Let x_0 be any integer in the interval $1 \leq x_0 \leq 1 + r$. Divide r by x_0, add x_0 to this quotient; then divide the result by 2 to get x_1. Repeat the process with x_n instead of x_0 to get x_{n+1}, for $n = 1, 2, 3, \ldots$. For example, if $r = 15$ and $x_0 = 4$, then Eq. (4) yields

$$x_1 = 3.875, \quad x_2 = 3.872984, \quad x_3 = 3.872983345,$$

and x_3 approximates $\sqrt{15}$ correctly to eight decimal places. If another choice is made for x_0, then the procedure might require more steps to equal this accuracy, indicating that a good initial guess will diminish the work involved.

To verify that the method will always work, we let $a = 1$, $b = 1 + r$, and check the conditions of Theorem 1. Note that $F(1) = 1 - r < 0$, $F(1 + r) = 1 + r + r^2 > 0$, $F'(x) = 2x > 0$ for $x > 1$, and $F''(x) = 2$, so conditions (i), (ii), and (iii) all hold. Since $F'(1) = 2 < 2 + 2r = F'(1 + r)$ and

$$\left|\frac{F(1)}{F'(1)}\right| = \frac{r-1}{2} \leq r = (r + 1) - 1,$$

condition (iv) also holds, and Newton's method will converge to a unique solution in the interval $1 \leq x \leq 1 + r$.

Although it is not necessary to check the conditions of Theorem 1 before applying Newton's method, failure to do so may result in:

1. Divergence of the sequence $\{x_n\}$, yielding no solution; or
2. Failure to locate additional solutions in the interval $[a, b]$.

Example 2   To find the kth root of a number $r > 1$, we solve

$$F(x) = x^k - r = 0, \quad x > 0,$$

by Newton's method, obtaining

$$x_{n+1} = x_n - \frac{x_n^k - r}{kx_n^{k-1}} = \left(1 - \frac{1}{k}\right)x_n + \frac{r}{kx_n^{k-1}}.$$

This formula will converge to $r^{1/k}$ for any choice of $x_0 > 1$.

Example 3   Find the roots of the polynomial

$$F(x) = x^3 + x^2 + 7x - 3. \tag{5}$$

We note that $F(0) = -3$ and $F(1) = 6$, so Eq. (5) has a root between 0 and 1. Letting $a = 0$, $b = 1$, we can easily verify conditions (i), (ii), (iii) of Theorem 1; and since $F'(0) = 7 < 12 = F'(1)$ and $3/7 < 1$, condition (iv) also holds. Thus

$$x_{n+1} = x_n - \frac{F(x_n)}{F'(x_n)} = \frac{2x_n^3 + x_n^2 + 3}{3x_n^2 + 2x_n + 7} \tag{6}$$

is Newton's formula for Eq. (5). An initial guess of $x_0 = 0$ yields $x_1 = 0.4286$, $x_2 = 0.3973$, $x_3 = 0.3971$, which is correct to four places.

Example 4   If we wish to find a reciprocal without dividing,† we can let $F(x) = 1/x - r$. Then $F'(x) = -1/x^2$, and Eq. (3) yields

$$x_{n+1} = x_n - \frac{x_n^{-1} - r}{-x_n^{-2}} = x_n(2 - rx_n).$$

This expression will converge to $1/r$ for any x_0 such that $0 < x_0 < 2/r$. To calculate $1/\pi$ for $\pi = 3.1415926$, let $x_0 = 0.5$. Then we have

$$x_0 = 0.5, \qquad x_2 = 0.2845, \qquad x_4 = 0.31827,$$
$$x_1 = 0.2146, \qquad x_3 = 0.3147, \qquad x_5 = 0.31830989,$$

the last of which is correct to eight decimal places.

Note that in Examples 1 and 4 the convergence is quite rapid. The rate of convergence in Newton's method is proportional to the quadratic $(x - x_n)^2$, which can be factored from each of the terms in Eq. (2) that we have omitted. For this reason, it is often called *quadratic convergence*.

EXERCISES 4.3

1. Using Newton's method, formulate an algorithm for calculating the cube root of a given positive number and then calculate $\sqrt[3]{6}$ to four decimal places.

2. Calculate $\frac{1}{6}$ without division to eight decimal places. Start the Newton iteration with 0.15.

3. Show by means of a graph that there is only one solution to the equation $x = e^{-x}$ and determine this solution to four decimal places by means of Newton's method.

4. For a suitable choice of x_0, formulate an al-

gorithm for finding the smallest positive root of $4 \cos x = e^x$ and calculate the root to four decimal places. (*Hint:* Draw graphs of $4 \cos x$ and e^x to see what is happening.)

5. Find to four decimal places the smallest positive root of $\frac{1}{2} \tan x = x$.

6. Find the single real root of $x^3 + 3x - 9 = 0$.

7. The derivative $F'(x_n)$ can be approximated by the difference quotient

$$\frac{F(x_n) - F(x_{n-1})}{x_n - x_{n-1}}.$$

---

† Some computers use this algorithm to do divisions.

Clearly, this quotient converges to the derivative as the difference between successive iterations approaches zero. Using the difference quotient instead of the derivative in Newton's method, derive a second-order difference equation that defines successive iterates. (*Note*: This defines a method, known as *regula falsi*, for the numerical solution of equations. The method is useful when calculation

of derivatives is undesirable.)

8. Using the method indicated in Exercise 7, formulate algorithms for calculating square roots and cube roots and calculate $\sqrt{15}$ and $\sqrt[3]{6}$. Compare these computations to those of Newton's method. (Note that two initial choices must be made.)

4.4 PROPERTIES OF SOLUTIONS TO LINEAR SECOND-ORDER EQUATIONS

We shall begin with the homogeneous equation

$$y_{n+2} + a_n y_{n+1} + b_n y_n = 0. \tag{1}$$

A *solution* to Eq. (1) consists of a sequence of real numbers $y_0, y_1, y_2, \ldots, y_n, \ldots$ that satisfy Eq. (1) for all integers $n \geq 0$. To avoid the cumbersome use of sequences, we shall denote a solution merely by the term y_n.

A *linear combination* of the solutions x_n and y_n of Eq. (1) is a sequence $Ax_0 + By_0, Ax_1 + By_1, \ldots, Ax_n + By_n, \ldots$, where A and B are real numbers. Two solutions x_n and y_n of Eq. (1) are said to be *linearly independent* if $Ax_n + By_n = 0$ only for $A = B = 0$. This is equivalent to saying that there is no constant c such that $x_n = cy_n$ for all n. These two definitions can be extended to apply to k solutions of Eq. (1) in the obvious way.

Theorem 1   Any linear combination of solutions of Eq. (1) is also a solution of Eq. (1).

Proof   We need only show that if x_n and y_n are solutions of Eq. (1), then so is $z_n = Ax_n + By_n$:

$$z_{n+2} + a_n z_{n+1} + b_n z_n$$
$$= Ax_{n+2} + By_{n+2} + a_n(Ax_{n+1} + By_{n+1}) + b_n(Ax_n + By_n)$$
$$= A(x_{n+2} + a_n x_{n+1} + b_n x_n) + B(y_{n+2} + a_n y_{n+1} + b_n y_n)$$
$$= 0. \ \blacksquare$$

We can now define the analog of the Wronskian for difference equations. Let x_n and y_n be two solutions of Eq. (1). Then the *Casoratian* of x_n and y_n is given by

$$C_n(x, y) = x_n y_{n+1} - x_{n+1} y_n. \tag{2}$$

In Section 3.1 we proved that homogeneous second-order linear differential equations have two linearly independent solutions. This is also true for homogeneous second-order linear difference equations, provided that none of the coefficients b_n in Eq. (1) is zero. The need for this condition is obvious in the case when all the coefficients b_n vanish, because then Eq. (1) is really a first-order difference equation and cannot have two linearly independent solutions. The next theorem, whose proof is left as an exercise, shows why every b_n must be nonzero.

Theorem 2　Suppose that some coefficient b_N in Eq. (1) is zero. Then Eq. (1) does not have two linearly independent solutions.

The next result is similar to Lemma 1 in Section 3.2.

Theorem 3　Let x_n and y_n be two solutions of Eq. (1) and suppose that $b_n \neq 0$ for every $n = 0, 1, 2, \ldots$. Then x_n and y_n are linearly independent if and only if $C_n(x, y) \neq 0$ for some integer n.

Proof　We shall begin by showing that $C_n(x, y)$ is never zero or $C_n(x, y)$ vanishes for all n. Using Eq. (2), we see that

$$C_{n+1} = x_{n+1}y_{n+2} - x_{n+2}y_{n+1}. \tag{3}$$

Since x_n and y_n are solutions of Eq. (1), we may replace x_{n+2} and y_{n+2} in Eq. (3) by

$$x_{n+2} = -a_n x_{n+1} - b_n x_n, \quad y_{n+2} = -a_n y_{n+1} - b_n y_n,$$

to obtain

$$\begin{aligned} C_{n+1} &= x_{n+1}(-a_n y_{n+1} - b_n y_n) - y_{n+1}(-a_n x_{n+1} - b_n x_n) \\ &= b_n[x_n y_{n+1} - x_{n+1} y_n] \end{aligned}$$

or

$$C_{n+1} = b_n C_n. \tag{4}$$

[Note the similarity between Eq. (4) and Eq. (3) in Section 3.2 for the Wronskian.] As we saw in Section 4.2, Eq. (4) has the solution

$$C_{n+1} = \left(\prod_{i=0}^{n} b_i\right) C_0.$$

Since $b_i \neq 0$ for every i by assumption, C_n is either always zero or never zero depending on whether C_0 is zero or not.

We can now prove the theorem by showing that the solutions x_n and y_n of Eq. (1) are linearly dependent if and only if $C_n(x, y) = 0$ (for all n).

If x_n and y_n are linearly dependent, then there is a constant c such that $y_n = cx_n$ for all n. Hence

$$C_n(x, y) = x_n y_{n+1} - y_n x_{n+1} = x_n(cx_{n+1}) - (cx_n)x_{n+1} = 0.$$

On the other hand, if $C_n(x, y) = 0$, then $C_0(x, y) = 0$ so that

$$x_0 y_1 = x_1 y_0. \tag{5}$$

There are two cases to consider, depending on whether $x_0 \neq 0$ or $x_0 = 0$.

CASE 1   If $x_0 \neq 0$, then Eq. (5) implies that

$$y_1 = \left(\frac{y_0}{x_0}\right)x_1.$$

Let $c = y_0/x_0$. Then

$$y_0 = \left(\frac{y_0}{x_0}\right)x_0 = cx_0.$$

By Eq. (1) it follows that

$$y_2 = -a_0 y_1 - b_0 y_0 = -a_0(cx_1) - b_0(cx_0)$$
$$= c(-a_0 x_1 - b_0 x_0) = cx_2.$$

Similarly, it follows that $y_3 = cx_3$, $y_4 = cx_4$, and so on, for every n. Thus $y_n = cx_n$, and x_n and y_n are linearly dependent.

CASE 2   If $x_0 = 0$, then either $x_1 = 0$ or $x_1 \neq 0$. If $x_1 = 0$, then Eq. (1) implies that $x_2 = 0$, $x_3 = 0$, and so on, for every n. Thus $x_n = 0 \cdot y_n$, and the solutions are dependent. If $x_1 \neq 0$, then Eq. (5) implies that

$$y_0 = \left(\frac{y_1}{x_1}\right)x_0.$$

Let $c = y_1/x_1$. We then note that

$$y_1 = \left(\frac{y_1}{x_1}\right)x_1 = cx_1.$$

The remaining proof follows as in Case 1. ∎

To complete the discussion of the homogeneous case, we shall prove:

Theorem 4   Let x_n and y_n be two linearly independent solutions to Eq. (1) and let z_n be another solution. Then z_n can be written as a linear combination of x_n and y_n.

Proof   Consider the linear system

$$x_0 c_1 + y_0 c_2 = z_0,$$
$$x_1 c_1 + y_1 c_2 = z_1,$$

where c_1 and c_2 are not known. The determinant of this system is $C_0(x, y)$, which is nonzero since x_n and y_n are linearly independent. Hence the system has a unique solution c_1 and c_2, and the sequence $z_n^* = c_1 x_n + c_2 y_n$ satisfies the conditions $z_0^* = z_0$ and $z_1^* = z_1$. Since the initial value problem has a unique solution, it follows that $z_n^* = z_n$, and the proof is complete. ∎

Once we have the above result, we can speak of the *general solution* of Eq. (1), which is given by

$$z_n = c_1 x_n + c_2 y_n,$$

where x_n and y_n are any two linearly independent solutions of Eq. (1).

Let us now turn briefly to the nonhomogeneous equation

$$y_{n+2} + a_n y_{n+1} + b_n y_n = f_n. \tag{6}$$

Theorem 5   Let y_n be a solution of Eq. (6) and let x_n be any other solution. Then $z_n = x_n - y_n$ is a solution of the homogeneous equation (1).

Proof   We have

$$z_{n+2} + a_n z_{n+1} + b_n z_n = (x_{n+2} - y_{n+2}) + a_n(x_{n+1} - y_{n+1}) + b_n(x_n - y_n)$$

$$= (x_{n+2} + a_n x_{n+1} + b_n x_n) - (y_{n+2} + a_n y_{n+1} + b_n y_n)$$

$$= f_n - f_n = 0. \quad \blacksquare$$

Given this theorem, it is evident that to obtain all solutions of the nonhomogeneous equation (6), it is necessary only to obtain one solution to Eq. (6) and the general solution to Eq. (1), as in the case of the corresponding differential equations.

EXERCISES 4.4

In Exercises 1 through 5, verify that x_n and y_n are solutions to each given difference equation and calculate their Casoratian.

1. $y_{n+2} - 3y_{n+1} + 2y_n = 0;$ $x_n = 2^n,$ $y_n = 1$
2. $y_{n+2} - 4y_{n+1} + 4y_n = 0;$ $x_n = 2^n,$ $y_n = n2^n$
3. $y_{n+2} + y_n = 0;$ $x_n = \cos\dfrac{n\pi}{2},$ $y_n = \sin\dfrac{n\pi}{2}$
4. $y_{n+2} - (n+2)(n+1)y_n = 0;$ $x_n = n!,$ $y_n = (-1)^n n!$
5. $y_{n+2} - 7y_{n+1} + 12y_n = 0;$ $x_n = 3^n,$ $y_n = 4^n$
6. Let x_n be a solution to

$$y_{n+2} + a_n y_{n+1} + b_n y_n = f_n$$

and let z_n be a solution to

$$y_{n+2} + a_n y_{n+1} + b_n y_n = g_n.$$

Show that $x_n + z_n$ is a solution to

$$y_{n+2} + a_n y_{n+1} + b_n y_n = f_n + g_n.$$

This is the *principle of superposition* for difference equations (see Exercise 15 in Section 3.2).

7. Consider the homogeneous third-order difference equation

$$y_{n+3} + a_n y_{n+2} + b_n y_{n+1} + c_n y_n = 0.$$

Show that if x_n, y_n, and z_n are three solutions to the equation, then any linear combination of them is also a solution.

8. Given the third-order equation of Exercise 7, again let x_n, y_n, and z_n be three solutions. Define the *Casoratian* $C_n(x, y, z)$ by

$$C_n(x, y, z) = \det \begin{vmatrix} x_n & y_n & z_n \\ x_{n+1} & y_{n+1} & z_{n+1} \\ x_{n+2} & y_{n+2} & z_{n+2} \end{vmatrix}.$$

Prove that $C_{n+1}(x, y, z) = c_n C_n(x, y, z)$ and conclude that if $c_n \neq 0$ for $n = 0, 1, 2, \ldots$, then $C_n(x, y, z)$ is either always zero or never zero.

9. Show that if, in Exercise 8, $c_n \neq 0$ for every n and if none of the solutions x_n, y_n, z_n is identically zero, then $C_n(x, y, z) \neq 0$ if and only if the three solutions are linearly independent.

10. Given that in Exercise 9 the three solutions are linearly independent and w_n is another solution, show that there exist constants α, β, and γ such that $w_n = \alpha x_n + \beta y_n + \gamma z_n$ for every n.

11. Show that if x_n and y_n are solutions to the third-order nonhomogeneous equation

$$y_{n+3} + a_n y_{n+2} + b_n y_{n+1} + c_n y_n = f_n,$$

then $z_n = x_n - y_n$ is a solution to the associated homogeneous equation.

12. Assume that some nonzero solution of

$$y_{n+2} + a_n y_{n+1} + b_n y_n = 0, \quad y_0 = 0 \qquad (7)$$

satisfies the condition $y_k = 0$ for some $k > 0$. Prove that $x_k = 0$ for any other solution x_n of Eq. (7).

*13. Prove Theorem 2.

4.5 USING ONE SOLUTION TO FIND ANOTHER

We shall consider the linear homogeneous equation

$$y_{n+2} + a_n y_{n+1} + b_n y_n = 0, \quad b_n \neq 0. \qquad (1)$$

If the sequences a_n and b_n are not constants, then there is no general method for obtaining solutions. However, as in the case of second-order homogeneous differential equations, if one solution is known, then another linearly independent solution can be found (see Section 3.3).

Suppose that x_n is a known nonzero solution to Eq. (1). We shall seek a second solution of the form

$$y_n = v_n x_n,$$

where v_n is a nonconstant sequence still to be determined. Define the sequence u_n by

$$u_n = v_{n+1} - v_n.$$

Recalling that the Casoratian $C_n(x, y)$ has the form $C_n(x, y) = x_n y_{n+1} - x_{n+1} y_n$ for any two solutions x_n and y_n of Eq. (1) and assuming that y_n is indeed a solution, we obtain, after some simple algebraic manipulations,

$$C_n(x, y) = x_{n+1} x_n \left(\frac{y_{n+1}}{x_{n+1}} - \frac{y_n}{x_n} \right)$$

$$= x_{n+1} x_n (v_{n+1} - v_n) = x_{n+1} x_n u_n$$

or

$$u_n = \frac{C_n(x, y)}{x_{n+1} x_n}.$$

Using the formula following Eq. (4) in Section 4.4 for the Casoratian, we can obtain

$$u_n = \frac{\prod_{i=0}^{n-1} b_i}{x_{n+1} x_n}, \qquad (2)$$

where we have assumed that $C_0 = 1$. The last assumption can be made since the unknown solution y_n is independent of x_n (implying $C_0 \neq 0$) and defined up to an arbitrary constant. Finally, from Eq. (2) we can obtain the first-order difference equation

$$v_{n+1} - v_n = \frac{\prod_{i=0}^{n-1} b_i}{x_{n+1} x_n} = d_n, \tag{3}$$

which by Eq. (5) in Section 4.2 has the solution

$$v_n = v_0 + \sum_{i=0}^{n-1} d_i.$$

Since neither x_n nor b_n is zero, d_n is not zero for any n and v_n is therefore not a constant. Hence $y_n = v_n x_n$ is a second linearly independent solution to Eq. (1).

Example 1   Solve $y_{n+2} - 4y_{n+1} + 4y_n = 0$.

One solution is easy to see: $x_n = 2^n$. (More will be said about constant-coefficient equations in the next two sections.) Let $y_n = v_n x_n$ be another solution. Then by Eq. (3) we see that

$$d_n = \frac{\prod_{i=0}^{n-1} b_i}{x_n x_{n+1}} = \frac{4^n}{2^n 2^{n+1}} = \frac{1}{2}$$

and thus

$$v_n = v_0 + \frac{n}{2}.$$

The choice of v_0 is arbitrary; so selecting $v_0 = 0$, we have

$$v_n = \frac{n}{2} \quad \text{and} \quad y_n = \frac{n}{2} x_n = \frac{n 2^n}{2}.$$

The general solution is therefore

$$y_n = c_1 2^n + c_2 n 2^n,$$

where the number 2 has been absorbed into the arbitrary constant c_2.

Example 2   Let $y_{n+2} - (n+2)(n+1)y_n = 0$. It is easy to verify that $x_n = n!$ is a solution. Since $b_n = -(n+2)(n+1)$,

$$d_n = \frac{\prod_{i=0}^{n-1} b_i}{x_n x_{n+1}} = \frac{(-1)^n (n+1)! n!}{(n+1)! n!} = (-1)^n.$$

Thus

$$v_n = v_0 + \sum_{i=0}^{n-1} d_i = v_0 + \frac{1 - (-1)^n}{2},$$

since the geometric progression

$$1 + a + a^2 + \cdots + a^{n-1} = (1 - a^n)/(1 - a).$$

As v_0 is arbitrary, we may set $v_0 = -\frac{1}{2}$ to obtain

$$y_n = v_n x_n = \frac{-(-1)^n}{2} n!,$$

and the general solution is given by

$$y_n = c_1 n! + c_2 (-1)^n n!.$$

Note that the solutions $n!$ and $(-1)^n n!$ are linearly independent, since $(-1)^n$ is not constant.

EXERCISES 4.5

In each of the following exercises, a difference equation is given with one solution. Find a second linearly independent solution.

1. $y_{n+2} - 2y_{n+1} + y_n = 0;$ $x_n = 7$

2. $y_{n+2} + 7y_{n+1} + 10y_n = 0;$ $x_n = (-2)^n$

3. $(n + 2)y_{n+2} - (n + 1)y_{n+1} - y_n = 0;$ $x_n = 3$

4. $y_{n+2} + 16y_n = 0;$ $x_n = 4^n \cos \dfrac{n\pi}{2}$

5. $y_{n+2} - 6y_{n+1} + 8y_n = 0;$ $x_n = 4^n$

6. $y_{n+2} + 6y_{n+1} + 9y_n = 0;$ $x_n = (5n)3^{n-1}$

7. $y_{n+2} - y_{n+1} - (n + 1)^2 y_n = 0;$ $x_n = n!$

8. $y_{n+2} - (n + 1)y_{n+1} - (n + 1)y_n = 0;$ $x_n = n!$

4.6 HOMOGENEOUS EQUATIONS WITH CONSTANT COEFFICIENTS: THE CASE OF REAL ROOTS

We shall now consider the linear homogeneous equation with constant coefficients

$$y_{n+2} + ay_{n+1} + by_n = 0, \quad b \neq 0, \tag{1}$$

and give a simple method for obtaining the general solution. In the case of the first-order equation $y_{n+1} = ay_n$, we saw in Section 4.2 that the general solution is $y_n = a^n y_0$. It is, then, not implausible to "guess" that there are solutions to Eq. (1) of the form $y_n = \lambda^n$ for some λ (real or complex). Substituting $y_n = \lambda^n$ into Eq. (1), we obtain

$$\lambda^{n+2} + a\lambda^{n+1} + b\lambda^n = 0.$$

Since this equation is true for all $n \geq 0$, it holds for $n = 0$, so that

$$\lambda^2 + a\lambda + b = 0. \tag{2}$$

This is the *characteristic equation* for the difference equation (1) and is identical to the characteristic equation for the second-order differential equation derived in Section 3.4. As before, the roots are

$$\lambda_1 = \frac{-a + \sqrt{a^2 - 4b}}{2} \quad \text{and} \quad \lambda_2 = \frac{-a - \sqrt{a^2 - 4b}}{2}. \tag{3}$$

Again there are three cases.

CASE 1 $a^2 - 4b > 0$. In this case there are two distinct real roots λ_1 and λ_2, given by Eqs. (3), and $x_n = \lambda_1^n$ and $y_n = \lambda_2^n$ are two solutions of Eq. (1). Since

$$C_n(x, y) = x_{n+1}y_n - x_n y_{n+1} = \lambda_1^n \lambda_2^n (\lambda_1 - \lambda_2),$$

$C_n(x, y)$ is not zero except in the special case of λ_1 or λ_2 being 0. This can only occur if $b = 0$, which has been ruled out. Thus we have proved:

Theorem 1   If $a^2 - 4b > 0$, then the general solution of Eq. (1) is given by

$$y_n = c_1 \lambda_1^n + c_2 \lambda_2^n,$$

where c_1 and c_2 are arbitrary constants and λ_1 and λ_2 are given by Eqs. (3).

Example 1   Consider the equation

$$x_{n+2} - 5x_{n+1} - 6x_n = 0.$$

The characteristic equation is $\lambda^2 - 5\lambda - 6 = 0$, with the roots $\lambda_1 = 6$ and $\lambda_2 = -1$. The general solution is given by $y_n = c_1(6)^n + c_2(-1)^n$. If we specify the initial conditions $y_0 = 3$, $y_1 = 11$, for example, then we obtain the system

$$c_1 + c_2 = 3,$$
$$6c_1 - c_2 = 11,$$

which has the unique solution $c_1 = 2$, $c_2 = 1$, and the specific solution $y_n = 2 \cdot 6^n + (-1)^n$.

CASE 2 $a^2 - 4b = 0$. Here the two roots of Eq. (2) are equal, and we have the solution $x_n = \lambda^n$ where $\lambda = -a/2$. We can obtain a second linearly independent solution by the method of the previous section. Letting $y_n = v_n x_n$ denote another solution, we have, by Eq. 3 in Section 4.5,

$$d_n = \frac{\prod_{i=0}^{n-1} b_i}{x_{n+1} x_n} = \frac{b^n}{\lambda^{n+1} \lambda^n} = \frac{b^n}{\lambda^{2n+1}}.$$

But $b = (a/2)^2$ and $\lambda = (-a/2)$, so that

$$d_n = \frac{(a/2)^{2n}}{(-a/2)^{2n+1}} = \frac{1}{(-a/2)} = \frac{1}{\lambda}.$$

Thus $v_n = v_0 + \sum_{i=0}^{n-1} d_i = n/\lambda$ (letting $v_0 = 0$) and $y_n = n\lambda^{n-1}$. We have thus shown the following result:

Theorem 2   Let $a^2 - 4b = 0$. Then the general solution of Eq. (1) is

$$y_n = c_1 \lambda^n + c_2 n \lambda^n,$$

where $\lambda = -a/2$ and c_1 and c_2 are arbitrary constants.

Example 2   Consider the equation

$$y_{n+2} - 6y_{n+1} + 9y_n = 0, \tag{4}$$

with initial conditions $y_0 = 5$, $y_1 = 12$. The characteristic equation is $\lambda^2 - 6\lambda + 9 = 0$ with the double root $\lambda = 3$. The general solution is therefore

$$y_n = c_1 3^n + c_2 n 3^n = 3^n(c_1 + nc_2).$$

Using the initial conditions, we obtain

$$c_1 = 5,$$

$$3c_1 + 3c_2 = 12.$$

The unique solution is $c_1 = 5$, $c_2 = -1$, and we have the specific solution to Eq. (4): $y_n = 5 \cdot 3^n - n \cdot 3^n = 3^n(5 - n)$.

We shall consider the third case in the next section.

EXERCISES 4.6

In Exercises 1 through 10, find the general solution to each given difference equation. When initial conditions are specified, find the unique solution that satisfies them.

1. $y_{n+2} - 3y_{n+1} - 4y_n = 0$

2. $y_{n+2} + 7y_{n+1} + 6y_n = 0$, $\quad y_0 = 0$, $\quad y_1 = 1$

3. $6y_{n+2} + 5y_{n+1} + y_n = 0$, $\quad y_0 = 1$, $\quad y_1 = 0$

4. $y_{n+2} + y_{n+1} - 6y_n = 0$, $\quad y_0 = 1$, $\quad y_1 = 2$

5. $y_{n+2} + 2y_{n+1} + y_n = 0$

6. $y_{n+2} + 16y_{n+1} + 64y_n = 0$, $\quad y_0 = 2$, $\quad y_1 = 0$

7. $y_{n+2} - \frac{2}{3}y_{n+1} + \frac{1}{9}y_n = 0$

8. $3y_{n+2} - 2y_{n+1} - y_n = 0$, $\quad y_0 = 0$, $\quad y_1 = 3$

9. $10y_{n+2} - y_{n+1} - y_n = 0$

10. $36y_{n+2} - 60y_{n+1} + 25y_n = 0$

11. In a study of infectious diseases a record is kept of outbreaks of measles in a particular school. It is estimated that the probability of at least one new infection occurring in the nth week after an outbreak is $P_n = P_{n-1} - \frac{1}{5}P_{n-2}$. If $P_0 = 0$ and $P_1 = 1$, what is P_n? After how many weeks will the probability of the occurrence of a new case of measles be less than ten percent?

12. The Fibonacci numbers are a sequence of num-

bers such that each one is the sum of its two predecessors. The first few Fibonacci numbers are 1, 1, 2, 3, 5, 8, 13, ...

a) Formulate an initial value difference equation that will generate the Fibonacci numbers.

b) Find the solution to this equation.

c) Show that the ratio of successive Fibonacci numbers tends to $(1 + \sqrt{5})/2$ as $n \to \infty$. This ratio, known as the *golden ratio*, was often used in ancient Greek architecture whenever rectangular structures were constructed. It was believed that when the ratio of the sides of a rectangle was this number, the resulting structure was most pleasing to the eye.

13. Two competing species of drosophila (fruit flies) are growing under favorable conditions. In each generation species A increases its population by 60 percent and species B increases by 40 percent. If initially there are 1000 flies of each species, what is the total population after n generations?

14. Consider the third-order difference equation

$$y_{n+3} + ay_{n+2} + by_{n+1} + cy_n = 0.$$

a) Show that $x_n = \lambda^n$ is a solution of the equation if λ satisfies the characteristic equation

$$\lambda^3 + a\lambda^2 + b\lambda + c = 0. \qquad (5)$$

b) Given that λ_1, λ_2, and λ_3 are distinct real roots of Eq. (5), show that the general solution is given by

$$y_n = c_1\lambda_1^n + c_2\lambda_2^n + c_3\lambda_3^n.$$

(See Exercises 8, 9, and 10 in Section 4.4.)

c) Given that λ_1 is a double root, show that the general solution

$$y_n = c_1\lambda_1^n + c_2 n\lambda_1^n + c_3\lambda_2^n.$$

d) Given that λ_1 is a triple root, show that the general solution is

$$y_n = c_1\lambda_1^n + c_2 n\lambda_1^n + c_3 n^2\lambda_1^n.$$

In the following exercises, use the results of Exercise 14 to obtain the general solution for each given equation.

15. $y_{n+3} - 6y_{n+2} + 11y_{n+1} - 6y_n = 0$

16. $y_{n+3} + 6y_{n+2} - 13y_{n+1} - 42y_n = 0$

17. $y_{n+3} - 3y_{n+1} + 2y_n = 0$

18. $y_{n+3} - 6y_{n+2} + 12y_{n+1} - 8y_n = 0$

19. $y_{n+3} - 3y_{n+2} + 3y_{n+1} - y_n = 0$

20. $y_{n+3} + 6y_{n+2} - 32y_n = 0$

4.7 HOMOGENEOUS EQUATIONS WITH CONSTANT COEFFICIENTS: THE COMPLEX CASE

CASE 3   When $a^2 - 4b < 0$, the roots of $\lambda^2 + a\lambda + b = 0$ are

$$\lambda_1 = \alpha + i\beta \quad \text{and} \quad \lambda_2 = \alpha - i\beta, \qquad (1)$$

where $\alpha = -a/2$ and $\beta = \sqrt{4b - a^2}/2$. Since solutions are of the form λ^n, we must describe how to calculate powers of complex numbers. This is very easy if the numbers are written in polar form. Let $z = re^{i\theta}$. Then $z^n = (re^{i\theta})^n = r^n e^{in\theta}$. But $e^{in\theta} = \cos n\theta + i \sin n\theta$. Thus we have obtained the *DeMoivre formula*

$$(\cos \theta + i \sin \theta)^n = \cos n\theta + i \sin n\theta. \qquad (2)$$

Example 1   Let $z = 1 + i$. Then $r = \sqrt{\alpha^2 + \beta^2} = \sqrt{2}$ and $\theta = \tan^{-1}(\beta/\alpha) = \tan^{-1} 1 = \pi/4$. So $z = \sqrt{2}e^{i\pi/4}$. Therefore,

$$z^3 = 2^{3/2}e^{i3\pi/4} = 2\sqrt{2}\left(\cos \frac{3\pi}{4} + i \sin \frac{3\pi}{4}\right) = -2 + 2i.$$

Of course, it is easier to cube $1 + i$ directly, but higher powers of $1 + i$ should be calculated this way.

Returning to the case where $a^2 - 4b < 0$, we can write the two roots λ_1 and λ_2 in Eq. (1) as

$$\lambda_1 = re^{i\theta}, \quad \lambda_2 = re^{-i\theta},$$

where $r = \sqrt{\alpha^2 + \beta^2}$ and $\theta = \tan^{-1}(\beta/\alpha)$, $0 < \theta < \pi$. The two linearly independent solutions are then

$$x_n = (re^{i\theta})^n = r^n e^{in\theta}, \quad y_n = r^n e^{-in\theta}.$$

Thus $\frac{1}{2}(x_n + y_n)$ is a solution, as is $(1/2i)(x_n - y_n)$. We saw in Section 3.5 that these solutions can be written as $x_n^* = r^n \cos n\theta$ and $y_n^* = r^n \sin n\theta$, respectively. They are clearly linearly independent, since one is not a constant multiple of the other. Alternatively, we show that the Casoratian $C_n(x^*, y^*)$ is nonzero:

$$C_0(x^*, y^*) = x_1^* y_0^* - x_0^* y_1^*$$
$$= r \cos \theta \cdot \sin 0 - \cos 0 \cdot r \sin \theta$$
$$= -r \sin \theta.$$

Since $\beta = \sqrt{4b - a^2}/2 \neq 0$, it follows that $r = \sqrt{\alpha^2 + \beta^2} \neq 0$, because $\alpha^2 + \beta^2$ must be positive. Also $\theta = \tan^{-1}(\beta/\alpha)$ cannot be zero or π, since $\tan 0 = \tan \pi = 0$ and $\tan \theta = \beta/\alpha \neq 0$. Thus $C_0(x^*, y^*) \neq 0$, which implies that $C_n(x^*, y^*)$ is nonzero and x_n^*, y_n^* are linearly independent. These results are summarized in Theorem 1.

Theorem 1   Let $a^2 - 4b < 0$. Then the general solution to the homogeneous equation $y_{n+2} + ay_{n+1} + by_n = 0$ is given by

$$y_n = c_1 r^n \cos n\theta + c_2 r^n \sin n\theta,$$

where $r = \sqrt{\alpha^2 + \beta^2}$, $\theta = \tan^{-1} \beta/\alpha$, $0 < \theta < \pi$, $\alpha = -a/2$, $\beta = \sqrt{4b - a^2}/2$, and c_1 and c_2 are arbitrary constants.

Example 2   Let $y_{n+2} + y_n = 0$. Then the characteristic equation is $\lambda^2 + 1 = 0$ with the roots $\pm i$. Here $\alpha = 0$ and $\beta = 1$, so $r = 1$ and $\theta = \pi/2$. The general solution is given by

$$y_n = c_1 \cos \frac{n\pi}{2} + c_2 \sin \frac{n\pi}{2}.$$

This is the equation for *discrete harmonic motion* which corresponds to ordinary harmonic motion as discussed in Example 1 of Section 3.5. If we specify $y_0 = 0$ and $y_1 = 1000$, we will obtain

$$c_1 = 0, \quad c_1 \cos \frac{\pi}{2} + c_2 \sin \frac{\pi}{2} = 1000,$$

with the solution $c_1 = 0$, $c_2 = 1000$, and the specific solution

$$y_n = 1000 \sin \frac{n\pi}{2}.$$

Example 3   Let P_n be the population in the nth generation of a species of bacteria. Assume the population in the nth generation depends on the two preceding generations:

$$P_{n+2} - rP_{n+1} - sP_n = 0, \tag{3}$$

where r and s are measures of the relative importance of the preceding two generations.

The characteristic equation is $\lambda^2 - r\lambda - s = 0$ with the roots

$$\lambda_1 = \frac{r + \sqrt{r^2 + 4s}}{2}, \quad \lambda_2 = \frac{r - \sqrt{r^2 + 4s}}{2}.$$

If $r^2 > -4s$, the roots are real and distinct, and the general solution is $P_n = c_1\lambda_1^n + c_2\lambda_2^n$. If $|\lambda_1| < 1$ and $|\lambda_2| < 1$, then $P_n \to 0$ as $n \to \infty$; but if either $|\lambda_1|$ or $|\lambda_2|$ is greater than 1, then $|P_n| \to \infty$. If $r^2 = -4s$ ($s < 0$), then the general solution is $P_n = c_1(r/2)^n + c_2 n(r/2)^{n-1}$, in which case $P_n \to 0$ if $|r| < 2$, but if $|r| \geqslant 2$, the solution tends to ∞. In the third case, $r^2 < -4s$, the general solution is

$$P_n = (-s)^{n/2}(c_1 \cos n\theta + c_2 \sin n\theta),$$

where $\theta = \tan^{-1}(\sqrt{-r^2 - 4s}/r)$. When $-s < 1$, the solution P_n tends to zero in an oscillatory manner. This is called *damped discrete harmonic motion* (see **Fig. 4**). If $-s = 1$, we have the harmonic motion of the previous example. Finally, if $-s > 1$, the solution grows in an oscillatory motion, called *force discrete harmonic motion* (see Fig. 5).

It is interesting to see that even in this very simple model, the behavior of solutions depends critically on the relative importance of the populations in the preceding two generations.

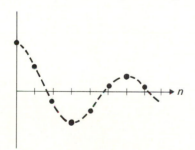

Figure 4

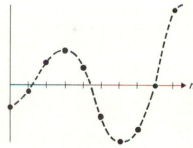

Figure 5

EXERCISES 4.7

In Exercises 1 through 4, find the general solution to each given difference equation. When initial conditions are specified, find the unique solution that satisfies them.

1. $y_{n+2} - \sqrt{2}\, y_{n+1} + y_n = 0$

2. $y_{n+2} - 2y_{n+1} + 2y_n = 0$, $\quad y_0 = 1$, $\quad y_1 = 2$

3. $y_{n+2} + 8y_n = 0$

4. $y_{n+2} - 2y_{n+1} + 4y_n = 0$, $\quad y_0 = 0$, $\quad y_1 = 1$

5. Discuss the properties of the solutions of
a) $x_{n+2} = x_{n+1} + \frac{1}{2}x_n$, and
b) $x_{n+2} = x_{n+1} - \frac{1}{2}x_n$,

as special cases of the model of population growth of Example 3.

6. Consider the integrals

$$I_n(\theta) = \int_0^\pi \frac{\cos nx - \cos n\theta}{\cos x - \cos \theta}\, dx.$$

a) Show that $I_{n+2}(\theta) - 2 \cos \theta\, I_{n+1}(\theta) + I_n(\theta) = 0$.

b) Solve this equation and obtain an explicit expression for $I_n(0)$. [*Hint*: It is first necessary to obtain the initial values $I_0(0)$ and $I_1(0)$.]

7. In Section 4.2 we discussed the nonlinear first-order Riccati equation

$$y_n y_{n-1} + a_n y_n + b_n y_{n-1} = c_n.$$

By making the substitution $y_n = x_n/x_{n+1} - b_n$, show that this equation becomes

$$(a_n b_n + c_n)x_{n+1} - (a_n - b_{n-1})x_n - x_{n-1} = 0.$$

Use the results of Exercise 7 to obtain the general solutions of the difference equations in Exercises 8 through 12.

8. $y_n y_{n-1} + 2y_n - 3y_{n-1} = 2$

9. $y_n y_{n-1} - y_n - y_{n-1} = 1$

10. $y_n y_{n-1} + y_n + y_{n-1} = 1$

11. $4y_n y_{n-1} + 6y_n - 3y_{n-1} = 0$

12. $2y_n y_{n-1} + 2y_n + 4y_{n-1} = -5$

Use the technique of Exercise 14 in Section 4.6 and the results of this section to obtain the general solutions of the difference equations in the following exercises.

13. $y_{n+3} - 2y_{n+2} + y_{n+1} - 2y_n = 0$

14. $y_{n+3} - y_{n+1} + \sqrt{2}y_n = 0$

15. $y_{n+3} - y_{n+2} + y_{n+1} - y_n = 0$

16. $y_{n+3} - 8y_{n+2} + 8y_{n+1} - 64y_n = 0$

17. $y_{n+3} + 4y_{n+2} - 8y_{n+1} + 24y_n = 0$

4.8 NONHOMOGENEOUS EQUATIONS: VARIATION OF CONSTANTS

There are two methods of solving nonhomogeneous difference equations—undetermined coefficients and variation of constants—which are analogous to the methods of solving nonhomogeneous differential equations. In this section we shall study the very powerful variation-of-constants method and discuss the technique of undetermined coefficients in the exercises.

As with differential equations, we assume a solution to

$$y_{n+2} + a_n y_{n+1} + b_n y_n = f_n, \quad b_n \neq 0, \tag{1}$$

of the form

$$z_n = c_n x_n + d_n y_n, \tag{2}$$

where x_n and y_n are linearly independent solutions of the homogeneous equation. From Eq. (2) we have

$$z_{n+1} = c_{n+1} x_{n+1} + d_{n+1} y_{n+1};$$

and adding and subtracting the quantities $c_n x_{n+1}$ and $d_n y_{n+1}$, we obtain

$$z_{n+1} = c_n x_{n+1} + d_n y_{n+1} + (c_{n+1} - c_n)x_{n+1} + (d_{n+1} - d_n)y_{n+1}.$$

As the first of two conditions that we will need to determine both c_n and d_n, it is convenient to assume, *for all n*, that

$$(c_{n+1} - c_n)x_{n+1} + (d_{n+1} - d_n)y_{n+1} = 0. \tag{3}$$

This requirement is analogous to that of Eq. (4) in Section 3.7 for differential equations. Thus

$$z_{n+1} = c_n x_{n+1} + d_n y_{n+1}$$

and

$$z_{n+2} = c_{n+1}x_{n+2} + d_{n+1}y_{n+2}.$$

Assuming that z_n is a solution of Eq. (1), we obtain

$$
\begin{aligned}
f_n &= z_{n+2} + a_n z_{n+1} + b_n z_n \\
&= (c_{n+1} - c_n)x_{n+2} + (d_{n+1} - d_n)y_{n+2} \\
&\quad + c_n[x_{n+2} + a_n x_{n+1} + b_n x_n] + d_n[y_{n+2} + a_n y_{n+1} + b_n y_n].
\end{aligned}
\tag{4}
$$

The bracketed expressions in Eq. (4) vanish, since x_n and y_n are solutions of Eq. (1), and thus we have the second condition [analogous to Eq. (5) in Section 3.7] that must hold for all n:

$$(c_{n+1} - c_n)x_{n+2} + (d_{n+1} - d_n)y_{n+2} = f_n. \tag{5}$$

Combining Eqs. (5) and (3), we obtain the following system of two equations in the two unknowns $(c_{n+1} - c_n)$ and $(d_{n+1} - d_n)$:

$$
\begin{aligned}
(c_{n+1} - c_n)x_{n+1} + (d_{n+1} - d_n)y_{n+1} &= 0, \\
(c_{n+1} - c_n)x_{n+2} + (d_{n+1} - d_n)y_{n+2} &= f_n.
\end{aligned}
$$

The determinant of this system, $C_{n+1}(x, y)$, is nonzero by Theorem 3 in Section 4.4 so that

$$c_{n+1} - c_n = -\frac{f_n y_{n+1}}{C_{n+1}(x, y)}, \quad d_{n+1} - d_n = \frac{f_n x_{n+1}}{C_{n+1}(x, y)}. \tag{6}$$

Equations (6) are first-order difference equations in the unknowns c_n and d_n that can be solved by means of Eq. (5) in Section 4.2. Thus

$$c_n = c_0 - \sum_{k=0}^{n-1} \frac{f_k y_{k+1}}{C_{k+1}(x, y)}, \quad d_n = d_0 + \sum_{k=0}^{n-1} \frac{f_k x_{k+1}}{C_{k+1}(x, y)},$$

and the general solution of Eq. (1) is given by

$$z_n = c_0 x_n + d_0 y_n - x_n \sum_{k=0}^{n-1} \frac{f_k y_{k+1}}{C_{k+1}(x, y)} + y_n \sum_{k=0}^{n-1} \frac{f_k x_{k+1}}{C_{k+1}(x, y)}, \tag{7}$$

where c_0 and d_0 are arbitrary constants.

Example 1 Solve

$$y_{n+2} - 3y_{n+1} + 2y_n = 1 + 5^{n+1}. \tag{8}$$

The characteristic equation has roots $\lambda = 1, 2$, so that the homogeneous equation has the independent solutions $x_n = 1$ and $y_n = 2^n$. The Casoratian is

$$
\begin{aligned}
C_{n+1}(x, y) &= x_{n+1}y_{n+2} - x_{n+2}y_{n+1} \\
&= 2^{n+2} - 2^{n+1} = 2^{n+1},
\end{aligned}
$$

and $f_n = 1 + 5^{n+1}$. Using these values in the sums of Eq. (7), we find that

$$\sum_{k=0}^{n-1} \frac{f_k y_{k+1}}{C_{k+1}(x, y)} = \sum_{k=0}^{n-1} (1 + 5^{k+1}) = n + \frac{5^{n+1}}{4} - \frac{5}{4},$$

$$\sum_{k=0}^{n-1} \frac{f_k x_{k+1}}{C_{k+1}(x, y)} = \sum_{k=0}^{n-1} \left[\left(\frac{1}{2}\right)^{k+1} + \left(\frac{5}{2}\right)^{k+1}\right] = \frac{2}{3}\left(\frac{5}{2}\right)^{n+1} - \left(\frac{1}{2}\right)^n - \frac{2}{3},$$

$$\tag{9}$$

where we have used the following fact about geometric progressions:

$$a + a^2 + a^3 + \cdots + a^n = \frac{a - a^{n+1}}{1 - a}.$$

Inserting Eqs. (9) into Eq. (7), combining like terms, and absorbing all stray coefficients into the arbitrary constants c_0 and d_0, we get the general solution of Eq. (8):

$$z_n = c_0 + d_0 2^n - n + \frac{5^{n+1}}{12}.$$

Example 2   Consider the equation

$$y_{n+2} + y_n = n + 1. \tag{10}$$

The roots of the characteristic equation are $\pm i$, so by Theorem 1 in Section 4.7 the homogeneous equation has the independent solutions $x_n = \cos n\pi/2$ and $y_n = \sin n\pi/2$ (see Example 2 in Section 4.7). The Casoratian is

$$C_{n+1}(x, y) = \cos\frac{(n + 1)\pi}{2} \sin\frac{(n + 2)\pi}{2} - \sin\frac{(n + 1)\pi}{2} \cos\frac{(n + 2)\pi}{2}$$

$$= \sin\frac{\pi}{2} = 1.$$

Therefore,

$$c_n = c_0 - \sum_{k=0}^{n-1} (k + 1) \sin\frac{(k + 1)\pi}{2} = c_0 - 1 + 3 - 5 + \cdots - n \sin\frac{n\pi}{2},$$

$$d_n = d_0 + \sum_{k=0}^{n-1} (k + 1) \cos\frac{(k + 1)\pi}{2} = d_0 - 2 + 4 - 6 + \cdots + n \cos\frac{n\pi}{2}.$$

Note that

$$c_{2m} = c_{2m-1} = c_0 + (-1)^m m, \quad \text{and} \quad d_{2m+1} = d_{2m} = d_0 + (-1)^m (m + 1) - 1,$$

so that the general solution of Eq. (10) is given by

$$z_n = c_n \cos\frac{n\pi}{2} + d_n \sin\frac{n\pi}{2},$$

where c_n and d_n are as given above. Note that this expression includes c_0 and d_0 as arbitrary constants.

Example 3   Solve

$$y_{n+2} - (n+2)(n+1)y_n = (n+3)!. \tag{11}$$

We saw in Example 2 in Section 4.5 that the homogeneous equation has the independent solutions $x_n = n!$ and $y_n = (-1)^n n!$. An easy computation yields the Casoratian $C_{n+1}(x, y) = 2(-1)^n(n+1)!(n+2)!$, so the sums in Eq. (7) are given by

$$\sum_{k=0}^{n-1} \frac{f_k y_{k+1}}{C_{k+1}(x, y)} = -\frac{1}{2}[3 + 4 + \cdots + (n+2)] = \frac{3}{2} - \frac{(n+3)(n+2)}{4},$$

$$\sum_{k=0}^{n-1} \frac{f_k x_{k+1}}{C_{k+1}(x, y)} = \frac{1}{2}[3 - 4 + 5 - 6 + \cdots + (-1)^{n+1}(n+2)]$$

$$= \frac{(-1)^{n-1}}{2}\left(\left[\frac{n+1}{2}\right] + 1 + (-1)^{n-1}\right),$$

where $[\frac{n}{2}]$ denotes the largest integer $\leq \frac{n}{2}$. The reader should verify this last equation. Thus absorbing constants into the c_0, d_0 terms and collecting like quantities, we obtain the general solution of Eq. (11):

$$z_n = c_0 n! + d_0(-1)^n n! + n!\left(\frac{n^2}{4} + \frac{5n}{4} - \frac{1}{2}\left[\frac{n+1}{2}\right]\right).$$

EXERCISES 4.8

Use the method of variation of constants to find particular solutions of the equations in Exercises 1 through 5.

1. $y_{n+2} - 5y_{n+1} + 6y_n = 5^{n+1}$

2. $y_{n+2} + y_{n+1} - 6y_n = e^{n+1} + 3e^n$

3. $y_{n+2} - 4y_{n+1} + 4y_n = n2^n$

4. $y_{n+2} - 2y_{n+1} + y_n = 2^n$

5. $y_{n+2} + 5y_n = \sin\dfrac{n\pi}{2}$

In the following exercises we shall develop the method of undetermined coefficients for difference equations. This method is easier to use than the variation-of-constants technique, but it applies only when $a_n = a$ and $b_n = b$ are constants (for all n) and f_n is of one of the following three forms: $f_n = A_0 a^n$, $A_1 \sin cn + A_2 \cos cn$, $A_0 + A_1 n + \cdots + A_k n^k$, or any combination of these terms. After finding the independent solutions x_n, y_n of the homogeneous equation, we proceed as follows: Write the expression z_n in the same form as f_n, with undetermined coefficients A_j. Then:

    i) If no part of z_n is in the general solution of the homogeneous equation, substitute z_n

for y_n in the equation

$$y_{n+2} + ay_{n+1} + by_n = f_n,$$

and solve for the coefficients A_j.

    ii) Otherwise, multiply z_n by the smallest integral power of n such that no part of the product belongs to the general solution of the homogeneous equation, and proceed as with z_n in step (i). (For example if the homogeneous solutions are 3^n and $n3^n$ and $f_n = 3^n$, then multiply z_n by n^2 so that $z_n = An^2 3^n$ is *not* a solution to the homogeneous equation.)

6.   Use $z_n = A_0 5^n$ to show that the equation in Exercise 1 has the general solution

$$y_n = c_0 2^n + c_1 3^n + \tfrac{1}{6}5^{n+1}.$$

7.   Solve the equation in Exercise 2 by the method of undetermined coefficients.

8.   Solve the equation in Exercise 4 by the method of undetermined coefficients.

9.   Solve the equation in Exercise 5 by the method of undetermined coefficients.

10.   Solve $y_{n+2} - 4y_{n+1} + 4y_n = 2^n$ by the method of undetermined coefficients.

In the following exercises, find the general solution of each equation by either of the two available methods. In some cases it may be useful to use the principle of superposition (see Exercise 6 in Section 4.4).

11. $y_{n+2} - 3y_{n+1} + 2y_n = 2^n + 2^{-n}$

12. $y_{n+2} - y_{n+1} - 6y_n = n + 3^n$

13. $y_{n+2} + y_n = \sin n$

14. $y_{n+3} - 6y_{n+2} + 11y_{n+1} - 6y_n = 2^n$

15. $y_{n+3} - 2y_{n+2} + 3y_n = \cos \dfrac{n\pi}{2}$

16. $y_{n+3} + y_{n+2} - 2y_n = n + n^2 + n^3$

17. $y_{n+2} - y_{n+1} - y_n = n^2 + 1$

18. $y_{n+2} + 2y_{n+1} + y_n = 2^n + 3^n + 4^n.$

4.9 AN APPLICATION TO GAMES AND QUALITY CONTROL

Suppose that two people, A and B, play a certain unspecified game several times in succession. One of the players must win on each play of the game (ties are ruled out). The probability that A wins is p ($\neq 0$), and the corresponding probability for B is q. Of course, $p + q = 1$. One dollar is bet by each competitor on each play of the game. Suppose that player A starts with k dollars and player B with j dollars. We let P_n denote the probability that A will bankrupt B (that is, win all B's money) when A has n dollars. Clearly $P_0 = 0$ (this is the probability that player A will wipe out player B when A has no money) and $P_{k+j} = 1$ (A has already eliminated B from further competition). To calculate P_n for other values of n between 0 and $k + j$, we have the following difference equation

$$P_n = qP_{n-1} + pP_{n+1}. \tag{1}$$

To understand this equation, we note that if A has n dollars at one turn, his probability of having $n - 1$ dollars at the next turn is q, and similarly for the other term in Eq. (1).

Equation (1) can be written in our usual format as

$$pP_{n+1} - P_n + qP_{n-1} = 0$$

or

$$P_{n+2} - \frac{1}{p} P_{n+1} + \frac{q}{p} P_n = 0.$$

The characteristic equation is

$$\lambda^2 - \frac{1}{p}\lambda + \frac{q}{p} = 0,$$

which has the roots

$$\frac{1}{2p}(1 \pm \sqrt{1 - 4pq}).$$

Since

$$\sqrt{1 - 4pq} = \sqrt{1 - 4p(1 - p)} = \sqrt{4p^2 - 4p + 1} = |1 - 2p|,$$

we discover that the roots of the characteristic equation are

$$\lambda_1 = \frac{1-p}{p} = \frac{q}{p}, \quad \lambda_2 = 1.$$

The general solution to Eq. (1) is therefore

$$P_n = c_1\left(\frac{q}{p}\right)^n + c_2$$

when $p \neq q$, and

$$P_n = c_1 + c_2 n$$

when $p = q = \frac{1}{2}$ (by the rules for repeated roots). Keeping in mind the fact that $0 \leqslant P_n \leqslant 1$ for all n and using the boundary conditions $P_0 = 0$ and $P_{k+j} = 1$, we can finally obtain

$$P_n = \frac{1-(q/p)^n}{1-(q/p)^{k+j}} \quad \text{if} \quad p \neq q, \tag{2}$$

and

$$P_n = \frac{n}{k+j} \quad \text{if} \quad p = q = \frac{1}{2}, \tag{3}$$

for all n such that $0 \leqslant n \leqslant k + j$.

Example 1 In a game of roulette a gambler bets against a casino. Suppose that the gambler bets one dollar on red each time. On a typical roulette wheel there are eighteen reds, eighteen blacks, a zero, and a double zero. If the wheel is honest, the probability that the casino will win is $p = \frac{20}{38} \approx 0.5263$. Then $q = 0.4737$ and $q/p = 0.9$. Suppose that both the gambler and the casino start with k dollars. Then the probability that the gambler will be cleaned out is

$$P_k = \frac{1-(q/p)^k}{1-(q/p)^{2k}} = \frac{1}{1+(q/p)^k} = \frac{1}{1+(0.9)^k}.$$

The second column in Table 1 shows the probability that the gambler will lose all his money for different initial amounts k. Note that the more money both start with, the more likely it is that the gamber will lose all his money. It is evident that as the gambler continues to play, the probability that he will be wiped out approaches a certainty. This is why even a very small advantage enables the casino, in almost every case, to break the gambler if he continues to bet.

The third column in Table 1 gives the probability that the gambler will lose all his money if he has one dollar and the casino has k dollars:

$$P_k^* = \frac{1-(q/p)^k}{1-(q/p)^{k+1}}.$$

Table 1

k	P_k	P_k^*
1	0.5263	0.5263
5	0.6287	0.8740
10	0.7415	0.9492
25	0.9330	0.9923
50	0.9949	0.9995
100	0.9999	0.9999

Thus, if the gambler has much less money than the casino, he is even more likely to lose it all. The combination of a small advantage, table limits, and huge financial resources makes running a casino a very profitable business indeed.

Example 2   The previous example can be used as a simple model of competition for resources between two species in a single ecological niche. Suppose that two species, A and B, control a combined "territory" of N resource units. The resource units may be such things as acres of grassland, number of trees, and so on. If species A controls k units, then species B will control the remaining $N - k$ units. Suppose that during each unit of time there is competition **for one unit of resource** between the two species. Let species A have the probability p of being successful. If we let P_n denote the probability that species B will lose all its resources when species A has n units of resource, then P_n is determined by Eq. (1) with initial conditions $P_0 = 0$ and $P_N = 1$. By Eqs. (2) and (3), the solution to this equation is

$$P_n = \begin{cases} \dfrac{1 - [(1 - p)/p]^n}{1 - [(1 - p)/p]^N} & \text{if } p \neq \dfrac{1}{2}, \\[2ex] \dfrac{n}{N} & \text{if } p = \dfrac{1}{2}. \end{cases}$$

As in the previous example, even a small competitive advantage will virtually ensure the extinction of the weaker species. For example, if $p = 0.55$, and species A has n of a total of 100 units, then we have Table 2.

Table 2

	P_n
1	0.1818
2	0.3306
3	0.4523
4	0.5519
5	0.6333
10	0.8656
25	0.9934

Note that even if the species with the competitive advantage starts with as few as 4 of the 100 units of resource, it has a better than even chance to supplant the weaker species. With one quarter of the resources, it is virtually certain to do so.

A process similar to the one discussed has been used with success to determine whether, in a manufacturing process, a batch of articles is satisfactory. Let us briefly describe this process here. More extensive details can be found in the paper by G. A. Barnard.†

To test whether a batch of articles is satisfactory, we introduce a scoring system. The score is initially set at N. If a randomly sampled item is found to be defective, we subtract k. If it is acceptable, we add 1. The procedure stops when the score reaches either $2N$ or becomes nonpositive. If $2N$, the batch is accepted; if nonpositive, it is rejected. Suppose that the probability of selecting an acceptable item is p, and $q = 1 - p$. Let P_n denote the probability that the batch will be rejected when the score is at n. Then after the next choice, the score will be either increased by 1 with probability p or decreased by k with probability q. Thus

$$P_n = pP_{n+1} + qP_{n-k},$$

which can be written as the $(k + 1)$st-order difference equation

$$P_{n+k+1} - \frac{1}{p} P_{n+k} + \frac{q}{p} P_n = 0$$

with boundary conditions

$$P_{1-k} = \cdots = P_0 = 1, \quad P_{2N} = 0.$$

The case of $k = 1$ reduces to Example 1 with the result that a batch is almost certain to be accepted or rejected depending on whether p is greater or less than $\frac{1}{2}$.

EXERCISES 4.9

1. In Example 1, assume that player A has a 10-percent competitive advantage. If player A starts with \$3, how much money must player B start with to have a better than even chance to win all of A's money? To have an 80-percent chance?

2. Answer the questions in Exercise 1 given that player A has

  a) a 2-percent advantage;

  b) a 20-percent advantage.

3. The games described in Examples 1 and 2 can be modified to allow for more than one possibility. Suppose that on each play of the game player A has the probability p to win one dollar, q to win two dollars, and r to lose one dollar, where $p + q + r = 1$. Let P_n be as before. Write down a difference equation that determines P_N, assuming that each player starts with N dollars.

4. Given that $p = q = \frac{1}{4}$ and $r = \frac{1}{2}$, solve the difference equation of Exercise 3.

† G. A. Barnard, "Sequential Tests in Industrial Statistics," Supplement to the *Journal of the Royal Statistical Society* **8**, No. 1 (1946).

5. Given that $p = q = r = \frac{1}{3}$, solve the difference equation of Exercise 3.

6. Suppose that player A has the probability p of winning one dollar, q of losing one dollar, and r of losing two dollars. Let P_n be the probability that A will bankrupt B when A has n dollars, and suppose A and B each have N dollars initially.

　　a) Obtain a difference equation with appropriate boundary conditions for this problem.

　　b) Solve the equation with $p = \frac{1}{6}$, $q = \frac{1}{3}$, $r = \frac{1}{2}$.

7. Analyze a game in which on each play player A has a $\frac{1}{3}$ probability of winning two dollars and a $\frac{2}{3}$ probability of losing one dollar.

　　a) Assume that A and B initially each have N dollars. Does A have an initial advantage? Suppose that $N = 10$. What is P_{10}?

　　b) If A has ten dollars and B has twenty dollars initially, what is the initial probability that A will bankrupt B?

8. Discuss each of the previous exercises in the context of two species competing for resources.

9. Formulate a model comparable to the one in Example 2 for three species competing for a single resource.

REVIEW EXERCISES FOR CHAPTER 4

In Exercises 1 through 8, find the general solution of the given first-order difference equation. Find the particular solution when an initial condition is specified.

1. $y_{n+1} = y_n + 1$

2. $y_{n+1} = 2y_n - 1$

3. $y_{n+1} = 3y_n + 2$

4. $y_{n+1} = 3y_n - 2$

5. $y_{n+1} = (n + 1)y_n + 1$

6. $y_{n+1} = ny_n + 1$

7. $y_{n+1} = 2y_n - 2$,　$y_0 = 7$

8. $y_{n+1} = 2y_n + 2^{n+1}$,　$y_0 = 0$

9. Use Newton's method to find the unique solution to

$$\ln x = 1 - x/2$$

to five significant figures.

10. Use Newton's method to find the single real root of

$$x^3 + 3x^2 + 6x - 5 = 0$$

to five significant figures.

In Exercises 11 through 16, find the general solution of the given second-order difference equation.

11. $3y_{n+2} - 8y_{n+1} + 5y_n = 0$

12. $y_{n+2} + 6y_{n+1} + 9y_n = 0$

13. $4y_{n+2} + 12y_{n+1} + 9y_n = 0$

14. $y_{n+2} - y_{n+1} + 2y_n = 0$

15. $y_{n+2} - y_{n+1} + y_n = 0$

16. $y_{n+2} - y_{n+1} - y_n = 0$

Use the method of variation of constants to find particular solutions to the equations in Exercises 17 through 20.

17. $y_{n+2} + 5y_{n+1} + 6y_n = 4^{n+1}$

18. $y_{n+2} - y_{n+1} - 6y_n = e^n$

19. $y_{n+2} + 2y_{n+1} + y_n = 3^n$

20. $y_{n+2} - y_{n+1} - y_n = 2^n$

Systems of linear difference equations can also be converted into a single higher-order difference equation by the method of elimination. Convert the given systems in Exercises 21 through 28 into a single higher-order equation and find its general solution. If initial conditions are given, determine the unique particular solution.

21. $x_{n+1} = 2x_n + y_n$,

　　$y_{n+1} = x_n + 2y_n$

22. $x_{n+1} = x_n + y_n$,

　　$y_{n+1} = -4x_n + 5y_n$

23. $x_{n+1} = -2x_n + y_n,$

   $y_{n+1} = 4x_n + y_n$

24. $x_{n+1} = -4x_n + y_n, \quad x_0 = 1,$

   $y_{n+1} = -10x_n + 2y_n, \quad y_0 = 4$

25. $x_{n+1} = 6x_n + 4y_n, \quad x_0 = 0,$

   $y_{n+1} = -4x_n - 2y_n, \quad y_0 = 1$

26. $x_{n+1} = x_n - y_n + n,$

   $y_{n+1} = 5x_n + y_n + 1$

27. $x_{n+1} = 2x_n - y_n - 1, \quad x_0 = 1,$

   $y_{n+1} = -x_n + 2y_n + 2, \quad y_0 = 0$

28. $x_{n+1} = -x_n + 2y_n + 5^{n+1}$

   $y_{n+1} = -3x_n + 4y_n + \frac{1}{2}$

*29. Snow geese mate in pairs in late spring of each year. Each female lays an average of five eggs, of which approximately twenty percent are claimed by predators and foul weather. The goslings, of which sixty percent are female, mature rapidly and are fully developed by the time the annual migration begins. Hunters and disease claim about 300,000 geese and 200,000 ganders annually. Are snow geese in danger of extinction?

Power Series Solutions of Differential Equations

In Chapter 3 we studied several methods for solving second- and higher-order differential equations. With the exception of the Euler equation and a few equations in which one solution was easily guessed, the techniques applied only to linear differential equations with *constant coefficients*. The case of linear differential equations with *variable coefficients* is much more complicated. Unfortunately many of the most important differential equations in applied mathematics—for example, Bessel's equation and Legendre's equation—are of this type. In this chapter we will consider a method for obtaining solutions to such equations. Since the solutions so obtained are in the form of power series, the procedure used is known as the *power series method*.

5.1 REVIEW OF POWER SERIES

In this section we will review some of the basic properties of power series. We take it for granted that most readers will have received some background in power series in an earlier course in calculus. A *power series* in $(x - a)$ is an infinite series of the form

$$\sum_{n=0}^{\infty} c_n (x - a)^n = c_0 + c_1 (x - a) + c_2 (x - a)^2 + \cdots, \tag{1}$$

where $c_0, c_1, \ldots$ are constants, called the *coefficients* of the series, a is a constant called the *center* of the series, and x is an independent variable. In particular, a power series centered at zero $(a = 0)$ has the form

$$\sum_{n=0}^{\infty} c_n x^n = c_0 + c_1 x + c_2 x^2 + c_3 x^3 + \cdots. \tag{2}$$

Note that polynomials are also power series, since they have this form.

A series of the form (1) can always be reduced to the form (2) by the substitution $X = x - a$. This substitution is merely a translation of the coordinate system. It is easy to see that the behavior of Eq. (2) near zero is exactly the same as the behavior of Eq. (1) near a. For this reason we need only study the properties of series of the form (2).

The expression

$$s_n(x) = c_0 + c_1 x + c_2 x^2 + \cdots + c_n x^n$$

is called the *nth partial sum* of the series (2); and the difference between (2) and (3),

$$R_n(x) = c_{n+1} x^{n+1} + c_{n+2} x^{n+2} + \cdots,$$

is called the *remainder after the nth term* of Eq. (2). Thus, in the case of the series

$$\sum_{n=0}^{\infty} (n + 1) x^n = 1 + 2x + 3x^2 + 4x^3 + \cdots,$$

we have

$$s_1(x) = 1 + 2x, \qquad R_1(x) = 3x^2 + 4x^3 + \cdots,$$

$$s_2(x) = 1 + 2x + 3x^2, \quad R_2(x) = 4x^3 + 5x^4 + \cdots, \quad \text{and so on.}$$

In this way we can generate a sequence of partial sums $s_1(x)$, $s_2(x)$, ... It often happens that for some particular value $x = x_0$, the sequence of partial sums evaluated at x_0 has a finite limit. When that occurs, we say that the series (2) *converges* (or *is convergent*) at x_0, and write

$$\sum_{n=0}^{\infty} c_n x_0^n = \lim_{n \to \infty} s_n(x_0) = s(x_0). \tag{3}$$

The number $s(x_0)$ obtained in Eq. (3) is called the *sum* of the series (2) at x_0. When the series is not convergent at x_0, we say it *diverges* (or *is divergent*) *at* x_0. In case of convergence, the partial sum $s_n(x_0)$ is an approximation of the sum $s(x_0)$, and the error of the approximation

$$|s(x_0) - s_n(x_0)| = |R_n(x_0)|$$

can be made as small as desired by using a sufficiently large n.

If a series (2) converges at x_0, then the terms $c_n x_0^n$ tend to zero:

$$\lim_{n \to \infty} c_n x_0^n = \lim_{n \to \infty} (s_n(x_0) - s_{n-1}(x_0)) = \lim_{n \to \infty} s_n(x_0) - \lim_{n \to \infty} s_{n-1}(x_0)$$

$$= s(x_0) - s(x_0) = 0. \tag{4}$$

However, even if the terms in the series tend to zero, the series may diverge (see Exercise 17).

If we let $x = 0$ in Eq. (2), then the series is reduced to the single term c_0 and thus converges. There may be other values at which the series converges. The values for which the series (2) converges lie in an interval centered at 0, called the *interval of convergence*. (This fact is proved in Theorem 1.) Hence to each series (2) corresponds a number $0 \leqslant R \leqslant \infty$, called the *radius of convergence*, with the property that the series converges if $|x| < R$ and diverges if $|x| > R$.

The radius of convergence can often be determined by means of the *root test* formula

$$\boxed{\frac{1}{R} = \lim_{n \to \infty} \sqrt[n]{|c_n|},} \tag{5}$$

provided that the limit exists. (If $\sqrt[n]{|c_n|} \to 0$, we set $R = \infty$.)

Example 1   Consider the *geometric series*

$$\sum_{n=0}^{\infty} x^n = 1 + x + x^2 + \cdots. \tag{6}$$

To find the sum of this series, we note that

$$s_n(x) = 1 + x + \cdots + x^{n-1} + x^n,$$

so that

$$x s_n(x) = x + x^2 + \cdots + x^n + x^{n+1}.$$

Taking the difference between these two expressions, we find that $(1 - x)s_n(x) = 1 - x^{n+1}$ or

$$s_n(x) = 1 + x + \cdots + x^n = \frac{1 - x^{n+1}}{1 - x}. \tag{7}$$

If $|x| < 1$, then the numerator in the right-hand term tends to 1 as n tends to infinity. Thus

$$s(x) = \lim_{n \to \infty} s_n(x) = \frac{1}{1 - x}, \tag{8}$$

for all x with $|x| < 1$.

If $|x| \geq 1$, then the sequence $\{s_n(x)\}$ does not have a finite limit, so the series (6) diverges.

Using the root test (5), we obtain $R = 1$, confirming the results above. The case $|x| = R$ must always be checked separately.

Theorem 1   Let R be determined by the root test formula (5). Then the series (2) converges for each x in $|x| < R$ and diverges for every x such that $|x| > R$.

Proof   Let $|x| < r < R$ so that $1/R < 1/r$. Since $\sqrt[n]{|c_n|} \to 1/R$, we must have $\sqrt[n]{|c_n|} < 1/r$ for all $n \geq n_0$, where n_0 is sufficiently large. Then using the triangle inequality,† we find that the remainder term $R_n(x)$ satisfies the inequality

$$|R_n(x)| \leq |c_{n+1}| |x|^{n+1} + |c_{n+2}| |x|^{n+2} + \cdots < \left| \frac{x}{r} \right|^{n+1} + \left| \frac{x}{r} \right|^{n+2} + \cdots. \tag{9}$$

Using Eq. (8), we can rewrite the last term in the inequality (9) in the form

$$|R_n(x)| < \left| \frac{x}{r} \right|^{n+1} \left(1 + \left| \frac{x}{r} \right| + \left| \frac{x}{r} \right|^2 + \cdots \right) = \frac{|x/r|^{n+1}}{1 - |x/r|}, \tag{10}$$

since $|x/r| < 1$. By Eq. (10), it is clear that the remainder term vanishes as n tends to infinity. Thus the series converges for each x such that $|x| < R$.

If $|x| > r > R$, we have $\sqrt[n]{|c_n|} > 1/r$, so that

$$|c_n x^n| > \left| \frac{x}{r} \right|^n > 1.$$

---

† The triangle inequality states that $|a + b| \leq |a| + |b|$.

Thus the terms in the series do not tend to zero. By Eq. (4) we see that the series must diverge for all x such that $|x| > R$. ∎

Another useful formula for determining the radius of convergence is given by the *ratio test*:

$$\frac{1}{R} = \lim_{n \to \infty} \left| \frac{c_{n+1}}{c_n} \right| \tag{11}$$

whenever the limit exists. The proof that this limit in fact yields the same value of R is left as an exercise (see Exercise 20).

Example 2   Find the radius of convergence of the series

$$\sum_{n=0}^{\infty} \frac{x^n}{n!} = 1 + x + \frac{x^2}{2!} + \frac{x^3}{3!} + \cdots.$$

Here $c_n = 1/n!$, so by the ratio test (11)

$$\frac{1}{R} = \lim_{n \to \infty} \frac{n!}{(n+1)!} = \lim_{n \to \infty} \frac{1}{n+1} = 0,$$

and $R = \infty$. Thus this series converges for all values of x.

Example 3   The series

$$\sum_{n=0}^{\infty} n! x^n = 1 + x + 2! x^2 + 3! x^3 + \cdots$$

diverges for all $x \neq 0$, since

$$\frac{1}{R} = \lim_{n \to \infty} \left| \frac{c_{n+1}}{c_n} \right| = \lim_{n \to \infty} \frac{(n+1)!}{n!} = \lim_{n \to \infty} (n+1) = \infty.$$

The most familiar power series are those that are obtained by the use of *Taylor's formula*:

$$f(x) = \sum_{n=0}^{N} \frac{f^{(n)}(x_0)}{n!} (x - x_0)^n + R_N(x - x_0) \tag{12}$$

If the function $f(x)$ has derivatives of all orders at the point x_0, and the remainder term $R_N(x - x_0)$ tends to zero as N tends to infinity, we say that $f(x)$ is *analytic at* x_0 and write

$$f(x) = \sum_{n=0}^{\infty} \frac{f^{(n)}(x_0)}{n!} (x - x_0)^n. \tag{13}$$

The series (13) is called the *Taylor series* of $f(x)$ at the point $x = x_0$. When

$x_0 = 0$, Eq. (13) is often called the *Maclaurin series* of $f(x)$. The following familiar expansions, valid for all x, may all be obtained by this method:

$$e^x = \sum_{n=0}^{\infty} \frac{x^n}{n!} = 1 + x + \frac{x^2}{2!} + \frac{x^3}{3!} + \cdots , \tag{14}$$

$$\sin x = \sum_{n=0}^{\infty} \frac{(-1)^n x^{2n+1}}{(2n+1)!} = x - \frac{x^3}{3!} + \frac{x^5}{5!} - \frac{x^7}{7!} + \cdots , \tag{15}$$

$$\cos x = \sum_{n=0}^{\infty} \frac{(-1)^n x^{2n}}{(2n)!} = 1 - \frac{x^2}{2!} + \frac{x^4}{4!} - \frac{x^6}{6!} + \cdots , \tag{16}$$

$$\sinh x = \sum_{n=0}^{\infty} \frac{x^{2n+1}}{(2n+1)!} = x + \frac{x^3}{3!} + \frac{x^5}{5!} + \frac{x^7}{7!} + \cdots , \tag{17}$$

$$\cosh x = \sum_{n=0}^{\infty} \frac{x^{2n}}{(2n)!} = 1 + \frac{x^2}{2!} + \frac{x^4}{4!} + \frac{x^6}{6!} + \cdots . \tag{18}$$

There are functions $f(x)$ that have derivatives of all orders at a given point x_0 and yet are not analytic. In these cases, the remainder term $R_N(x - x_0)$ does not tend to zero as N tends to ∞. An example of such a function is given in Exercise 24.

Let us now consider four operations on power series; all will be used in applying the power series method to differential equations.

1. *Two power series may be added term by term.* To be precise, if the series

$$\sum_{n=0}^{\infty} b_n (x - x_0)^n \quad \text{and} \quad \sum_{n=0}^{\infty} c_n (x - x_0)^n$$

have radii of convergence R_b and R_c and sums $b(x)$ and $c(x)$, respectively, then the series

$$\sum_{n=0}^{\infty} (b_n + c_n)(x - x_0)^n$$

converges to $b(x) + c(x)$ for all x such that $|x - x_0| < R$, where $R = \min(R_b, R_c)$.

2. *Two power series may be multiplied term by term.* Indeed, given the preceding two series, we have

$$b(x)c(x) = \left(\sum_{n=0}^{\infty} b_n (x - x_0)^n \right)\left(\sum_{n=0}^{\infty} c_n (x - x_0)^n \right)$$

$$= \sum_{n=0}^{\infty} (b_0 c_n + b_1 c_{n-1} + \cdots + b_n c_0)(x - x_0)^n$$

for all x such that $|x - x_0| < R$, where again $R = \min(R_b, R_c)$.

3. *A power series may be differentiated term by term.* Thus

$$b'(x) = \frac{d}{dx}\left(\sum_{n=0}^{\infty} b_n(x - x_0)^n\right) = \sum_{n=1}^{\infty} nb_n(x - x_0)^{n-1} \qquad \textbf{(19)}$$

for all x such that $|x - x_0| < R_b$.

4. *A power series may be integrated term by term.* That is,

$$\int b(x)\,dx = \int \sum_{n=0}^{\infty} b_n(x - x_0)^n\,dx = \sum_{n=0}^{\infty} \frac{b_n(x - x_0)^{n+1}}{n + 1} \qquad \textbf{(20)}$$

for all x such that $|x - x_0| < R_b$.

We note that *the radius of convergence is unaffected by differentiation or integration.*

We will leave the proofs of the first two properties as exercises (see Exercises 18 and 19). To show that Eq. (19) is indeed true, we observe that

$$\frac{b(x + h) - b(x)}{h} = \sum_{n=0}^{\infty} b_n \frac{(x + h - x_0)^n - (x - x_0)^n}{h}. \qquad \textbf{(21)}$$

Expanding the term

$$(x - x_0 + h)^n = (x - x_0)^n + nh(x - x_0)^{n-1} + \cdots + h^n,$$

we see that Eq. (21) becomes

$$\sum_{n=1}^{\infty} b_n \frac{nh(x - x_0)^{n-1} + \cdots + h^n}{h} = \sum_{n=1}^{\infty} b_n[n(x - x_0)^{n-1} + \cdots + h^{n-1}], \qquad \textbf{(22)}$$

since the first term drops out. Interchanging the limit and sum† and letting h tend to zero, we note that all but the first term in the brackets vanish in Eq. (22). Therefore, we obtain the right-hand side of Eq. (19). To see that the series (19) has the same radius of convergence, we may use the limit (11) (if it exists):

$$\lim_{n\to\infty} \left|\frac{(n + 1)b_{n+1}}{nb_n}\right| = \lim_{n\to\infty} \frac{n + 1}{n} \lim_{n\to\infty} \left|\frac{b_{n+1}}{b_n}\right| = \lim_{n\to\infty} \left|\frac{b_{n+1}}{b_n}\right| = \frac{1}{R_b}.$$

Finally, we prove Eq. (20) by means of Eq. (19), noting that

$$\frac{d}{dx} \sum_{n=0}^{\infty} b_n \frac{(x - x_0)^{n+1}}{n + 1} = \sum_{n=0}^{\infty} \frac{d}{dx} b_n \frac{(x - x_0)^{n+1}}{n + 1} = \sum_{n=0}^{\infty} b_n(x - x_0)^n = b(x).$$

Thus Eq. (20) is, indeed, an integral of $b(x)$. ∎

---

† Interchanging limits and sums requires justification. In this case there is no difficulty, since power series are *uniformly convergent* on closed bounded subsets of $|x| < R_b$. The proof may be found in most advanced calculus texts.

EXERCISES 5.1

Obtain each of the following Taylor series by repeated differentiations.

1. Eq. (14)

2. Eq. (15)

3. Eq. (16)

4. Eq. (17)

5. Eq. (18)

6. $\ln(1+x) = x - \dfrac{x^2}{2} + \dfrac{x^3}{3} - \dfrac{x^4}{4} + \cdots, \quad |x| < 1$

7. $\sin^{-1} x = x + \dfrac{1}{2} \cdot \dfrac{x^3}{3} + \dfrac{1}{2} \cdot \dfrac{3}{4} \cdot \dfrac{x^5}{5} + \dfrac{1}{2} \cdot \dfrac{3}{4} \cdot \dfrac{5}{6} \cdot \dfrac{x^7}{7}$
$+ \cdots, \quad |x| < 1$

8. $\ln x = (x-1) - \dfrac{(x-1)^2}{2} + \dfrac{(x-1)^3}{3} - \dfrac{(x-1)^4}{4}$
$+ \cdots, \quad 0 < x < 2$

9. $\dfrac{1}{2-x} = 1 + (x-1) + (x-1)^2 + (x-1)^3$
$+ \cdots, \quad 0 < x < 2$

10. Use Eq. (8) to show that

$$\frac{1}{1+x} = 1 - x + x^2 - x^3 + \cdots, \quad |x| < 1.$$

Then prove that:

a) $\ln(1+x) = x - \dfrac{x^2}{2} + \dfrac{x^3}{3} - \dfrac{x^4}{4} + \cdots,$
$|x| < 1;$

b) $\tan^{-1} x = x - \dfrac{x^3}{3} + \dfrac{x^5}{5} - \dfrac{x^7}{7} + \cdots, \quad |x| < 1;$

c) $\dfrac{1}{(1+x)^2} = 1 - 2x + 3x^2 - 4x^3 + \cdots,$
$|x| < 1.$

Find the radius and interval of convergence of each given series in Exercises 11 through 16.

11. $\displaystyle\sum_{n=1}^{\infty} \dfrac{x^n}{n^2}$

12. $\displaystyle\sum_{n=1}^{\infty} \left(\dfrac{x-2}{n}\right)^n$

13. $\displaystyle\sum_{n=1}^{\infty} n^n x^n$

14. $\displaystyle\sum_{n=0}^{\infty} \dfrac{n^2(x-1)^n}{2^n}$

15. $\displaystyle\sum_{n=0}^{\infty} \dfrac{(2n)! x^n}{(n!)^2}$

16. $\displaystyle\sum_{n=0}^{\infty} \dfrac{(k+n)!(x+1)^n}{k!n!}$

17. Show that the series

$$\sum_{n=1}^{\infty} \frac{x^n}{n} = x + \frac{x^2}{2} + \frac{x^3}{3} + \frac{x^4}{4} + \cdots$$

diverges at $x = 1$ by proving that the partial sums satisfy the inequality

$$s_{2^k}(1) \geqslant 1 + k/2.$$

(This exercise shows that even though the terms in a series may tend to zero, the series itself may diverge, in this case at $x = 1$.)

18. Prove that two power series may be added term by term and determine the appropriate interval of convergence.

19. Prove that two power series may be multiplied term by term and determine the appropriate interval of convergence.

20. Prove that formulas (11) and (5) yield the same result when both limits exist.

21. Prove that the remainder term $R_n(x - x_0)$ of Taylor's formula satisfies the equation

$$R_n(x - x_0) = \frac{f^{(n+1)}(\bar{x})}{(n+1)!}(x - x_0)^{n+1},$$

where $\bar{x}$ is some value between x_0 and x. (*Hint*: Use the mean value theorem of differential calculus.)

22. Use the result of Exercise 21 to verify that e^x, $\sin x$, and $\cos x$ are analytic for all x.

23. Use the result of Exercise 21 to prove that $\ln(1+x)$ and $\tan^{-1} x$ are analytic for all x such that $|x| < 1$.

24. Consider the function

$$f(x) = \begin{cases} e^{-1/x^2}, & x \neq 0, \\ 0, & x = 0. \end{cases}$$

a) Show that f has derivatives of all orders at $x = 0$ and that

$$f'(0) = f''(0) = \cdots = 0.$$

b) Conclude that $f(x)$ does not have a Taylor series expansion at $x = 0$, even though it is infinitely differentiable there. Thus f is not analytic at $x = 0$.

25. Using Taylor's formula, prove the *binomial formula*

$$(1+x)^p = 1 + px + \frac{p(p-1)}{1 \cdot 2}x^2$$
$$+ \frac{p(p-1)(p-2)}{1 \cdot 2 \cdot 3}x^3 + \cdots.$$

5.2 THE POWER SERIES METHOD: EXAMPLES

The fundamental assumption used in solving a differential equation by the power series method is that the solution of the differential equation can be expressed in the form of a power series, say,

$$y = \sum_{n=0}^{\infty} c_n x^n. \tag{1}$$

Once this assumption has been made, power series expansions for y', y'', ... can be obtained by differentiating Eq. (1) term by term:

$$y' = \sum_{n=1}^{\infty} n c_n x^{n-1}, \tag{2}$$

$$y'' = \sum_{n=2}^{\infty} n(n-1) c_n x^{n-2}, \quad \text{etc.,} \tag{3}$$

and these may then be substituted into the given differential equation. After all the indicated operations have been carried out, and like powers of x have been collected, we obtain an expression of the form

$$k_0 + k_1 x + k_2 x^2 + \cdots = \sum_{n=0}^{\infty} k_n x^n = 0, \tag{4}$$

where the coefficients $k_0, k_1, k_2, \ldots$ are expressions involving the unknown coefficients $c_0, c_1, c_2, \ldots$. Since Eq. (4) must hold for all values of x in some interval, all the coefficients $k_0, k_1, k_2, \ldots$ must vanish. From the equations

$$k_0 = 0, \quad k_1 = 0, \quad k_2 = 0, \ldots$$

it is then possible to determine successively the coefficients $c_0, c_1, c_2, \ldots$. In this section we will illustrate this procedure by means of several examples, without concerning ourselves with questions of the convergence of the power series under consideration or the inherent limitations of the method. We will see that power series provide a powerful method for solving certain linear differential equations with variable coefficients. First, however, in order to check that the power series method does provide the required solution, we shall solve three problems that could be solved more easily by other methods.

Example 1   Consider the initial value problem

$$y' = y + x^2, \quad y(0) = 1. \tag{5}$$

Inserting Eqs. (1) and (2) into the equation, we have

$$c_1 + 2c_2 x + 3c_3 x^2 + 4c_4 x^3 + \cdots = (c_0 + c_1 x + c_2 x^2 + c_3 x^3 + \cdots) + x^2.$$

Collecting like powers of x, we obtain

$$(c_1 - c_0) + (2c_2 - c_1)x + (3c_3 - c_2 - 1)x^2 + (4c_4 - c_3)x^3 + \cdots = 0.$$

Equating each of the coefficients to zero, we obtain the identities

$$c_1 - c_0 = 0, \quad 2c_2 - c_1 = 0, \quad 3c_3 - c_2 - 1 = 0, \quad 4c_4 - c_3 = 0, \ldots,$$

from which we find that

$$c_1 = c_0, \quad c_2 = \frac{c_1}{2} = \frac{c_0}{2!}, \quad c_3 = \frac{c_2 + 1}{3} = \frac{c_0 + 2}{3!}, \quad c_4 = \frac{c_3}{4} = \frac{c_0 + 2}{4!}, \ldots.$$

With these values, Eq. (1) becomes

$$y = c_0 + c_0 x + \frac{c_0}{2!} x^2 + \frac{c_0 + 2}{3!} x^3 + \frac{c_0 + 2}{4!} x^4 + \frac{c_0 + 2}{5!} x^5 + \cdots$$

$$= (c_0 + 2)\left[1 + x + \frac{x^2}{2!} + \frac{x^3}{3!} + \frac{x^4}{4!} + \cdots\right] - 2\left[1 + x + \frac{x^2}{2!}\right].$$

Looking carefully at the series in square brackets, we recognize the expansion for e^x given in Eq. (14) in Section 5.1, so we have the general solution

$$y = (c_0 + 2)e^x - x^2 - 2x - 2.$$

To solve the initial value problem, we set $x = 0$ to obtain

$$1 = y(0) = c_0 + 2 - 2 = c_0.$$

Thus the solution of the initial value problem (5) is given by the equation

$$y = 3e^x - x^2 - 2x - 2.$$

Example 2   Solve

$$y'' + y = 0. \tag{6}$$

Using Eqs. (1) and (3), we have

$$(2c_2 + 3 \cdot 2c_3 x + 4 \cdot 3c_4 x^2 + \cdots) + (c_0 + c_1 x + c_2 x^2 + \cdots) = 0.$$

Gathering like powers of x yields

$$(2c_2 + c_0) + (3 \cdot 2c_3 + c_1)x + (4 \cdot 3c_4 + c_2)x^2 + \cdots = 0.$$

Setting each of the coefficients to zero, we obtain

$$2c_2 + c_0 = 0, \quad 3 \cdot 2c_3 + c_1 = 0, \quad 4 \cdot 3c_4 + c_2 = 0, \quad 5 \cdot 4c_5 + c_3 = 0, \ldots,$$

and

$$c_2 = -\frac{c_0}{2!}, \quad c_3 = -\frac{c_1}{3!}, \quad c_4 = -\frac{c_2}{4 \cdot 3} = \frac{c_0}{4!}, \quad c_5 = -\frac{c_3}{5 \cdot 4} = \frac{c_1}{5!}, \ldots.$$

Substituting these values into the power series (1) for y yields

$$y = c_0 + c_1 x - \frac{c_0}{2!} x^2 - \frac{c_1}{3!} x^3 + \frac{c_0}{4!} x^4 + \frac{c_1}{5!} x^5 + \cdots.$$

Splitting this series into two parts, we have

$$y = c_0\left(1 - \frac{x^2}{2!} + \frac{x^4}{4!} - \cdots\right) + c_1\left(x - \frac{x^3}{3!} + \frac{x^5}{5!} - \cdots\right).$$

Using Eqs. (15) and (16) in Section 5.1 reveals the familiar general solution
$$y = c_0 \cos x + c_1 \sin x.$$

We observe that in this case the power series method produces two arbitrary constants c_0, c_1, and yields the general solution for Eq. (6).

So far we have considered only linear equations with constant coefficients. We turn now to linear equations with variable coefficients.

Example 3   Consider the initial value problem
$$(1 + x^2)y' = 2pxy, \quad y(0) = 1, \tag{7}$$

where p is a constant. Applying Eqs. (1) and (2), we have

$$(1 + x^2)\sum_{n=1}^{\infty} nc_n x^{n-1} = 2px\sum_{n=0}^{\infty} c_n x^n.$$

We use the summation notation in this example in order to develop the skill in manipulating power series that will be required later on. Equation (7) may be rewritten in the form

$$\sum_{n=1}^{\infty} nc_n x^{n-1} + \sum_{n=1}^{\infty} nc_n x^{n+1} = \sum_{n=0}^{\infty} 2pc_n x^{n+1}. \tag{8}$$

We would like to rewrite each of the sums in Eq. (8) so that each general term will contain the same power of x. This can be done by assuming that each general term contains the term x^k. For the first sum, this amounts to substituting $k = n - 1$. Since n ranges from 1 to ∞, $k = n - 1$ will range from 0 to ∞. Substituting $k = n + 1$ with k ranging from 2 to ∞ into the second sum, and $k = n + 1$ with k ranging from 1 to ∞ into the third sum, allows us to rewrite these sums so that the general term will involve the power x^k. We then obtain

$$\sum_{k=0}^{\infty} (k + 1)c_{k+1} x^k + \sum_{k=2}^{\infty} (k - 1)c_{k-1} x^k = \sum_{k=1}^{\infty} 2pc_{k-1} x^k.$$

Now we can gather like terms in x:

$$c_1 + (2c_2 - 2pc_0)x + \sum_{k=2}^{\infty} \{(k + 1)c_{k+1} + [(k - 1) - 2p]c_{k-1}\}x^k = 0.$$

Equating each coefficient to zero yields
$$c_1 = 0, \quad 2c_2 - 2pc_0 = 0, \quad 3c_3 + (1 - 2p)c_1 = 0,$$
and in general
$$(k + 1)c_{k+1} + [(k - 1) - 2p]c_{k-1} = 0, \quad k \geq 1. \tag{9}$$

We note that Eq. (9) is a difference equation with variable coefficients. This equation is called a *recursion formula* and may be used to evaluate the constants $c_0, c_1, c_2, \ldots$ successively. We see that

$$c_1 = 0, \quad c_2 = pc_0, \quad c_3 = 0,$$

and by Eq. (9), in general

$$c_{k+1} = \frac{(2p - k + 1)}{k + 1} c_{k-1},$$

so that

$$c_4 = \frac{2p - 2}{4} c_2 = \frac{p(p - 1)}{1 \cdot 2} c_0, \quad c_5 = 0,$$

$$c_6 = \frac{2p - 4}{6} c_4 = \frac{p(p - 1)(p - 2)}{1 \cdot 2 \cdot 3} c_0, \quad c_7 = 0, \ldots,$$

since $c_3 = 0$. Thus the coefficients with odd-numbered subscripts vanish and the power series for y is given by

$$y = c_0 + \frac{p}{1} c_0 x^2 + \frac{p(p - 1)}{1 \cdot 2} c_0 x^4 + \frac{p(p - 1)(p - 2)}{1 \cdot 2 \cdot 3} c_0 x^6 + \cdots$$

$$= c_0 \left(1 + \frac{p}{1} x^2 + \frac{p(p - 1)}{1 \cdot 2} x^4 + \frac{p(p - 1)(p - 2)}{1 \cdot 2 \cdot 3} x^6 + \cdots \right).$$

Replacing x by x^2 in the binomial formula (see Exercise 22 in Section 5.1), we have

$$(1 + x)^p = 1 + \frac{p}{1} x + \frac{p(p - 1)}{1 \cdot 2} x^2 + \frac{p(p - 1)(p - 2)}{1 \cdot 2 \cdot 3} x^3 + \cdots,$$

which yields the general solution of the differential equation:

$$y = c_0(1 + x^2)^p.$$

Since $y(0) = 1$, it follows that $c_0 = 1$ and $y = (1 + x^2)^p$.

Example 4 Consider the differential equation

$$y'' + xy' + y = 0. \tag{10}$$

Using Eqs. (1), (2), and (3), we obtain the equation

$$\sum_{n=2}^{\infty} n(n - 1)c_n x^{n-2} + x \sum_{n=1}^{\infty} nc_n x^{n-1} + \sum_{n=0}^{\infty} c_n x^n = 0.$$

Reindexing to obtain equal powers of x, we have

$$\sum_{k=0}^{\infty} (k + 2)(k + 1)c_{k+2} x^k + \sum_{k=1}^{\infty} kc_k x^k + \sum_{k=0}^{\infty} c_k x^k = 0.$$

Note that the second sum can also be allowed to range from 0 to ∞.

Gathering like terms in x produces the equation

$$\sum_{k=0}^{\infty} [(k + 2)(k + 1)c_{k+2} + (k + 1)c_k]x^k = 0.$$

Setting the coefficients equal to zero, we obtain the general recursion formula

$$(k + 2)(k + 1)c_{k+2} + (k + 1)c_k = 0.$$

Therefore $(k + 2)c_{k+2} = -c_k$, and

$$c_2 = -\frac{c_0}{2}, \quad c_3 = -\frac{c_1}{3}, \quad c_4 = -\frac{c_2}{4} = \frac{c_0}{2 \cdot 4},$$

$$c_5 = -\frac{c_3}{5} = \frac{c_1}{3 \cdot 5}, \quad c_6 = -\frac{c_4}{6} = -\frac{c_0}{2 \cdot 4 \cdot 6}, \quad \text{etc.}$$

Hence the power series for y can be written in the form

$$y = c_0 + c_1 x - \frac{c_0}{2} x^2 - \frac{c_1}{3} x^3 + \frac{c_0}{2 \cdot 4} x^4 + \frac{c_1}{3 \cdot 5} x^5 - \cdots$$

$$= c_0\left(1 - \frac{x^2}{2} + \frac{x^4}{2 \cdot 4} - \frac{x^6}{2 \cdot 4 \cdot 6} + \cdots\right) + c_1\left(x - \frac{x^3}{3} + \frac{x^5}{3 \cdot 5} - \frac{x^7}{3 \cdot 5 \cdot 7} + \cdots\right)$$

$$\tag{11}$$

by separating the terms that involve c_0 and c_1. At this point we try to see whether we recognize the two series that have been obtained by the power series method. Very frequently this is an unproductive task, but in this instance we are fortunate:

$$1 - \frac{x^2}{2} + \frac{x^4}{2 \cdot 4} - \frac{x^6}{2 \cdot 4 \cdot 6} + \cdots = 1 + \left(-\frac{x^2}{2}\right) + \frac{1}{2!}\left(-\frac{x^2}{2}\right)^2 + \frac{1}{3!}\left(-\frac{x^2}{2}\right)^3 + \cdots$$

$$= e^{-x^2/2}.$$

We can't recognize the second series, so we use the method given in Section 3.3 of finding one solution when another is known. By Eq. (4) in Section 3.3 we have

$$y_2 = y_1 \int \frac{e^{-\int x\, dx}}{y_1^2} \, dx = e^{-x^2/2} \int \frac{e^{-x^2/2}}{(e^{-x^2/2})^2} \, dx$$

$$= e^{-x^2/2} \int e^{x^2/2} \, dx \tag{12}$$

The integral in Eq. (12) does not have a closed-form solution. That this is indeed the second series in Eq. (11) can be verified by integrating the series for $e^{x^2/2}$ term by term and multiplying the result by the series for $e^{-x^2/2}$. Hence the general solution of Eq. (10) is given by

$$y = c_0 e^{-x^2/2} + c_1 e^{-x^2/2} \int e^{x^2/2} \, dx.$$

Example 5   Solve the equation

$$xy'' + y' + xy = 0. \tag{13}$$

Using the power series (1), (2), and (3) for Eq. (13) yields the equation

$$\sum_{n=2}^{\infty} n(n-1)c_n x^{n-1} + \sum_{n=1}^{\infty} nc_n x^{n-1} + \sum_{n=0}^{\infty} c_n x^{n+1} = 0.$$

Reindexing the series to obtain like powers of x, we have

$$\sum_{k=1}^{\infty} (k+1)kc_{k+1}x^k + \sum_{k=0}^{\infty} (k+1)c_{k+1}x^k + \sum_{k=1}^{\infty} c_{k-1}x^k = 0.$$

Condensing the three series in one yields, after some algebra,

$$c_1 + \sum_{k=1}^{\infty} [(k+1)^2 c_{k+1} + c_{k-1}]x^k = 0.$$

Setting the coefficients to zero, we have $c_1 = 0$ and

$$(k+1)^2 c_{k+1} = -c_{k-1}, \quad k = 1, 2, 3, \ldots. \tag{14}$$

The recursion formula (14) together with $c_1 = 0$ imply that all coefficients with odd-numbered subscripts vanish, and

$$c_2 = -\frac{c_0}{2^2}, \quad c_4 = -\frac{c_2}{4^2} = \frac{c_0}{2^2 4^2}, \quad c_6 = -\frac{c_4}{6^2} = -\frac{c_0}{2^2 4^2 6^2}, \ldots.$$

Hence

$$y = c_0 - \frac{c_0}{2^2}x^2 + \frac{c_0}{2^2 4^2}x^4 - \frac{c_0}{2^2 4^2 6^2}x^6 + \cdots$$

$$= c_0 \sum_{n=0}^{\infty} \frac{1}{(n!)^2}\left(-\frac{x^2}{4}\right)^n. \tag{15}$$

It is unlikely that the reader is familiar with the series in Eq. (15). This series is often used in applied mathematics and is known as the *Bessel function of index zero*, $J_0(x)$. (We will study the properties of Bessel functions in Section 5.4.) Note also that the power series method has produced only *one* of the solutions of Eq. (13). To find the other solution, we can again proceed as in Example 4 (see also Exercise 12 in Section 3.3). Thus

$$y_2(x) = J_0(x) \int \frac{dx}{xJ_0^2(x)}.$$

Finally, the general solution of Eq. (13) is given by

$$y(x) = AJ_0(x) + BJ_0(x) \int \frac{dx}{xJ_0^2(x)}.$$

In our next example we will meet a situation in which the power series method fails to yield any solution.

Example 6   Consider the Euler equation

$$x^2 y'' + xy' + y = 0. \tag{16}$$

Making use of the series (1), (2), and (3), and multiplying by the appropriate powers of x, we have

$$\sum_{n=2}^{\infty} n(n-1)c_n x^n + \sum_{n=1}^{\infty} nc_n x^n + \sum_{n=0}^{\infty} c_n x^n = 0$$

or

$$\sum_{n=0}^{\infty} (n^2 + 1)c_n x^n = 0. \tag{17}$$

Clearly, if we equate each of the coefficients of Eq. (17) to zero, all the coefficients c_n will vanish and $y \equiv 0$. Thus in this case the power series method fails completely in helping us find the general solution

$$y = A \cos(\ln|x|) + B \sin(\ln|x|)$$

of Eq. (16) (check!).

When initial conditions are given, there is another method based on the Taylor series [see Eq. (13) in Section 5.1] that can also be used.

Example 1 (revisited)   Consider the initial value problem

$$y' = y + x^2, \quad y(0) = 1. \tag{18}$$

Differentiating both sides of the differential equation repeatedly and successively evaluating each derivative at the initial value of $x = 0$, we have

$$y' = y + x^2 \big|_{x=0} = y(0) + (0)^2 = 1,$$
$$y'' = y' + 2x \big|_{x=0} = y'(0) + 2(0) = 1,$$
$$y^{(3)} = y'' + 2 \big|_{x=0} = y''(0) + 2 = 3,$$
$$y^{(4)} = y^{(3)} \big|_{x=0} = y^{(3)}(0) = 3, \ldots.$$

Substituting these derivatives in the Taylor series

$$y(x) = \sum_{n=0}^{\infty} \frac{y^{(n)}(x_0)}{n!} (x - x_0)^n \tag{19}$$

with $x_0 = 0$, we have

$$y(x) = 1 + x + \frac{x^2}{2!} + \frac{3x^3}{3!} + \frac{3x^4}{4!} + \cdots = 3e^x - 2 - 2x - x^2,$$

which is the result that we obtained before.

Taylor's method is easily adapted to higher-order initial value problems by rewriting the differential equation so that the highest-order derivative is expressed in terms of the other derivatives and the independent variable. Successive differentiations will again yield the values $y^{(n)}(x_0)$ for substitution into the Taylor series.

EXERCISES 5.2

In Exercises 1 through 16, find the general solution of each equation by the power series method. When initial conditions are specified, give the solution that satisfies them.

1. $y' = y - x, \quad y(0) = 2$

2. $y' = x^3 - 2xy, \quad y(0) = 1$

3. $y'' + y = x$

4. $y'' + 4y = 0, \quad y(0) = 1, \quad y'(0) = 0$

5. $(1 + x^2)y'' + 2xy' - 2y = 0$

6. $xy'' - xy' + y = e^x, \quad y(0) = 1, \quad y'(0) = 2$

7. $xy'' - x^2y' + (x^2 - 2)y = 0, \quad y(0) = 0,$
$\quad y'(0) = 1$

8. $(1 - x)y'' - y' + xy = 0, \quad y(0) = y'(0) = 1$

9. $y'' - 2xy' + 4y = 0, \quad y(0) = 1, \quad y'(0) = 0$

10. $(1 - x^2)y'' - xy' + y = 0, \quad y(0) = 0, \quad y'(0) = 1$

11. $y'' - xy' + y = -x \cos x, \quad y(0) = 0, \quad y'(0) = 2$

12. $y'' - xy' + xy = 0, \quad y(0) = 2, \quad y'(0) = 1$

13. $(1 - x)^2y'' - (1 - x)y' - y = 0,$
$\quad y(0) = y'(0) = 1$

14. $y'' - 2xy' + 2y = 0$

15. $y'' - 2xy' - 2y = x, \quad y(0) = 1, \quad y'(0) = -\frac{1}{4}$

16. $y'' - x^2y = 0$

17. Airy's equation

$$y'' - xy = 0$$

has applications in the theory of diffraction. Find the general solution of this equation.

18. Hermite's equation

$$y'' - 2xy' + 2py = 0,$$

where p is constant, arises in quantum mechanics in connection with the Schrödinger equation for a harmonic oscillator. Show that if p is a positive integer, one of the two linearly independent solutions of Hermite's equation is a polynomial, called the *Hermite polynomial* $H_p(x)$.

19. Use the Taylor series method to solve Airy's equation

$$y'' - xy = 0, \quad y(1) = 1, \quad y'(1) = 0.$$

20. Use the Taylor series method to solve

$$y'' - xy' - y = 0, \quad y(0) = 1, \quad y'(0) = 0.$$

21. Does the power series method yield a solution to the equation

    a) $x^2y' = y$?

    b) $x^3y' = y$?

*22. Solve $y' = y\sqrt{y^2 - 1}$ by squaring the power series for y.

23. Show that the power series method fails for

$$x^2y'' + x^2y' + y = 0.$$

5.3 ORDINARY AND SINGULAR POINTS

The reader must have noticed in the last section that the power series method sometimes fails to yield a solution for one equation while working very well for an apparently similar equation. In this section we shall analyze this anomaly and discover its cause.

    The main clue to the puzzle can be obtained by making the coefficient of the highest-order derivative equal to 1. Thus, if we write each of the second-order homogeneous equations in the examples of Section 5.2 in the form

$$y'' + a(x)y' + b(x)y = 0, \tag{1}$$

then the equations given in Examples 5 and 6 in Section 5.2 become, respectively,

$$y'' + \frac{1}{x}y' + y = 0, \tag{2}$$

and

$$y'' + \frac{1}{x}y' + \frac{1}{x^2}y = 0. \tag{3}$$

Note that in each of these equations one or both of the terms $a(x)$ and $b(x)$ are not defined at $x = 0$. The important fact about Eq. (1) is that the behavior of its solution near the point $x = x_0$ depends on the behavior of the functions $a(x)$ and $b(x)$ near x_0. When both of the functions $a(x)$ and $b(x)$ are analytic at $x = x_0$ [that is, both $a(x)$ and $b(x)$ can be expressed as a power series in $(x - x_0)$ with positive radius of convergence], we call x_0 an *ordinary point* of Eq. (1). Any point that is not an ordinary point is called a *singular point* of Eq. (1).

Ordinary Points

Suppose that x_0 is an ordinary point of Eq. (1). Then both $a(x)$ and $b(x)$ can be expressed as power series in $(x - x_0)$ in some interval $|x - x_0| < R$. The next theorem asserts that under these circumstances the power series method will yield a power series expansion of the solution $y(x)$.

Theorem 1   Let x_0 be an ordinary point of the differential equation

$$y'' + a(x)y' + b(x)y = 0, \tag{4}$$

and let α and β be arbitrary constants. Then there exists a unique function $y(x)$, analytic at x_0, which satisfies Eq. (4) and the initial conditions $y(x_0) = \alpha$ and $y'(x_0) = \beta$. Furthermore, if the power series representations of $a(x)$ and $b(x)$ are valid for all x such that $|x - x_0| < R$, then so is the power series expansion of the solution $y(x)$.

The proof of the theorem is complicated, and its principal details are sketched in Exercise 27 at the end of this section.

Theorem 1 provides the justification for the use of the power series method in solving differential equations at an ordinary point. Examples 1 through 4 in Section 5.2 satisfy the hypotheses of Theorem 1 and in each case have $x = 0$ as an ordinary point.

Regular Singular Points

Consider the differential equation

$$y'' + \frac{2}{x}y' - y = 0,$$

which has a singular point at $x = 0$. It can easily be shown that $y = e^x/x$ is a solution of this equation. Although it is impossible to expand e^x/x as a power series in x, we can write it as a power of x times a power series in x:

$$\frac{e^x}{x} = \frac{1}{x}\left(1 + x + \frac{x^2}{2!} + \frac{x^3}{3!} + \cdots\right).$$

This suggests that we should try to find solutions of the form

$$y = x^r(c_0 + c_1x + c_2x^2 + c_3x^3 + \cdots),$$

where r is some real or complex number, whenever $x = 0$ is a singular point of the differential equation. For one class of singular points, this modification of the power series method does yield solutions.

A *regular singular point* is a point x_0 such that the functions $(x - x_0)a(x)$ and $(x - x_0)^2b(x)$ are analytic. For example, $x = 0$ is a regular singular point of both Eqs. (2) and (3), since in Eq. (2)

$$xa(x) = 1, \quad x^2b(x) = x^2, \tag{5}$$

and in Eq. (3)

$$xa(x) = 1, \quad x^2b(x) = 1. \tag{6}$$

All the functions in Eqs. (5) and (6) are power series in x with all but one of the coefficients equal to zero, and are therefore analytic functions at $x = 0$.

A singular point that is not regular is called *irregular*. For example, the point $x = 0$ is an irregular singular point of the two equations

$$y'' + \frac{1}{x^2}y' + y = 0,$$

$$y'' + \frac{1}{x}y' + \frac{1}{x^3}y = 0.$$

To simplify the explanation of the modified power series method, called the *method of Frobenius*, we shall assume that $x = 0$ is a regular singular point of the equation

$$y'' + a(x)y' + b(x)y = 0. \tag{7}$$

[If $x_0 \neq 0$ is a regular singular point, then the substitution $X = x - x_0$ will transform power series in $(x - x_0)$ into power series in X. The point $X = 0$ is then a regular singular point of the transformed differential equation.] We now assume that Eq. (7) has a solution of the form

$$y = x^r(c_0 + c_1x + c_2x^2 + \cdots) = \sum_{n=0}^{\infty} c_nx^{r+n}, \quad c_0 = 1, \quad x > 0, \tag{8}$$

where r is some real or complex number. We can assume that $c_0 = 1$, since the smallest power of x can always be factored out of an expression of the form (8) and any constant multiple of a solution is again a solution of the differential equation. In addition, the choice $c_0 = 1$ simplifies much of the following discussion. The restriction $x > 0$ is necessary to prevent difficulties for certain values of r, such as $r = \frac{1}{2}$ and $-\frac{1}{4}$, since we are not interested in imaginary solutions. [If we need to find a solution valid for $x < 0$, we can change variables by substituting $X = -x$ into Eq. (7) and solve the resulting equation for $X > 0$.] Since

$$y' = \sum_{n=0}^{\infty} c_n(r + n)x^{r+n-1} \tag{9}$$

and

$$y'' = \sum_{n=0}^{\infty} c_n(r + n)(r + n - 1)x^{r+n-2}, \tag{10}$$

Eq. (4) can be rewritten as

$$\sum_{n=0}^{\infty} c_n(r + n)(r + n - 1)x^{r+n-2} + a(x) \sum_{n=0}^{\infty} c_n(r + n)x^{r+n-1}$$
$$+ b(x) \sum_{n=0}^{\infty} c_n x^{r+n} = 0$$

or

$$\sum_{n=0}^{\infty} c_n[(r + n)(r + n - 1) + (r + n)xa(x) + x^2 b(x)]x^{r+n-2} = 0. \tag{11}$$

Since $x = 0$ is a regular singular point, both $xa(x)$ and $x^2 b(x)$ can be expressed as power series in x with positive radii of convergence:

$$xa(x) = a_0 + a_1 x + a_2 x^2 + \cdots, \tag{12}$$
$$x^2 b(x) = b_0 + b_1 x + b_2 x^2 + \cdots.$$

But $n \geq 0$, so that x^{r-2} is the smallest power of x in Eq. (11). Since the coefficients of a power series whose sum is zero must vanish, we have, for $n = 0$,

$$c_0[r(r - 1) + a_0 r + b_0] = 0.$$

By hypothesis $c_0 = 1$, so that we obtain the *indicial equation*

$$\boxed{r(r - 1) + a_0 r + b_0 = 0,} \tag{13}$$

whose roots, r_1 and r_2, are called the *exponents* of the differential equation (4). In what follows we shall see that one of the solutions of Eq. (4) will always be of the form (8) and that there are three possible forms for the second linearly independent solution corresponding to the following cases:

CASE 1 r_1 and r_2 do not differ by an integer.

CASE 2 $r_1 = r_2$.

CASE 3 r_1 and r_2 differ by a nonzero integer.

We shall consider the three cases separately.

CASE 1   *r_1 and r_2 do not differ by an integer.* This is the easiest case, since Eq. (4) will have two solutions, for $x > 0$, of the forms

$$y_1(x) = x^{r_1}(c_0 + c_1 x + c_2 x^2 + \cdots), \quad c_0 = 1,$$
$$y_2(x) = x^{r_2}(c_0^* + c_1^* x + c_2^* x^2 + \cdots), \quad c_0^* = 1.$$

That y_1 and y_2 are linearly independent follows easily from the fact that y_1/y_2 cannot be constant, since if it were, the roots r_1 and r_2 would coincide. The coefficients $c_1, c_2, \ldots$ are obtained, as in Section 5.2, by replacing r by r_1 and setting the coefficients of each power of x equal to zero in Eq. (11). Similarly, to find $c_1^*, c_2^*, \ldots$, we repeat the process above for $r = r_2$. The procedure is demonstrated in the following examples.

Example 1   Consider the Euler equation

$$y'' + \frac{1}{4x} y' + \frac{1}{8x^2} y = 0.$$

Since $xa(x) = \frac{1}{4}$ and $x^2 b(x) = \frac{1}{8}$, the point $x = 0$ is a regular singular point and $a_0 = \frac{1}{4}$, $b_0 = \frac{1}{8}$. Thus the indicial equation is

$$r(r - 1) + \tfrac{1}{4} r + \tfrac{1}{8} = r^2 - \tfrac{3}{4} r + \tfrac{1}{8} = (r - \tfrac{1}{2})(r - \tfrac{1}{4}) = 0,$$

with roots $r = \frac{1}{4}$ and $r = \frac{1}{2}$ that do not differ by an integer. Assuming a solution of the form

$$y = x^{1/4}(c_0 + c_1 x + c_2 x^2 + \cdots),$$

Eq. (11) becomes

$$\sum_{n=0}^{\infty} c_n[(\tfrac{1}{4} + n)(\tfrac{1}{4} + n - 1) + (\tfrac{1}{4} + n)\tfrac{1}{4} + \tfrac{1}{8}]x^{1/4+n-2} = 0,$$

or

$$\sum_{n=0}^{\infty} c_n\left[n^2 - \frac{n}{4}\right]x^{n-7/4} = 0.$$

Equating *all* terms of this series to zero, we get $n(n - \frac{1}{4})c_n = 0$, which holds only if $c_n = 0$, for $n > 0$. Thus $y_1(z) = c_0 x^{1/4} = x^{1/4}$.

To find the second solution we set $r = \frac{1}{2}$ in Eq. (11), obtaining

$$\sum_{n=0}^{\infty} c_n^*[(\tfrac{1}{2} + n)(\tfrac{1}{2} + n - 1) + (\tfrac{1}{2} + n)\tfrac{1}{4} + \tfrac{1}{8}]x^{1/2+n-2} = 0,$$

from which we get $n(n + \frac{1}{4})c_n^* = 0$. Thus $c_n^* = 0$ for $n > 0$, so that $y_2(x) = c_0^* \sqrt{x}$. Hence the general solution is

$$y = Ax^{1/4} + Bx^{1/2}.$$

The roots of the indicial equation may also be complex, as the following example illustrates.

Example 2   Consider Eq. (3):

$$y'' + \frac{1}{x} y' + \frac{1}{x^2} y = 0.$$

By Eq. (6), the Maclaurin series for $xa(x)$ and $x^2b(x)$ consist only of the term 1, so $a_0 = b_0 = 1$. Thus the indicial equation of (3) is

$$r(r - 1) + r + 1 = r^2 + 1 = 0,$$

with the roots $r_1 = i$, $r_2 = -i$, which do not differ by an integer. Setting $r = i$ in Eq. (11), we have

$$\sum_{n=0}^{\infty} c_n[(i + n)(i + n - 1) + (i + n) + 1]x^{i+n-2} = 0.$$

Equating all coefficients of this series to zero, we have, after combining terms,

$$0 = c_n[(i + n)^2 + 1] = c_n(n^2 + 2in),$$

which holds only if $c_n = 0$ for $n > 0$. Thus

$$y_1(x) = c_0 x^i = e^{i(\ln x)} = [\cos(\ln x) + i \sin(\ln x)].$$

Similarly, substituting $r = -i$ into Eq. (11) yields the series

$$\sum_{n=0}^{\infty} c_n^*[(-i + n)(-i + n - 1) + (-i + n) + 1]x^{-i+n-2} = 0,$$

whose coefficients satisfy the condition

$$c_n^*[n^2 - 2in] = 0.$$

Thus $c_n^* = 0$ for $n > 0$. Hence

$$y_2(x) = c_0^* x^{-i} = [\cos(\ln x) - i \sin(\ln x)].$$

Finally, since linear combinations of solutions are solutions, the real and imaginary parts of y_1 and y_2,

$$y_1^*(x) = \frac{1}{2}(y_1 + y_2) = \cos(\ln x), \quad y_2^*(x) = \frac{1}{2i}(y_1 - y_2) = \sin(\ln x),$$

are solutions of the equation (3). That y_1^* and y_2^* are linearly independent follows obviously by reason of the fact that $y_2^*/y_1^* = \tan(\ln x)$, which is nonconstant. Hence Eq. (3) has the general solution

$$y = A\cos(\ln x) + B\sin(\ln x), \quad x > 0.$$

(Compare this proof with that of Exercise 28 in Section 3.5.)

CASE 2 $r_1 = r_2$. Here we set $r = r_1$ and determine the coefficients $c_1, c_2, \ldots$ as in Case 1. We can then use formula (4) in Section 3.3 to find the second linearly independent solution, since one solution is known. Consider the following example.

Example 3   Recall Eq. (2):

$$y'' + \frac{1}{x}y' + y = 0.$$

By Eq. (5), the Maclaurin series are $xa(x) = 1$ and $x^2b(x) = x^2$; thus $a_0 = 1$ and $b_0 = 0$. Hence the indicial equation is

$$r(r-1) + r = r^2 = 0$$

with the double root $r = 0$. Thus Eq. (2) has a power series solution, which was found in Example 5 in Section 5.2:

$$y_1(x) = J_0(x) = \sum_{n=0}^{\infty} \frac{1}{(n!)^2}\left(\frac{-x^2}{4}\right)^n.$$

Finally, as in Example 5 in Section 5.2,

$$y_2(x) = J_0(x)\int \frac{dx}{xJ_0^2(x)}.$$

Example 4   Consider the equation

$$y'' + y' + \frac{1}{4x^2}y = 0. \tag{14}$$

Here $xa(x) = x$ and $x^2b(x) = \frac{1}{4}$, so that $a_0 = 0$ and $b_0 = \frac{1}{4}$. Hence the indicial equation is

$$r(r-1) + \tfrac{1}{4} = (r - \tfrac{1}{2})^2 = 0$$

with $r = \frac{1}{2}$ as a double root. Setting $r = \frac{1}{2}$ in Eq. (11), we obtain

$$\sum_{n=0}^{\infty} c_n[(n + \tfrac{1}{2})(n - \tfrac{1}{2}) + (n + \tfrac{1}{2})x + \tfrac{1}{4}]x^{n-3/2} = 0$$

or

$$\sum_{n=0}^{\infty} c_n n^2 x^{n-3/2} + \sum_{n=0}^{\infty} c_n(n + \tfrac{1}{2})x^{n-1/2} = 0.$$

Since the first term of the first series vanishes, we can reindex this series by setting $n = k + 1$ and combine like powers of x to obtain

$$\sum_{k=0}^{\infty} [c_{k+1}(k + 1)^2 + c_k(k + \tfrac{1}{2})]x^{k-1/2} = 0. \tag{15}$$

Equating the coefficients of Eq. (15) to zero, we have the recurrence formula

$$c_{k+1}(k + 1)^2 + c_k(k + \tfrac{1}{2}) = 0.$$

Hence

$$c_1 = -\frac{c_0}{2}, \quad c_2 = -\frac{c_1(\tfrac{3}{2})}{2^2} = \frac{3c_0}{2^2 \cdot 2^2}, \quad c_3 = -\frac{5c_2}{2 \cdot 3^2} = -\frac{3 \cdot 5c_0}{2^3 \cdot 2^2 \cdot 3^2},$$

$$c_4 = -\frac{7c_3}{2 \cdot 4^2} = \frac{3 \cdot 5 \cdot 7c_0}{2^4 \cdot 2^2 \cdot 3^2 \cdot 4^2}, \dots,$$

so that

$$y_1(x) = x^{1/2}\left(c_0 - \frac{c_0}{2}x + \frac{3c_0}{2^2 \cdot 2^2}x^2 - \frac{3 \cdot 5c_0}{2^3 \cdot 2^2 \cdot 3^2}x^3 + \frac{3 \cdot 5 \cdot 7c_0}{2^4 \cdot 2^2 \cdot 3^2 \cdot 4^2}x^4 - \cdots\right)$$

$$= c_0 x^{1/2}\left[1 - \left(\frac{x}{2}\right) + \frac{3}{2^2}\left(\frac{x}{2}\right)^2 - \frac{3 \cdot 5}{2^2 \cdot 3^2}\left(\frac{x}{2}\right)^3 + \frac{3 \cdot 5 \cdot 7}{2^2 \cdot 3^2 \cdot 4^2}\left(\frac{x}{2}\right)^4 - \cdots\right]$$

$$= x^{1/2} \sum_{n=0}^{\infty} \frac{(2n)!}{(n!)^3}\left(-\frac{x}{4}\right)^n, \quad x > 0. \tag{16}$$

To find the radius of convergence of the series in Eq. (16), we use the ratio test:

$$\frac{1}{R} = \lim_{n \to \infty}\left|\frac{(n!)^3 4^n(2n + 2)!}{(2n)!(n + 1)!^3 4^{n+1}}\right|$$

$$= \lim_{n \to \infty}\left|\frac{(2n + 2)(2n + 1)}{4(n + 1)^3}\right|$$

$$= \lim_{n \to \infty}\left|\frac{2n + 1}{2(n + 1)^2}\right| = 0.$$

So the radius of convergence $R = \infty$. We can now use formula (4) in Section 3.3 to produce the second linearly independent solution or use the alternate procedure sketched below. We recall that in deriving that formula we let $y_2 = vy_1$, where v satisfies the differential equation (3) in Section 3.3 or, in our case,

$$\frac{v''}{v'} = -2\frac{y_1'}{y_1} - 1 = \frac{-2\left(\frac{1}{2\sqrt{x}}\right)\left[1 - 3\left(\frac{x}{2}\right) + \frac{3 \cdot 5}{2^2}\left(\frac{x}{2}\right)^2 - \cdots\right]}{\sqrt{x}\left[1 - \left(\frac{x}{2}\right) + \frac{3}{2^2}\left(\frac{x}{2}\right)^2 + \cdots\right]} - 1.$$

After finding the first few terms by long division (carried out exactly as in the division of one polynomial by another), we have

$$\frac{v''}{v'} = \frac{-1}{x}\left(1 - x + \frac{x^2}{4} - \cdots\right) - 1 = \frac{-1}{x} - \frac{x}{4} + \cdots. \tag{17}$$

Integrating both sides of Eq. (17), we obtain

$$\ln v' = -\ln x - \frac{x^2}{8} + \cdots$$

or

$$v' = \frac{1}{x}\exp\left(-\frac{x^2}{8} + \cdots\right) = \frac{1}{x}\left[1 + \left(\frac{-x^2}{8} + \cdots\right) + \frac{1}{2!}\left(\frac{-x^2}{8} + \cdots\right)^2 + \cdots\right].$$

After expanding the exponential as a power series in x, we integrate once more and find that v has the form

$$v = \ln x - \frac{x^2}{16} + \cdots.$$

Then

$$y_2 = vy_1 = \left(\ln x - \frac{x^2}{16} + \cdots\right) \cdot \sqrt{x}\left[1 - \left(\frac{x}{2}\right) + \frac{3}{2^2}\left(\frac{x}{2}\right)^2 - \cdots\right]$$

$$= (\ln x)y_1 + \sqrt{x}\left(-\frac{x^2}{16} + \cdots\right),$$

and the general solution of Eq. (14) has the form

$$y_1(x) = \sqrt{x}\left\{(A + B\ln x)\left[1 - \left(\frac{x}{2}\right) + \cdots\right] + B\left(-\frac{x^2}{16} + \cdots\right)\right\}, \quad x > 0.$$

Indeed, it is always true in such a case that the general solution has the form

$$y(x) = x^r\left(\sum_{n=0}^{\infty} c_n x^n + \ln x \sum_{n=0}^{\infty} c_n^* x^n\right), \quad x > 0. \tag{18}$$

To verify this fact, we note that by long division

$$\frac{y_1'}{y_1} = \frac{(rc_0 x^{r-1} + (r+1)c_1 x^r + \cdots)}{c_0 x^r + c_1 x^{r+1} + \cdots} = \left(\frac{r}{x} + \frac{c_1}{c_0} + \cdots\right), \quad c_0 = 1, \quad \textbf{(19)}$$

and by Eq. (12),

$$a(x) = \frac{a_0}{x} + a_1 + a_2 x + \cdots. \qquad \textbf{(20)}$$

Substituting Eqs. (19) and (20) into Eq. (3) in Section 3.3, we have

$$-\frac{v''}{v'} = \frac{a_0 + 2r}{x} + (a_1 + 2c_1) + \cdots,$$

and integrating both sides of this equation, we obtain

$$-\ln v' = (a_0 + 2r)\ln x + (a_1 + 2c_1)x + \cdots. \qquad \textbf{(21)}$$

Since the indicial equation (13) has a double root

$$r = \frac{1 - a_0}{2},$$

it follows that $a_0 + 2r = 1$, so that we can rewrite Eq. (21) as

$$\frac{1}{v'} = x \exp\left[(a_1 + 2c_1)x + \cdots\right]$$

or

$$v' = \frac{1}{x} \exp\left[-(a_1 + 2c_1)x + \cdots\right].$$

Expanding the exponential as a power series in x and integrating once more, we finally obtain

$$v(x) = \ln x - (a_1 + 2c_1)x + \cdots.$$

Since $y_2 = vy_1$ and y_1 has the form (8), the form of the general solution (18) is immediately obvious.

CASE 3 *r_1 and r_2 differ by a nonzero integer.* Suppose that $r_1 > r_2$. Then one solution of Eq. (4) will have the form

$$y_1 = x^{r_1}(c_0 + c_1 x + c_2 x^2 + \cdots), \quad c_0 = 1, \quad x > 0,$$

as in Case 1. In some instances it is not possible to determine y_2 as was done in Case 1, because the procedure regenerates the same series expansion we obtained for y_1 (in this case, the first $r_1 - r_2$ coefficients c_i^* vanish). When this occurs, we proceed as in Case 2. These two possibilities are illustrated in the following two examples.

Example 5   *Bessel's equation of order $\frac{1}{2}$ is*

$$x^2 y'' + xy' + [x^2 - (\tfrac{1}{2})^2]y = 0$$

or, after division by x^2,

$$y'' + \frac{1}{x}y' + \left(1 - \frac{1}{4x^2}\right)y = 0. \tag{22}$$

Clearly $x = 0$ is a regular singular point, since the functions $xa(x) = 1$ and $x^2 b(x) = x^2 - \frac{1}{4}$ are both analytic at $x = 0$. The indicial equation for Eq. (22) is

$$r(r - 1) + r - \tfrac{1}{4} = r^2 - \tfrac{1}{4} = 0$$

with the roots $r_1 = \frac{1}{2}$ and $r_2 = -\frac{1}{2}$. Here the roots differ by the nonzero integer 1. Substituting $r = r_1$ in Eq. (11), we obtain

$$\sum_{n=0}^{\infty} c_n[(n + \tfrac{1}{2})(n - \tfrac{1}{2}) + (n + \tfrac{1}{2}) + (x^2 - \tfrac{1}{4})]x^{n-3/2} = 0$$

or

$$\sum_{n=0}^{\infty} c_n(n^2 + n)x^{n-3/2} + \sum_{n=0}^{\infty} c_n x^{n+1/2} = 0. \tag{23}$$

Noting that the first term of the first series vanishes, we can reindex the series (23) to obtain

$$\sum_{k=-1}^{\infty} c_{k+2}(k + 2)(k + 3)x^{k+1/2} + \sum_{k=0}^{\infty} c_k x^{k+1/2}$$

$$= 2c_1 x^{-1/2} + \sum_{k=0}^{\infty} [(k + 2)(k + 3)c_{k+2} + c_k]x^{k+1/2} = 0.$$

Setting the coefficients of this series equal to zero, we obtain $c_1 = 0$ and the recurrence relation

$$c_{k+2} = -\frac{c_k}{(k + 2)(k + 3)}.$$

Clearly all the coefficients with odd-numbered subscripts will vanish, and

$$c_2 = -\frac{c_0}{3!}, \quad c_4 = -\frac{c_2}{4 \cdot 5} = \frac{c_0}{5!}, \quad c_6 = -\frac{c_4}{6 \cdot 7} = -\frac{c_0}{7!}, \dots,$$

and we have the solution

$$y_1(x) = \sqrt{x}\left(c_0 - \frac{c_0}{3!}x^2 + \frac{c_0}{5!}x^4 - \frac{c_0}{7!}x^6 + \cdots\right)$$

$$= c_0\sqrt{x}\left(1 - \frac{x^2}{3!} + \frac{x^4}{5!} - \frac{x^6}{7!} + \cdots\right)$$

or, since $c_0 = 1$,

$$y_1(x) = \frac{1}{\sqrt{x}}\left(x - \frac{x^3}{3!} + \frac{x^5}{5!} - \frac{x^7}{7!} + \cdots\right).$$

Applying Eq. (15) in Section 5.1, we find that

$$y_1(x) = \frac{\sin x}{\sqrt{x}}, \quad x > 0.$$

Now we set $r = r_2$ in Eq. (11) to obtain

$$\sum_{n=0}^{\infty} c_n[(n - \tfrac{1}{2})(n - \tfrac{3}{2}) + (n - \tfrac{1}{2}) + (x^2 - \tfrac{1}{4})]x^{n-5/2} = 0$$

or

$$\sum_{n=0}^{\infty} c_n n(n - 1)x^{n-5/2} + \sum_{n=0}^{\infty} c_n x^{n-1/2} = 0.$$

Since the first two terms of the first series vanish, reindexing and gathering like powers of x yields

$$\sum_{k=0}^{\infty} [(k + 2)(k + 1)c_{k+2} + c_k]x^{k-1/2},$$

from which we obtain the recurrence relation

$$c_{k+2} = -\frac{c_k}{(k + 1)(k + 2)}. \tag{24}$$

Now by Eq. (24), we have

$$c_2 = -\frac{c_0}{2!}, \quad c_4 = -\frac{c_2}{3\cdot 4} = \frac{c_0}{4!}, \quad c_6 = -\frac{c_4}{5\cdot 6} = -\frac{c_0}{6!}, \dots,$$

$$c_3 = -\frac{c_1}{3!}, \quad c_5 = -\frac{c_3}{4\cdot 5} = \frac{c_1}{5!}, \quad c_7 = -\frac{c_5}{6\cdot 7} = -\frac{c_1}{7!}, \dots,$$

and

$$y_2(x) = x^{-1/2}\left[c_0 + c_1 x - c_0\frac{x^2}{2!} - c_1\frac{x^3}{3!} + c_0\frac{x^4}{4!} + c_1\frac{x^5}{5!} - \cdots\right]$$

$$= \frac{1}{\sqrt{x}}(c_0 \cos x + c_1 \sin x), \quad c_0 = 1.$$

Since the last term of y_2 is a multiple of y_1 and we are looking for linearly independent solutions, we may set $c_1 = 0$ to obtain

$$y_2 = \frac{\cos x}{\sqrt{x}}, \quad x > 0.$$

That y_1 and y_2 are linearly independent follows from the fact that $y_1/y_2 = \tan x$, which is nonconstant. Thus the general solution of Eq. (22) is

$$y = \frac{A}{\sqrt{x}} \cos x + \frac{B}{\sqrt{x}} \sin x, \quad x > 0.$$

Example 6 Consider *Bessel's equation of order 1*:

$$x^2 y'' + xy' + (x^2 - 1)y = 0$$

or

$$y'' + \frac{1}{x} y' + \left(1 - \frac{1}{x^2}\right)y = 0. \tag{25}$$

Again $x = 0$ is a regular singular point of Eq. (25), and the indicial equation for Eq. (25) is

$$r(r - 1) + r - 1 = r^2 - 1 = 0,$$

with roots $r_1 = 1$, $r_2 = -1$ that differ by 2. Setting $r = 1$ in Eq. (11) yields

$$\sum_{n=0}^{\infty} c_n [n(n + 1) + (n + 1) + (x^2 - 1)]x^{n-1} = 0$$

or

$$3c_1 + \sum_{k=0}^{\infty} [c_{k+2}(k + 2)(k + 4) + c_k]x^{k+1} = 0. \tag{26}$$

By setting the coefficients of Eq. (26) to zero, we obtain $c_1 = 0$ and the recurrence relation

$$c_{k+2} = -\frac{c_k}{(k + 2)(k + 4)}.$$

Thus all the coefficients with odd-numbered subscripts vanish, and

$$c_2 = -\frac{c_0}{2 \cdot 4}, \quad c_4 = -\frac{c_2}{4 \cdot 6} = \frac{c_0}{2 \cdot 4^2 \cdot 6}, \quad c_6 = -\frac{c_4}{6 \cdot 8} = -\frac{c_0}{2 \cdot 4^2 \cdot 6^2 \cdot 8}, \cdots$$

Hence, since $c_0 = 1$,

$$y_1(x) = x\left(c_0 - \frac{c_0}{2 \cdot 4} x^2 + \frac{c_0}{2 \cdot 4^2 \cdot 6} x^4 - \frac{c_0}{2 \cdot 4^2 \cdot 6^2 \cdot 8} x^6 + \cdots\right)$$

$$= x\left(1 - \frac{1}{1!2!}\left(\frac{x}{2}\right)^2 + \frac{1}{2!3!}\left(\frac{x}{2}\right)^4 - \frac{1}{3!4!}\left(\frac{x}{2}\right)^6 + \cdots\right). \tag{27}$$

Note that the series

$$1 - \frac{t}{1!2!} + \frac{t^2}{2!3!} - \frac{t^3}{3!4!} + \cdots + \frac{(-1)^n t^n}{n!(n + 1)!} + \cdots$$

has a radius of convergence $R = \infty$ since by the ratio test

$$\frac{1}{R} = \lim_{n\to\infty} \left| \frac{1/(n + 1)!(n + 2)!}{1/n!(n + 1)!} \right| = \lim_{n\to\infty} \frac{n!(n + 1)!}{(n + 1)!(n + 2)!}$$

$$= \lim_{n\to\infty} \frac{1}{(n + 1)(n + 2)} = 0.$$

Thus Eq. (27) is valid for all values of x.

Now we shall see that the Frobenius method will not work for the second root $r_2 = -1$ of the indicial equation. Setting $r = -1$ in Eq. (11), we have

$$\sum_{n=0}^{\infty} c_n[(n - 1)(n - 2) + (n - 1) + x^2 - 1]x^{n-3} = 0$$

or

$$-c_1x^{-2} + c_0x^{-1} + \sum_{k=0}^{\infty} [c_{k+3}(k + 1)(k + 3) + c_{k+1}]x^k = 0.$$

If we set all the coefficients in this series to zero, we will find that $c_0 = 0$, which contradicts the assumption that $c_0 = 1$ made in Eq. (8). Thus the method of Frobenius fails for this root. However, applying the method of Case 2, we obtain

$$-\frac{v''}{v'} = 2\frac{y_1'}{y_1} + a(x) = \frac{3}{x} - \frac{x}{2} - \cdots.$$

Integrating both ends of this equation, we have

$$-\ln v' = 3\ln x - \frac{x^2}{4} - \cdots$$

or

$$v' = x^{-3}\exp\left[\frac{x^2}{4} + \cdots\right] = x^{-3} + \frac{1}{4}x^{-1} + \cdots.$$

Integrating once more, we get

$$v = -\tfrac{1}{2}x^{-2} + \tfrac{1}{4}\ln x + \cdots,$$

so that

$$y_2 = vy_1 = \frac{1}{4}y_1\ln x - \frac{1}{2}x^{-1} + \frac{x}{16} + \cdots, \quad x > 0.$$

In general, if the method of Case 1 fails for r_2, the procedure above will yield the solution

$$y_2 = k_{-1}(\ln x)y_1 + x^{r_2}(k_0 + k_1x + \cdots), \quad x > 0,$$

where k_{-1} may equal zero.

We gather all the facts we have proved in this section in one theorem:

Theorem 2 Let $x = 0$ be a regular singular point of the differential equation

$$y'' + a(x)y' + b(x)y = 0, \quad x \neq 0, \tag{28}$$

and let r_1 and r_2 be the roots of the indicial equation

$$r(r - 1) + a_0 r + b_0 = 0,$$

where a_0 and b_0 are given by the power series expansions

$$xa(x) = a_0 + a_1 x + a_2 x^2 + \cdots,$$

$$x^2 b(x) = b_0 + b_1 x + b_2 x^2 + \cdots.$$

Then Eq. (28) has two linearly independent solutions y_1 and y_2 whose form depends on r_1 and r_2 as follows:

CASE 1 If r_1 and r_2 do not differ by an integer, then

$$y_1(x) = |x|^{r_1} \left(\sum_{n=0}^{\infty} c_n x^n \right), \quad c_0 = 1,$$

$$y_2(x) = |x|^{r_2} \left(\sum_{n=0}^{\infty} c_n^* x^n \right), \quad c_0^* = 1.$$

(The absolute-value signs are needed to avoid the assumption that $x > 0$.)

CASE 2 If $r_1 = r_2 = r$, then

$$y_1(x) = |x|^r \left(\sum_{n=0}^{\infty} c_n x^n \right), \quad c_0 = 1,$$

$$y_2(x) = |x|^r \left(\sum_{n=1}^{\infty} c_n^* x^n \right) + y_1(x) \ln |x|.$$

CASE 3 If $r_1 - r_2$ is a positive integer, then

$$y_1(x) = |x|^{r_1} \left(\sum_{n=0}^{\infty} c_n x^n \right), \quad c_0 = 1,$$

$$y_2(x) = |x|^{r_2} \left(\sum_{n=0}^{\infty} c_n^* x^n \right) + c_{-1}^* y_1(x) \ln |x|, \quad c_0^* = 1,$$

and c_{-1}^* may equal zero.

Furthermore, if the power series expansions for $xa(x)$ and $x^2 b(x)$ are valid for x such that $|x| < R$, then the solutions y_1 and y_2 are valid for $0 < |x| < R$. The proof of this fact is left as an exercise for the reader (see Exercise 28).

EXERCISES 5.3

Find the general solutions of the differential equations in Exercises 1 through 22 by the method of Frobenius.

1. $y'' + \dfrac{1}{2x} y' + \dfrac{1}{4x} y = 0$

2. $y'' + \dfrac{2(1 - 2x)}{x(1 - x)} y' - \dfrac{2}{x(1 - x)} y = 0$

3. $y'' + \dfrac{6}{x} y' + \left(\dfrac{6}{x^2} - 1 \right) y = 0$

4. $y'' + \dfrac{4}{x} y' + \left(1 + \dfrac{2}{x^2} \right) y = 0$

5. $y'' + \dfrac{3}{x} y' + 4x^2 y = 0$

6. $(x - 1)y'' - \left(\dfrac{4x^2 - 3x + 1}{2x} \right) y'$
$$+ \left(\dfrac{2x^2 - x + 2}{2x} \right) y = 0$$

7. $y'' + \dfrac{2}{x} y' - \dfrac{2}{x^2} y = 0$

8. $4xy'' + 2y' + y = 0$

9. $xy'' + 2y' + xy = 0$

10. $xy'' - y' + 4x^3 y = 0$

11. $xy'' + (1 - 2x)y' - (1 - x)y = 0$

12. $x(x + 1)^2 y'' + (1 - x^2)y' - (1 - x)y = 0$

13. $y'' - 2y' + \left(1 + \dfrac{1}{4x^2} \right) y = 0$

14. (*Euler's equation*) $x^2 y'' + Axy' + By = 0$, A and B constant

15. $x(x - 1)y'' - (1 - 3x)y' + y = 0$

16. $x^2(x^2 - 1)y'' - x(x^2 + 1)y' + (x^2 + 1)y = 0$

17. $y'' + \dfrac{y'}{x} - y = 0$

18. $2xy'' - (x - 3)y' - y = 0$

19. $y'' + \dfrac{x + 1}{2x} y' + \dfrac{3}{2x} y = 0$

20. $y'' + \dfrac{1}{2x} y' - \dfrac{x + 1}{2x^2} y = 0$

21. $x^2 y'' + x(x - 1)y' - (x - 1)y = 0$

22. $xy'' - (3 + x)y' + 2y = 0$

23. Prove by means of Eq. (3) in Section 3.3 that the second linearly independent solution in Example 3 has the form

$$y_2(x) = J_0(x) \ln x$$
$$+ \sum_{n=1}^{\infty} \dfrac{(-1)^{n+1}}{2^{2n}(n!)^2} \left(1 + \dfrac{1}{2} + \cdots + \dfrac{1}{n} \right) x^{2n}, \quad x > 0.$$

24. Can the method of Frobenius be used to solve Exercise 21 in Section 5.2?

25. Consider the differential equation

$$y'' - \dfrac{1}{x^2} y' + \dfrac{1}{x^3} y = 0.$$

a) Show that $x = 0$ is an irregular singular point of this equation.

b) Use the fact that $y_1 = x$ is a solution to find a second independent solution.

c) Show that the solution y_2 cannot be expressed as a series of the form (8). Thus this solution cannot be found by the method of Frobenius.

26. The differential equation

$$x^2 y'' + (4x - 1)y' + 2y = 0$$

has $x = 0$ as an irregular singular point.

a) Suppose that Eq. (8) is inserted into this equation. Show that $r = 0$ and the corresponding Frobenius method "solution" is

$$y = \sum_{n=0}^{\infty} (n + 1)! x^n.$$

b) Prove that the series above has radius of convergence $R = 0$. Hence even though a Frobenius series may formally satisfy a differential equation, it may not be a valid solution at an irregular singular point.

*27. Let $x_0 = 0$ and suppose that the Maclaurin series

$$a(x) = \sum_{n=0}^{\infty} a_n x^n, \quad b(x) = \sum_{n=0}^{\infty} b_n x^n$$

are valid for $|x| < R$.

a) Show that if Eq. (4) has a power series solution

$$y(x) = \sum_{n=0}^{\infty} c_n x^n, \quad c_0 = 1,$$

then the coefficients c_n satisfy the recursion formula

$$(n + 1)(n + 2)c_{n+2}$$
$$= -\sum_{k=0}^{n} [(k + 1)a_{n-k}c_{k+1} + b_{n-k}c_k].$$

b) Use the root test formula (5) in Section 5.1 for finding the radius of convergence to show that for any r such that $0 < r < R$ there is a constant $M > 0$ such that

$$(n + 1)(n + 2)|c_{n+2}|$$
$$\leq \frac{M}{r^n} \sum_{k=0}^{\infty} [(k + 1)|c_{k+1}| + |c_k|]r^k + M|c_{n+1}|r.$$

c) Use the ratio test to prove that the series

$$\sum_{n=0}^{\infty} |c_n|x^n$$

converges for $|x| < r$. Then by the comparison test for series, it follows that the series $y(x)$ converges for $|x| < r$. Since r is arbitrary, it follows that the series representation of the solution is valid for $|x| < R$.

*28. Modify the argument in Exercise 27 to justify the last statement of Theorem 2.

5.4 BESSEL FUNCTIONS

The differential equation

$$x^2 y'' + xy' + (x^2 - p^2)y = 0, \tag{1}$$

which is known as *Bessel's equation of order p* (≥ 0), is one of the most important differential equations in applied mathematics. The equation was first investigated in 1703 by Jakob Bernoulli (1654–1705) in connection with the oscillatory behavior of a hanging chain, and later by Friedrich Wilhelm Bessel (1784–1846) in his studies of planetary motion. Since then, the Bessel functions have been used in the studies of elasticity, fluid motion, potential theory, diffusion, and the propagation of waves. We shall present a few applications of the Bessel functions in Chapter 12 when we study the solutions of partial differential equations. (See Section 12.4.)

The reader may recall that in Section 5.3 we found the solution of Bessel's equation for $p = 0, \frac{1}{2}$, and 1 (see Examples 3, 5, and 6 there). In each of these examples, the method of Frobenius was an important tool, so we anticipate again the successful application of this procedure. We assume that a solution of the form

$$y(x) = |x|^r \sum_{n=0}^{\infty} c_n x^n, \quad x \neq 0, \quad c_0 \neq 0, \tag{2}$$

exists for Bessel's equation of order p. Then substituting Eq. (2) into Eq. (1), we have

$$|x|^r \left[\sum_{n=0}^{\infty} c_n (r + n)(r + n - 1)x^n + \sum_{n=0}^{\infty} c_n (r + n)x^n + (x^2 - p^2) \sum_{n=0}^{\infty} c_n x^n \right] = 0$$

or

$$|x|^r \left[\sum_{n=0}^{\infty} c_n[(r + n)^2 - p^2]x^n + \sum_{n=0}^{\infty} c_n x^{n+2} \right] = 0. \tag{3}$$

The indicial equation is $r^2 - p^2 = 0$ with the roots $r_1 = p(\geqslant 0)$ and $r_2 = -p$. For any $p \geqslant 0$ we can obtain a first solution $y_1(x)$ for Eq. (1) by the method of Frobenius. Letting $r = p$ in Eq. (3), we have

$$|x|^p \left[(1 + 2p)c_1 x + \sum_{n=2}^{\infty} c_n n(n + 2p)x^n + \sum_{n=0}^{\infty} c_n x^{n+2} \right] = 0$$

or

$$|x|^p \left[(1 + 2p)c_1 x + \sum_{k=0}^{\infty} [c_{k+2}(k + 2)(k + 2 + 2p) + c_k]x^{k+2} \right] = 0. \tag{4}$$

Since the sum of the series in Eq. (4) is zero, the coefficients must all vanish, yielding $c_1 = 0$ and the recurrence relation

$$c_{k+2} = \frac{-c_k}{(k + 2)(k + 2 + 2p)}. \tag{5}$$

Hence all the coefficients with odd-numbered subscripts $c_{2j+1} = 0$, since by Eq. (5) they can all be expressed as a multiple of c_1. Letting $k = 2j$, we see that the coefficients with even-numbered subscripts satisfy the equation

$$c_{2(j+1)} = \frac{-c_{2j}}{2^2(j + 1)(p + j + 1)},$$

which yields

$$c_2 = \frac{-c_0}{2^2(p + 1)}, \quad c_4 = \frac{-c_2}{2^2 \cdot 2(p + 2)} = \frac{c_0}{2^4 2!(p + 1)(p + 2)},$$

$$c_6 = \frac{-c_4}{2^2 \cdot 3(p + 3)} = \frac{-c_0}{2^6 3!(p + 1)(p + 2)(p + 3)}, \ldots$$

Hence the series (2) becomes

$$y_1(x) = |x|^p \left[c_0 - \frac{c_0}{2^2(p + 1)} x^2 + \frac{c_0}{2^4 2!(p + 1)(p + 2)} x^4 - \cdots \right]$$

$$= c_0 |x|^p \sum_{n=0}^{\infty} (-1)^n \frac{x^{2n}}{2^{2n} n!(p + 1)(p + 2) \cdots (p + n)}. \tag{6}$$

To write Eq. (6) in a more compact form, we define the *gamma function* for all values $p > -1$:

$$\Gamma(p + 1) = \int_0^{\infty} e^{-t} t^p \, dt. \tag{7}$$

Integrating $\Gamma(p + 1)$ by parts, we have

$$\Gamma(p + 1) = \int_0^\infty e^{-t} t^p \, dt = -e^{-t} t^p \big|_0^\infty + p \int_0^\infty e^{-t} t^{p-1} \, dt.$$

The first expression on the right is zero, and the integral on the right-hand side is $\Gamma(p)$. We thus have the basic property of gamma functions:

$$\Gamma(p + 1) = p\Gamma(p). \tag{8}$$

Since

$$\Gamma(1) = \int_0^\infty e^{-t} \, dt = -e^{-t} \big|_0^\infty = 1,$$

it follows that $\Gamma(2) = \Gamma(1) = 1!$, $\Gamma(3) = 2\Gamma(2) = 2!, \ldots$, and in general, $\Gamma(n + 1) = n!$. Thus, the gamma function is the extension to real numbers $p > -1$, of the factorial function.

It is customary in Eq. (6) to let $c_0 = [2^p \Gamma(p + 1)]^{-1}$. Then Eq. (6) becomes

$$J_p(x) = \left|\frac{x}{2}\right|^p \sum_{n=0}^\infty (-1)^n \frac{(x/2)^{2n}}{n!\Gamma(p + n + 1)}, \quad x \neq 0, \tag{9}$$

which is known as the *Bessel function of the first kind of order p*. Thus $J_p(x)$ is the first solution of Eq. (1) guaranteed by Theorem 2 in Section 5.3.

To find the second solution promised by that theorem we must consider the difference $r_1 - r_2 = 2p$. By Case 1 of the theorem, if p is *not* a multiple of $\frac{1}{2}$, we will again be able to apply the method of Frobenius with $r = -p$ to find the second solution. And the results of Examples 5 and 6 in Section 5.3 make it appear likely that we will obtain $\ln|x|$ terms only when p is an integer. Therefore, we set $r = -p$ in Eq. (3) and assume p is not an integer. Then we have

$$|x|^{-p}\left[(1 - 2p)c_1 x + \sum_{k=0}^\infty [c_{k+2}(k + 2)(k + 2 - 2p) + c_k]x^{k+2}\right] = 0.$$

Setting the coefficients of this series equal to zero, we note that when p is not a multiple of $\frac{1}{2}$, all the coefficients c_k with odd-numbered subscripts will be zero. If $p = (2m + 1)/2$, then c_{2m+1} is arbitrary and the recurrence relation

$$c_{k+2} = \frac{-c_k}{(k + 2)(k + 2 - 2p)} \tag{10}$$

will yield the coefficients

$$c_{2m+3} = \frac{-c_{2m+1}}{2^2(p + 1)}, \quad c_{2m+5} = \frac{c_{2m+1}}{2^4 2!(p + 1)(p + 2)}, \ldots.$$

Thus, the odd-numbered coefficients generate the series

$$|x|^{-p} \left[c_{2m+1} x^{2m+1} - \frac{c_{2m+1}}{2^2(p+1)} x^{2m+3} + \frac{c_{2m+1} x^{2m+5}}{2^4 2!(p+1)(p+2)} - \cdots \right]$$

$$= c_{2m+1} |x|^p \left[1 - \frac{x^2}{2^2(p+1)} + \frac{x^4}{2^4 2!(p+1)(p+2)} - \cdots \right],$$

which is a multiple of $J_p(x)$. Thus, we can ignore the odd-numbered coefficients and concentrate on using Eq. (10) to calculate the coefficients with even-numbered subscripts. Then

$$c_2 = \frac{-c_0}{2^2(1-p)}, \quad c_4 = \frac{-c_2}{2^2 \cdot 2(2-p)} = \frac{c_0}{2^4 2!(1-p)(2-p)}, \ldots,$$

and the second solution is

$$J_{-p}(x) = \left| \frac{x}{2} \right|^{-p} \sum_{n=0}^{\infty} (-1)^n \frac{(x/2)^{2n}}{n! \Gamma(n-p+1)}. \tag{11}$$

To see that Eqs. (9) and (11) are linearly independent, we obtain by long division

$$\frac{J_p(x)}{J_{-p}(x)} = \frac{|x/2|^p / \Gamma(p+1) - |x/2|^{p+2}/2! \Gamma(p+3) + \cdots}{|x/2|^{-p} / \Gamma(1-p) - |x/2|^{2-p}/2! \Gamma(3-p) + \cdots}$$

$$= \frac{|x/2|^{2p}}{\Gamma(1+p)/\Gamma(1-p)} + \frac{3p|x/2|^{2p+2}}{\Gamma(3+p)/\Gamma(1-p)} + \cdots,$$

which clearly is not a constant function.

The radius of convergence of the series

$$\sum_{n=0}^{\infty} (-1)^n \frac{t^n}{n! \Gamma(n \pm p + 1)}$$

is easily found by the ratio test:

$$\frac{1}{R} = \lim_{n \to \infty} \frac{n! \Gamma(n \pm p + 1)}{(n+1)! \Gamma(n \pm p + 2)} = \lim_{n \to \infty} \frac{1}{(n+1)(n \pm p + 1)} = 0,$$

implying that $R = \infty$. Hence Eqs. (9) and (11) converge for all values. We have proved the following result.

Theorem 1   If p is not an integer, then

$$y(x) = A J_p(x) + B J_{-p}(x),$$

is the general solution of Bessel's equation for all values $x \neq 0$.

If p is an integer, then the term $(k + 2 - 2p)$ in the recurrence relation (10) will vanish for some even integer $k = 2m$. Since

$$(k+2)(k+2-p)c_{k+2} = -c_k, \tag{12}$$

c_{2m} will vanish, and iterating Eq. (12) repeatedly, we see that $c_{2m-2} = c_{2m-4} = \cdots = c_2 = c_0 = 0$. But this contradicts the assumed form (2) of the solution. Thus the method of Frobenius cannot be used when p is a positive integer. By Theorem 2 in Section 5.3, the second linearly independent solution of Eq. (1) must have the form

$$y_2(x) = J_p(x) \ln |x| + |x|^{-p} \sum_{n=0}^{\infty} c_n^* x^n, \quad c_0^* \neq 0. \tag{13}$$

After an extremely long (but straightforward) calculation we obtain

$$y_2(x) = J_p(x) \ln |x| - \frac{1}{2}\left[\sum_{k=0}^{p-1} \frac{(p-k-1)!}{k!} \left(\frac{x}{2}\right)^{2k-p} + \frac{h_p}{p!}\left(\frac{x}{2}\right)^p \right.$$
$$\left. + \sum_{k=1}^{\infty} \frac{(-1)^k [h_k + h_{p+k}]}{k!(p+k)!} \left(\frac{x}{2}\right)^{2k+p} \right], \tag{14}$$

where

$$h_p = 1 + \frac{1}{2} + \frac{1}{3} + \cdots + \frac{1}{p} \tag{15}$$

and p is a positive integer. A similar procedure will yield the result in Exercise 23 in Section 5.3 for $p = 0$.

It is customary to replace Eq. (14) by the combination

$$Y_p(x) = \frac{2}{\pi} [y_2(x) + (\gamma - \ln 2)J_p(x)], \quad p = 0, 1, 2, \ldots, \tag{16}$$

where

$$\gamma = \lim_{p \to \infty} (h_p - \ln p) = 0.57721\,56649 \ldots \tag{17}$$

is the *Euler constant*. This particular solution is obviously independent of $J_p(x)$ and is called the *Bessel function of the second kind of order p* or *Neumann's function of order p*. It is defined by the formula

$$Y_p(x) = \frac{2}{\pi} J_p(x)\left(\ln \frac{x}{2} + \gamma\right)$$
$$- \frac{1}{\pi}\left[\sum_{k=0}^{p-1} \frac{(p-k-1)!}{k!}\left(\frac{x}{2}\right)^{2k-p} + \frac{h_p}{p!}\left(\frac{x}{2}\right)^p + \sum_{k=1}^{\infty} (-1)^k \frac{[h_k + h_{p+k}]}{k!(p+k)!} \left(\frac{x}{2}\right)^{2k+p} \right],$$

for all integers $p = 0, 1, 2, \ldots$.

The function Y_p may be extended to all *real* numbers $p \geq 0$ (see Exercise 24) by the formula

$$Y_p(x) = \frac{1}{\sin p\pi} [J_p(x) \cos p\pi - J_{-p}(x)], \quad p \neq 0, 1, 2, \ldots. \tag{18}$$

Using this definition of Y_p, we have the following result:

Theorem 2   A general solution of Bessel's equation of order p is

$$y(x) = AJ_p(x) + BY_p(x), \quad x \neq 0.$$

Graphs of the functions Y_0, Y_1, and Y_2 are given in Fig. 1.

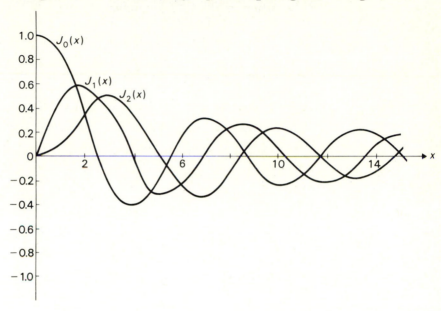

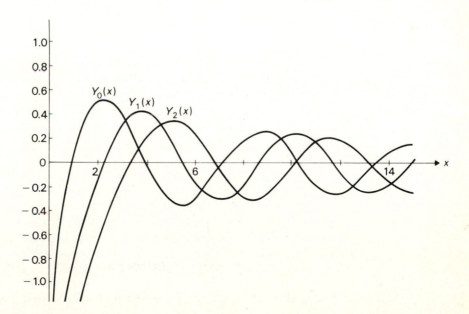

Figure 1

Properties of Bessel's Functions

Now that we have the expansions for $J_p(x)$ and $Y_p(x)$, we can derive a number of important formulas involving Bessel functions and their derivatives. For simplicity we shall assume $x > 0$. The first two identities are immediate consequences of Eq. (9):

$$\frac{d}{dx}[x^p J_p(x)] = x^p J_{p-1}(x), \tag{19}$$

$$\frac{d}{dx}[x^{-p} J_p(x)] = -x^{-p} J_{p+1}(x). \tag{20}$$

To prove Eq. (19), we differentiate the product $x^p J_p$ term by term:

$$\frac{d}{dx} \sum_{n=0}^{\infty} (-1)^n \frac{2^p (x/2)^{2n+2p}}{n!\,\Gamma(p+n+1)} = \sum_{n=0}^{\infty} (-1)^n \frac{2^{p-1}(x/2)^{2n+2p-1}2(n+p)}{n!\,\Gamma(p+n+1)}$$

$$= x^p \sum_{n=0}^{\infty} (-1)^n \frac{(x/2)^{2n+p-1}}{n!\,\Gamma(p+n)} = x^p J_{p-1}(x),$$

since $\Gamma(p+n+1) = (p+n)\Gamma(p+n)$. The proof of Eq. (20) is similar (see Exercise 4). Expanding the left-hand sides of Eqs. (19) and (20), we have

$$x^p J'_p + px^{p-1} J_p = x^p J_{p-1}$$

and

$$x^{-p} J'_p - px^{-p-1} J_p = -x^{-p} J_{p+1},$$

which may be simplified to yield the identities

$$x J'_p = x J_{p-1} - p J_p, \tag{21}$$

$$x J'_p = p J_p - x J_{p+1}. \tag{22}$$

Subtracting Eq. (22) from Eq. (21), we obtain the recursion relation

$$x J_{p+1} - 2p J_p + x J_{p-1} = 0. \tag{23}$$

Adding the two together yields

$$2 J'_p = J_{p-1} - J_{p+1}. \tag{24}$$

Formulas (19) through (24) are extremely important in solving problems involving the Bessel functions, since they allow us to express Bessel functions of higher order in terms of lower-order functions. Note that for fixed x, $J_p(x)$ is a number, so that Eq. (23) is a second-order homogeneous linear difference equation with nonconstant coefficients. Since $Y_p(x)$ also satisfies Eq. (23), this equation can be used for calculating $Y_p(x)$ by the method of Section 4.4.

Example 1   Express $J_3(x)$ in terms of $J_0(x)$ and $J_1(x)$. We let $p = 2$ in Eq. (23):

$$xJ_3 = 4J_2 - xJ_1.$$

Applying formula (23) with $p = 1$ to J_2 yields

$$xJ_2 = 2J_1 - xJ_0.$$

Thus

$$J_3(x) = \frac{4}{x} J_2 - J_1 = \frac{4}{x^2}(2J_1 - xJ_0) - J_1$$

$$= \left(\frac{8}{x^2} - 1\right)J_1(x) - \frac{4}{x} J_0(x).$$

Example 2   Evaluate the integral

$$\int x^4 J_1(x)\, dx. \qquad (25)$$

Integrating Eq. (25) by parts, we have by Eq. (19)

$$\int x^2[x^2 J_1(x)]\, dx = x^2(x^2 J_2) - \int x^2 J_2 \cdot 2x\, dx$$

$$= x^4 J_2(x) - 2\int x^3 J_2\, dx.$$

Again applying Eq. (19) to the last integral, we obtain

$$\int x^4 J_1(x)\, dx = x^4 J_2(x) - 2x^3 J_3(x) + c.$$

In general, an integral of the form

$$\int x^m J_n(x)\, dx,$$

where m and n are integers such that $m + n \geqslant 0$, can be completely integrated if $m + n$ is odd. But if $m + n$ is even, then the result depends on the residual integral $\int J_0(x)\, dx$. It is not possible to reduce $\int J_0(x)\, dx$ [or $\int Y_0(x)\, dx$] any further and for this reason the functions

$$\int_0^x J_0(x)\, dx \quad \text{and} \quad \int_0^x Y_0(x)\, dx$$

have been tabulated.†

---

† A. N. Lowan and M. Abramwitz, "Tables of Integrals of $\int_0^x J_0(t)\, dt$ and $\int_0^x Y_0(t)\, dt$," *J. Math. Phys.* **22**: 3–12 (1943).

Example 3   Express $J_{3/2}(x)$ in terms of $\sin x$ and $\cos x$. We recall from Example 5 in Section 5.3 that the general solution of Bessel's equation of order $\frac{1}{2}$ can be written in terms of sines and cosines. Multiplying $y_1(x)$ and $y_2(x)$ by $c_0 = [\sqrt{2}\Gamma(\frac{3}{2})]^{-1}$, we have

$$J_{1/2}(x) = \frac{1}{\sqrt{2}\Gamma(\frac{3}{2})} \frac{\sin x}{\sqrt{x}} = \sqrt{\frac{2}{\pi x}} \sin x \qquad (26)$$

and

$$J_{-1/2}(x) = \frac{1}{\sqrt{2}\Gamma(\frac{3}{2})} \frac{\cos x}{\sqrt{x}} = \sqrt{\frac{2}{\pi x}} \cos x, \qquad (27)$$

since $\Gamma(\frac{3}{2}) = (\frac{1}{2})\Gamma(\frac{1}{2}) = \sqrt{\pi}/2$ (see Appendix 1, Formulas 55 and 56). By Eq. (23),

$$J_{3/2}(x) = \frac{1}{x} J_{1/2} - J_{-1/2} = \sqrt{\frac{2}{\pi x}} \left(\frac{\sin x}{x} - \cos x \right).$$

Similar results hold for $Y_p(x)$ (see Exercises 5, 6, and 7).

Many differential equations with variable coefficients can be reduced to Bessel equations.

Example 4   Consider the equation

$$y'' + k^2 x y = 0. \qquad (28)$$

The following substitution will reduce Eq. (28) to a Bessel equation. Let $u = y/\sqrt{x}$ and $z = 2kx^{3/2}/3$. Then

$$\frac{du}{dz} = \frac{du/dx}{dz/dx} = \frac{y'}{kx} - \frac{y}{2kx^2}$$

and

$$\frac{d^2u}{dz^2} = \frac{\frac{d}{dx}\left(\frac{du}{dz}\right)}{dz/dx} = \frac{y''}{k^2 x^{3/2}} - \frac{3y'}{2k^2 x^{5/2}} + \frac{y}{k^2 x^{7/2}}.$$

Hence

$$z^2 \frac{d^2u}{dz^2} + z \frac{du}{dz} = \frac{4}{9} x^{3/2} y'' + \frac{1}{9} \frac{y}{\sqrt{x}},$$

and using Eq. (28) for y'', we obtain

$$z^2 \frac{d^2u}{dz^2} + z \frac{du}{dz} = -\frac{4}{9} k^2 x^3 \left(\frac{y}{\sqrt{x}} \right) + \frac{1}{9} \frac{y}{\sqrt{x}} = -\left(z^2 - \frac{1}{9} \right) u$$

or

$$z^2 \frac{d^2u}{dz^2} + z \frac{du}{dz} + \left(z^2 - \frac{1}{9}\right)u = 0, \tag{29}$$

the Bessel equation of order $\frac{1}{3}$. Since Eq. (29) has the general solution

$$u(z) = AJ_{1/3}(z) + BJ_{-1/3}(z),$$

Eq. (28) has the solution

$$y(x) = \sqrt{x}\,[AJ_{1/3}(\tfrac{2}{3}kx^{3/2}) + BJ_{-1/3}(\tfrac{2}{3}kx^{3/2})].$$

Additional facts concerning the orthogonality and zeros of Bessel functions will be developed in Chapter 11.

EXERCISES 5.4

1. Express $J_5(x)$ in terms of $J_0(x)$ and $J_1(x)$.

2. Express $J_{5/2}(x)$ in terms of $\sin x$ and $\cos x$.

3. Show that:

  a) $4J_p''(x) = J_{p+2}(x) - 2J_p(x) + J_{p-2}(x)$;

  b) $-8J_p'''(x) = J_{p+3}(x) - 3J_{p+1}(x) + 3J_{p-1}(x) - J_{p-3}(x)$.

4. Prove that $[x^{-p}J_p(x)]' = x^{-p}J_{p+1}(x)$.

5. Show that $[x^p Y_p(x)]' = x^p Y_{p-1}(x)$.

6. Prove that $[x^{-p}Y_p(x)]' = -x^{-p}Y_{p+1}(x)$.

7. Using the equations of Exercises 5 and 6, show that:

  a) $x(Y_{p+1} + Y_{p-1}) = 2pY_p$;

  b) $2Y_p' = Y_{p-1} - Y_{p+1}$.

8. Prove the following identities.

  a) $\int J_1(x)\,dx = -J_0(x) + c$

  b) $\int x^2 J_1(x)\,dx = 2xJ_1(x) - x^2 J_0(x) + c$

  c) $\int xJ_0(x)\,dx = xJ_1(x) + c$

  d) $\int x^3 J_0(x)\,dx = (x^3 - 4x)J_1(x) + 2x^2 J_0(x) + c$

  e) $\int J_0(x)\cos x\,dx = xJ_0(x)\cos x + xJ_1(x)\sin x + c$

  f) $\int J_0(x)\sin x\,dx = xJ_0(x)\sin x - xJ_1(x)\cos x + c$

  g) $\int J_1(x)\cos x\,dx = xJ_1(x)\cos x - (x\sin x + \cos x)J_0(x) + c$

  h) $\int J_1(x)\sin x\,dx = xJ_1(x)\sin x + (x\cos x - \sin x)J_0(x) + c$

9. Verify the following identities.

  a) $\int x^2 J_0(x)\,dx = x^2 J_1(x) + xJ_0(x) - \int J_0(x)\,dx + c$

  b) $\int x^{-1}J_1(x)\,dx = -J_1(x) + \int J_0(x)\,dx + c$

  c) $\int xJ_1(x)\,dx = -xJ_0(x) + \int J_0(x)\,dx + c$

  d) $\int x^3 J_1(x)\,dx = 3x^2 J_1(x) - (x^3 - 3x)J_0(x) - 3\int J_0(x)\,dx + c$

10. Show that $\int J_0(\sqrt{x})\,dx = 2xJ_1(\sqrt{x}) + c$.

11. Show that

$$\int xJ_0(x)\sin x\,dx = \tfrac{1}{3}\{x^2[J_0(x)\sin x - J_1(x)\cos x] + xJ_1(x)\sin x\} + c.$$

12. Show that

$$\int xJ_1(x)\cos x\,dx = \tfrac{1}{3}\{x^2[J_1(x)\cos x - J_0(x)\sin x] + 2xJ_1(x)\sin x\} + c.$$

13. Show that

$$\int J_0(x)\,dx = 2[J_1(x) + J_3(x) + J_5(x) + \cdots] + c.$$

In Exercises 14 through 21 reduce each given equation to a Bessel equation and solve it.

14. $x^2 y'' + xy' + (a^2 x^2 - p^2)y = 0$

15. $4x^2 y'' + 4xy' + (x^2 - p^2)y = 0$

16. $x^2 y'' + xy' + 4(x^4 - p^2)y = 0$

17. $xy'' - y' + xy = 0$

18. $x^2 y'' + (x^2 + \tfrac{1}{4})y = 0$

19. $xy'' + (1 + 2k)y' + xy = 0$

20. $y'' + k^2 x^2 y = 0$

21. $y'' + k^2 x^4 y = 0$

22. Obtain the result of Exercise 23 in Section 5.3 by the methods of this section.

23. Obtain formula (14) for $p = 1$ by the methods of this section.

*24. Prove that if $p \geq 0$ is an integer,

$$\lim_{q \to p} \frac{J_q(x) \cos q\pi - J_{-q}(x)}{\sin q\pi} = Y_p(x).$$

This is the extension (18) of Y_q to all real values $q \geq 0$.

25. a) Expand $e^{(x/2)[t-(1/t)]}$ as a power series in t by multiplying the series for $e^{xt/2}$ and $e^{-x/2t}$.

    b) Show that the coefficient of t^n in the expansion obtained in part (a) is $J_n(x)$.

    c) Conclude that

$$e^{(x/2)[t-(1/t)]} = J_0(x) + \sum_{n=1}^{\infty} J_n(x)[t^n + (-t)^{-n}].$$

    This function is called the *generating function* of the Bessel functions.

    d) Set $t = e^{i\theta}$ in the expression in part (c) and obtain the identities

$$\cos(x \sin \theta) = J_0(x) + 2 \sum_{n=1}^{\infty} J_{2n}(x) \cos 2n\theta$$

and

$$\sin(x \sin \theta) = 2 \sum_{n=1}^{\infty} J_{2n-1}(x) \sin(2n-1)\theta.$$

26. Show that $J_0(x) = (1/\pi) \int_0^\pi \cos(x \cos t)\, dt$.

27. Show that $J_n(x) = (1/\pi) \int_0^\pi \cos(nt - x \sin t)\, dt$.

28. *Modified Bessel functions.* The function $I_p(x) = i^{-p} J_p(ix)$, $i^2 = -1$ is called the *modified Bessel function of the first kind of order p*. Show

that $I_p(x)$ is a solution of the differential equation

$$x^2 y'' + xy' - (x^2 + p^2)y = 0,$$

and obtain its series representation by the method of Frobenius.

29. Show that another solution of the differential equation in Exercise 28 is the *modified Bessel function of the second kind of order p*:

$$K_p(x) = \frac{\pi}{2 \sin p\pi} [I_{-p}(x) - I_p(x)].$$

30. Prove (see Exercise 25) that

$$e^{(x/2)[t+(1/t)]} = I_0(x) + \sum_{n=1}^{\infty} I_n(x)[t^n + t^{-n}].$$

31. Prove the following identities.

    a) $\dfrac{d}{dx}[x^p I_p(x)] = x^p I_{p-1}(x)$

    b) $\dfrac{d}{dx}[x^{-p} I_p(x)] = x^{-p} I_{p+1}(x)$

    c) $x(I_{p-1} - I_{p+1}) = 2p I_p$

32. a) Prove for all integers $n > 0$ that

$$\int_0^\infty J_{n+1}(x)\, dx = \int_0^\infty J_{n-1}(x)\, dx$$

by means of Eq. (24), given the approximation

$$J_n(x) \approx \sqrt{\frac{2}{\pi x}} \cos\left(x - \frac{\pi}{4} - \frac{n\pi}{2}\right).$$

    b) Prove a similar fact for Y_n given the approximation

$$Y_n(x) \approx \sqrt{\frac{2}{\pi x}} \sin\left(x - \frac{\pi}{4} - \frac{n\pi}{2}\right).$$

    c) Show that $\int_0^\infty J_n(x)\, dx = 1$.

    d) Prove that $\int_0^\infty (J_n(x)/x)\, dx = 1/n$.

5.5 LEGENDRE POLYNOMIALS

Another very important differential equation that arises in many applications (see, for example, Sections 11.2 and 12.4) is *Legendre's differential equation*

$$(1 - x^2)y'' - 2xy' + p(p+1)y = 0, \tag{1}$$

where p is a given real number. Any solution of Eq. (1) is called a *Legendre function.*†

Dividing Eq. (1) by $(1 - x^2)$, we obtain the equation

$$y'' - \frac{2x}{1 - x^2} y' + \frac{p(p + 1)}{1 - x^2} y = 0,$$

and we observe, using the geometric series, that the coefficient functions $a(x)$ and $b(x)$ of the form of Eq. (1) in Section 5.3 are both analytic at $x = 0$ with radius of convergence $R = 1$:

$$a(x) = \frac{-2x}{1 - x^2} = -2x(1 + x^2 + x^4 + x^6 + \cdots)$$

and

$$b(x) = p(p + 1)(1 + x^2 + x^4 + x^6 + \cdots).$$

By Theorem 1 in Section 5.3 we can apply the power series method to obtain the general solution of Eq. (1). In addition, the general solution will have a power series representation valid in the interval $|x| < 1$. Substituting $y = \sum_{n=0}^{\infty} c_n x^n$, and its derivatives into Eq. (1), we have

$$(1 - x^2) \sum_{n=2}^{\infty} c_n n(n - 1)x^{n-2} - 2x \sum_{n=1}^{\infty} c_n n x^{n-1} + p(p + 1) \sum_{n=0}^{\infty} c_n x^n = 0$$

or

$$\sum_{n=0}^{\infty} \{(n + 2)(n + 1)c_{n+2} - c_n[n(n + 1) - p(p + 1)]\}x^n = 0. \qquad (2)$$

Setting the coefficients of the sum (2) to zero, we obtain the recurrence relation

$$(n + 2)(n + 1)c_{n+2} = c_n(n^2 + n - p^2 - p) = c_n(n - p)(n + p + 1).$$

Thus we have

$$c_{n+2} = -\frac{(p - n)(p + n + 1)}{(n + 2)(n + 1)} c_n. \qquad (3)$$

Therefore

$$c_2 = -\frac{p(p + 1)}{2!} c_0, \quad c_3 = -\frac{(p - 1)(p + 2)}{3!} c_1,$$

$$c_4 = -\frac{(p - 2)(p + 3)}{4 \cdot 3} c_2 = \frac{(p - 2)p(p + 1)(p + 3)}{4!} c_0,$$

$$c_5 = -\frac{(p - 3)(p + 4)}{5 \cdot 4} c_3 = \frac{(p - 3)(p - 1)(p + 2)(p + 4)}{5!} c_1, \quad \text{etc.}$$

---

† Named after a famous French mathematician Adrien Marie Legendre (1752–1833).

Inserting these values for the coefficients into the power series expansion for $y(x)$ yields

$$y(x) = c_0 y_1(x) + c_1 y_2(x), \tag{4}$$

where

$$y_1(x) = 1 - p(p + 1)\frac{x^2}{2!} + (p - 2)p(p + 1)(p + 3)\frac{x^4}{4!} - \cdots, \tag{5}$$

$$y_2(x) = x - (p - 1)(p + 2)\frac{x^3}{3!} + (p - 3)(p - 1)(p + 2)(p + 4)\frac{x^5}{5!} - \cdots. \tag{6}$$

Dividing Eq. (6) by Eq. (5), we have

$$\frac{y_2(x)}{y_1(x)} = x + \frac{(p^2 + p + 1)}{3}x^3 + \cdots,$$

which obviously is nonconstant, implying that y_1 and y_2 are linearly independent. Thus Eq. (4) is the general solution of Legendre's equation (1) for $|x| < 1$.

In many applications the parameter p in Legendre's equation is a nonnegative integer. When this occurs, the right-hand side of Eq. (3) will vanish for $n = p$, implying that $c_{p+2} = c_{p+4} = c_{p+6} = \cdots = 0$. Thus one of the equations (5) or (6) reduces to a polynomial of degree p. (For even p, it is y_1; for odd p, it is y_2.) These polynomials, multiplied by an appropriate constant, are called the *Legendre polynomials*. Because of their importance, we shall study these polynomials in greater detail. It is customary to set

$$c_p = \frac{(2p)!}{2^p(p!)^2}, \quad p = 0, 1, 2, \ldots, \tag{7}$$

so that

$$c_{p-2} = -\frac{p(p - 1)}{2(2p - 1)}c_p = -\frac{(2p - 2)!}{2^p(p - 1)!(p - 2)!},$$

$$c_{p-4} = -\frac{(p - 2)(p - 3)}{4(2p - 3)}c_{p-2} = \frac{(2p - 4)!}{2^p 2!(p - 2)!(p - 4)!}, \cdots$$

and in general

$$c_{p-2k} = \frac{(-1)^k(2p - 2k)!}{2^p k!(p - k)!(p - 2k)!}.$$

Then the *Legendre polynomials of degree p* are given by

$$P_p(x) = \sum_{k=0}^{M} \frac{(-1)^k(2p - 2k)!}{2^p k!(p - k)!(p - 2k)!}x^{p-2k}, \quad p = 0, 1, 2, \ldots, \tag{8}$$

where M is the largest integer not greater than $p/2$. In particular, we have $P_0(x) = 1$, $P_1(x) = x$, $P_2(x) = \frac{1}{2}(3x^2 - 1)$, $P_3(x) = \frac{1}{2}(5x^3 - 3x)$, $P_4(x) = \frac{1}{8}(35x^4 - 30x^2 + 3)$, etc. As these particular results illustrate, as a consequence of the choice (7) of the value of c_p, we have $P_p(1) = 1$ and $P_p(-1) = (-1)^p$ for all integers $p \geq 0$. This fact will be proved in Example 3.

To obtain an even more concise form than Eq. (8) for the Legendre polynomials, we observe that we can write

$$P_p(x) = \sum_{k=0}^{M} \frac{(-1)^k}{2^p k!(p-k)!} \frac{d}{dx^p}(x^{2p-2k}),$$

since

$$\frac{d}{dx^p}(x^{2p-2k}) = (2p-2k)\frac{d}{dx^{p-1}}(x^{2p-2k-1}) = \cdots$$

$$= (2p-2k)\cdots(p-2k+1)x^{p-2k} = \frac{(2p-2k)!}{(p-2k)!}x^{p-2k}.$$

Hence

$$P_p(x) = \frac{1}{2^p p!} \frac{d^p}{dx^p} \sum_{k=0}^{M} (-1)^k \frac{p!}{k!(p-k)!}(x^2)^{p-k}.$$

We may now extend the range of this sum by letting k range from 0 to n. This extension will not affect the result, since the added terms are a polynomial of degree $<p$ so that the pth derivative will vanish. Thus

$$P_p(x) = \frac{1}{2^p p!} \frac{d^p}{dx^p} \sum_{k=0}^{n} \frac{p!}{k!(p-k)!}(x^2)^{p-k}(-1)^k,$$

and by the binomial formula we have

$$P_p(x) = \frac{1}{2^p p!} \frac{d^p}{dx^p}(x^2-1)^p, \quad p = 0, 1, 2, \ldots. \tag{9}$$

This formula is called *Rodrigues' formula*† and provides an easy way of computing successive Legendre polynomials.

Example 1   Show that $P_2(x) = \frac{1}{2}(3x^2 - 1)$.

By Rodrigues' formula

$$P_2(x) = \frac{1}{2^2 2!} \frac{d^2}{dx^2}(x^4 - 2x^2 + 1) = \frac{1}{8}(12x^2 - 4) = \frac{1}{2}(3x^2 - 1).$$

We can use Rodrigues' formula to obtain several useful recurrence relations. Observe that

$$P'_{p+1} = \frac{d}{dx}\left[\frac{1}{2^{p+1}(p+1)!} \frac{d^{p+1}}{dx^{p+1}}(x^2-1)^{p+1}\right]$$

$$= \frac{d}{dx}\left\{\frac{1}{2^p p!} \frac{d^p}{dx^p}[x(x^2-1)^p]\right\} = \frac{1}{2^p p!} \frac{d^{p+1}}{dx^{p+1}}[x(x^2-1)^p]. \tag{10}$$

---

† Named after the French mathematician and banker Olinde Rodrigues (1794–1851).

Hence taking the derivative of the term in brackets, we have

$$P'_{p+1} = \frac{1}{2^p p!} \frac{d^p}{dx^p} [(x^2 - 1)^p + 2px^2(x^2 - 1)^{p-1}]$$

$$= \frac{1}{2^p p!} \frac{d^p}{dx^p} [(2p + 1)(x^2 - 1)^p + 2p(x^2 - 1)^{p-1}]$$

$$= (2p + 1)P_p + P'_{p-1}, \quad p = 1, 2, 3, \ldots.$$

We can get another recurrence relation from Eq. (10) if we consider the effect of repeated differentiations on a product of the form $xf(x)$. Note that

$$\frac{d}{dx} [xf(x)] = x\frac{d}{dx} f(x) + f(x),$$

$$\frac{d^2}{dx^2} [xf(x)] = x\frac{d^2}{dx^2} f(x) + 2\frac{d}{dx} f(x),$$

and in general

$$\frac{d^{p+1}}{dx^{p+1}} [xf(x)] = x\frac{d^{p+1}}{dx^{p+1}} f(x) + (p + 1)\frac{d^p}{dx^p} f(x). \tag{11}$$

Applying Eq. (11) to the expression in brackets in Eq. (10), we obtain

$$P'_{p+1} = \frac{1}{2^p p!}\left[x\frac{d^{p+1}}{dx^{p+1}} (x^2 - 1)^p + (p + 1)\frac{d^p}{dx^p} (x^2 - 1)^p\right]$$

$$= xP'_p + (p + 1)P_p, \quad p = 0, 1, 2, \ldots.$$

Thus we have proved the identities

$$(p + 1)P_p = P'_{p+1} - xP'_p,$$

$$(2p + 1)P_p = P'_{p+1} - P'_{p-1}. \tag{12}$$

Subtracting the top identity in Eq. (12) from the bottom one yields

$$pP_p = xP'_p - P'_{p-1}, \quad p = 1, 2, \ldots. \tag{13}$$

Finally, we note that from Eqs. (12) and (13) we can get

$$(p + 1)P_{p+1} - (2p + 1)xP_p + pP_{p-1}$$

$$= (xP'_{p+1} - P'_p) - x(P'_{p+1} - P'_{p-1}) + (P'_p - xP'_{p-1}),$$

so that we can eliminate all derivatives and obtain the relation

$$(p + 1)P_{p+1} + pP_{p-1} = (2p + 1)xP_p, \quad p = 1, 2, \ldots. \tag{14}$$

The second-order homogeneous linear difference equation (14) can be used to generate all the Legendre polynomials if P_0 and P_1 are given (see Chapter 4). We shall illustrate this iterative technique in the next example.

Example 2   Starting with $P_0 = 1$ and $P_1 = x$, calculate the polynomials P_2, P_3, and P_4. By Eq. (14),

$$P_{p+1} = \frac{(2p + 1)xP_p - pP_{p-1}}{p + 1},$$

so that

$$P_2 = \frac{3xP_1 - P_0}{2} = \frac{3x^2 - 1}{2},$$

$$P_3 = \frac{5xP_2 - 2P_1}{3} = \frac{15x^3 - 5x - 4x}{6} = \frac{5x^3 - 3x}{2},$$

$$P_4 = \frac{7xP_3 - 3P_2}{4} = \frac{35x^4 - 21x^2 - 9x^2 + 3}{8} = \frac{35x^4 - 30x^2 + 3}{8}.$$

Another extremely important identity, called the *generating function* for Legendre polynomials, is given in the following theorem.

Theorem 1 $$\frac{1}{\sqrt{1 - 2xz + z^2}} = P_0(x) + P_1(x)z + P_2(x)z^2 + \cdots + P_n(x)z^n + \cdots.$$

$$\textbf{(15)}$$

Proof   Using the binomial theorem (see Exercise 25 in Section 5.1), we expand the expression

$$[1 - (2xz - z^2)]^{-1/2} = 1 + \frac{1}{2}(2xz - z^2) + \frac{(\frac{1}{2})(\frac{3}{2})}{2!}(2xz - z^2)^2 + \cdots$$

$$+ \frac{(\frac{1}{2})(\frac{3}{2})(\frac{5}{2}) \cdots [(2p - 1)/2]}{p!}(2xz - z^2)^p + \cdots.$$

The power z^p can only occur in the terms going from the pth term $(2xz - z^2)^p[= z^p(2x - z)^p]$ down. Thus by expanding the various powers of $(2x - z)$, we find that the coefficient of z^p is

$$\frac{(\frac{1}{2})(\frac{3}{2}) \cdots [(2p - 1)/2]}{p!}(2x)^p - \frac{(\frac{1}{2})(\frac{3}{2}) \cdots [(2p - 3)/2]}{(p - 1)!}(p - 1)(2x)^{p-2}$$

$$+ \frac{(\frac{1}{2})(\frac{3}{2}) \cdots [(2p - 5)/2]}{(p - 2)!}\frac{(p - 2)(p - 3)}{2!}(2x)^{p-4} - \cdots$$

or

$$\frac{(2p)!}{2^p(p!)^2}x^p - \frac{(2p - 2)!x^{p-2}}{2^p(p - 1)!(p - 2)!} + \frac{(2p - 4)!x^{p-4}}{2^p 2!(p - 2)!(p - 4)!} - \cdots. \quad \textbf{(16)}$$

Let M be the largest integer not greater than $p/2$. Note now that the highest power of z in the term $(2xz - z^2)^{M-1}$ is z^{2M-2}, and $2M - 2 \leqslant$

$p - 2$. Thus the sum (16) includes only the terms

$$\sum_{k=0}^{M} \frac{(-1)^k (2p - 2k)! x^{p-2k}}{2^p k! (p - k)! (p - 2k)!} = P_p(x). \quad \blacksquare$$

Example 3   For all integers $p \geqslant 0$ we have the identities

$$P_p(1) = 1 \quad \text{and} \quad P_p(-1) = (-1)^p.$$

To verify this fact, we set $x = \pm 1$ in Eq. (15), thus obtaining

$$\frac{1}{\sqrt{1 \mp 2z + z^2}} = P_0(\pm 1) + P_1(\pm 1)z + P_2(\pm 1)z^2 + \cdots + P_n(\pm 1)z^n + \cdots.$$

But $1 \mp 2z + z^2 = (1 \mp z)^2$, and the geometric series

$$\frac{1}{1 \mp z} = 1 \pm z + z^2 \pm \cdots + (\pm z)^n + \cdots$$

by Eq. (8) in Section 5.1. Thus the coefficients of the two series must agree, yielding the desired result.

Some additional properties of Legendre polynomials will be developed in Chapter 11 when we discuss the zeros and orthogonality of these functions. In that chapter we will show in particular that the Legendre polynomials give the best "least-squares" polynomial approximation to a given continuous function.

EXERCISES 5.5

1. Calculate P_5, P_6, P_7, and P_8 by means of Eq. (14).

2. Prove that the series (5) has a radius of convergence $R = 1$.

3. Prove that the series (6) has a radius of convergence $R = 1$.

4. Calculate P_4 by means of Rodrigues' formula.

5. Prove that $P_{2p+1}(0) = 0$ for all integers $p \geqslant 0$.

6. Prove that

$$P_{2p}(0) = \frac{(-1)^p (2p)!}{2^{2p} (p!)^2},$$

for all $p \geqslant 0$.

7. Prove that for all integers $p \geqslant 0$

   a) $P'_{2p}(0) = 0$;

   b) $P'_{2p+1}(0) = \dfrac{(-1)^p (2p + 1)!}{2^{2p} (p!)^2}$.

8. Show that for all integers $p > 0$:

   a) $\displaystyle\int_0^1 P_p(x)\, dx = \frac{1}{p + 1} P_{p-1}(0)$;

   b) $\displaystyle\int_0^1 P_{2p}(x)\, dx = 0$;

   c) $\displaystyle\int_0^1 P_{2p+1}(x)\, dx = (-1)^p \frac{(2p)!(4p + 3)}{2^{2p+1} p!(p + 1)!}$.

   d) Compute these integrals for $p = 0$.

9. Consider the differential equation

$$y'' - 2xy' + 2py = 0, \tag{17}$$

which is known as *Hermite's equation*,

a) Use the method of Frobenius to show that all solutions of Eq. (17) are of the form

$$c_0\left[1 + \sum_{n=1}^{\infty} \frac{2^n(-p)(2-p)\cdots(2n-2-p)x^{2n}}{(2n)!}\right]$$

$$+ c_1\left[x + \sum_{n=1}^{\infty} \frac{2^n(1-p)(3-p)\cdots(2n-1-p)x^{2n+1}}{(2n+1)!}\right],$$

where c_0 and c_1 are arbitrary functions.

b) Show that Eq. (17) has a polynomial solution of degree p for a nonnegative integer p. These polynomials, denoted by $H_p(x)$, are called the *Hermite polynomials of degree p*.

c) Show that

$$H_p(x) = \sum_{n=0}^{M} \frac{(-1)^n p!(2x)^{p-2n}}{n!(p-2n)!},$$

where M is the greatest integer $\leq p/2$.

d) Calculate H_0, H_1, H_2, H_3, and H_4.

10. Consider *Laguerre's equation*

$$xy'' + (1-x)y' + py = 0. \qquad (18)$$

a) Show that if p is a nonnegative integer, then there is a polynomial solution to Eq. (18) of the form

$$L_p(x) = \sum_{n=0}^{p} \frac{(-1)^n p!x^n}{(p-n)!(n!)^2}.$$

The functions $L_p(x)$ are known as the *Laguerre polynomials*.

b) Calculate $L_0(x)$, $L_1(x)$, $L_2(x)$, $L_3(x)$, and $L_4(x)$.

REVIEW EXERCISES

1. By considering the partial sums, determine whether the following series converge or diverge.

a) $\displaystyle\sum_{n=1}^{\infty} \frac{1}{n(n+1)}$ b) $\displaystyle\sum_{n=1}^{\infty} \frac{n}{(n+1)!}$

c) $\displaystyle\sum_{n=1}^{\infty} nx^n$ d) $\displaystyle\sum_{n=1}^{\infty} \frac{n^n}{n!}$

2. Show that for $|x-1| < 1$.

$$\ln x = (x-1) - \tfrac{1}{2}(x-1)^2 + \tfrac{1}{3}(x-1)^3 \cdots.$$

3. Show that the series

$$1 + \tfrac{1}{2} - \tfrac{1}{3} + \tfrac{1}{4} + \tfrac{1}{5} - \tfrac{1}{6} + \tfrac{1}{7} + \tfrac{1}{8} - \tfrac{1}{9} + \cdots$$

diverges.

4. Show that

$$\ln \frac{x^2}{x^2-1} = \frac{1}{x^2} + \frac{1}{2x^4} + \frac{1}{3x^6} + \cdots, \quad \text{for } |x| > 1.$$

5. Use Taylor's theorem to show that

$$e^{\tan x} = 1 + x + \frac{x^2}{2!} + \frac{3x^3}{3!} + \frac{9x^4}{4!} + \frac{37x^5}{5!} + \cdots.$$

$$\text{for } |x| < \frac{\pi}{2}.$$

In Exercises 6 through 11, use power series to find the solution of the given initial value problem.

6. $xy'' + xy' - y = e^{-x}$, $y(0) = 1$, $y'(0) = 0$

7. $xy'' - y' + (1-x)y = x^2(1-x)$,
$y(0) = y'(0) = 1$

8. $(1+x)y'' + (2-x-x^2)y' + y = 0$,
$y(0) = 0$, $y'(0) = 1$

9. $xy'' - 2y' + xy = x^2 - 2 - 2\sin x$,
$y(0) = 0$, $y'(0) = 1$

10. $y'' - 3x^2y' - 6xy = 0$, $y(0) = 1$, $y'(0) = 0$

11. $y'' + 2xy' + 2y = 0$, $y(0) = 1$, $y'(0) = 0$

In Exercises 12 through 17, use the method of Frobenius to solve the given differential equations.

12. $4xy'' + 2y' - y = 0$

13. $2x(1-2x)y'' + (1+4x^2)y' - (1+2x)y = 0$

14. $2x(1-2x)y'' + (1+x)y' - y = 0$

15. $x(1-x)y'' + 2(1-2x)y' - 2y = 0$

16. $2x(1-x)y'' + (1-x)y' + 3y = 0$

17. $2x^2y'' + x(1-x)y' - y = 0$

18. Gauss's hypergeometric equation is given by

$$x(1-x)y'' + [c - (a+b+1)x]y' - aby = 0,$$

where a, b, and c are constants. Show that it has a solution of the form

$$y_1(x) = 1 + \frac{ab}{c}x + \frac{a(a+1)b(b+1)}{c(c+1)}\frac{x^2}{2!}$$

$$+ \frac{a(a+1)(a+2)b(b+1)(b+2)}{c(c+1)(c+2)}\frac{x^3}{3!} + \cdots.$$

This series is called the *hypergeometric series* and denoted by the symbol $F(a, b, c; x)$.

19. Prove, using the result of Exercise 18, that:

a) $F(-a, b, b; -x) = (1+x)^a$;

b) $xF(1, 1, 2; -x) = \ln(1+x)$.

20. Show that Chebyshev's equation

$$(1 - x^2)y'' - xy' + p^2y = 0$$

has a polynomial solution when p is an integer.

21. Prove the following identities.

a) $\displaystyle\int_0^1 xJ_0(ax)J_0(bx)\,dx = 0, \quad a \neq b$

b) $\displaystyle\int_0^1 xJ_0^2(ax)\,dx = \tfrac{1}{2}J_1^2(ax)$

c) $x^2J_0'(x) = x[J_1(x) - J_0(x)] - (x^2 - 1)J_1(x)$

d) $[xJ_0(x)J_1(x)]' = x[J_0^2(x) - J_1^2(x)]$

22. Find solutions in terms of Bessel functions for the following differential equations.

a) $x^2y'' + (x^2 - 2)y = 0$

b) $x^2y'' - xy' + (1 + x^2 - k^2)y = 0$

23. Using the method of Frobenius, find a solution to

$$x^2y'' - xy' + (x^2 + 1)y = 0.$$

24. Prove the following identities for integral values of n

a) $\displaystyle\int_{-1}^1 xP_n(x)P_{n-1}(x)\,dx = \frac{2n}{4n^2 - 1}$

b) $\displaystyle\int_{-1}^1 (1 - x^2)[P_n'(x)]^2\,dx = \frac{2n(n+1)}{2n+1}$

c) $(m + n + 1)\displaystyle\int_0^1 x^m P_n(x)\,dx$

$$= m\int_0^1 x^{m-1}P_{n-1}(x)\,dx.$$

25. Find a solution for the differential equation

$$y'' + (\cot x)y' + n(n+1)y = 0$$

(*Hint*: Make a trigonometric substitution.)

Laplace Transforms

6.1 INTRODUCTION: DEFINITION AND BASIC PROPERTIES OF THE LAPLACE TRANSFORM

One of the most efficient methods of solving certain ordinary and partial differential equations is to use Laplace† transforms. The effectiveness of the Laplace transform is due to its ability to convert a differential equation into an algebraic equation, whose solution yields the solution of the differential equation when the transformation is reversed. In many ways, this procedure is similar to the use of logarithms in performing multiplications and divisions.

As we shall see in a moment, the Laplace transform is defined as a certain integral over the range from zero to infinity. We recall that such an integral is called an *improper integral*. Formally, if t_0 is a given real number, then for any function $f(t)$, we define

$$\int_{t_0}^{\infty} f(t)\, dt = \lim_{A \to \infty} \int_{t_0}^{A} f(t)\, dt.$$

If this limit exists and is finite, we say that the improper integral *converges*. Otherwise, it *diverges*.

Example 1   Let $f(t) = e^{at}$, where $a \neq 0$. Then

$$\int_{0}^{\infty} e^{at}\, dt = \lim_{A \to \infty} \int_{0}^{A} e^{at}\, dt = \lim_{A \to \infty} \frac{1}{a} e^{at}\Big|_{0}^{A} = \lim_{A \to \infty} \frac{1}{a}(e^{aA} - 1).$$

Clearly this limit is finite (and is equal to $-1/a$) if $a < 0$ and diverges to $+\infty$ if $a > 0$.

Example 2   Let $f(t) = \cos t$. Then

$$\int_{0}^{\infty} \cos t\, dt = \lim_{A \to \infty} \int_{0}^{A} \cos t\, dt = \lim_{A \to \infty} \sin t\Big|_{0}^{A} = \lim_{A \to \infty} \sin A.$$

But $\sin A$ has no limit as $A \to \infty$. Therefore, $\int_{0}^{\infty} \cos t\, dt$ diverges, even though $-1 \leq \int_{0}^{A} \cos t\, dt \leq 1$ for every $A \geq 0$.

Example 3   Let $f(t) = 1/t^p$, $p \neq 1$. Then

$$\int_{1}^{\infty} t^{-p}\, dt = \lim_{A \to \infty} \int_{1}^{A} t^{-p}\, dt$$

$$= \lim_{A \to \infty} \frac{1}{1-p} t^{1-p}\Big|_{1}^{A} = \lim_{A \to \infty} \frac{1}{1-p}(A^{1-p} - 1),$$

which converges to $1/(p - 1)$ if $p > 1$, and diverges if $p < 1$.

There are other kinds of improper integrals.

---

† Named after the French mathematician P. S. Laplace (1749–1827).

Example 4   Let $f(t) = t^{-1/2}$ and consider $\int_0^1 t^{-1/2}\, dt$. Since $f(t)$ is not defined at $t = 0$, we define

$$\int_0^1 t^{-1/2}\, dt = \lim_{A \to 0} \int_A^1 t^{-1/2}\, dt$$

$$= \lim_{A \to 0} 2t^{1/2}\Big|_A^1 = \lim_{A \to 0} 2(1 - \sqrt{A}) = 2.$$

Therefore, $\int_0^1 t^{-1/2}\, dt$ converges.

Example 5   Let $f(t) = t^{-1}$. Then $\int_0^1 t^{-1}\, dt$ is an improper integral and

$$\int_0^1 t^{-1}\, dt = \lim_{A \to 0} \int_A^1 t^{-1}\, dt = \lim_{A \to 0} \ln t\Big|_A^1$$

$$= \lim_{A \to 0} (\ln 1 - \ln A) = \lim_{A \to 0} (-\ln A) = +\infty.$$

Therefore, this integral diverges.

In the rest of this chapter we shall not formally calculate improper integrals as we did in these five examples, but the reader should always keep in mind the definition of an improper integral as a limit.

Let $f(t)$ be a real-valued function that is defined for $t \geq 0$. Suppose that $f(t)$ is multiplied by e^{-st} and the result is integrated with respect to t from zero to infinity. If the integral converges, it is a function of s:†

$$F(s) = \int_0^\infty e^{-st} f(t)\, dt, \tag{1}$$

and it is called the *Laplace transform* of $f(t)$. *We shall denote the original function by a lower-case letter and the transform by the same letter in capitals or by $\mathscr{L}\{f(t)\}$:*

$$\boxed{F(s) = \mathscr{L}\{f(t)\}(s) = \int_0^\infty e^{-st} f(t)\, dt.} \tag{2}$$

It should now be apparent why the word *transform* is associated with this operation. The operation "transforms" the original function $f(t)$ into a new function $\mathscr{L}\{f(t)\}(s)$. Since we shall be interested in reversing the procedure, we call the original function $f(t)$ the *inverse transform* of $F = \mathscr{L}\{f(t)\}$ and denote it by $f(t) = \mathscr{L}^{-1}\{F\}$. The term "inverse transform" is similar in meaning to the term "inverse of a function." For example, if $f(x) = \sqrt{x}$, then the inverse of f, denoted by $f^{-1}(x)$, is the function $f^{-1}(x) = x^2$. The meaning here is clear. If $x > 0$ and we take the positive square root of x

---

† In general, the variable s is complex, but in this chapter we need only consider real values of s.

and then square it, we will end up with the original number. In mathematical symbols, we have $f^{-1}(f(x)) = x$. Similarly for the Laplace transform, we may say that the inverse transform of F, $\mathscr{L}^{-1}\{F\}$, is the function whose transform is F. Note that the last statement translates into the mathematical symbols $\mathscr{L}^{-1}\{F\} = \mathscr{L}^{-1}\{\mathscr{L}\{f\}\} = f$.

Example 6   Let $f(t) = e^{at}$, where a is constant. Then

$$\mathscr{L}\{e^{at}\} = \int_0^\infty e^{-st}e^{at}\, dt = \left. \frac{e^{-(s-a)t}}{a-s} \right|_0^\infty ,$$

which converges, if $s - a > 0$, to

$$\mathscr{L}\{e^{at}\} = \frac{1}{s-a} . \tag{3}$$

Thus the Laplace transform of the function e^{at} is the function $F(s) = 1/(s-a)$ for $s > a$. Note that we can also conclude that $\mathscr{L}^{-1}\{F(s)\} = e^{at}$.

The last example shows that $\mathscr{L}\{f(t)\}$ may not be defined for all values of s, but if it is defined, then it will exist for suitably large values of s. Indeed, Eq. (3) holds only for values $s > a$.

Example 7   Let $f(t) = 1/t$. Then

$$\int_0^\infty \frac{e^{-st}}{t}\, dt = \int_0^1 \frac{e^{-st}}{t}\, dt + \int_1^\infty \frac{e^{-st}}{t}\, dt.$$

But for t in the interval $0 \le t \le 1$, $e^{-st} \ge e^{-s}$ if $s > 0$. Thus,

$$\int_0^\infty \frac{e^{-st}}{t}\, dt \ge e^{-s}\int_0^1 \frac{dt}{t} + \int_1^\infty \frac{e^{-st}}{t}\, dt.$$

However, as we saw earlier, $\int_0^1 t^{-1}\, dt$ diverges. Thus $f(t) = 1/t$ has no Laplace transform.

This example and the preceding discussion pinpoint the need for answers to the following questions:

1. Which functions $f(t)$ have Laplace transforms?
2. Can two functions $f(t)$ and $g(t)$ have the same Laplace transform?

In answering these questions, we shall be satisfied if a class of functions, large enough to contain virtually all functions that arise in practice, can be found for which the Laplace transforms exist and whose inverses are unique. The need for a unique inverse arises from the fact that we need to reverse the transformation to find the solution of a given problem and this step is not possible if the inverses within the given class of functions are not unique. We shall see in Section 6.2 that certain differential equations can be solved by first taking the Laplace transform of both sides of the equation, then finding the Laplace transform of the solution, and finally taking the unique inverse transform.

In order to give simple conditions that guarantee the existence of a Laplace transform, we shall require the following definitions.

A function $f(t)$ has a *jump discontinuity* at a point t^* if the function has different (finite) limits as it approaches t^* from the left and from the right or if the two limits are equal but different from $f(t^*)$. Note that $f(x_0)$ may not be equal to either

$$\lim_{x \to x_0^+} f(x) \quad \text{or} \quad \lim_{x \to x_0^-} f(x).$$

In fact, $f(x_0)$ may not even be defined. A function $f(t)$ defined on $[0, \infty)$ is *piecewise continuous* if it is continuous on every finite interval $0 \le x \le b$, except possibly at finitely many points where it has jump discontinuities. Such a function is illustrated in Fig. 1. The class of piecewise continuous functions includes every continuous function, as well as many important discontinuous functions, such as the unit step function, square waves, and the staircase function, which we shall encounter later in the chapter.

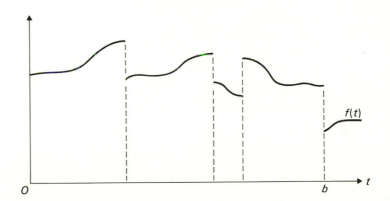

Figure 1

Theorem 1   *Existence theorem.* Let $f(t)$ be piecewise continuous on $t \ge 0$ and satisfy the condition

$$|f(t)| \le M e^{at} \tag{4}$$

for $t \ge T$ and for fixed nonnegative constants a, M, and T. Then $\mathscr{L}\{f(t)\}$ exists for all $s > a$.

Proof   Since $f(t)$ is piecewise continuous, $e^{-st}f(t)$ is integrable over any finite interval on $t \ge 0$, and

$$|\mathscr{L}\{f(t)\}| = \left| \int_0^\infty e^{-st} f(t)\, dt \right| \le \left| \int_0^T e^{-st} f(t)\, dt \right| + \int_T^\infty e^{-st} |f(t)|\, dt. \tag{5}$$

The first integral on the right-hand side of Eq. (5) exists, and by Eq. (4)

$$\int_T^\infty e^{-st}|f(t)|\,dt \leqslant M\int_T^\infty e^{-(s-a)t}\,dt = \frac{Me^{-(s-a)t}}{a-s}\bigg|_T^\infty$$

converges to $Me^{-(s-a)T}/(s-a)$ as $t \to \infty$ if $s > a$. Thus it follows by the comparison theorem of integrals that $\mathscr{L}\{f(t)\}$ exists. ∎

The conditions in Theorem 1 are easy to test. For example,

$$\sinh t \leqslant e^t, \quad t^n \leqslant n!e^t, \quad \text{for } t > 0,$$

but

$$e^{t^2} > Me^{at}$$

for sufficiently large t, regardless of the choice of M and a.

These facts are easily shown as follows:

1. $\sinh t = \dfrac{e^t - e^{-t}}{2} < \dfrac{e^t}{2} < e^t$, since $-\dfrac{e^{-t}}{2} < 0$.

2. $e^t = 1 + t + \dfrac{t^2}{2!} + \cdots + \dfrac{t^n}{n!} + \cdots$, so that for $t > 0$, $\dfrac{t^n}{n!} \leqslant e^t$, or

$$t^n \leqslant n!e^t.$$

3. Let M and a be any fixed constants. Clearly, for sufficiently large t, $t > a + \ln M/t$ and

$$t^2 > \ln M + at.$$

Exponentiation now yields

$$e^{t^2} > e^{\ln M + at} = e^{\ln M}e^{at} = Me^{at}.$$

It should also be noted that there are functions having Laplace transforms that do not satisfy the hypotheses of Theorem 1. For example, $f(t) = 1/\sqrt{t}$ is infinite at $t = 0$; but setting $x^2 = st$, we have

$$\mathscr{L}\{t^{-1/2}\} = \int_0^\infty e^{-st}t^{-1/2}\,dt = \frac{2}{\sqrt{s}}\int_0^\infty e^{-x^2}\,dx = \sqrt{\frac{\pi}{s}},$$

according to Formula 58 in Appendix 1.

The proof of uniqueness would take us too far afield at this point. However, it can be shown† that *two functions having the same Laplace transform cannot differ on an interval of positive length*, although they may differ at several isolated points. Thus two different piecewise continuous functions having the same Laplace transform can differ only at isolated

---

† See, for example, I. S. Sokolnikoff and R. M. Redheffer, *Mathematics of Physics and Modern Engineering*, p. 217. New York: McGraw-Hill (1966).

points. Such differences are generally of no importance in applications. Hence the Laplace transform has an essentially unique inverse. In particular, different continuous functions have different Laplace transforms.

One of the most important properties of the Laplace transform is stated in the following theorem.

Theorem 2 *Linearity.*

$$\mathcal{L}\{af(t) + bg(t)\} = a\mathcal{L}\{f(t)\} + b\mathcal{L}\{g(t)\}.$$

Proof By definition

$$\mathcal{L}\{af(t) + bg(t)\} = \int_0^\infty e^{-st}[af(t) + bg(t)]\, dt$$

$$= a\int_0^\infty e^{-st}f(t)\, dt + b\int_0^\infty e^{-st}g(t)\, dt$$

$$= a\mathcal{L}\{f(t)\} + b\mathcal{L}\{g(t)\}. \blacksquare$$

The linearity property allows us to deal with an equation term by term in order to obtain its Laplace transform.

It is essential that we begin to recognize the Laplace transforms of many different functions as quickly as possible. We list in Table 1 the transforms of seven basic functions. A much more extensive list can be found in Appendix 2. Note that, by definition, $0! = 1$.

Table 1

$f(t)$	$\mathcal{L}\{f(t)\}$	Range of definition	
e^{at}	$\dfrac{1}{s - a}$	$s > a$ (real)	**(6)**
c (a constant)	$\dfrac{c}{s}$	$s > 0$	**(7)**
t^n	$\dfrac{n!}{s^{n+1}}$	$s > 0$	**(8)**
$\sin at$	$\dfrac{a}{s^2 + a^2}$	$s > 0$	**(9)**
$\cos at$	$\dfrac{s}{s^2 + a^2}$	$s > 0$	**(10)**
$\sinh at$	$\dfrac{a}{s^2 - a^2}$	$s > |a|$	**(11)**
$\cosh at$	$\dfrac{s}{s^2 - a^2}$	$s > |a|$	**(12)**

Equation (6) has already been obtained in Example 6. The derivations of the other six transforms are given below. For Eq. (7), we have

$$\mathcal{L}\{c\} = \int_0^\infty e^{-st}c\,dt = \frac{ce^{-st}}{-s}\bigg|_0^\infty = \frac{c}{s}, \quad \text{for} \quad s > 0.$$

Example 8   Let n be a positive integer. Then Eq. (8) is obtained by integrating

$$\mathcal{L}\{t^n\} = \int_0^\infty e^{-st}t^n\,dt$$

by parts with $u = t^n$ and $dv = e^{-st}\,dt$. We have $du = nt^{n-1}\,dt$ and $v = -(1/s)e^{-st}$:

$$\mathcal{L}\{t^n\} = \frac{-e^{-st}t^n}{s}\bigg|_0^\infty + \frac{n}{s}\int_0^\infty e^{-st}t^{n-1}\,dt$$

$$= \frac{n}{s}\mathcal{L}\{t^{n-1}\}, \quad \text{for} \quad s > 0.$$

Thus

$$\mathcal{L}\{t^n\} = \frac{n}{s}\mathcal{L}\{t^{n-1}\} = \frac{n(n-1)}{s^2}\mathcal{L}\{t^{n-2}\} = \cdots = \frac{n!}{s^n}\mathcal{L}\{t^0\}.$$

But $t^0 = 1$, so by Eq. (7) we have $\mathcal{L}\{1\} = 1/s$ and

$$\mathcal{L}\{t^n\} = \frac{n!}{s^{n+1}}.$$

Example 9   The Laplace transform of $\sin at$ is also obtained by integrating by parts. Let $u = \sin at$ and $dv = e^{-st}\,dt$; then $du = a\cos at\,dt$ and $v = -(1/s)e^{-st}$, so that

$$\mathcal{L}\{\sin at\} = \int_0^\infty e^{-st}\sin at\,dt = \frac{-e^{-st}\sin at}{s}\bigg|_0^\infty + \frac{a}{s}\int_0^\infty e^{-st}\cos at\,dt,$$

or

$$\mathcal{L}\{\sin at\} = \frac{a}{s}\mathcal{L}\{\cos at\}. \tag{13}$$

We must integrate this last integral again by parts with $u = \cos at$ and $dv = e^{-st}\,dt$, so that $du = -a\sin at\,dt$ and $v = -(1/s)e^{-st}$, yielding

$$\mathcal{L}\{\sin at\} = \frac{a}{s}\int_0^\infty e^{-st}\cos at\,dt = \frac{a}{s}\left[-\frac{e^{-st}\cos at}{s}\bigg|_0^\infty - \frac{a}{s}\int_0^\infty e^{-st}\sin at\,dt\right]$$

or

$$\mathcal{L}\{\sin at\} = \frac{a}{s^2} - \frac{a^2}{s^2}\mathcal{L}\{\sin at\}. \tag{14}$$

Moving the last term on the right-hand side of Eq. (14) to the left-hand side, we get

$$\left(1 + \frac{a^2}{s^2}\right)\mathscr{L}\{\sin at\} = \frac{a}{s^2},$$

or

$$\frac{s^2 + a^2}{s^2}\mathscr{L}\{\sin at\} = \frac{a}{s^2}.$$

Dividing both sides by $s^2/(s^2 + a^2)$, we obtain

$$\mathscr{L}\{\sin at\} = \frac{a}{s^2 + a^2}.$$

Equation (10) follows at once from Eqs. (9) and (13) since

$$\mathscr{L}\{\cos at\} = \frac{s}{a}\mathscr{L}\{\sin at\} = \frac{s}{s^2 + a^2}.$$

Explain why these computations are valid only if $s > 0$.

Example 10   Since $\sinh at = (e^{at} - e^{-at})/2$, we can use Theorem 2 and Eq. (6) to obtain

$$\mathscr{L}\{\sinh at\} = \mathscr{L}\left\{\frac{e^{at} - e^{-at}}{2}\right\} = \frac{1}{2}(\mathscr{L}\{e^{at}\} - \mathscr{L}\{e^{-at}\})$$

$$= \frac{1}{2}\left(\frac{1}{s - a} - \frac{1}{s + a}\right) = \frac{a}{s^2 - a^2}.$$

Similarly,

$$\mathscr{L}\{\cosh at\} = \mathscr{L}\left\{\frac{e^{at} + e^{-at}}{2}\right\} = \frac{1}{2}(\mathscr{L}\{e^{at}\} + \mathscr{L}\{e^{-at}\})$$

$$= \frac{1}{2}\left(\frac{1}{s - a} + \frac{1}{s + a}\right) = \frac{s}{s^2 - a^2}.$$

Example 11   Compute $\mathscr{L}\{3t^5 - t^8 + 4 - 5e^{2t} + 6\cos 3t\}$.

Using the linearity property and the results in Table 1, we have

$$\mathscr{L}\{3t^5 - t^8 + 4 - 5e^{2t} + \cos 3t\}$$

$$= 3\mathscr{L}\{t^5\} - \mathscr{L}\{t^8\} + \mathscr{L}\{4\} - 5\mathscr{L}\{e^{2t}\} + \mathscr{L}\{6\cos 3t\}$$

$$= 3\frac{5!}{s^6} - \frac{8!}{s^9} + \frac{4}{s} - \frac{5}{s - 2} + \frac{6s}{s^2 + 9}$$

$$= \frac{360}{s^6} - \frac{40{,}320}{s^9} + \frac{4}{s} - \frac{5}{s - 2} + \frac{6s}{s^2 + 9}.$$

There are many other facts that can be used to facilitate the computation of Laplace transforms. One of these is given below. Other facts will be given in the exercises and in the next three sections.

The next theorem presents a quick way of computing the Laplace transform $\mathcal{L}\{e^{at}f(t)\}$ when $\mathcal{L}\{f(t)\}$ is known.

Theorem 3   *First shifting property of the Laplace transform.* Suppose that $F(s) = \mathcal{L}\{f(t)\}$ exists for $s > b$. If a is a real number, then

$$\boxed{\mathcal{L}\{e^{at}f(t)\}(s) = F(s - a), \quad \text{for} \quad s > a + b.}$$ **(15)**

Proof   By definition,

$$\mathcal{L}\{e^{at}f(t)\} = \int_0^\infty e^{-st}e^{at}f(t)\,dt = \int_0^\infty e^{-(s-a)t}f(t)\,dt$$

$$= \mathcal{L}\{f(t)\}(s - a) = F(s - a),$$

if $s - a > b$ or $s > a + b$. As the formula suggests, to find $\mathcal{L}\{e^{at}f(t)\}$, we simply replace each s in $\mathcal{L}\{f(t)\}$ by $s - a$. ∎

Example 12   Compute $\mathcal{L}\{e^{2t}\cos 3t\}$.

Since

$$F(s) = \mathcal{L}\{\cos 3t\} = \frac{s}{s^2 + 9}$$

and $a = 2$, we have

$$\mathcal{L}\{e^{2t}\cos 3t\} = F(s - 2) = \frac{s - 2}{(s - 2)^2 + 9}.$$

If we apply the First Shifting Property to the Laplace transforms in Table 1, we obtain the results shown in Table 2.

Table 2

$f(t)$	$\mathcal{L}\{f(t)\}$	Range of definition
$e^{at}t^n$	$\dfrac{n!}{(s - a)^{n+1}}$	$s > a$
$e^{at}\sin bt$	$\dfrac{b}{(s - a)^2 + b^2}$	$s > a$
$e^{at}\cos bt$	$\dfrac{s - a}{(s - a)^2 + b^2}$	$s > a$
$e^{at}\sinh bt$	$\dfrac{b}{(s - a)^2 - b^2}$	$s > a + |b|$
$e^{at}\cosh bt$	$\dfrac{s - a}{(s - a)^2 - b^2}$	$s > a + |b|$

In Section 6.2 we will have frequent need to reverse the process of taking a Laplace transform. The following example demonstrates the technique we will use in finding the inverse Laplace transform.

Example 13   Compute

$$\mathscr{L}^{-1}\left\{\frac{s + 9}{s^2 + 6s + 13}\right\}.$$

Example 12 provides a hint. We begin by completing the square in the denominator:

$$\frac{s + 9}{s^2 + 6s + 13} = \frac{s + 9}{(s + 3)^2 + 4}.$$

But $4 = 2^2$ and $s + 9 = (s + 3) + 6$, so that we can write

$$\frac{s + 9}{s^2 + 6s + 13} = \frac{(s + 3) + 6}{(s + 3)^2 + 2^2}.$$

Since by Theorem 2 the Laplace transform of a sum of terms is the sum of the Laplace transforms of the individual terms, the inverse transform also satisfies this linearity property:

$$\mathscr{L}^{-1}\{aF(s) + bG(s)\} = a\mathscr{L}^{-1}\{F(s)\} + b\mathscr{L}^{-1}\{G(s)\}.$$

Hence

$$\mathscr{L}^{-1}\left\{\frac{(s + 3) + 6}{(s + 3)^2 + 2^2}\right\} = \mathscr{L}^{-1}\left\{\frac{(s + 3)}{(s + 3)^2 + 2^2}\right\} + 3\mathscr{L}^{-1}\left\{\frac{2}{(s + 3)^2 + 2^2}\right\}$$

and using Table 2 (or the First Shifting Property and Table 1), we have

$$\mathscr{L}^{-1}\left\{\frac{(s + 3) + 6}{(s + 3)^2 + 2^2}\right\} = e^{-3t}\cos 2t + 3e^{-3t}\sin 2t.$$

EXERCISES 6.1

Find the Laplace transforms of the following functions, where a, b, and c are real constants. For what values of s are the transforms defined?

1. $5t + 2$
2. $7t - 8$
3. $9t^2 - 7$
4. $16t^2 - 4t$
5. $t^2 + 8t - 16$
6. $27t^3 - 9t + 4$
7. $\dfrac{t^3}{8} + \dfrac{t^2}{4} + \dfrac{t}{2} + 1$
8. $\dfrac{t^5}{120} + \dfrac{t^2}{6} + 1$
9. $at + b$
10. $at^2 + bt + c$
11. e^{5t+2}
12. e^{7t-8}
13. $e^{t/2}$
14. $e^{-t/3}$
15. $e^{-t-1/2}$
16. e^{at+b}
17. $\sin (3t)$
18. $\sin \dfrac{t}{2}$
19. $\cos (7t)$
20. $\cos (-t/3)$
21. $\sin (5t + 2)$
22. $\cos (7t - 8)$
23. $\cos (at + b)$
24. $\sin (at + b)$
25. $\cosh (t/2)$
26. $\sinh (-t/3)$
27. $\cosh (5t - 2)$
28. $\sinh (7t + 8)$
29. $\sinh (at + b)$
30. $\cosh (at + b)$
31. te^t
32. $t^2 e^{2t}$
33. $(t^3 - 1)e^{-t}$
34. $e^{3t}(t^2 + t)$
35. $e^t \sin t$
36. $e^{-t} \sin 2t$

37. $e^{4t}(\cos 2t)$　　　　**38.** $e^{-t}\sinh 2t$

39. $e^{-t}(\sin t + \cos t)$　　　**40.** $e^{2t}(t + \cosh t)$

41. Recall [Eq. (3) in Section 3.5] that $e^{iat} = \cos at + i\sin at$.

　　a) Show that $\mathcal{L}\{e^{iat}\} = \dfrac{1}{s - ia}$.

　　b) Show that $\dfrac{1}{s - ia} = \dfrac{s + ia}{s^2 + a^2}$.

　　c) Use parts (a) and (b) to derive (without integration by parts) the formulas for $\mathcal{L}\{\sin at\}$ and $\mathcal{L}\{\cos at\}$. (*Hint*: Equate real and imaginary parts.)

In Exercises 42 through 55, find $f(t)$ where $F(s) = \mathcal{L}\{f(t)\}$ is given. If necessary, complete the square in the denominator.

42. $\dfrac{7}{s^2}$

43. $\dfrac{18}{s^3} + \dfrac{7}{s}$

44. $\dfrac{a_1}{s} + \dfrac{a_2}{s^2} + \cdots + \dfrac{a_{n+1}}{s^{n+1}}$

45. $\dfrac{s + 1}{s^2 + 1}$

46. $\dfrac{7}{s - 3}$

47. $\dfrac{s - 2}{s^2 - 2}$

48. $\dfrac{s - 2}{s^2 + 3}$

49. $\dfrac{1}{(s - 1)^2}$

50. $\dfrac{1}{s^2 + 2s + 2}$

51. $\dfrac{3}{s^2 + 4s + 9}$

52. $\dfrac{s + 12}{s^2 + 10s + 35}$

53. $\dfrac{2s - 1}{s^2 + 2s + 8}$

54. $\dfrac{7s - 8}{s^2 + 9s + 25}$

55. $\dfrac{cs + d}{s^2 + 2as + b}$　　$\begin{array}{l} b > a^2 > 0; \\ a, b, c, d \text{ are real} \end{array}$

In Exercises 56 through 61, express each given hyperbolic function in terms of exponentials and apply the first shifting theorem to show the following.

56. $\mathcal{L}\{\cosh^2 at\} = \dfrac{s^2 - 2a^2}{s(s^2 - 4a^2)}$

57. $\mathcal{L}\{\sinh^2 at\} = \dfrac{2a^2}{s(s^2 - 4a^2)}$

58. $\mathcal{L}\{\cosh at \sin at\} = \dfrac{a(s^2 + 2a^2)}{s^4 + 4a^4}$

59. $\mathcal{L}\{\cosh at \cos at\} = \dfrac{s^3}{s^4 + 4a^4}$

60. $\mathcal{L}\{\sinh at \sin at\} = \dfrac{2a^2 s}{s^4 + 4a^4}$

61. $\mathcal{L}\{\sinh at \cos at\} = \dfrac{a(s^2 - 2a^2)}{s^4 + 4a^4}$

Using the method above, find the Laplace transforms in Exercises 62 through 67.

62. $\mathcal{L}\{\cosh at \cosh bt\}$　　**63.** $\mathcal{L}\{\sinh at \sinh bt\}$

64. $\mathcal{L}\{\cosh at \sin bt\}$　　**65.** $\mathcal{L}\{\cosh at \cos bt\}$

66. $\mathcal{L}\{\sinh at \sin bt\}$　　**67.** $\mathcal{L}\{\sinh at \cos bt\}$

68. Suppose that $F(s) = \mathcal{L}\{f(t)\}$ exists for $s > a$. Show that

$$\mathcal{L}\{tf(t)\} = -F'(s), \quad \text{for} \quad s > a. \qquad \textbf{(16)}$$

[*Hint*: Assume that you can interchange the derivative and integral on the right-hand side of Eq. (16).]

69. Use Eq. (16) to show that

$$\mathcal{L}\{t^n f(t)\} = (-1)^n \frac{d^n}{ds^n} F(s), \quad \text{for} \quad s > a. \qquad \textbf{(17)}$$

Use Eqs. (16) and (17) to compute the Laplace transform of the functions given in Exercises 70 through 78. Assume a and b are real.

70. te^t　　　　　　　**71.** $t^3 e^{-t}$

72. $t \sin t$　　　　　　**73.** $t^2 \cos 3t$

74. $te^t \sin t$　　　　　**75.** $te^{at} \cos bt$

76. $te^{at} \sin bt$　　　　**77.** $3te^{-t} \cosh t$

78. $te^{-t} \sinh 2t$

79. Suppose that $f(t) = \mathcal{L}^{-1}\{F(s)\}$ and that $g(t) =$

$\mathcal{L}^{-1}\{G(s)\}$. Prove that

$$\alpha f(t) + \beta g(t) = \mathcal{L}^{-1}\{\alpha F(s) + \beta G(s)\},$$

where α and β are any constants. This property is called the *linearity property* of the inverse Laplace transform.

*80. Let $\sum_{n=1}^{\infty} f_n(t)$ be a uniformly convergent series of functions, each of which has a Laplace transform defined for $s \geq a$ (that is, $\mathcal{L}\{f_n(t)\}$ exists for $s \geq a$). Prove that

$$f(t) = \sum_{n=1}^{\infty} f_n(t)$$

has a Laplace transform for $s \geq a$ defined by

$$\mathcal{L}\{f(t)\} = \sum_{n=1}^{\infty} \mathcal{L}\{f_n(t)\}.$$

81. The *gamma function* is defined by

$$\Gamma(x) = \int_0^{\infty} e^{-u} u^{x-1} \, du, \quad x > 0.$$

a) Show that $\Gamma(x + 1) = \int_0^{\infty} e^{-u} u^x \, dx$.

b) By integrating by parts, show that
$$\Gamma(x + 1) = x\Gamma(x).$$

c) Show that $\Gamma(1) = 1$.

d) Using the results of parts (b) and (c), show that if n is a positive integer, then
$$\Gamma(n + 1) = n!.$$

e) By making the substitution $u = st$ in part (a), show that
$$\mathcal{L}\{t^x\} = \frac{\Gamma(x + 1)}{s^{x+1}}, \quad s > 0, \quad x > -1.$$

82. It can be shown that $\Gamma(1/2) = \sqrt{\pi}$. Use this fact and the results of Exercise 81 to compute:

a) $\mathcal{L}\left\{\dfrac{1}{\sqrt{t}}\right\}$;   b) $\mathcal{L}\{\sqrt{t}\}$;

c) $\mathcal{L}\{t^{5/2}\}$.

6.2 SOLVING INITIAL VALUE PROBLEMS BY LAPLACE TRANSFORM METHODS

In this section we will show how the theory developed in Section 6.1 can be applied to solve linear initial value problems. We will see that the Laplace transform converts linear initial value problems with constant coefficients into algebraic equations whose solution is the Laplace transform of the solution to the initial value problem.

The most important property of Laplace transforms for solving differential equations concerns the transform of the derivative of a function $f(t)$. We prove below that differentiation of $f(t)$ roughly corresponds to multiplication of the transform by s.

Theorem 1   *Differentiation property.* Let $f(t)$ satisfy the condition

$$|f(t)| \leq Me^{at} \tag{1}$$

for $t \geq T$, for fixed nonnegative constants a, M, and T, and suppose that $f'(t)$ is piecewise continuous for $t \geq 0$. Then the Laplace transform of $f'(t)$ exists for all $s > a$, and

$$\boxed{\mathcal{L}\{f'(t)\} = s\mathcal{L}\{f(t)\} - f(0).} \tag{2}$$

Proof   Since f is differentiable, it is also continuous, hence satisfies the conditions of the existence theorem (1) in Section 6.1, and has a Laplace transform.

Suppose, first, that $f'(t)$ is continuous on $t \geqslant 0$. Then integrating the definition of $\mathcal{L}\{f'(t)\}$ by parts, we set $u = e^{-st}$, $dv = f'(t)\,dt$ so that $du = -se^{-st}\,dt$, $v = f(t)$, and

$$\mathcal{L}\{f'(t)\} = \int_0^\infty e^{-st} f'(t)\,dt = e^{-st} f(t) \Big|_0^\infty + s \int_0^\infty e^{-st} f(t)\,dt. \qquad (3)$$

Since $f(t)$ satisfies Eq. (1), the first term on the right-hand side in Eq. (3) vanishes at the upper limit when $s > a$, and by definition we obtain $\mathcal{L}\{f'\} = s\mathcal{L}\{f\} - f(0)$. When $f'(t)$ is piecewise continuous, the proof is similar. We simply break up the range of integration into parts on each of which $f'(t)$ is continuous, and integrate by parts as in Eq. (3). All first terms will cancel out or vanish except $-f(0)$, and the second terms will combine to yield $s\mathcal{L}\{f\}$. ∎

Theorem 1 may be extended to apply to piecewise continuous functions $f(t)$ (see Exercise 50 at the end of this section).

Equation (2) may be applied repeatedly to obtain the Laplace transform of higher-order derivatives:

$$\mathcal{L}\{f''\} = s\mathcal{L}\{f'\} - f'(0) = s[s\mathcal{L}\{f\} - f(0)] - f'(0)$$

or

$$\boxed{\mathcal{L}\{f''\} = s^2 \mathcal{L}\{f\} - sf(0) - f'(0).} \qquad (4)$$

Similarly,

$$\mathcal{L}\{f'''\} = s^3 \mathcal{L}\{f\} - s^2 f(0) - sf'(0) - f''(0),$$

leading by induction to the following extension of Theorem 1.

Theorem 2   Let $f^{(k)}(t)$ satisfy Eq. (1) for $k = 0, 1, 2, \ldots, n - 1$ and suppose that $f^{(n)}(t)$ is piecewise continuous on $t \geqslant 0$. Then $\mathcal{L}\{f^{(n)}(t)\}$ exists and is given by

$$\boxed{\mathcal{L}\{f^{(n)}(t)\} = s^n \mathcal{L}\{f\} - s^{n-1} f(0) - s^{n-2} f'(0) - \cdots - f^{(n-1)}(0).} \qquad (5)$$

Theorems 1 and 2 are important, since they are used to reduce the Laplace transform of a differential equation into an equation involving only the transform of the solution. Several such applications will be considered in this section. However, these theorems are also useful in determining the transforms of certain functions.

Example 1   Compute $\mathcal{L}\{\sin^2 at\}$.

Let $f(t) = \sin^2 at$. Then

$$f'(t) = 2a \sin at \cos at = a \sin 2at,$$

so

$$\frac{2a^2}{s^2 + 4a^2} = \mathscr{L}\{f'\} = s\mathscr{L}\{f\} - f(0).$$

Since $f(0) = 0$, it follows that

$$\mathscr{L}\{\sin^2 at\} = \frac{2a^2}{s(s^2 + 4a^2)}, \quad s > 0.$$

Example 2   Compute $\mathscr{L}\{t \sin at\}$.

Suppose that $f(t) = t \sin at$. Then

$$f'(t) = \sin at + at \cos at, \quad f''(t) = 2a \cos at - a^2 t \sin at.$$

Thus, since $f(0) = f'(0) = 0$,

$$2a\mathscr{L}\{\cos at\} - a^2\mathscr{L}\{f(t)\} = \mathscr{L}\{f''\} = s^2\mathscr{L}\{f\},$$

so that

$$(s^2 + a^2)\mathscr{L}\{f\} = 2a\mathscr{L}\{\cos at\} = \frac{2as}{s^2 + a^2}$$

or

$$\mathscr{L}\{f(t)\} = \frac{2as}{(s^2 + a^2)^2}, \quad s > 0.$$

We now apply Theorems 1 and 2 to solve initial value problems. In what follows, we will take Laplace transforms without worrying about their existence. Any solution so obtained must be checked by substitution into the original equation.

Example 3   Find the solution of the initial value problem

$$y'' - 4y = 0, \quad y(0) = 1, \quad y'(0) = 2. \tag{6}$$

Taking the Laplace transform of both sides of the differential equation in (6) and using the differentiation property, we transform Eq. (6) into the algebraic equation

$$[s^2\mathscr{L}\{y\} - sy(0) - y'(0)] - 4\mathscr{L}\{y\} = [s^2\mathscr{L}\{y\} - s - 2] - 4\mathscr{L}\{y\} = 0,$$

so that

$$\mathscr{L}\{y\} = \frac{s + 2}{s^2 - 4} = \frac{1}{s - 2}.$$

Thus, by Table 1 in Section 6.1, we have

$$y(t) = e^{2t}$$

which satisfies all the conditions in Eq. (6).

Example 4 Solve

$$y'' + 4y = 0, \quad y(0) = 1, \quad y'(0) = 2. \tag{7}$$

Using the differentiation property, we obtain

$$s^2\mathscr{L}\{y\} - sy(0) - y'(0) + 4\mathscr{L}\{y\} = s^2\mathscr{L}\{y\} - s - 2 + 4\mathscr{L}\{y\} = 0.$$

Solving for $\mathscr{L}\{y\}$, we have

$$\mathscr{L}\{y\} = \frac{s + 2}{s^2 + 4} = \left(\frac{s}{s^2 + 4}\right) + \left(\frac{2}{s^2 + 4}\right).$$

By reference to Table 1 in Section 6.1, we find that

$$y(t) = \cos 2t + \sin 2t,$$

which can readily be verified to be the solution of Eq. (7). In calculating the inverse transform, we used the linearity of $\mathscr{L}^{-1}$ (see Exercise 79 in Section 6.1).

This example indicates the necessity of writing $\mathscr{L}\{y\}$ as a linear combination of terms for which the inverse Laplace transforms are known.

Example 5 Find the solution of the initial value problem

$$y'' - 3y' + 2y = 4t - 6, \quad y(0) = 1, \quad y'(0) = 3. \tag{8}$$

Taking the Laplace transform of both sides and using the differentiation property we have from Table 1 in Section 6.1

$$[s^2\mathscr{L}\{y\} - s - 3] - 3[s\mathscr{L}\{y\} - 1] + 2\mathscr{L}\{y\} = \frac{4}{s^2} - \frac{6}{s},$$

so that

$$(s^2 - 3s + 2)\mathscr{L}\{y\} = s + \frac{4}{s^2} - \frac{6}{s} = \frac{s^3 - 6s + 4}{s^2}.$$

Hence, factoring the numerator, we obtain

$$\mathscr{L}\{y\} = \frac{s^3 - 6s + 4}{s^2(s^2 - 3s + 2)}$$

$$= \frac{(s - 2)(s^2 + 2s - 2)}{s^2(s - 2)(s - 1)} = \frac{s^2 + 2s - 2}{s^2(s - 1)}.$$

But

$$\frac{s^2 + 2s - 2}{s^2(s - 1)} = \frac{s^2}{s^2(s - 1)} + \frac{2s - 2}{s^2(s - 1)} = \frac{1}{s - 1} + \frac{2}{s^2},$$

so that

$$\mathcal{L}\{y\} = \frac{1}{s-1} + \frac{2}{s^2}.$$

Using Table 1 in Section 6.1, we obtain the solution

$$y = e^t + 2t$$

to the initial value problem in Eq. (8).

We now discuss the most general second-order linear initial value problem with constant coefficients. Suppose that we wish to solve the nonhomogeneous differential equation with constant coefficients

$$y'' + ay' + by = f(t), \quad y(0) = y_0, \quad y'(0) = y_1. \tag{9}$$

The general existence–uniqueness theorem (Theorem 1 in Section 3.1) states that the initial value problem (9) will have a unique solution if $f(t)$ is continuous. Assuming this is the case, and taking the Laplace transforms of both sides, we obtain

$$\mathcal{L}\{y''\} + a\mathcal{L}\{y'\} + b\mathcal{L}\{y\} = \mathcal{L}\{f(t)\}.$$

Now by Theorems 1 and 2 (differentiation properties) we have

$$[s^2\mathcal{L}\{y\} - sy(0) - y'(0)] + a[s\mathcal{L}\{y\} - y(0)] + b\mathcal{L}\{y\} = \mathcal{L}\{f(t)\}.$$

Then

$$[s^2 + as + b]\mathcal{L}\{y\} - [sy(0) + ay(0) + y'(0)] = \mathcal{L}\{f(t)\},$$

so that

$$\mathcal{L}\{y\} = \frac{(s+a)y(0) + y'(0) + \mathcal{L}\{f(t)\}}{s^2 + as + b}. \tag{10}$$

Three facts are evident from Eq. (10):

1. Initial conditions must be given.

2. The function $f(t)$ must have a Laplace transform.

3. We must be able to find $\mathcal{L}^{-1}$ of the right-hand side.

Thus Laplace transform methods are primarily intended for the solution of linear initial value problems with constant coefficients.

It should be clear that the major difficulty in solving problem (9) lies in finding the inverse transform of the right-hand side of Eq. (10). There is a general formula that provides the solution as an integral, but some knowledge of complex variable theory is required to take full advantage of this formula. Fortunately, many of the transforms you will encounter in solving initial value problems can be inverted using techniques from calculus. We illustrate with some examples.

Example 6   Solve

$$y'' - 5y' + 4y = e^{2t}, \quad y(0) = 1, \quad y'(0) = 0.$$

Making use of the differentiation property and Table 1 in Section 6.1, we have

$$[s^2 \mathscr{L}\{y\} - sy(0) - y'(0)] - 5[s\mathscr{L}\{y\} - y(0)] + 4\mathscr{L}\{y\} = \mathscr{L}\{e^{2t}\}$$

or

$$[s^2 \mathscr{L}\{y\} - s] - 5[s\mathscr{L}\{y\} - 1] + 4\mathscr{L}\{y\} = \frac{1}{s - 2},$$

so that

$$(s^2 - 5s + 4)\mathscr{L}\{y\} = s - 5 + \frac{1}{s - 2} = \frac{s^2 - 7s + 11}{s - 2}.$$

Then

$$\mathscr{L}\{y\} = \frac{s^2 - 7s + 11}{(s - 2)(s^2 - 5s + 4)} = \frac{s^2 - 7s + 11}{(s - 2)(s - 1)(s - 4)}. \tag{11}$$

At this point we pause. Remember that when you studied techniques of integration in calculus, you integrated functions like the right-hand side of Eq. (11) by using the method of *partial fractions*. This method is useful here. We seek constants A, B, and C such that

$$\frac{A}{s - 2} + \frac{B}{s - 1} + \frac{C}{s - 4} = \frac{s^2 - 7s + 11}{(s - 2)(s - 1)(s - 4)}. \tag{12}$$

Why? Because we know that $\mathscr{L}^{-1}\{1/(s - 2)\} = e^{2t}$ so that $\mathscr{L}^{-1}\{A/(s - 2)\} = Ae^{2t}$, and so on.

There is an easy method for finding these constants:

$$A = \frac{s^2 - 7s + 11}{(s - 1)(s - 4)}\bigg|_{s=2} = -\frac{1}{2}; \quad B = \frac{s^2 - 7s + 11}{(s - 2)(s - 4)}\bigg|_{s=1} = \frac{5}{3};$$

$$C = \frac{s^2 - 7s + 11}{(s - 2)(s - 1)}\bigg|_{s=4} = -\frac{1}{6}.$$

Observe that we eliminate the denominator $(s - a)$ of each term on the left-hand side of Eq. (12) from the right-hand side of Eq. (12), and evaluate the resulting equation at $s = a$ to obtain the desired constant.

To understand why this procedure works, let us multiply both sides of Eq. (12) by $(s - 2)$. Then we have

$$A + (s - 2)\left[\frac{B}{s - 1} + \frac{C}{s - 4}\right] = \frac{s^2 - 7s + 11}{(s - 1)(s - 4)}. \tag{13}$$

Setting $s = 2$ on both sides eliminates all but the constant A on the left-hand side of Eq. (13), and therefore

$$A = \left.\frac{s^2 - 7s + 11}{(s-1)(s-4)}\right|_{s=2}.$$

Returning to our problem, we see that

$$\mathcal{L}\{y\} = \frac{(-\frac{1}{2})}{s-2} + \frac{(\frac{5}{3})}{s-1} + \frac{(-\frac{1}{6})}{s-4},$$

which implies, according to Table 1 in Section 6.1, that

$$y(t) = -\frac{e^{2t}}{2} + \frac{5e^t}{3} - \frac{e^{4t}}{6}.$$

Example 7   Solve

$$y'' + 2y' + 2y = t, \quad y(0) = y'(0) = 1.$$

Using the differentiation property, we obtain

$$[s^2\mathcal{L}\{y\} - s - 1] + 2[s\mathcal{L}\{y\} - 1] + 2\mathcal{L}\{y\} = \frac{1}{s^2},$$

or

$$(s^2 + 2s + 2)\mathcal{L}\{y\} = \frac{1}{s^2} + s + 3 = \frac{s^3 + 3s^2 + 1}{s^2}$$

and

$$\mathcal{L}\{y\} = \frac{s^3 + 3s^2 + 1}{s^2(s^2 + 2s + 2)}. \tag{14}$$

The term $s^2 + 2s + 2$ can't be factored [since $2^2 - 4(1)(2) = -4 < 0$], so we write the right-hand side of Eq. (14) as

$$\frac{s^3 + 3s^2 + 1}{s^2(s^2 + 2s + 2)} = \frac{As + B}{s^2 + 2s + 2} + \frac{C}{s} + \frac{D}{s^2}. \tag{15}$$

Why do we do this? Because

$$\frac{s+1}{s^2 + 2s + 2} = \frac{s+1}{(s+1)^2 + 1},$$

so that

$$\mathcal{L}^{-1}\left\{\frac{s+1}{s^2 + 2s + 1}\right\} = \mathcal{L}^{-1}\left\{\frac{s+1}{(s+1)^2 + 1}\right\} = e^{-t}\cos t$$

by Table 2 in Section 6.1 as a consequence of the first shifting theorem. Similarly,

$$\mathcal{L}^{-1}\left\{\frac{1}{(s+1)^2 + 1}\right\} = e^{-t}\sin t.$$

Also, by Table 1 in Section 6.1,

$$\mathscr{L}^{-1}\left\{\frac{1}{s}\right\} = 1 \quad \text{and} \quad \mathscr{L}^{-1}\left\{\frac{1}{s^2}\right\} = t.$$

There are "tricks" for finding the constants A, B, C, and D in Eq. (15), but these are more complicated than the method we used in Example 6. We can find these constants directly by combining terms:

$$\frac{(As + B)s^2 + C(s^2 + 2s + 2)s + D(s^2 + 2s + 2)}{s^2(s^2 + 2s + 1)} = \frac{s^3 + 3s^2 + 1}{s^2(s^2 + 2s + 2)},$$

so that, equating coefficients of like powers of s, we obtain:

$$A \quad + \quad C + \qquad = 1 \quad \text{(these are the coefficients of } s^3\text{);}$$
$$B + 2C + \quad D = 3 \quad \text{(these are the coefficients of } s^2\text{);}$$
$$2C + 2D = 0 \quad \text{(these are the coefficients of } s\text{);}$$
$$2D = 1 \quad \text{(these are the constant terms).}$$

From the last equation we see that $D = \frac{1}{2}$, so working backward, we obtain $C = -\frac{1}{2}$, $B = \frac{7}{2}$, and $A = \frac{3}{2}$. Then

$$y = \mathscr{L}^{-1}\left\{\frac{s^3 + 3s^2 + 1}{s^2(s^2 + 2s + 2)}\right\}$$

$$= \mathscr{L}^{-1}\left\{\frac{\frac{3}{2}s + \frac{7}{2}}{s^2 + 2s + 2} + \frac{(-\frac{1}{2})}{s} + \frac{(\frac{1}{2})}{s^2}\right\}$$

$$= \mathscr{L}^{-1}\left\{\frac{(\frac{3}{2})(s + 1)}{(s + 1)^2 + 1} + \frac{2}{(s + 1)^2 + 1} + \frac{(-\frac{1}{2})}{s} + \frac{(\frac{1}{2})}{s^2}\right\}$$

or

$$y = \tfrac{3}{2}e^{-t}\cos t + 2e^{-t}\sin t - \tfrac{1}{2} + \tfrac{1}{2}t,$$

which is the solution to our differential equation.

The methods used in the last two equations apply to the problem of inverting a Laplace transform obtained in trying to solve an initial value problem with constant coefficients. In some special cases, we can use these techniques to solve linear problems with variable coefficients. First, however, we need to prove the identities that were stated in Exercises 68 and 69 in Section 6.1.

Consider the derivative

$$\frac{d}{ds}\mathscr{L}\{f(t)\} = \frac{d}{ds}\int_0^\infty e^{-st}f(t)\,dt. \tag{16}$$

If we reverse the order in which the operations of differentiation and integration are performed on the right-hand side of Eq. (16), we obtain

$$\frac{d}{ds}\mathscr{L}\{f(t)\} = \int_0^\infty \frac{d}{ds}e^{-st}f(t)\,dt = \int_0^\infty -te^{-st}f(t)\,dt = -\mathscr{L}\{tf(t)\}.$$

Hence

$$\mathscr{L}\{tf(t)\} = -\frac{d}{ds}\mathscr{L}\{f(t)\}, \tag{17}$$

and using Eq. (17) repeatedly, we obtain

$$\mathscr{L}\{t^n f(t)\} = -\frac{d}{ds}\mathscr{L}\{t^{n-1}f(t)\} = (-1)^2\frac{d^2}{ds^2}\mathscr{L}\{t^{n-2}f(t)\}$$

$$= \cdots = (-1)^n \frac{d^n}{ds^n}\mathscr{L}\{f(t)\}. \tag{18}$$

Of course, it may not be legitimate to interchange the order of differentiation and integration in Eq. (16) (pathological examples do exist), but if the method succeeds in providing a correct solution to our problem, we need not be concerned. This lack of rigor reemphasizes the need of checking the final solution when solving problems by Laplace transform techniques.

The following example illustrates how Eqs. (17) and (18) can be used in conjunction with the differentiation property to solve some initial value problems with variable coefficients.

Example 8 Solve the equation with variable coefficients

$$ty'' - ty' - y = 0, \quad y(0) = 0, \quad y'(0) = 3.$$

If we let $Y(s) = \mathscr{L}\{y(t)\}$, then by the differentiation property and Eq. (17)

$$\mathscr{L}\{ty''\} = -\frac{d}{ds}\mathscr{L}\{y''\} = -\frac{d}{ds}\{s^2 Y(s) - sy(0) - y'(0)\}$$

$$= -s^2 Y' - 2sY$$

and

$$\mathscr{L}\{ty'\} = -\frac{d}{ds}\mathscr{L}\{y'\} = -\frac{d}{ds}\{sY - y(0)\} = -sY' - Y.$$

Substituting these expressions into the Laplace transform of the original equation yields

$$-s^2 Y' - 2sY + sY' + Y - Y = 0.$$

Rearranging and canceling terms, we have

$$(s^2 - s)Y' + 2sY = 0.$$

We now divide both sides by $s^2 - s = s(s-1)$ to obtain

$$Y' + \frac{2}{s-1}Y = 0.$$

Separating variables, we have

$$\frac{dY}{Y} = -\frac{2}{s-1}\,ds,$$

and an integration yields

$$\ln Y = -2\ln(s-1) + c$$

or

$$Y(s) = \frac{c}{(s-1)^2}.$$

Thus, by Table 2 in Section 6.1,

$$y(t) = cte^t.$$

Note that $y(0) = 0$. To find c, we differentiate and use the second initial condition to obtain

$$3 = y'(0) = c(t+1)e^t\Big|_{t=0} = c.$$

Thus, the unique solution to the initial value problem is given by

$$y(t) = 3te^t.$$

We caution the reader not to expect to be able to solve all variable coefficient equations by this method. It will work only when

a)   the coefficients $a_i(t)$ are polynomials in t,

b)   the differential equation involving $Y(s)$ can be solved, and

c)   the inverse transform of $Y(s)$ can be found.

It is rare that all these conditions can be met (see Exercise 49).

Example 9   In Section 3.9 we applied Kirchhoff's law to obtain [see Eq. (1)] the following differential equation relating the current (I), charge (Q), resistance (R), inductance (L), and capacitance (C) of the electric circuit shown in Fig. 2:

$$L\frac{dI}{dt} + RI + \frac{Q}{C} = E. \tag{19}$$

We then differentiated Eq. (19) using the fact that

$$\frac{dQ}{dt} = I \tag{20}$$

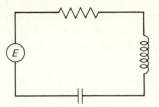

Figure 2

and, assuming that E was constant, obtained a homogeneous, second-order equation that we then solved. Now we make our model more realistic by assuming that the electromotive force (emf) $E = E(t)$ is a nonconstant function of time. Replacing each I in Eq. (19) by the identity in Eq. (20), we obtain

$$L\frac{dQ^2}{dt^2} + R\frac{dQ}{dt} + \frac{Q}{C} = E(t). \tag{21}$$

If $Q(0) = a$ and $Q'(0) = I(0) = b$, we can solve Eq. (21) by Laplace transform methods and use that solution to point out a feature common to many physical and biological systems.

We set $\hat{Q}(s) = \mathscr{L}\{Q(t)\}$, $\hat{E}(s) = \mathscr{L}\{E(t)\}$, and take the transform of both sides of Eq. (21), using the differentiation property, to obtain

$$L[s^2\hat{Q}(s) - as - b] + R[s\hat{Q}(s) - a] + \frac{1}{C}\hat{Q}(s) = \hat{E}(s),$$

or

$$\hat{Q}(s)\left[Ls^2 + Rs + \frac{1}{C}\right] = [Las + Lb + Ra] + \hat{E}(s). \tag{22}$$

Now let $U(s) = Ls^2 + Rs + 1/C$ and $V(s) = Las + Lb + Ra$ and rewrite Eq. (22) as

$$\hat{Q}(s) = \frac{\hat{E}(s) + V(s)}{U(s)} = \hat{E}(s)\left[\frac{1 + V(s)/\hat{E}(s)}{U(s)}\right]. \tag{23}$$

Defining $T(s) = (1 + V/\hat{E})/U$, we can rewrite Eq. (23) in the form

$$\hat{Q}(s) = \hat{E}(s)T(s). \tag{24}$$

Engineers like to talk about "black boxes." In a black box, something goes in (the input) and is transformed into something that comes out (the output). In the system under discussion we have the "black-box" setup shown in Fig. 3. In Eq. (24), we have a relationship between the transforms of the input and the output. The function $T(s)$ is called a *transfer*

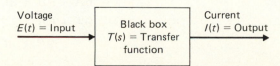

Figure 3

function and describes, precisely, the inner workings of the black box. It tells us exactly what we get out in terms of what we put in and gives us a simple equation relating input to output.

Example 10 Suppose the circuit in Fig. 2 is connected at $t = 0$ to the emf $E(t) = \cos t$, so that $Q(0) = 0$ and $I(0) = 0$. Assume that $L = 1$ henry, $R = 6$ ohms, and $C = \frac{1}{9}$ farad. Then we have the initial value problem

$$\frac{dI}{dt} + 6I + 9Q = \cos t, \quad Q(0) = 0, \quad I(0) = 0.$$

Using the identity (20) we obtain

$$\frac{d^2Q}{dt^2} + 6\frac{dQ}{dt} + 9Q = \cos t, \quad Q(0) = Q'(0) = 0, \tag{25}$$

and if we use the differentiation property of Laplace transforms, Eq. (25) becomes

$$s^2\hat{Q} + 6s\hat{Q} + 9\hat{Q} = \frac{s}{s^2 + 1}$$

or

$$\hat{Q}(s) \cdot [s^2 + 6s + 9] = \frac{s}{s^2 + 1}. \tag{26}$$

Comparing Eqs. (22) and (26), we note that $U(s) = s^2 + 6s + 9 = (s + 3)^2$ and $V(s) = 0$, so that the transfer function $T(s) = 1/U(s)$. Solving for $\hat{Q}$ we have

$$\hat{Q}(s) = \frac{s}{s^2 + 1} \cdot \frac{1}{(s + 3)^2},$$

which we wish to write in partial fraction form:

$$\frac{s}{(s^2 + 1)(s + 3)^2} = \frac{As + B}{s^2 + 1} + \frac{C}{s + 3} + \frac{D}{(s + 3)^2}. \tag{27}$$

Getting the common divisor on the right-hand side of Eq. (27), we have

$$s = (As + B)(s + 3)^2 + C(s + 3)(s^2 + 1) + D(s^2 + 1)$$

$$= (A + C)s^3 + (6A + B + 3C + D)s^2 + (9A + 6B + C)s$$
$$+ (9B + 3C + D).$$

Equating like powers of s on both sides of the equation, we obtain the system

$$\begin{aligned} A \qquad + C \qquad\ &= 0, \\ 6A + B + 3C + D &= 0, \\ 9A + 6B + C \qquad\ &= 1, \\ 9B + 3C + D &= 0. \end{aligned} \tag{28}$$

Subtracting the first equation from the third and the fourth from the second, we get

$$8A + 6B = 1,$$
$$6A - 8B = 0,$$

from which we obtain $A = 0.08$, $B = 0.06$, $C = -0.08$, and $D = -0.3$. Hence

$$\hat{Q}(s) = \frac{0.08s}{s^2 + 1} + \frac{0.06}{s^2 + 1} - \frac{0.08}{s + 3} - \frac{0.3}{(s + 3)^2}$$

which, by Tables 1 and 2 in Section 6.1, yields

$$Q(t) = 0.08 \cos t + 0.06 \sin t - 0.08e^{-3t} - 0.3te^{-3t}. \tag{29}$$

Differentiating Eq. (29) we obtain the expression for the current:

$$I(t) = -0.08 \sin t + 0.06 \cos t - 0.06e^{-3t} + 0.9te^{-3t}.$$

There are many other situations that can be modeled using the abstract of a black box and an appropriate transfer function relating output to input.

The following brief list of Laplace transforms will be useful in doing the exercises.

$f(t)$	$\mathscr{L}\{f(t)\}$	$f(t)$	$\mathscr{L}\{f(t)\}$
c	$\dfrac{c}{s}$	e^{at}	$\dfrac{1}{(s - a)}$
t^n	$\dfrac{n!}{s^{n+1}}$	$e^{at}t^n$	$\dfrac{n!}{(s - a)^{n+1}}$
$\sin bt$	$\dfrac{b}{s^2 + b^2}$	$e^{at} \sin bt$	$\dfrac{b}{(s - a)^2 + b^2}$
$\cos bt$	$\dfrac{s}{s^2 + b^2}$	$e^{at} \cos bt$	$\dfrac{s - a}{(s - a)^2 + b^2}$
$\sinh bt$	$\dfrac{b}{s^2 - b^2}$	$e^{at} \sinh bt$	$\dfrac{b}{(s - a)^2 - b^2}$
$\cosh bt$	$\dfrac{s}{s^2 - b^2}$	$e^{at} \cosh bt$	$\dfrac{s - a}{(s - a)^2 - b^2}$

$$\mathscr{L}\{f'(t)\} = s\mathscr{L}\{f(t)\} - f(0), \quad \mathscr{L}\{f''(t)\} = s^2\mathscr{L}\{f(t)\} - sf(0) - f'(0)$$

EXERCISES 6.2

In Exercises 1 through 20, solve the given initial value problems.

1. $y'' + y = 0$, $y(0) = 1$, $y'(0) = 0$

2. $y'' + y' = 0$, $y(0) = 0$, $y'(0) = 1$

3. $y'' - a^2 y = 0$, $y(0) = A$, $y'(0) = B$

4. $y'' - ay' = 0$, $y(0) = 1$, $y'(0) = a$

5. $y'' + 2y' + 5y = 0$, $y(0) = y'(0) = 1$

6. $y'' - y' + y = 0$, $y(0) = y'(0) = 1$

7. $y'' - 4y' + 3y = 1$, $y(0) = 1$, $y'(0) = 4$

8. $y'' - 2y' - 3y = 5$, $y(0) = 0$, $y'(0) = 1$

9. $y'' - 9y = t$, $y(0) = 1$, $y'(0) = 2$

10. $y'' - 3y' - 4y = t^2$, $y(0) = 2$, $y'(0) = 1$

11. $y''' + y = 0$, $y(0) = y''(0) = 1$, $y'(0) = -1$

12. $y^{iv} - y = 0$, $y(0) = y''(0) = 1$, $y'(0) = y'''(0) = 0$

13. $y^{iv} - y = 0$, $y(0) = y''(0) = 0$, $y'(0) = y'''(0) = 1$

14. $y''' - 3y' - 2y = e^{2t}$, $y(0) = y'(0) = 0$, $y''(0) = 1$

15. $y'' + k^2 y = \cos kt$, $y(0) = 0$, $y'(0) = k$

16. $y'' + 4y = \cos t$, $y(0) = y'(0) = 0$

17. $y'' + a^2 y = \sin at$, $y(0) = a$, $y'(0) = a^2$

18. $y'' - y = te^t$, $y(0) = y'(0) = 1$

19. $y^{iv} - y = \cos t$, $y(0) = y''(0) = 1$, $y'(0) = y'''(0) = 0$

20. $y^{iv} - y = \sinh t$, $y(0) = y''(0) = 0$, $y'(0) = y'''(0) = 1$

In Exercises 21 through 29, find the Laplace transform of each function by using the differentiation property or Eq. (18).

21. $\cos^2 at$ 22. $t \cos at$

23. $t^2 \sin at$ 24. $t^2 \cos at$

25. $t \sin^2 t$ 26. $t \cos^2 t$

27. $t \sin^2 at$ 28. $t^2 \cos^2 3t$

29. $t^2 \sin^2 2t$

30. By reversing the order of integration, show that if $F(s) = \mathcal{L}\{f(t)\}$, then

$$\int_s^\infty F(s)\, ds = \mathcal{L}\left\{\frac{f(t)}{t}\right\}. \tag{30}$$

31. Let $g(t) = \int_0^t f(u)\, du$. Using calculus and the differentiation property (Theorem 1), show that:

*a) $g'(t) = f(t)$ at all points of continuity of $f(t)$;

b) $\mathcal{L}\{f(t)\} = s\mathcal{L}\{g(t)\} - g(0)$;

c) $g(0) = 0$.

Finally, using parts (b) and (c) conclude that

$$\mathcal{L}\left\{\int_0^t f(u)\, du\right\} = \frac{1}{s}\, \mathcal{L}\{f(t)\}. \tag{31}$$

In Exercises 32 through 44, use the results (30) and (31) of Exercises 30 and 31 to compute the Laplace transform of the given function.

32. $\dfrac{\cos t - 1}{t}$

33. $\dfrac{\sin t}{t}$

34. $\dfrac{\sin t}{t}$

35. $\dfrac{\sin 3t}{t}$

36. $\dfrac{\sinh kt}{t}$

37. $\dfrac{\sin kt}{t}$

38. $\dfrac{1 - \cos at}{t}$

39. $\dfrac{1 - \cosh at}{t}$

40. $\displaystyle\int_0^t \frac{\sin ku}{u}\, du$

41. $\displaystyle\int_0^t \frac{1 - \cos au}{u}\, du$

42. $\displaystyle\int_0^t \frac{1 - \cosh au}{u}\, du$

43. $\operatorname{erf}(t) = \dfrac{2}{\sqrt{\pi}} \displaystyle\int_0^t e^{-u^2}\, du$

44. $\dfrac{e^{-k^2/4t}}{\sqrt{\pi t}}$

Find the inverse Laplace transform of the functions

in Exercises 45 through 48. Use derivatives and integrals.

45. $\ln\left(1 + \dfrac{a^2}{s^2}\right)$ **46.** $\ln\dfrac{s-a}{s-b}$

47. $\arctan\dfrac{1}{s}$ **48.** $\dfrac{1}{s}\arctan\dfrac{1}{s}$

49. Consider the equation

$$y'' + t^2 y = 0, \quad y(0) = 0, \quad y'(0) = 1.$$

  a) Use the result of Exercise 41 to obtain a differential equation for $Y(s) = \mathcal{L}\{y(t)\}$.

  b) Solve the differential equation and find $Y(s)$. (Note that it is not possible to invert this transform by the methods we have discussed.)

*__50.__ Let $f(t)$ be continuous, except for a jump discontinuity at $t = a\,(>0)$, and let it satisfy all other conditions of Theorem 1. Prove that

$$\mathcal{L}\{f'(t)\} = s\mathcal{L}\{f(t)\} - f(0)$$
$$- e^{-as}[f(a+0) - f(a-0)],$$

where $f(a+0) = \lim_{h\to 0+} f(a+h)$ and $f(a-0) = \lim_{h\to 0-} f(a+h)$.

51. In Example 9, find $I(t)$ if $E(t) = \sin t$, $Q(0) = I(0) = 0$, $L = 2$ henrys, $R = 20$ ohms, and $C = 0.02$ farad.

52. Let $L = 1$ henry, $R = 100$ ohms, $C = 10^{-4}$ farad, and $E = 1000 \sin t$ volts in the circuit in Fig. 2. Suppose that no charge and current is initially present. Find the current and charge at all times t.

53. Let L, R, and C be as in Exercise 51 but let $E(t) = 10 \sin 10t$. If $Q(0) = I(0) = 0$, find $Q(t)$.

54. A 50-kg mass is suspended from a spring with spring constant 20 N/m. When the system is vibrating freely, the maximum displacement of each consecutive cycle decreases by 20 percent. Assume a force equal to $10 \cos \omega t$ N acts upon the system. Find the amplitude of the resultant steady-state motion if:

  a) $\omega = 8$ rad/s;   b) $\omega = 10$ rad/s;

  c) $\omega = 12$ rad/s;   d) $\omega = 14$ rad/s;

  e) $\omega = 18$ rad/s.

6.3 STEP FUNCTIONS AND IMPULSE FUNCTIONS

In Section 6.2 we saw how to solve linear differential equations in which the *forcing function* $f(t)$ was continuous. In a great number of applications, however, the forcing function is either a step function or an impulse function. We shall define these terms and show how to compute the Laplace transforms of these two important types of functions in this section. In Section 6.4 we will give some examples of differential equations with discontinuous forcing functions.

The following function, which is extremely important for practical applications (for example, as a unit impulse in a mechanical control system), is known as the *unit step function* or *Heaviside function*:

$$H(t - a) = \begin{cases} 0, & t < a, \\ 1, & t > a, \end{cases} \tag{1}$$

where a is any fixed constant. In particular, if $a = 0$, we have

$$H(t) = \begin{cases} 0, & t < 0, \\ 1, & t > 0. \end{cases} \tag{2}$$

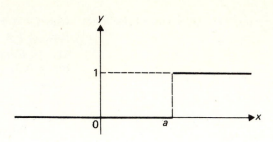

Figure 4

For $a \geqslant 0$ and $s > 0$, we obtain

$$\mathscr{L}\{H(t - a)\} = \int_0^\infty e^{-st}H(t - a)\, dt = \int_a^\infty e^{-st}\, dt = \frac{e^{-as}}{s}. \qquad (3)$$

A sketch of $H(t - a)$ is given in Fig. 4. Note that $H(t - a)$ has a jump discontinuity at $t = a$. In fact, $H(t - a)$ is not defined at $t = a$.

The following theorem shows that multiplying a function by a unit step function has the effect of multiplying its transform by an exponential function.

Theorem 1   *The Second Shifting Property of Laplace Transforms.* Let $a > 0$. Then

$$\mathscr{L}\{f(t - a)H(t - a)\} = e^{-as}\mathscr{L}\{f(t)\}. \qquad (4)$$

Proof   Using the definition and the substitution $x = t - a$, we find that

$$\mathscr{L}\{f(t - a)H(t - a)\} = \int_0^\infty e^{-st}f(t - a)H(t - a)\, dt = \int_a^\infty e^{-st}f(t - a)\, dt$$

$$= \int_0^\infty e^{-s(x+a)}f(x)\, dx = e^{-as}\mathscr{L}\{f(t)\}.$$

In this theorem, we are shifting the function a units to the right and truncating it at zero. ∎

Example 1 $\mathscr{L}\{\sin a(t - b)H(t - b)\} = e^{-bs}\mathscr{L}\{\sin at\} = ae^{-bs}/(s^2 + a^2).$

Example 2   Compute $\mathscr{L}\{f(t)\}$ when
$$f(t) = \begin{cases} e^t, & 0 \leqslant t < 2\pi, \\ e^t + \cos t, & t > 2\pi. \end{cases}$$

The function $f(t)$ has a jump discontinuity at $t = 2\pi$. We may write
$$f(t) = e^t + H(t - 2\pi)\cos(t - 2\pi),$$
since
$$H(t - 2\pi)\cos(t - 2\pi) = \begin{cases} 0, & \text{if } t < 2\pi, \\ \cos(t - 2\pi) = \cos t, & \text{if } t > 2\pi. \end{cases}$$

Thus, by the second shifting property (Theorem 1),

$$\mathcal{L}\{f(t)\} = \mathcal{L}\{e^t\} + e^{-2\pi s}\mathcal{L}\{\cos t\}$$

$$= \frac{1}{s} + \frac{se^{-2\pi s}}{1 + s^2}.$$

Example 3   Compute

$$\mathcal{L}^{-1}\left\{\frac{1 - e^{(-\pi s/2)}}{1 + s^2}\right\}.$$

Observe that

$$\mathcal{L}^{-1}\left\{\frac{1 - e^{(-\pi s/2)}}{1 + s^2}\right\} = \mathcal{L}^{-1}\left\{\frac{1}{1 + s^2}\right\} - \mathcal{L}^{-1}\left\{\frac{e^{(-\pi s/2)}}{1 + s^2}\right\}$$

$$= \sin t - H(t - \pi/2) \sin (t - \pi/2)$$

$$= \sin t + H(t - \pi/2) \cos t.$$

The unit step function can be used as a building block in the construction of other functions. For example,

$$f_1(t) = H(t - a) - H(t - b), \quad a < b, \tag{5}$$

is a square wave between a and b, whereas

$$f_2(t) = H(t - a) + H(t - 2a) + H(t - 3a), \quad a > 0,$$

yields a three-step staircase. (See Fig. 5.) By the linearity property, we obtain

$$\mathcal{L}\{f_1(t)\} = \frac{1}{s}(e^{-as} - e^{-bs}),$$

and

$$\mathcal{L}\{f_2(t)\} = \frac{1}{s}(e^{-as} + e^{-2as} + e^{-3as}).$$

Figure 5

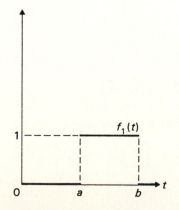
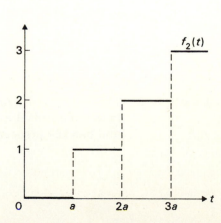

Example 4   Compute the Laplace transform of the infinite staircase

$$f(t) = H(t) + H(t - a) + H(t - 2a) + H(t - 3a) + \cdots, \quad a > 0. \quad \textbf{(6)}$$

Since $e^{-as} < 1$, if $as > 0$, we can use the formula for the sum of a geometric series

$$\sum_{n=0}^{\infty} x^n = 1 + x + x^2 + \cdots = \frac{1}{1 - x}, \quad |x| < 1. \quad \textbf{(7)}$$

Then, for $s > 0$, by Table 1 in Section 6.1,

$$\mathscr{L}\{f(t)\} = \frac{1}{s}(1 + e^{-as} + e^{-2as} + e^{-3as} + \cdots) = \frac{1}{s(1 - e^{-as})}. \quad \textbf{(8)}$$

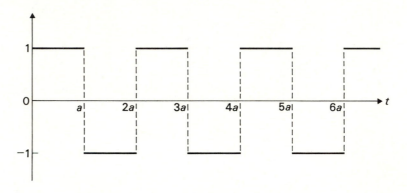

Figure 6

Example 5   Let $f(t)$ be the periodic square wave shown in Fig. 6. Then we can write $f(t)$ in the form

$$f(t) = H(t) - 2H(t - a) + 2H(t - 2a) - 2H(t - 3a) + \cdots,$$

from which it follows that

$$\mathscr{L}\{f(t)\} = \frac{1}{s}(1 - 2e^{-as} + 2e^{-2as} - 2e^{-3as} + \cdots)$$

$$= \frac{1}{s}\left(\frac{2}{1 + e^{-as}} - 1\right) = \frac{1 - e^{-as}}{s(1 + e^{-as})}.$$

Example 6   The *unit impulse function* (also called the *Dirac delta function*) $\delta(t - a)$ is loosely described as a "function" that is zero everywhere except at $t = a$ and has the property that

$$\int_{-\infty}^{\infty} \delta(t - a)\, dt = 1. \quad \textbf{(9)}$$

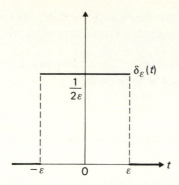

Figure 7

As an illustration, we describe the Dirac delta function for $a = 0$. For any $\varepsilon > 0$, consider the function (see Fig. 7)

$$\delta_\varepsilon(t) = \begin{cases} 1/2\varepsilon, & -\varepsilon < t < \varepsilon, \\ 0, & |t| > \varepsilon. \end{cases}$$

Clearly, $\delta_\varepsilon(t)$ is piecewise continuous and

$$\int_{-\infty}^{\infty} \delta_\varepsilon(t)\, dt = \int_{-\varepsilon}^{\varepsilon} \frac{1}{2\varepsilon}\, dt = 1.$$

Then $\delta(t)$ may be defined by

$$\delta(t) = \lim_{\varepsilon \to 0} \delta_\varepsilon(t).$$

Of course, $\delta(t)$ is not a function. However, because it is the limit of piecewise continuous functions, we may treat $\delta(t)$ as if it were a legitimate function. We shall not prove this fact here but shall nevertheless make use of it in all further discussions of the delta function.

Since $\delta(t - a)$ concentrates all its "mass" at $t = a$, we see that

$$H(t - a) = \int_{-\infty}^{t} \delta(u - a)\, du, \qquad (10)$$

since the integral in Eq. (10) is zero if $t < a$ and equals 1 when $t > a$. By the integration property, if $a \geqslant 0$,

$$\frac{1}{s}\mathcal{L}\{\delta(t - a)\} = \mathcal{L}\left\{ \int_0^t \delta(u - a)\, du \right\} = \mathcal{L}\{H(t - a)\} = \frac{e^{-as}}{s}.$$

Thus

$$\mathcal{L}\{\delta(t - a)\} = e^{-as}, \text{ for } a \geqslant 0 \quad \text{and} \quad s > 0. \qquad (11)$$

Before going further, we prove a result that is very useful for finding the Laplace transform of a wide variety of functions.

Theorem 2   *Periodicity Property of the Laplace Transform.* Let $f(t)$ be continuous in $[0, \omega]$ and periodic with period ω ($\omega > 0$), that is, $f(t + \omega) = f(t)$, for each $t \geq 0$. Then $f(t)$ has a Laplace transform

$$F(s) = \mathscr{L}\{f(t)\} = \frac{\int_0^\omega e^{-st}f(t)\, dt}{1 - e^{-\omega s}} \tag{12}$$

valid for every $s > 0$.

Proof   By definition,

$$F(s) = \int_0^\infty e^{-st}f(t)\, dt$$

$$= \int_0^\omega e^{-st}f(t)\, dt + \int_\omega^{2\omega} e^{-st}f(t)\, dt + \cdots$$

$$= \sum_{k=0}^\infty \int_{k\omega}^{(k+1)\omega} e^{-st}f(t)\, dt. \tag{13}$$

Now, making the substitution $u = t - k\omega$, we obtain

$$\int_{k\omega}^{(k+1)\omega} e^{-st}f(t)\, dt = \int_0^\omega e^{-s(u+k\omega)}f(u + k\omega)\, du$$

$$= e^{-sk\omega} \int_0^\omega e^{-su}f(u)\, du, \tag{14}$$

because of the periodicity of f. Thus, substituting Eq. (14) into Eq. (13) and using Eq. (7) with $x = e^{-s\omega}$, we have

$$F(s) = \sum_{k=0}^\infty e^{-sk\omega} \int_0^\omega e^{-su}f(u)\, du$$

$$= \left[\int_0^\omega e^{-su}f(u)\, du \right] \cdot \sum_{k=0}^\infty (e^{-\omega s})^k$$

$$= \frac{\int_0^\omega e^{-su}f(u)\, du}{1 - e^{-\omega s}}.$$

Note that if $s > 0$, then $\omega s > 0$ and $e^{-\omega s} < 1$ so that the use of formula (7) is valid. ∎

Example 7   Find the Laplace transform of the function

$$f(t) = |\sin at|, \quad a > 0.$$

Note that $f(t)$ has period $\omega = \pi/a$. By Theorem 2 we have

$$\mathcal{L}\{|\sin at|\} = \frac{\int_0^{\pi/a} e^{-st} \sin at \, dt}{1 - e^{-\pi s/a}},$$

since $|\sin at| = \sin at$ in $[0, \pi/a]$. Now, using Formula 50 of Appendix 1, we have

$$\int_0^{\pi/a} e^{-st} \sin at \, dt = \frac{e^{-st}}{s^2 + a^2} (-s \sin at - a \cos at) \Big|_0^{\pi/a}$$

$$= \frac{a(e^{-\pi s/a} + 1)}{s^2 + a^2},$$

so that

$$\mathcal{L}\{|\sin at|\} = \frac{a}{s^2 + a^2} \frac{1 + e^{-\pi s/a}}{1 - e^{-\pi s/a}},$$

which can be simplified by using hyperbolic functions to

$$\mathcal{L}\{|\sin at|\} = \frac{a}{s^2 + a^2} \coth\left(\frac{\pi s}{2a}\right).$$

Example 8   Solve the differential equation

$$y'' + 2y' + y = \delta(t - 1), \quad y(0) = 2, \quad y'(0) = 3.$$

Taking Laplace transforms and using Example 6, we obtain

$$[s^2 \mathcal{L}\{y\} - 2s - 3] + 2[s\mathcal{L}\{y\} - 2] + \mathcal{L}\{y\} = e^{-s}$$

or

$$(s^2 + 2s + 1)\mathcal{L}\{y\} = 2s + 7 + e^{-s}.$$

Hence, we get

$$\mathcal{L}\{y\} = \frac{2s + 7 + e^{-s}}{s^2 + 2s + 1} = \frac{2(s + 1)}{(s + 1)^2} + \frac{5}{(s + 1)^2} + \frac{e^{-s}}{(s + 1)^2}$$

$$= \frac{2}{(s + 1)} + \frac{5}{(s + 1)^2} + \frac{e^{-s}}{(s + 1)^2}.$$

Since $\mathcal{L}\{te^{-t}\} = (s + 1)^{-2}$, it follows from Theorem 1 that

$$\frac{e^{-s}}{(s + 1)^2} = e^{-s}\mathcal{L}\{te^{-t}\} = \mathcal{L}\{(t - 1)e^{-(t-1)}H(t - 1)\}.$$

Finally, the solution is

$$y(t) = 2e^{-t} + 5te^{-t} + (t - 1)e^{-(t-1)}H(t - 1)$$

$$= e^{-t}[2 + 5t + e(t - 1)H(t - 1)].$$

EXERCISES 6.3

In Exercises 1 through 8, use the second shifting theorem to show the following.

1. $\mathscr{L}\{tH(t-1)\} = e^{-s}\left(\dfrac{1}{s^2} + \dfrac{1}{s}\right)$

2. $\mathscr{L}\{t^2\,H(t-1)\} = e^{-s}\left(\dfrac{2}{s^3} + \dfrac{2}{s^2} + \dfrac{1}{s}\right)$

3. $\mathscr{L}\{e^t\,H(t-1)\} = \dfrac{e^{-(s-1)}}{s-1}$

4. $\mathscr{L}\{e^{at}\,H(t-b)\} = \dfrac{e^{-b(s-a)}}{s-a}$

5. $\mathscr{L}\left\{\sin t \cdot H\left(t-\dfrac{\pi}{2}\right)\right\} = \dfrac{se^{-\pi s/2}}{s^2+1}$

6. $\mathscr{L}\{\cos a(t-b)\,H(t-b)\} = \dfrac{e^{-bs}s}{s^2+a^2}$

7. $\mathscr{L}\{\sinh a(t-b)\,H(t-b)\} = \dfrac{e^{-bs}a}{s^2-a^2}$

8. $\mathscr{L}\{\cosh a(t-b)\,H(t-b)\} = \dfrac{e^{-bs}s}{s^2-a^2}$

In Exercises 9 through 11, represent the graphed functions in terms of unit step functions and find their respective Laplace transform.

9.

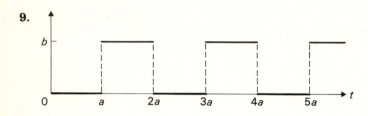

10.

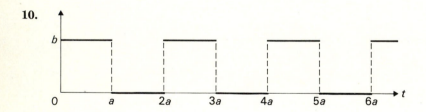

11.

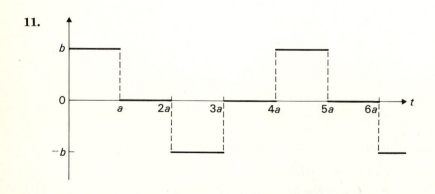

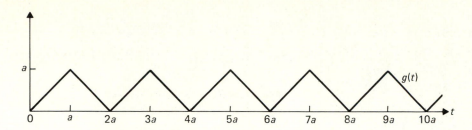

12. Let $g(t)$ be the sawtooth function shown above.

    a) Show that $g'(t)$ is piecewise continuous and that $g'(t) = f(t)$, where f is the step function of Example 5.

    b) Use the differentiation property to compute $\mathcal{L}\{g(t)\}$.

In Exercises 13 through 15, use the methods of Exercise 12 to find the Laplace transform of the given functions.

13.

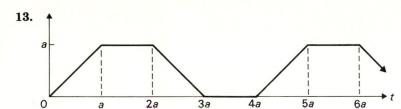

14.

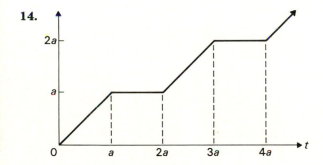

15.

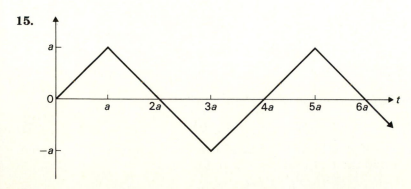

16. Let $f(t) = \begin{cases} \sin t, & t < 4\pi, \\ \sin t + \cos t, & t > 4\pi. \end{cases}$

Compute $\mathcal{L}\{f(t)\}$.

17. Let $f(t) = \begin{cases} \cos t, & t < 3\pi/2, \\ \cos t + \sin t, & t > 3\pi/2. \end{cases}$

Compute $\mathcal{L}\{f(t)\}$.

In Exercises 18 through 23, compute the inverse of the given Laplace transform.

18. $\dfrac{e^{-\pi s}}{1 + s^2}$

19. $\dfrac{se^{-3\pi s}}{1 + s^2}$

20. $\dfrac{s - se^{-\pi s}}{1 + s^2}$

21. $\dfrac{1 - e^{-2s}}{s^2}$

22. $\dfrac{1 + e^{-4s}}{s^5}$

23. $\dfrac{e^{-2s}}{s^2 - 1}$

(*Hint:* Use partial fractions.)

24. Let $f(t) = \begin{cases} 1, & t < 1, \\ 3, & 1 < t < 7, \\ 5, & t > 7. \end{cases}$

Write $f(t)$ as a step function and compute $\mathcal{L}\{f(t)\}$.

25. Do the same for the function

$$f(t) = \begin{cases} -2, & 0 < t < 1, \\ 0, & 1 < t < 10, \\ 2, & t > 10. \end{cases}$$

6.4 SOME DIFFERENTIAL EQUATIONS WITH DISCONTINUOUS FORCING FUNCTIONS

There are many physical models that give rise to differential equations with discontinuous forcing functions. In this section, we discuss several models involving electrical circuits. We begin with the *RLC* circuit discussed in Sections 3.9 and 6.2.

Consider the differential equation

$$L\frac{dI}{dt} + RI + \frac{Q}{C} = E. \tag{1}$$

[See Eq. (1) in Section 3.9 and Eq. (19) in Section 6.2.] This is the equation that describes the circuit shown (again) in Fig. 8.

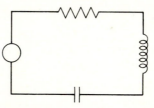

Figure 8

We assume that the voltage source, which may be a battery, is controlled by a switch that, initially, is turned off, and $Q(0) = I(0) = 0$. At some later time, t_1, the switch is turned on and the voltage is then equal to some constant value, E_0. In this situation it is easy to see that

$$E(t) = E_0 H(t - t_1). \tag{2}$$

To find the current at all times $t > 0$, we use the technique of Example 9 in Section 6.2 and the fact that $s\hat{Q} = \hat{I}$ to find that

$$\hat{I}(s) = T(s)\hat{E}(s) \tag{3}$$

where

$$T(s) = \frac{s/L}{s^2 + (R/L)s + (1/LC)}. \tag{4}$$

Here

$$\hat{E}(s) = \mathcal{L}\{E_0 H(t - t_1)\}$$

$$= \frac{E_0}{s} e^{-t_1 s}.$$

We can use this to solve for $\hat{I}(s)$ in Eq. (3).

Remark $E(t)$ is not defined at $t = t_1$ and, evidently, is not differentiable at that point. Therefore, the use of Eq. (3) is not strictly valid. However, we can get around this difficulty by observing that, according to Eq. (7) in Section 6.3, $H'(t - t_1) = \delta(t - t_1)$. Of course, $\delta(t - t_1)$ is not a function in the traditional sense but, since $\delta(t - t_1)$ has a Laplace transform [see Eq. (8) in Section 6.3], we will not worry about this difficulty.

Example 1   An *RLC* circuit with $R = 10$ ohms, $L = 1$ henry, and $C = 0.01$ farad is hooked up to a battery that delivers a steady voltage of 20 volts when switched on. If the switch, initially off, is turned on after 10 seconds, find the current for all future values of t.

Using Eqs. (3) and (4) and the values given above, we have

$$\hat{I}(s) = \frac{s}{s^2 + 10s + 100}\left(\frac{E_0}{s} e^{-10s}\right)$$

$$= \frac{E_0 e^{-10s}}{s^2 + 10s + 100} = \frac{20 e^{-10s}}{(s + 5)^2 + 75}.$$

From the second shifting theorem, we obtain

$$\frac{e^{-10s}}{(s + 5)^2 + 75} = \mathcal{L}\{f(t - 10)\, H(t - 10)\},$$

where $f(t)$ is the function whose Laplace transform is $[(s + 5)^2 + 75]^{-1}$. Thus

$$f(t) = \mathcal{L}^{-1}\left\{\frac{1}{(s + 5)^2 + 75}\right\}$$

$$= \frac{1}{\sqrt{75}}\, \mathcal{L}^{-1}\left\{\frac{\sqrt{75}}{(s + 5)^2 + 75}\right\} = \frac{1}{\sqrt{75}} e^{-5t} \sin \sqrt{75}t.$$

Next,

$$f(t - 10) = \frac{1}{\sqrt{75}} e^{-5(t-10)} \sin \sqrt{75}(t - 10)$$

so, finally, we have

$$I(t) = \frac{20}{\sqrt{75}}\, e^{-5(t-10)} \sin \sqrt{75}(t - 10)\, H(t - 10).$$

Note that there is no current if $t < 10$.

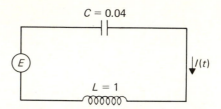

Figure 9

Example 2   Consider the LC circuit given in Fig. 9 with $I(0) = I'(0) = 0$. The voltage is given by

$$E(t) = \begin{cases} 25t, & 0 \leqslant t \leqslant 4, \\ 100, & t > 4. \end{cases}$$

Find the current for all values of $t \geqslant 0$.
    Using Eq. (1) we have (since $1/0.04 = 25$)

$$\frac{dI}{dt} + 25Q = E$$

and, differentiating,

$$\frac{d^2I}{dt^2} + 25I = E'(t) = \begin{cases} 25, & 0 \leqslant t \leqslant 4, \\ 0, & t > 4, \end{cases}$$

or

$$\frac{d^2I}{dt^2} + 25I = 25 - 25H(t - 4), \quad I(0) = I'(0) = 0.$$

Then, taking Laplace transforms and using $I(0) = I'(0) = 0$, we have

$$s^2\hat{I}(s) + 25\hat{I}(s) = \frac{25}{s} - \frac{25e^{-4s}}{s} = \frac{-25}{s}(e^{-4s} - 1)$$

so that

$$\hat{I}(s) = \frac{-25(e^{-4s} - 1)}{s\,(s^2 + 25)}.$$

Note that

$$\frac{25}{s(s^2 + 25)} = \frac{1}{s} - \frac{s}{s^2 + 25}$$

and

$$\hat{I}(s) = (e^{-4s} - 1)\left(\frac{-1}{s} + \frac{s}{s^2 + 25}\right)$$

$$= \frac{-e^{-4s}}{s} + e^{-4s}\frac{s}{s^2 + 25} + \frac{1}{s} - \frac{s}{s^2 + 25}.$$

Thus

$$I(t) = 1 - \cos 5t + H(t - 4)[\cos 5(t - 4) - 1].$$

Example 3   Consider the parallel electric circuit shown in Fig. 10, where the arrows denote the direction of current flow over each component of the circuit. We assume that $I(t) = CE_0\delta(t - t_1)$. Clearly there is no current except at $t = t_1$. Show that if $E(0) = 0$, then $I(t)$ yields enough current to charge the capacitor to the voltage E_0 immediately.

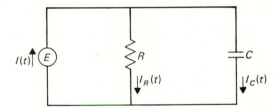

Figure 10

We refer to Kirchhoff's laws given in Section 3.13. We have the system

$$E = RI_R, \tag{5}$$

$$E = \frac{1}{C}Q_C,$$

or, differentiating,

$$E' = \frac{1}{C}\frac{dQ_C}{dt} = \frac{1}{C}I_C(t), \tag{6}$$

so that

$$I = I_R + I_C, \tag{7}$$

Thus,

$$I(t) = I_R(t) + I_C(t) = \frac{E}{R} + CE'$$

or

$$E'(t) + \frac{1}{RC}E(t) = \frac{1}{C}I(t) = E_0\delta(t - t_1).$$

Then, taking transforms and using the fact that $E(0) = 0$, we have

$$s\hat{E}(s) + \frac{1}{RC}\hat{E}(s) = E_0 e^{-st_1}$$

or

$$\hat{E}(s) = \frac{E_0 e^{-st_1}}{s + 1/RC} = \mathcal{L}\{H(t - t_1)f(t - t_1)\},$$

where

$$\mathcal{L}\{f(t)\} = \frac{E_0}{s + 1/RC}.$$

Thus

$$f(t) = E_0 e^{-(1/RC)t},$$

and

$$E(t) = E_0 e^{-(1/RC)(t-t_1)}H(t - t_1).$$

Note that the voltage on the capacitor is zero before time $t = t_1$. At that time it jumps to the value E_0.

Example 4   In Example 3, what happens after time t_1?

For $t > t_1$, $I(t) = 0$. Thus, for $t > t_1$ the only current is the current through the resistor and capacitor. From Eq. (5), we have, for $t > t_1$,

$$I_R(t) = \frac{1}{R}E(t) = \frac{1}{R}E_0 e^{-(1/RC)(t-t_1)}H(t - t_1)$$

$$= \frac{E_0}{R}e^{-(1/RC)(t-t_1)}.$$

Thus the current through the resistor decreases exponentially after the time $t = t_1$; that is, the current "bleeds off" through the resistor after the instant at which the capacitor is charged.

EXERCISES 6.4

1. Find the current for all t in the RLC circuit of Example 1, if $R = 20$ ohms, $L = \frac{1}{2}$ henry, and $C = 0.002$ farad, and a steady voltage 50-volt battery that is initially off is turned on after 30 seconds.

2. Answer the question in Exercise 1 if $R = 15$ ohms, $L = 2$ henrys, $C = 0.04$ farad, and E is a steady volt battery of 25 volts that is turned on after one minute.

In Exercises 3 through 5, find the current for all values of t in the LC circuit of Example 2 using the given data.

3. $L = 1$, $C = \frac{1}{16}$, $E(t) = \begin{cases} 16t, & 0 \leq t \leq 5, \\ 80, & t > 5. \end{cases}$

4. $L = 1$, $C = 0.04$, $E(t) = \begin{cases} 0, & 0 \leq t < 2, \\ 20t, & 2 \leq t \leq 4, \\ 80, & t > 4. \end{cases}$

5. $L = 1$, $C = 0.1$, $E(t) = \begin{cases} 10t, & 0 \leqslant t \leqslant 2, \\ 20, & 2 \leqslant t \leqslant 4, \\ 20t, & t > 4. \end{cases}$

6. In Example 3 find the voltage across the resistor after 20 seconds if $E_0 = 10$ volts, $t_1 = 10$ seconds, $R = 10$ ohms, and $C = 0.1$ farad.

7. An undamped spring (see Section 3.8) supports an object of 1-kg mass. The spring constant of the spring is 4 N/m. Suppose that a force $f(t)$ is applied to the object where

$$f(t) = \begin{cases} 2t, & 0 \leqslant t < \pi/2, \\ 0, & t \geqslant \pi/2, \end{cases} \quad \text{N.}$$

a) Find the equation of motion of the mass.

b) Assuming that, initially, the mass is displaced downward 1 m before $f(t)$ is applied, find the position of the object for all $t > 0$.

8. Answer the questions in Exercise 7 if

$$f(t) = \begin{cases} 0, & t < \pi/2, \\ 4, & t > \pi/2, \end{cases} \quad \text{N.}$$

6.5 THE TRANSFORM OF CONVOLUTION INTEGRALS

It often occurs that in the process of solving a linear differential equation by transforms, we end up with a transform that is the product of two other transforms. Although we proved in Exercise 79 in Section 6.1 that

$$\mathcal{L}^{-1}\{F + G\} = \mathcal{L}^{-1}\{F\} + \mathcal{L}^{-1}\{G\},$$

it is not true that $\mathcal{L}^{-1}\{FG\} = \mathcal{L}^{-1}\{F\}\mathcal{L}^{-1}\{G\}$. Almost any function you might try will illustrate this. For example, if $F(s) = 1/s$ and $G(s) = 1/s^2$, then $F(s)G(s) = 1/s^3$, but

$$\mathcal{L}^{-1}\{FG\} = \mathcal{L}^{-1}\left\{\frac{1}{s^3}\right\} = \frac{t^2}{2}, \quad \mathcal{L}^{-1}\{F\} = 1, \quad \text{and} \quad \mathcal{L}^{-1}\left\{\frac{1}{s^2}\right\} = t$$

and, clearly, $\mathcal{L}^{-1}\{FG\} \neq \mathcal{L}^{-1}\{F\}\mathcal{L}^{-1}\{G\}$.

In this section we shall define the convolution of two functions f and g and show that $\mathcal{L}^{-1}\{FG\}$ is equal to the convolution of $\mathcal{L}^{-1}\{F\}$ and $\mathcal{L}^{-1}\{G\}$. We shall then apply this fact in a variety of ways.

Definition   If $f(t)$ and $g(t)$ are piecewise continuous functions, then the *convolution* of f and g, written $f * g(t)$, is defined by

$$f * g(t) = \int_0^t f(t - u)g(u)\, du. \tag{1}$$

The notation $f * g(t)$ indicates that the convolution $f * g$ is a function of the independent variable t.

Using the change of variables $v = t - u$, we see that

$$f * g(t) = -\int_t^0 f(v)g(t - v)\, dv = \int_0^t g(t - v)f(v)\, dv$$

$$= g * f(t). \tag{2}$$

Hence $f * g(t) = g * f(t)$, and we can take the convolution in either order without altering the result. We may now state the main result of this section.

Theorem 1   *Convolution Theorem for Laplace Transforms.* Let $F(s) = \mathscr{L}\{f(t)\}$ and $G(s) = \mathscr{L}\{g(t)\}$. Then

$$\boxed{\mathscr{L}\{f * g(t)\} = F(s)G(s).}$$

Proof   By definition

$$F(s)G(s) = \left(\int_0^\infty e^{-su}f(u)\,du\right)\left(\int_0^\infty e^{-sv}g(v)\,dv\right)$$

$$= \int_0^\infty \int_0^\infty e^{-s(u+v)}f(u)g(v)\,dv\,du. \tag{3}$$

If we make the change of variables $t = u + v$, then $dt = dv$ and the integral (3) is equal to

$$F(s)G(s) = \int_0^\infty \int_u^\infty e^{-st}f(u)g(t-u)\,dt\,du. \tag{4}$$

Changing the order of integration† and noting that

$$\int_0^\infty \int_u^\infty dt\,du = \int_0^\infty \int_0^t du\,dt,$$

(check!), we have the integral in (4) equal to

$$F(s)G(s) = \int_0^\infty \int_0^t e^{-st}f(u)g(t-u)\,du\,dt$$

$$= \int_0^\infty e^{-st}\left[\int_0^t g(t-u)f(u)\,du\right]dt$$

$$= \int_0^\infty e^{-st}g * f(t)\,dt = \int_0^\infty e^{-st}f * g(t)\,dt$$

$$= \mathscr{L}\{f * g\}. \quad\blacksquare$$

Our first applications of this theorem are in the computation of inverse transforms.

Example 1   Compute $\mathscr{L}^{-1}\{s/(s^2 + 1)^2\}$.
          Since

$$\mathscr{L}\{\cos at\} = \frac{s}{s^2 + 1} \quad\text{and}\quad \mathscr{L}\{\sin t\} = \frac{1}{s^2 + 1},$$

---

† This may not always be possible. Conditions under which reversing the order of integration is permissible are found in most advanced calculus texts.

we have

$$\mathscr{L}^{-1}\left\{\frac{s}{(s^2 + 1)^2}\right\} = \mathscr{L}^{-1}\left\{\frac{s}{s^2 + 1} \cdot \frac{1}{s^2 + 1}\right\}.$$

By Theorem 1, this is the convolution of $\cos t$ and $\sin t$. But

$$\sin t * \cos t = \int_0^t \sin(t - u)\cos u\,du$$

$$= \int_0^t (\sin t \cos u - \cos t \sin u)\cos u\,du$$

$$= \sin t \int_0^t \cos^2 u\,du - \cos t \int_0^t \sin u \cos u\,du,$$

which, according to the table of integrals (Appendix 1), is equal to

$$\left[\sin t\left(\frac{\sin u \cos u + u}{2}\right) - \cos t\,\frac{\sin^2 u}{2}\right]\Bigg|_{u=0}^{u=t} = \frac{t \sin t}{2}.$$

Therefore,

$$\mathscr{L}^{-1}\left\{\frac{s}{(s^2 + 1)^2}\right\} = \frac{t \sin t}{2}. \qquad (5)$$

Example 2 Compute $\mathscr{L}^{-1}\{1/s^2(s + 1)^2\}$.
We have

$$\frac{1}{s^2} = \mathscr{L}\{t\} \quad \text{and} \quad \frac{1}{(s + 1)^2} = \mathscr{L}\{te^{-t}\}.$$

Therefore,

$$\mathscr{L}^{-1}\left\{\frac{1}{s^2(s + 1)^2}\right\} = \mathscr{L}^{-1}\left\{\frac{1}{s^2} \cdot \frac{1}{(s + 1)^2}\right\} = t * te^{-t}.$$

But

$$t * te^{-t} = \int_0^t (t - u)ue^{-u}\,du = t \int_0^t ue^{-u}\,du - \int_0^t u^2 e^{-u}\,du.$$

Integrating by parts, we obtain

$$t * te^{-t} = \{-te^{-u}(1 + u) + e^{-u}[u^2 + 2u + 2]\}\Bigg|_0^t$$

$$= t - 2 + (t + 2)e^{-t}$$

or

$$\mathscr{L}^{-1}\left\{\frac{1}{s^2(s + 1)^2}\right\} = t - 2 + (t + 2)e^{-t}.$$

Example 3   Compute $\mathcal{L}^{-1}\{e^{-as}/s^{n+1}\}$, where $n \geqslant 1$ is an integer and a is a real number. Note that

$$\frac{1}{s^{n+1}}e^{-as} = \frac{1}{s^n}\frac{e^{-as}}{s} = \mathcal{L}\left\{\frac{t^{n-1}}{(n-1)!}\right\}\mathcal{L}\{H(t-a)\}.$$

Thus

$$\mathcal{L}^{-1}\left\{\frac{1}{s^{n+1}}e^{-as}\right\} = \int_0^t \frac{(t-u)^{n-1}}{(n-1)!} H(u-a)\, du.$$

If $t < a$, then $H(u - a) = 0$, but if $t > a$, then

$$\int_0^t \frac{(t-u)^{n-1}}{(n-1)!} H(u-a)\, du = \int_a^t \frac{(t-u)^{n-1}}{(n-1)!}\, du$$

$$= -\frac{(t-u)^n}{n!}\bigg|_a^t = \frac{(t-a)^n}{n!}.$$

Thus

$$\mathcal{L}^{-1}\left\{\frac{1}{s^{n+1}}e^{-as}\right\} = \begin{cases} 0, & \text{if } t < a, \\ \dfrac{(t-a)^n}{n!}, & \text{if } t > a, \end{cases}$$

or

$$\boxed{\mathcal{L}^{-1}\left\{\frac{1}{s^{n+1}}e^{-as}\right\} = \frac{(t-a)^n}{n!} H(t-a).} \tag{6}$$

This formula is very useful in solving differential equations with discontinuous right-hand sides.

Although the convolution theorem is obviously very useful in calculating inverse transforms, it also has important applications in a very different area. In 1931 the Italian mathematician Vito Volterra[†] published a book that contained a fairly sophisticated model of population growth. It would be beyond the scope of this book to go into a derivation of Volterra's model. However, a central equation in this model is of the form

$$\boxed{x(t) = f(t) + \int_0^t a(t-u)x(u)\, du.} \tag{7}$$

[†] V. Volterra, *Leçons sur la Théorie Mathématique de la Lutte pour la Vie.* Paris: Gauthier-Villars (1931).

An equation of this type, where $f(t)$ and $a(t)$ can be assumed to be continuous, is called a *Volterra integral equation*. Since the publication of Volterra's papers, many diverse phenomena in thermodynamics, electrical systems theory, nuclear reactor theory, and chemotherapy have been modeled with Volterra integral equations.

It is quite easy to see how Laplace transforms can be used to solve an equation in the form of Eq. (7). Taking transforms on both sides of Eq. (7), using the convolution theorem, and denoting transforms by the appropriate capital letters, we obtain

$$X(s) = F(s) + A(s)X(s)$$

or

$$X(s) = \frac{F(s)}{1 - A(s)}. \tag{8}$$

Looking at Eq. (8), we immediately see that if $F(s)$ and $A(s)$ are defined for $s \geq s_0$, then $X(s)$ is similarly defined so long as $A(s) \neq 1$. Once $X(s)$ is known, we may (if possible) calculate the solution $x(t) = \mathscr{L}^{-1}\{X(s)\}$.

Example 4   Consider the integral equation

$$x(t) = t^2 + \int_0^t \sin(t - u)x(u)\, du. \tag{9}$$

Taking transforms, we have

$$X(s) = \frac{2}{s^3} + \frac{1}{s^2 + 1} \cdot X(s)$$

or

$$X(s) = \frac{2/s^3}{1 - 1/(s^2 + 1)}$$

$$= \frac{2(s^2 + 1)}{s^5}$$

$$= \frac{2}{s^3} + \frac{2}{s^5}.$$

Hence the solution to Eq. (9) is given by

$$x(t) = t^2 + \tfrac{1}{12}t^4.$$

There are other applications of the very useful convolution theorem given in the exercises. The student, however, should always keep in mind that the greatest difficulty in using any of these methods is that it is frequently difficult to calculate inverse transforms. Unfortunately, most problems that arise lead to inverting transforms that do not fit into familiar patterns. For this reason methods have been devised for estimating such inverses. The interested reader should consult a more advanced book on Laplace transforms, such as the excellent book by Widder.†

EXERCISES 6.5

In Exercises 1 through 5, find the Laplace transform of each given convolution integral.

1. $f(t) = \int_0^t (t-u)^3 \sin u\, du$

2. $f(t) = \int_0^t e^{-(t-u)} \cos 2u\, du$

3. $f(t) = \int_0^t (t-u)^3 u^5\, du$

4. $f(t) = \int_0^t \sinh 4(t-u) \cosh 5u\, du$

5. $f(t) = \int_0^t e^{17(t-u)} u^{19}\, du$

In Exercises 6 through 12, use the convolution theorem to calculate the inverse Laplace transforms of the given functions.

6. $F(s) = \dfrac{3}{s^4(s^2+1)}$

7. $F(s) = \dfrac{a}{s^2(s^2+a^2)}$

8. $F(s) = \dfrac{1}{(s^2+1)^2}$

9. $F(s) = \dfrac{1}{s(s^2+a^2)}$

10. $F(s) = \dfrac{1}{(s^2+1)^3}$

11. $F(s) = \dfrac{e^{-3s}}{s^3}$

12. $F(s) = \dfrac{e^{-10s}}{s^5}$

13. Solve the Volterra integral equation
$$x(t) = e^{-t} - 2\int_0^t \cos(t-u)x(u)\, du.$$

14. Solve the Volterra integral equation
$$x(t) = t + \tfrac{1}{6}\int_0^t (t-u)^3 x(u)\, du.$$

15. Find the solution of the initial value problem
$$y'' + 4y' + 13y = f(t), \quad y(0) = y'(0) = 0,$$
where
$$f(t) = \begin{cases} 1, & t < \pi, \\ 0, & t > \pi. \end{cases}$$

16. Find the solution of the initial value problem
$$y'' - 2y' + 2y = f(t), \quad y(0) = y'(0) = 0,$$
where
$$f(t) = \begin{cases} 0, & t < \pi/2, \\ 1, & \pi/2 < t < 3\pi/2, \\ 2, & t > 3\pi/2. \end{cases}$$

6.6 LAPLACE TRANSFORM METHODS FOR SYSTEMS

Laplace transform techniques are very useful for solving systems of differential equations with given initial conditions. Consider the system

$$\frac{dx}{dt} = a_{11}x + a_{12}y + f(t),$$

$$\frac{dy}{dt} = a_{21}x + a_{22}y + g(t),$$

$$(1)$$

† D. V. Widder, *The Laplace Transformation*. Princeton, N. J.: Princeton University Press (1941).

with initial conditions $x(0) = x_0$, $y(0) = y_0$. Taking the Laplace transform of both equations in the system (1) and letting the corresponding capital letter represent the Laplace transforms of the functions x, y, f, and g, we obtain

$$sX - x_0 = a_{11}X + a_{12}Y + F,$$
$$sY - y_0 = a_{21}X + a_{22}Y + G. \tag{2}$$

Gathering all the terms involving X and Y on the left-hand side, we obtain from (2) the system of simultaneous equations

$$(s - a_{11})X - a_{12}Y = F + x_0,$$
$$-a_{21}X + (s - a_{22})Y = G + y_0. \tag{3}$$

If $F + x_0$ and $G + y_0$ are not both identically zero, we may solve Eqs. (3) simultaneously, obtaining

$$X = \frac{(s - a_{22})(F + x_0) + a_{12}(G + y_0)}{s^2 - (a_{11} + a_{22})s + (a_{11}a_{22} - a_{12}a_{21})},$$
$$Y = \frac{(s - a_{11})(G + y_0) + a_{21}(F + x_0)}{s^2 - (a_{11} + a_{22})s + (a_{11}a_{22} - a_{12}a_{21})}. \tag{4}$$

Note that the denominators of the fractions in Eqs. (4) are identical to the characteristic equation for the system (1) which we obtained in Section 3.12. Thus we may rewrite Eqs. (4) in the form

$$X = \frac{(s - a_{22})(F + x_0) + a_{12}(G + y_0)}{(s - \lambda_1)(s - \lambda_2)},$$
$$Y = \frac{(s - a_{11})(G + y_0) + a_{21}(F + x_0)}{(s - \lambda_1)(s - \lambda_2)}, \tag{5}$$

where λ_1 and λ_2 are the solutions of the characteristic equation

$$\lambda^2 - (a_{11} + a_{22})\lambda + (a_{11}a_{22} - a_{12}a_{21}) = 0.$$

We can now find the solution $\{x, y\}$ of the system (1) with given initial conditions by inverting (if possible) the equations (5).

It should be apparent from the discussion above that the Laplace transform allows us to convert a system of differential equations with given initial conditions to a system of simultaneous equations. This method clearly can be generalized to apply to systems of n linear first-order differential equations with constant coefficients, thus yielding a corresponding system of n simultaneous linear equations. As in the case of a single differential equation (see Section 6.2), Laplace transform methods are primarily intended for the solution of systems of linear differential equations with constant coefficients and given initial conditions. Any deviation from these conditions can so complicate the problem as to make no solution obtainable.

Example 1   Consider the initial value problem

$$x' = x - y + e^t, \qquad x(0) = 1,$$
$$y' = 2x + 3y + e^{-t}, \quad y(0) = 0. \tag{6}$$

Using the differentiation property of Laplace transforms, we have

$$s\,X - 1 = X - Y + 1/(s - 1),$$
$$s\,Y = 2X + 3Y + 1/(s + 1). \tag{7}$$

The system (7) may be rewritten as

$$(s - 1)X + Y = s/(s - 1),$$
$$-2X + (s - 3)Y = 1/(s + 1), \tag{8}$$

from which we find that

$$X = \frac{s^2 - 3s - 1}{(s + 1)[(s - 2)^2 + 1]} = \frac{A_1}{s + 1} + \frac{A_2(s - 2) + A_3}{(s - 2)^2 + 1},$$

$$Y = \frac{3s - 1}{(s + 1)[(s - 2)^2 + 1]} = \frac{B_1}{s + 1} + \frac{B_2(s - 2) + B_3}{(s - 2)^2 + 1}. \tag{9}$$

Using the methods developed in Sections 6.1 and 6.2, we obtain $A_1 = \frac{3}{10}$, $A_2 = \frac{7}{10}$, $A_3 = -\frac{11}{10}$, $B_1 = -\frac{2}{5}$, $B_2 = \frac{2}{5}$, and $B_3 = \frac{9}{5}$. Therefore, we have the solution

$$\{x, y\} = \left\{ \frac{3}{10}e^{-t} + \frac{e^{2t}}{10}(7\cos t - 11\sin t), -\frac{2}{5}e^{-t} + \frac{e^{2t}}{5}(2\cos t + 9\sin t) \right\}.$$

Example 2   We give here a far more complicated model, which describes the motion of a particle projected from the earth, where we do not ignore the effects on the particle caused by the earth's rotation.[†] To begin, we set up the needed three-dimensional coordinate system.

Assume the positive x-axis points south, and the positive y-axis points east, and the positive z-axis points in the direction opposite to the direction of the acceleration, g, due to gravity.

This model was first studied by the German physicist B. M. Planck.[‡]

[†] This example is computationally very difficult. Skip it if you balk at lengthy calculations. Unfortunately, real problems rarely have easy solutions. This problem is typical of those encountered when you graduate from textbook examples.

[‡] B. M. Planck, *Einführung in die Allgemeine Mechanik*, 4th ed., p. 81. Leipsig: S. Hirzel (1928).

Planck took the origin to have latitude β and the angular velocity of the earth to be ω. Assuming the mass of the particle to be negligible, Planck derived the following system of second-order equations:

$$\frac{d^2x}{dt^2} = 2\omega \sin \beta \frac{dy}{dt}, \tag{10}$$

$$\frac{d^2y}{dt^2} = -2\omega\left(\sin \beta \frac{dx}{dt} + \cos \beta \frac{dz}{dt}\right), \tag{11}$$

$$\frac{d^2z}{dt^2} = 2\cos \beta \frac{dy}{dt} - g, \tag{12}$$

with

$$0 = x(0) = y(0) = z(0), \quad x'(0) = u, \quad y'(0) = v, \quad z'(0) = w. \tag{13}$$

Now, taking transforms of both sides of Eq. (10), we obtain

$$s^2\hat{x} - sx(0) - x'(0) = 2\omega \sin \beta(s\hat{y} - y(0)),$$

or, using the conditions in Eq. (13),

$$s^2\hat{x} - u = 2\omega(\sin \beta)s\hat{y},$$

or

$$s^2\hat{x} - 2\omega(\sin \beta)s\hat{y} = u. \tag{14}$$

Similarly (see Exercise 13), we obtain

$$2\omega(\sin \beta)s\hat{x} + s^2\hat{y} + 2\omega(\cos \beta)\hat{z} = v, \tag{15}$$

and

$$-2\omega(\cos \beta)\hat{y} + s^2\hat{z} = w - \frac{g}{s}. \tag{16}$$

The equations (14), (15), and (16) constitute a system of three equations in the three unknowns $\hat{x}$, $\hat{y}$, and $\hat{z}$, and have a unique solution if and only if the determinant of the system is nonzero. This determinant is (see Appendix 4)

$$D = \begin{vmatrix} s^2 & -2\omega(\sin \beta)s & 0 \\ 2\omega(\sin \beta)s & s^2 & 2\omega(\cos \beta)s \\ 0 & -2\omega(\cos \beta)s & s^2 \end{vmatrix}$$

$$= s^6 + 4\omega^2(\sin^2 \beta)s^4 + 4\omega^2(\cos^2 \beta)s^4$$

$$= s^6 + 4\omega^2 s^4 = s^4(s^2 + 4\omega^2).$$

Thus, for $s > 0$ the determinant is nonzero and the system has a unique solution. Using Cramer's rule (Theorem A4.4), we obtain

$$
\hat{x}(s) = \frac{\begin{vmatrix} u & -2\omega(\sin\beta)s & 0 \\ v & s^2 & 2\omega(\cos\beta)s \\ w - \dfrac{g}{s} & -2\omega(\cos\beta)s & s^2 \end{vmatrix}}{D}
$$

$$
= \frac{us^4 - 4\omega^2\sin\beta(\cos\beta)s^2\left(w - \dfrac{g}{s}\right) + 2\omega(\sin\beta)vs^3 + 4\omega^2(\cos^2\beta)s^2 u}{s^4(s^2 + 4\omega^2)}
$$

$$
= u\left(\frac{1}{s^2 + 4\omega^2} + \frac{4\omega^2\cos^2\beta}{s^2(s^2 + 4\omega^2)}\right) + v\left(\frac{2\omega\sin\beta}{s(s^2 + 4\omega^2)}\right)
$$

$$
- w\left(\frac{4\omega^2\sin\beta\cos\beta}{s^2(s^2 + 4\omega^2)}\right) + g\left(\frac{4\omega^2\sin\beta\cos\beta}{s^3(s^2 + 4\omega^2)}\right). \tag{17}
$$

Similarly (see Exercise 14), we obtain

$$
\hat{y}(s) = -u\left(\frac{2\omega\sin\beta}{s(s^2 + 4\omega^2)}\right) + v\left(\frac{1}{s^2 + 4\omega^2}\right)
$$

$$
- w\left(\frac{2\omega\cos\beta}{s(s^2 + 4\omega^2)}\right) + g\left(\frac{2\omega\cos\beta}{s(s^2 + 4\omega^2)}\right), \tag{18}
$$

and

$$
\hat{z}(s) = -u\left(\frac{4\omega^2\sin\beta\cos\beta}{s(s^2 + 4\omega^2)}\right) + v\left(\frac{2\omega\cos\beta}{s(s^2 + 4\omega^2)}\right)
$$

$$
+ w\left(\frac{1}{s^2 + 4\omega^2} + \frac{4\omega^2\sin^2\beta}{s^2(s^2 + 4\omega^2)}\right) - g\left(\frac{1}{s(s^2 + 4\omega^2)} + \frac{4\omega^2\sin^2\beta}{s^3(s^2 + 4\omega^2)}\right). \tag{19}
$$

Next (see Exercise 15), Eqs. (17), (18), and (19) can be inverted, and using the trigonometric identity $2\sin^2 A = 1 - \cos 2A$, we obtain

$$
x(t) = \frac{u}{2\omega}(2\omega t\cos^2\beta + \sin^2\beta\sin 2\omega t) + \frac{v}{\omega}\sin\beta\sin^2\omega t
$$

$$
- \frac{w}{2\omega}\sin\beta\cos\beta(2\omega t - \sin^2\omega t) + \frac{g}{2\omega^2}\sin\beta\cos\beta(\omega^2 t^2 - \sin^2\omega t); \tag{20}
$$

$$
y(t) = -\frac{u}{\omega}\sin\beta\sin^2\omega t + \frac{v}{2\omega}\sin 2\omega t
$$

$$
- \frac{w}{\omega}\cos\beta\sin^2\omega t + \frac{g}{4\omega^2}\cos\beta(2\omega t - \sin 2\omega t); \tag{21}
$$

$$z(t) = -\frac{u}{2\omega}\sin\beta\cos\beta(2\omega t - \sin 2\omega t) + \frac{v}{\omega}\cos\beta\sin^2\omega t$$

$$+ \frac{w}{2\omega}(2\omega t \sin^2\beta + \sin 2\omega t \cos^2\beta)$$

$$- \frac{g}{2\omega^2}(\omega^2 t^2 \sin^2\beta + \cos^2\beta \sin^2\omega t). \tag{22}$$

These are the equations of motion of the projectile when the earth's rotation is taken into account. Finally, we note by L'Hôpital's rule that

$$\lim_{\omega\to 0}\frac{\sin 2\omega t}{2\omega} = \lim_{\omega\to 0}\frac{2t \cos\omega t}{2} = t,$$

and

$$\lim_{\omega\to 0}\frac{\sin^2\omega t}{\omega} = \lim_{\omega\to 0}\frac{2t\sin\omega t\cos\omega t}{1} = 0.$$

Thus,

$$\lim_{\omega\to 0}x(t) = ut, \quad \lim_{\omega\to 0}y(t) = vt, \quad \text{and} \quad \lim_{\omega\to 0}z(t) = wt - \tfrac{1}{2}gt^2, \tag{23}$$

showing that Eqs. (20), (21), and (22) reduce to the usual equations of motion when the earth's rotation is ignored.

EXERCISES 6.6

In Exercises 1 through 12, solve the initial value problems involving systems of differential equations by the Laplace transform method.

1. $x' = y$, $x(0) = 1$
    $y' = x$, $y(0) = 0$

2. $x' = -3x + 4y$, $x(0) = 3$
    $y' = -2x + 3y$, $y(0) = 2$

3. $x' = 4x - 2y$, $x(0) = 2$
    $y' = 5x + 2y$, $y(0) = -2$

4. $x' = x - 2y$, $x(0) = 1$
    $y' = 4x + 5y$, $y(0) = -2$

5. $x' = -3x + 4y + \cos t$, $x(0) = 0$
    $y' = -2x + 3y + t$, $y(0) = 1$

6. $x' = 4x - 2y + e^t$, $x(0) = 1$
    $y' = 5x + 2y - t$, $y(0) = 0$

7. $x' = x - 2y + t^2$, $x(0) = 1$
    $y' = 4x + 5y - e^t$, $y(0) = -1$

8. $x'' + x + y = 0$, $x(0) = x'(0) = 0$
    $x' + y' = 0$, $y(0) = 1$

9. $x'' = y + \sin t$, $x(0) = 1$, $x'(0) = 0$
    $y'' = -x' + \cos t$, $y(0) = -1$, $y'(0) = -1$

10. $x'' = 2y + 2$, $x(0) = 2$, $x'(0) = 2$,
    $y' = -x + 5e^{2t} + 1$, $y(0) = 1$

11. $x = z'$, $x(0) = y(0) = z(0) = 1$
    $x' + y + z = 1$
    $-x + y' + z = 2\sin t$

12. $x'' = y - z$, $x(0) = x'(0) = 0$
    $y'' = x' + z'$, $y(0) = -1$, $y'(0) = 1$
    $z'' = -(1 + x + y)$, $z(0) = 0$, $z'(0) = 1$

13. Beginning with Eqs. (11) and (12), use the differentiation property to obtain Eqs. (15) and (16).

14. Use Cramer's rule in the system (14), (15), and (16) to obtain the expressions (18) and (19) for y and z.

15. Invert the transforms in Eqs. (17), (18), and (19) to solve for $x(t)$, $y(t)$, and $z(t)$.

REVIEW EXERCISES FOR CHAPTER 6

In Exercises 1 through 17, find the Laplace transform of the given function.

1. $3t - 2$

2. $t^3 + 4t^2 - 2t + 1$

3. e^{2t-1}

4. $\cos(2t + 1)$

5. te^{-t}

6. $e^{-t}\cos 2t$

7. $\sinh(3t - 4)$

8. $t^3 e^{2t}$

9. $te^t \cos t$

10. $\cosh^2 2t$

11. $\cos^2 t$

12. $\int_0^t u \cos u \, du$

13. $t^2 \cos 2t$

14. $\cos t \cdot H(t - 2\pi)$

15. $\delta(t - 3)$

16. The function shown in the figure below

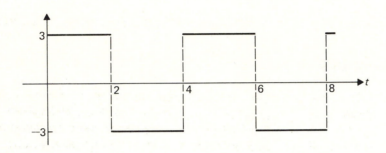

17. $f(t) = \begin{cases} \sin t, & t < 2\pi \\ \sin t + \cos t, & t > 2\pi \end{cases}$

In Exercises 18 through 32, find the inverse of the given Laplace transform.

18. $\dfrac{3}{s^2}$

19. $\dfrac{-14}{s}$

20. $\dfrac{s + 2}{s^2 + 4}$

21. $\dfrac{1}{(s - 2)^2}$

22. $\dfrac{s - 3}{s^2 - 3}$

23. $\dfrac{1}{s^2 + 4s + 5}$

24. $\dfrac{s + 3}{s^2 + 8s + 17}$

25. $\dfrac{s}{s^2 - 3s + 2}$

26. $\dfrac{s + 2}{s(s^2 + 4)}$

27. $\dfrac{s^2 + 8s - 3}{(s^2 + 2s + 1)(s^2 + 1)}$

28. $\ln \dfrac{s - 3}{s - 2}$

29. $\ln\left(1 + \dfrac{4}{s^2}\right)$

30. $\dfrac{se^{-(\pi/2)s}}{1 + s^2}$

31. $\dfrac{s - se^{-(\pi/2)s}}{1 + s^2}$

32. $\dfrac{e^{-3s}}{s^2 - 1}$

In Exercises 33 through 41, solve the given initial value problem by Laplace transform methods.

33. $y'' + y = 0, \quad y(0) = 1, \quad y'(0) = 3$

34. $y'' - 4y = 0, \quad y(0) = 2, \quad y'(0) = -5$

35. $y'' - 5y' + 6y = 0, \quad y(0) = 2, \quad y'(0) = 1$

36. $y'' + 4y' + 4y = 0, \quad y(0) = -1, \quad y'(0) = 2$

37. $y'' - y = te^{2t}, \quad y(0) = 0, \quad y'(0) = 1$

38. $y'' + 9y = \sin t, \quad y(0) = y'(0) = 0$

39. $y'' + 2y' + 2y = H(t - 3), \quad y(0) = y'(0) = 0$

40. $y' - 6y = H(t - 2), \quad y(0) = 0$

41. $y'' - 4y' + 4y = \delta(t - 1), \quad y(0) = 0,$ $\quad y'(0) = 1$

In Exercises 42 through 44, find the Laplace transform of the given convolution integral.

42. $\int_0^t (t - u)^2 \sin u \, du$

43. $\int_0^t (t - u)^4 u^7 \, du$

44. $\int_0^t e^{15(t-u)} u^{25} \, du$

45. Use the convolution theorem to compute the inverse Laplace transform of:

a) $F(s) = \dfrac{2}{s^3(s^2+1)}$; b) $F(s) = \dfrac{1}{s(s^2+4)}$.

46. Solve the initial value problem

$$y'' + 6y' + 18y = f(t), \quad y(0) = y'(0) = 0,$$

where

$$f(t) = \begin{cases} 2, & t < \pi, \\ 0, & t > \pi. \end{cases}$$

In Exercises 47 through 50, solve the given system by Laplace transform methods.

47. $2x' - 3y' = 2e^t$, $x(0) = 2$
$x' - 2y' = 0$, $y(0) = 1$

48. $x'' - 3x' - y' + 2y = 14t + 3$,
$\qquad\qquad\qquad\qquad x(0) = 0, \quad x'(0) = 0$
$x' - 3x + y' = 1$, $y(0) = \frac{13}{2}$

49. $x' + x + 2y = 0$, $x(0) = 1$,
$3x + 2y + y' = 0$, $y(0) = 2$

50. $x' = y - z' + 2t$, $x(0) = 0$
$2x = y'' + z'$, $y(0) = 1$, $y'(0) = 0$
$y = z''/2$, $z(0) = z'(0) = 0$

Numerical Methods

In the preceding chapters we developed several techniques for solving differential and difference equations. Unfortunately, these methods are not always applicable to the equations that arise in practical problems. Additionally, even when they do apply, the computational labor of solving, for example, a system of many simultaneous first-order equations may be formidable. It is for these reasons that techniques have been developed for computing the numerical solution of almost any such problem. In this chapter we shall discuss some of these methods.

Before discussing particular numerical methods, we stress that care must always be exercised in the utilization of any scheme for the numerical solution of an equation. The accuracy of any solution depends not only on the "correctness" of the numerical method being used, but also on the precision of the hand calculator or computer used for the tedious arithmetic computations. A detailed discussion of the kinds of error one can expect to encounter will appear in Sections 7.1, 7.2, and 7.5.

7.1 FIRST-ORDER EQUATIONS

In this section we shall assume that the initial value problem

$$\frac{dy}{dx} = f(x, y), \quad y(x_0) = y_0 \tag{1}$$

has a unique solution $y(x)$. The three techniques we will describe below approximate this solution $y(x)$ only at a finite number of points

$$x_0, \quad x_1 = x_0 + h, \quad x_2 = x_0 + 2h, \ldots, \quad x_n = x_0 + nh,$$

where h is some (nonzero) real number. The methods provide a value y_k that is an approximation to the exact value $y(x_k)$ for $k = 0, 1, \ldots, n$. As the notation suggests, what we are doing is approximating the equation (1) by a suitable difference equation.

Euler's Method

This procedure is crude but very simple. The idea is to obtain y_1 by assuming that $f(x, y)$ varies so little on the interval $x_0 \le x \le x_1$ that only a very small error is made by replacing it by the constant value $f(x_0, y_0)$. Integrating

$$\frac{dy}{dx} = f(x, y)$$

from x_0 to x_1, we obtain

$$y(x_1) - y_0 = y(x_1) - y(x_0)$$

$$= \int_{x_0}^{x_1} f(x, y) \, dx \approx f(x_0, y_0)(x_1 - x_0) \tag{2}$$

or, since $h = x_1 - x_0$,

$$y_1 = y_0 + hf(x_0, y_0).$$

Repeating the process with (x_1, y_1) to obtain y_2, etc., we obtain the difference equation

$$y_{n+1} = y_n + hf(x_n, y_n). \tag{3}$$

We shall solve Eq. (3) iteratively, that is, by first finding y_1, then using it to find y_2, and so on.

The geometric meaning of Eq. (3) is shown in Fig. 1, where the smooth curve is the unknown exact solution of Eq. (1), which is being approximated by the broken line. Remember that $f(x_0, y_0)$ is the slope of the tangent to $y = y(x)$ at the point (x_0, y_0). The differences Δ_k are errors at the kth stage in the process.

Figure 1

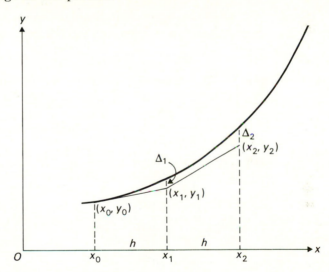

Example 1   Solve

$$\frac{dy}{dx} = y + x^2, \quad y(0) = 1. \tag{4}$$

We wish to find $y(1)$ by approximating the solution at $x = 0.0, 0.2, 0.4, 0.6,$ 0.8, and 1.0. Here $h = 0.2$, $f(x_n, y_n) = y_n + x_n^2$, and Euler's method [Eq. (3)] yields

$$y_{n+1} = y_n + h \cdot f(x_n, y_n) = y_n + h(y_n + x_n^2).$$

Since $y_0 = y(0) = 1$, we obtain

$$y_1 = y_0 + h \cdot (y_0 + x_0^2) = 1 + 0.2(1 + 0^2) = 1.2,$$
$$y_2 = y_1 + h \cdot (y_1 + x_1^2) = 1.2 + 0.2[1.2 + (0.2)^2] = 1.448 \approx 1.45,$$

and so on. We arrange our work as shown in Table 1. The value $y_5 = 2.77$, corresponding to $x_5 = 1.0$, is our approximate value for $y(1)$.

Table 1

x_n	y_n	$f(x_n, y_n) = y_n + x_n^2$	$y_{n+1} = y_n + h \cdot f(x_n, y_n)$
0.0	1.00	1.00	1.20
0.2	1.20	1.24	1.45
0.4	1.45	1.61	1.77
0.6	1.77	2.13	2.20
0.8	2.20	2.84	2.77
1.0	2.77		

If we solve the equation, we will obtain $y = 3e^x - x^2 - 2x - 2$, so that $y(1) = 3e - 5 \approx 3.154$. Thus the Euler's method estimate was off by about twelve percent. This is not surprising because we treated the derivative as a constant over intervals of length of 0.2 unit. The error that arises in this way is called *discretization error*, because the "discrete" function $f(x_n, y_n)$ was substituted for the "continuously valued" function $f(x, y)$. It should be intuitively obvious that if we reduce the step size h, then we can improve the accuracy of our answer, since, then, the "discretized" function $f(x_n, y_n)$ will be closer to the true value of $f(x, y)$ over the interval $[0, 1]$. This is illustrated in Fig. 2 with $h = 0.2$ and $h = 0.1$. Indeed, carrying out similar calculations with $h = 0.1$ yields an approximation of $y(1)$ of 3.07, which is a good deal more accurate (an error of about three percent).

Figure 2

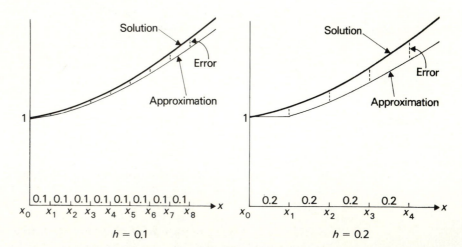

If we solve the equation

Thus, in general, reducing step size will improve accuracy. However, a warning must be attached to this. Reducing the step size will obviously increase the amount of work that must be done. Moreover, at every stage of the computation *round-off errors* are introduced. For example, in our calculations with $h = 0.2$, we rounded off the exact value 1.448 to the value 1.45 (correct to two decimal places). The rounded-off value was then used to calculate further values of y_n. It is not unusual for a computer solution of a more complicated differential equation to take several thousand individual computations, thus having several thousand round-off errors. In some problems (see Section 7.5) the accumulated round-off error can be so large that the resulting computed solution will be sufficiently inaccurate to invalidate the result. Fortunately, this usually does not occur since round-off errors can be positive or negative and tend to cancel one another out. This statement is made under the assumption (usually true) that the average of the round-off errors is zero. In any event, it should be clear that reducing the step size, thereby increasing the number of computations, is a procedure that should be carried out carefully. In general, each problem has an optimal step size, and a smaller than optimal step size will yield a greater error due to accumulated round-off errors.

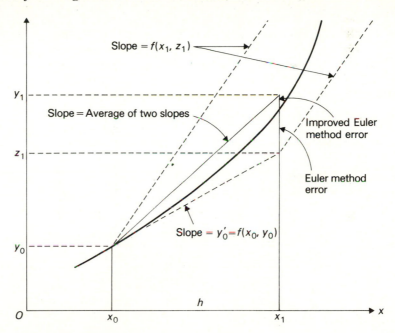

Figure 3

Improved Euler Method

This method has better accuracy than Euler's method and so is more valuable for hand computation. It is based on the intuitively evident fact that an improvement will result if we average the values of the slope at the left and right endpoints of the interval, thereby reducing the difference between $f(x, y)$ and $f(x_n, y_n)$ in each interval of the form $x_n \leqslant x < x_{n+1}$ (see Fig. 3). This amounts to approximating the integral in Eq. (2) by the *trapezoidal rule*:

$$\int_{x_0}^{x_1} f(x, y)\, dx \approx \frac{h}{2} \{f(x_0, y_0) + f(x_1, y(x_1))\}.$$

Since $y(x_1)$ is not known, we will replace it by the value found by Euler's method, which we call z_1; then Eq. (2) can be replaced by the system of equations

$$z_1 = y_0 + hf(x_0, y_0),$$

$$y_1 = y_0 + \frac{h}{2}[f(x_0, y_0) + f(x_1, z_1)].$$

This gives us the general procedure

$$z_{n+1} = y_n + hf(x_n, y_n),$$

$$y_{n+1} = y_n + \frac{h}{2}[f(x_n, y_n) + f(x_{n+1}, z_{n+1})].$$

(5)

Using $x_0 = 0$ and $y_0 = 1$ in Example 1, we obtain, with $h = 0.2$,

$$z_1 = y_0 + hf(x_0, y_0) = 1 + 0.2(1 + 0^2) = 1.2,$$

$$y_1 = y_0 + \frac{h}{2}[f(x_0, y_0) + f(x_1, z_1)] = 1 + 0.1[(1 + 0^2) + 1.2 + 0.2^2]$$

$$= 1 + 0.1[2.24] = 1.224 \approx 1.22,$$

$$z_2 = y_1 + hf(x_1, y_1) = 1.22 + 0.2[1.22 + (0.2)^2] = 1.472 \approx 1.47,$$

$$y_2 = y_1 + \frac{h}{2}[f(x_1, y_1) + f(x_2, z_2)]$$

$$= 1.22 + 0.1[1.22 + (0.2)^2 + 1.47 + (0.4)^2] = 1.509 \approx 1.51,$$

and so on. Table 2 shows the approximate values of the solution of Eq. (4) used in Example 1. The error this time is less than one percent.

Table 2

x_n	y_n	$f(x_n, y_n) = y_n + x_n^2$	z_{n+1}	$f(x_{n+1}, z_{n+1}) = z_{n+1} + x_{n+1}^2$	y_{n+1}
0.0	1.0	1.0	1.20	1.24	1.22
0.2	1.22	1.26	1.47	1.63	1.51
0.4	1.51	1.67	1.84	2.20	1.90
0.6	1.90	2.26	2.35	2.99	2.43
0.8	2.43	3.07	3.04	4.04	3.14
1.0	3.14				

Runge-Kutta Method

This powerful method gives accurate results without a large number of steps (that is, without the need to make the step size too small). The efficiency is obtained by using a version of Simpson's rule (a frequently used method of numerical integration) in evaluating the integral in Eq.

(2). We will derive the formula in Section 7.3, but for now we merely describe its use. Let

$$y_{n+1} = y_n + \tfrac{1}{6}(m_1 + 2m_2 + 2m_3 + m_4), \tag{6}$$

where

$$
\begin{aligned}
m_1 &= hf(x_n, y_n), \\
m_2 &= hf\left(x_n + \frac{h}{2}, y_n + \frac{m_1}{2}\right), \\
m_3 &= hf\left(x_n + \frac{h}{2}, y_n + \frac{m_2}{2}\right), \\
m_4 &= hf(x_n + h, y_n + m_3).
\end{aligned}
\tag{7}
$$

Note that the values m_1/h, m_2/h, m_3/h, and m_4/h are four slopes between $x_n \le x \le x_{n+1}$, so that Eq. (6) is a weighted average of these slopes—a procedure similar to the one we used in the improved Euler method. Observe that when $f(x, y)$ is a function of x alone, $m_2 = m_3$ and Eq. (6) becomes *Simpson's rule*:

$$\int_x^{x+h} f(x)\, dx \approx \frac{(h/2)}{3}\left[f(x) + 4f\left(x + \frac{h}{2}\right) + f(x + h)\right].$$

We apply the Runge-Kutta method to Eq. (4) of Example 1 with $h = 1$ and $n = 1$:

$$
\begin{aligned}
m_1 &= f(0, 1) = 1, \\
m_2 &= f(\tfrac{1}{2}, \tfrac{3}{2}) = \tfrac{7}{4}, \\
m_3 &= f(\tfrac{1}{2}, \tfrac{15}{8}) = \tfrac{17}{8}, \\
m_4 &= f(1, \tfrac{25}{8}) = \tfrac{33}{8}.
\end{aligned}
$$

Thus

$$y_1 = 1 + \tfrac{1}{6}(1 + \tfrac{7}{2} + \tfrac{17}{4} + \tfrac{33}{8}) = \tfrac{151}{48} \approx 3.146.$$

In one step this method got us even closer to the correct value than the improved Euler method.

The three methods described in this section illustrate some of the many different numerical schemes available for finding approximate solutions to differential equations. The Euler method is the easiest to apply but requires many steps (a small step size) to achieve any reasonable degree of accuracy. The accuracy of the Euler method as a function of step size will be discussed in detail in the next section. The improved Euler method is more accurate (with the same step size) but involves more arithmetic calculations at each iteration. Finally, the Runge-Kutta method usually yields greater accuracy at the cost of a great deal more work at each step. The choice of method often is determined by the accuracy needed. If only an approximate (one or two decimal place) answer is needed, then the Euler method or the improved Euler method will be sufficient. However, for greater accuracy, a more sophisticated numerical scheme is required.

It is not difficult to write short programs in BASIC or FORTRAN that will do the many calculations that arise when we select a small step size. In fact, it is even possible to use programmable hand-calculators. Appendix 3 contains three highly efficient HP-25 routines for the three methods we have discussed in this section. These routines can easily be modified for use on other programmable calculators.

EXERCISES 7.1

In Exercises 1 through 10, solve each problem exactly using the methods of Chapter 2. Then:

a) Use the Euler method and the indicated value of h;

b) Use the improved Euler method and the given value of h;

c) Use the Runge-Kutta method with the given h.

Compare the accuracy of the three methods with the exact answer.

1. $\dfrac{dy}{dx} = x + y$, $y(0) = 1$. Find $y(1)$ with $h = 0.2$.

2. $\dfrac{dy}{dx} = x - y$, $y(1) = 2$. Find $y(3)$ with $h = 0.4$.

3. $\dfrac{dy}{dx} = \dfrac{x - y}{x + y}$, $y(2) = 1$. Find $y(1)$ with $h = -0.2$.

4. $\dfrac{dy}{dx} = \dfrac{y}{x} + \left(\dfrac{y}{x}\right)^2$, $y(1) = 1$. Find $y(2)$ with $h = 0.2$.

5. $\dfrac{dy}{dx} = x\sqrt{1 + y^2}$, $y(1) = 0$. Find $y(3)$ with $h = 0.4$.

6. $\dfrac{dy}{dx} = x\sqrt{1 - y^2}$, $y(1) = 0$. Find $y(2)$ with $h = 0.125$.

7. $\dfrac{dy}{dx} = \dfrac{y}{x} - \dfrac{5}{2}x^2y^3$, $y(1) = \dfrac{1}{\sqrt{2}}$. Find $y(2)$ with $h = 0.125$.

8. $\dfrac{dy}{dx} = \dfrac{-y}{x} + x^2y^2$, $y(1) = \dfrac{2}{9}$. Find $y(3)$ with $h = \frac{1}{3}$.

9. $\dfrac{dy}{dx} = ye^x$, $y(0) = 2$. Find $y(2)$ with $h = 0.2$.

10. $\dfrac{dy}{dx} = xe^y$, $y(0) = 0$. Find $y(1)$ with $h = 0.1$.

In Exercises 11 through 20, use (a) the improved Euler method, or (b) the Runge-Kutta method to graph approximately the solution of the given initial value problem by plotting the points (x_k, y_k) over the indicated range, where $x_k = x_0 + kh$.

11. $y' = xy^2 + y^3$, $y(0) = 1$, $h = 0.02$, $0 \leq x \leq 0.1$

12. $y' = x + \sin(\pi y)$, $y(1) = 0$, $h = 0.2$, $1 \leq x \leq 2$

13. $y' = x + \cos(\pi y)$, $y(0) = 0$, $h = 0.4$, $0 \leq x \leq 2$

14. $y' = \cos(xy)$, $y(0) = 0$, $h = \pi/4$, $0 \leq x \leq \pi$

15. $y' = \sin(xy)$, $y(0) = 1$, $h = \pi/4$, $0 \leq x \leq 2\pi$

16. $y' = \sqrt{x^2 + y^2}$, $y(0) = 1$, $h = 0.5$, $0 \leq x \leq 5$

17. $y' = \sqrt{y^2 - x^2}$, $y(0) = 1$, $h = 0.1$, $0 \leq x \leq 1$

18. $y' = \sqrt{x + y^2}$, $y(0) = 1$, $h = 0.2$, $0 \leq x \leq 1$

19. $y' = \sqrt{x + y^2}$, $y(1) = 2$, $h = -0.2$, $0 \leq x \leq 1$

20. $y' = \sqrt{x^2 + y^2}$, $y(1) = 5$, $h = -0.2$, $0 \leq x \leq 1$

21. Let
$$\dfrac{dy}{dx} = \dfrac{x - y}{x + y}, \quad y(2) = 0.$$

Use the improved Euler method and the Runge-Kutta method to approximate $y(1)$ with $h = -0.2$. Compare your answer with the exact value and explain why both methods failed.

22. Use the improved Euler method and the Runge-Kutta method to approximate $y(3)$ with $h = 0.4$ for the initial value problem

$$\frac{dy}{dx} + \frac{3}{x}y = x^2y^2, \quad y(1) = 2.$$

Compare your answer to the exact answer and

explain why the numerical techniques failed.

23. Repeat Exercise 22 for the initial value problem

$$\frac{dy}{dx} + \frac{y}{x} = x^3y^3, \quad y(1) = 1.$$

24. Let $y' = e^{xy}$, $y(0) = 1$, and obtain a value for $y(4)$ with $h = 0.5$ using the improved Euler method and the Runge-Kutta method. What difficulties are encountered? How much confidence do you have in your answer?

7.2 AN ERROR ANALYSIS FOR EULER'S METHOD (Optional)

In this section we discuss only the discretization errors encountered in the use of Euler's method. Round-off errors depend not only on the method and the number of steps in the calculation, but also on the type of instrument (hand-calculator, slide rule, computer, pencil and paper, etc.) used for computing the answer. Round-off error will not be discussed in this section (it will be discussed in Section 7.5), although it never should be ignored.

Let us again consider the first-order initial value problem

$$y' = f(x, y), \quad y(x_0) = y_0, \tag{1}$$

and use the iteration scheme

$$y_{n+1} = y_n + hf(x_n, y_n), \tag{2}$$

where h is a fixed step size.

We shall assume for the remainder of this section that $f(x, y)$ possesses continuous first partial derivatives. Then, on any finite interval, $\partial f(x, y)/\partial y$ is bounded by some constant that we denote by L (a continuous function is always bounded on a closed, bounded interval). Since $y'(x) = f(x, y)$, we obtain, by the chain rule,

$$y''(x) = \frac{\partial f}{\partial x}(x, y) + \frac{\partial f}{\partial y}(x, y)y'(x),$$

which must be continuous since it is the sum of continuous functions. Hence $y''(x)$ must be bounded on the interval $x_0 \leq x \leq a$. So we assume that $|y''(x)| < M$ for some positive constant M.

We now wish to estimate the error e_n at the nth step of the iteration defined by Eq. (2). Since $y(x_n)$ is the exact value of the solution $y(x)$ at the point $x_n = x_0 + nh$, and y_n is the approximate value at that point, the error at the nth step is given by

$$e_n = y_n - y(x_n). \tag{3}$$

Note that $y_0 = y(x_0)$, so that $e_0 = 0$.

Now $y(x_{n+1}) = y(x_n + h)$ and $y''(x)$ is continuous. So we may use Taylor's theorem with remainder to obtain

$$y(x_{n+1}) = y(x_n + h) = y(x_n) + hy'(x_n) + \frac{h^2}{2} y''(\xi_n), \tag{4}$$

where $x_n \leq \xi_n \leq x_{n+1}$. We may now state the main result of this section.

Theorem 1   Let $f(x, y)$ have continuous first partial derivatives and let y_n be the approximate solution of Eq. (1) generated by Euler's method [Eq. (2)]. Suppose that $y(x)$ is defined and the inequalities

$$\left| \frac{\partial f}{\partial y} (x, y) \right| < L \quad \text{and} \quad |y''(x)| < M$$

hold on the bounded interval $x_0 \leq x \leq a$. Then the error $e_n = y_n - y(x_n)$ satisfies the inequality

$$\boxed{|e_n| \leq \frac{hM}{2L} (e^{(x_n - x_0)L} - 1) = \frac{hM}{2L} (e^{nhL} - 1).} \tag{5}$$

In particular, since $x_n - x_0 \leq a - x_0$ (which is finite), every $|e_n|$ tends to zero as h tends to zero.

Proof   Subtracting Eq. (4) from Eq. (2) yields

$$y_{n+1} - y(x_{n+1}) = y_n - y(x_n) + h[f(x_n, y_n) - y'(x_n)] - \frac{h^2}{2} y''(\xi_n)$$

or

$$e_{n+1} = e_n + h[f(x_n, y_n) - f(x_n, y(x_n))] - \frac{h^2}{2} y''(\xi_n). \tag{6}$$

By the mean value theorem of differential calculus,

$$f(x_n, y_n) - f(x_n, y(x_n)) = \frac{\partial f}{\partial y} (x_n, \hat{y}_n)[y_n - y(x_n)]$$

$$= \frac{\partial f}{\partial y} (x_n, \hat{y}_n) e_n, \tag{7}$$

where $\hat{y}_n$ is between y_n and $y(x_n)$. We substitute Eq. (7) into Eq. (6) to obtain

$$e_{n+1} = e_n + h \frac{\partial f}{\partial y} (x_n, \hat{y}_n) e_n - \frac{h^2}{2} y''(\xi_n). \tag{8}$$

But $|\partial f / \partial y| \leq L$ and $|y''| \leq M$, so that taking the absolute value of both sides of Eq. (8) and using the triangle inequality, we obtain

$$|e_{n+1}| \leq |e_n| + hL |e_n| + \frac{h^2}{2} M = (1 + hL) |e_n| + \frac{h^2}{2} M. \tag{9}$$

We now consider the first-order difference equation

$$r_{n+1} = (1 + hL)r_n + \frac{h^2}{2} M, \quad r_0 = 0, \tag{10}$$

and claim that if r_n is the solution to Eq. (10), then $|e_n| \leq r_n$. We show this by induction. It is true for $n = 0$, since $e_0 = r_0 = 0$. We assume it is true for $n = k$ and prove it for $n = k + 1$. That is, we assume that $|e_m| \leq r_m$, for $m = 0, 1, \ldots, k$. Then

$$r_{k+1} = (1 + hL)r_k + \frac{h^2}{2} M \geq (1 + hL)|e_k| + \frac{h^2}{2} M \geq |e_{k+1}|,$$

and the claim is proved. [The last step follows from Eq. (9).] We can solve the constant-coefficient first-order nonhomogeneous difference equation (10) by proceeding inductively: $r_1 = h^2M/2 = [(1 + hL) - 1]hM/2$, $r_2 = [(1 + hL) + 1]h^2M/2 = [(1 + hL)^2 - 1]hM/2L$, and, using the geometrical progression (Eq. (7) of Section 5.1),

$$r_n = \frac{hM}{2L}(1 + hL)^n - \frac{hM}{2L}.$$

Now, $e^{hL} = 1 + hL + h^2L^2/2! + \cdots$, so that

$$1 + hL \leq e^{hL} \quad \text{and} \quad (1 + hL)^n \leq (e^{hL})^n = e^{nhL}.$$

Thus

$$|e_n| \leq r_n \leq \frac{hM}{2L} e^{nhL} - \frac{hM}{2L} = \frac{hM}{2L}(e^{nhL} - 1). \tag{11}$$

But $x_n = x_0 + nh$, so that $x_n - x_0 = nh$ and Eq. (11) becomes

$$|e_n| \leq \frac{hM}{2L}(e^{(x_n - x_0)L} - 1),$$

and the theorem is proved. ∎

Theorem 1 not only shows that the errors get small as h tends to zero, but also tells us *how fast* the errors decrease. If we define the constant k by

$$k = \frac{M}{2L} |e^{(a - x_0)L} - 1|, \tag{12}$$

then we have

$$|e_n| \leq kh. \tag{13}$$

Thus the error is bounded by a *linear* function of h. (Note that $|e_n|$ is bounded by a term that depends only on h, not on n.) Roughly speaking, this implies that the error decreases at a rate proportional to the decrease in the step size. If, for example, we halve the step size, then we can expect at least to halve the error. Actually, since the estimates used in arriving at

Eq. (13) were very crude, we can often do better, as in Example 1 in Section 7.1, where we halved the step size and decreased the error by a factor of four. Nevertheless, it is useful to have an upper bound for the error. It should be noted, however, that this bound may be difficult to obtain, since it is frequently difficult to find a bound for $y''(x)$.

Example 1   Consider the equation $y' = y$, $y(0) = 1$. We have

$$f(x, y) = y \quad \text{and} \quad \left| \frac{\partial f}{\partial y}(x, y) \right| = 1 = L.$$

Since the solution of the problem is $y(x) = e^x$, we have $|y''| \leq e^1 = M$ on the interval $0 \leq x \leq 1$. Then Eq. (12) becomes

$$k = \frac{e}{2} |e - 1| = \frac{e^2 - e}{2} \approx 2.34,$$

so that

$$|e_n| \leq 2.34h.$$

Therefore, using a step size of $h = 0.1$, say, we can expect to have an error at each step of less than 0.234 (see Table 1). We note that the greatest actual error is about half of the maximum possible error according to Eq. (13).

Table 1

x_n	$y'_n = f(x_n, y_n)$	$y_{n+1} = y_n + hy'_n$	$y(x_n) = e^{x_n}$	$e_n = y_n - y(x_n)$
0.0	1	1.1	1	0
0.1	1.1	1.21	1.11	−0.01
0.2	1.21	1.33	1.22	−0.01
0.3	1.33	1.46	1.35	−0.02
0.4	1.46	1.61	1.49	−0.03
0.5	1.61	1.77	1.65	−0.04
0.6	1.77	1.95	1.82	−0.05
0.7	1.95	2.15	2.01	−0.06
0.8	2.15	2.37	2.23	−0.08
0.9		2.61	2.46	−0.09
1.0	2.61		2.72	−0.11

It turns out that it is possible to derive error estimates like Eq. (11) or (13) for every method we shall discuss in this chapter for solving differential equations numerically. Actually, to derive these estimates would take us beyond the scope of this book,† but we should mention that for the

---

† For a more detailed analysis, see, for example, C. W. Gear, *Numerical Initial Value Problems in Ordinary Differential Equations.* Englewood Cliffs, N. J.: Prentice-Hall (1971).

Runge-Kutta method discussed in Section 7.1, the discretization error e_n is of the form

$$|e_n| \leqslant kh^4,$$

for some appropriate constant k. Thus halving the step size, for example, has the effect of decreasing the bound on the error by a factor of $2^4 = 16$. However, the price for this greater accuracy is to have to calculate $f(x, y)$ at four points [see Eq. (7) in Section 7.1] for each step in the iteration.

EXERCISES 7.2

1. Consider the differential equation $y' = -y$, $y(0) = 1$. We wish to find $y(1)$.

a) Calculate an upper bound on the error of Euler's method as a function of h.

b) Calculate this bound for $h = 0.1$ and $h = 0.2$.

c) Perform the iterations for $h = 0.2$ and $h = 0.1$ and compare the actual error with the maximum error.

2. Consider the equation of Exercise 1. If we ignore round-off error, how many iterations would have to be performed in order to guarantee that the calculation of $y(1)$ obtained by Euler's method be correct to:

a) five decimal places?

b) six decimal places?

3. Answer the questions in Exercise 2 for the equation

$$y' = 3y - x^2, \quad y(1) = 2$$

if we wish to find $y(1.5)$.

7.3 RUNGE-KUTTA FORMULAS

In this section we will derive some techniques similar to the Runge-Kutta method [see Eqs. (6) and (7) in Section 7.1] for the numerical calculation of a solution to an initial value problem. In Euler's method we used one value for the derivative $y' = f(x, y)$ for each iteration. In the improved Euler's method we used two values. In the Runge-Kutta formulas we shall discuss, we must make use of four values of the derivative for each iteration. We will show how to find the four "best" values in a sense to be made precise later.

To begin, we need to recall the Taylor series expansions of functions of one or two variables:

$$y(x_0 + h) = y(x_0) + hy'(x_0) + \frac{h^2}{2!} y''(x_0) + \frac{h^3}{3!} y'''(x_0) + \cdots, \tag{1}$$

$$f(x_0 + mh, y_0 + nh) = f(x_0, y_0) + h(mf_x + nf_y)$$

$$+ \frac{h^2}{2!} (m^2 f_{xx} + 2mn f_{xy} + n^2 f_{yy})$$

$$+ \frac{h^3}{3!} (m^3 f_{xxx} + 3m^2 n f_{xxy} + 3mn^2 f_{xyy} + n^3 f_{yyy})$$

$$+ \cdots, \tag{2}$$

where the partials are all evaluated at the point (x_0, y_0). Since

$$y' = f(x, y), \tag{3}$$

we find that

$$y'' = f_x + (f_y)y' = f_x + ff_y,$$
$$y''' = f_{xx} + 2ff_{xy} + f^2 f_{yy} + f_y(f_x + ff_y),$$

and so on. (Note that $f_{xy} = f_{yx}$ when these derivatives are continuous.) Thus Eq. (1) can be written in the form

$$y_1 - y_0 = hf + \frac{h^2}{2}(f_x + ff_y) + \frac{h^3}{6}[f_{xx} + 2ff_{xy} + f^2 f_{yy} + f_y(f_x + ff_y)] + \cdots. \tag{4}$$

The main idea is somehow to select several points (x, y) so that the Taylor series expansions [Eq. (2)] of the corresponding $f(x, y)$ terms coincide with the terms on the right-hand side of Eq. (4). Suppose we let

$$m_1 = hf(x_0, y_0),$$
$$m_2 = hf(x_0 + nh, y_0 + nm_1),$$
$$m_3 = hf(x_0 + ph, y_0 + pm_2),$$
$$m_4 = hf(x_0 + qh, y_0 + qm_3).$$

(The reason for doing this will be made clear shortly.) Using Eq. (2), we may write these values as

$$m_1 = hf,$$
$$m_2 = h\left[f + nh(f_x + ff_y) + \frac{(nh)^2}{2}(f_{xx} + 2ff_{xy} + f^2 f_{yy}) + \cdots\right],$$
$$m_3$$
$$= h\left\{f + ph(f_x + ff_y) + \frac{h^2}{2}[p^2(f_{xx} + 2ff_{xy} + f^2 f_{yy}) + 2npf_y(f_x + ff_y)] + \cdots\right\},$$
$$m_4$$
$$= h\left\{f + qh(f_x + ff_y) + \frac{h^2}{2}[q^2(f_{xx} + 2ff_{xy} + f^2 f_{yy}) + 2pqf_y(f_x + ff_y)] + \cdots\right\},$$

where all functions are evaluated at the point (x_0, y_0).

We now consider an expression of the form

$$am_1 + bm_2 + cm_3 + dm_4$$

and try to equate it to the right-hand side of Eq. (4). This will have the effect of giving us a numerical scheme that agrees with the solution to Eq. (3) up to and including third-order terms. Then the error will be no greater than terms like kh^4, and so on. Matching like expressions, we find that

$$
\begin{aligned}
a + b \quad + c \quad + d \quad &= 1, \\
bn + cp \quad + dq &= \tfrac{1}{2}, \\
bn^2 + cp^2 + dq^2 &= \tfrac{1}{3}, \\
cnp + dpq &= \tfrac{1}{6}.
\end{aligned}
\tag{5}
$$

Now any solution of these equations will produce a method in which there is no error up to the third-order terms. Suppose we take $n = p = \tfrac{1}{2}$ and $q = 1$. Then Eq. (5) reduces to the system of equations

$$
\begin{aligned}
a + b + \quad c + \quad d &= 1, \\
b + \quad c + \quad 2d &= 1, \\
3b + 3c + 12d &= 4, \\
3c + \quad 6d &= 2,
\end{aligned}
$$

which has the solution $a = d = \tfrac{1}{6}$, $b = c = \tfrac{1}{3}$. Thus the Runge-Kutta formula [Eq. (6) of Section 7.1] agrees with $y_1 - y_0$ for all terms up to and including the terms in h^3. Actually, with quite a bit more work, one can show that they agree in the h^4 terms, too. Thus the error (if any) involves only terms in h^5 and higher. Hence, for small h, we should expect to get very good results.

Other formulas are also readily derivable. Suppose we choose $n = \tfrac{1}{3}$, $p = \tfrac{2}{3}$, $q = 1$. Then Eq. (5) yields

$$
\begin{aligned}
a + b + \quad c + \quad d &= 1, \\
2b + 4c + \quad 6d &= 3, \\
b + 4c + \quad 9d &= 3, \\
4c + 12d &= 3,
\end{aligned}
$$

which has the solution $a = d = \tfrac{1}{8}$, $b = c = \tfrac{3}{8}$. The formula, known as the *Kutta-Simpson $\tfrac{3}{8}$-rule*, may be written as

$$
y_1 = y_0 + \tfrac{1}{8}(m_1 + 3m_2 + 3m_3 + m_4),
$$

where

$$
\begin{aligned}
m_1 &= hf(x_0, y_0), \\
m_2 &= hf(x_0 + h/3, y_0 + m_1/3), \\
m_3 &= hf(x_0 + 2h/3, y_0 + 2m_2/3), \\
m_4 &= hf(x_0 + h, y_0 + m_3).
\end{aligned}
\tag{6}
$$

Similarly, the choice $n = \tfrac{1}{3}$, $p = \tfrac{2}{3}$, $q = 1$ yields the solution $a = c = 0$, $b = \tfrac{3}{4}$, $d = \tfrac{1}{4}$; hence

$$
y_1 = y_0 + \tfrac{1}{4}(3m_2 + m_4),
$$

where m_2 and m_4 are defined as in Eq. (6). Since the number of possible choices of n, p, and q is infinite, the reader may be amused by solving Eq. (5) for a, b, c, and d with whatever values of n, p, and q that he or she selects.

EXERCISES 7.3

1. Set $d = 0$ in Eq. (5) and let $n = \frac{1}{3}$, $p = \frac{2}{3}$. Then find the coefficients a, b, and c for these choices. The resulting formula is called *Heun's formula*.

2. Set $a = d = 0$, $b = \frac{3}{4}$, $c = \frac{1}{4}$ and find n and p.

3. Set $a = \frac{2}{8}$, $b = c = \frac{3}{8}$, $d = 0$ and find n and p.

4. Prove that the Runge-Kutta formula agrees with Eq. (4) up to and including the h^4 terms.

5. Explain why the choice $n = \frac{1}{3}$, $p = \frac{2}{3}$, $q = 1$ yielded two sets of solutions a, b, c, and d. Are other solutions possible? Does the choice $n = p = \frac{1}{2}$, $q = 1$ allow for multiple solutions?

7.4 PREDICTOR-CORRECTOR FORMULAS

The simplest type of predictor-corrector formula is one that we have already used, namely, the improved Euler method. Recall that with this method, we first obtain a value for y_n by Euler's method (the *predicting* part of the process) and then improve on the accuracy of the method by applying a trapezoidal rule (the *correcting* phase of the process). In this section we will indicate how such methods are derived, and provide several procedures that will perform their tasks with a high degree of accuracy.

We begin by developing a procedure for obtaining *quadrature formulas*. These formulas are designed to obtain the approximate value of a definite integral by using equally spaced values of the integrand. Two well-known quadrature formulas are the trapezoidal rule and Simpson's rule,† which can be written in the forms

$$y_1 - y_0 = \frac{h}{2}[y_0' + y_1'], \tag{1}$$

$$y_2 - y_0 = \frac{h}{3}[y_0' + 4y_1' + y_2'], \tag{2}$$

respectively, where h is the step size, $x_n = x_0 + nh$, $y_n = y(x_n)$, and $y_n' = f(x_n, y_n)$. Note that, unlike in previously discussed methods, here we have slightly shifted the point of view by representing the right-hand side as a sum of derivatives instead of values of the function f.

In Eq. (1) we are using only the points y_0' and y_1' whereas in Eq. (2) we also use y_2'. For this reason, Eq. (1) is called a 2-*point quadrature formula*, while Eq. (2) is a 3-*point quadrature formula*. In general, the more points involved, the higher the accuracy. In the present case, Eq. (1) provides the

---

† These rules can be found in most calculus books.

exact integral only for straight lines, whereas Eq. (2) is also exact for quadratic polynomials (see Exercises 15 and 16).

We shall now develop a method for obtaining 3-point quadrature formulas. The method is easily adapted to n-point quadrature formulas.

3-Point Quadrature Formulas

Assume that the function $y(x)$ is a quadratic polynomial

$$y(x) = a_0 + a_1 x + a_2 x^2. \tag{3}$$

Let h and x_0 be fixed real numbers and define $x_k = x_0 + kh$, for all integers k. Let $y_k = y(x_k)$. We wish to find coefficients A_1, A_2, A_3 such that

$$y_j - y_i = h[A_0 y_0' + A_1 y_1' + A_2 y_2'], \tag{4}$$

where $i, j = 0, 1, 2$ and $i \neq j$. This will lead to an integration scheme that is exact for quadratic polynomials. For example, if $i = 0$, then the left-hand side of Eq. (4) becomes

$$y_j - y_0 = a_1(x_j - x_0) + a_2(x_j^2 - x_0^2)$$
$$= a_1 jh + a_2[2x_0 jh + (jh)^2] = j(a_1 h + 2a_2 x_0 h) + j^2(a_2 h^2). \tag{5}$$

On the other hand, using the facts that $y' = a_1 + 2a_2 x$ and $x_k = x_0 + kh$, we find that the right-hand side of Eq. (4) becomes

$$h[A_0 y_0' + A_1 y_1' + A_2 y_2'] = h[A_0(a_1 + 2a_2 x_0) + A_1(a_1 + 2a_2 x_1)$$
$$+ A_2(a_1 + 2a_2 x_2)]$$
$$= (A_0 + A_1 + A_2)(a_1 h + 2a_2 x_0 h)$$
$$+ (2A_1 + 4A_2)(a_2 h^2). \tag{6}$$

Equating Eqs. (5) and (6), we obtain the simultaneous equations

$$A_0 + A_1 + A_2 = j,$$
$$2A_1 + 4A_2 = j^2. \tag{7}$$

Since this system is underdetermined, it has an infinite number of solutions A_0, A_1, A_2, each leading to a different quadrature formula. For example, if $j = 1$, we can pick $A_0 = \frac{5}{6}$, $A_1 = -\frac{1}{6}$, $A_2 = \frac{1}{3}$ and arrive at the formula

$$y_1 - y_0 = \frac{h}{6}(5y_0' - y_1' + 2y_2'). \tag{8}$$

If $j = 2$, then selecting $A_0 = \frac{1}{3}$, $A_1 = \frac{4}{3}$, $A_2 = \frac{1}{3}$ will yield Simpson's rule (2). In addition, quadrature formulas may be added or subtracted to yield new formulas. For example, subtracting Eq. (8) from Eq. (2) yields the *Adams-Bashforth formula*

$$y_2 - y_1 = \frac{h}{2}[-y_0' + 3y_1']. \tag{9}$$

Predictor-Corrector Methods

Let us now illustrate how predictor-corrector formulas are used. Suppose we are given the initial value problem

$$\frac{dy}{dx} = f(x, y), \quad y(x_0) = y_0. \tag{10}$$

The value y_0 is given, and y'_0 can be obtained by evaluating Eq. (10) at $x = x_0$, $y = y_0$. We next perform an improved Euler method computation to obtain y_1 [and y'_1 by means of Eq. (10)]. At this point it is often desirable to apply repeatedly the trapezoidal rule to the process until the value of y_1 stabilizes (that is, remains unchanged to a given number of decimal places; see Example 1). Then since y_0, y'_0, y_1, and y'_1 are all known, we may use Eq. (9) to *predict* the value of y_2. This value is then used in Eq. (10) to obtain y'_2, and the trapezoidal rule [Eq. (1)] is used to *correct* the y_2 value previously determined. The process is now repeated to predict and correct y_3 and y'_3 in terms of the known values y_1, y'_1, y_2, y'_2. We use

$$y_{n+1} = y_n + \frac{h}{2}[-y'_{n-1} + 3y'_n] \tag{11}$$

to *predict* the value of y_{n+1}, Eq. (10) to obtain y'_{n+1},

$$y_{n+1} = y_n + \frac{h}{2}[y'_{n+1} + y'_n] \tag{12}$$

to *correct* the value of y_{n+1}, and Eq. (10) again to obtain y'_{n+1}.

Example 1 Let $dy/dx = y + x^2$, $y(0) = 1$, and suppose we wish to find $y(1)$, with $h = 0.2$, by using the predictor-corrector formulas (11) and (12).

   The predictor formula (11) requires that we know the values of y'_0, y_1, and y'_1 before it can be used to generate y_2. At this point, the only one of these three values that we know is

$$y'_0 = f(x_0, y_0) = y_0 + x_0^2 = 1,$$

since $x_0 = 0$, $y_0 = y(x_0) = y(0) = 1$. Therefore, before we can begin using the predictor formula (11), we must determine y_1. [Once we know y_1 we can compute $y'_1 = f(x_1, y_1)$.] The usual method for obtaining y_1 is to use the improved Euler method *repeatedly*. We illustrate this procedure below:

x_0	y_0	y'_0	$\bar{y}_1$	$\bar{y}'_1$	y_1
0.0	1.0	1.0	1.20	1.24	1.22
			1.22	1.26	1.23
			1.23	1.27	1.23

The first entry in the $\bar{y}_1$ column is obtained by Euler's formula: $y_1 = y_0 + hy_0'$. The entries in the $\bar{y}_1'$ column are obtained from the differential equation $\bar{y}_1' = f(x_1, \bar{y}_1) = \bar{y}_1 + x_1^2$. The last column is determined by the improved Euler formula

$$y_1 = y_0 + \frac{h}{2}(y_0' + \bar{y}_1'),$$

and the resulting value for y_1 is transferred to the next row in the $\bar{y}_1$ column. We then repeat the steps in the $\bar{y}_1'$ and y_1 columns. We see that the process stabilizes with $y_1 = 1.23$ and $y_1' = 1.27$ (provided that we are using two decimal place accuracy).

We now apply Eqs. (11) and (12) where we have arranged the calculations in Table 1. The result is better than the answer obtained by the improved Euler method (with slightly more work).

Table 1

x_n	y_n	$y_n' = f(x_n, y_n)$	Predictor $y_{n+1} = y_n + \frac{h}{2}(-y_{n-1}' + 3y_n')$	y_{n+1}'	Corrector $y_{n+1} = y_n + \frac{h}{2}(y_{n+1}' + y_n')$
0.0	1.0	1.00			
0.2	1.23	1.27	$1.23 + (0.1)(-1.0 + 3.81) = 1.51$	1.67	$1.23 + (0.1)(1.67 + 1.27) = 1.52$
0.4	1.52	1.68	$1.52 + (0.1)(-1.27 + 5.04) = 1.90$	2.26	$1.52 + (0.1)(2.26 + 1.68) = 1.91$
0.6	1.91	2.27	$1.91 + (0.1)(-1.68 + 6.81) = 2.42$	3.06	$1.91 + (0.1)(3.06 + 2.27) = 2.44$
0.8	2.44	3.08	$2.44 + (0.1)(-2.27 + 9.24) = 3.14$	4.14	$2.44 + (0.1)(4.14 + 3.08) = 3.16$
1.0	3.16				

A very accurate predictor-corrector method due to Milne uses a 4-point quadrature formula as a predictor and Simpson's rule as a corrector:

$$\text{P:} \quad y_{n+4} - y_n = \frac{4h}{3}[2y_{n+1}' - y_{n+2}' + 2y_{n+3}'],$$

$$\text{C:} \quad y_{n+4} - y_{n+2} = \frac{h}{3}[y_{n+2}' + 4y_{n+3}' + y_{n+4}']. \tag{13}$$

To apply this method, it is necessary to have good values for y_0, y_0', y_1, y_1', y_2, y_2', y_3, and y_3'.

Predictor-corrector methods have many advantages from the point of view of accuracy and the amount of work involved. The extra step involved in "correcting" dramatically improves the accuracy, without requiring an inordinate amount of extra work.

EXERCISES 7.4

In Exercises 1 through 10, solve each problem exactly using the methods of Chapter 2. Then:

a) Use the predictor-corrector method of Example 1 [formulas (11) and (12)] and the indicated value of h to find an approximate solution to the given value of y;

b) Use the predictor-corrector method in Eq. (13) with the given h to find the indicated value of y. Use the values generated in part (a) to initialize Milne's method.

Compare the accuracy of these methods with the exact answer.

1. $y' = x + y$, $y(0) = 1$. Find $y(1)$ with $h = 0.2$.

2. $y' = x - y$, $y(1) = 2$. Find $y(3)$ with $h = 0.4$.

3. $y' = \dfrac{x - y}{x + y}$, $y(2) = 1$. Find $y(1)$ with $h = -0.2$.

4. $y' = (y/x) + (y/x)^2$, $y(1) = 1$. Find $y(2)$ with $h = 0.2$.

5. $y' = x\sqrt{1 + y^2}$, $y(1) = 0$. Find $y(3)$ with $h = 0.4$.

6. $y' = x\sqrt{1 - y^2}$, $y(1) = 0$. Find $y(2)$ with $h = \frac{1}{8}$.

7. $y' = (y/x) - (5x^2y^3/2)$, $y(1) = 1/\sqrt{2}$. Find $y(2)$ with $h = \frac{1}{8}$.

8. $y' = (-y/x) + x^2y^2$, $y(1) = \frac{2}{9}$. Find $y(3)$ with $h = \frac{1}{3}$.

9. $y' = ye^x$, $y(0) = 2$. Find $y(2)$ with $h = 0.2$.

10. $y' = xe^y$, $y(0) = 0$. Find $y(1)$ with $h = 0.1$.

11. Obtain the trapezoidal rule (1) by using the 3-point quadrature formulas (4) and (7).

12. Obtain the 3-point quadrature formulas:

a) $y_1 - y_0 = \dfrac{h}{12}(5y_0' + 8y_1' - y_2')$;

b) $y_2 - y_0 = \dfrac{h}{8}(y_0' + 14y_1' + y_2')$;

c) $y_2 - y_0 = \dfrac{h}{4}(y_0' + 6y_1' + y_2')$.

13. Obtain the 3-point quadrature formula

$$y_3 - y_0 = \frac{h}{2}[-y_0' + 5y_1' + 2y_2'].$$

14. Use the formula obtained in Exercise 13 and Simpson's rule as a predictor-corrector to solve the initial value problem

$$y' = x + y, \quad y(0) = 1,$$

for $y(1)$ with $h = 0.2$. Use the improved Euler method to find y_1 and y_2.

15. Let $y(x) = ax + b$. Show that the trapezoidal rule (1) provides the exact value for $\int_0^1 y(x)\,dx$ for step sizes $h = \frac{1}{2}$ and $\frac{1}{5}$.

16. Let $y(x) = ax^2 + bx + c$. Show that Simpson's rule (2) provides the exact value for $\int_0^1 y(x)\,dx$ for step sizes $h = \frac{1}{4}$ and $\frac{1}{8}$.

17. Show that the equations for 4-point quadrature formulas analogous to Eq. (7) are

$$A_0 + A_1 + A_2 + A_3 = j,$$
$$2A_1 + 4A_2 + 6A_3 = j^2,$$
$$3A_1 + 12A_2 + 27A_3 = j^3.$$

Use these equations to derive Milne's equation (13).

18. Obtain the underdetermined system of equations for 5-point quadrature formulas analogous to those in Exercise 17.

7.5 THE PROPAGATION OF ROUND-OFF ERROR: AN EXAMPLE OF NUMERICAL INSTABILITY (Optional)

In this section we will show how a theoretically very accurate method can produce results that are useless. A *multistep method* is a method (such as a predictor-corrector formula) that involves information about the solution at more than one point. Consider the multistep method given by the equation

$$y_{n+1} = y_{n-1} + 2hf(x_n, y_n). \tag{1}$$

Here it is necessary to use both the nth and the $(n - 1)$st iterate to obtain the $(n + 1)$st iterate. It can be shown† that this method has the following error estimate:

$$|e_n| = |y_n - y(x_n)| \leqslant kh^2.$$

Since the error for Euler's method is $|e_n| \leqslant kh$, we would theoretically expect more accuracy in solving our initial value problem by using Eq. (1) than by using Euler's method. However, this does not always turn out to be the case.

Example 1   Consider the initial value problem

$$y' = -y + 2, \quad y(0) = 1.$$

The solution to this equation is easily obtained: $y(x) = 2 - e^{-x}$. Let us obtain $y(5)$ by Euler's method and the method of Eq. (1). To use the latter, we need two initial values y_0 and y_1. Since we know the solution, we use the exact value $y_1 = y(x_1) = 2 - e^{-x_1}$. Table 1 illustrates the computation

Table 1

x_n	$y(x_n) = 2 - e^{-x_n}$	$y_n^{(E)} = y_{n-1}^{(E)} + h(2 - y_{n-1}^{(E)})$	$y_n^{(2s)} = y_{n-2}^{(2s)} + 2h(2 - y_{n-1}^{(2s)})$	$e_n^{(E)}$	$e_n^{(2s)}$
0.00	1.0000	1.0000	1.0000	0.0000	0.0000
0.25	1.2212	1.2500	1.2212	0.0288	0.0000
0.50	1.3935	1.4375	1.3894	0.0440	−0.0041
0.75	1.5276	1.5781	1.5265	0.0505	−0.0011
1.00	1.6321	1.6836	1.6262	0.0515	−0.0059
1.25	1.7135	1.7627	1.7134	0.0492	−0.0001
1.50	1.7769	1.8220	1.7695	0.0453	−0.0074
1.75	1.8262	1.8665	1.8287	0.0403	+0.0025
2.00	1.8647	1.8999	1.8552	0.0352	−0.0095
2.25	1.8946	1.9249	1.9011	0.0303	+0.0065
2.50	1.9179	1.9437	1.9047	0.0258	−0.0132
2.75	1.9361	1.9578	1.9488	0.0217	+0.0127
3.00	1.9502	1.9684	1.9303	0.0182	−0.0199
3.25	1.9612	1.9763	1.9837	0.0151	+0.0225
3.50	1.9698	1.9822	1.9385	0.0124	−0.0313
3.75	1.9765	1.9867	2.0145	0.0102	+0.0380
4.00	1.9817	1.9900	1.9313	0.0083	−0.0504
4.25	1.9857	1.9925	2.0489	0.0068	+0.0632
4.50	1.9889	1.9944	1.9069	0.0055	−0.0820
4.75	1.9913	1.9958	2.0955	0.0045	+0.1042
5.00	1.9933	1.9969	1.8952	0.0036	−0.0981

† See S. D. Conte, *Elements of Numerical Analysis*, Section 6.6. New York: McGraw-Hill (1965).

with a step size $h = 0.25$. The second column is the correct value of $y(x_n)$ to four decimal places. Column three gives the Euler iterates, and column four gives the iterates obtained by the two-step method (1). Column five is the Euler error, $e_n^{(\text{Euler})} = y_n^{(\text{Euler})} - y(x_n)$, and column six is the error of the two-step method, $e_n^{(2s)} = y_n^{(2s)} - y(x_n)$.

It is evident that the two-step method (1) produces a smaller error for small values of x_n than Euler's method. However, as x_n increases, the error in Euler's method decreases, whereas the error in the two-step method not only increases but does so with oscillating sign. This phenomenon is called *numerical instability*. As we shall see, it is due to a propagation of round-off errors.

Let us now explain what will lead to this instability. In the example, $f(x_n, y_n) = -y_n + 2$, so that Eq. (1) is

$$y_{n+1} = y_{n-1} + 2h(2 - y_n)$$

or

$$y_{n+1} + 2hy_n - y_{n-1} = 4h, \quad y_0 = 1. \tag{2}$$

Equation (2) is a linear nonhomogeneous second-order difference equation with constant coefficients that can be solved by the methods of Section 4.8 of the long version of this text. The general solution is given by

$$y_n = c_1\lambda_1^n + c_2\lambda_2^n + 2, \tag{3}$$

where λ_1 and λ_2 are the roots of the characteristic equation

$$\lambda^2 + 2h\lambda - 1 = 0.$$

Thus,

$$\lambda_1 = \frac{-2h + \sqrt{4h^2 + 4}}{2} = -h + \sqrt{1 + h^2}$$

and

$$\lambda_2 = -h - \sqrt{1 + h^2}. \tag{4}$$

By the binomial theorem (see Exercise 25 in Section 5.1),

$$(1 + h^2)^{1/2} = 1 + \tfrac{1}{2}h^2 - \tfrac{1}{8}h^4 + \tfrac{1}{16}h^6 - \cdots,$$

where the omitted terms are higher powers of h. Hence the roots (4) of the characteristic equation can be written as

$$\lambda_1 = 1 - h + \alpha(h) \quad \text{and} \quad \lambda_2 = -1 - h - \alpha(h), \tag{5}$$

where

$$\alpha(h) = \frac{h^2}{2} - \frac{h^4}{8} + \frac{h^6}{16} - \cdots.$$

Substituting Eqs. (5) into Eq. (3) yields

$$y_n = c_1[1 - h + \alpha(h)]^n + c_2(-1)^n[1 + h + \alpha(h)]^n + 2. \tag{6}$$

From calculus we know that

$$\lim_{k \to 0}\left(1 + \frac{1}{k}\right)^k = \lim_{h \to 0}(1 + h)^{1/h} = e.$$

Therefore, since $x_n = 0 + nh = nh$, we have

$$\lim_{h \to 0}(1 - h)^n = \lim_{h \to 0}(1 - h)^{x_n/h} = e^{-x_n} \quad \text{and} \quad \lim_{h \to 0}(1 + h)^n = e^{x_n}.$$

Hence as $h \to 0$, we may ignore the higher-order terms $\alpha(h)$ in Eq. (6) to obtain

$$y_n = c_1 e^{-x_n} + 2 + c_2(-1)^n e^{x_n}. \tag{7}$$

Here lies the problem. The exact solution of the problem requires that $c_1 = -1$ and $c_2 = 0$. However, even a small round-off error may cause c_2 to be nonzero and this error will grow exponentially while the real solution is approaching the constant two. This is the phenomenon we observed in Table 1. Note that the $(-1)^n$ in Eq. (7) causes the errors to oscillate (as we also observed).

The problem arose because we approximated a *first*-order differential equation by a *second*-order difference equation. Such approximations do not always lead to this kind of instability, but it is a possibility that cannot be ignored. In general, to analyze the effectiveness of a given method, we must not only estimate the discretization error, but also show that the method is not numerically unstable (that is, *it is numerically stable*), for the given problem.

7.6 SYSTEMS AND BOUNDARY VALUE PROBLEMS

The methods developed in Sections 7.1, 7.3, and 7.4 can be extended very easily to apply to higher-order equations and systems of equations.

Euler Methods

For this technique and the improved Euler method, it is necessary only to reinterpret the formulas

$$y_{n+1} = y_n + hf(x_n, y_n) \tag{1}$$

and

$$y_{n+1} = y_n + \frac{h}{2}[f(x_n, y_n) + f(x_{n+1}, y_{n+1})], \tag{2}$$

with y_n a vector with as many entries as there are dependent variables. In this case, the function f consists of a vector of functions also. The methods are best illustrated by examples.

Example 1   Consider the initial value problem

$$\frac{dx}{dt} = -3x + 4y, \quad x(0) = 1,$$

$$\frac{dy}{dt} = -2x + 3y, \quad y(0) = 2. \tag{3}$$

Suppose we are seeking the values $x(1)$ and $y(1)$. In this problem t is the independent variable, and x and y are the dependent variables. If we wish to use Euler's method, formula (1) translates into the equations

$$x_{n+1} = x_n + hx'_n = x_n + h(-3x_n + 4y_n),$$

$$y_{n+1} = y_n + hy'_n = y_n + h(-2x_n + 3y_n).$$

The initial values are $x_0 = 1$, $y_0 = 2$, and $h = 0.2$, and the procedure is essentially the same as before (see Table 1).

Table 1

t_n	x_n	y_n	x'_n	y'_n	$x_{n+1} = x_n + hx'_n$	$y_{n+1} = y_n + hy'_n$
0.0	1.00	2.00	5.00	4.00	2.00	2.80
0.2	2.00	2.80	5.20	4.40	3.04	3.68
0.4	3.04	3.68	5.60	4.96	4.16	4.67
0.6	4.16	4.67	6.20	5.69	5.40	5.81
0.8	5.40	5.81	7.04	6.63	6.81	7.14
1.0	6.81	7.14				

The solution of Eqs. (3) is given by

$$x(t) = 3e^t - 2e^{-t}, \quad y(t) = 3e^t - e^{-t},$$

so $x(1) = 3e - 2e^{-1} \approx 7.419$ and $y(1) = 3e - e^{-1} \approx 7.787$, implying that our method has an error of about ten percent. The accuracy may be improved by selecting smaller values of h.

No additional difficulty is caused by having a nonhomogeneous or even nonlinear system of equations.

Predictor-Corrector Methods

Example 2   Adapt the predictor-corrector formulas (11) and (12) in Section 7.4 to the system in Example 1.

We will assume from the calculations in Example 1 that $x_0 = 1$, $x_0' = 5$, $x_1 = 2$, $x_1' = 5.2$, $y_0 = 2$, $y_0' = 4$, $y_1 = 2.8$, $y_1' = 4.4$, and $h = 0.2$. With these values we first predict

$$x_{n+2} = x_{n+1} + \frac{h}{2}(-x_n' + 3x_{n+1}'),$$

$$y_{n+2} = y_{n+1} + \frac{h}{2}(-y_n' + 3y_{n+1}'),$$

(4)

and then use these values to compute x_{n+2}', y_{n+2}', using the system of differential equations (3). Then, to correct these values, we use the trapezoidal rules:

$$x_{n+2} = x_{n+1} + \frac{h}{2}(x_{n+2}' + x_{n+1}'),$$

$$y_{n+2} = y_{n+1} + \frac{h}{2}(y_{n+2}' + y_{n+1}')$$

(5)

and recalculate x_{n+2}', y_{n+2}' with Eqs. (3).

Table 2

					Predictor				Corrector	
t_{n+1}	x_{n+1}	y_{n+1}	x_{n+1}'	y_{n+1}'	x_{n+2}	y_{n+2}	x_{n+2}'	y_{n+2}'	x_{n+2}	y_{n+2}
0.0	1.00	2.00	5.00	4.00						
0.2	2.00	2.80	5.20	4.40	3.06	3.72	5.70	5.04	3.09	3.74
0.4	3.09	3.74	5.69	5.04	4.28	4.81	6.40	5.87	4.30	4.83
0.6	4.30	4.83	6.42	5.89	5.66	6.09	7.38	6.95	5.68	6.11
0.8	5.68	6.11	7.40	6.97	7.26	7.61	8.66	8.31	7.29	7.64
1.0	7.29	7.64								

It is clear that such methods are laborious, but they are easily carried out on a computer. The calculations are shown in Table 2 and agree far better with the exact values

$$x(1) \approx 7.419, \quad y(1) \approx 7.787.$$

(6)

Runge-Kutta Method

The Runge-Kutta formula for a system of differential equations is a direct generalization of Eqs. (6) and (7) in Section 7.1. Suppose that we are given the system

$$\frac{dx}{dt} = f(t, x, y), \quad x(t_0) = x_0,$$

$$\frac{dy}{dt} = g(t, x, y), \quad y(t_0) = y_0.$$

(7)

Then the rule becomes

$$x_1 = x_0 + \tfrac{1}{6}(m_1 + 2m_2 + 2m_3 + m_4),$$
$$y_1 = y_0 + \tfrac{1}{6}(n_1 + 2n_2 + 2n_3 + n_4),$$

(8)

where

$$m_1 = hf(t_0, x_0, y_0) \qquad\qquad n_1 = hg(t_0, x_0, y_0),$$

$$m_2 = hf\left(t_0 + \frac{h}{2}, x_0 + \frac{m_1}{2}, y_0 + \frac{n_1}{2}\right), \quad n_2 = hg\left(t_0 + \frac{h}{2}, x_0 + \frac{m_1}{2}, y_0 + \frac{n_1}{2}\right),$$

$$m_3 = hf\left(t_0 + \frac{h}{2}, x_0 + \frac{m_2}{2}, y_0 + \frac{n_2}{2}\right), \quad n_3 = hg\left(t_0 + \frac{h}{2}, x_0 + \frac{m_2}{2}, y_0 + \frac{n_2}{2}\right),$$

$$m_4 = hf(t_0 + h, x_0 + m_3, y_0 + n_3), \qquad n_4 = hg(t_0 + h, x_0 + m_3, y_0 + n_3).$$

(9)

It should now be apparent how this procedure is generalized for systems involving more dependent variables. We apply the formulas above to the system (3) in Example 1 with $h = 1$:

$$m_1 = 5, \quad n_1 = 4,$$

$$m_2 = \frac{11}{2}, \quad n_2 = 5,$$

$$m_3 = \frac{27}{4}, \quad n_3 = 6,$$

$$m_4 = \frac{35}{4}, \quad n_4 = \frac{17}{2}.$$

We obtain

$$x_1 \approx 7.375, \quad y_1 \approx 7.750.$$

Even though this process involves more complicated computations at each step, it involves less work than predictor-corrector methods. Since it is also quite accurate, it is thus the preferred method for hand calculations.

All of these methods can be applied to higher-order differential equations by converting each higher-order equation into a system of first-order equations using the procedure outlined in Section 3.10.

Boundary Value Problems

Consider the differential equation

$$y'' = f(x, y, y'),$$

(10)

with boundary conditions $y(a) = y_a$ and $y(b) = y_b$. We now describe a procedure, sometimes called the *shooting method*, that is often used to solve such problems. The idea is to convert Eq. (10) into an initial value problem, with initial conditions $y(a) = y_a$ and $y'(a) = M_0$, where the number M_0 is arbitrarily selected. Using one of the previously described techniques (Euler method, Runge-Kutta, or predictor-corrector method), we now calculate the value $y(b) = N_0$ for the initial value problem. This number will undoubtedly be different from the required value y_b, so we again solve Eq. (10) as an initial value problem with $y(a) = y_a$ and $y'(a) = M_1$, obtaining $y(b) = N_1$. The assumption is now made that $y(b)$ varies linearly with the values $y'(a)$, so the next value we choose for $y'(a)$ $(= M_2)$ is selected by solving the equation

$$\frac{M_2 - M_1}{M_0 - M_1} = \frac{y_b - N_1}{N_0 - N_1} \tag{11}$$

or

$$M_2 = M_1 + \frac{y_b - N_1}{N_0 - N_1}(M_0 - M_1). \tag{12}$$

Equation (12) will yield very accurate information if the user is prepared to repeat the process several times. Again, it is clear that since this process is very laborious, it is best performed by using a computer.

Finally, it should be noted that although shooting methods are useful in finding approximate solutions for many boundary value problems, they do not work, for a variety of reasons, for all such problems. Other methods, some very complex, are available to deal with these situations.

EXERCISES 7.6

In Exercises 1 through 8, find $x(1)$ and $y(1)$ with $h = 0.2$ using the

a) Euler method,

b) improved Euler method, and

c) Runge-Kutta method

for each initial value system. Check your accuracy by calculating the exact value.

1. $x' = 4x - 2y,$　$x(0) = 1$
$\quad y' = 5x + 2y,$　$y(0) = 2$

2. $x' = x + y,$　$x(0) = 1$
$\quad y' = x - y,$　$y(0) = 0$

3. $x' = x + 2y,$　$x(0) = 0$
$\quad y' = 3x + 2y,$　$y(0) = 1$

4. $x' = -4x - y,$　$x(0) = 0$
$\quad y' = x - 2y,$　$y(0) = 1$

5. $x' = 2x + y + t,$　$x(0) = 1$
$\quad y' = x + 2y + t^2,$　$y(0) = 0$

6. $x' = x + 2y + t - 1,$　$x(0) = 0$
$\quad y' = 3x + 2y - 5t - 2,$　$y(0) = 4$

7. $x' = 3x + 3y + t,$　$x(0) = 0$
$\quad y' = -x - y + 1,$　$y(0) = 2$

8. $x' = 4x - 3y + t,$　$x(0) = 1$
$\quad y' = 5x - 4y - 1,$　$y(0) = -1$

9. Solve the initial value problem

$$y'' = y' + xy^2, \quad y(0) = 1, \quad y'(0) = 0,$$

for $y(1)$ with $h = 0.2$ by Euler's method.

10. Use the "shooting method" to determine the value of $y'(0)$ for the boundary value problem

$$y'' = -y^2, \quad y(0) = y(1) = 0,$$

in such a way that y is positive over the interval $0 < x < 1$. Use the Runge-Kutta method [Eqs. (8) and (9)] with $h = 1$.

11. Find the maximum value of y over the interval $0 \leqslant x \leqslant 1$ for the boundary value problem

$$y'' + yy' + 1 = 0, \quad y(0) = y(1) = 0.$$

12. Develop a BASIC (or FORTRAN) program to perform the "shooting method" using the improved Euler method for an equation of the form

$$y'' = f(x, y, y'), \quad y(a) = y_a, \quad y(b) = y_b.$$

Use it to find the maximum value of y over the interval $0 \leqslant x \leqslant 1$ for the boundary value problem

$$y'' + \sin y = 0, \quad y(0) = y(1) = 0.$$

REVIEW EXERCISES FOR CHAPTER 7

In Exercises 1 through 6, solve the given initial value problem using the methods of Chapter 2. Then use the

a) improved Euler method or

b) Runge-Kutta method

and the given value of h to obtain an approximate solution at the indicated value of x. Compare the numerical answer with the exact answer.

1. $\dfrac{dy}{dx} = \dfrac{e^x}{y}, \quad y(0) = 2.$ Find $y(3)$ with $h = \frac{1}{2}$.

2. $\dfrac{dy}{dx} = \dfrac{e^y}{x}, \quad y(1) = 0.$ Find $y(\frac{1}{2})$ with $h = -0.1$.

3. $\dfrac{dy}{dx} = \dfrac{y}{\sqrt{1 + x^2}}, \quad y(0) = 1.$ Find $y(3)$ with $h = \frac{1}{2}$.

4. $xy\dfrac{dy}{dx} = y^2 - x^2, \quad y(1) = 2.$ Find $y(3)$ with $h = \frac{1}{2}$.

5. $\dfrac{dy}{dx} = y - xy^3, \quad y(0) = 1.$ Find $y(3)$ with $h = \frac{1}{2}$.

6. $\dfrac{dy}{dx} = \dfrac{2xy}{3x^2 - y^2}, \quad y(-\frac{3}{8}) = -\frac{3}{4}.$ Find $y(6)$ with $h = \frac{3}{8}$.

7. Consider the differential equation in Exercise 6 with the initial condition $y(0) = -1$. Use the Runge-Kutta method or the improved Euler method to calculate $y(6)$ with $h = 1$. Why does the numerical solution differ from the exact answer?

8. Suppose the initial condition in Exercise 4 is $y(1) = 1$. Can any of the three methods of Section 7.1 provide the correct answer for $y(3)$?

9. Consider the initial value problem

$$y' = 1 + y^2, \quad y(0) = 0.$$

Can any of the methods in Section 7.1 be used to obtain $y(2)$?

In Exercises 10 through 13, find the dependent function(s) value at 2 with $h = 0.2$ using the

a) Euler method,

b) Runge-Kutta method, and

c) improved Euler method as predictor, trapezoidal rule as corrector

to numerically solve the following initial value problems. Compare the numerical answer to the exact solution.

10. $x^2 y'' + xy' + y = 0,$
$y(1) = 1, \quad y'(1) = 0$

11. $x^2 y'' + xy' + y = 0,$
$y(1) = 1, \quad y'(1) = 1$

12. $x' = x - 2y, \quad x(0) = 1$
$y' = 2x + 5y, \quad y(0) = 0$

13. $x' = x + 2y, \quad x(0) = 1$
$y' = 2x + 5y, \quad y(0) = 0$

Matrices and Systems of Linear First-Order Equations

8.1 INTRODUCTION

In this chapter we use the powerful tools of matrix theory to describe the behavior of solutions to systems of differential equations.

We shall assume, from here on, that the reader is familiar with the elementary properties of vectors and matrices,† including vector and matrix addition and scalar multiplication, matrix multiplication, the notion of linear dependence and independence of vectors, and the calculation of the inverse of an invertible matrix.

Because we will use row operations in Section 8.3, it would not be amiss to give an example of matrix inversion by *Gaussian elimination*. Using this method we append an $n \times n$ identity matrix I to the right of the $n \times n$ matrix A that we wish to invert, obtaining the augmented matrix $(A \mid I)$. Then, by using *row operations*—that is,

---

1. any two rows may be interchanged;
2. any row may be multiplied by a nonzero constant;
3. any multiple of a row may be added to another row—

---

we try to transform $(A \mid I)$ into an augmented matrix whose first n columns **form the $n \times n$ identity matrix. If we fail in our attempt, the** matrix A has no inverse; but if we succeed in obtaining an identity matrix in the first n columns, then the last n columns will be the inverse of the matrix A:

$$(A \mid I) \xrightarrow{\text{row operations}} (I \mid A^{-1}).$$

For example, consider the 3×3 matrix

$$A = \begin{pmatrix} 0 & 3 & 8 \\ 1 & 2 & 0 \\ 1 & 0 & -5 \end{pmatrix},$$

with augmented matrix

$$(A \mid I) = \begin{pmatrix} 0 & 3 & 8 & 1 & 0 & 0 \\ 1 & 2 & 0 & 0 & 1 & 0 \\ 1 & 0 & -5 & 0 & 0 & 1 \end{pmatrix}.$$

Interchanging the top and bottom rows, we have

$$\begin{pmatrix} 1 & 0 & -5 & 0 & 0 & 1 \\ 1 & 2 & 0 & 0 & 1 & 0 \\ 0 & 3 & 8 & 1 & 0 & 0 \end{pmatrix}.$$

---

† In the remainder of this chapter, vectors will be represented by boldface lower-case letters and matrices by italic upper-case letters.

Adding -1 times the top row to the middle row, we obtain

$$\begin{pmatrix} 1 & 0 & -5 & | & 0 & 0 & 1 \\ 0 & 2 & 5 & | & 0 & 1 & -1 \\ 0 & 3 & 8 & | & 1 & 0 & 0 \end{pmatrix}.$$

Multiplying the middle row by $\frac{1}{2}$ yields

$$\begin{pmatrix} 1 & 0 & -5 & | & 0 & 0 & 1 \\ 0 & 1 & \frac{5}{2} & | & 0 & \frac{1}{2} & -\frac{1}{2} \\ 0 & 3 & 8 & | & 1 & 0 & 0 \end{pmatrix}.$$

Adding -3 times the middle row to the bottom row, we obtain

$$\begin{pmatrix} 1 & 0 & -5 & | & 0 & 0 & 1 \\ 0 & 1 & \frac{5}{2} & | & 0 & \frac{1}{2} & -\frac{1}{2} \\ 0 & 0 & \frac{1}{2} & | & 1 & -\frac{3}{2} & \frac{3}{2} \end{pmatrix}.$$

Next, we multiply the bottom row by 2:

$$\begin{pmatrix} 1 & 0 & -5 & | & 0 & 0 & 1 \\ 0 & 1 & \frac{5}{2} & | & 0 & \frac{1}{2} & -\frac{1}{2} \\ 0 & 0 & 1 & | & 2 & -3 & 3 \end{pmatrix}.$$

Finally, we add 5 times the bottom row to the top row and $-\frac{5}{2}$ times the bottom row to the middle row, obtaining

$$\begin{pmatrix} 1 & 0 & 0 & | & 10 & -15 & 16 \\ 0 & 1 & 0 & | & -5 & 8 & -8 \\ 0 & 0 & 1 & | & 2 & -3 & 3 \end{pmatrix}.$$

We can easily check that

$$A^{-1} = \begin{pmatrix} 10 & -15 & 16 \\ -5 & 8 & -8 \\ 2 & -3 & 3 \end{pmatrix}$$

is the inverse of A by multiplying A and A^{-1} together.

Before discussing the relationship between matrices and systems of equations, let us consider the notion of a vector and matrix function.

An n-component *vector function*

$$\mathbf{v}(t) = \begin{pmatrix} v_1(t) \\ v_2(t) \\ \cdot \\ \cdot \\ \cdot \\ v_n(t) \end{pmatrix} \tag{1}$$

is an n-vector, each of whose components is a function (usually assumed to be continuous). An $n \times n$ *matrix function* $A(t)$ is an $n \times n$ matrix

$$A(t) = \begin{pmatrix} a_{11}(t) & a_{12}(t) & \cdots & a_{1n}(t) \\ a_{21}(t) & a_{22}(t) & \cdots & a_{2n}(t) \\ \cdot & \cdot & & \cdot \\ \cdot & \cdot & & \cdot \\ \cdot & \cdot & & \cdot \\ a_{n1}(t) & a_{n2}(t) & \cdots & a_{nn}(t) \end{pmatrix}, \tag{2}$$

each of whose n^2 components is a function. We may add and multiply vector and matrix functions in the same way that we add and multiply constant vectors and matrices. Thus if, for example,

$$A(t) = \begin{pmatrix} a_{11}(t) & a_{12}(t) \\ a_{21}(t) & a_{22}(t) \end{pmatrix} \quad \text{and} \quad B(t) = \begin{pmatrix} b_{11}(t) & b_{12}(t) \\ b_{21}(t) & b_{22}(t) \end{pmatrix},$$

then

$$A(t)B(t) = \begin{pmatrix} a_{11}(t)b_{11}(t) + a_{12}(t)b_{21}(t) & a_{11}(t)b_{12}(t) + a_{12}(t)b_{22}(t) \\ a_{21}(t)b_{11}(t) + a_{22}(t)b_{21}(t) & a_{21}(t)b_{12}(t) + a_{22}(t)b_{22}(t) \end{pmatrix}.$$

We may also differentiate and integrate vector and matrix functions, componentwise. Thus if $\mathbf{v}(t)$ is given by Eq. (1), then

$$\mathbf{v}'(t) = \begin{pmatrix} v_1'(t) \\ v_2'(t) \\ \cdot \\ \cdot \\ \cdot \\ v_n'(t) \end{pmatrix} \quad \text{and} \quad \int_{t_0}^{t} \mathbf{v}(s)\,ds = \begin{pmatrix} \int_{t_0}^{t} v_1(s)\,ds \\ \int_{t_0}^{t} v_2(s)\,ds \\ \cdot \\ \cdot \\ \cdot \\ \int_{t_0}^{t} v_n(s)\,ds \end{pmatrix}.$$

Similarly, if $A(t)$ is given by Eq. (2), then

$$A'(t) = \begin{pmatrix} a_{11}'(t) & a_{12}'(t) & \cdots & a_{1n}'(t) \\ a_{21}'(t) & a_{22}'(t) & \cdots & a_{2n}'(t) \\ \cdot & \cdot & & \cdot \\ \cdot & \cdot & & \cdot \\ \cdot & \cdot & & \cdot \\ a_{n1}'(t) & a_{n2}'(t) & \cdots & a_{nn}'(t) \end{pmatrix}$$

and

$$\int_{t_0}^{t} A(s)\, ds = \begin{pmatrix} \int_{t_0}^{t} a_{11}(s)\, ds & \int_{t_0}^{t} a_{12}(s)\, ds & \cdots & \int_{t_0}^{t} a_{1n}(s)\, ds \\ \int_{t_0}^{t} a_{21}(s)\, ds & \int_{t_0}^{t} a_{22}(s)\, ds & \cdots & \int_{t_0}^{t} a_{2n}(s)\, ds \\ \cdot & \cdot & & \cdot \\ \cdot & \cdot & & \cdot \\ \cdot & \cdot & & \cdot \\ \int_{t_0}^{t} a_{n1}(s)\, ds & \int_{t_0}^{t} a_{n2}(s)\, ds & \cdots & \int_{t_0}^{t} a_{nn}(s)\, ds \end{pmatrix}.$$

Example 1 Let

$$\mathbf{v}(t) = \begin{pmatrix} t \\ t^2 \\ \sin t \\ e^t \end{pmatrix}.$$

Then

$$\mathbf{v}'(t) = \begin{pmatrix} 1 \\ 2t \\ \cos t \\ e^t \end{pmatrix} \quad \text{and} \quad \int_{0}^{t} \mathbf{v}(s)\, ds = \begin{pmatrix} t^2/2 \\ t^3/3 \\ 1 - \cos t \\ e^t - 1 \end{pmatrix}.$$

In Section 3.10 we discussed the general system of n first-order equations

$$\begin{aligned} x_1' &= a_{11}(t)x_1 + a_{12}(t)x_2 + \cdots + a_{1n}(t)x_n + f_1(t), \\ x_2' &= a_{21}(t)x_1 + a_{22}(t)x_2 + \cdots + a_{2n}(t)x_n + f_2(t), \\ &\ \vdots \\ x_n' &= a_{n1}(t)x_1 + a_{n2}(t)x_2 + \cdots + a_{nn}(t)x_n + f_n(t), \end{aligned} \tag{3}$$

which is nonhomogeneous if at least one of the functions $f_i(t)$, $i = 1, 2, \ldots, n$, is not the zero function, and the associated homogeneous system

$$\begin{aligned} x_1' &= a_{11}(t)x_1 + a_{12}(t)x_2 + \cdots + a_{1n}(t)x_n, \\ x_2' &= a_{21}(t)x_1 + a_{22}(t)x_2 + \cdots + a_{2n}(t)x_n, \\ &\ \vdots \\ x_n' &= a_{n1}(t)x_1 + a_{n2}(t)x_2 + \cdots + a_{nn}(t)x_n. \end{aligned} \tag{4}$$

As was shown in Section 3.10, systems containing higher-order equations can always be reduced to systems of first-order equations. Hence we shall restrict our discussion to the systems of first-order equations (3) and (4).

We now define the vector function $\mathbf{x}(t)$, the matrix function $A(t)$, and the vector function $\mathbf{f}(t)$ as follows:

$$\mathbf{x}(t) = \begin{pmatrix} x_1(t) \\ x_2(t) \\ \cdot \\ \cdot \\ \cdot \\ x_n(t) \end{pmatrix}, \quad A(t) = \begin{pmatrix} a_{11}(t) & a_{12}(t) & \cdots & a_{1n}(t) \\ a_{21}(t) & a_{22}(t) & \cdots & a_{2n}(t) \\ \cdot & \cdot & & \cdot \\ \cdot & \cdot & & \cdot \\ \cdot & \cdot & & \cdot \\ a_{n1}(t) & a_{n2}(t) & \cdots & a_{nn}(t) \end{pmatrix}, \quad \mathbf{f}(t) = \begin{pmatrix} f_1(t) \\ f_2(t) \\ \cdot \\ \cdot \\ \cdot \\ f_n(t) \end{pmatrix}.$$

$$(5)$$

Then, using Eqs. (5), we can rewrite the system (3) as the *vector differential equation*

$$\boxed{\mathbf{x}'(t) = A(t)\mathbf{x}(t) + \mathbf{f}(t).}$$

$$(6)$$

The system (4) becomes

$$\boxed{\mathbf{x}'(t) = A(t)\mathbf{x}(t).}$$

$$(7)$$

It is clear from what has already been said that any linear differential equation or system can be written in the form (7) if it is homogeneous, and in the form (6) if it is nonhomogeneous. The reason for writing a system in these forms is that, besides the obvious advantage of compactness of notation, Eqs. (6) and (7) behave very much like first-order linear differential equations, as we shall see. It will be very easy to work with systems of equations in this way once we get used to the notation.

Example 2   Consider the system

$$x_1' = (2t)x_1 + (\sin t)x_2 - e^t x_3 - e^t,$$
$$x_2' = -t^3 x_1 + e^{\sin t} x_2 - (\ln t)x_3 + \cos t,$$
$$x_3' = 2x_1 - 5t x_2 + 2t x_3 + \tan t.$$

It can be rewritten as

$$\begin{pmatrix} x_1 \\ x_2 \\ x_3 \end{pmatrix}' = \begin{pmatrix} 2t & \sin t & -e^t \\ -t^3 & e^{\sin t} & -\ln t \\ 2 & -5t & 2t \end{pmatrix} \begin{pmatrix} x_1 \\ x_2 \\ x_3 \end{pmatrix} + \begin{pmatrix} -e^t \\ \cos t \\ \tan t \end{pmatrix}.$$

Example 3   Consider the general second-order linear differential equation

$$x'' + a(t)x' + b(t)x = f(t).$$

Defining $x_1 = x$ and $x_2 = x'$, we obtain the equivalent system

$$x_1' = x_2,$$
$$x_2' = -b(t)x_1 - a(t)x_2 + f(t),$$

which can be rewritten as

$$\mathbf{x}' = A(t)\mathbf{x} + \mathbf{f}(t),$$

where

$$\mathbf{x} = \begin{pmatrix} x_1 \\ x_2 \end{pmatrix}, \quad A(t) = \begin{pmatrix} 0 & 1 \\ -b(t) & -a(t) \end{pmatrix}, \quad \mathbf{f}(t) = \begin{pmatrix} 0 \\ f(t) \end{pmatrix}.$$

Example 4   Consider the third-order equation with constant coefficients

$$x''' - 6x'' + 11x' - 6x = 0. \tag{8}$$

Defining $x_1 = x$, $x_2 = x'$, and $x_3 = x''$, we obtain the system

$$x_1' = x_2,$$
$$x_2' = x_3,$$
$$x_3' = 6x_1 - 11x_2 + 6x_3,$$

or

$$\mathbf{x}' = A\mathbf{x}, \tag{9}$$

where

$$\mathbf{x} = \begin{pmatrix} x_1 \\ x_2 \\ x_3 \end{pmatrix} \quad \text{and} \quad A = \begin{pmatrix} 0 & 1 & 0 \\ 0 & 0 & 1 \\ 6 & -11 & 6 \end{pmatrix}.$$

Let us now consider the initial value problem

$$\mathbf{x}'(t) = A(t)\mathbf{x}(t) + \mathbf{f}(t), \quad \mathbf{x}(t_0) = \mathbf{x}_0, \tag{10}$$

where

$$\mathbf{x}(t) = \begin{pmatrix} x_1(t) \\ x_2(t) \\ \cdot \\ \cdot \\ \cdot \\ x_n(t) \end{pmatrix} \quad \text{and} \quad \mathbf{x}_0 = \begin{pmatrix} x_{10} \\ x_{20} \\ \cdot \\ \cdot \\ \cdot \\ x_{n0} \end{pmatrix}.$$

We say that a vector function

$$\boldsymbol{\varphi}(t) = \begin{pmatrix} \varphi_1(t) \\ \cdot \\ \cdot \\ \cdot \\ \varphi_n(t) \end{pmatrix}$$

is a *solution* to Eqs. (10) if φ is differentiable and satisfies the differential equation and the given initial condition. The following theorem will be proved in Chapter 10.

Theorem 1   Let $A(t)$ and $\mathbf{f}(t)$ be continuous matrix and vector functions, respectively, on some interval $[a, b]$ (that is, the component functions of both $A(t)$ and $\mathbf{f}(t)$ are continuous). Then there exists a unique vector function $\varphi(t)$ that is a solution to the initial value problem (10) on the entire interval $[a, b]$.

Example 5   Referring to Example 4, we find by the methods of Chapter 3 that e^t, e^{2t}, and e^{3t} are solutions of Eq. (8). Since a solution vector for this problem is

$$\varphi(t) = \begin{pmatrix} x(t) \\ x'(t) \\ x''(t) \end{pmatrix},$$

we see that three vector solutions of Eq. (9) are

$$\varphi_1(t) = \begin{pmatrix} e^t \\ e^t \\ e^t \end{pmatrix} = e^t\begin{pmatrix} 1 \\ 1 \\ 1 \end{pmatrix}, \quad \varphi_2(t) = \begin{pmatrix} e^{2t} \\ 2e^{2t} \\ 4e^{2t} \end{pmatrix} = e^{2t}\begin{pmatrix} 1 \\ 2 \\ 4 \end{pmatrix},$$

and

$$\varphi_3(t) = \begin{pmatrix} e^{3t} \\ 3e^{3t} \\ 9e^{3t} \end{pmatrix} = e^{3t}\begin{pmatrix} 1 \\ 3 \\ 9 \end{pmatrix}.$$

If we specify the initial condition

$$\mathbf{x}(0) = \begin{pmatrix} 2 \\ -3 \\ 5 \end{pmatrix},$$

then the unique solution vector is easily verified to be

$$\varphi = 16\varphi_1 - 23\varphi_2 + 9\varphi_3,$$

or

$$\begin{pmatrix} 16e^t - 23e^{2t} + 9e^{3t} \\ 16e^t - 46e^{2t} + 27e^{3t} \\ 16e^t - 92e^{2t} + 81e^{3t} \end{pmatrix}.$$

Example 6   The system

$$x_1' = -4x_1 - x_2, \quad x_1(0) = 1,$$
$$x_2' = x_1 - 2x_2, \quad x_2(0) = 2,$$

can be written as

$$\begin{pmatrix} x_1 \\ x_2 \end{pmatrix} = \begin{pmatrix} -4 & -1 \\ 1 & -2 \end{pmatrix}\begin{pmatrix} x_1 \\ x_2 \end{pmatrix}, \quad \begin{pmatrix} x_1(0) \\ x_2(0) \end{pmatrix} = \begin{pmatrix} 1 \\ 2 \end{pmatrix}.$$

It can easily be verified that

$$\varphi_1(t) = \begin{pmatrix} e^{-3t} \\ -e^{-3t} \end{pmatrix} \quad \text{and} \quad \varphi_2(t) = \begin{pmatrix} (1-t)e^{-3t} \\ te^{-3t} \end{pmatrix}$$

are solution vectors. It can also be immediately verified that the unique solution vector that satisfies the given initial conditions is

$$\varphi(t) = \begin{pmatrix} (1-3t)e^{-3t} \\ (2+3t)e^{-3t} \end{pmatrix}.$$

The central problem of the remainder of the chapter is to derive properties of vector solutions and, where possible, to calculate them. In the next section we will show how all solutions to the homogeneous system $\mathbf{x}' = A\mathbf{x}$ can be represented in a convenient form, and in Section 8.6 how information about the solutions to this homogeneous system can be used to find a particular solution to the nonhomogeneous system $\mathbf{x}' = A\mathbf{x} + \mathbf{f}$.

EXERCISES 8.1

In Exercises 1 through 6, write each given equation or system in the matrix-vector form (6), (7), or (10).

1. $x_1' = 2x_1 + 3x_2,$
$x_2' = 4x_1 - 6x_2$

2. $x_1' = (\cos t)x_1 - (\sin t)x_2 + e^{t^2},$
$x_2' = e^t x_1 + 2tx_2 - \ln t,$
$x_1(2) = 3, x_2(2) = 7$

3. $x''' - 2x'' + 4tx' - x = \sin t$

4. $x^{(iv)} + 2x''' - 3x'' + 4x' - 7x = 0,$
$x(0) = 1, x'(0) = 2, x''(0) = 3, x'''(0) = 4$

5. $x_1' = 2tx_1 - 3t^2 x_2 + (\sin t)x_3,$
$x_2' = 2x_1 - 4x_3 - \sin t,$
$x_3' = 17x_2 + 4tx_3 + e^t$

6. $x''' + a(t)x'' + b(t)x' + c(t)x = f(t),$
$x(t_0) = d_1, x'(t_0) = d_2, x''(t_0) = d_3$

In Exercises 7 through 14, verify that each given vector function is a solution to the given system.

7. $\mathbf{x}' = \begin{pmatrix} 1 & 1 \\ -3 & -1 \end{pmatrix}\mathbf{x},$

$\varphi(t) = \begin{pmatrix} \cos\sqrt{2}t \\ \sqrt{2}\sin\sqrt{2}t - \cos\sqrt{2}t \end{pmatrix}$

8. $\mathbf{x}' = \begin{pmatrix} 2 & 1 \\ 1 & 2 \end{pmatrix}\mathbf{x} + \begin{pmatrix} t \\ t^2 \end{pmatrix},$

$\varphi(t) = \begin{pmatrix} e^t + \frac{1}{3}t^2 + \frac{2}{9}t + \frac{11}{27} \\ -e^t - \frac{2}{3}t^2 - \frac{7}{9}t - \frac{16}{27} \end{pmatrix}$

9. $\mathbf{x}' = \begin{pmatrix} -1 & 6 \\ 1 & -2 \end{pmatrix}\mathbf{x}, \quad \varphi(t) = \begin{pmatrix} 3e^t \\ e^t \end{pmatrix}$

10. $\mathbf{x}' = \begin{pmatrix} -4 & -1 \\ 1 & -2 \end{pmatrix}\mathbf{x}, \quad \varphi(t) = \begin{pmatrix} (1+t)e^{-3t} \\ (-2-t)e^{-3t} \end{pmatrix}$

11. $\mathbf{x}' = \begin{pmatrix} 4 & 1 \\ -8 & 8 \end{pmatrix}\mathbf{x}, \quad \varphi(t) = \begin{pmatrix} e^{6t}(\cos 2t - \frac{1}{2}\sin 2t) \\ e^{6t}(\cos 2t - 3\sin 2t) \end{pmatrix}$

12. $\mathbf{x}' = \begin{pmatrix} 1 & 1 & 1 \\ -1 & -1 & 0 \\ -1 & 0 & 1 \end{pmatrix}\mathbf{x}, \quad \varphi(t) = \begin{pmatrix} \sin t - \cos t \\ \cos t \\ \cos t \end{pmatrix}$

13. $\mathbf{x}' = \begin{pmatrix} 1 & -1 & 1 & -1 \\ 0 & -1 & 2 & -2 \\ 0 & 0 & 2 & -3 \\ 0 & 0 & 0 & -2 \end{pmatrix}\mathbf{x}, \quad \varphi(t) = \begin{pmatrix} e^{-2t} \\ 2e^{-2t} \\ 3e^{-2t} \\ 4e^{-2t} \end{pmatrix}$

14. $\mathbf{x}' = \begin{pmatrix} 3 & 2 & 1 \\ -1 & 0 & -1 \\ 1 & 1 & 2 \end{pmatrix}\mathbf{x}, \quad \varphi(t) = \begin{pmatrix} e^{2t} + te^{2t} \\ -te^{2t} \\ te^{2t} \end{pmatrix}$

15. Let $\varphi_1(t)$ and $\varphi_2(t)$ be any two vector solutions of the homogeneous system $\mathbf{x}' = A(t)\mathbf{x}$. Show that $\varphi(t) = c_1\varphi_1(t) + c_2\varphi_2(t)$ is also a solution.

16. Let $\varphi_1(t)$ and $\varphi_2(t)$ be vector solutions of the nonhomogeneous system (6). Show that their difference,

$$\varphi(t) = \varphi_1(t) - \varphi_2(t),$$

is a solution to the homogeneous system (7).

17. Find the derivative and integral of each of the following vector and matrix functions:

a) $\mathbf{x}(t) = (t, \sin t)$;

b) $\mathbf{y}(t) = \begin{pmatrix} e^t \\ \cos t \\ \tan t \end{pmatrix}$;

c) $A(t) = \begin{pmatrix} \sqrt{t} & t^2 \\ e^{2t} & \sin 2t \end{pmatrix}$;

d) $B(t) = \begin{pmatrix} \ln t & e^t \sin t & e^t \cos t \\ t^{5/2} & -\cos t & -\sin t \\ 1/t & te^{t^2} & t^2 e^{t^3} \end{pmatrix}$.

8.2 FUNDAMENTAL SETS AND FUNDAMENTAL MATRIX SOLUTIONS OF A HOMOGENEOUS SYSTEM OF DIFFERENTIAL EQUATIONS

In this section we will discuss properties of the homogeneous system

$$\mathbf{x}' = A(t)\mathbf{x}, \tag{1}$$

where $\mathbf{x}(t)$ is an n-vector and $A(t)$ is an $n \times n$ matrix.

Let $\boldsymbol{\varphi}_1(t), \boldsymbol{\varphi}_2(t), \ldots, \boldsymbol{\varphi}_m(t)$ be m vector solutions of the system (1). We say that they are *linearly independent* if the equation

$$c_1\boldsymbol{\varphi}_1(t) + c_2\boldsymbol{\varphi}_2(t) + \cdots + c_m\boldsymbol{\varphi}_m(t) = \mathbf{0}$$

holds only for $c_1 = c_2 = \cdots = c_m = 0$. Since the system (1) is equivalent to an nth-order equation, it is natural for us to seek n linearly independent solutions to the system. *Any set of n linearly independent solutions of (1) is called a fundamental set of solutions.*

In Sections 3.11 and 3.12 we saw how a fundamental set of solutions (that is, two linearly independent solutions) could be found in the case where A was a 2×2 constant matrix. In particular, by Theorem 5 in Section 3.11, the vectors

$$\boldsymbol{\varphi}_1(t) = \begin{pmatrix} x_1(t) \\ y_1(t) \end{pmatrix} \quad \text{and} \quad \boldsymbol{\varphi}_2(t) = \begin{pmatrix} x_2(t) \\ y_2(t) \end{pmatrix}$$

are a fundamental set of solutions if and only if the Wronskian $W(t)$, defined by Eq. (6) in Section 3.11, is nonzero.

Example 1 Let $\mathbf{x}' = A\mathbf{x}$ where

$$A = \begin{pmatrix} -1 & 6 \\ 1 & -2 \end{pmatrix}.$$

In Example 1 in Section 3.12 we verified that

$$\boldsymbol{\varphi}_1(t) = \begin{pmatrix} -2e^{-4t} \\ e^{-4t} \end{pmatrix} \quad \text{and} \quad \boldsymbol{\varphi}_2(t) = \begin{pmatrix} 3e^t \\ e^t \end{pmatrix}$$

are solution vectors. To show that they are fundamental (as we did in Example 1 in Section 3.12), suppose that $c_1\boldsymbol{\varphi}_1(t) + c_2\boldsymbol{\varphi}_2(t) = \mathbf{0}$ for every t.

Then, in particular, the second component yields $c_1 e^{-4t} + c_2 e^t = 0$ for all t. For $t = 0$, this implies that $c_1 + c_2 = 0$ or $c_1 = -c_2$. Then $c_1(e^{-4t} - e^t) = 0$ for all t. This is impossible unless $c_1 = -c_2 = 0$, which proves the independence of φ_1 and φ_2.

Example 2   Let $\mathbf{x}' = A\mathbf{x}$ where

$$A = \begin{pmatrix} -4 & -1 \\ 1 & -2 \end{pmatrix}.$$

In Example 2 in Section 3.12 we obtained the two solution vectors

$$\varphi_1(t) = \begin{pmatrix} e^{-3t} \\ -e^{-3t} \end{pmatrix} \quad \text{and} \quad \varphi_2(t) = \begin{pmatrix} (1 + t)e^{-3t} \\ (-2 - t)e^{-3t} \end{pmatrix}.$$

If we set $c_1\varphi_1(t) + c_2\varphi_2(t) = 0$, then the first component yields

$$e^{-3t}[c_1 + c_2(1 + t)] = 0$$

for all t. Since $e^{-3t} \neq 0$ if $t = 0$, we have $c_1 + c_2 = 0$, while $t = 1$ yields the equation $c_1 + 2c_2 = 0$. These equations are satisfied only when $c_1 = c_2 = 0$, so that $\varphi_1(t)$ and $\varphi_2(t)$ form a fundamental set of solutions.

Example 3   Consider the system $\mathbf{x}' = A\mathbf{x}$ where

$$A = \begin{pmatrix} 4 & 1 \\ -8 & 8 \end{pmatrix}$$

(see Example 3 in Section 3.12). Two solution vectors are

$$\varphi_1(t) = \begin{pmatrix} e^{6t}(\cos 2t - \tfrac{1}{2}\sin 2t) \\ e^{6t}(\cos 2t - 3\sin 2t) \end{pmatrix}, \quad \varphi_2(t) = \begin{pmatrix} e^{6t}(\sin 2t + \tfrac{1}{2}\cos 2t) \\ e^{6t}(\sin 2t + 3\cos 2t) \end{pmatrix}.$$

To show that they are linearly independent, let $c_1\varphi_1(t) + c_2\varphi_2(t) = 0$ for every t. Then for $t = 0$, we have

$$\begin{pmatrix} c_1 \\ c_1 \end{pmatrix} + \begin{pmatrix} \tfrac{1}{2}c_2 \\ 3c_2 \end{pmatrix} = 0$$

or

$$c_1 + \tfrac{1}{2}c_2 = 0,$$
$$c_1 + 3c_2 = 0.$$

Clearly the only solution of this system is $c_1 = c_2 = 0$, and so φ_1 and φ_2 are, indeed, linearly independent.

Example 4   Let $\mathbf{x}' = A\mathbf{x}$ where

$$A = \begin{pmatrix} 1 & 1 & -2 \\ -1 & 2 & 1 \\ 0 & 1 & -1 \end{pmatrix}.$$

Then it is easy to show that

$$\boldsymbol{\varphi}_1(t) = \begin{pmatrix} e^{-t} \\ 0 \\ e^{-t} \end{pmatrix} = e^{-t}\begin{pmatrix} 1 \\ 0 \\ 1 \end{pmatrix}, \quad \boldsymbol{\varphi}_2(t) = \begin{pmatrix} 3e^t \\ 2e^t \\ e^t \end{pmatrix} = e^t\begin{pmatrix} 3 \\ 2 \\ 1 \end{pmatrix},$$

$$\boldsymbol{\varphi}_3(t) = \begin{pmatrix} e^{2t} \\ 3e^{2t} \\ e^{2t} \end{pmatrix} = e^{2t}\begin{pmatrix} 1 \\ 3 \\ 1 \end{pmatrix}$$

are a fundamental set of solutions.

Let $\boldsymbol{\varphi}_1, \boldsymbol{\varphi}_2, \ldots, \boldsymbol{\varphi}_n$ be n-vector solutions of $\mathbf{x}' = A(t)\mathbf{x}$. Let $\Phi(t)$ be the matrix whose columns are the vectors $\boldsymbol{\varphi}_1, \boldsymbol{\varphi}_2, \ldots, \boldsymbol{\varphi}_n$. That is,

$$\Phi(t) = (\boldsymbol{\varphi}_1(t), \ldots, \boldsymbol{\varphi}_n(t)) = \begin{pmatrix} \varphi_{11}(t) & \varphi_{12}(t) & \cdots & \varphi_{1n}(t) \\ \varphi_{21}(t) & \varphi_{22}(t) & \cdots & \varphi_{2n}(t) \\ \cdot & & & \cdot \\ \cdot & & \cdot & \cdot \\ \cdot & & \cdot & \cdot \\ \varphi_{n1}(t) & \varphi_{n2}(t) & \cdots & \varphi_{nn}(t) \end{pmatrix}. \tag{2}$$

Such a matrix is called a *matrix solution* of the system $\mathbf{x}' = A\mathbf{x}$. Equivalently, *an $n \times n$ matrix function $\Phi(t)$ is a matrix solution of $\mathbf{x}' = A\mathbf{x}$ if and only if each of its columns is a solution vector of $\mathbf{x}' = A\mathbf{x}$.* If the vectors $\boldsymbol{\varphi}_1, \boldsymbol{\varphi}_2, \ldots, \boldsymbol{\varphi}_n$ form a fundamental set of solutions (that is, if they are linearly independent), then $\Phi(t)$ is called a *fundamental matrix solution*. In what follows, we shall show that fundamental matrix solutions play a central role in the theory of linear systems of differential equations.

Example 5 In the four previous examples of this section, fundamental matrix solutions were found to be, respectively:

1. $\begin{pmatrix} -2e^{-4t} & 3e^t \\ e^{-4t} & e^t \end{pmatrix}$

2. $\begin{pmatrix} e^{-3t} & (1+t)e^{-3t} \\ -e^{-3t} & (-2-t)e^{-3t} \end{pmatrix}$

3. $\begin{pmatrix} e^{6t}(\cos 2t - \frac{1}{2}\sin 2t) & e^{6t}(\sin 2t + \frac{1}{2}\cos 2t) \\ e^{6t}(\cos 2t - 3\sin 2t) & e^{6t}(\sin 2t + 3\cos 2t) \end{pmatrix}$

4. $\begin{pmatrix} e^{-t} & 3e^t & e^{2t} \\ 0 & 2e^t & 3e^{2t} \\ e^{-t} & e^t & e^{2t} \end{pmatrix}$

Note that fundamental matrix solutions are not unique, due to the fact that a solution vector may be multiplied by any constant and still remain a solution. In addition, any linear combination of solutions is again a solution (see Exercise 6). However, we have uniqueness for the *principal matrix solution* $\Psi(t)$, which is defined as that fundamental matrix solution which satisfies the condition

$$\Psi(t_0) = I, \tag{3}$$

where I is the $n \times n$ identity matrix.

We will show later in this section that if $A(t)$ is continuous, then $\mathbf{x}' = A\mathbf{x}$ always has a unique principal matrix solution. But first, we will demonstrate an easy way to determine whether or not a given matrix solution is a fundamental matrix solution.

Let $\Phi(t)$ be a matrix solution of $\mathbf{x}' = A(t)\mathbf{x}$. We define the *Wronskian of* $\Phi(t)$, written $W(t)$, *as*

$$W(t) = \det \Phi(t). \tag{4}$$

We should remind the reader of two facts from matrix theory. First, a matrix A is invertible if and only if $\det A \neq 0$. Second, $\det A \neq 0$ if and only if the columns of A are linearly independent. From these facts it follows that $\Phi(t)$ will be a fundamental matrix solution if and only if $W(t)$ is nonzero for some t. We will see in the next theorem that $W(t)$ is either always zero or never zero, so that we can calculate $W(t)$ for some especially simple value of t, say $t = 0$, to determine whether Φ is a fundamental matrix solution. Note that many of these theorems are similar to those proven in Chapter 3. In particular, the reader should compare the present definition (4) of the Wronskian with the definitions of the Wronskian in Sections 3.2 and 3.11.

Theorem 1 *Abel's Formula*. Let $W(t)$ be the Wronskian of the matrix solution $\Phi(t)$ of the system $\mathbf{x}' = A(t)\mathbf{x}$. Then

$$W(t) = W(t_0) \exp\left(\int_{t_0}^{t} \operatorname{tr} A(s)\, ds\right), \tag{5}$$

where the trace of A, written $\operatorname{tr} A(t)$, is the sum of the diagonal elements of the matrix $A(t)$:

$$\operatorname{tr} A(t) = a_{11}(t) + a_{22}(t) + \cdots + a_{nn}(t). \tag{6}$$

Proof We prove this theorem for the case of $A(t)$ being a 2×2 matrix (see Theorem 4 in Section 3.11). The proof for the $n \times n$ case is similar (but more complicated) and is left as an exercise. In the 2×2 case, the system

$\mathbf{x}' = A\mathbf{x}$ and the matrix solution may be written as

$$\begin{pmatrix} x_1 \\ x_2 \end{pmatrix}' = \begin{pmatrix} a_{11}(t) & a_{12}(t) \\ a_{21}(t) & a_{22}(t) \end{pmatrix}\begin{pmatrix} x_1 \\ x_2 \end{pmatrix}, \quad \Phi(t) = (\boldsymbol{\varphi}_1, \boldsymbol{\varphi}_2) = \begin{pmatrix} \varphi_{11} & \varphi_{12} \\ \varphi_{21} & \varphi_{22} \end{pmatrix}.$$

Since $W(t) = \varphi_{11}\varphi_{22} - \varphi_{12}\varphi_{21}$, the derivative

$$W' = \varphi_{11}\varphi'_{22} + \varphi'_{11}\varphi_{22} - \varphi_{12}\varphi'_{21} - \varphi'_{12}\varphi_{21}$$

may be written in determinant form as

$$W' = \begin{vmatrix} \varphi_{11} & \varphi_{12} \\ \varphi'_{21} & \varphi'_{22} \end{vmatrix} + \begin{vmatrix} \varphi'_{11} & \varphi'_{12} \\ \varphi_{21} & \varphi_{22} \end{vmatrix}. \tag{7}$$

But $\varphi'_{11} = a_{11}\varphi_{11} + a_{12}\varphi_{21}$, since $\boldsymbol{\varphi}_1$ is a vector solution, and similarly for φ'_{12}, φ'_{21}, and φ'_{22}. Replacing these derivatives in (7), we obtain

$$W' = \begin{vmatrix} \varphi_{11} & \varphi_{12} \\ a_{21}\varphi_{11} + a_{22}\varphi_{21} & a_{21}\varphi_{12} + a_{22}\varphi_{22} \end{vmatrix}$$

$$+ \begin{vmatrix} a_{11}\varphi_{11} + a_{12}\varphi_{21} & a_{11}\varphi_{12} + a_{12}\varphi_{22} \\ \varphi_{21} & \varphi_{22} \end{vmatrix}$$

$$= D_1 + D_2. \tag{8}$$

But according to the theory of determinants (see Appendix 4), a determinant is unchanged when a multiple of one row is added to another row. In addition, multiplication of every element in one row by a given constant is equivalent to multiplying the determinant by that constant. Hence we may multiply the first row of D_1 by $-a_{21}$ and add it to the second row. Then

$$D_1 = \begin{vmatrix} \varphi_{11} & \varphi_{12} \\ a_{22}\varphi_{21} & a_{22}\varphi_{22} \end{vmatrix} = a_{22}\begin{vmatrix} \varphi_{11} & \varphi_{12} \\ \varphi_{21} & \varphi_{22} \end{vmatrix} = a_{22}W.$$

Similarly, $D_2 = a_{11}W$. Thus

$$W'(t) = [a_{11}(t) + a_{22}(t)]W(t) = [\operatorname{tr} A(t)]W(t). \tag{9}$$

Equation (9) is a first-order (scalar) differential equation that has the solution

$$W(t) = W(t_0)\exp\left(\int_{t_0}^{t} \operatorname{tr} A(s)\,ds\right).$$

This completes the proof for the 2×2 case. Although the proof is much longer than that of Theorem 4 in Section 3.11, it can be immediately extended to the $n \times n$ case (see Exercises 11 and 12). ∎

Example 6 We consider the four matrix solutions of Example 5. Evaluating each at $t = 0$, we obtain:

1. $W(0) = \begin{vmatrix} -2 & 3 \\ 1 & 1 \end{vmatrix} = -5;$

2. $W(0) = \begin{vmatrix} 1 & 1 \\ -1 & -2 \end{vmatrix} = -1;$

3. $W(0) = \begin{vmatrix} 1 & \frac{1}{2} \\ 1 & 3 \end{vmatrix} = \frac{5}{2};$

4. $W(0) = \begin{vmatrix} 1 & 3 & 1 \\ 0 & 2 & 3 \\ 1 & 1 & 1 \end{vmatrix} = 6.$

Therefore, without direct verification of linear independence, we can see that all four matrix solutions are fundamental matrix solutions.

We are now ready to prove the theorem mentioned earlier, namely, that principal matrix solutions exist and are unique. Since principal matrix solutions are fundamental matrix solutions, this theorem also proves the existence of fundamental matrix solutions.

Theorem 2   Let $A(t)$ be continuous on some interval $[a, b]$. Then for any t_0, $a \le t_0 \le b$, there exists a unique fundamental matrix solution $\Psi(t)$ of the system $\mathbf{x}' = A(t)\mathbf{x}$ satisfying the condition $\Psi(t_0) = I$.

Proof   Let $\boldsymbol{\delta}_i$, $i = 1, 2, \ldots, n$, denote the n-column vector that has a one in the ith position (row) and a zero everywhere else:

$$\boldsymbol{\delta}_1 = \begin{pmatrix} 1 \\ 0 \\ 0 \\ \cdot \\ \cdot \\ \cdot \\ 0 \end{pmatrix}, \quad \boldsymbol{\delta}_2 = \begin{pmatrix} 0 \\ 1 \\ 0 \\ \cdot \\ \cdot \\ \cdot \\ 0 \end{pmatrix}, \quad \ldots, \quad \boldsymbol{\delta}_n = \begin{pmatrix} 0 \\ 0 \\ \cdot \\ \cdot \\ \cdot \\ 0 \\ 1 \end{pmatrix}.$$

By the basic existence–uniqueness Theorem 1 in Section 8.1 with $\mathbf{f}(t) \equiv \mathbf{0}$, there exists a unique vector solution $\boldsymbol{\varphi}_i(t)$ of $\mathbf{x}' = A\mathbf{x}$ that satisfies $\boldsymbol{\varphi}_i(t_0) = \boldsymbol{\delta}_i$, $i = 1, 2, \ldots, n$. Define the matrix function

$$\Psi(t) = [\boldsymbol{\varphi}_1(t), \boldsymbol{\varphi}_2(t), \ldots, \boldsymbol{\varphi}_n(t)]. \tag{10}$$

Then $\Psi(t)$ is the matrix whose columns are the vector solutions $\boldsymbol{\varphi}_i$, $i = 1, 2, \ldots, n$. Clearly $\Psi(t)$ is a matrix solution and $\Psi(t_0) = (\boldsymbol{\varphi}_1(t_0), \ldots, \boldsymbol{\varphi}_n(t_0)) = (\boldsymbol{\delta}_1, \boldsymbol{\delta}_2, \ldots, \boldsymbol{\delta}_n) = I$. It remains to be shown that $\Psi(t)$ is a fundamental matrix solution. This is easy to do. We simply note that $\det \Psi(t_0) = \det I = 1 \ne 0$. ∎

The calculation of a fundamental or principal matrix solution is generally impossible if $A(t)$ is nonconstant. If $A(t)$ is a constant matrix, then, as we shall see in Section 8.5, a principal matrix solution can always be obtained. In the remainder of this section we will show how all solutions of $\mathbf{x}' = A(t)\mathbf{x}$ can be expressed in terms of a single fundamental matrix solution. First, we define the *associated matrix equation* to the system $\mathbf{x}' = A(t)\mathbf{x}$:

$$X'(t) = A(t)X(t). \tag{11}$$

We now seek a matrix (instead of a vector) solution of Eq. (11). The following fact is easy to prove and is left as an exercise: $X(t)$ *is a solution of the associated matrix equation* (11) *if and only if every column of $X(t)$ is a solution of the system* $\mathbf{x}' = A(t)\mathbf{x}$.

Theorem 3   Let Φ be a matrix solution of $\mathbf{x}' = A(t)\mathbf{x}$ and let C be any constant matrix. Then $\Phi_1 = \Phi C$ is also a matrix solution of $\mathbf{x}' = A(t)\mathbf{x}$.

Proof   Since a matrix solution of $\mathbf{x}' = A(t)\mathbf{x}$ is also a solution of Eq. (11), and conversely, Φ is a solution of Eq. (11), we must show that Φ_1 is also a solution of Eq. (11). But $\Phi_1' = (\Phi C)' = \Phi'C + \Phi C' = \Phi'C$, since $C' = 0$, C being constant. Finally, since Φ is a solution,

$$\Phi_1' = \Phi'C = A\Phi C = A\Phi_1. \ \blacksquare$$

Example 7   Consider Example 1, with the fundamental matrix solution

$$\Phi(t) = \begin{pmatrix} -2e^{-4t} & 3e^t \\ e^{-4t} & e^t \end{pmatrix}.$$

Let

$$C_1 = \begin{pmatrix} 1 & 2 \\ 3 & 4 \end{pmatrix} \quad \text{and} \quad C_2 = \begin{pmatrix} 1 & 2 \\ 2 & 4 \end{pmatrix}.$$

Then

$$\Phi_1 = \Phi C_1 = \begin{pmatrix} -2e^{-4t} + 9e^t & -4e^{-4t} + 12e^t \\ e^{-4t} + 3e^t & 2e^{-4t} + 4e^t \end{pmatrix}$$

and

$$\Phi_2 = \Phi C_2 = \begin{pmatrix} -2e^{-4t} + 6e^t & -4e^{-4t} + 12e^t \\ e^{-4t} + 2e^t & 2e^{-4t} + 4e^t \end{pmatrix}.$$

It is easily verified that both Φ_1 and Φ_2 are matrix solutions. Note that although Φ_1 is another fundamental matrix solution, Φ_2 is not, since $\det \Phi_2(0) = 0$. Can you explain this fact (see Exercise 10)?

Theorem 3 gives us an easy way of finding a principal matrix solution when a fundamental matrix solution is known. To see this, let $\Phi(t)$ be a fundamental matrix solution. Since $\det \Phi(t_0) \neq 0$, $\Phi(t_0)$ is invertible, and we define $C = \Phi^{-1}(t_0)$ and $\Psi(t) = \Phi(t)C$. By Theorem 3, $\Psi(t)$ is a matrix solution and $\Psi(t_0) = \Phi(t_0)C = \Phi(t_0)\Phi^{-1}(t_0) = I$ so that $\Psi(t)$ is a principal matrix solution. Thus, if $\Phi(t)$ is a fundamental matrix solution, we can always obtain a principal matrix solution by multiplying $\Phi(t)$ on the right-hand side by $\Phi^{-1}(t_0)$.

Example 8   A fundamental matrix solution of the system of Example 1 is [see Example 5(1)]:

$$\Phi(t) = \begin{pmatrix} -2e^{-4t} & 3e^t \\ 3^{-4t} & e^t \end{pmatrix} \quad \text{and} \quad \Phi(0) = \begin{pmatrix} -2 & 3 \\ 1 & 1 \end{pmatrix}.$$

Then

$$C = \Phi^{-1}(0) = \begin{pmatrix} -\frac{1}{5} & \frac{3}{5} \\ \frac{1}{5} & \frac{2}{5} \end{pmatrix} = \frac{1}{5}\begin{pmatrix} -1 & 3 \\ 1 & 2 \end{pmatrix},$$

so that

$$\Psi(t) = \Phi(t)C = \frac{1}{5}\begin{pmatrix} 2e^{-4t} + 3e^t & -6e^{-4t} + 6e^t \\ -e^{-4t} + e^t & 3e^{-4t} + 2e^t \end{pmatrix}$$

is a principal matrix solution.

Theorem 4   Let $\Phi(t)$ be a fundamental matrix solution and let $X(t)$ be any other matrix solution of the system $\mathbf{x}' = A(t)\mathbf{x}$. Then there exists a constant matrix C such that $X(t) = \Phi(t)C$. That is, *any solution vector of* $\mathbf{x}' = A(t)\mathbf{x}$ *can be written as a linear combination of vectors in a fundamental set.* (Compare this theorem with Theorem 2 in Section 3.2.)

Before giving the proof, we should warn the reader that it is important to state on which side we are multiplying the matrix Φ by C, since matrix multiplication is not, in general, commutative.

Proof   Since $\Phi(t)$ is a fundamental matrix solution, $\det \Phi(t) \neq 0$ and $\Phi^{-1}(t)$ exists for every t. We will show that

$$\frac{d}{dt}[\Phi^{-1}(t)X(t)] = 0.$$

This will imply that $\Phi^{-1}(t)X(t)$ is a constant matrix C and the theorem will be proved. First, we calculate

$$\frac{d}{dt}[\Phi^{-1}(t)].$$

Using the product rule of differentiation (which can easily be shown to apply to matrix products), we have

$$0 = \frac{dI}{dt} = \frac{d}{dt}(\Phi\Phi^{-1}) = \frac{d\Phi}{dt}\Phi^{-1} + \Phi\frac{d\Phi^{-1}}{dt} \qquad \textbf{(12)}$$

or, after multiplying both sides of Eq. (12) on the left by Φ^{-1} and solving for $d\Phi^{-1}/dt$,

$$\frac{d\Phi^{-1}}{dt} = -\Phi^{-1}\frac{d\Phi}{dt}\Phi^{-1}. \tag{13}$$

Note the analogy between Eq. (13) and the identity

$$\frac{d}{dt}\left(\frac{1}{f(t)}\right) = -\frac{f'(t)}{[f(t)]^2}.$$

Now, by the product formula of derivatives,

$$\frac{d}{dt}(\Phi^{-1}X) = \left(\frac{d}{dt}\Phi^{-1}\right)X + \Phi^{-1}\frac{dX}{dt}, \tag{14}$$

and since both Φ and X are solutions of Eq. (11), Eq. (14) becomes

$$\frac{d}{dt}(\Phi^{-1}X) = \left(-\Phi^{-1}\frac{d\Phi}{dt}\Phi^{-1}\right)X + \Phi^{-1}(AX)$$

$$= -\Phi^{-1}A\Phi\Phi^{-1}X + \Phi^{-1}AX$$

$$= -\Phi^{-1}AX + \Phi^{-1}AX = 0. \quad\blacksquare$$

Example 9   Consider the system $\mathbf{x}' = A\mathbf{x}$ where

$$A = \begin{pmatrix} 1 & -2 \\ 2 & -3 \end{pmatrix}.$$

It is easy to verify that

$$\Phi_1(t) = \begin{pmatrix} e^{-t} & (2t+2)e^{-t} \\ e^{-t} & (2t+1)e^{-t} \end{pmatrix} = e^{-t}\begin{pmatrix} 1 & 2t+2 \\ 1 & 2t+1 \end{pmatrix}$$

is a fundamental matrix solution. Another matrix solution is

$$\Phi_2(t) = e^{-t}\begin{pmatrix} 4t+7 & 8t+1 \\ 4t+5 & 8t-3 \end{pmatrix}.$$

There is a matrix C such that $\Phi_2 = \Phi_1 C$. But $\Phi_1^{-1}(t)\Phi_2(t) = C$ holds for every value of t, in particular for $t = 0$. Thus

$$C = \Phi_1^{-1}(0)\Phi_2(0) = \begin{pmatrix} -1 & 2 \\ 1 & -1 \end{pmatrix}\begin{pmatrix} 7 & 1 \\ 5 & -3 \end{pmatrix} = \begin{pmatrix} 3 & -7 \\ 2 & 4 \end{pmatrix}.$$

Example 10   Consider the system $\mathbf{x}' = A\mathbf{x}$ where

$$A = \begin{pmatrix} 3 & -1 & 1 \\ -1 & 5 & -1 \\ 1 & -1 & 3 \end{pmatrix}.$$

A fundamental matrix solution is

$$\Phi(t) = \begin{pmatrix} e^{2t} & e^{3t} & e^{6t} \\ 0 & e^{3t} & -2e^{6t} \\ -e^{2t} & e^{3t} & e^{6t} \end{pmatrix}.$$

Another matrix solution is

$$X(t) = \begin{pmatrix} e^{2t} + 2e^{3t} + 3e^{6t} & e^{2t} - 3e^{3t} - 2e^{6t} & 2e^{2t} + 5e^{3t} + 7e^{6t} \\ 2e^{3t} - 6e^{6t} & -3e^{3t} + 4e^{6t} & 5e^{3t} - 14e^{6t} \\ -e^{2t} + 2e^{2t} + 3e^{6t} & -e^{2t} - 3e^{3t} - 2e^{6t} & -2e^{2t} + 5e^{3t} + 7e^{6t} \end{pmatrix}.$$

As in the previous example, a matrix C such that $X(t) = \Phi(t)C$ is given by

$$C = \Phi^{-1}(0)X(0) = \frac{1}{6}\begin{pmatrix} 3 & 0 & -3 \\ 2 & 2 & 2 \\ 1 & -2 & 1 \end{pmatrix}\begin{pmatrix} 6 & -4 & 14 \\ -4 & 1 & -9 \\ 4 & -6 & 10 \end{pmatrix}$$

$$= \frac{1}{6}\begin{pmatrix} 6 & 6 & 12 \\ 12 & -18 & 30 \\ 18 & -12 & 42 \end{pmatrix} = \begin{pmatrix} 1 & 1 & 2 \\ 2 & -3 & 5 \\ 3 & -2 & 7 \end{pmatrix}.$$

Theorem 5   Let $\Phi(t)$ be a fundamental matrix solution and let $\mathbf{x}(t)$ be any solution of $\mathbf{x}' = A(t)\mathbf{x}$. Then there exists a constant vector $\mathbf{c}$ such that

$$\mathbf{x}(t) = \Phi(t)\mathbf{c}. \tag{15}$$

Proof   This theorem is an immediate consequence of Theorem 4, if we form the matrix solution $X(t) = (\mathbf{x}(t), \mathbf{x}(t), \dots, \mathbf{x}(t))$ whose n columns are each the vector solution $\mathbf{x}(t)$. Then a matrix C exists such that $X(t) = \Phi(t)C$. Every column of C is a vector $\mathbf{c}$. ∎

Example 11   In Example 3 we found the fundamental matrix solution

$$\Phi(t) = e^{6t}\begin{pmatrix} \cos 2t - \frac{1}{2}\sin t & \sin 2t + \frac{1}{2}\cos 2t \\ \cos 2t - 3\sin 2t & \sin 2t + 3\cos 2t \end{pmatrix}.$$

The vector

$$\mathbf{x}(t) = e^{6t}\begin{pmatrix} -5\sin 2t \\ -10\cos 2t - 10\sin 2t \end{pmatrix}$$

is easily seen to be a solution. From Eq. (15) we obtain

$$\mathbf{c} = \Phi^{-1}(t)\mathbf{x}(t) = \Phi^{-1}(0)\mathbf{x}(0) = \frac{2}{5}\begin{pmatrix} 3 & -\frac{1}{2} \\ -1 & 1 \end{pmatrix}\begin{pmatrix} 0 \\ -10 \end{pmatrix}$$

$$= \frac{2}{5}\begin{pmatrix} 5 \\ -10 \end{pmatrix} = \begin{pmatrix} 2 \\ -4 \end{pmatrix}.$$

Example 12   Consider the system

$$x_1' = \frac{-t}{1-t^2} x_1 + \frac{1}{1-t^2} x_2,$$

$$x_2' = \frac{1}{1-t^2} x_1 - \frac{t}{1-t^2} x_2$$

or

$$\mathbf{x}' = \begin{pmatrix} \dfrac{-t}{1-t^2} & \dfrac{1}{1-t^2} \\ \dfrac{1}{1-t^2} & \dfrac{-t}{1-t^2} \end{pmatrix} \mathbf{x}. \tag{16}$$

It is easy to verify that

$$\Phi_1(t) = \begin{pmatrix} t \\ 1 \end{pmatrix} \quad \text{and} \quad \Phi_2(t) = \begin{pmatrix} 1 \\ t \end{pmatrix}$$

are linearly independent solutions and that

$$\Phi(t) = \begin{pmatrix} t & 1 \\ 1 & t \end{pmatrix}$$

is a fundamental matrix solution. First, note that although $W(0) = -1 \neq 0$, we also have $W(1) = 0$. A cursory inspection will help to explain this apparent contradiction of Theorem 1. The matrix $A(t)$ is undefined at $t = 1$; thus there cannot even be a solution to Eq. (16) at $t = 1$. The theorem about Wronskians is, of course, only valid in an interval over which the solution is defined. Continuing with the example, let us find a solution $\mathbf{x}(t)$ that satisfies the initial conditions

$$\mathbf{x}(0) = \begin{pmatrix} x_1(0) \\ x_2(0) \end{pmatrix} = \begin{pmatrix} 2 \\ -3 \end{pmatrix}.$$

Then

$$\mathbf{c} = \Phi^{-1}(0)\mathbf{x}(0) = \begin{pmatrix} 0 & 1 \\ 1 & 0 \end{pmatrix} \begin{pmatrix} 2 \\ -3 \end{pmatrix} = \begin{pmatrix} -3 \\ 2 \end{pmatrix}.$$

[Note that $\Phi(0) = \begin{pmatrix} 0 & 1 \\ 1 & 0 \end{pmatrix}$ is a matrix that is its own inverse.] Thus

$$\mathbf{x}(t) = \Phi(t)\mathbf{c} = \begin{pmatrix} t & 1 \\ 1 & t \end{pmatrix} \begin{pmatrix} -3 \\ 2 \end{pmatrix} = \begin{pmatrix} 2-3t \\ -3+2t \end{pmatrix}$$

is a solution vector of Eq. (16) that satisfies the given initial conditions.

EXERCISES 8.2

In Exercises 1 through 5, decide whether each given set of solution vectors constitutes a fundamental set of the given system by (a) determining whether the vectors are linearly independent, and (b) using the method of Wronskians to determine whether or not $W(t)$ is zero.

1. $\mathbf{x}' = \begin{pmatrix} 2 & 5 \\ 0 & 2 \end{pmatrix}\mathbf{x}, \quad \varphi_1(t) = \begin{pmatrix} e^{2t}(1 + 10t) \\ 2e^{2t} \end{pmatrix},$

$\varphi_2(t) = \begin{pmatrix} e^{2t}(-3 + 20t) \\ 4e^{2t} \end{pmatrix}$

2. $\mathbf{x}' = \begin{pmatrix} 4 & -13 \\ 2 & -6 \end{pmatrix}\mathbf{x},$

$\varphi_1(t) = \begin{pmatrix} e^{-t}(13 \cos t - 26 \sin t) \\ e^{-t}(7 \cos t - 9 \sin t) \end{pmatrix},$

$\varphi_2(t) = \begin{pmatrix} e^{-t}(26 \cos t - 52 \sin t) \\ e^{-t}(14 \cos t - 18 \sin t) \end{pmatrix}$

3. $\mathbf{x}' = \begin{pmatrix} 1 & 1 \\ 4 & 1 \end{pmatrix}\mathbf{x}, \quad \varphi_1(t) = \begin{pmatrix} e^{3t} - e^{-t} \\ 2e^{3t} + 2e^{-t} \end{pmatrix},$

$\varphi_2(t) = \begin{pmatrix} 2e^{3t} \\ 4e^{3t} \end{pmatrix}$

4. $\mathbf{x}' = \begin{pmatrix} 1 & -1 & 4 \\ 3 & 2 & -1 \\ 2 & 1 & -1 \end{pmatrix}\mathbf{x},$

$\varphi_1(t) = \begin{pmatrix} e^t + 2e^{-t} + 3e^{3t} \\ -4e^t - 2e^{-2t} + 6e^{3t} \\ -e^t - 2e^{-2t} + 3e^{3t} \end{pmatrix},$

$\varphi_2(t) = \begin{pmatrix} -2e^t + 2e^{-2t} \\ 8e^t - 2e^{-2t} \\ 2e^t - 2e^{-2t} \end{pmatrix},$

$\varphi_3(t) = \begin{pmatrix} 3e^t - 6e^{-2t} + 3e^{3t} \\ -12e^t + 6e^{-2t} + 6e^{3t} \\ -3e^t + 6e^{-2t} + 3e^{3t} \end{pmatrix}$

5. $\mathbf{x}' = \begin{pmatrix} 3 & 2 & 1 \\ -1 & 0 & -1 \\ 1 & 1 & 2 \end{pmatrix}\mathbf{x},$

$\varphi_1(t) = \begin{pmatrix} -e^t + te^{2t} + e^{2t} \\ e^t - te^{2t} \\ te^{2t} \end{pmatrix},$

$\varphi_2(t) = \begin{pmatrix} 2e^{2t} + te^{2t} \\ -e^{2t} - te^{2t} \\ e^{2t} + te^{2t} \end{pmatrix},$

$\varphi_3(t) = \begin{pmatrix} -e^t + 3e^{2t} + 2te^{2t} \\ e^t - e^{2t} - 2te^{2t} \\ e^{2t} + 2te^{2t} \end{pmatrix}$

6. Let $\varphi_1(t), \varphi_2(t), \ldots, \varphi_m(t)$ be m solutions of the homogeneous system (1). Show that

$$\varphi(t) = c_1\varphi_1(t) + c_2\varphi(t) + \cdots + c_m\varphi_m(t)$$

is also a solution.

In each of Exercises 7 through 9, two matrix functions Φ_1 and Φ_2 are given. Find a matrix C such that $\Phi_2(t) = \Phi_1(t)C$.

7. $\Phi_1(t) = e^{6t}\begin{pmatrix} \cos 2t - \frac{1}{2}\sin 2t & \sin 2t + \frac{1}{2}\cos 2t \\ \cos 2t - 3\sin 2t & \sin 2t + 3\cos 2t \end{pmatrix},$

$\Phi_2(t)$

$= e^{6t}\begin{pmatrix} \frac{1}{2}\cos 2t - \frac{3}{2}\sin 2t & -\frac{3}{2}\cos 2t + 2\sin 2t \\ -2\cos 2t - 4\sin 2t & \cos 2t + 7\sin 2t \end{pmatrix}$

8. $\Phi_1(t) = \begin{pmatrix} \sin e^t & \cos e^t \\ e^t \cos e^t & -e^t \sin e^t \end{pmatrix},$

$\Phi_2(t) = \begin{pmatrix} \cos e^t & 3\sin e^t + 2\cos e^t \\ -e^t \sin e^t & 3e^t \cos e^t - 2e^t \sin e^t \end{pmatrix}$

9. $\Phi_1(t) = \begin{pmatrix} e^{-t} & 3e^t & e^{2t} \\ 0 & 2e^t & 3e^{2t} \\ e^{-t} & e^t & e^{2t} \end{pmatrix},$

$\Phi_2(t) = \begin{pmatrix} e^{-t} + e^{2t} & -e^{-t} + 3e^t & e^{-t} + 3e^t \\ 3e^{2t} & 2e^t & 2e^t \\ e^{-t} + e^{2t} & -e^{-t} + e^t & e^{-t} + e^t \end{pmatrix}$

10. Let $\Phi_1(t)$ be a fundamental matrix solution of $\mathbf{x}' = A\mathbf{x}$. Then $\Phi_2 = \Phi_1 C$ is a matrix solution for any constant matrix C. Show that Φ_2 is a fundamental matrix solution if and only if C is nonsingular.

11. Let $\Phi(t)$ be a matrix solution of the system $\mathbf{x}' = A(t)\mathbf{x}$ where $A(t)$ is a 3×3 matrix. Prove that

$$W(t) = W(t_0)\exp\left[\int_{t_0}^t [a_{11}(s) + a_{22}(s) + a_{33}(s)]\,ds\right].$$

12. Using the result of Exercise 11, prove

Theorem 1 for the case of $A(t)$ being an $n \times n$ matrix.

In Exercises 13 through 16, find the principal matrix solution $\Psi(t)$ for each given fundamental matrix solution $\Phi(t)$. Assume that $t_0 = 0$.

13. $\Phi(t) = e^{6t} \begin{pmatrix} \cos 2t - \frac{1}{2}\sin 2t & \sin 2t + \frac{1}{2}\cos 2t \\ \cos 2t - 3\sin 2t & \sin 2t + 3\cos 2t \end{pmatrix}$

14. $\Phi(t) = \begin{pmatrix} \sin e^t & \cos e^t \\ e^t \cos e^t & -e^t \sin e^t \end{pmatrix}$

15. $\Phi(t) = \begin{pmatrix} e^{-t} & 3e^t & e^{2t} \\ 0 & 2e^t & 3e^{2t} \\ e^{-t} & e^t & e^{2t} \end{pmatrix}$

16. $\Phi(t) = \begin{pmatrix} 2e^t + te^t & te^t + e^t & e^t \\ 0 & e^t & e^t \\ -3e^t - te^t & -te^t - 2e^t & -e^t \end{pmatrix}$

17. Consider the system

$$\mathbf{x}' = \begin{pmatrix} 3 & -2 \\ 2 & -1 \end{pmatrix} \mathbf{x}.$$

It is easy to verify that

$$\Phi(t) = \begin{pmatrix} 2te^t + e^t & 2te^t \\ 2te^t & -e^t + 2te^t \end{pmatrix}$$

is a fundamental matrix solution. Find a solution that satisfies each of the following initial conditions:

a) $\mathbf{x}(0) = \begin{pmatrix} 1 \\ 2 \end{pmatrix}$;   b) $\mathbf{x}(0) = \begin{pmatrix} -2 \\ 3 \end{pmatrix}$;

c) $\mathbf{x}(1) = \begin{pmatrix} 0 \\ 1 \end{pmatrix}$;   d) $\mathbf{x}(-1) = \begin{pmatrix} 2 \\ 1 \end{pmatrix}$;

e) $\mathbf{x}(3) = \begin{pmatrix} 3 \\ 3 \end{pmatrix}$;   f) $\mathbf{x}(a) = \begin{pmatrix} b \\ c \end{pmatrix}$.

18. In Example 5 we saw that a fundamental matrix solution to the system

$$\mathbf{x}' = \begin{pmatrix} 1 & 1 & -2 \\ -1 & 2 & 1 \\ 0 & 1 & -1 \end{pmatrix} \mathbf{x}$$

of Example 4 was

$$\Phi(t) = \begin{pmatrix} e^{-t} & 3e^t & e^{2t} \\ 0 & 2e^t & 3e^{2t} \\ e^{-t} & e^t & e^{2t} \end{pmatrix}.$$

Find particular solutions that satisfy the following conditions:

a) $\mathbf{x}(0) = \begin{pmatrix} 1 \\ -1 \\ 2 \end{pmatrix}$;   b) $\mathbf{x}(0) = \begin{pmatrix} 3 \\ 1 \\ 2 \end{pmatrix}$;

c) $\mathbf{x}(1) = \begin{pmatrix} 1 \\ 0 \\ 1 \end{pmatrix}$;   d) $\mathbf{x}(-1) = \begin{pmatrix} 2 \\ -3 \\ 5 \end{pmatrix}$.

19. Consider the second-order equation

$$x'' + a(t)x' + b(t)x = 0. \tag{17}$$

a) Write Eq. (17) in the form $\mathbf{x}' = A(t)\mathbf{x}$.

b) Given that

$$\Phi(t) = \begin{pmatrix} \varphi_1 & \varphi_2 \\ \varphi_1' & \varphi_2' \end{pmatrix}$$

is a fundamental matrix solution, show that

$$\det \Phi(t) = \det \Phi(t_0) \exp\left[-\int_{t_0}^t a(s)\, ds \right].$$

c) Show that the formula in part (b) can be rearranged as

$$\varphi_2' - \frac{\varphi_1'}{\varphi_1}\varphi_2 \tag{18}$$
$$= \frac{\det \Phi(t_0)}{\varphi_1} \exp\left[-\int_{t_0}^t a(s)\, ds \right].$$

Therefore, if one solution $\varphi_1(t)$ of Eq. (17) is known, then another solution can be calculated by solving this equation.

20. Given that $\varphi_1(t) = \sin(\ln t)$, find a second linearly independent solution of

$$x'' + \frac{1}{t}x' + \frac{1}{t^2}x = 0.$$

21. Given that $\varphi_1(t) = e^{t^2}$ is a solution of

$$x'' - 2tx' - 2x = 0,$$

find a second linearly independent solution.

22. Given that $\varphi_1(t) = \sin t^2$ is a solution of

$$tx'' - x' + 4t^3 x = 0,$$

find a second linearly independent solution.

8.3 EIGENVALUES AND EIGENVECTORS

In this and the next two sections we will present two methods for computing the principal matrix solution of the system

$$x' = Ax, \qquad (1)$$

when the matrix A is constant. The method in this section involves the use of the eigenvalues and corresponding eigenvectors of the matrix A.

Definition 1   Let A be an $n \times n$ matrix with real† components. The number λ (real or complex) is called an *eigenvalue* of A if there is a *nonzero* vector $\mathbf{v}$ with real or complex entries such that

$$A\mathbf{v} = \lambda\mathbf{v}. \qquad (2)$$

The vector $\mathbf{v} \neq 0$ is called an *eigenvector of A corresponding to the eigenvalue* λ.

Note   "Eigen" is the German word for "own" or "proper." Eigenvalues are also called *proper values* or *characteristic values* and eigenvectors are called *proper vectors* or *characteristic vectors*.

Remark   As we shall see (for example, in Example 6), a matrix with real components can have complex eigenvalues and eigenvectors. That is why, in the definition, we have asserted that λ and the components of $\mathbf{v}$ may be complex.

Example 1   Let

$$A = \begin{pmatrix} 10 & -18 \\ 6 & -11 \end{pmatrix}.$$

Then

$$A\begin{pmatrix} 2 \\ 1 \end{pmatrix} = \begin{pmatrix} 10 & -18 \\ 6 & -11 \end{pmatrix}\begin{pmatrix} 2 \\ 1 \end{pmatrix} = \begin{pmatrix} 2 \\ 1 \end{pmatrix}.$$

Thus $\lambda_1 = 1$ is an eigenvalue of A with corresponding eigenvector $\mathbf{v}_1 = \begin{pmatrix} 2 \\ 1 \end{pmatrix}$. Similarly,

$$A\begin{pmatrix} 3 \\ 2 \end{pmatrix} = \begin{pmatrix} 10 & -18 \\ 6 & -11 \end{pmatrix}\begin{pmatrix} 3 \\ 2 \end{pmatrix} = \begin{pmatrix} -6 \\ -4 \end{pmatrix} = -2\begin{pmatrix} 3 \\ 2 \end{pmatrix},$$

so that $\lambda_2 = -2$ is an eigenvalue of A with corresponding eigenvector $\mathbf{v}_2 = \begin{pmatrix} 3 \\ 2 \end{pmatrix}$. As we shall soon see, these are the only eigenvalues of A.

---

† This definition is also valid if A has complex components but since the matrices we will deal with will, for the most part, have real components, the definition is sufficient for our purposes.

Example 2   Let $A = I$. Then for any $\mathbf{v}$, $A\mathbf{v} = I\mathbf{v} = \mathbf{v}$. Thus 1 is the only eigenvalue of A and every $\mathbf{v}$ is an eigenvector of I.

We will compute the eigenvalues and eigenvectors of many matrices in this section. But first we need to prove some facts that will simplify our computations.

Suppose that λ is an eigenvalue of A. Then there exists a nonzero vector

$$\mathbf{v} = \begin{pmatrix} x_1 \\ x_2 \\ \cdot \\ \cdot \\ \cdot \\ x_n \end{pmatrix} \neq \mathbf{0}$$

such that $A\mathbf{v} = \lambda\mathbf{v} = \lambda I\mathbf{v}$.

Rewriting this, we have

$$(A - \lambda I)\mathbf{v} = \mathbf{0}. \tag{3}$$

If A is an $n \times n$ matrix, Eq. (3) is a homogeneous system of n equations in the unknowns $x_1, x_2, \ldots, x_n$. Since, by assumption, the system has nontrivial solutions, we conclude that $\det(A - \lambda I) = 0$. Conversely, if $\det(A - \lambda I) = 0$, then Eq. (3) has nontrivial solutions and λ is an eigenvalue of A. On the other hand, if $\det(A - \lambda I) \neq 0$, then Eq. (3) has only the solution $\mathbf{v} = 0$ so that λ is *not* an eigenvalue of A. Summing up these facts, we have the following.

Theorem 1   Let A be an $n \times n$ matrix. Then λ is an eigenvalue of A if and only if

$$\boxed{p(\lambda) = \det(A - \lambda I) = 0.} \tag{4}$$

Definition 2   Equation (4) is called the *characteristic equation* of A and $p(\lambda)$ is called the *characteristic polynomial* of A.

As will become apparent in the examples, $p(\lambda)$ is a polynomial of degree n in λ. For example, if

$$A = \begin{pmatrix} a & b \\ c & d \end{pmatrix},$$

then

$$A - \lambda I = \begin{pmatrix} a & b \\ c & d \end{pmatrix} - \begin{pmatrix} \lambda & 0 \\ 0 & \lambda \end{pmatrix} = \begin{pmatrix} a - \lambda & b \\ c & d - \lambda \end{pmatrix}$$

and

$$p(\lambda) = \det(A - \lambda I) = (a - \lambda)(d - \lambda) - bc$$
$$= \lambda^2 - (a + d)\lambda + (ad - bc).$$

Similarly, if

$$A = \begin{pmatrix} a_{11} & a_{12} & \cdots & a_{1n} \\ a_{21} & a_{22} & \cdots & a_{2n} \\ \cdot & \cdot & & \cdot \\ \cdot & \cdot & & \cdot \\ \cdot & \cdot & & \cdot \\ a_{n1} & a_{n2} & \cdots & a_{nn} \end{pmatrix},$$

then

$$p(\lambda) = \det(A - \lambda I) = \begin{vmatrix} a_{11} - \lambda & a_{12} & \cdots & a_{1n} \\ a_{21} & a_{22} - \lambda & \cdots & a_{2n} \\ \cdot & \cdot & & \cdot \\ \cdot & \cdot & & \cdot \\ \cdot & \cdot & & \cdot \\ a_{n1} & a_{n2} & \cdots & a_{nn} - \lambda \end{vmatrix},$$

and $p(\lambda)$ can be written in the form

$$p(\lambda) = \lambda^n + b_{n-1}\lambda^{n-1} + \cdots + b_1\lambda + b_0 = 0. \tag{5}$$

By the fundamental theorem of algebra, any polynomial of degree n with real or complex coefficients has exactly n roots (counting multiplicities). By this we mean, for example, that the polynomial $(\lambda - 1)^5$ has five roots, all equal to the number 1. Since any eigenvalue of A is a root of the characteristic equation of A, an $n \times n$ matrix has n eigenvalues, some of which may be repeated. If $\lambda_1, \lambda_2, \ldots, \lambda_m$ are the distinct roots of Eq. (5) with multiplicities $r_1, r_2, \ldots, r_m$, respectively, then Eq. (5) may be factored to obtain

$$p(\lambda) = (\lambda - \lambda_1)^{r_1}(\lambda - \lambda_2)^{r_2}\cdots(\lambda - \lambda_m)^{r_m} = 0. \tag{6}$$

The numbers $r_1, r_2, \ldots, r_m$ are called the *algebraic multiplicities* of the eigenvalues $\lambda_1, \lambda_2, \ldots, \lambda_m$, respectively.

Theorem 2   Let λ be an eigenvalue of the $n \times n$ matrix A and let $E_\lambda = \{v: Av = \lambda v\}$. Then E is a subspace of C^n.†

---

† C^n is the vector space of complex n-tuples.

Proof   Let $\mathbf{v}_1$ and $\mathbf{v}_2$ be in E_λ. Then

$$A(\mathbf{v}_1 + \mathbf{v}_2) = A\mathbf{v}_1 + A\mathbf{v}_2 = \lambda\mathbf{v}_1 + \lambda\mathbf{v}_2 = \lambda(\mathbf{v}_1 + \mathbf{v}_2),$$

so that $\mathbf{v}_1 + \mathbf{v}_2 \in E_\lambda$. Similarly, for any scalar $\alpha \neq 0$,

$$A(\alpha\mathbf{v}_1) = \alpha A\mathbf{v}_1 = \alpha\lambda\mathbf{v}_1 = \lambda(\alpha\mathbf{v}_1),$$

so that $\alpha\mathbf{v}_1 \in E_\lambda$. This shows that E_λ is a subspace of C^n. ∎

Definition 3   Let λ be an eigenvalue of A. The subspace E_λ is called the *eigenspace* of A corresponding to the eigenvalue λ.

We now prove another useful result.

Theorem 3   Let A be an $n \times n$ matrix and let $\lambda_1\lambda_2, \ldots, \lambda_m$ be distinct eigenvalues of A with corresponding eigenvectors $\mathbf{v}_1, \mathbf{v}_2, \ldots, \mathbf{v}_m$. Then $\mathbf{v}_1, \mathbf{v}_2, \ldots, \mathbf{v}_m$ are linearly independent. That is, *eigenvectors corresponding to distinct eigenvalues are linearly independent.*

Proof   We prove this by mathematical induction. We start with $m = 2$. Suppose that

$$c_1\mathbf{v}_1 + c_2\mathbf{v}_2 = \mathbf{0}. \tag{7}$$

Then, multiplying both sides of Eq. (7) by A, we have

$$\mathbf{0} = A(c_1\mathbf{v}_1 + c_2\mathbf{v}_2) = c_1A\mathbf{v}_1 + c_2A\mathbf{v}_2$$

or

$$c_1\lambda_1\mathbf{v}_1 + c_2\lambda_2\mathbf{v}_2 = \mathbf{0}. \tag{8}$$

We then multiply Eq. (7) by λ_1 and subtract it from Eq. (8) to obtain

$$(c_1\lambda_1\mathbf{v}_1 + c_2\lambda_2\mathbf{v}_2) - (c_1\lambda_1\mathbf{v}_1 + c_2\lambda_1\mathbf{v}_2) = \mathbf{0}$$

or

$$c_2(\lambda_2 - \lambda_1)\mathbf{v}_2 = \mathbf{0}.$$

Since $\mathbf{v}_2 \neq \mathbf{0}$ (by the definition of an eigenvector) and since $\lambda_2 \neq \lambda_1$, we conclude that $c_2 = 0$. Then inserting $c_2 = 0$ in Eq. (7), we obtain $c_1 = 0$, which proves the theorem in the case $m = 2$. Now suppose that the theorem is true for $m = k$. That is, we assume that any k eigenvectors corresponding to distinct eigenvalues are linearly independent. We prove the theorem for $m = k + 1$. So we assume that

$$c_1\mathbf{v}_1 + c_2\mathbf{v}_2 + \cdots + c_k\mathbf{v}_k + c_{k+1}\mathbf{v}_{k+1} = \mathbf{0}. \tag{9}$$

Then, multiplying both sides of Eq. (9) by A and using the fact that $A\mathbf{v}_i = \lambda_i\mathbf{v}_i$, we obtain

$$c_1\lambda_1\mathbf{v}_1 + c_2\lambda_2\mathbf{v}_2 + \cdots + c_k\lambda_k\mathbf{v}_k + c_{k+1}\lambda_{k+1}\mathbf{v}_{k+1} = \mathbf{0}. \tag{10}$$

We multiply both sides of Eq. (9) by λ_{k+1} and subtract it from Eq. (10):

$$c_1(\lambda_1 - \lambda_{k+1})\mathbf{v}_1 + c_2(\lambda_2 - \lambda_{k+1})\mathbf{v}_2 + \cdots + c_k(\lambda_k - \lambda_{k+1})\mathbf{v}_k = \mathbf{0}.$$

But, by the induction assumption, $\mathbf{v}_1, \mathbf{v}_2, \ldots, \mathbf{v}_k$ are linearly independent. Thus

$$c_1(\lambda_1 - \lambda_{k+1}) = c_2(\lambda_2 - \lambda_{k+1}) = \cdots = c_k(\lambda_k - \lambda_{k+1}) = 0,$$

and, since $\lambda_i \neq \lambda_{k+1}$ for $i = 1, 2, \ldots, k$, we conclude that $c_1 = c_2 = \cdots = c_k = 0$. But, from Eq. (9), this means that $c_{k+1} = 0$. Thus the theorem is true for $m = k + 1$ and the proof is complete. ∎

We now proceed to calculate eigenvalues and corresponding eigenspaces. We do this using a three-step procedure:

1. Find $p(\lambda) = \det(A - \lambda I)$.	**(11)**
2. Find the roots $\lambda_1, \lambda_2, \ldots, \lambda_m$ of $p(\lambda) = 0$.	**(12)**
3. Corresponding to each eigenvalue λ_i, solve the homogeneous system $(A - \lambda_i I)\mathbf{v} = \mathbf{0}$.	**(13)**

Step 2 is often the hardest one to carry out.

Example 3   Let

$$A = \begin{pmatrix} 4 & 2 \\ 3 & 3 \end{pmatrix}.$$

Then

$$\det(A - \lambda I) = \begin{vmatrix} 4 - \lambda & 2 \\ 3 & 3 - \lambda \end{vmatrix} = (4 - \lambda)(3 - \lambda) - 6$$

$$= \lambda^2 - 7\lambda + 6 = (\lambda - 1)(\lambda - 6) = 0.$$

Thus the eigenvalues of A are $\lambda_1 = 1$ and $\lambda_2 = 6$. For $\lambda_1 = 1$, we solve $(A - I)\mathbf{v} = \mathbf{0}$ or

$$\begin{pmatrix} 3 & 2 \\ 3 & 2 \end{pmatrix}\begin{pmatrix} x_1 \\ x_2 \end{pmatrix} = \begin{pmatrix} 0 \\ 0 \end{pmatrix}.$$

Clearly, any eigenvector corresponding to $\lambda_1 = 1$ satisfies $3x_1 + 2x_2 = 0$. One such eigenvector is

$$\mathbf{v}_1 = \begin{pmatrix} 2 \\ -3 \end{pmatrix}.$$

Thus

$$E_1 = \text{span}\left\{ \begin{pmatrix} 2 \\ -3 \end{pmatrix} \right\}.$$

Similarly, the equation $(A - 6I)\mathbf{v} = \mathbf{0}$ means that

$$\begin{pmatrix} -2 & 2 \\ 3 & -3 \end{pmatrix} \begin{pmatrix} x_1 \\ x_2 \end{pmatrix} = \begin{pmatrix} 0 \\ 0 \end{pmatrix},$$

or $x_1 = x_2$. Thus $\mathbf{v}_2 = \begin{pmatrix} 1 \\ 1 \end{pmatrix}$ is an eigenvector corresponding to $\lambda_2 = 6$ and $E_6 = \text{span}\{\begin{pmatrix} 1 \\ 1 \end{pmatrix}\}$. Note that $\mathbf{v}_1$ and $\mathbf{v}_2$ are linearly independent since one is not a multiple of the other.

Example 4   Let

$$A = \begin{pmatrix} 1 & -1 & 4 \\ 3 & 2 & -1 \\ 2 & 1 & -1 \end{pmatrix}.$$

Then

$$\det (A - \lambda I) = \begin{vmatrix} 1 - \lambda & -1 & 4 \\ 3 & 2 - \lambda & -1 \\ 2 & 1 & -1 - \lambda \end{vmatrix} = -(\lambda^3 - 2\lambda^2 - 5\lambda + 6)$$

$$= -(\lambda - 1)(\lambda + 2)(\lambda - 3) = 0.$$

Thus the eigenvalues of A are $\lambda_1 = 1$, $\lambda_2 = -2$, and $\lambda_3 = 3$. Corresponding to $\lambda_1 = 1$, we have

$$(A - I)\mathbf{v} = \begin{pmatrix} 0 & -1 & 4 \\ 3 & 1 & -1 \\ 2 & 1 & -2 \end{pmatrix} \begin{pmatrix} x_1 \\ x_2 \\ x_3 \end{pmatrix} = \begin{pmatrix} 0 \\ 0 \\ 0 \end{pmatrix}.$$

Solving by row reduction, we obtain, successively,†

$$\begin{pmatrix} 0 & -1 & 4 & | & 0 \\ 3 & 1 & -1 & | & 0 \\ 2 & 1 & -2 & | & 0 \end{pmatrix} \xrightarrow[A_{1,3}(1)]{A_{1,2}(1)} \begin{pmatrix} 0 & -1 & 4 & | & 0 \\ 3 & 0 & 3 & | & 0 \\ 2 & 0 & 2 & | & 0 \end{pmatrix}$$

$$\xrightarrow{M_2(\frac{1}{3})} \begin{pmatrix} 0 & -1 & 4 & | & 0 \\ 1 & 0 & 1 & | & 0 \\ 2 & 0 & 2 & | & 0 \end{pmatrix} \xrightarrow{A_{2,3}(-2)} \begin{pmatrix} 0 & -1 & 4 & | & 0 \\ 1 & 0 & 1 & | & 0 \\ 0 & 0 & 0 & | & 0 \end{pmatrix},$$

Thus $x_1 = -x_3$, $x_2 = 4x_3$, an eigenvector is

$$\mathbf{v}_1 = \begin{pmatrix} -1 \\ 4 \\ 1 \end{pmatrix},$$

---

† The notation is as follows:

$A_{i,j}(c)$ means to multiply the ith row by c and add it to the jth row.

$M_i(c)$ means to multiply the ith row by c.

and $E_1 = \text{span } \{v_1\}$. For $\lambda_2 = -2$, we have

$$[A - (-2I)]v = (A + 2I)v = 0$$

or

$$\begin{pmatrix} 3 & -1 & 4 \\ 3 & 4 & -1 \\ 2 & 1 & 1 \end{pmatrix} \begin{pmatrix} x_1 \\ x_2 \\ x_3 \end{pmatrix} = \begin{pmatrix} 0 \\ 0 \\ 0 \end{pmatrix}.$$

This leads to

$$\begin{pmatrix} 3 & -1 & 4 & | & 0 \\ 3 & 4 & -1 & | & 0 \\ 2 & 1 & 1 & | & 0 \end{pmatrix} \xrightarrow[\substack{A_{1,2}(4) \\ A_{1,3}(1)}]{} \begin{pmatrix} 3 & -1 & 4 & | & 0 \\ 15 & 0 & 15 & | & 0 \\ 5 & 0 & 5 & | & 0 \end{pmatrix}$$

$$\xrightarrow[M_2(\frac{1}{15})]{} \begin{pmatrix} 3 & -1 & 4 & | & 0 \\ 1 & 0 & 1 & | & 0 \\ 5 & 0 & 5 & | & 0 \end{pmatrix} \xrightarrow[\substack{A_{2,1}(-4) \\ A_{2,3}(-5)}]{} \begin{pmatrix} -1 & -1 & 0 & | & 0 \\ 1 & 0 & 1 & | & 0 \\ 0 & 0 & 0 & | & 0 \end{pmatrix}.$$

Thus $x_2 = -x_1$, $x_3 = -x_1$, an eigenvector is

$$v_2 = \begin{pmatrix} 1 \\ -1 \\ -1 \end{pmatrix},$$

and $E_{-2} = \text{span } \{v_2\}$. Finally, for $\lambda_3 = 3$, we have

$$(A - 3I)v = \begin{pmatrix} -2 & -1 & 4 \\ 3 & -1 & -1 \\ 2 & 1 & -4 \end{pmatrix} \begin{pmatrix} x_1 \\ x_2 \\ x_3 \end{pmatrix} = \begin{pmatrix} 0 \\ 0 \\ 0 \end{pmatrix}$$

and

$$\begin{pmatrix} -2 & -1 & 4 & | & 0 \\ 3 & -1 & -1 & | & 0 \\ 2 & 1 & -4 & | & 0 \end{pmatrix} \xrightarrow[\substack{A_{1,2}(-1) \\ A_{1,3}(1)}]{} \begin{pmatrix} 0 & 0 & 0 & | & 0 \\ 5 & 0 & -5 & | & 0 \\ 2 & 1 & -4 & | & 0 \end{pmatrix}$$

$$\xrightarrow[M_2(\frac{1}{5})]{} \begin{pmatrix} 0 & 0 & 0 & | & 0 \\ 1 & 0 & -1 & | & 0 \\ 2 & 1 & -4 & | & 0 \end{pmatrix} \xrightarrow[A_{2,3}(-4)]{} \begin{pmatrix} 0 & 0 & 0 & | & 0 \\ 1 & 0 & -1 & | & 0 \\ -2 & 1 & 0 & | & 0 \end{pmatrix},$$

so that $x_3 = x_1$, $x_2 = 2x_1$,

$$v_3 = \begin{pmatrix} 1 \\ 2 \\ 1 \end{pmatrix},$$

and $E_3 = \text{span } \{v_3\}$.

Remark   In this and every other example, there is always an infinite number of choices for each eigenvector. We arbitrarily choose a simple one by setting one or more of the x_i's equal to 1.

Example 5   Let

$$A = \begin{pmatrix} 2 & -1 \\ -4 & 2 \end{pmatrix}.$$

Then

$$\det(A - \lambda I) = \begin{vmatrix} 2 - \lambda & -1 \\ -4 & 2 - \lambda \end{vmatrix} = \lambda^2 - 4\lambda = \lambda(\lambda - 4).$$

Thus the eigenvalues are $\lambda_1 = 0$ and $\lambda_2 = 4$. The eigenspace corresponding to zero is called the *kernel* of A. We calculate

$$\begin{pmatrix} 2 & -1 \\ -4 & 2 \end{pmatrix}\begin{pmatrix} x_1 \\ x_2 \end{pmatrix} = \begin{pmatrix} 0 \\ 0 \end{pmatrix},$$

or $2x_1 = x_2$ and an eigenvector is $\mathbf{v}_1 = \binom{1}{2}$ so that $\ker A = E_0 = \text{span}\{\binom{1}{2}\}$.
     Corresponding to $\lambda_2 = 4$, we have

$$\begin{pmatrix} -2 & -1 \\ -4 & -2 \end{pmatrix}\begin{pmatrix} x_1 \\ x_2 \end{pmatrix} = \begin{pmatrix} 0 \\ 0 \end{pmatrix}$$

so that

$$E_4 = \text{span}\left\{\begin{pmatrix} 1 \\ -2 \end{pmatrix}\right\}.$$

Example 6   Let

$$A = \begin{pmatrix} 3 & -5 \\ 1 & -1 \end{pmatrix}.$$

Then

$$\det(A - I) = \begin{vmatrix} 3 - \lambda & -5 \\ 1 & -1 - \lambda \end{vmatrix} = \lambda^2 - 2\lambda + 2 = 0.$$

Then

$$\begin{matrix} \lambda_1 \\ \lambda_2 \end{matrix}\Bigg\} = \frac{-(-2) \pm \sqrt{4 - 4(1)(2)}}{2} = \frac{2 \pm \sqrt{-4}}{2} = \frac{2 \pm 2i}{2} = 1 \pm i.$$

Thus $\lambda_1 = 1 + i$ and $\lambda_2 = 1 - i$. Then

$$[A - (1 + i)I]\mathbf{v} = \begin{pmatrix} 2 - i & -5 \\ 1 & -2 - i \end{pmatrix}\begin{pmatrix} x_1 \\ x_2 \end{pmatrix} = \begin{pmatrix} 0 \\ 0 \end{pmatrix}$$

and we obtain $(2 - i)x_1 - 5x_2 = 0$ and $x_1 + (-2 - i)x_2 = 0$.† Thus $x_1 = (2 + i)x_2$, which yields the eigenvector

$$\mathbf{v}_1 = \begin{pmatrix} 2 + i \\ 1 \end{pmatrix} \quad \text{and} \quad E_{1+i} = \text{span}\left\{\begin{pmatrix} 2 + i \\ 1 \end{pmatrix}\right\}.$$

Similarly,

$$[A - (1 - i)I]\mathbf{v} = \begin{pmatrix} 2 + i & -5 \\ 1 & -2 + i \end{pmatrix}\begin{pmatrix} x_1 \\ x_2 \end{pmatrix} = \begin{pmatrix} 0 \\ 0 \end{pmatrix}$$

or $x_1 + (-2 + i)x_2 = 0$, which yields $x_1 = (2 - i)x_2$,

$$\mathbf{v}_2 = \begin{pmatrix} 2 - i \\ 1 \end{pmatrix}, \quad \text{and} \quad E_{1-i} = \text{span}\left\{\begin{pmatrix} 2 - i \\ 1 \end{pmatrix}\right\}.$$

Remark   This example illustrates that a real matrix may have complex eigenvalues and eigenvectors. It should be pointed out that some texts define eigenvalues of real matrices to be the *real* roots of the characteristic equation. With this definition, the matrix of the last example has *no* eigenvalues. This might make the computations simpler, but it also significantly reduces the usefulness of the theory of eigenvalues and eigenvectors. We shall see an important illustration of the use of complex eigenvalues in Example 11 and in Section 8.5 in our computation of fundamental matrix solution.

Example 7   Let

$$A = \begin{pmatrix} 4 & 0 \\ 0 & 4 \end{pmatrix}.$$

Then

$$\det(A - \lambda I) = \begin{vmatrix} 4 - \lambda & 0 \\ 0 & 4 - \lambda \end{vmatrix} = (\lambda - 4)^2 = 0$$

so that $\lambda = 4$ is an eigenvalue of algebraic multiplicity two. It is obvious that $A\mathbf{v} = 4\mathbf{v}$ for every vector $\mathbf{v} \in R^2$ so that

$$E_4 = R^2 = \text{span}\left\{\begin{pmatrix} 1 \\ 0 \end{pmatrix}, \begin{pmatrix} 0 \\ 1 \end{pmatrix}\right\}.$$

Example 8   Let

$$A = \begin{pmatrix} 4 & 1 \\ 0 & 4 \end{pmatrix}.$$

---

† Note that

$$(-2 - i)\begin{pmatrix} 2 - i \\ 1 \end{pmatrix} = \begin{pmatrix} -5 \\ -2 - i \end{pmatrix}.$$

Then

$$\det(A - \lambda I) = \begin{vmatrix} 4 - \lambda & 1 \\ 0 & 4 - \lambda \end{vmatrix} = (\lambda - 4)^2 = 0$$

so that $\lambda = 4$ is again an eigenvalue of algebraic multiplicity two. But this time we have

$$(A - 4I)\mathbf{v} = \begin{pmatrix} 0 & 1 \\ 0 & 0 \end{pmatrix} \begin{pmatrix} x_1 \\ x_2 \end{pmatrix} = \begin{pmatrix} x_2 \\ 0 \end{pmatrix}.$$

Thus $x_2 = 0$, $\mathbf{v}_1 = \binom{1}{0}$ is an eigenvector, and $E_4 = \text{span}\{\binom{1}{0}\}$.

You may have noticed in Examples 7 and 8 that the algebraic multiplicity of the eigenvalue $\lambda = 4$ was $r = 2$. In Example 7 we found *two* linearly independent eigenvectors corresponding to $\lambda = 4$, but in Example 8 there was only *one* eigenvector corresponding to $\lambda = 4$. Thus the number of linearly independent eigenvectors need not equal the algebraic multiplicity of the eigenvalue. If we consider this statement in conjunction with Theorem 3, we immediately deduce that:

1. the $n \times n$ matrix A has n linearly independent eigenvectors if all of its eigenvalues have algebraic multiplicity equal to 1;

2. the $n \times n$ matrix A need not have n linearly independent eigenvectors if some eigenvalue has algebraic multiplicity greater than 1.

We now prove that the principal matrix solution of the system

$$\mathbf{x}' = A\mathbf{x} \tag{14}$$

for constant matrix A can easily be found using eigenvectors and eigenvalues if the $n \times n$ matrix A has n linearly independent eigenvectors.

Theorem 4   Suppose that the constant $n \times n$ matrix A has n linearly independent eigenvectors $\mathbf{v}_1, \mathbf{v}_2, \ldots, \mathbf{v}_n$ corresponding to the eigenvalues $\lambda_1, \lambda_2, \ldots, \lambda_n$ (not necessarily distinct), respectively. Then there exists a fundamental set of solutions to the system (14) of the form

$$\boldsymbol{\varphi}_1(t) = \mathbf{v}_1 e^{\lambda_1 t}, \quad \boldsymbol{\varphi}_2(t) = \mathbf{v}_2 e^{\lambda_2 t}, \ldots, \boldsymbol{\varphi}_n = \mathbf{v}_n e^{\lambda_n t}, \tag{15}$$

so that the matrix $\Phi(t)$ whose columns are $\boldsymbol{\varphi}_1(t), \ldots, \boldsymbol{\varphi}_n(t)$ is a fundamental matrix solution for Eq. (14).

Proof   We first show that $\boldsymbol{\varphi}_i(t)$ is a solution of Eq. (14) for $i = 1, 2, \ldots, n$. We have

$$\boldsymbol{\varphi}_i'(t) = (\mathbf{v}_i e^{\lambda_i t})' = \lambda_i \mathbf{v}_i e^{\lambda_i t}$$
$$= A\mathbf{v}_i e^{\lambda_i t} = A\boldsymbol{\varphi}_i(t),$$

since $\mathbf{v}_i$ is an eigenvector of A corresponding to the eigenvalue λ_i. To show that $\Phi(t)$ is a fundamental matrix solution, we simply note that

$$\det \Phi(0) = \det (\mathbf{v}_1, \mathbf{v}_2, \ldots, \mathbf{v}_n) \neq 0,$$

since the eigenvectors $\mathbf{v}_i$ are linearly independent. ∎

Example 9   Consider the system

$$\begin{pmatrix} x_1 \\ x_2 \end{pmatrix}' = \begin{pmatrix} 4 & 2 \\ 3 & 3 \end{pmatrix} \begin{pmatrix} x_1 \\ x_2 \end{pmatrix}. \tag{16}$$

It was shown in Example 3 that the eigenvalues of this system are $\lambda_1 = 1$ and $\lambda_2 = 6$ with corresponding linearly independent eigenvectors

$$\mathbf{v}_1 = \begin{pmatrix} 2 \\ -3 \end{pmatrix} \quad \text{and} \quad \mathbf{v}_2 = \begin{pmatrix} 1 \\ 1 \end{pmatrix}.$$

Therefore a fundamental set of solutions of Eq. (16) is

$$\boldsymbol{\varphi}_1(t) = \begin{pmatrix} 2 \\ -3 \end{pmatrix} e^t = \begin{pmatrix} 2e^t \\ -3e^t \end{pmatrix} \quad \text{and} \quad \boldsymbol{\varphi}_2(t) = \begin{pmatrix} 1 \\ 1 \end{pmatrix} e^{6t} = \begin{pmatrix} e^{6t} \\ e^{6t} \end{pmatrix},$$

so that a fundamental matrix solution is

$$\Phi(t) = \begin{pmatrix} 2e^t & e^{6t} \\ -3e^t & e^{6t} \end{pmatrix}.$$

Example 10   Consider the system

$$\begin{pmatrix} x_1 \\ x_2 \\ x_3 \end{pmatrix}' = \begin{pmatrix} 1 & -1 & 4 \\ 3 & 2 & -1 \\ 2 & 1 & -1 \end{pmatrix} \begin{pmatrix} x_1 \\ x_2 \\ x_3 \end{pmatrix}. \tag{17}$$

As was shown in Example 4, the eigenvalues of A are $\lambda_1 = 1$, $\lambda_2 = -2$, and $\lambda_3 = 3$ with corresponding eigenvectors

$$\mathbf{v}_1 = \begin{pmatrix} -1 \\ 4 \\ 1 \end{pmatrix}, \quad \mathbf{v}_2 = \begin{pmatrix} 1 \\ -1 \\ -1 \end{pmatrix}, \quad \mathbf{v}_3 = \begin{pmatrix} 1 \\ 2 \\ 1 \end{pmatrix}.$$

Therefore a fundamental set of solutions to Eq. (17) is

$$\boldsymbol{\varphi}_1(t) = \begin{pmatrix} -1 \\ 4 \\ 1 \end{pmatrix} e^t = \begin{pmatrix} -e^t \\ 4e^t \\ e^t \end{pmatrix}, \quad \boldsymbol{\varphi}_2(t) = \begin{pmatrix} 1 \\ -1 \\ -1 \end{pmatrix} e^{-2t} = \begin{pmatrix} e^{-2t} \\ -e^{-2t} \\ -e^{-2t} \end{pmatrix},$$

and

$$\boldsymbol{\varphi}_3(t) = \begin{pmatrix} 1 \\ 2 \\ 1 \end{pmatrix} e^{3t} = \begin{pmatrix} e^{3t} \\ 2e^{3t} \\ e^{3t} \end{pmatrix},$$

yielding the fundamental matrix solution

$$\Phi(t) = \begin{pmatrix} -e^t & e^{-2t} & e^{3t} \\ 4e^t & -e^{-2t} & 2e^{3t} \\ e^t & -e^{-2t} & e^{3t} \end{pmatrix}.$$

Example 11   Consider the system

$$\begin{pmatrix} x_1 \\ x_2 \end{pmatrix}' = \begin{pmatrix} 3 & -5 \\ 1 & -1 \end{pmatrix} \begin{pmatrix} x_1 \\ x_2 \end{pmatrix}. \tag{18}$$

As was shown in Example 6, the eigenvalues of this system are $\lambda_1 = 1 + i$ and $\lambda_2 = 1 - i$ with corresponding eigenvectors

$$\mathbf{v}_1 = \begin{pmatrix} 2 + i \\ 1 \end{pmatrix} \quad \text{and} \quad \mathbf{v}_2 = \begin{pmatrix} 2 - i \\ 1 \end{pmatrix}.$$

A fundamental set of solutions to system (18) is

$$\varphi_1(t) = \begin{pmatrix} 2 + i \\ 1 \end{pmatrix} e^{(1+i)t} = \begin{pmatrix} (2 + i)e^{(1+i)t} \\ e^{(1+i)t} \end{pmatrix},$$

and

$$\varphi_2(t) = \begin{pmatrix} 2 - i \\ 1 \end{pmatrix} e^{(1-i)t} = \begin{pmatrix} (2 - i)e^{(1-i)t} \\ e^{(1-i)t} \end{pmatrix},$$

with fundamental matrix solution

$$\Phi(t) = \begin{pmatrix} (2 + i)e^{(1+i)t} & (2 - i)e^{(1-i)t} \\ e^{(1+i)t} & e^{(1-i)t} \end{pmatrix}. \tag{19}$$

The complex terms in Eq. (19) make this fundamental matrix solution somewhat unpleasant. We can use Theorem 3 of Section 8.2 to produce a fundamental matrix solution involving only real terms, by multiplying Eq. (19) by a suitably chosen constant matrix. To see how this is done, write Eq. (19) as the product

$$\Phi(t) = \begin{pmatrix} 2 + i & 2 - i \\ 1 & 1 \end{pmatrix} \begin{pmatrix} e^{(1+i)t} & 0 \\ 0 & e^{(1-i)t} \end{pmatrix}, \tag{20}$$

or $\Phi(t) = V \cdot E(t)$, where

$$V = (\mathbf{v}_1, \mathbf{v}_2) \quad \text{and} \quad E(t) = \begin{pmatrix} e^{\lambda_1 t} & 0 \\ 0 & e^{\lambda_2 t} \end{pmatrix}.$$

To eliminate the complex terms in Eq. (20), multiply both sides by the inverse of the matrix V (see Exercise 30):

$$V^{-1} = \frac{1}{2i} \begin{pmatrix} 1 & -2 + i \\ -1 & 2 + i \end{pmatrix},$$

which yields

$$\Phi_1(t) = \Phi(t)V^{-1} = \frac{1}{2i} \begin{pmatrix} 2 + i & 2 - i \\ 1 & 1 \end{pmatrix} \begin{pmatrix} e^{(1+i)t} & 0 \\ 0 & e^{(1-i)t} \end{pmatrix} \begin{pmatrix} 1 & -2 + i \\ -1 & 2 + i \end{pmatrix},$$

or, after multiplication

$$\Phi_1(t) = \begin{pmatrix} 2\left(\dfrac{e^{(1+i)t} - e^{(1-i)t}}{2i}\right) + \left(\dfrac{e^{(1+i)t} + e^{(1-i)t}}{2}\right) & -5\left(\dfrac{e^{(1+i)t} - e^{(1-i)t}}{2i}\right) \\[3mm] \left(\dfrac{e^{(1+i)t} - e^{(1-i)t}}{2i}\right) & -2\left(\dfrac{e^{(1+i)t} - e^{(1-i)t}}{2i}\right) + \left(\dfrac{e^{(1+i)t} + e^{(1-i)t}}{2}\right) \end{pmatrix}.$$

Now using the identity in Eq. (3) of Section 3.5 we have

$$\frac{1}{2}(e^{(\alpha+i\beta)t} + e^{(\alpha-i\beta)t}) = e^{\alpha t}\cos\beta t,$$

$$\frac{1}{2i}(e^{(\alpha+i\beta)t} - e^{(\alpha-i\beta)t}) = e^{\alpha t}\sin\beta t.$$

(21)

Thus,

$$\Phi_1(t) = \begin{pmatrix} 2e^t\sin t + e^t\cos t & -5e^t\sin t \\ e^t\sin t & -2e^t\sin t + e^t\cos t \end{pmatrix}$$

$$= e^t\begin{pmatrix} 2\sin t + \cos t & -5\sin t \\ \sin t & \cos t - 2\sin t \end{pmatrix}.$$

(22)

Note that det $\Phi_1(0) = \det I = 1$, so $\Phi_1(t)$ is the principal matrix solution of system (18).

Examples 9 through 11 illustrate the power of the eigenvalue method for solving the homogeneous system $\mathbf{x}' = A\mathbf{x}$. Note that the technique of Theorem 4 applies only to $n \times n$ matrices A having n linearly independent eigenvectors. In Sections 8.4 and 8.5 we will develop an alternative method, based on the Cayley-Hamilton theorem, that can be used to solve *any* homogeneous system $\mathbf{x}' = A\mathbf{x}$. By using the Cayley–Hamilton theorem, we will be able to avoid the more tedious and difficult development of Jordan canonical forms.

EXERCISES 8.3

In Exercises 1 through 23, calculate the eigenvalues and eigenspaces of the given matrix.

1. $\begin{pmatrix} -2 & -2 \\ -5 & 1 \end{pmatrix}$

2. $\begin{pmatrix} -12 & 7 \\ -7 & 2 \end{pmatrix}$

3. $\begin{pmatrix} 2 & -1 \\ 5 & -2 \end{pmatrix}$

4. $\begin{pmatrix} -3 & 0 \\ 0 & -3 \end{pmatrix}$

5. $\begin{pmatrix} -3 & 2 \\ 0 & -3 \end{pmatrix}$

6. $\begin{pmatrix} 3 & 2 \\ -5 & 1 \end{pmatrix}$

7. $\begin{pmatrix} 1 & -1 & 0 \\ -1 & 2 & -1 \\ 0 & -1 & 1 \end{pmatrix}$

8. $\begin{pmatrix} 1 & 1 & -2 \\ -1 & 2 & 1 \\ 0 & 1 & -1 \end{pmatrix}$

9. $\begin{pmatrix} 5 & 4 & 2 \\ 4 & 5 & 2 \\ 2 & 2 & 2 \end{pmatrix}$

10. $\begin{pmatrix} 1 & 2 & 2 \\ 0 & 2 & 1 \\ -1 & 2 & 2 \end{pmatrix}$

11. $\begin{pmatrix} 0 & 1 & 0 \\ 0 & 0 & 1 \\ 1 & -3 & 3 \end{pmatrix}$

12. $\begin{pmatrix} -3 & -7 & -5 \\ 2 & 4 & 3 \\ 1 & 2 & 2 \end{pmatrix}$

13. $\begin{pmatrix} 1 & -1 & -1 \\ 1 & -1 & 0 \\ 1 & 0 & -1 \end{pmatrix}$

14. $\begin{pmatrix} 7 & -2 & -4 \\ 3 & 0 & -2 \\ 6 & -2 & -3 \end{pmatrix}$

15. $\begin{pmatrix} 4 & 6 & 6 \\ 1 & 3 & 2 \\ -1 & -5 & -2 \end{pmatrix}$

16. $\begin{pmatrix} 3 & 2 & 4 \\ 2 & 0 & 2 \\ 4 & 2 & 3 \end{pmatrix}$

17. $\begin{pmatrix} -5 & -5 & -9 \\ 8 & 9 & 18 \\ -2 & -3 & -7 \end{pmatrix}$

18. $\begin{pmatrix} -1 & -3 & -9 \\ 0 & 5 & 18 \\ 0 & -2 & -7 \end{pmatrix}$

19. $\begin{pmatrix} 4 & 1 & 0 & 1 \\ 2 & 3 & 0 & 1 \\ -2 & 1 & 2 & -3 \\ 2 & -1 & 0 & 5 \end{pmatrix}$

20. $\begin{pmatrix} a & 0 & 0 & 0 \\ 0 & a & 0 & 0 \\ 0 & 0 & a & 0 \\ 0 & 0 & 0 & a \end{pmatrix}$

21. $\begin{pmatrix} a & b & 0 & 0 \\ 0 & a & 0 & 0 \\ 0 & 0 & a & 0 \\ 0 & 0 & 0 & a \end{pmatrix}, \quad b \neq 0$

22. $\begin{pmatrix} a & b & 0 & 0 \\ 0 & a & c & 0 \\ 0 & 0 & a & 0 \\ 0 & 0 & 0 & a \end{pmatrix}, \quad bc \neq 0$

23. $\begin{pmatrix} a & b & 0 & 0 \\ 0 & a & c & 0 \\ 0 & 0 & a & d \\ 0 & 0 & 0 & a \end{pmatrix}, \quad bcd \neq 0$

In Exercises 24 through 32, compute a fundamental matrix solution of the homogeneous system $\mathbf{x}' = A\mathbf{x}$, where A is the given constant matrix.

24. $\begin{pmatrix} 10 & -18 \\ 6 & -11 \end{pmatrix}$

25. $\begin{pmatrix} 4 & -3 \\ 5 & -4 \end{pmatrix}$

26. $\begin{pmatrix} 7 & 6 \\ 2 & 6 \end{pmatrix}$

27. $\begin{pmatrix} 2 & -1 \\ -4 & 2 \end{pmatrix}$

28. $\begin{pmatrix} 4 & -3 \\ 8 & -6 \end{pmatrix}$

29. $\begin{pmatrix} -1 & 1 \\ -5 & 3 \end{pmatrix}$

30. $\begin{pmatrix} 3 & -1 & 1 \\ -1 & 5 & -1 \\ 1 & -1 & 3 \end{pmatrix}$

31. $\begin{pmatrix} 1 & 1 & -2 \\ -1 & 2 & 1 \\ 0 & 1 & -1 \end{pmatrix}$

32. $\begin{pmatrix} 1 & -1 & 0 \\ -1 & 2 & -1 \\ 0 & -1 & 1 \end{pmatrix}$

33. Show that the inverse of the constant 2×2 matrix

$$A = \begin{pmatrix} a & b \\ c & d \end{pmatrix}, \quad ad - bc \neq 0,$$

is

$$A^{-1} = \frac{1}{ad - bc} \begin{pmatrix} d & -b \\ -c & a \end{pmatrix}.$$

34. Show that for any real numbers a and b, the matrix

$$A = \begin{pmatrix} a & b \\ -b & a \end{pmatrix}$$

has the eigenvectors

$$\begin{pmatrix} 1 \\ i \end{pmatrix} \quad \text{and} \quad \begin{pmatrix} 1 \\ -i \end{pmatrix}.$$

In Exercises 35 through 41, assume that the matrix A has the eigenvalues $\lambda_1, \lambda_2, \ldots, \lambda_k$.

35. Show that the eigenvalues of A^t are $\lambda_1, \lambda_2, \ldots, \lambda_k$.

36. Show that the eigenvalues of αA are $\lambda_1, \lambda_2, \ldots, \lambda_k$.

37. Show that A^{-1} exists if and only if $\lambda_1 \cdot \lambda_2 \cdot \cdots \cdot \lambda_k \neq 0$.

***38.** If A^{-1} exists, show that the eigenvalues of A^{-1} are $1/\lambda_1, 1/\lambda_2, \ldots, 1/\lambda_k$. [*Hint*: Show that

$$\det(A^{-1} - (1/\lambda i)I) = 0.]$$

39. Show that the matrix $A - \alpha I$ has the eigenvalues, $\lambda_1 - \alpha, \lambda_2 - \alpha, \ldots, \lambda_k - \alpha$.

***40.** Show that the eigenvalues of A^2 are $\lambda_1^2, \lambda_2^2, \ldots, \lambda_k^2$. [*Hint*: Show that the $\det(A^2 - \lambda_i^2 I) = 0$ by factoring $A^2 - \lambda_i^2 I$.]

***41.** Show that the eigenvalues of A^m are $\lambda_1^m, \lambda_2^m, \ldots, \lambda_k^m$ for $m = 1, 2, 3, \ldots$.

42. Let λ be an eigenvalue of A with corresponding eigenvector $\mathbf{v}$. Let $p(\lambda) = a_0 + a_1\lambda + a_2\lambda^2 + \cdots + a_n\lambda^n$. Define the matrix $p(A)$ by $p(A) = a_0 I + a_1 A + a_2 A^2 + \cdots + a_n A^n$. Show that

$$p(A)\mathbf{v} = p(\lambda)\mathbf{v}.$$

43. Using the result of Exercise 42, show that if $\lambda_1, \lambda_2, \ldots, \lambda_k$ are eigenvalues of A, then $p(\lambda_1), p(\lambda_2), \ldots, p(\lambda_k)$ are eigenvalues of $p(A)$.

44. Show that if A is an upper triangular matrix, then the eigenvalues of A are the diagonal components of A.

45. Let

$$A_1 = \begin{pmatrix} 2 & 0 & 0 & 0 \\ 0 & 2 & 0 & 0 \\ 0 & 0 & 2 & 0 \\ 0 & 0 & 0 & 2 \end{pmatrix}, \qquad A_2 = \begin{pmatrix} 2 & 1 & 0 & 0 \\ 0 & 2 & 0 & 0 \\ 0 & 0 & 2 & 0 \\ 0 & 0 & 0 & 2 \end{pmatrix},$$

$$A_3 = \begin{pmatrix} 2 & 1 & 0 & 0 \\ 0 & 2 & 1 & 0 \\ 0 & 0 & 2 & 0 \\ 0 & 0 & 0 & 2 \end{pmatrix}, \qquad A_4 = \begin{pmatrix} 2 & 1 & 0 & 0 \\ 0 & 2 & 1 & 0 \\ 0 & 0 & 2 & 1 \\ 0 & 0 & 0 & 2 \end{pmatrix}.$$

Show that, for each matrix, $\lambda = 2$ is an eigenvalue of algebraic multiplicity 4. In each case, compute the eigenspace of $\lambda = 2$.

*46. Let A be a real $n \times n$ matrix. Show that if λ_1 is a complex eigenvalue of A with eigenvector $\mathbf{v}_1$, then $\bar{\lambda}_1$ is an eigenvalue of A with eigenvector $\bar{\mathbf{v}}_1$.

*47. A probability matrix is an $n \times n$ matrix having two properties:

   i) $a_{ij} \geqslant 0$ for every i and j;

   ii) the sum of the components in every column is 1.

Prove that 1 is an eigenvalue of every probability matrix.

8.4 THE CAYLEY–HAMILTON THEOREM

There are many other interesting and useful facts about eigenvectors and eigenvalues. In this section we present a very important result that will enable us to compute the principal matrix solution of *any* homogeneous differential equation

$$\mathbf{x}'(t) = A\mathbf{x}(t).$$

Let $p(\lambda) = \lambda^m + a_{m-1}\lambda^{m-1} + \cdots + a_1\lambda + a_0$ be a polynomial and let A be an $n \times n$ matrix. Since powers of A are also $n \times n$ matrices, we define

$$\boxed{p(A) = A^m + a_{m-1}A^{m-1} + \cdots + a_1A + a_0I.} \qquad \textbf{(1)}$$

Example 1   Let

$$A = \begin{pmatrix} -1 & 4 \\ 3 & 7 \end{pmatrix}$$

and $p(\lambda) = \lambda^2 - 5\lambda + 3$. Then

$$p(A) = A^2 - 5A + 3I = \begin{pmatrix} 13 & 24 \\ 18 & 61 \end{pmatrix} + \begin{pmatrix} 5 & -20 \\ -15 & -35 \end{pmatrix} + \begin{pmatrix} 3 & 0 \\ 0 & 3 \end{pmatrix} = \begin{pmatrix} 21 & 4 \\ 3 & 29 \end{pmatrix}.$$

Expression (1) is a polynomial with scalar coefficients defined for a matrix variable. We can also define a polynomial with $n \times n$ matrix coefficients by

$$Q(\lambda) = B_0 + B_1\lambda + B_2\lambda^2 + \cdots + B_m\lambda^m. \qquad \textbf{(2)}$$

If A is an $n \times n$ matrix, then we define

$$Q(A) = B_0 + B_1A + B_2A^2 + \cdots + B_mA^m. \qquad \textbf{(3)}$$

We must be careful in writing Eq. (3) since matrices do not commute under multiplication.

Theorem 1   If $P(\lambda)$ and $Q(\lambda)$ are polynomials in the scalar variable λ with $n \times n$ matrix coefficients and if $P(\lambda) = Q(\lambda)(A - \lambda I)$, then $P(A) = 0$.

Proof   If $Q(\lambda)$ is given by Eq. (2), then

$$P(\lambda) = (B_0 + B_1\lambda + B_2\lambda^2 + \cdots + B_m\lambda^m)(A - \lambda I)$$

$$= B_0A + B_1A\lambda + B_2A\lambda^2 + \cdots + B_mA\lambda^m$$

$$- B_0\lambda - B_1\lambda^2 - B_2\lambda^3 - \cdots - B_m\lambda^{m+1}. \tag{4}$$

Substituting A for λ in Eq. (4), we obtain

$$P(A) = B_0A + B_1A^2 + B_2A^3 + \cdots + B_mA^{m+1}$$

$$- B_0A - B_1A^2 - B_2A^3 - \cdots - B_mA^{m+1} = 0. \blacksquare$$

Note   We cannot prove this theorem by simply substituting $\lambda = A$ to obtain $P(A) = Q(A)(A - A) = 0$. This is because it is possible to find polynomials $Q(\lambda)$ and $R(\lambda)$ with matrix coefficients such that $P(\lambda) = Q(\lambda)R(\lambda)$ but $P(A) \neq Q(A)R(A)$. (See Exercise 10.)

We can now state the main theorem.

Theorem 2   *The Cayley–Hamilton Theorem.*† Every square matrix satisfies its own characteristic equation. That is, if $p(\lambda) = 0$ is the characteristic equation of A, then $p(A) = 0$.

Proof   We have

$$p(\lambda) = \det(A - \lambda I) = \begin{vmatrix} a_{11} - \lambda & a_{12} & \cdots & a_{1n} \\ a_{21} & a_{22} - \lambda & \cdots & a_{2n} \\ \vdots & & & \vdots \\ a_{n1} & a_{n2} & \cdots & a_{nn} - \lambda \end{vmatrix} = 0.$$

The *adjoint* of $A - \lambda I$ is an $n \times n$ matrix, denoted by adj $(A - \lambda I)$, whose component in the ith row and jth column equals $(-1)^{i+j}(A - \lambda I)_{ji}$, where $(A - \lambda I)_{ji}$ is the determinant of the $(n - 1) \times (n - 1)$ matrix obtained by deleting the jth row and ith column of $A - \lambda I$. The most important property of adjoints is the identity (see Exercise 11):

$$\det(A - \lambda I)I = [\text{adj}(A - \lambda I)](A - \lambda I). \tag{5}$$

Because the components of adj $(A - \lambda I)$ are determinants of $(n - 1) \times (n - 1)$ submatrices of $A - \lambda I$, each component of adj $(A - \lambda I)$ is a polyno-

---

† Named after Sir William Rowan Hamilton (1805–1865) and Arthur Cayley (1821–1895). Cayley published the first discussion of this famous theorem in 1858. Independently, Hamilton discovered the result in his work on quaternions.

mial in λ. Thus, we can write

$$\text{adj}\,(A - \lambda I) = \begin{pmatrix} p_{11}(\lambda) & p_{12}(\lambda) & \cdots & p_{1n}(\lambda) \\ p_{21}(\lambda) & p_{22}(\lambda) & \cdots & p_{2n}(\lambda) \\ \vdots & \vdots & & \vdots \\ p_{n1}(\lambda) & p_{n2}(\lambda) & \cdots & p_{nn}(\lambda) \end{pmatrix}.$$

This means that we can think of $\text{adj}\,(A - \lambda I)$ as a polynomial, $Q(\lambda)$, in λ with $n \times n$ matrix coefficients. To see this, look at the following example:

$$\begin{pmatrix} -\lambda^2 - 2\lambda + 1 & 2\lambda^2 - 7\lambda - 4 \\ 4\lambda^2 + 5\lambda - 2 & -3\lambda^2 - \lambda + 3 \end{pmatrix} = \begin{pmatrix} -1 & 2 \\ 4 & -3 \end{pmatrix}\lambda^2 + \begin{pmatrix} -2 & -7 \\ 5 & -1 \end{pmatrix}\lambda + \begin{pmatrix} 1 & -4 \\ -2 & 3 \end{pmatrix}.$$

Replacing $\text{adj}\,(A - \lambda I)$ by the polynomial $Q(\lambda)$, we have

$$\det\,(A - \lambda I)I = [\text{adj}\,(A - \lambda I)](A - \lambda I) = Q(\lambda)(A - \lambda I).$$

But the determinant $\det\,(A - \lambda I)$ is also a polynomial in λ:

$$\det\,(A - \lambda I) = p(\lambda) = \lambda^n + a_{n-1}\lambda^{n-1} + \cdots + a_1\lambda + a_0.$$

Defining

$$P(\lambda) = p(\lambda)I = \lambda^n I + a_{n-1}\lambda^{n-1}I + \cdots + a_1\lambda I + a_0 I,$$

we have $P(\lambda) = Q(\lambda)(A - \lambda I)$. Finally, from Theorem 1, we find that $P(A) = 0$. But $P(A) = p(A)$. ∎

Example 2 Let

$$A = \begin{pmatrix} 1 & -1 & 4 \\ 3 & 2 & -1 \\ 2 & 1 & -1 \end{pmatrix}.$$

In Example 4 in Section 8.3, we computed A's characteristic equation $\lambda^3 - 2\lambda^2 - 5\lambda + 6 = 0$. Since

$$A^2 = \begin{pmatrix} 6 & 1 & 1 \\ 7 & 0 & 11 \\ 3 & -1 & 8 \end{pmatrix}$$

and

$$A^3 = \begin{pmatrix} 11 & -3 & 22 \\ 29 & 4 & 17 \\ 16 & 3 & 5 \end{pmatrix},$$

we have

$$A^3 - 2A^2 - 5A + 6I = \begin{pmatrix} 11 & -3 & 22 \\ 29 & 4 & 17 \\ 16 & 3 & 5 \end{pmatrix} + \begin{pmatrix} -12 & -2 & -2 \\ -14 & 0 & -22 \\ -6 & 2 & -16 \end{pmatrix}$$

$$+ \begin{pmatrix} -5 & 5 & -20 \\ -15 & -10 & 5 \\ -10 & -5 & 5 \end{pmatrix} + \begin{pmatrix} 6 & 0 & 0 \\ 0 & 6 & 0 \\ 0 & 0 & 6 \end{pmatrix}$$

$$= \begin{pmatrix} 0 & 0 & 0 \\ 0 & 0 & 0 \\ 0 & 0 & 0 \end{pmatrix}.$$

The Cayley–Hamilton theorem can be used to calculate the inverse of a matrix if A^{-1} exists. If $p(\lambda) = \lambda^n + a_{n-1}\lambda^{n-1} + \cdots + a_1\lambda + a_0$, then

$$p(A) = A^n + a_{n-1}A^{n-1} + \cdots + a_1A + a_0I = 0,$$

and

$$A^{-1}p(A) = A^{n+1} + a_{n-1}A^{n-2} + \cdots + a_2A + a_1I + a_0A^{-1} = 0.$$

Thus,

$$A^{-1} = \frac{1}{a_0}(-A^{n-1} - a_{n-1}A^{n-2} - \cdots - a_2A - a_1I). \qquad \textbf{(6)}$$

Note that $a_0 \neq 0$ because $a_0 = \det A$ (why?) and we assumed that A was invertible.

Example 3   Let

$$A = \begin{pmatrix} 1 & -1 & 4 \\ 3 & 2 & -1 \\ 2 & 1 & -1 \end{pmatrix}.$$

Then $p(\lambda) = \lambda^3 - 2\lambda^2 - 5\lambda + 6$. Here $n = 3$, $a_2 = -2$, $a_1 = -5$, $a_0 = 6$, and

$$A^{-1} = \frac{1}{6}(-A^2 + 2A + 5I)$$

$$= \frac{1}{6}\left[\begin{pmatrix} -6 & -1 & -1 \\ -7 & 0 & -11 \\ -3 & 1 & -8 \end{pmatrix} + \begin{pmatrix} 2 & -2 & 8 \\ 6 & 4 & -2 \\ 4 & 2 & -2 \end{pmatrix} + \begin{pmatrix} 5 & 0 & 0 \\ 0 & 5 & 0 \\ 0 & 0 & 5 \end{pmatrix} \right]$$

$$= \frac{1}{6}\begin{pmatrix} 1 & -3 & 7 \\ -1 & 9 & -13 \\ 1 & 3 & -5 \end{pmatrix}.$$

Note that we computed A^{-1} with a single division and with only one calculation of a determinant [in order to find $p(\lambda) = \det(A - \lambda I)$]. This method is sometimes very efficient on a computer.

EXERCISES 8.4

In Exercises 1 through 9, (a) find the characteristic equation $p(\lambda) = 0$ of the given matrix; (b) verify that $p(A) = 0$; and (c) use part (b) to compute A^{-1} if it exists.

1. $\begin{pmatrix} -2 & -2 \\ -5 & 1 \end{pmatrix}$ **2.** $\begin{pmatrix} 2 & -1 \\ 5 & -2 \end{pmatrix}$

3. $\begin{pmatrix} 1 & -1 & 0 \\ -1 & 2 & -1 \\ 0 & -1 & 1 \end{pmatrix}$ **4.** $\begin{pmatrix} 1 & 2 & 2 \\ 0 & 2 & 1 \\ -1 & 2 & 2 \end{pmatrix}$

5. $\begin{pmatrix} 0 & 1 & 0 \\ 0 & 0 & 1 \\ 1 & -3 & 3 \end{pmatrix}$ **6.** $\begin{pmatrix} -3 & -7 & -5 \\ 2 & 4 & 3 \\ 1 & 2 & 2 \end{pmatrix}$

7. $\begin{pmatrix} 2 & -1 & 3 \\ 4 & 1 & 6 \\ 1 & 5 & 3 \end{pmatrix}$ **8.** $\begin{pmatrix} 1 & 0 & 1 & 0 \\ 2 & -1 & 0 & 2 \\ -1 & 0 & 0 & 1 \\ 4 & 1 & -1 & 0 \end{pmatrix}$

9. $\begin{pmatrix} a & b & 0 & 0 \\ 0 & a & c & 0 \\ 0 & 0 & a & d \\ 0 & 0 & 0 & a \end{pmatrix}$, $bcd \neq 0$

10. Let $R(\lambda) = B_0 + B_1\lambda$ and $Q(\lambda) = C_0 + C_1\lambda$, where B_0, B_1, C_0, and C_1 are $n \times n$ matrices.

a) Compute $P(\lambda) = R(\lambda)Q(\lambda)$.

b) Let A be an $n \times n$ matrix. Show that $P(A) = R(A)Q(A)$ if and only if A commutes with both C_0 and C_1.

11. Let $A = (a_{ij})$ be an $n \times n$ matrix, and let A_{ij} be the determinant of the $(n-1) \times (n-1)$ matrix obtained by deleting the ith row and jth column of A.

a) Show that if two rows of A are identical, then $\det A = 0$. (*Hint*: See Fig. 1 in Appendix 4.)

b) Prove using part (a) and Eq. (10) in Appendix 4 that $(-1)^{1+j}a_{1i}A_{1j} + (-1)^{2+j}a_{2i}A_{2j} + \cdots + (-1)^{n+j}a_{ni}A_{nj} = (\det A)\delta_{ij}$, where

$$\delta_{ij} = \begin{cases} 0, & \text{if } i \neq j, \\ 1, & \text{if } i = j. \end{cases}$$

c) Use part (b) to show that

$$(\text{adj } A)A = (\det A)I.$$

d) Show that if A^{-1} exists, then

$$A^{-1} = \frac{1}{\det A}(\text{adj } A).$$

Show the connection between this result and Cramer's rule (Theorem 4 in Appendix 4).

8.5 FUNDAMENTAL MATRIX SOLUTIONS IN THE CONSTANT-COEFFICIENT CASE

In this section we shall use the Cayley–Hamilton theorem to calculate a fundamental matrix solution for any system

$$\mathbf{x}' = A\mathbf{x}, \tag{1}$$

when the matrix A is constant. In fact, the method described below will give us the principal matrix solution, that is, the fundamental matrix solution $\Psi(t)$ that satisfies $\Psi(0) = I$. Recall that we began a systematic study of solutions to linear differential equations in Chapter 2 with the equation (with $n = 1$)

$$x'(t) = ax(t), \tag{2}$$

which has a solution

$$\psi(t) = e^{at}. \tag{3}$$

The function $\psi(t)$ is the principal 1×1 matrix solution to Eq. (2) since $\psi(0) = 1$. By analogy, we shall define the matrix function e^{At} in the case where A is an $n \times n$ matrix.

We recall [see Eq. (16) in Section 5.1] that the exponential function can be defined as the power series

$$e^{at} = 1 + at + \frac{(at)^2}{2!} + \cdots + \frac{(at)^m}{m!} + \cdots. \tag{4}$$

We use this expansion to define the matrix function

$$e^{At} = I + At + \frac{(At)^2}{2!} + \frac{(At)^3}{3!} + \cdots + \frac{(At)^m}{m!} + \cdots. \tag{5}$$

Note that since powers of the matrix A are $n \times n$ matrices, the right side of Eq. (5) will be an $n \times n$ matrix if the series converges.

Example 1 Let

$$A = \begin{pmatrix} 1 & 0 & 0 \\ 0 & 2 & 0 \\ 0 & 0 & 3 \end{pmatrix}. \tag{6}$$

Then

$$A^2 = \begin{pmatrix} 1 & 0 & 0 \\ 0 & 2^2 & 0 \\ 0 & 0 & 3^2 \end{pmatrix}, \quad A^3 = \begin{pmatrix} 1 & 0 & 0 \\ 0 & 2^3 & 0 \\ 0 & 0 & 3^3 \end{pmatrix}, \ldots, \quad A^m = \begin{pmatrix} 1 & 0 & 0 \\ 0 & 2^m & 0 \\ 0 & 0 & 3^m \end{pmatrix},$$

so that

$$e^{At} = I + At + \frac{A^2 t^2}{2} + \cdots + \frac{A^m t^m}{m} + \cdots = \begin{pmatrix} 1 & 0 & 0 \\ 0 & 1 & 0 \\ 0 & 0 & 1 \end{pmatrix} + \begin{pmatrix} t & 0 & 0 \\ 0 & 2t & 0 \\ 0 & 0 & 3t \end{pmatrix}$$

$$+ \cdots + \begin{pmatrix} \dfrac{t^m}{m!} & 0 & 0 \\ 0 & \dfrac{(2t)^m}{m!} & 0 \\ 0 & 0 & \dfrac{(3t)^m}{m!} \end{pmatrix} + \cdots$$

$$= \begin{pmatrix} 1 + t + \cdots + \dfrac{t^m}{m!} + \cdots & 0 & 0 \\ 0 & 1 + 2t + \cdots + \dfrac{(2t)^m}{m!} + \cdots & 0 \\ 0 & 0 & 1 + 3t + \cdots + \dfrac{(3t)^m}{m!} + \cdots \end{pmatrix}.$$

Using Eq. (4), we finally obtain

$$e^{At} = \begin{pmatrix} e^t & 0 & 0 \\ 0 & e^{2t} & 0 \\ 0 & 0 & e^{3t} \end{pmatrix}. \tag{7}$$

Note that $\Psi(t) = e^{At}$ satisfies $\Psi(0) = I$ and

$$\Phi'(t) = (e^{At})' = \begin{pmatrix} e^t & 0 & 0 \\ 0 & 2e^{2t} & 0 \\ 0 & 0 & 3e^{3t} \end{pmatrix} = \begin{pmatrix} 1 & 0 & 0 \\ 0 & 2 & 0 \\ 0 & 0 & 3 \end{pmatrix}\begin{pmatrix} e^t & 0 & 0 \\ 0 & e^{2t} & 0 \\ 0 & 0 & e^{3t} \end{pmatrix}$$

$$= A(e^{At}) = A\Psi(t). \tag{8}$$

Thus, $\Psi(t) = e^{At}$ is the principal matrix solution of the system $\mathbf{x}' = A\mathbf{x}$, when A is the matrix in Eq. (6).

The question of convergence for the series in Eq. (5) for an arbitrary $n \times n$ matrix A is settled in the following theorem.

Theorem 1   The series

$$e^{At} = I + At + \frac{(At)^2}{2!} + \frac{(At)^3}{3!} + \cdots \tag{9}$$

converges for all t, can be differentiated term by term, and is the principal matrix solution of the system $\mathbf{x}' = A\mathbf{x}$.

Note   We are assuming in this section that $t_0 = 0$ so that the principal matrix solution, $\Psi(t)$, satisfies $\Psi(0) = I$. If $t_0 \neq 0$, then the principal matrix solution is given by $\Psi(t) = e^{A(t-t_0)}$.

Proof   It is not difficult to show that each of the n^2 components of e^{At}, as defined by Eq. (9), is a power series in t. If *each* of these power series can be shown to converge, then the entire right-hand side of Eq. (9) will coverage. To do this, we define the norm of a matrix

$$\|A\| = \sum_{i=1}^{n} \sum_{j=1}^{n} |a_{ij}|. \tag{10}$$

It can be shown (see Exercise 23) that

$$\|AB\| \leq \|A\| \|B\| \tag{11}$$

and, in particular,

$$\|A^2\| = \|A \cdot A\| \leq \|A\| \|A\| = \|A\|^2.$$

Proceeding inductively, we have

$$\|A^m\| \leq \|A\|^m \tag{12}$$

for all integers m; hence

$$\left\| \frac{(At)^m}{m!} \right\| \le \frac{\|A\|^m |t|^m}{m!}.$$

But, since the norm of a matrix is the sum of the absolute values of the components of that matrix, we see immediately that if $a_{ij}^{(m)}(t)$ denotes the ijth component of the matrix $(At)^m/m!$, then by Eq. (12)

$$|a_{ij}^{(m)}(t)| \le \frac{\|A\|^m |t|^m}{m!}.$$

Since

$$\sum_{m=0}^{\infty} \frac{\|A\|^m |t|^m}{m!} = e^{\|A\| |t|}$$

(which is an ordinary scalar exponential since $\|A\|$ is a scalar), we see, by the comparison test for series, that the power series in the ijth position, $\sum_{m=0}^{\infty} |a_{ij}^{(m)}(t)|$ converges for every value of t. From Section 5.1 recall that a power series may be differentiated term by term; hence

$$\frac{d}{dt}(e^{At}) = \frac{d}{dt} \sum_{m=0}^{\infty} \frac{A^m t^m}{m!} = \sum_{m=1}^{\infty} \frac{A^m t^{m-1}}{(m-1)!} = Ae^{At}.$$

This shows, since $e^{A0} = e^0 = I$, that e^{At} is the principal matrix solution of the matrix equation $\mathbf{x}' = A\mathbf{x}$. ∎

The problem of calculating the principal matrix solution, therefore, reduces to the calculation of the matrix e^{At}. In general, this is a very tedious calculation. However, when A is a diagonal matrix, then e^{At} is easily calculated as in Example 1:

If

$$A = \begin{pmatrix} \lambda_1 & 0 & \cdots & 0 \\ 0 & \lambda_2 & \cdots & 0 \\ \cdot & \cdot & & \cdot \\ \cdot & \cdot & & \cdot \\ \cdot & \cdot & & \cdot \\ 0 & 0 & \cdots & \lambda_n \end{pmatrix},$$

then

$$e^{At} = \begin{pmatrix} e^{\lambda_1 t} & 0 & \cdots & 0 \\ 0 & e^{\lambda_2 t} & \cdots & 0 \\ \cdot & \cdot & & \cdot \\ \cdot & \cdot & & \cdot \\ \cdot & \cdot & & \cdot \\ 0 & 0 & \cdots & e^{\lambda_n t} \end{pmatrix}. \tag{13}$$

The "brute-force" method of calculating e^{At}, given by the infinite series in Eq. (9), is useful only for particularly simple matrices A. We now give a procedure, using the Cayley–Hamilton theorem (Theorem 2 in

Section 8.4), that can be used to calculate e^{At} for any square matrix A. Although the procedure may appear to be complicated, it is very easy to use.

Before explaining the procedure, we will define the notation we plan to use. Let $p(\lambda) = \det(A - \lambda I)$ be the characteristic polynomial of the $n \times n$ matrix A, and suppose that

$$p(\lambda) = (\lambda - \lambda_1)^{r_1} \cdot (\lambda - \lambda_2)^{r_2}, \cdots, (\lambda - \lambda_k)^{r_k}, \qquad \textbf{(14)}$$

where $\lambda_1, \lambda_2, \ldots, \lambda_k$ are the eigenvalues of A of multiplicities $r_1, r_2, \ldots, r_k$, respectively. Using partial fractions, we can write

$$\frac{1}{p(\lambda)} = \frac{a_1(\lambda)}{(\lambda - \lambda_1)^{r_1}} + \frac{a_2(\lambda)}{(\lambda - \lambda_2)^{r_2}} + \cdots + \frac{a_k(\lambda)}{(\lambda - \lambda_k)^{r_k}}, \qquad \textbf{(15)}$$

where for each polynomial $a_i(\lambda)$

$$\deg a_i(\lambda) \le r_i - 1. \qquad \textbf{(16)}$$

Multiplying both sides of Eq. (15) by $p(\lambda)$, we get

$$\boxed{1 = a_1(\lambda)q_1(\lambda) + a_2(\lambda)q_2(\lambda) + \cdots + a_k(\lambda)q_k(\lambda),} \qquad \textbf{(17)}$$

where $q_i(\lambda)$ is the polynomial consisting of all but the $(\lambda - \lambda_i)^{r_i}$ term of $p(\lambda)$:

$$\boxed{p(\lambda) = q_i(\lambda)(\lambda - \lambda_i)^{r_i}.} \qquad \textbf{(18)}$$

We are now ready to begin the procedure for calculating e^{At} for any $n \times n$ matrix A. We shall illustrate each step in the procedure by applying it to the matrix

$$A = \begin{pmatrix} 1 & 2 & 3 \\ 0 & 0 & 4 \\ 0 & 0 & 0 \end{pmatrix}.$$

STEP 1   *Find the characteristic polynomial $p(\lambda)$ and use it to determine the polynomials $a_i(\lambda)$ and $q_i(\lambda)$ in Eqs. (17) and (18).*

In this case we have

$$p(\lambda) = \det(A - \lambda I) = \det\begin{pmatrix} 1 - \lambda & 2 & 3 \\ 0 & -\lambda & 4 \\ 0 & 0 & -\lambda \end{pmatrix} = -\lambda^2(\lambda - 1),$$

so that $\lambda_1 = 0$ and $\lambda_1 = 1$ with $r_1 = 2$ and $r_2 = 1$, respectively. By Eq. (18)

we easily obtain

$$q_1(\lambda) = 1 - \lambda \quad \text{and} \quad q_2(\lambda) = -\lambda^2. \tag{19}$$

Using Eq. (16) we note that $\deg a_1(\lambda) \leq 1$ and $\deg a_2(\lambda) \leq 0$, so that the general forms of the polynomials a_1 and a_2 are

$$a_1(\lambda) = a\lambda + b \quad \text{and} \quad a_2(\lambda) = c.$$

Substituting these polynomials into Eq. (17) and equating like powers of λ, we obtain

$$a_1(\lambda) = \lambda + 1 \quad \text{and} \quad a_2(\lambda) = -1. \tag{20}$$

At this point we need to develop some additional facts. Recall the Cayley–Hamilton theorem. Since A satisfies its characteristic equation, Eq. (18) becomes

$$0 = p(A) = q_i(A)(A - \lambda_i I)^{r_i}. \tag{21}$$

Equation (17) is also satisfied by the matrix A, since it was derived from the characteristic equation. Thus,

$$I = a_1(A)q_1(A) + a_2(A)q_2(A) + \cdots + a_k(A)q_k(A). \tag{22}$$

We can easily check Eq. (22) for our particular example:

$$I = (A + I)(I - A) + IA^2.$$

Using Eq. (13), we observe that $e^{\lambda_i tI} = e^{\lambda_i t}I$ so that by Eq. (9), we have

$$e^{At} = e^{\lambda_i tI}e^{(A - \lambda_i I)t} = e^{\lambda_i t}\sum_{j=0}^{\infty}\frac{(A - \lambda_i I)^j t^j}{j!}. \tag{23}$$

Multiplying both ends of Eq. (23) on the left by $q_i(A)$, we obtain

$$q_i(A)e^{At} = e^{\lambda_i t}\sum_{j=0}^{\infty}\frac{q_i(A)(A - \lambda_i I)^j t^j}{j!}. \tag{24}$$

By Eq. (21), all the terms in the series for $j \geq r_i$ are equal to the zero matrix so Eq. (24) reduces to

$$q_i(A)e^{At} = e^{\lambda_i t}\sum_{j=0}^{r_i-1}\frac{q_i(A)(A - \lambda_i I)^j t^j}{j!}. \tag{25}$$

Multiplying each side of Eq. (25) on the left by $a_i(A)$ yields

$$a_i(A)q_i(A)e^{At} = e^{\lambda_i t}\sum_{j=0}^{r_i-1}\frac{a_i(A)q_i(A)(A - \lambda_i I)^j t^j}{j!}. \tag{26}$$

Finally, summing Eq. (26) over all the indices i and using Eq. (22), we conclude that

$$e^{At} = Ie^{At} = \sum_{i=1}^{k} a_i(A)q_i(A)e^{At}$$

or

$$e^{At} = \sum_{i=1}^{k} \left\{ e^{\lambda_i t} a_i(A) q_i(A) \sum_{j=0}^{r_i-1} \frac{(A - \lambda_i I)^j t^j}{j!} \right\}.$$

Although this equation looks formidable, we shall see that for most applications it is very easy to use. Thus, the final step in computing e^{At} is:

STEP 2   *Using the polynomials $a_i(\lambda)$, $q_i(\lambda)$, and the eigenvalues λ_i with multiplicities r_i that were obtained in Step 1, compute:*

$$e^{At} = \sum_{i=1}^{k} \left\{ e^{\lambda_i t} a_i(A) q_i(A) \sum_{j=0}^{r_i-1} \frac{(A - \lambda_i I)^j t^j}{j!} \right\}. \tag{27}$$

For the particular matrix A we are considering, we have

$$\lambda_1 = 0, \quad r_1 = 2, \quad \lambda_2 = 1, \quad r_2 = 1,$$

and

$$q_1(A) = I - A, \quad q_2(A) = -A^2, \quad a_1(A) = A + I, \quad a_2(A) = -I.$$

Substituting these values in Eq. (27), we get

$$e^{At} = \left\{ e^{0t}(A + I)(I - A) \sum_{j=0}^{1} \frac{A^j t^j}{j!} \right\} + \left\{ e^{t} I A^2 \sum_{j=0}^{0} \frac{(A - I)^j t^j}{j!} \right\}$$

$$= (A + I)(I - A)(I + At) + e^{t} A^2$$

$$= (I - A^2)(I + At) + e^{t} A^2.$$

Since

$$A^2 = \begin{pmatrix} 1 & 2 & 3 \\ 0 & 0 & 4 \\ 0 & 0 & 0 \end{pmatrix} \begin{pmatrix} 1 & 2 & 3 \\ 0 & 0 & 4 \\ 0 & 0 & 0 \end{pmatrix} = \begin{pmatrix} 1 & 2 & 11 \\ 0 & 0 & 0 \\ 0 & 0 & 0 \end{pmatrix},$$

we have

$$e^{At} = \begin{pmatrix} 0 & -2 & -11 \\ 0 & 1 & 0 \\ 0 & 0 & 1 \end{pmatrix} \begin{pmatrix} 1+t & 2t & 3t \\ 0 & 1 & 4t \\ 0 & 0 & 1 \end{pmatrix} + e^{t} \begin{pmatrix} 1 & 2 & 11 \\ 0 & 0 & 0 \\ 0 & 0 & 0 \end{pmatrix}$$

$$= \begin{pmatrix} 0 & -2 & -8t - 11 \\ 0 & 1 & 4t \\ 0 & 0 & 1 \end{pmatrix} + \begin{pmatrix} e^{t} & 2e^{t} & 11e^{t} \\ 0 & 0 & 0 \\ 0 & 0 & 0 \end{pmatrix}$$

$$= \begin{pmatrix} e^{t} & 2(e^{t} - 1) & 11e^{t} - 8t - 11 \\ 0 & 1 & 4t \\ 0 & 0 & 1 \end{pmatrix}.$$

Summarizing, we find that the procedure reduces to two steps:

---

1. Find the characteristic polynomial for the matrix A

$$p(\lambda) = \det(A - \lambda I)$$
$$= (\lambda - \lambda_1)^{r_1}(\lambda - \lambda_2)^{r_2} \cdots (\lambda - \lambda_k)^{r_k},$$

and use it first to determine the polynomials

$$q_i(\lambda) = \frac{p(\lambda)}{(\lambda - \lambda_i)^{r_i}},$$

and then the polynomials $a_i(\lambda)$ that satisfy

$$a_1(\lambda)q_1(\lambda) + a_2(\lambda)q_2(\lambda) + \cdots + a_k(\lambda)q_k(\lambda) = 1.$$

2. Replace each λ^m by A^m in the expressions for $a_i(\lambda)$ and $q_i(\lambda)$ and compute

$$e^{At} = \sum_{i=1}^{k} \left\{ e^{\lambda_i t} a_i(A) q_i(A) \sum_{j=0}^{r_i - 1} \frac{(A - \lambda_i I)^j t^j}{j!} \right\}.$$

We illustrate the procedure with several examples.

Example 2   Find the principal matrix solution of the system

$$\begin{pmatrix} x_1 \\ x_2 \end{pmatrix}' = \begin{pmatrix} 4 & 2 \\ 3 & 3 \end{pmatrix}\begin{pmatrix} x_1 \\ x_2 \end{pmatrix}.$$

By Example 3 in Section 8.3, we know that the characteristic polynomial is

$$p(\lambda) = (\lambda - 1)(\lambda - 6) = 0.$$

Thus $\lambda_1 = 1$, $r_1 = 1$, $\lambda_2 = 6$, $r_2 = 1$, $q_1(\lambda) = \lambda - 6$, $q_2(\lambda) = \lambda - 1$, and $\deg a_1(\lambda) = \deg a_2(\lambda) \leq 0$, implying that a_1 and a_2 are constants:

$$1 = a_1(\lambda - 6) + a_2(\lambda - 1) = (a_1 + a_2)\lambda - (6a_1 + a_2).$$

Solving the system
$$a_1 + a_2 = 0,$$
$$-6a_1 - a_2 = 1,$$

we get $a_1 = -\frac{1}{5}$ and $a_2 = \frac{1}{5}$. Hence, the principal matrix solution is

$$\Psi(t) = e^{At} = \left\{ e^t\left(-\frac{1}{5}\right)I(A - 6I)\right\} + \left\{e^{6t}\left(\frac{1}{5}\right)I(A - I)\right\}$$

$$= \frac{-e^t}{5}(A - 6I) + \frac{e^{6t}}{5}(A - I) = \frac{-e^t}{5}\begin{pmatrix} -2 & 2 \\ 3 & -3 \end{pmatrix} + \frac{e^{6t}}{5}\begin{pmatrix} 3 & 2 \\ 3 & 2 \end{pmatrix}$$

$$= \frac{1}{5}\begin{pmatrix} 3e^{6t} + 2e^t & 2e^{6t} - 2e^t \\ 3e^{6t} - 3e^t & 2e^{6t} + 3e^t \end{pmatrix}.$$

Note that this differs from the fundamental matrix solution we derived in Example 9 in Section 8.3. To obtain that solution, we need only multiply $\Psi(t)$ by $\Phi(0)$:

$$\Phi(t) = \Psi(t)\Phi(0) = \frac{1}{5}\begin{pmatrix} 3e^{6t} + 2e^t & 2e^{6t} - 2e^t \\ 3e^{6t} - 3e^t & 2e^{6t} + 3e^t \end{pmatrix}\begin{pmatrix} 2 & 1 \\ -3 & 1 \end{pmatrix}$$

$$= \begin{pmatrix} 2e^t & e^{6t} \\ -3e^t & e^{6t} \end{pmatrix}.$$

Example 3 Find the principal matrix solution for

$$\mathbf{x}' = \begin{pmatrix} 4 & 1 \\ 0 & 4 \end{pmatrix}\mathbf{x}.$$

This is the matrix of Example 8 in Section 8.3 with characteristic polynomial $p(\lambda) = (\lambda - 4)^2$ and eigenspace spanned by the single vector $\binom{1}{0}$. Theorem 4 of Section 8.3 does not apply to this situation. However, the method used in this section will yield a quick result. There is only one eigenvalue $\lambda_1 = 4$ with $r_1 = 2$, so $q_1(\lambda) = 1 = a_1(\lambda)$. Thus

$$\Psi(t) = e^{At} = e^{4t}I \cdot I \sum_{j=0}^{1} \frac{(A - 4I)^j t^j}{j!}$$

$$= e^{4t}[I + (A - 4I)t] = e^{4t}\left[\begin{pmatrix} 1 & 0 \\ 0 & 1 \end{pmatrix} + \begin{pmatrix} 0 & 1 \\ 0 & 0 \end{pmatrix}t\right]$$

$$= \begin{pmatrix} e^{4t} & te^{4t} \\ 0 & e^{4t} \end{pmatrix}.$$

Example 4 Find the principal matrix solution of

$$\mathbf{x}' = \begin{pmatrix} 3 & -5 \\ 1 & -1 \end{pmatrix}\mathbf{x}.$$

In Example 6 of Section 8.3 we found the characteristic polynomial $p(\lambda) = \lambda^2 - 2\lambda + 2$ with eigenvalues $\lambda_1 = 1 + i$ and $\lambda_2 = 1 - i$ of algebraic multiplicity $r_1 = r_2 = 1$. Thus $p(\lambda) = (\lambda - 1 - i)(\lambda - 1 + i)$, $q_1(\lambda) = \lambda - 1 + i$, $q_2(\lambda) = \lambda - 1 - i$, and a_1 and a_2 are both constants satisfying

$$1 = a_1(\lambda - 1 + i) + a_2(\lambda - 1 - i).$$

Solving, we get $a_1 = 1/2i$, $a_2 = -1/2i$, and

$$\Psi(t) = e^{At} = \left\{e^{(1+i)t}\left(\frac{1}{2i}\right)(A - (1 - i)I)\right\} + \left\{e^{(1-i)t}\left(\frac{-1}{2i}\right)(A - (1 + i)I)\right\}$$

$$= e^t\begin{pmatrix} 2\left(\dfrac{e^{it} - e^{-it}}{2i}\right) + \left(\dfrac{e^{it} + e^{-it}}{2}\right) & -5\left(\dfrac{e^{it} - e^{-it}}{2i}\right) \\ \dfrac{e^{it} - e^{-it}}{2i} & -2\left(\dfrac{e^{it} - e^{-it}}{2i}\right) + \left(\dfrac{e^{it} + e^{-it}}{2}\right) \end{pmatrix}$$

$$= e^t\begin{pmatrix} 2\sin t + \cos t & -5\sin t \\ \sin t & -2\sin t + \cos t \end{pmatrix}.$$

Note that this is the solution we obtained with considerably more difficulty in **Example 11** in Section 8.3 [see Eq. (22) there].

Example 5   Find the principal matrix solution to the system

$$\mathbf{x}' = \begin{pmatrix} 3 & 2 & 4 \\ 2 & 0 & 2 \\ 4 & 2 & 3 \end{pmatrix} \mathbf{x}.$$

The characteristic polynomial

$$p(\lambda) = -\lambda^3 + 6\lambda^2 + 15\lambda + 8 = (\lambda + 1)^2(8 - \lambda) = 0$$

has eigenvalues $\lambda_1 = -1$ and $\lambda_2 = 8$ with multiplicities $r_1 = 2$ and $r_2 = 1$, respectively. Thus $q_1(\lambda) = 8 - \lambda$, $q_2(\lambda) = (\lambda + 1)^2$, deg $a_1(\lambda) \le 1$, and deg $a_2(\lambda) \le 0$. Setting $a_1(\lambda) = a\lambda + b$ and $a_2(\lambda) = c$, we have

$$1 = (a\lambda + b)(8 - \lambda) + c(\lambda + 1)^2,$$

which has the solution $a = c = \frac{1}{81}$ and $b = \frac{10}{81}$. Thus

$$\Psi(t) = e^{At} = \left\{ e^{-t}\left(\frac{1}{81}\right)(A + 10I)(8I - A) \sum_{j=0}^{1} \frac{(A + I)^j t^j}{j!} \right\} + \left\{ \frac{e^{8t}}{81}(A + I)^2 I \right\}$$

$$= \frac{e^{-t}}{81}(80I - 2A - A^2)(I + (A + I)t) + \frac{e^{8t}}{81}(A^2 + 2A + I)$$

$$= \frac{e^{-t}}{81}\begin{pmatrix} 45 & -18 & -36 \\ -18 & 72 & -18 \\ -36 & -18 & 45 \end{pmatrix}\begin{pmatrix} 1 + 4t & 2t & 4t \\ 2t & 1 + t & 2t \\ 4t & 2t & 1 + 4t \end{pmatrix}$$

$$+ \frac{e^{8t}}{81}\begin{pmatrix} 36 & 18 & 36 \\ 18 & 9 & 18 \\ 36 & 18 & 36 \end{pmatrix}$$

$$= \frac{1}{9}\begin{pmatrix} 4e^{8t} + 5e^{-t} & 2(e^{8t} - e^{-t}) & 4(e^{8t} - e^{-t}) \\ 2(e^{8t} - e^{-t}) & e^{8t} + 8e^{-t} & 2(e^{8t} - e^{-t}) \\ 4(e^{8t} - e^{-t}) & 2(e^{8t} - e^{-t}) & 4e^{8t} + 5e^{-t} \end{pmatrix}.$$

Example 6   Solve the initial value problem

$$\mathbf{x}' = \begin{pmatrix} 2 & -1 \\ -4 & 2 \end{pmatrix}\mathbf{x}, \quad \mathbf{x}(0) = \begin{pmatrix} 0 \\ 4 \end{pmatrix}.$$

The characteristic polynomial $p(\lambda) = \lambda(\lambda - 4)$ has the eigenvalues $\lambda_1 = 0$ and $\lambda_2 = 4$, both with algebraic multiplicity $r_1 = r_2 = 1$. The polynomials $q_1(\lambda) = \lambda - 4$, $q_2(\lambda) = \lambda$, and deg $a_1 = $ deg $a_2 \le 0$ imply that a_1 and a_2 are constants satisfying

$$1 = a_1 \cdot (\lambda - 4) + a_2\lambda,$$

so that $a_1 = -a_2 = -\frac{1}{4}$. Hence, the principal matrix solution is

$$\Psi(t) = e^{At} = \left\{ -\frac{1}{4}(A - 4I) \right\} + \left\{ \frac{e^{4t}}{4} A \right\} = I + \left(\frac{e^{4t} - 1}{4} \right) A$$

$$= \begin{pmatrix} \dfrac{1 + e^{4t}}{2} & \dfrac{1 - e^{4t}}{4} \\ 1 - e^{4t} & \dfrac{1 + e^{4t}}{2} \end{pmatrix}.$$

To solve the initial value problem we simply multiply the principal matrix solution by $\mathbf{x}(0)$, which yields the solution

$$\mathbf{x}(t) = \begin{pmatrix} 1 - e^{4t} \\ 2 + 2e^{4t} \end{pmatrix}.$$

EXERCISES 8.5

Use the methods of this section to calculate the principal matrix solution of the system $\mathbf{x}' = A\mathbf{x}$, where A is the given constant matrix. If initial conditions are given, find the solution of the initial value problem.

1. $\begin{pmatrix} -2 & -2 \\ -5 & 1 \end{pmatrix}$

2. $\begin{pmatrix} -12 & 7 \\ -7 & 2 \end{pmatrix}$

3. $\begin{pmatrix} 2 & -1 \\ 5 & -2 \end{pmatrix}$

4. $\begin{pmatrix} 3 & 2 \\ -5 & 1 \end{pmatrix}$

5. $\begin{pmatrix} 3 & -2 \\ 8 & -5 \end{pmatrix}$

6. $\begin{pmatrix} 1 & 1 \\ 1 & -1 \end{pmatrix}$

7. $\begin{pmatrix} 3 & -2 \\ 8 & -5 \end{pmatrix}, \quad \mathbf{x}(0) = \begin{pmatrix} \frac{3}{4} \\ 1 \end{pmatrix}$

8. $\begin{pmatrix} 3 & -2 \\ 8 & -5 \end{pmatrix}, \quad \mathbf{x}(0) = \begin{pmatrix} 1 \\ 2 \end{pmatrix}$

9. $\begin{pmatrix} 3 & -2 \\ 8 & -5 \end{pmatrix}, \quad \mathbf{x}(0) = \begin{pmatrix} 2 \\ 5 \end{pmatrix}$

10. $\begin{pmatrix} 4 & 1 \\ -8 & 8 \end{pmatrix}, \quad \mathbf{x}(0) = \begin{pmatrix} 1 \\ 0 \end{pmatrix}$

11. $\begin{pmatrix} 1 & -1 & 0 \\ -1 & 2 & -1 \\ 0 & -1 & 1 \end{pmatrix}$

12. $\begin{pmatrix} 1 & 1 & -2 \\ -1 & 2 & 1 \\ 0 & 1 & -1 \end{pmatrix}$

13. $\begin{pmatrix} 4 & 6 & 6 \\ 1 & 3 & 2 \\ -1 & -5 & -2 \end{pmatrix}$

14. $\begin{pmatrix} 7 & -2 & -4 \\ 3 & 0 & -2 \\ 6 & -2 & -3 \end{pmatrix}$

15. $\begin{pmatrix} 5 & 4 & 2 \\ 4 & 5 & 2 \\ 2 & 2 & 2 \end{pmatrix}$

16. $\begin{pmatrix} -3 & 0 & 2 \\ 1 & -1 & 0 \\ -2 & -1 & 0 \end{pmatrix}$

17. $\begin{pmatrix} 4 & 1 & 0 & 1 \\ 2 & 3 & 0 & 1 \\ -2 & 1 & 2 & -3 \\ 2 & -1 & 0 & 5 \end{pmatrix}$

18. $\begin{pmatrix} 0 & -1 & -2 \\ 1 & 0 & 1 \\ 2 & -1 & 0 \end{pmatrix}$

19. $\begin{pmatrix} 1 & -1 & 0 \\ -1 & 2 & -1 \\ 0 & -1 & 1 \end{pmatrix}$, $\mathbf{x}(0) = \begin{pmatrix} 1 \\ 0 \\ 1 \end{pmatrix}$

20. $\begin{pmatrix} 5 & 4 & 2 \\ 4 & 5 & 2 \\ 2 & 2 & 2 \end{pmatrix}$, $\mathbf{x}(0) = \begin{pmatrix} 1 \\ 2 \\ 3 \end{pmatrix}$

21. $\begin{pmatrix} 4 & 6 & 6 \\ 1 & 3 & 2 \\ -1 & -5 & -2 \end{pmatrix}$, $\mathbf{x}(0) = \begin{pmatrix} -1 \\ 0 \\ 2 \end{pmatrix}$

22. $\begin{pmatrix} 4 & 1 & 0 & 1 \\ 2 & 3 & 0 & 1 \\ -2 & 1 & 2 & -3 \\ 2 & -1 & 0 & 5 \end{pmatrix}$, $\mathbf{x}(0) = \begin{pmatrix} 4 \\ 5 \\ 6 \\ 2 \end{pmatrix}$

*23. Let A and B be two $n \times n$ matrices. Show that $\|AB\| \leq \|A\| \|B\|$ where $\|A\|$ is given by Eq. (10). [*Hint:* Write the components of AB and repeatedly use the triangle inequality.]

8.6 NONHOMOGENEOUS SYSTEMS

We shall now present a method for solving the nonhomogeneous system

$$\mathbf{x}' = A(t)\mathbf{x} + \mathbf{f}(t), \tag{1}$$

given that a fundamental matrix solution $\Phi(t)$ for the homogeneous system

$$\mathbf{x}' = A(t)\mathbf{x} \tag{2}$$

is known. Such a solution can always be found if $A(t)$ is a constant matrix (by the methods of Section 8.5).

Theorem 1   Let $\boldsymbol{\varphi}_p(t)$ and $\boldsymbol{\varphi}_q(t)$ be two solutions of the system (1). Then their difference,

$$\boldsymbol{\varphi}(t) = \boldsymbol{\varphi}_p(t) - \boldsymbol{\varphi}_q(t),$$

is a solution of Eq. (2).

Proof $\boldsymbol{\varphi}' = (\boldsymbol{\varphi}_p - \boldsymbol{\varphi}_q)' = (A\boldsymbol{\varphi}_p + \mathbf{f}) - (A\boldsymbol{\varphi}_q + \mathbf{f}) = A(\boldsymbol{\varphi}_p - \boldsymbol{\varphi}_q) = A\boldsymbol{\varphi}$. Thus, as in the case of linear scalar equations (Chapter 3), it is necessary only to find one particular solution of Eq. (1). ∎

If $\boldsymbol{\varphi}_p(t)$ is such a solution, then *the general solution to the nonhomogeneous system* (1) *is of the form*

$$\boxed{\boldsymbol{\varphi}(t) = \Phi(t)\mathbf{c} + \boldsymbol{\varphi}_p(t),} \tag{3}$$

where $\mathbf{c}$ *is a vector of arbitrary constants and* $\Phi(t)$ *is a fundamental matrix solution of the homogeneous equation* (2). That Eq. (3) is a solution can be verified as follows:

$$\boldsymbol{\varphi}'(t) = \Phi'(t)\mathbf{c} + \boldsymbol{\varphi}_p'(t)$$
$$= [A(t)\Phi(t)\mathbf{c}] + [A(t)\boldsymbol{\varphi}_p(t) + \mathbf{f}(t)],$$

since Φ is a solution of the associated matrix equation and $\boldsymbol{\varphi}_p$ is a particular solution of Eq. (2). Combining terms, we have

$$\varphi'(t) = A(t)[\Phi(t)\mathbf{c} + \varphi_p(t)] + \mathbf{f}(t) = A(t)\varphi(t) + \mathbf{f}(t),$$

and φ is a solution of Eq. (2).

We now derive a *variation-of-constants* formula for the nonhomogeneous system

$$\mathbf{x}' = A(t)\mathbf{x} + f(t). \tag{4}$$

All variation-of-constants formulas begin by assuming that a solution to the homogeneous equation $\mathbf{x}' = A(t)\mathbf{x}$ is known. Assuming that Φ is a fundamental matrix solution of the homogeneous equation, we seek a particular solution to Eq. (4) of the form

$$\varphi_p(t) = \Phi(t)\mathbf{c}(t), \tag{5}$$

where $\mathbf{c}(t)$ is a vector function in t. Differentiating both sides of Eq. (5) with respect to t, we have

$$\varphi_p' = \Phi'\mathbf{c} + \Phi\mathbf{c}' = A\Phi\mathbf{c} + \Phi\mathbf{c}' = A\varphi_p + \Phi\mathbf{c}'.$$

Since φ_p is a particular solution of Eq. (4), it follows that $\Phi\mathbf{c}' = \mathbf{f}$. But every fundamental matrix solution has an inverse, so that we can integrate $\mathbf{c}' = \Phi^{-1}\mathbf{f}$, obtaining

$$\varphi_p(t) = \Phi(t)\mathbf{c}(t) = \Phi(t)\int \Phi^{-1}(t)\mathbf{f}(t)\,dt. \tag{6}$$

This is the *variation-of-constants* formula for a particular solution to the nonhomogeneous system (4). Thus, the general solution to the system (4) has the form

$$\boxed{\varphi(t) = \Phi(t)\mathbf{c} + \Phi(t)\int \Phi^{-1}(t)\mathbf{f}(t)\,dt,} \tag{7}$$

where $\mathbf{c}$ is an arbitrary *constant* vector.

For the initial value problem

$$\mathbf{x}' = A(t)\mathbf{x} + \mathbf{f}(t), \quad \mathbf{x}(t_0) = \mathbf{x}_0, \tag{8}$$

it is convenient to choose a particular solution $\varphi_p(t)$ that vanishes at t_0. This can be done by selecting the limits of integration in Eq. (6) to be from t_0 to t, so that

$$\varphi(t) = \Phi(t)\mathbf{c} + \Phi(t)\int_{t_0}^{t} \Phi^{-1}(s)\mathbf{f}(s)\,ds.$$

Substituting $t = t_0$ in this equation, we obtain

$$\mathbf{x}_0 = \varphi(t_0) = \Phi(t_0)\mathbf{c},$$

which implies that $\mathbf{c} = \Phi^{-1}(t_0)\mathbf{x}_0$. Hence, the solution of the initial value problem (8) is

$$
\boxed{
\begin{aligned}
\boldsymbol{\varphi}(t) &= \Phi(t)\Phi^{-1}(t_0)\mathbf{x}_0 + \Phi(t)\int_{t_0}^{t}\Phi^{-1}(s)\mathbf{f}(s)\,ds \\
&= \boldsymbol{\varphi}_{\mathrm{h}}(t) + \boldsymbol{\varphi}_{\mathrm{p}}(t),
\end{aligned}
}
\tag{9}
$$

where $\boldsymbol{\varphi}_{\mathrm{h}}$ and $\boldsymbol{\varphi}_{\mathrm{p}}$ are the homogeneous and particular solutions, respectively. Note that if $\Psi(t)$ is the principal matrix solution of $\mathbf{x}' = A\mathbf{x}$, then $\Psi(t_0) = \Psi^{-1}(t_0) = I$. Thus, Eq. (9) takes the simpler form

$$
\boxed{
\boldsymbol{\varphi}(t) = \Psi(t)\mathbf{x}_0 + \Psi(t)\int_{t_0}^{t}\Psi^{-1}(s)\mathbf{f}(s)\,ds,
}
\tag{10}
$$

when the principal matrix solution $\Psi(t)$ of $\mathbf{x}' = A(t)\mathbf{x}$ is used. We summarize these results in the theorem below.

Theorem 2   Let $\Phi(t)$ be a fundamental matrix solution of the homogeneous system

$$
\mathbf{x}' = A(t)\mathbf{x}.
\tag{11}
$$

Then the solution to the initial value problem

$$
\mathbf{x}' = A(t)\mathbf{x} + \mathbf{f}(t), \quad \mathbf{x}(t_0) = \mathbf{x}_0,
\tag{12}
$$

is given by

$$
\boldsymbol{\varphi}(t) = \Phi(t)\Phi^{-1}(t_0)\mathbf{x}_0 + \boldsymbol{\varphi}_{\mathrm{p}}(t),
$$

where

$$
\boldsymbol{\varphi}_{\mathrm{p}}(t) = \Phi(t)\int_{t_0}^{t}\Phi^{-1}(s)\mathbf{f}(s)\,ds
\tag{13}
$$

is a particular solution of the nonhomogeneous system

$$
\mathbf{x}' = A(t)\mathbf{x} + \mathbf{f}(t).
$$

If $\Psi(t)$ is the principal matrix solution of the homogeneous system (11), then the solution of the initial value problem (12) is

$$
\boldsymbol{\varphi}(t) = \Psi(t)\mathbf{x}_0 + \Psi(t)\int_{t_0}^{t}\Psi^{-1}(s)\mathbf{f}(s)\,ds.
\tag{14}
$$

As we have already seen, the situation is simplest when $A(t)$ is a constant matrix. To deal with this case most effectively, we need the following theorem.

Theorem 3   Let

$$\Phi(t) = e^{At}.$$

Then

$$\boxed{\Phi^{-1}(t) = e^{-At}.}$$ **(15)**

Proof   From Eq. (9) in Section 8.5, we have

$$e^{-At} = I - At + \frac{(At)^2}{2!} - \frac{(At)^3}{3!} + \cdots = \sum_{k=0} \frac{(-At)^k}{k!}.$$

Thus,

$$e^{At}e^{-At} = \left(I + At + \frac{(At)^2}{2!} + \frac{(At)^3}{3!} + \cdots\right)\left(I - At + \frac{(At)^2}{2!} - \frac{(At)^3}{3!} + \cdots\right).$$

The first term in this product is I. What are the other terms? The term involving At is $(At)I + I(-At) = 0$. The term involving $(At)^2$ is

$$\frac{(At)^2}{2!}I + \frac{(At)^2}{2!}I - (At)(At) = 0.$$

In general, the term involving $(At)^n$ is

$$\sum_{k=0}^{n} \frac{(At)^k}{k!}\frac{(-At)^{n-k}}{(n-k)!} = (At)^n \sum_{k=0}^{n} \frac{(-1)^{n-k}}{k!(n-k)!}.$$

Now, the binomial theorem states that

$$(x + y)^n = \sum_{k=0}^{n} \frac{n!}{k!(n-k)!} x^k y^{n-k}.$$

Thus,

$$0 = (1 + (-1))^n = \sum_{k=0}^{n} \frac{n!}{k!(n-k)!} 1^k (-1)^{n-k} = n! \sum_{k=0}^{n} \frac{(-1)^{n-k}}{k!(n-k)!},$$

and

$$\sum_{k=0}^{n} \frac{(-1)^{n-k}}{k!(n-k)!} = 0,$$

which shows that $e^{At}e^{-At} = I$. A similar expansion shows that $e^{-At}e^{At} = I$. Thus,

$$e^{-At} = (e^{At})^{-1}. \quad \blacksquare$$

From Theorem 3, we see that $e^{At}(e^{As})^{-1} = e^{At}e^{-As} = e^{A(t-s)}$ so that, together with Theorem 2, we have:

Corollary 4   The unique solution to the nonhomogeneous system with constant matrix A

$$\mathbf{x}' = A\mathbf{x} + \mathbf{f}(t), \quad \mathbf{x}(t_0) = \mathbf{x}_0, \tag{16}$$

is given by

$$\boxed{\boldsymbol{\varphi}(t) = e^{At}\mathbf{x}_0 + \int_{t_0}^{t} e^{A(t-s)}\mathbf{f}(s)\,ds.} \tag{17}$$

Example 1   Find the unique solution to the system

$$\mathbf{x}' = \begin{pmatrix} x_1 \\ x_2 \end{pmatrix}' = \begin{pmatrix} 4 & 2 \\ 3 & 3 \end{pmatrix}\begin{pmatrix} x_1 \\ x_2 \end{pmatrix} + \begin{pmatrix} e^t \\ e^{2t} \end{pmatrix} = A\mathbf{x} + \mathbf{f}(t), \quad \mathbf{x}(0) = \begin{pmatrix} 1 \\ 2 \end{pmatrix}.$$

A fundamental matrix solution for the homogeneous system is (see **Example 9 in Section 8.3**)

$$\Phi(t) = \begin{pmatrix} 2e^t & e^{6t} \\ -3e^t & e^{6t} \end{pmatrix}.$$

Then

$$\Phi^{-1}(t) = \frac{1}{5}\begin{pmatrix} e^{-t} & -e^{-t} \\ 3e^{-6t} & 2e^{-6t} \end{pmatrix},$$

and by Eq. (12), we have the particular solution

$$\boldsymbol{\varphi}_p = \frac{1}{5}\begin{pmatrix} 2e^t & e^{6t} \\ -3e^t & e^{6t} \end{pmatrix}\int_0^t \begin{pmatrix} e^{-s} & -e^{-s} \\ 3e^{-6s} & 2e^{-6s} \end{pmatrix}\begin{pmatrix} e^s \\ e^{2s} \end{pmatrix}ds$$

$$= \frac{1}{5}\begin{pmatrix} 2e^t & e^{6t} \\ -3e^t & e^{6t} \end{pmatrix}\int_0^t \begin{pmatrix} 1 - e^s \\ 3e^{-5s} + 2e^{-4s} \end{pmatrix}ds.$$

Since the integral of a vector function is the vector of integrals,

$$\boldsymbol{\varphi}_p(t) = \frac{1}{5}\begin{pmatrix} 2e^t & e^{6t} \\ -3e^t & e^{6t} \end{pmatrix}\begin{pmatrix} t - e^t + 1 \\ \dfrac{11}{10} - \dfrac{3}{5}e^{-5t} - \dfrac{e^{-4t}}{2} \end{pmatrix}$$

$$= \begin{pmatrix} \dfrac{2}{5}te^t - \dfrac{1}{2}e^{2t} + \dfrac{7}{25}e^t + \dfrac{11}{50}e^{6t} \\ \dfrac{-3}{5}te^t + \dfrac{1}{2}e^{2t} - \dfrac{18}{25}e^t + \dfrac{11}{50}e^{6t} \end{pmatrix}.$$

Note that $\boldsymbol{\varphi}_p(0) = \mathbf{0}$, which must be the case from the way in which we found φ_p. Next, from Eq. (9), we have that the unique solution is

$$\varphi(t) = \Phi(t)\Phi^{-1}(0)\mathbf{x}_0 + \varphi_p(t)$$

$$= \frac{1}{5}\begin{pmatrix} 2e^t & e^{6t} \\ -3e^t & e^{6t} \end{pmatrix}\begin{pmatrix} 1 & -1 \\ 3 & 2 \end{pmatrix}\begin{pmatrix} 1 \\ 2 \end{pmatrix} + \varphi_p$$

$$= \frac{1}{5}\begin{pmatrix} 2e^t & e^{6t} \\ -3e^t & e^{6t} \end{pmatrix}\begin{pmatrix} -1 \\ 7 \end{pmatrix} + \varphi_p$$

$$= \begin{pmatrix} -\dfrac{2}{5}e^t + \dfrac{7}{5}e^{6t} \\ \dfrac{3}{5}e^t + \dfrac{7}{5}e^{6t} \end{pmatrix} + \begin{pmatrix} \dfrac{2}{5}te^t - \dfrac{1}{2}e^{2t} + \dfrac{7}{25}e^t + \dfrac{11}{50}e^{6t} \\ \dfrac{-3}{5}te^t + \dfrac{1}{2}e^{2t} - \dfrac{18}{25}e^t + \dfrac{11}{50}e^{6t} \end{pmatrix}$$

$$= \begin{pmatrix} \dfrac{2}{5}te^t - \dfrac{1}{2}e^{2t} - \dfrac{3}{25}e^t + \dfrac{81}{50}e^{6t} \\ \dfrac{-3}{5}te^t + \dfrac{1}{2}e^{2t} - \dfrac{3}{25}e^t + \dfrac{81}{50}e^{6t} \end{pmatrix}.$$

Note, as a check, that $\varphi(0) = \binom{1}{2}$.

Example 2 Consider the initial value problem (see Example 2 in Section 3.7)

$$x'' + x = 2\cos t, \quad x(0) = 5, \quad x'(0) = 2.$$

Using the substitution $x_1 = x$, $x_2 = x'$, we can write this in matrix form

$$\begin{pmatrix} x_1 \\ x_2 \end{pmatrix}' = \begin{pmatrix} 0 & 1 \\ -1 & 0 \end{pmatrix}\begin{pmatrix} x_1 \\ x_2 \end{pmatrix} + \begin{pmatrix} 0 \\ 2\cos t \end{pmatrix},$$

where the homogeneous system has the principal matrix solution

$$\Psi(t) = \begin{pmatrix} \cos t & \sin t \\ -\sin t & \cos t \end{pmatrix}.$$

Then

$$\Psi^{-1}(t) = \begin{pmatrix} \cos t & -\sin t \\ \sin t & \cos t \end{pmatrix},$$

and

$$\int_0^t \Psi^{-1}(s)\mathbf{f}(s)\,ds = \int_0^t \begin{pmatrix} \cos s & -\sin s \\ \sin s & \cos s \end{pmatrix}\begin{pmatrix} 0 \\ 2\cos s \end{pmatrix} ds$$

$$= \int_0^t \begin{pmatrix} -2\sin s \cos s \\ 2\cos^2 s \end{pmatrix} ds = \begin{pmatrix} \cos^2 t - 1 \\ t + \sin t \cos t \end{pmatrix}.$$

Thus, since the solution $\varphi(t)$ satisfies the initial conditions

$$\varphi(0) = \begin{pmatrix} 5 \\ 2 \end{pmatrix},$$

we obtain from Eq. (14)

$$\varphi(t) = \begin{pmatrix} \cos t & \sin t \\ -\sin t & \cos t \end{pmatrix} \begin{pmatrix} 5 \\ 2 \end{pmatrix} + \begin{pmatrix} \cos t & \sin t \\ -\sin t & \cos t \end{pmatrix} \begin{pmatrix} \cos^2 t - 1 \\ t + \sin t \cos t \end{pmatrix}$$

$$= \begin{pmatrix} 5 \cos t + 2 \sin t + t \sin t \\ -4 \sin t + 2 \cos t + t \cos t \end{pmatrix},$$

where we have used the fact that

$$\cos^3 t + \sin^2 t \cos t = \cos t \, (\cos^2 t + \sin^2 t) = \cos t.$$

Example 3   Consider the system

$$\begin{pmatrix} x_1 \\ x_2 \\ x_3 \end{pmatrix}' = \begin{pmatrix} 0 & 1 & 0 \\ 0 & 0 & 1 \\ -2/t^3 & 2/t^3 & 1/t \end{pmatrix} \begin{pmatrix} x_1 \\ x_2 \\ x_3 \end{pmatrix} + \begin{pmatrix} 2t^2 \\ -t^3 \\ t^5 \end{pmatrix} \tag{18}$$

with initial conditions $x_1(1) = 2$, $x_2(1) = 0$, and $x_3(1) = -1$. A fundamental matrix solution (check!) is

$$\Phi(t) = \begin{pmatrix} t & 1/t & t^2 \\ 1 & -1/t^2 & 2t \\ 0 & 2/t^3 & 2 \end{pmatrix}.$$

Note that this solution is valid only for $t > 0$ since $\Phi(t)$ is not defined at $t = 0$. Then

$$\Phi^{-1}(t) = \frac{1}{6} \begin{pmatrix} 6/t & 0 & -3t \\ 2t & -2t^2 & t^3 \\ -2/t^2 & 2/t & 2 \end{pmatrix}.$$

Hence, by Eq. (9), the solution to the initial value problem (18) is

$$\varphi(t) = \Phi(t)\Phi^{-1}(1) \begin{pmatrix} 2 \\ 0 \\ -1 \end{pmatrix} + \Phi(t) \int_1^t \Phi^{-1}(s)\mathbf{f}(s) \, ds = \Phi(t)\mathbf{c} + \Phi_p(t).$$

Setting $t = 1$, we have

$$\Phi^{-1}(1) = \frac{1}{6} \begin{pmatrix} 6 & 0 & -3 \\ 2 & -2 & 1 \\ -2 & 2 & 2 \end{pmatrix}$$

so that

$$\Phi(t)\Phi^{-1}(1) \begin{pmatrix} 2 \\ 0 \\ -1 \end{pmatrix} = \frac{1}{6} \begin{pmatrix} 9t - 5/t - 2t^2 \\ 9 - 5/t^2 - 4t \\ 10/t^3 - 4 \end{pmatrix}.$$

Therefore, after a great deal of arithmetic, we have

$$\varphi(t) = \frac{1}{6}\begin{pmatrix} 9t - 5/t - 2t^2 \\ 9 - 5/t^2 - 4t \\ 10/t^3 - 4 \end{pmatrix} + \frac{1}{6}\begin{pmatrix} t & 1/t & t^2 \\ 1 & -1/t^2 & 2t \\ 0 & 2/t^3 & 2 \end{pmatrix} \int_1^t \begin{pmatrix} 12s - 3s^6 \\ 4s^3 + 2s^5 + s^8 \\ -4 - 2s^2 + 2s^5 \end{pmatrix} ds$$

$$= \begin{pmatrix} \dfrac{7}{27t} + \dfrac{33}{21}t - \dfrac{5}{18}t^2 + \dfrac{1}{2}t^3 - \dfrac{t^5}{18} + \dfrac{t^8}{378} \\[3mm] \dfrac{-7}{27t^2} + \dfrac{33}{21} - \dfrac{5}{9}t + \dfrac{3}{2}t^2 - \dfrac{5}{18}t^4 + \dfrac{4}{189}t^7 \\[3mm] \dfrac{14}{27t^3} - \dfrac{5}{9} + 3t - \dfrac{10}{9}t^3 + \dfrac{4}{27}t^6 \end{pmatrix}.$$

EXERCISES 8.6

In each of Exercises 1 through 9, calculate a fundamental matrix solution for the associated homogeneous system and then use Eq. (13) and the variation-of-constants formula (9) to obtain a particular solution to the given nonhomogeneous system. Where initial conditions are given, find the unique solution that satisfies them.

1. $\mathbf{x}' = \begin{pmatrix} -2 & -2 \\ -5 & 1 \end{pmatrix}\mathbf{x} + \begin{pmatrix} e^t \\ e^{2t} \end{pmatrix}$

2. $\mathbf{x}' = \begin{pmatrix} -12 & 7 \\ -7 & 2 \end{pmatrix}\mathbf{x} + \begin{pmatrix} t \\ 2 \end{pmatrix},\quad x_1(0) = 1,\quad x_2(0) = 0$

3. $\mathbf{x}' = \begin{pmatrix} 2 & -1 \\ 5 & -2 \end{pmatrix}\mathbf{x} + \begin{pmatrix} \sin t \\ \cos t \end{pmatrix},\quad x_1(0) = 0,\quad x_2(0) = 1$

4. $\mathbf{x}' = \begin{pmatrix} 3 & 2 \\ -5 & 1 \end{pmatrix}\mathbf{x} + \begin{pmatrix} 2\sin 3t \\ \cos 3t \end{pmatrix}$

5. $\mathbf{x}' = \begin{pmatrix} 1 & 1 & -2 \\ -1 & 2 & 1 \\ 0 & 1 & -1 \end{pmatrix}\mathbf{x} + \begin{pmatrix} e^t \\ e^{2t} \\ e^{3t} \end{pmatrix},$
$x_1(0) = 0,\quad x_2(0) = 1,\quad x_3(0) = -1$

6. $\mathbf{x}' = \begin{pmatrix} 0 & 1 & 0 \\ 0 & 0 & 1 \\ 1 & -3 & 3 \end{pmatrix}\mathbf{x} + \begin{pmatrix} t^2 \\ 0 \\ 1 \end{pmatrix}$

7. $\mathbf{x}' = \begin{pmatrix} 4 & 6 & 6 \\ 1 & 3 & 2 \\ -1 & -5 & -2 \end{pmatrix}\mathbf{x} + \begin{pmatrix} 1 - 4t - 6t^2 - 6t^4 \\ t - 3t^2 - 2t^4 \\ t + 5t^2 + 4t^3 + 2t^4 \end{pmatrix}$

8. $\mathbf{x}' = \begin{pmatrix} 1 & -1 & -1 \\ 1 & -1 & 0 \\ 1 & 0 & -1 \end{pmatrix}\mathbf{x} + \begin{pmatrix} 2 \\ e^{-t} \\ e^{-t} \end{pmatrix},$
$x_1(0) = 1,\quad x_2(0) = -1,\quad x_3(0) = 0$

9. $\mathbf{x}' = \begin{pmatrix} 2 & -5 \\ 1 & -2 \end{pmatrix}\mathbf{x} + \begin{pmatrix} 0 \\ \cot t \end{pmatrix},\quad 0 < t < \pi$

In each of Exercises 10 through 12, one homogeneous solution to a given system is given. Use the method of Exercise 19 in Section 8.2 to obtain a fundamental matrix solution. Then use this solution to find the general solution of the nonhomogeneous system.

10. $\mathbf{x}' = \begin{pmatrix} 0 & 1 \\ -1/4t^2 & 0 \end{pmatrix}\mathbf{x} + \begin{pmatrix} \sqrt{t} \\ 2 \end{pmatrix},\quad \varphi_1(t) = \begin{pmatrix} \sqrt{t} \\ 1/2\sqrt{t} \end{pmatrix}$

11. $\mathbf{x}' = \begin{pmatrix} 0 & 1 \\ -1/t^2 & -3/t \end{pmatrix}\mathbf{x} + \begin{pmatrix} t \\ e^t \end{pmatrix},\quad \varphi_1(t) = \begin{pmatrix} 1/t \\ -1/t^2 \end{pmatrix}$

12. $\mathbf{x}' = \begin{pmatrix} \dfrac{-t}{1-t^2} & \dfrac{1}{1-t^2} \\[2mm] \dfrac{1}{1-t^2} & \dfrac{-t}{1-t^2} \end{pmatrix}\mathbf{x} + \begin{pmatrix} t^2 \\ t^3 \end{pmatrix},\quad \varphi_1(t) = \begin{pmatrix} 1 \\ t \end{pmatrix},$
$-1 < t < 1,$

13. Let $\varphi_1(t)$ be a solution to $\mathbf{x}'(t) = A\mathbf{x}(t) + \mathbf{b}_1(t)$, $\varphi_2(t)$ a solution to $\mathbf{x}'(t) = A\mathbf{x}(t) + \mathbf{b}_2(t), \ldots,$ and $\varphi_n(t)$ a solution to $\mathbf{x}'(t) = A\mathbf{x}(t) + \mathbf{b}_n(t)$. Prove that $\varphi_1(t) + \varphi_2(t) + \cdots + \varphi_n(t)$ is a solution to

$$\mathbf{x}'(t) = A\mathbf{x}(t) + \mathbf{b}_1(t) + \mathbf{b}_2(t) + \cdots + \mathbf{b}_n(t).$$

This again is called the *principle of superposition*.

8.7 AN APPLICATION OF NONHOMOGENEOUS SYSTEMS: FORCED OSCILLATIONS (Optional)

Consider the nonhomogeneous system with constant coefficients

$$\mathbf{x}'(t) = A\mathbf{x}(t) + \mathbf{b}(t). \tag{1}$$

The system (1) can be considered in the following way. If A is fixed, then given an *input vector* $\mathbf{b}(t)$, we can obtain an *output vector* $\mathbf{x}(t)$. That is, with fixed A, the output of the system (the solution) is determined by the input to the system. In this context, vector $\mathbf{b}(t)$ is called the *forcing vector* of the system. With this terminology, the system (1) is called an *input-output system*.

It often occurs in practice that the forcing term is periodic in nature (for example, electrical circuits forced by an alternating current, such as in Examples 2 in Section 2.5, and 1 and 2 in Section 3.9). An important question may now be asked: If the forcing term is periodic, does there exist a periodic solution to Eq. (1) with the same period? An affirmative answer to this question would tell us that an oscillatory input function (an alternating current, for example) will lead to oscillatory behavior of the system governed by the differential equation.

Accordingly, we suppose that

$$\mathbf{b}(t) = e^{i\beta t}\mathbf{b} = (\cos \beta t + i \sin \beta t)\mathbf{b}, \tag{2}$$

where $\mathbf{b}$ is a constant vector and $e^{i\beta t}$ is periodic with period $2\pi/\beta$. Suppose that there is a solution $\mathbf{x}(t)$ to Eq. (1) that is periodic with period $2\pi/\beta$. Then we may write

$$\mathbf{x}(t) = e^{i\beta t}\mathbf{x}, \tag{3}$$

where $\mathbf{x}$ is a constant vector. Substituting Eqs. (2) and (3) into (1), we obtain

$$i\beta e^{i\beta t}\mathbf{x} = (e^{i\beta t}\mathbf{x})' = e^{i\beta t}A\mathbf{x} + e^{i\beta t}\mathbf{b}. \tag{4}$$

Dividing both sides of Eq. (4) by $e^{i\beta t}$ and rearranging terms, we obtain

$$(A - i\beta I)\mathbf{x} = -\mathbf{b}. \tag{5}$$

Equation (5) is a nonhomogeneous system of n equations in n unknowns that has a unique solution if and only if

$$\det (A - i\beta I) \neq 0.$$

In other words, there is a unique solution if and only if $i\beta$ is *not* an eigenvalue of the matrix A. We therefore have the following theorem.

Theorem 1   In the system $\mathbf{x}' = A\mathbf{x} + \mathbf{b}$, let the forcing term $\mathbf{b}(t)$ be periodic with the form $\mathbf{b}(t) = e^{i\beta t}\mathbf{b}$. Then, if $i\beta$ is not an eigenvalue of the matrix A, there exists a unique periodic solution $\mathbf{x}(t) = e^{i\beta t}\mathbf{x}$ of $\mathbf{x}' = A\mathbf{x} + \mathbf{b}$ such that

$x = -(A - i\beta I)^{-1}\mathbf{b}$. If $i\beta$ is an eigenvalue of A, then there are either no periodic solutions or an infinite number of them.

Note   The differential equation will always have a solution. This theorem tells us something about the nature of the solutions.

Remark   If $i\beta$ is not an eigenvalue of A, then a periodic (or oscillatory) input will give rise to a periodic output. This phenomenon is called *forced oscillations* (see Section 3.8).

Example 1   Consider the system

$$\mathbf{x}'(t) = \begin{pmatrix} x_1 \\ x_2 \end{pmatrix}' = \begin{pmatrix} 2 & 1 \\ 1 & 0 \end{pmatrix}\begin{pmatrix} x_1 \\ x_2 \end{pmatrix} + e^{2it}\begin{pmatrix} 2 \\ 1 \end{pmatrix} = A\mathbf{x}(t) + \mathbf{b}(t).$$

Here the forcing term is periodic with period π. Since $2i$ is not an eigenvalue of A, we may use Eq. (5) to obtain a periodic solution of period π:

$$\mathbf{x}(t) = e^{2it}\mathbf{x},$$

where

$$\mathbf{x} = -(A - 2iI)^{-1}\begin{pmatrix} 2 \\ 1 \end{pmatrix} = -\begin{pmatrix} 2 - 2i & 1 \\ 1 & -2i \end{pmatrix}^{-1}\begin{pmatrix} 2 \\ 1 \end{pmatrix}$$

$$= \frac{-1}{5 + 4i}\begin{pmatrix} 2i & 1 \\ 1 & -2 + 2i \end{pmatrix}\begin{pmatrix} 2 \\ 1 \end{pmatrix}.$$

Multiplying the numerator and denominator by $5 - 4i$, we have

$$\mathbf{x} = \frac{-5 + 4i}{41}\begin{pmatrix} 1 + 4i \\ 2i \end{pmatrix} = \frac{-1}{41}\begin{pmatrix} 21 + 16i \\ 8 + 10i \end{pmatrix}.$$

We would like to write this solution in a more illuminating form. We recall (see Section 3.5) that

$$A + Bi = \sqrt{A^2 + B^2}\left(\frac{A}{\sqrt{A^2 + B^2}} + i\frac{B}{\sqrt{A^2 + B^2}}\right) = \sqrt{A^2 + B^2}\,e^{i\theta},$$

where $\tan\theta = B/A$ (and $\cos\theta = A/\sqrt{A^2 + B^2}$, $\sin\theta = B/\sqrt{A^2 + B^2}$). Therefore, we have

$$\mathbf{x} = \frac{-1}{41}\begin{pmatrix} \sqrt{697}\,e^{i\theta_1} \\ \sqrt{164}\,e^{i\theta_2} \end{pmatrix},$$

where $\tan\theta_1 = \frac{16}{21}$ and $\tan\theta_2 = \frac{5}{4}$. Hence

$$\mathbf{x}(t) = \frac{-1}{41}\begin{pmatrix} \sqrt{697}\,e^{i(\theta_1 + 2t)} \\ \sqrt{164}\,e^{i(\theta_2 + 2t)} \end{pmatrix}.$$

Although $\mathbf{x}(t)$ has the same period, π, as the forcing term, the coordinate functions have been shifted by θ_1 and θ_2, respectively. Such a phenomenon is called a *phase shift*.

Now we answer the question, "What happens if $i\beta$ is an eigenvalue of A?" According to the discussion in Section 8.5, the principal matrix solution e^{At} of the homogeneous system $\mathbf{x}' = A\mathbf{x}$ contains terms of the form $e^{i\beta t}$ so that $\Phi^{-1}(t)$ contains terms of the form $e^{-i\beta t}$ (since $\Phi\Phi^{-1} = I$). Using Eq. (13) in Section 8.6, we find a particular solution of Eq. (1):

$$\boldsymbol{\varphi}_p(t) = \Phi(t) \int_{t_0}^{t} \Phi^{-1}(s)\mathbf{b}e^{i\beta s} \, ds.$$

But the product of $\Phi^{-1}(s)$ and $e^{i\beta s}$ will contain constant terms (since $e^{-i\beta s}e^{i\beta s} = 1$) and the integral of these constant terms will be of the form ct, which becomes unbounded as t tends to $\pm\infty$. Such a phenomenon is called *resonance* (see Section 3.8). If $i\beta$ is an eigenvalue of A, then β is called a *natural frequency* of the system. We can summarize the above discussion by stating that *in general, resonance will occur when the frequency of the input vector is a natural frequency of the system.*

Example 2   Consider the circuit shown in Fig. 1. Applying Kirchhoff's voltage law (see Section 2.5), we obtain the second-order nonhomogeneous equation

$$L\frac{d^2I}{dt^2} + \frac{I}{C} = E'(t). \tag{6}$$

Letting $x_1 = I$ and $x_2 = I'$, we have

$$x_2' = I'' = \frac{E'}{L} - \frac{I}{LC} = \frac{E'}{L} - \frac{x_1}{LC},$$

so we may rewrite Eq. (6) in the form

$$\begin{pmatrix} x_1 \\ x_2 \end{pmatrix}' = \begin{pmatrix} 0 & 1 \\ -1/LC & 0 \end{pmatrix}\begin{pmatrix} x_1 \\ x_2 \end{pmatrix} + \begin{pmatrix} 0 \\ E'/L \end{pmatrix}. \tag{7}$$

Suppose that $E = E_0 e^{i\omega t}$ (see Exercise 16 in Section 3.9). Then Eq. (7) may be treated by the method of this section, and the solution $\mathbf{x}(t)$ is of the form $e^{i\omega t}\mathbf{x}$, where

$$\mathbf{x} = -(A - i\omega I)^{-1}\mathbf{b} \quad \text{and} \quad \mathbf{b} = \begin{pmatrix} 0 \\ i\omega E_0/L \end{pmatrix}.$$

But

$$\det(A - i\omega I) = \det\begin{pmatrix} -i\omega & 1 \\ -1/LC & -i\omega \end{pmatrix} = \frac{1}{LC} - \omega^2,$$

which is nonzero if $\omega \neq 1/\sqrt{LC}$. Therefore,

$$\mathbf{x} = \frac{-1}{(1/LC) - \omega^2}\begin{pmatrix} -i\omega & -1 \\ 1/LC & -i\omega \end{pmatrix}\begin{pmatrix} 0 \\ i\omega E_0/L \end{pmatrix} = \frac{\omega C E_0}{LC\omega^2 - 1}\begin{pmatrix} -i \\ \omega \end{pmatrix}$$

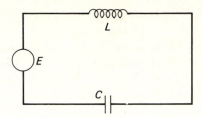

Figure 1

and

$$\mathbf{x}(t) = \frac{\omega C E_0}{LC\omega^2 - 1} \begin{pmatrix} -i \\ \omega \end{pmatrix} e^{i\omega t}.$$

Thus the current is

$$x_1(t) = I(t) = -i\omega C E_0 e^{i\omega t}$$

or

$$I(t) = \omega C E_0 (\sin \omega t - i \cos \omega t).$$

Of course, currents are not imaginary. The complex term here simply tells us that the real and imaginary parts of the solution are the responses to the real and imaginary parts of the forcing function.

If $\omega = 1/\sqrt{LC}$ (the natural frequency), then the circuit is in resonance. Since $A^2 = (-1/LC)I$, it follows after a short computation that the principal matrix solution e^{At} is

$$\boldsymbol{\Psi}(t) = \begin{pmatrix} \cos (t/\sqrt{LC}) & \sqrt{LC} \sin (t/\sqrt{LC}) \\ (-1/\sqrt{LC}) \sin (t/\sqrt{LC}) & \cos (t/\sqrt{LC}) \end{pmatrix},$$

and by Eq. (14) in Section 8.6,

$$\mathbf{x}(t) = \boldsymbol{\Psi}(t)\mathbf{x}(0) + \boldsymbol{\Psi}(t) \int_0^t \boldsymbol{\Psi}^{-1}(s)\mathbf{b}(s)\, ds. \tag{8}$$

To calculate the integral, we observe that since $\cos(-s) = \cos s$ and $\sin(-s) = -\sin s$, we have

$$\boldsymbol{\Psi}^{-1}(s)\mathbf{b}(s) = \begin{bmatrix} \cos \dfrac{s}{\sqrt{LC}} & -\sqrt{LC} \sin \dfrac{s}{\sqrt{LC}} \\ \dfrac{1}{\sqrt{LC}} \sin \dfrac{s}{\sqrt{LC}} & \cos \dfrac{s}{\sqrt{LC}} \end{bmatrix} \begin{bmatrix} 0 \\ \dfrac{iE_0 e^{is/\sqrt{LC}}}{L\sqrt{LC}} \end{bmatrix}$$

$$= \begin{bmatrix} \dfrac{E_0}{L} \sin \dfrac{s}{\sqrt{LC}} \left(\sin \dfrac{s}{\sqrt{LC}} - i \cos \dfrac{s}{\sqrt{LC}} \right) \\ \dfrac{E_0}{L\sqrt{LC}} \cos \dfrac{s}{\sqrt{LC}} \left(-\sin \dfrac{s}{\sqrt{LC}} + i \cos \dfrac{s}{\sqrt{LC}} \right) \end{bmatrix}.$$

Using Formulas 19, 24, and 27 of Appendix 1, we see that the integral in

Eq. (8) becomes

$$\int_0^t \Psi^{-1}(s)\mathbf{b}(s)\,ds = \frac{E_0}{2L}\begin{bmatrix} t - \sqrt{LC}\sin\dfrac{t}{\sqrt{LC}}\,e^{it/\sqrt{LC}} \\[2mm] \dfrac{t}{\sqrt{LC}} - 1 + \cos\dfrac{t}{\sqrt{LC}}\,e^{it/\sqrt{LC}} \end{bmatrix}. \tag{9}$$

Adding this vector to $\mathbf{x}(0)$ and multiplying $\Psi(t)$ by the result will give the solution of the system (7). Note that the vector (9) has components that become arbitrarily large as t approaches $+\infty$. This is an effect of resonance on the system.

EXERCISES 8.7

In Exercises 1 through 4, find a solution $\mathbf{x}(t)$, if possible, of each given system that has the same period of oscillation as the forcing term. If the natural and forcing frequencies coincide, show that a particular solution is unbounded as t approaches $\pm\infty$ (that is, resonance occurs).

1. $\mathbf{x}' = \begin{pmatrix} 2 & -5 \\ 0 & 3 \end{pmatrix}\mathbf{x} + \begin{pmatrix} 1 \\ 4 \end{pmatrix}e^{it}$

2. $\mathbf{x}' = \begin{pmatrix} 1 & -2 \\ \frac{5}{2} & -1 \end{pmatrix}\mathbf{x} + \begin{pmatrix} 2 \\ 3 \end{pmatrix}e^{2it}$

3. $\mathbf{x}' = \begin{pmatrix} 3 & 4 \\ -1 & -2 \end{pmatrix}\mathbf{x} + \begin{pmatrix} -1 \\ 4 \end{pmatrix}e^{-5it}$

4. $\mathbf{x}' = \begin{pmatrix} -1 & -7 \\ 5 & 1 \end{pmatrix}\mathbf{x} + \begin{pmatrix} -2 \\ 7 \end{pmatrix}e^{4it}$

5. Suppose that $\mathbf{b}(t) = \sum_{k=1}^m \mathbf{b}_k e^{i\beta_k t}$ (a finite sum of periodic inputs). Assume that $i\beta_k$ is not a root of the characteristic equation of A for $k = 1, 2, \ldots, m$. Use the principle of superposition (see Exercise 13 in Section 8.6) to find a solution $\mathbf{x}(t)$ for Eq. (1) that can be written in the form

$$\mathbf{x}(t) = \sum_{k=1}^m \mathbf{x}_k e^{i\beta_k t}.$$

6. Use Euler's formula (3) in Section 3.5 to show that

$$2\cos\beta t = e^{i\beta t} + e^{-i\beta t} \quad \text{and} \quad 2i\sin\beta t = e^{i\beta t} - e^{-i\beta t}.$$

Then use the results of Exercise 5 to obtain periodic solutions to the following equations (if possible):

  a) $x'' - x' - 2x = \sin t$;

  b) $x'' + 4x = \cos t$;

  c) $x'' + 4x = \cos 2t$;

  d) $x'' + 2x' - 15x = \sin 4t$.

7. Verify the form of the principal matrix solution $\Psi(t)$ if ω equals the natural frequency in Example 2.

8. Verify Eq. (9).

9. a) Express the forced vibration equation (11) in Section 3.8 for a spring-mass system with $\mu = 0$ as a 2×2 system of differential equations.

  b) Obtain a solution by the method of this section, given that $\omega \neq \sqrt{k/m}$.

  c) What happens if $\omega = \sqrt{k/m}$? Justify your answer.

REVIEW EXERCISES FOR CHAPTER 8

In Exercises 1 through 4, write the given system of equations in vector-matrix form.

1. $x_1' = 3x_1 - 4x_2,$
   $x_2' = -2x_1 + 7x_2$

2. $x_1' = (\sin t)x_1 + e^t x_2,$
   $x_2' = -x_1 + (\tan t)x_2$

3. $x_1' = x_1 + x_2 + e^t,$
   $x_2' = -3x_1 + 2x_2 + e^{2t}$

4. $x_1' = -tx_1 + t^2 x_2 + t^3,$

  $x_2' = -\sqrt{t}\, x_1 + \sqrt[3]{t}\, x_2 + t^{3/5}$

5. Consider the system

$$\mathbf{x}' = \begin{pmatrix} 4 & 2 \\ 3 & 3 \end{pmatrix}\mathbf{x}.$$

A fundamental matrix solution is

$$\Phi(t) = \begin{pmatrix} 2e^t & e^{6t} \\ -3e^t & e^{6t} \end{pmatrix}.$$

Find a solution that satisfies each of the following initial conditions.

a) $\mathbf{x}(0) = \begin{pmatrix} 2 \\ 3 \end{pmatrix}$;

b) $\mathbf{x}(0) = \begin{pmatrix} -1 \\ 0 \end{pmatrix}$;

c) $\mathbf{x}(0) = \begin{pmatrix} 0 \\ 0 \end{pmatrix}$;

d) $\mathbf{x}(0) = \begin{pmatrix} 7 \\ -2 \end{pmatrix}$;

e) $\mathbf{x}(0) = \begin{pmatrix} a \\ b \end{pmatrix}$.

In Exercises 6 through 11, calculate the eigenvalues and eigenspaces of the given matrix.

6. $\begin{pmatrix} 5 & -1 \\ 8 & 1 \end{pmatrix}$ **7.** $\begin{pmatrix} 2 & 5 \\ 0 & 2 \end{pmatrix}$

8. $\begin{pmatrix} 1 & 0 & 0 \\ 3 & 7 & 0 \\ -2 & 4 & -5 \end{pmatrix}$ **9.** $\begin{pmatrix} 1 & -1 & 0 \\ 1 & 2 & 1 \\ -2 & 1 & -1 \end{pmatrix}$

10. $\begin{pmatrix} 5 & -2 & 0 & 0 \\ 4 & -1 & 0 & 0 \\ 0 & 0 & 3 & -1 \\ 0 & 0 & 2 & 3 \end{pmatrix}$ **11.** $\begin{pmatrix} -2 & 1 & 0 \\ 0 & -2 & 1 \\ 0 & 0 & -2 \end{pmatrix}$

In Exercises 12 through 23, calculate the matrix e^{At} for each given matrix A.

12. $\begin{pmatrix} 2 & 5 \\ -1 & -2 \end{pmatrix}$ **13.** $\begin{pmatrix} 3 & -5 \\ 2 & 1 \end{pmatrix}$

14. $\begin{pmatrix} -9 & 4 \\ -25 & 11 \end{pmatrix}$ **15.** $\begin{pmatrix} -4 & 4 \\ -1 & 0 \end{pmatrix}$

16. $\begin{pmatrix} 4 & 2 & 0 \\ 2 & 4 & 0 \\ 0 & 0 & -3 \end{pmatrix}$ **17.** $\begin{pmatrix} -3 & 2 & 1 \\ -7 & 4 & 2 \\ -5 & 3 & 2 \end{pmatrix}$

18. $\begin{pmatrix} 8 & 0 & 12 \\ 0 & -2 & 0 \\ 12 & 0 & -2 \end{pmatrix}$ **19.** $\begin{pmatrix} 1 & 1 & 1 \\ -1 & -1 & 0 \\ -1 & 0 & -1 \end{pmatrix}$

20. $\begin{pmatrix} 0 & -18 & -7 \\ 1 & -12 & -4 \\ -1 & 25 & 9 \end{pmatrix}$ **21.** $\begin{pmatrix} 2 & 2 & 0 \\ 2 & 2 & 0 \\ 0 & 0 & -3 \end{pmatrix}$

22. $\begin{pmatrix} 4 & 2 & -2 & 2 \\ 1 & 3 & 1 & -1 \\ 0 & 0 & 2 & 0 \\ 1 & 1 & -3 & 5 \end{pmatrix}$ **23.** $\begin{pmatrix} 3 & 1 & 0 & 0 \\ 0 & 3 & 0 & 0 \\ 0 & 0 & -6 & 1 \\ 0 & 0 & 0 & -6 \end{pmatrix}$

In Exercises 24 through 28, find the principal matrix solution of the given system.

24. $\mathbf{x}' = \begin{pmatrix} -3 & 4 \\ -2 & 3 \end{pmatrix}\mathbf{x}$

25. $\mathbf{x}' = \begin{pmatrix} 3 & -1 \\ -2 & 4 \end{pmatrix}\mathbf{x}$

26. $\mathbf{x}' = \begin{pmatrix} -3 & -4 \\ -2 & 1 \end{pmatrix}\mathbf{x}$

27. $\mathbf{x}' = \begin{pmatrix} -1 & -18 & -7 \\ 1 & -13 & -4 \\ -1 & 25 & 8 \end{pmatrix}\mathbf{x}$

28. $\mathbf{x}' = \begin{pmatrix} 2 & 1 & 0 \\ -2 & -1 & 2 \\ 1 & 1 & 1 \end{pmatrix}\mathbf{x}$

29. Solve the system

$$\mathbf{x}' = \begin{pmatrix} 2 & 1 \\ -4 & 2 \end{pmatrix}\mathbf{x} + \begin{pmatrix} 3 \\ t \end{pmatrix}e^{2t}, \quad \mathbf{x}(0) = \begin{pmatrix} 3 \\ 2 \end{pmatrix}$$

30. Solve the system

$$\mathbf{x}' = \begin{pmatrix} 2 & 1 & 0 \\ -2 & -1 & 2 \\ 1 & 1 & 1 \end{pmatrix}\mathbf{x} + \begin{pmatrix} 0 \\ 1 \\ e^t \end{pmatrix}, \quad \mathbf{x}(0) = \begin{pmatrix} 1 \\ 2 \\ 3 \end{pmatrix}$$

Nonlinear Equations
and Stability

9.1 INTRODUCTION

In the preceding chapters we have seen that there are large classes of differential equations and systems having solutions defined in some interval. However, if an equation is nonlinear, then there is usually not any way to find its solution. For this reason, it is necessary to seek methods for describing the nature of a solution without explicitly solving the equation.

First, it is necessary to ask, "what kind of information about a solution is it useful to have?" We indicate a partial answer by considering our old standby: second-order linear equations with constant coefficients.

Example 1   Consider the three equations

a) $x'' + 3x' + 2x = 0$,

b) $x'' - 3x' + 2x = 0$,

c) $x'' + x = 0$.

The general solutions to these equations are

a) $x(t) = c_1 e^{-t} + c_2 e^{-2t}$,

b) $x(t) = c_1 e^t + c_2 e^{2t}$,

c) $x(t) = c_1 \cos t + c_2 \sin t$.

It is clear that all solutions of (a) approach zero as t tends to ∞, all solutions of (b) approach ∞ as t tends to ∞, and all solutions of (c) remain bounded but do not approach any constant as t tends to ∞. Furthermore, the solutions of (c) are periodic of period 2π.

Nonlinear equations, too, may approach zero, become unbounded, or remain bounded as t becomes large. They also may be periodic. It is fair to say that a major portion of modern research in the theory of ordinary differential equations is concerned with finding conditions that will ensure that the solution of a nonlinear equation have one of these properties. There is no general method for analyzing *all* nonlinear equations. In this chapter we will discuss some of the oldest known and most elementary ways of obtaining this information.

One of these methods is to consider the nonlinear equation as a *perturbation* of some linear equation; that is, attempt to approximate a nonlinear equation by a "related" linear equation. We shall illustrate this method with some examples.

Example 2   Consider the freely swinging (frictionless) pendulum of length l shown in Fig. 1. In Exercise 14 of Section 3.8 we indicated that Newton's law of motion yields the nonlinear second-order equation

$$\frac{d^2\theta}{dt^2} + \omega^2 \sin \theta = 0, \tag{1}$$

where $\omega^2 = g/l$. However, since

$$\lim_{\theta \to 0} \frac{\sin \theta}{\theta} = 1,$$

we may approximate Eq. (1) for small values of θ by the linear equation

$$\frac{d^2\theta}{dt^2} + \omega^2\theta = 0. \tag{2}$$

The general solution of Eq. (2) is periodic:

$$\theta(t) = c_1 \cos \omega t + c_2 \sin \omega t.$$

How similar in behavior are the solutions of these two equations? This question will be answered in Section 9.3.

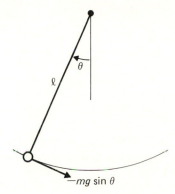

Figure 1

Example 3   Consider the nonlinear first-order scalar equation

$$x' = -x + x^2. \tag{3}$$

This equation has two constant solutions,

$$x = 0 \quad \text{and} \quad x = 1,$$

easily verified by substitution into Eq. (3). For x close to zero, the nonlinear term x^2 is relatively small compared to the linear term $-x$, since

$$\lim_{x \to 0} \frac{x^2}{x} = 0.$$

Thus we wish to compare the solutions of Eq. (3) to those of the linear equation

$$x' = -x, \tag{4}$$

whose general solution is

$$x(t) = x(0)e^{-t}.$$

The nonlinear equation (3) can be solved by a separation of variables:

$$\int \frac{dx}{-x + x^2} = \int dt = t + C.$$

By using partial fractions we have

$$\int \frac{dx}{-x + x^2} = \int \left(\frac{1}{x - 1} - \frac{1}{x}\right) dx = \ln(x - 1) - \ln(x) = \ln\left(\frac{x - 1}{x}\right),$$

which implies that

$$\frac{x - 1}{x} = Ce^t \tag{5}$$

for some new constant C.

We may assume that $x(0) \neq 0$, because if $x(0) = 0$, we already have the unique solution $x(t) \equiv 0$. Then, for $t = 0$, Eq. (5) yields

$$\frac{x(0) - 1}{x(0)} = C.$$

Thus

$$\frac{x(t) - 1}{x(t)} = \frac{x(0) - 1}{x(0)} e^t$$

or, after some simple algebra,

$$x(t) = \frac{x(0)}{x(0)(1 - e^t) + e^t}. \tag{6}$$

This solution is defined so long as the denominator is not zero; that is, so long as

$$x(0)(1 - e^t) + e^t \neq 0$$

or

$$e^t \neq \frac{x(0)}{x(0) - 1} = \frac{1}{C}$$

or

$$t \neq \ln \frac{x(0)}{x(0) - 1} = -\ln C.$$

Note that for small values of t, $1 - e^t$ is close to zero so that the solution $x(t)$, given by Eq. (6), is close to $x(0)e^{-t}$, which is the solution to the linear equation (4).

Now suppose that $0 < x(0) < 1$. Then by Eq. (5), $C < 0$. Thus $Ce^t \neq 1$ for all $t \geqslant 0$, and the solution of Eq. (3) [given by Eq. (6)] approaches zero as t tends to ∞. Hence for $0 < x(0) < 1$, Eq. (4) is a "good" approximation to Eq. (3) in the sense that the solution to the two equations exhibit the

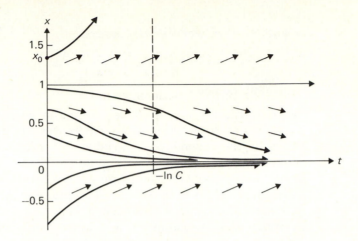

Figure 2

same asymptotic behavior. When $x(0) \geqslant 1$, we are no longer "near" the zero solution, and Eq. (4) is not a good approximation. If $x(0) = 1$, we obtain the constant solution $x \equiv 1$. If $x(0) > 1$, then $0 < C < 1$ and $-\ln C > 0$, so that the solution (5) approaches ∞ as t tends to $-\ln C$. This situation is illustrated in Fig. 2. In the terminology to be introduced in the next section, we may say that the solution $x \equiv 0$ of Eq. (3) is *asymptotically stable*, whereas the solution $x \equiv 1$ is *unstable*.

In earlier chapters we introduced a terminology for classifying certain types of differential equations. Although nonlinear equations and systems can take many different forms, they can be roughly classified into two different categories. To illustrate this, we consider the system of two first-order equations

$$x' = f(t, x, y), \tag{7}$$
$$y' = g(t, x, y),$$

where f and g are assumed to be continuously differentiable functions of t, x, and y over some region

$$D: a < t < b, \quad c < x < d, \quad e < y < h$$

in three-dimensional space. By Theorems 3 and 5 of Section 10.1, this is enough to guarantee that there is a unique solution (defined over some interval in t) that passes through any initial point (t_0, x_0, y_0) in D.

The system (7) is said to be *autonomous* (time independent) if the functions f and g do not depend on t. Otherwise, Eq. (7) is said to be *nonautonomous*. Hence Eq. (7) is autonomous if $f(t, x, y) = f(x, y)$ and $g(t, x, y) = g(x, y)$.

Example 4   The system

$$x' = -x^2 + y,$$
$$y' = -x + y^2$$

is autonomous, whereas the system

$$x' = ty,$$
$$y' = -x$$

is nonautonomous.

In previous chapters, we wrote the solutions of a system of two equations as a pair $(x(t), y(t))$, where each of the solution functions depends on the independent variable t. A graph of such a solution would require three dimensions for t, x, and y. However, it is often of interest to treat t as a parameter and express the solution as a curve in the xy-plane. Then the xy-plane is called the *phase plane* of the system, and a curve that expresses the relation between x and y is called an *orbit* (or *phase portrait*) of the system. It is often possible to derive a great deal of information from an examination of the orbits of the system.

For example, let $x(t)$ and $y(t)$ denote the respective populations of two species competing for the same limited resources. A model for the interaction between the two species is given by the Lotka-Volterra equations (see Example 5 in Section 1.1)

$$x' = \beta_1 x - \delta_{11}x^2 - \delta_{12}xy,$$
$$y' = \beta_2 y - \delta_{21}xy - \delta_{22}y^2.$$

We shall examine this system more closely in Section 9.3. At this point, we merely remark that an orbit of this system would give us very useful information. Increases or decreases in the population of one of the two species will affect the population of the other species. An orbit will graphically depict this effect. Consider, for example, the orbit shown in Fig. 3. We can derive a great deal of information from such an orbit. When $x = a$ units, an increase in x will cause a decrease in y until $y = c$. Then both x and y will increase until x reaches its maximum sustainable population of b units. The second population will continue to rise until it reaches a population of d units, and so on. Moreover, both populations are

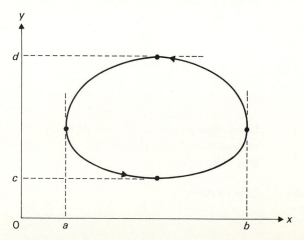

Figure 3

periodic, that is, all population levels recur continually. Note that all this information can be obtained (if the orbits can be drawn) *without actually solving the system*!

We shall illustrate the calculation of orbits in the next few examples of linear systems and return to the discussion of nonlinear systems (such as the Lotka-Volterra equations) in Section 9.3.

Example 5   Consider the equation of the harmonic oscillator

$$x'' + x = 0,$$

with initial conditions $x(0) = 1$, $x'(0) = 0$. We may rewrite it as the autonomous system

$$x' = y, \quad x(0) = 1,$$
$$y' = -x, \quad y(0) = 0.$$

There are two ways of finding the orbit. First, we observe that the unique solution of the initial value problem is the solution pair $(\cos t, -\sin t)$. Since $\cos^2 t + \sin^2 t = 1$, the orbit satisfies the equation

$$x^2 + y^2 = 1,$$

which is the unit circle in the xy-plane (see Fig. 4). The arrows in the figure indicate the direction in which the solutions move about the orbit as t increases. Note that as t increases, $\cos t$ (the x-coordinate) moves from 1 (when $t = 0$) to 0 (when $t = \pi/2$), to -1 (when $t = \pi$), to 0 (when $t = 3\pi/2$), and back to 1 (at $t = 2\pi$). Similarly, $-\sin t$ (the y-coordinate) moves from 0 to -1, to 0, to $+1$, and back to 0. This phenomenon explains the direction indicated by the arrows in Fig. 4. Therefore, starting at the point $(1, 0)$ (corresponding to $t = 0$), x decreases while y decreases.

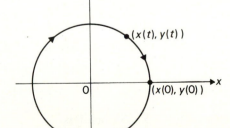

Figure 4

We can also find this orbit without solving the system. By the chain rule, we have

$$\frac{dy}{dx} = \frac{dy/dt}{dx/dt} = -\frac{x}{y}.$$

Separating the variables, we find that

$$y \, dy = -x \, dx$$

or, after an integration,

$$x^2 + y^2 = C.$$

To evaluate the constant C, we note that at $t = 0$, $x = 1$ and $y = 0$, so that $C = x^2(0) + y^2(0) = 1$. (Thus the radius of the orbit depends on the initial conditions.)

Example 6   Again consider the harmonic oscillator with the new initial condition

$$x(t_0) = 1, \quad y(t_0) = 0.$$

The unique solution pair is

$$(x(t), y(t)) = (\cos(t - t_0), -\sin(t - t_0)).$$

But then

$$x^2 + y^2 = \cos^2(t - t_0) + \sin^2(t - t_0) = 1,$$

which is the *same* orbit as in the previous example. In other words, *the orbit is independent of the initial value of t* [but not, of course, of the initial values $x(t_0)$ and $y(t_0)$]. This is a property shared by *all autonomous systems*. This fact will be assumed for the remainder of this chapter. Its proof can be found in most advanced differential equations tests.† The property does not hold for nonautonomous systems, as is easily illustrated by the next example.

Example 7   Consider the nonautonomous system

$$x' = \frac{1}{t} x, \quad x(t_0) = 1,$$

$$y' = y, \quad y(t_0) = 2.$$

Since these equations are uncoupled, it is easy to calculate the solution pair

$$(x(t), y(t)) = \left(\frac{t}{t_0}, 2e^{t - t_0} \right).$$

Since $t = t_0 x$, the orbit is

$$y = 2e^{t_0(x-1)}.$$

Thus different values of the initial value of t lead to different orbits. Figure 5 shows the orbits for $t_0 = 1$, $t_0 = 2$.

---

† See, for example, H. K. Wilson, *Ordinary Differential Equations*. Reading, Mass.: Addison-Wesley (1972).

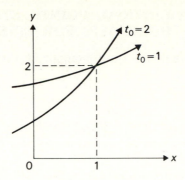

Figure 5

In light of the properties of autonomous systems illustrated in Examples 5 and 6, we will deal with them exclusively in the remainder of this chapter. As we saw earlier (see Example 2), autonomous systems can and do arise naturally in applications. A discussion of the properties of nonautonomous systems is more complicated (one reason being the necessity to worry about the initial value of t). It can be found in many intermediate and advanced textbooks on differential equations.

EXERCISES 9.1

In each of Exercises 1 through 6, (a) find a related linear equation (as in Examples 2 and 3), (b) find all constant solutions of the nonlinear equation, (c) solve the nonlinear equation, and (d) determine the behavior of the solutions to the nonlinear equation for values of $x(0)$ in the indicated range.

1. $x' = x - x^2$, $-\infty < x(0) < \infty$

2. $x' = -2x + 3x^2$, $x(0) \geq 0$

3. $x' = 2x + 3x^2$, $x(0) \geq 0$

4. $x' = 2x - 3x^2$, $-\infty < x(0) < \infty$

5. $x' = x(x - 1)(x - 2)$, $x(0) \geq 0$

6. $x' = -x(x - 1)(x - 2)$, $x(0) \geq 0$

7. a) Draw the orbits for the initial value problem
$$x' = y, \quad x(0) = a,$$
$$y' = -x, \quad y(0) = b.$$

   b) Show that these orbits are identical to those for the same system with the initial conditions
$$x(t_0) = a, \quad y(t_0) = b.$$

8. Show that the orbits for the equation
$$x'' + \omega^2 x = 0$$
are ellipses centered at the origin.

9. Find the orbits for the system
$$x' = tx, \quad x(t_0) = 1,$$
$$y' = -y, \quad y(t_0) = 1,$$
and graph these orbits for $t_0 = 0$, $t_0 = 1$, and $t_0 = 2$.

*10. Suppose that the differential equations $x' = f(x, y)$ and $y' = g(x, y)$ have unique solutions whenever an initial condition is given for each. Show that no two orbits of the autonomous system
$$x' = f(x, y), \quad y' = g(x, y) \qquad (8)$$
can ever intersect.

*11. Use the result of Exercise 10 to show that if (x_0, y_0) is a point having the property that $f(x_0, y_0) = g(x_0, y_0) = 0$ and if $(x(t), y(t))$ is a nonzero solution pair of the system (8), then there is no value of t for which $(x(t), y(t)) = (x_0, y_0)$.

9.2 CRITICAL POINTS, STABILITY, AND PHASE PORTRAITS FOR LINEAR SYSTEMS

The general autonomous system of two first-order equations is given by

$$x' = f(x, y),$$
$$y' = g(x, y). \tag{1}$$

Since orbits are independent of t_0, we shall assume that $t_0 = 0$.

A point (x_0, y_0) is called a *critical point* of the system (1) if

$$f(x_0, y_0) = g(x_0, y_0) = 0.$$

Any critical point (x_0, y_0) is a constant solution pair of (1), since the derivative of a constant is zero:

$$x_0' = 0 = f(x_0, y_0),$$
$$y_0' = 0 = g(x_0, y_0).$$

A critical point (x_0, y_0) of the system (1) is a point of *equilibrium*, since once we reach this point we can never leave it, the derivatives of both $x(t)$ and $y(t)$ being zero there. Physically, a critical point is often a point at which the potential energy is at a minimum. For instance, in Example 2 of Section 9.1, if we use the substitution $\mu = d\theta/dt$, we can write the system (1) of Section 9.1 as

$$\theta' = \mu,$$
$$\mu' = -\omega^2 \sin \theta.$$

From Fig. 1, it is clear that the potential energy is a minimum when $\theta = 0$. The point $(0, 0)$ is a point of equilibrium of the system. Of course, there are other critical points (see the next example). This situation will be discussed in great detail in **Example 4 of Section 9.3**.

Example 1 Consider the system

$$x' = y,$$
$$y' = -\omega^2 \sin x,$$

which was just obtained from Eq. (1) of Section 9.1. This system has infinitely many critical points, since $(k\pi, 0)$ is critical for all integers k.

Example 2 Consider the system

$$x' = -x^2 + y,$$
$$y' = x - y^2.$$

The two critical points are $(0, 0)$ and $(1, 1)$.

The notion of stability is central to any discussion of the behavior of differential equations. Roughly, a solution $\varphi(t)$ to a system of equations is *stable* if whenever we start "close" to $\varphi(t)$, we will stay close to $\varphi(t)$ for all future values of t. It is *asymptotically stable* if it is stable and the solutions that start close to $\varphi(t)$ approach $\varphi(t)$ as t tends to ∞. Finally, $\varphi(t)$ is *unstable* if it is not stable.

We already saw an example of a system that is stable. In Example 5 of Section 9.1 the orbits (see Fig. 4) were circles centered at the origin of radius $\sqrt{x^2(0) + y^2(0)}$. If the initial conditions are changed by a small amount, then the radius of the circular orbit is changed by a small amount, and thus the new orbit stays close to the original one.

To define "closeness" more precisely, we make use of the Pythagorean distance between two points in the plane. If (x_1, y_1) and (x_2, y_2) are the two points, then the distance between them is

$$d = [(x_1 - x_2)^2 + (y_1 - y_2)^2]^{1/2}.$$

We denote by $(x(t, x^*, y^*), y(t, x^*, y^*))$ the unique solution pair to the system (1) that satisfies the initial conditions

$$x(0) = x^*, \quad y(0) = y^*.$$

Now we can give formal definitions of the above concepts. The constant solution (or critical point) (x_0, y_0) is said to be:

---

1. *Stable* if for every number $\varepsilon > 0$ there is a number $\delta > 0$ such that whenever

$$[(x_0 - x^*)^2 + (y_0 - y^*)^2]^{1/2} < \delta,$$

we have

$$[(x_0 - x(t, x^*, y^*))^2 + (y_0 - y(t, x^*, y^*))^2]^{1/2} < \varepsilon,$$

for all $t \geq 0$ (that is, if you start close, you stay close);

2. *Asymptotically stable* if it is stable and there exists a number $A > 0$ such that whenever

$$[(x_0 - x^*)^2 + (y_0 - y^*)^2]^{1/2} < A,$$

we have

$$\lim_{t \to \infty} [(x_0 - x(t, x^*, y^*))^2 + (y_0 - y(t, x^*, y^*))^2] = 0$$

(that is, if you start close enough, the solution will approach the critical point as t tends to ∞);

3. *Unstable* if it is not stable (that is, no matter how close to the constant solution you start, there are solutions that will move away from the constant solution).

The requirement that the solution be stable is part of the definition of asymptotic stability. There are examples, which we shall not cite here, of systems where all solutions eventually tend to zero but each gets very large, no matter how close to zero it starts. The zero solution for such a system is unstable.

The foregoing ideas are sketched in Fig. 6, where the critical point is taken to be the origin.

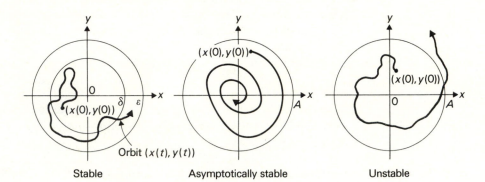

Figure 6   Stable   Asymptotically stable   Unstable

Example 3   Consider again the harmonic oscillator

$$x' = y, \quad y' = -x.$$

Clearly $(0, 0)$ is a constant solution. The solution pair with the initial conditions $x(0) = x^*$, $y(0) = y^*$ is

$$(x(t, x^*, y^*), y(t, x^*, y^*)) = (x^* \cos t + y^* \sin t, -x^* \sin t + y^* \cos t),$$

so that

$$(x(t, x^*, y^*) - 0)^2 + (y(t, x^*, y^*) - 0)^2$$
$$= (x^* \cos t + y^* \sin t)^2 + (-x^* \sin t + y^* \cos t)^2 = 2(x^{*2} + y^{*2}).$$

Thus $\delta = \varepsilon/\sqrt{2}$ satisfies the definition of stability and the zero solution is stable.

Example 4   Consider the system

$$x' = y,$$
$$y' = -2x - 3y.$$

Again $(0, 0)$ is a critical point. The solution pair that satisfies $x(0) = x^*$, $y(0) = y^*$ is given by

$$(x(t, x^*, y^*), y(t, x^*, y^*))$$
$$= ((2x^* + y^*)e^{-t} - (x^* + y^*)e^{-2t}, -(2x^* + y^*)e^{-t} + 2(x^* + y^*)e^{-2t}),$$

which tends to zero as t tends to ∞ no matter how large x^* and y^* are.

Hence the zero solution is asymptotically stable. As in this example, any situation in which A can be arbitrarily large is called *global asymptotic stability*.

Example 5   The system

$$x' = y,$$
$$y' = -2x + 3y$$

has $(0, 0)$ as a critical point. However, the zero solution is unstable, since for any $x^* \neq 0$ and $y^* \neq 0$ (no matter how small), the solution pair is

$$(x(t, x^*, y^*), y(t, x^*, y^*))$$
$$= ((2x^* - y^*)e^t + (y^* - x^*)e^{2t}, (2x^* - y^*)e^t + 2(y^* - x^*)e^{2t}),$$

which becomes arbitrarily large as t tends to ∞.

The three examples considered above were all linear. The analysis of stability properties for nonlinear systems is much more difficult, since, in general, solutions to such systems cannot be found. We will consider a class of nonlinear systems in the next section, but in the remainder of this section we will classify all possible linear systems† so that we may have some basis of comparison when we get to the nonlinear ones.

The linear system we will consider is

$$x' = a_{11}x + a_{12}y, \qquad a_{11}a_{22} - a_{12}a_{21} \neq 0, \qquad \textbf{(2)}$$
$$y' = a_{21}x + a_{22}y,$$

where the coefficients a_{ij} are real constants. As in Section 3.12, we derive the characteristic equation of the system

$$\lambda^2 - (a_{11} + a_{22})\lambda + (a_{11}a_{22} - a_{21}a_{12}) = 0, \qquad \textbf{(3)}$$

with the roots λ_1 and λ_2.‡ The orbits of the system (2) will depend on the nature of these two roots. We shall therefore consider each case separately. We note that in most cases $(0, 0)$ will be the only constant solution (critical point) of the system (why?), so that we shall restrict our attention to the nature of the orbits around the origin. This restriction also means that none of the roots of the characteristic equation (3) will be zero (see Exercise 11).

---

† Except those in which as least one of the roots of the characteristic equation (3) is zero.
‡ For those of you who covered the material in Chapter 8, λ_1 and λ_2 are the eigenvalues of the matrix

$$A = \begin{pmatrix} a_{11} & a_{12} \\ a_{21} & a_{22} \end{pmatrix}.$$

Although we avoid the eigenvalue terminology to make this chapter accessible to students who have not covered Chapter 8, the material *should* be regarded in terms of eigenvalues.

In the following discussion, we shall examine the different possibilities for the roots of Eq. (3) and draw representative orbits of the system for each case. Thus, merely knowing the roots of the characteristic equation is enough to determine the nature of the orbits.

CASE 1 λ_1 *and* λ_2 *are real, distinct, and of the same sign.* We may assume, for simplicity, that $\lambda_1 > \lambda_2$. Then by Theorem 1 of Section 3.12 each solution pair has the form

$$(x(t), y(t)) = (c_1\alpha_1 e^{\lambda_1 t} + c_2\alpha_2 e^{\lambda_2 t}, c_1\beta_1 e^{\lambda_1 t} + c_2\beta_2 e^{\lambda_2 t}), \tag{4}$$

where c_1 and c_2 are arbitrary.

CASE 1(a). $\lambda_2 < \lambda_1 < 0$ (both roots are negative). Clearly all solutions tend to $(0, 0)$ as t tends to ∞. First, we assume that $c_1 = 0$ and $c_2 \neq 0$. Then $y = (\beta_2/\alpha_2)x$, which means that the orbit is a straight line with slope β_2/α_2. If $c_1 \neq 0$ and $c_2 = 0$, then the situation is similar and we obtain the line $y = (\beta_1/\alpha_1)x$. To obtain the other orbits, we assume that c_1 and c_2 are both nonzero. Then

$$\frac{y(t)}{x(t)} = \frac{c_1\beta_1 e^{\lambda_1 t} + c_2\beta_2 e^{\lambda_2 t}}{c_1\alpha_1 e^{\lambda_1 t} + c_2\alpha_2 e^{\lambda_2 t}},$$

and dividing the numerator and denominator by $e^{\lambda_1 t}$, we have

$$\frac{y(t)}{x(t)} = \frac{c_1\beta_1 + c_2\beta_2 e^{(\lambda_2 - \lambda_1)t}}{c_1\alpha_1 + c_2\alpha_2 e^{(\lambda_2 - \lambda_1)t}} \to \frac{c_1\beta_1}{c_1\alpha_1} = \frac{\beta_1}{\alpha_1}$$

as t tends to ∞. Thus all orbits approach the origin with the slope β_1/α_1. Similarly, as t tends to $-\infty$, all solutions become asymptotic to the line with the slope β_2/α_2. This situation is illustrated in Fig. 7 for three different values of the slopes β_1/α_1 and β_2/α_2. It is clear that in this case the zero solution is asymptotically stable. Here the origin is called a *stable node*.

CASE 1(b). $\lambda_1 > \lambda_2 > 0$ (both roots are positive). Then all solutions (except the zero solution) approach ∞ as t tends to ∞. Hence the zero solution is unstable. The orbits are the same as in the previous case except that the direction of motion is reversed. The origin here is called an *unstable node*. As t tends to $-\infty$, the orbits approach zero with the slope β_2/α_2 and as t tends to ∞, the orbits become asymptotic to the line with the slope β_1/α_1.

CASE 2 λ_1 *and* λ_2 *are real with opposite signs.* We assume that $\lambda_1 > 0 > \lambda_2$. The situation here is very different. If $c_1 = 0$ and $c_2 \neq 0$, we obtain, as before,

$$\frac{y}{x} = \frac{\beta_2}{\alpha_2} \quad \text{or} \quad y = \frac{\beta_2}{\alpha_2} x.$$

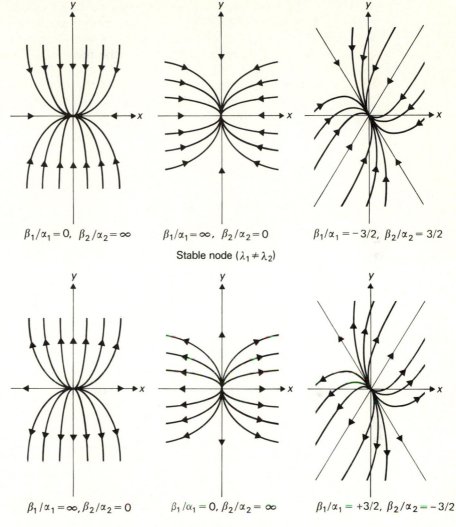

$\beta_1/\alpha_1 = 0, \ \beta_2/\alpha_2 = \infty$ $\beta_1/\alpha_1 = \infty, \ \beta_2/\alpha_2 = 0$ $\beta_1/\alpha_1 = -3/2, \ \beta_2/\alpha_2 = 3/2$

Stable node $(\lambda_1 \neq \lambda_2)$

$\beta_1/\alpha_1 = \infty, \beta_2/\alpha_2 = 0$ $\beta_1/\alpha_1 = 0, \beta_2/\alpha_2 = \infty$ $\beta_1/\alpha_1 = +3/2, \beta_2/\alpha_2 = -3/2$

Figure 7   Unstable node $(\lambda_1 \neq \lambda_2)$

As t tends to ∞, $x(t)$ and $y(t)$ approach zero. If $c_1 \neq 0$ and $c_2 = 0$, then $y = (\beta_1/\alpha_1)x$ and both x and y approach ∞ as t tends to ∞, and approach zero as t tends to $-\infty$. These two orbits are sketched in Fig. 8. When both c_1 and c_2 are nonzero, the situation is more complicated. Again

$$\frac{y(t)}{x(t)} = \frac{c_1\beta_1 e^{\lambda_1 t} + c_2\beta_2 e^{\lambda_2 t}}{c_1\alpha_1 e^{\lambda_1 t} + c_2\alpha_2 e^{\lambda_2 t}} = \frac{c_1\beta_1 + c_2\beta_2 e^{(\lambda_2 - \lambda_1)t}}{c_1\alpha_1 + c_2\alpha_2 e^{(\lambda_2 - \lambda_1)t}},$$

Figure 8

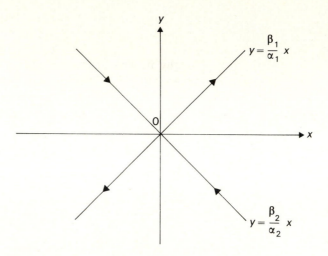

which approaches β_1/α_1 as t tends to ∞. Hence all orbits are asymptotic to the line $y = (\beta_1/\alpha_1)x$ as t tends to ∞. Also

$$\frac{y(t)}{x(t)} = \frac{c_1\beta_1 e^{(\lambda_1-\lambda_2)t} + c_2\beta_2}{c_1\alpha_1 e^{(\lambda_1-\lambda_2)t} + c_2\alpha_2},$$

which approaches β_2/α_2 as t tends to $-\infty$. Hence all orbits are asymptotic to the line $y = (\beta_2/\alpha_2)x$ as t tends to $-\infty$. Finally, we observe that both $x(t)$ and $y(t)$ approach ∞ as t tends to $\pm\infty$, and by uniqueness, no orbit can pass through the origin. The orbits are therefore as shown in Fig. 9.

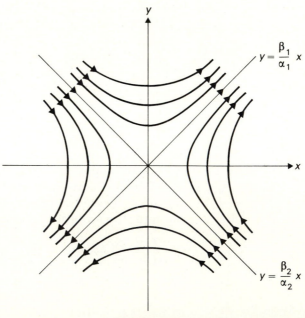

Figure 9   Saddle point

It is clear here that the origin is unstable. In this situation, the origin is called (for obvious reasons) a *saddle point*. We note that a saddle point has the property that exactly one orbit approaches the origin and all others are "repelled" by it. The physical behavior corresponding to a saddle point is illustrated in Example 4 in Section 9.3.

CASE 3 $\lambda_1 = \lambda_2 = \lambda$. Here either $\lambda < 0$ or $\lambda > 0$.

CASE 3(a). $\lambda < 0$. There are two ways in which the characteristic equation (3) can yield a double root. One possibility is

$$a_{11} = a_{22} \neq 0, \quad a_{21} = a_{12} = 0. \tag{5}$$

Then the characteristic equation is

$$\lambda^2 - 2a_{11}\lambda + a_{11}^2 = 0,$$

or $\lambda = a_{11}$ is the double root. Then the system (2) becomes

$$x' = \lambda x,$$
$$y' = \lambda y.$$

The solutions are obviously of the form

$$(x(t), y(t)) = (c_1 e^{\lambda t}, c_2 e^{\lambda t}),$$

so that

$$\frac{y}{x} = \frac{c_2}{c_1} \quad \text{or} \quad y = \frac{c_2}{c_1} x.$$

Thus all orbits are straight lines with the slope c_2/c_1. Since $\lambda < 0$, all solutions approach zero as t tends to ∞, and the zero solution is asymptotically stable. The situation is graphed in Fig. 10. The origin in this case is also called a node. Sometimes the nodes shown in Fig. 6 are called *improper nodes*, whereas the node in Fig. 10 is called a *proper node*. We

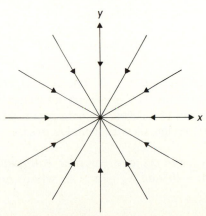

Figure 10   (Star-shaped) stable node $(\lambda_1 = \lambda_2)$

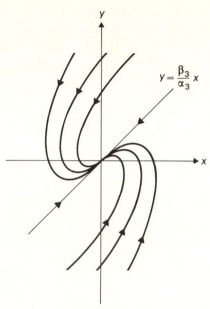

Figure 11

Stable node ($\lambda_1 = \lambda_2$)

will not use this terminology. Also, we should add that the node of Fig. 10 is sometimes called a *star-shaped node*.

If $\lambda < 0$ is a double root but the equalities (5) do not hold, then the equations are coupled and the general solution is, according to Theorem 2 of Section 3.12,

$$(x(t), y(t)) = ([c_1\alpha_1 + c_2(\alpha_2 + \alpha_3 t)]e^{\lambda t}, [c_1\beta_1 + c_2(\beta_2 + \beta_3 t)]e^{\lambda t}). \quad \textbf{(6)}$$

Then

$$\frac{y}{x} = \frac{c_1\beta_1 + c_2\beta_2 + c_2\beta_3 t}{c_1\alpha_1 + c_2\alpha_2 + c_2\alpha_3 t} = \frac{c_1\beta_1/t + c_2\beta_2/t + c_2\beta_3}{c_1\alpha_1/t + c_2\alpha_2/t + c_2\alpha_3},$$

which approaches β_3/α_3 as t tends to $\pm\infty$. Since both $x(t)$ and $y(t)$ approach zero as t tends to ∞, the zero solution is asymptotically stable. Also all orbits are asymptotic to the line $y = (\beta_3/\alpha_3)x$ as t tends to $\pm\infty$, as illustrated in Fig. 11.

CASE 3(b). $\lambda > 0$. The orbits are the same but with the arrows reversed, since now all solutions approach ∞ as t tends to ∞. (See Figs. 12 and 13.) In these two cases the origin is unstable. Cases 3(a) and 3(b) provide another situation in which nodes arise.

CASE 4 λ_1 *and* λ_2 *are complex conjugates but not pure imaginary.* Then $\lambda_1 = a + ib$ and $\lambda_2 = a - ib$ where neither a nor b is zero.

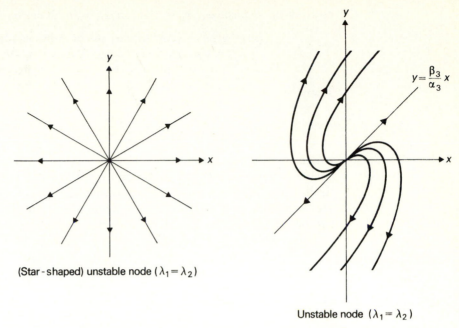

(Star - shaped) unstable node ($\lambda_1 = \lambda_2$)

Figure 12   **Figure 13**

Unstable node ($\lambda_1 = \lambda_2$)

CASE 4(a). $a < 0$. According to Theorem 3 of Section 3.12, all solutions have the form

$$\{x(t), y(t)\} = \{e^{at}[c_1(A_1 \cos bt - A_2 \sin bt) + c_2(A_1 \sin bt + A_2 \cos bt)], \\ e^{at}[c_1(B_1 \cos bt - B_2 \sin bt) + c_2(B_1 \sin bt + B_2 \cos bt)]\}. \tag{7}$$

To simplify the notation, we define

$$k_1 = c_1A_1 + c_2A_2, \quad k_2 = -c_1A_2 + c_2A_1,$$
$$k_3 = c_1B_1 + c_2B_2, \quad k_4 = -c_1B_2 + c_2B_1,$$

so that Eq. (7) becomes

$$\{x(t), y(t)\} = \{e^{at}(k_1 \cos bt + k_2 \sin bt), e^{at}(k_3 \cos bt + k_4 \sin bt)\}. \tag{8}$$

We now define $A = \sqrt{k_1^2 + k_2^2}$ and $B = \sqrt{k_3^2 + k_4^2}$. Then we define α_1 and α_2 by

$$\cos \alpha_1 = \frac{k_1}{A}, \qquad \cos \alpha_2 = \frac{k_3}{B},$$

$$\sin \alpha_1 = -\frac{k_2}{A}, \quad \sin \alpha_2 = -\frac{k_4}{B}, \tag{9}$$

so that $k_1 = A \cos \alpha_1$, $k_2 = -A \sin \alpha_1$, $k_3 = B \cos \alpha_2$, $k_4 = -B \sin \alpha_4$, and

$$\{x(t), y(t)\} = \{Ae^{at}(\cos \alpha_1 \cos bt - \sin \alpha_1 \sin bt),$$
$$Be^{at}(\cos \alpha_2 \cos bt - \sin \alpha_2 \sin bt)\}$$
$$= \{Ae^{at} \cos (bt + \alpha_1), Be^{at} \cos (bt + \alpha_2)\}. \qquad (10)$$

Then

$$\frac{y}{x} = \frac{B \cos (bt + \alpha_1)}{A \cos (bt + \alpha_2)},$$

which is defined whenever $\cos (bt + \alpha_2) \neq 0$. Since this expression is periodic, it is clear that as t tends to ∞, the ratio y/x does not approach a limit, but the orbits must circle around the origin. Since $a < 0$, $x(t)$ and $y(t)$ approach zero as t tends to ∞. Hence the orbits must spiral in toward the origin. The zero solution is asymptotically stable, and the origin is called a *stable focus* (or *spiral point*). See Fig. 14.

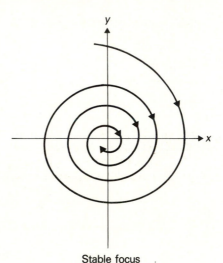

Figure 14

Stable focus

CASE 4(b). $a > 0$. Here the analysis is as before except that all solutions approach ∞ as t tends to ∞. See Fig. 15.

CASE 5 λ_1 *and* λ_2 *are pure imaginary.* Then $\lambda_1 = ib$ and $\lambda_2 = -ib$, and we can use the same analysis as above with $a = 0$: We have

$$\{x(t), y(t)\} = \{A \cos (bt + \alpha_1), B \cos (bt + \alpha_2)\}. \qquad (11)$$

Clearly $x(t)$ and $y(t)$ are periodic with period $2\pi/b$ so that every orbit beginning at the point (x^*, y^*) when $t = t^*$ will return to the *same point* when $t = t^* + 2\pi/b$. Thus the orbits are closed curves. To get a feeling for the nature of these curves, we set $k_2 = k_3 = 0$ in Eq. (8) so that

$$x(t) = k_1 \cos bt \quad \text{and} \quad y(t) = k_4 \sin bt.$$

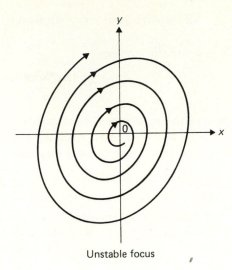

Unstable focus

Figure 15

Then

$$\frac{x^2}{k_1^2} + \frac{y^2}{k_4^2} = \cos^2 bt + \sin^2 bt = 1,$$

which is the equation of an ellipse centered about $(0, 0)$ with the x-axis as its axis of symmetry. If k_2 and k_3 are nonzero, then we obtain ellipses that have a rotated axis of symmetry. In this situation the zero solution is stable but not asymptotically stable, since solutions do not approach zero. Then the origin is called a *center*, which is illustrated in Fig. 16.

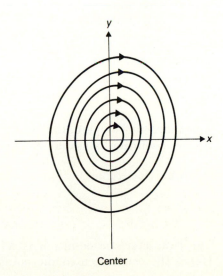

Center

Figure 16

The entire preceding analysis is summarized in the theorem below.

Theorem 1   Consider the system

$$x' = a_{11}x + a_{12}y,$$
$$y' = a_{21}x + a_{22}y,$$

where the a_{ij} are real constants and $a_{11}a_{22} - a_{12}a_{21} \neq 0$ so that the origin $(0, 0)$ is the only critical point (see Exercise 11). Let λ_1 and λ_2 be the two roots of the characteristic equation (3). Then

a) the origin is stable if λ_1 and λ_2 are pure imaginary,

b) the origin is asymptotically stable if $\text{Re } \lambda_1 < 0$ and $\text{Re } \lambda_2 < 0$,

c) the origin is unstable in all other cases. Moreover, the behavior of the orbits near the origin is as indicated in Table 1.

Table 1

λ_1, λ_2	Type of critical point
real, distinct, negative	stable node
real, distinct, positive	unstable node
real, distinct, opposite signs	saddle point (unstable)
real, equal, negative	stable node
real, equal, positive	unstable node
complex conjugate, not pure imaginary, negative real parts	stable focus
complex conjugate, not pure imaginary, positive real parts	unstable focus
pure imaginary	center (stable)

Example 6   Consider the system

$$x' = x - 3y,$$
$$y' = x - y.$$

The characteristic equation is $\lambda^2 + 2 = 0$ with the roots $\pm\sqrt{2}i$. Therefore, the zero solution is stable and the origin is a center.

Example 7   Consider the system

$$x' = 4x - y,$$
$$y' = 6x - 3y.$$

The characteristic equation is $\lambda^2 - \lambda - 6 = 0$ with the roots 3 and -2. Hence the origin is a saddle point and the zero solution is unstable.

Example 8　Consider the system

$$x' = -4x - y,$$
$$y' = x - 2y.$$

The characteristic equation is $\lambda^2 + 6\lambda + 9 = 0$ with the double root $\lambda = -3$. Hence the origin is a stable node and the zero solution is asymptotically stable.

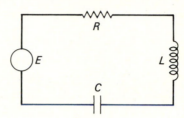

Figure 17

Example 9　Consider the RLC circuit shown in Fig. 17. If $E = 0$, then from Section 3.9 we obtain the differential equation

$$\frac{d^2I}{dt^2} + \frac{R}{L}\frac{dI}{dt} + \frac{I}{CL} = 0 \tag{12}$$

for the description of this circuit. Writing the equation as a system, we obtain

$$I' = y,$$
$$y' = -\frac{1}{CL}I - \frac{R}{L}y.$$

The characteristic equation is

$$\lambda^2 + \frac{R}{L}\lambda + \frac{1}{CL} = 0$$

with the roots

$$\lambda_1 = \frac{-R + \sqrt{R^2 - 4L/C}}{2L} \quad \text{and} \quad \lambda_2 = \frac{-R - \sqrt{R^2 - 4L/C}}{2L}. \tag{13}$$

There are three cases to consider, according to whether $R^2 - 4L/C$ is greater than zero, less than zero, or equal to zero.

1. If $R^2 - 4L/C > 0$, then λ_1 and λ_2 are real, distinct, and negative, so that the origin is a stable node.
2. If $R^2 - 4L/C = 0$, then $\lambda_1 = \lambda_2 = -R/2L$, so that the zero solution is again a stable node.
3. If $R^2 - 4L/C < 0$, then λ_1 and λ_2 are complex conjugates with negative real parts, so that the origin is a stable focus.

In all three cases the critical point $(0, 0)$ is asymptotically stable, and the transient current tends to zero as $t \to \infty$. Of course, the emf E is generally nonzero, but it affects only the steady state current. By superposition, the current $I(t)$ is the sum of the steady state and transient currents.

EXERCISES 9.2

In Exercises 1 through 8, describe the nature of the critical point $(0, 0)$ of each system and sketch the orbits.

1. $x' = 4x - 3y$,
   $y' = 5x - 4y$

2. $x' = -2x + 3y$,
   $y' = x - 3y$

3. $x' = -x + y$,
   $y' = -5x + 3y$

4. $x' = x + y$,
   $y' = -x - 3y$

5. $x' = -4x - 2y$,
   $y' = 5x + 2y$

6. $x' = 4x - 3y$,
   $y' = 8x + 5y$

7. $x' = 2x + y$,
   $y' = -4x + 2y$

8. $x' = 2x$,
   $y' = 2y$

9. Consider the system

$$x' = a_{11}x + a_{12}y,$$
$$y' = a_{21}x + a_{22}y.$$

Let $T = a_{11} + a_{22}$, $D = a_{11}a_{22} - a_{12}a_{21}$, and $C = T^2 - 4D$. Show that the origin is:

a) a node if $D > 0$ and $C \geqslant 0$;

b) a saddle point if $D < 0$;

c) a focus if $T \neq 0$ and $C < 0$;

d) a center if $T = 0$ and $D > 0$.

10. Show that the zero solution in Exercise 9 is:

a) asymptotically stable if $D > 0$ and $T < 0$;

b) stable if $T = 0$ and $D > 0$;

c) unstable if $T > 0$ or $D < 0$.

11. Show that $(0, 0)$ is the only critical point of the system (2) if and only if $\lambda = 0$ is *not* a root of the characteristic equation (3). [Hint: See Appendix 4.]

12. Let $L = 2$ henries, $R = 50$ ohms, and $C = 0.0003$ farad. Locate graphically the position on the orbit of Eq. (12) at $t = 1$ if $I(0) = 0$, and $I'(0)$ is one of the values 10, 100, and 1000.

13. Let $L = 0.44$ henry, $R = 1200$ ohms, and $C = 10^{-6}$ farad. Locate graphically the position of the solution on the orbit at $t = 1$ if $I(0) = 0$, and $I'(0)$ is one of the values 10, 100, and 1000.

14. Consider the mass-spring system which is damped so that Eq. (6) of Section 3.8 holds. That is,

$$x'' + \frac{\mu}{m}x' + \frac{\lambda}{m}x = 0.$$

Following the analysis of Example 9, describe the behavior of the orbits near the origin for different positive values of m, λ, and μ.

15. Consider the system

$$x' = 0,$$
$$y' = -x + y.$$

a) Solve the system.

b) Show that $\lambda_1 = 0$ and $\lambda_2 = 1$ are the roots of the characteristic equation (3).

c) Find all the critical points of the system.

d) Show that all the orbits are straight lines.

e) Show that the origin is an unstable equilibrium point.

16. Consider the system

$$x' = 0,$$
$$y' = -x - y.$$

a) Solve the system.

b) Show that the roots of Eq. (3) for this system are $\lambda_1 = 0$ and $\lambda_2 = -1$.

c) Graph the orbits.

d) Show that the zero solution is stable but *not* asymptotically stable.

9.3 STABILITY OF NONLINEAR SYSTEMS

In this section we shall discuss the stability properties of the autonomous nonlinear system

$$x' = f(x, y),$$
$$y' = g(x, y), \tag{1}$$

where $f(0, 0) = g(0, 0) = 0$ so that the origin is a critical point. We assume that $f(x, y)$ and $g(x, y)$ possess continuous third partial derivatives so that they can each be expanded in a Taylor series:

$$f(x, y) = f(0, 0) + \frac{\partial f}{\partial x}(0, 0)x + \frac{\partial f}{\partial y}(0, 0)y + \frac{\partial^2 f}{\partial x^2}(0, 0)\frac{x^2}{2}$$

$$+ \frac{\partial^2 f}{\partial x \, \partial y}(0, 0)xy + \frac{\partial^2 f}{\partial y^2}(0, 0)\frac{y^2}{2} + \cdots,$$

$$g(x, y) = g(0, 0) + \frac{\partial g}{\partial x}(0, 0)x + \frac{\partial g}{\partial y}(0, 0)y + \frac{\partial^2 g}{\partial x^2}(0, 0)\frac{x^2}{2}$$

$$+ \frac{\partial^2 g}{\partial x \, \partial y}(0, 0)xy + \frac{\partial^2 g}{\partial y^2}(0, 0)\frac{y^2}{2} + \cdots, \tag{2}$$

where the omitted terms all involve higher powers of x and y. Now we define

$$a_{11} = \frac{\partial f}{\partial x}(0, 0), \quad a_{12} = \frac{\partial f}{\partial y}(0, 0), \quad a_{21} = \frac{\partial g}{\partial x}(0, 0), \quad a_{22} = \frac{\partial g}{\partial y}(0, 0).$$

and assume that

$$a_{11}a_{22} - a_{12}a_{21} \neq 0 \tag{3}$$

(see Exercise 11 of Section 9.2). Then using the fact that $f(0, 0) = g(0, 0) = 0$, we can write $f(x, y)$ and $g(x, y)$ as

$$f(x, y) = a_{11}x + a_{12}y + f_1(x, y),$$
$$g(x, y) = a_{21}x + a_{22}y + g_1(x, y),$$

where

$$\lim_{x,y \to 0} \frac{f_1(x, y)}{\sqrt{x^2 + y^2}} = \lim_{x,y \to 0} \frac{g_1(x, y)}{\sqrt{x^2 + y^2}} = 0. \tag{4}$$

The last property simply says that the point $(f_1(x, y), g_1(x, y))$ approaches the point $(0, 0)$ "faster" than the point (x, y) does. In one dimension, this is easily visualized by noting, for example, that the function $f_1(x) = x^2$ goes to zero faster than x, or

$$\lim_{x \to 0} \frac{x^2}{x} = 0.$$

We now show that condition (4) holds for the function x^2. Once this has been done, it will be clear that the condition holds for xy, y^2, and higher powers of x and y (such as x^3, x^2y, xy^2, and y^3, etc.). Now,

$$\lim_{x,y \to 0} \frac{x^2}{\sqrt{x^2 + y^2}} = \lim_{x,y \to 0} \frac{x}{\sqrt{1 + y^2/x^2}}$$

(obtained by dividing the numerator and denominator by x). We may let x and y tend to zero in a variety of ways. For convenience, we let $y = x$ as they both tend to zero. Then $y^2/x^2 = 1$ and

$$\lim_{x,y \to 0} \frac{x}{\sqrt{1 + y^2/x^2}} = \lim_{x,y \to 0} \frac{x}{\sqrt{2}} = 0.$$

Note that condition (3) will be satisfied if the determinant

$$\begin{vmatrix} \partial f/\partial x & \partial f/\partial y \\ \partial g/\partial x & \partial g/\partial y \end{vmatrix}$$

is nonzero at $(0, 0)$.

Example 1 The system

$$x' = 2x + 3y + x^3,$$
$$y' = x - 2y - y^{3/2}$$

satisfies the conditions (3) and (4) since (prove this)

$$\lim_{x,y \to 0} \frac{x^3}{\sqrt{x^2 + y^2}} = \lim_{x,y \to 0} \frac{y^{3/2}}{\sqrt{x^2 + y^2}} = 0.$$

In the rest of this section we shall consider the system

$$x' = a_{11}x + a_{12}y + f_1(x, y),$$
$$y' = a_{21}x + a_{22}y + g_1(x, y),$$
(5)

where Eqs. (3) and (4) are satisfied, and the *associated linear system*

$$x' = a_{11}x + a_{12}y,$$
$$y' = a_{21}x + a_{22}y.$$
(6)

The following theorem enables us to determine the nature of the unique critical point $(0, 0)$ of Eq. (5) by indicating the behavior of the solutions of the linear system (6) near the origin. The proof of this theorem is difficult and beyond the scope of this text.†

Theorem 1   Let λ_1 and λ_2 be the roots of the characteristic equation of the linear system (6).

   i) The nonlinear system (5) has the same type of critical point at the origin as the linear system (6) whenever:

     (a) $\lambda_1 \neq \lambda_2$ and $(0, 0)$ is a node of the system (6),

     (b) $\lambda_1 = \lambda_2$ and $(0, 0)$ is not a star-shaped node of the system (6),

     (c) $(0, 0)$ is a saddle point of the system (6),

     (d) $(0, 0)$ is a focus of the system (6).

   ii) The origin is not necessarily the same type of critical point for the two systems:

     (e) If $\lambda_1 = \lambda_2$ and $(0, 0)$ is a star-shaped node of the system (6), then $(0, 0)$ is either a node or a focus of the system (5).

     (f) If $(0, 0)$ is a center of the system (6), then $(0, 0)$ is either a center or a focus of the system (5).

The next theorem relates the stability of the nonlinear system to that of the associated linear system. As before, the proof is omitted. The proof of part (i), however, is suggested in Exercise 11 of Section 9.4.

Theorem 2   i) If the zero solution of the system (6) is asymptotically stable, then the zero solution of the system (5) is asymptotically stable.

   ii) If the zero solution of the system (6) is unstable, then the zero solution of the system (5) is unstable.

   iii) If the zero solution of the system (6) is stable but not asymptotically stable, then the zero solution of the system (5) may be asymptotically stable, stable, or unstable.

Remark   Part (ii) of this theorem holds even when Eq. (3) is not satisfied. We shall use this fact in Example 3.

Theorems 1 and 2 are often called *perturbation* theorems, because we may consider the nonlinear system (5) as a small perturbation of the linear system (6) *near the origin*.

Example 2   In Example 5 in Section 1.1, we discussed the Lotka-Volterra equations as a model for the interaction of two competing species:

$$x' = \beta_1 x - \delta_{11} x^2 - \delta_{12} xy,$$
$$y' = \beta_2 y - \delta_{21} xy - \delta_{22} y^2. \tag{7}$$

---

† For a proof, see J. K. Hale, *Ordinary Differential Equations*. New York: Wiley (1969).

We can think of this system as a perturbation of the associated uncoupled linear system

$$x' = \beta_1 x,$$
$$y' = \beta_2 y. \tag{8}$$

The system (8) has the obvious solution

$$(x(t), y(t)) = (c_1 e^{\beta_1 t}, c_2 e^{\beta_2 t}),$$

and

$$\lim_{x,y \to 0} \frac{x^2}{\sqrt{x^2 + y^2}} = \lim_{x,y \to 0} \frac{xy}{\sqrt{x^2 + y^2}} = \lim_{x,y \to 0} \frac{y^2}{\sqrt{x^2 + y^2}} = 0.$$

Hence Theorems 1 and 2 apply in the following cases:

1. If β_1 and β_2 are negative, then the critical point $(0, 0)$ is asymptotically stable for both systems (7) and (8). In both systems the origin is a stable node. This means that both populations will become extinct, in the absence of other factors, if the initial populations are small [that is, we start near $(0, 0)$]. Thus small initial populations cannot sustain themselves.

2. If β_1 and β_2 have opposite signs, then the origin in both cases is a saddle point, and the zero solution is unstable. This situation implies that one of the populations will become extinct while the other will grow without bound (since the asymptotes of the saddle point are the x- and y-axes).

3. If β_1 and β_2 are unequal and positive, then the origin in both cases is an unstable node. Hence both populations will increase if they start near $(0, 0)$. However, the orbits of (7) need not increase without bound, since as we move away from the origin the orbits may approach other critical points of (7) exhibiting a different type of behavior.

This is not a complete analysis of the system (7), since we can expect different and perhaps more interesting types of behavior near other critical points (see Exercise 16). We shall illustrate a similar situation in the next example.

Example 3   Consider the system

$$x' = -2xy = f(x, y),$$
$$y' = -x + y + xy - y^3 = g(x, y). \tag{9}$$

Setting $-2xy = -x + y + xy - y^3 = 0$, we find the three critical points $(0, 0)$, $(0, 1)$, and $(0, -1)$. We shall treat each of these separately.

1. $(0, 0)$. The associated linear system is

$$x' = 0,$$
$$y' = -x + y. \tag{10}$$

The characteristic equation for (10) is

$$\lambda^2 - \lambda = 0,$$

with the roots $\lambda_1 = 0$, $\lambda_2 = 1$. Hence the origin of (10) is unstable (see Exercise 15 of Section 9.2), and therefore the zero solution of (9) is unstable by the remark following Theorem 2.

   2. $(0, 1)$. To obtain the associated linear system, we need to use Taylor's theorem to expand the right-hand sides of (9) around the point $(0, 1)$. Then

$$-2xy = f(0, 1) + \left.\frac{\partial f}{\partial x}\right|_{(0, 1)} (x - 0) + \left.\frac{\partial f}{\partial y}\right|_{(0, 1)} (y - 1) + \cdots$$

$$= -2x + \cdots [= -2x - 2x(y - 1)]$$

and

$$-x + y + xy - y^3 = g(0, 1) + \left.\frac{\partial g}{\partial x}\right|_{(0, 1)} (x - 0) + \left.\frac{\partial g}{\partial y}\right|_{(0, 1)} (y - 1) + \cdots$$

$$= -2(y - 1) + \cdots$$

$$[= -2(y - 1) + x(y - 1) - 6(y - 1)^2 - 6(y - 1)^3].$$

Selecting only the first-degree terms of these expansions, we obtain the associated linear system

$$\begin{aligned} x' &= -2x, \\ y' &= -2(y - 1), \end{aligned} \tag{11}$$

Here we treat the "new" phase plane variables as x and $z = y - 1$. Then the roots of the characteristic equation of (11) are $\lambda_1 = \lambda_2 = -2$, which means that the point $(0, 1)$ is a stable star-shaped node and the critical point $(0, 1)$ is an asymptotically stable solution of (9). By Theorem 1(e), the point $(0, 1)$ is either a stable node or a stable focus of (9).

   3. $(0, -1)$. Expanding $f(x, y)$ and $g(x, y)$ around $(0, -1)$, we obtain

$$-2xy = f(0, -1) + \left.\frac{\partial f}{\partial x}\right|_{(0, -1)} (x - 0) + \left.\frac{\partial f}{\partial y}\right|_{(0, -1)} (y + 1) + \cdots$$

$$= 2x + \cdots [= 2x - 2x(y + 1)]$$

and

$$-x + y + xy - y^3 = g(0, -1) + \left.\frac{\partial g}{\partial x}\right|_{(0, -1)} (x - 0) + \left.\frac{\partial g}{\partial y}\right|_{(0, -1)} (y + 1) + \cdots$$

$$= -2x + \cdots$$

$$[= -2x - 2(y + 1) + x(y + 1) + 6(y + 1)^2 - 6(y - 1)^3].$$

so that the associated linear system around the point $(0, -1)$ is

$$\begin{aligned} x' &= 2x, \\ y' &= -2x - 2(y + 1). \end{aligned} \tag{12}$$

Letting $z = y + 1$, we find the roots of the characteristic equation for the system

$$x' = 2x,$$
$$z' = -2x - 2z$$

to be $\lambda_1 = 2$, $\lambda_2 = -2$, so that the solution $(0, -1)$ is a saddle point (unstable) of (9). This situation is illustrated in Fig. 18, where the critical point $(0, 1)$ is shown as a node, although the theory only asserts that it is a node or a focus.

Figure 18

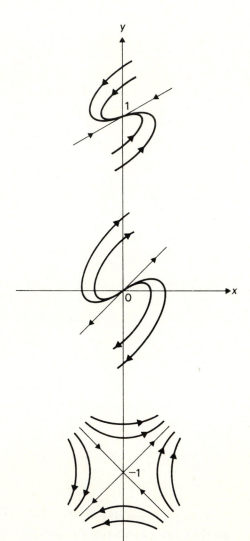

Example 4   In Example 2 of Section 9.1 we discussed the equation of motion of a frictionless pendulum given by

$$\theta'' + \omega^2 \sin\theta = 0.$$

Defining $\mu = \theta'$, we have the system

$$\begin{aligned} \theta' &= \mu, \\ \mu' &= -\omega^2 \sin\theta. \end{aligned} \tag{13}$$

This system has an infinite number of critical points of the form $(k\pi, 0)$, $k = \pm 1, \pm 2, \pm 3, \ldots$. The associated linear system near the critical point $(0, 0)$ is

$$\begin{aligned} \theta' &= \mu, \\ \mu' &= -\omega^2 \theta, \end{aligned} \tag{14}$$

since the Taylor series of $\sin\theta$ is

$$\sin\theta = \theta - \frac{\theta^3}{3!} + \frac{\theta^5}{5!} - \cdots .$$

This is the system of the familiar harmonic oscillator. The origin of (14) is a center, so that we cannot conclude anything about the stability of the origin of (13). The results are more definitive for the critical point $(\pi, 0)$. Expanding $\sin\theta$ around $\theta = \pi$, we have

$$\sin\theta = \sin\pi + (\sin\theta)'|_{\theta=\pi}(\theta - \pi) + \cdots$$

$$= (\pi - \theta) - \frac{1}{3!}(\pi - \theta)^3 + \frac{1}{5!}(\pi - \theta)^5 - \cdots .$$

Thus the associated linear system is

$$\begin{aligned} \theta' &= \mu, \\ \mu' &= \omega^2(\theta - \pi). \end{aligned} \tag{15}$$

Letting $z = \theta - \pi$, the roots of the characteristic equation $\lambda^2 - \omega^2 = 0$ are $\lambda_1 = \omega$, $\lambda_2 = -\omega$, so that $(\pi, 0)$ is a saddle point. Hence we may conclude that the critical point $(\pi, 0)$ of the system (13) is an unstable saddle point. Figure 1 illustrates intuitively what is happening. When $\theta = \pi$ the pendulum is pointing vertically upward, which is a position at which the potential energy is at a maximum and the kinetic energy is zero. Clearly such a position is unstable, and a small displacement will cause large deviations from the initial position. On the other hand, it is just as clear that $\theta = 0$ (the vertically downward position) is a stable center. An initial displacement of θ_0 of a frictionless pendulum will lead to periodic oscillations with a maximum displacement of θ_0. It is evident that all critical points of the form $(k\pi, 0)$ will be of the same type as $(0, 0)$ if k is even and of the type $(\pi, 0)$ if k is odd. Before drawing the orbits, we can show that the zero solution of (13) really is a center. By Theorem 1 it must be a center or a focus. But the system is *conservative* (there is no loss or gain of energy), whereas a stable focus would imply that the energy was decreasing to zero and an unstable focus would imply an increase in the total energy. Hence, a focus is ruled out, and the origin must be a center. This is all illustrated in Fig. 19.

Figure 19

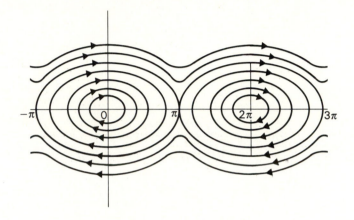

Example 5 We shall consider the pendulum of the previous example, this time including the effect of friction. We assume that the frictional force is proportional to the angular velocity θ'. Denoting this constant of proportionality by $\varepsilon > 0$, we obtain the equation

$$\theta'' + \varepsilon\theta' + \omega^2 \sin \theta = 0$$

or, equivalently,

$$\theta' = \mu,$$
$$\mu' = -\omega^2 \sin \theta - \varepsilon\mu. \tag{16}$$

Again the origin is a critical point. However, in this case it is clear from physical considerations that the origin is asymptotically stable, since the friction will cause initial deviations from the vertical to damp out. We can prove this easily by considering the zero solution of the associated linear system

$$\theta' = \mu,$$
$$\mu' = -\omega^2\theta - \varepsilon\mu. \tag{17}$$

The characteristic equation is $\lambda^2 + \varepsilon\lambda + \omega^2 = 0$ with the roots

$$\lambda_1 = \frac{-\varepsilon + \sqrt{\varepsilon^2 - 4\omega^2}}{2} \quad \text{and} \quad \lambda_2 = \frac{-\varepsilon - \sqrt{\varepsilon^2 - 4\omega^2}}{2}.$$

Hence the origin of (17) is a stable node (if $\varepsilon > 2\omega$), a star-shaped node (if $\varepsilon = 2\omega$), or a stable focus (if $\varepsilon < 2\omega$). In all cases, by **Theorem 2**, the origin of the system (16) is asymptotically stable. The last case is the most interesting. The "focal behavior" near the origin implies that the pendulum will continue to oscillate, but with constantly decreasing amplitudes and constantly increasing frequency.

Example 6   Consider the *RLC* circuit of **Example 9** in Section 9.2. **Equation** (12) is an idealized description of the circuit, since there may very well be nonlinear terms present (such as induced currents from other sources). To take this factor into account, we have the equation

$$I'' + \frac{R}{L}I' + \frac{1}{CL}I + f(I, I') = 0, \tag{18}$$

where $f(x, y)$ is a nonlinear function such that

$$f(0, 0) = \left.\frac{\partial f}{\partial x}\right|_{(0,0)} = \left.\frac{\partial f}{\partial y}\right|_{(0,0)} = 0.$$

Equation (18) can be written in the form

$$I' = y,$$
$$y' = -\frac{1}{CL}I - \frac{R}{L}y - f(I, y).$$

The associated linear system is

$$I' = y,$$
$$y' = -\frac{1}{CL}I - \frac{R}{L}y. \tag{19}$$

But as we showed in **Example 9** in Section 9.2, the zero solution of (19) is asymptotically stable, and so by **Theorem 2**, the zero solution of (18) is also asymptotically stable. Therefore, in analyzing the circuit, we may safely ignore the nonlinear terms for small initial values of I and I'.

EXERCISES 9.3

In Exercises 1 through 6, verify that in each case $(0, 0)$ is a critical point and determine the asymptotic behavior of solutions near that point.

1. $x' = 3\sin x + e^y - 1,$
$y' = xy - y$

2. $x' = \ln(1 + y) + \cosh x - 1,$
$y' = \tan y + 2x$

3. $x' = 1 - y - e^{-x},$
$y' = y - \sin x$

4. $x' = 2\cos y - \frac{1}{2}y + e^x - 3 - \sin 2x,$
$y' = 2\tan x - y$

5. $x' = (\sin x)(\cos x) + y^2,$
$y' = y^2 - x - x^3 + 3y$

6. $x' = -y + \varepsilon x(1 - y^2), \quad \varepsilon > 0,$
$y' = x$

In Exercises 7 through 13, determine the critical points of each nonlinear equation; find the associated linear system for each of these critical points; determine, if possible, the nature of each critical point and its stability properties; and sketch the orbits near each such point.

7. $x' = x + x^3,$
$y' = y + y^3$

8. $x' = -\sin x + x^2,$
$y' = \sin y$

9. $x' = x - x^2 + xy,$
$y' = 2y - xy - 6y^2$

10. $x' = -e^y + 1,$
$y' = e^x - 1$

11. $x' = -xy^2 + y^2 - 7xy - x^2 - 6x,$
$y' = x^2 + y$

12. $x' = 1 - xy,$
$y' = x - y^3$

13. $x' = 2y,$
$y' = -2x - y + y^4$

14. a) Convert the equation

$$x'' + ax' + bx + x^2 = 0, \quad a, b > 0,$$

into a system.

b) Show that the origin is a stable focus and the point $(0, -b)$ is a saddle point.

c) Conclude that the orbits have the form shown in Fig. 20.

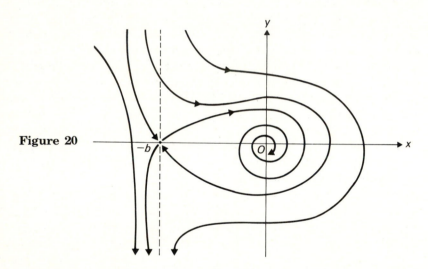

Figure 20

15. The *Van der Pol equation*

$$x'' + \varepsilon(x^2 - 1)x' + x = 0 \qquad \textbf{(20)}$$

arises in the study of a vacuum tube with three internal elements (triode). Show that if $\varepsilon < 0$, then the origin is asymptotically stable. [It can also be shown that if $\varepsilon > 0$, then Eq. (20) has a periodic solution that is approached by all other solutions as t tends to ∞. This phenomenon is called a *limit cycle*.†]

16. Consider the following special case of the Lotka-Volterra equations (7):

$$x' = -x - 2x^2 + xy, \qquad \textbf{(21)}$$
$$y' = -y + 7xy - 2y^2,$$

where x and y are measured in hundreds of organisms.

a) Show that the system (21) has four critical points but that only two of them have any biological meaning (negative populations

---

† See, for example, H. K. Wilson, *Ordinary Differential Equations*. Reading, Mass.: Addison-Wesley (1971).

are not permissible).

b) Show that if both populations are small initially, then both species will become extinct.

c) Show that one biologically meaningful crit-

ical point is a saddle point, indicating that larger initial populations may lead to continued existence without the threat of extinction.

9.4 LYAPUNOV'S METHOD (Optional)

In the preceding section we introduced a method for deriving the stability of nonlinear systems by comparing them with linear ones. This procedure, while often useful, has two obvious drawbacks. First, in the case of a center, no information can be obtained. Second, and much more serious, the method fails to yield information concerning the behavior of nonlinear systems that cannot easily be treated as perturbations of linear systems. Landmark work to resolve these difficulties was done by the Russian mathematician A. A. Lyapunov.† Lyapunov reasoned intuitively as follows: Suppose we have a system of differential equations that arises from a description of a physical system. If a critical point corresponds to a point of minimum potential energy of the system, and if the energy in the system is constant or decreasing, then it is reasonable to "guess" that the critical point will be stable. On the other hand, if the critical point corresponds to a maximum of potential energy, then the point will be unstable.

Example 1   Consider the vibrations of a mass attached to a coiled spring, the upper end of which is securely fastened (see Section 3.8). If we make the natural assumption that damping forces (friction, air resistance, etc.) are present, then the equation of motion is of the form [from Eq. (6) of Section 3.8]

$$x'' + \varepsilon x' + \mu x = 0. \tag{1}$$

For simplicity, we assume $\mu = 1$ so that the system (1) can be written as

$$\begin{aligned} x' &= y, \\ y' &= -x - \varepsilon y. \end{aligned} \tag{2}$$

From the discussion in Section 9.3 it is obvious that the origin of this system is asymptotically stable. We shall use this simple problem to motivate the subsequent discussion.

Physically the potential energy of the system is proportional to the square of x, the distance from the mass to the origin, whereas the kinetic

---

† Lyapunov's original paper on this subject appeared in 1892. His work was essentially unknown until a French translation appeared in 1907 under the title "Problème général de la stabilité du mouvement."

energy is proportional to the square of the velocity x'. This is so because potential energy is usually given as an integral of position. Here the position is represented by x, so that the potential energy is proportional to $\int x\,dx = x^2/2$. Kinetic energy is given by the formula

$$KE = mv^2 = m\left(\frac{dx}{dt}\right)^2 = my^2.$$

Thus the function $V(x, y)$, defined by

$$V(x, y) = \tfrac{1}{2}(x^2 + y^2), \tag{3}$$

where $y = x'$, is representative of the total energy of the system. Now, at the origin potential energy is a minimum, so that the origin can be expected to be stable. The function $V(x, y)$ defined in Eq. (3) will be used shortly to prove that the origin is indeed stable.

We can generalize these remarks. Let us consider the autonomous system

$$\begin{aligned} x' &= f(x, y), \\ y' &= g(x, y), \end{aligned} \tag{4}$$

where we assume that the origin is a critical point. Let $V(x, y)$ be a continuous real-valued function on the xy-plane with continuous first partial derivatives. Let D be a region containing the origin and suppose that $V(0, 0) = 0$ and $V(x, y) > 0$ for all other points (x, y) in D. Then $V(x, y)$ is said to be *positive definite* in D. If $V(0, 0) = 0$ and $V(x, y) < 0$ for all other points (x, y) in D, we say that $V(x, y)$ is *negative definite* in D. If $V(x, y) \geqslant 0$ [or $V(x, y) \leqslant 0$], then the function is said to be *positive semidefinite* [or *negative semidefinite*] in D. If $V(x, y)$ satisfies none of these conditions, then V is said to be *indefinite* in D.

Example 2   a) The function $V(x, y)$ given in (3) is positive definite for all real values of x and y, since $x^2 + y^2$ is the square of the distance from (x, y) to the origin.

b) The function $-(x^2 + y^2)$ is negative definite.

c) The function $V(x, y) = x^2$ is positive semidefinite, since $V(0, a) = 0$ for any real value of a.

d) The function $V(x, y) = -y^2$ is negative semidefinite.

e) The function $V(x, y) = xy$ is indefinite, since $V(a, a) = a^2 > 0$ and $V(a, -a) = -a^2 < 0$ for all numbers $a > 0$.

Often the total energy of a system is a polynomial in x and y, in which case the following theorem is useful.

Theorem 1   The function

$$V(x, y) = x^2 + axy + by^2$$

is (a) positive definite if and only if $4b - a^2 > 0$; (b) positive semidefinite if and only if $4b - a^2 \geqslant 0$.

Proof   If $4b - a^2 > 0$, then completing the squares, we find that

$$x^2 + axy + by^2 = \left(x + \frac{a}{2}y\right)^2 + \left(b - \frac{a^2}{4}\right)y^2. \tag{5}$$

If $y \neq 0$, then $[b - (a^2/4)]y^2 > 0$ by assumption and $V(x, y)$ is positive definite. On the other hand, suppose that $[b - (a^2/4)] \leq 0$. Then choosing any nonzero y and $x = -(a/2)y$, we find the expression (5) to be less than or equal to zero, which is a contradiction, since V is positive definite. Thus $4b - a^2 > 0$, and the first part of the theorem is proved. The second part follows in the same way. ∎

Note that $V(x, y)$ is negative definite if and only if $-V(x, y)$ is positive definite, so that Theorem 1 is also a theorem about negative definiteness (and semidefiniteness).

Example 3   a) The function $x^2 - xy + 2y^2$ is positive definite, since $4b - a^2 = 7 > 0$.

b) The function $V(x, y) = -x^2 + 4xy - 4y^2$ is negative semidefinite, since $-V(x, y) = x^2 - 4xy + 4y^2$, $4b - a^2 = 0$, and $-V$ is positive semidefinite.

c) The function $x^2 + 4xy - 4y^2$ is indefinite, since neither V nor $-V$ belongs to any of the other four categories.

Now let $V(x, y)$ be a continuously differentiable, positive definite function. We define the *derivative of V along the orbits of the system* (4) by

$$V'(x, y) = \frac{\partial V}{\partial x}x' + \frac{\partial V}{\partial y}y' = \frac{\partial V}{\partial x}f(x, y) + \frac{\partial V}{\partial y}g(x, y). \tag{6}$$

When this association between $V(x, y)$ and the system (4) holds, $V(x, y)$ is called a *Lyapunov function* for the system. We emphasize that in order for it to be a Lyapunov function for the system (4), $V(x, y)$ must be continuously differentiable and positive definite, and have its derivative along the orbits defined by Eq. (6). We should also emphasize that $V(x, y)$ is a Lyapunov function for (4) only when $V'(x, y)$ is defined with respect to (4) according to (6). There will always be many choices for a Lyapunov function. Often, however, most of these functions will not be useful. The great importance of defining the derivative of V along the orbits of (4) is given in the next theorem.

Theorem 2   Let $V(x, y)$ be a Lyapunov function for the system (4). Then:

> i) if $V'(x, y)$ is negative semidefinite, the origin is stable;
> ii) if $V'(x, y)$ is negative definite, the origin is asymptotically stable;
> iii) if $V'(x, y)$ is positive definite, the origin is unstable.

Proof†   i) Let $\varepsilon > 0$ be given. We must show that there is a $\delta > 0$ such that if (x_0, y_0) is in D and $\sqrt{x_0^2 + y_0^2} < \delta$, then the solution pair $(x(t, x_0, y_0), y(t, x_0, y_0))$ (see Section 9.2) satisfies the inequality

$$\sqrt{[x(t, x_0, y_0)]^2 + [y(t, x_0, y_0)]^2} < \varepsilon$$

for all $t \geqslant 0$. We define

$$m = \min_{\sqrt{x^2 + y^2} = \varepsilon} V(x, y).$$

This minimum exists since $V(x, y)$ is continuous on the circle $x^2 + y^2 = \varepsilon^2$. Furthermore, by the continuity of V and the fact that $V(0, 0) = 0$, there exists a $\delta > 0$ such that $V(x, y) < m$ whenever $\sqrt{x_0^2 + y_0^2} < \delta$. (See Fig. 21.) Suppose that there is a number $t^* > 0$ for which $x(t^*, x_0, y_0)^2 + y(t^*, x_0, y_0)^2 = \varepsilon^2$. Since $dV/dt = V'(x, y) \leqslant 0$, we have $V(x(t, x_0, y_0), y(t, x_0, y_0)) \leqslant V(x_0, y_0)$ for all $t \geqslant 0$. Then

$$V(x(t^*, x_0, y_0), y(t^*, x_0, y_0)) \leqslant V(x_0, y_0) < m \leqslant V(x(t^*, x_0, y_0), y(t^*, x_0, y_0)),$$

since m is a minimum on the circle $x^2 + y^2 = \varepsilon^2$. This contradiction establishes (i), since it shows that $x(t, x_0, y_0)^2 + y(t, x_0, y_0)^2 < \varepsilon^2$ for all $t > 0$.

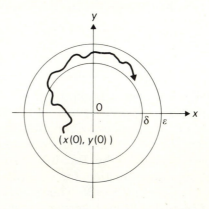

Figure 21

---

† This proof is difficult and may be omitted without loss of continuity.

ii) By hypothesis, $V(x, y)$ decreases as t increases. Since V is positive for all x and y and decreasing along the orbits,

$$\lim_{t \to \infty} V(x(t), y(t)) = \lambda \geqslant 0$$

exists. We must show that $\lambda = 0$ since, then, $(0, 0)$ being the only point for which V is zero, we will necessarily have

$$\lim_{t \to \infty} x(t) = \lim_{t \to \infty} y(t) = 0.$$

Suppose $\lambda > 0$. Then, as before, there is a $\eta > 0$ such that $V(x_0, y_0) < \lambda$ whenever $\sqrt{x_0^2 + y_0^2} < \eta$, meaning that the orbit $(x(t), y(t))$ never enters the circular region described by $x^2 + y^2 < \eta^2$. Let ε be as in part (i) and let

$$m_1 = \min_{\eta \leqslant \sqrt{x^2+y^2} \leqslant \varepsilon} - V'(x, y).$$

Since $\eta > 0$ and V' is negative definite, we have $m_1 > 0$. Then, since $m_1 \leqslant -V'(x, y)$, we have $V'(x(t), y(t)) \leqslant -m_1$ for all $t \geqslant 0$. Therefore, we obtain upon integration

$$\int_0^t V'(x(s), y(s)) \, ds \leqslant \int_0^t - m_1 \, ds$$

or

$$V(x(t), y(t)) - V(x_0, y_0) \leqslant -m_1 t$$

or

$$V(x(t), y(t)) \leqslant V(x_0, y_0) - m_1 t.$$

But the right-hand side of the last inequality becomes negative when t approaches ∞, thereby contradicting the positive definiteness of V unless $m_1 = 0$. But $m_1 = 0$ if and only if $\eta = 0$, which holds if and only if $\lambda = 0$. Therefore, (ii) is proved.

iii) The proof of part (iii) is similar and therefore left as an exercise (see **Exercise 6**). ∎

The rest of this section indicates the wide range of applicability of Theorem 2.

Example 4 In Example 1, the function $V(x, y) = \frac{1}{2}(x^2 + y^2)$ is a Lyapunov function. In addition, by Eq. (2),

$$V'(x, y) = \frac{\partial V}{\partial x} x' + \frac{\partial V}{\partial y} y' = xy + y(-x - \varepsilon y) = -\varepsilon y^2,$$

which is negative semidefinite. Hence Theorem 2 implies that the origin is stable. Observe that Theorem 2 does not provide the best possible result since we know the origin to be asymptotically stable. Stronger results are known and can be found in many advanced differential equations books.†

Example 5   In our example of the movement of a mass attached to a frictionless spring, we assumed that the restoring force was proportional to the distance of the mass to the origin. Generally, we may assume the restoring force to be a nonlinear function $-f(x)$ of the distance to the origin. The equation of motion is then

$$x'' + f(x) = 0. \tag{7}$$

To analyze this equation, we make the assumptions that

$$f(0) = 0 \quad \text{and} \quad xf(x) > 0 \quad \text{for } x \neq 0; \tag{8}$$

that is, $f(x)$ and x have the same sign. Equation (7), together with the conditions (8), is often called the equation of a *nonlinear spring*. We now write Eq. (7) as

$$\begin{aligned} x' &= y, \\ y' &= -f(x). \end{aligned} \tag{9}$$

Clearly the origin is the only critical point of the system. The kinetic energy of this system is proportional to the square of the velocity $x' (= y)$, whereas the potential energy at any point x is given by

$$F(x) = \int_0^x f(x) \, dx.$$

Hence the total energy of the system is

$$V(x, y) = F(x) + \frac{y^2}{2}.$$

Since $f(x)$ and x have the same sign, $F \geq 0$ and $V(x, y)$ is positive definite. Moreover, $V'(x, y)$ is negative semidefinite since

$$V'(x, y) = F'(x)x' + yy' = f(x)y + y(-f(x)) = 0,$$

implying by Theorem 2 that the origin is stable. In this case, as in the linear case $x'' + x = 0$, it can be shown that the origin is a center.

Example 6   Consider the system

$$\begin{aligned} x' &= -x - \frac{x^3}{3} - x \sin y, \\ y' &= -y - \frac{y^3}{3}. \end{aligned} \tag{10}$$

---

† See, for example, J. P. LaSalle and S. Lefshetz, *Stability by Lyapunov's Direct Method.* New York: Academic Press (1961).

Here the origin is the only critical point. We define $V(x, y) = \frac{1}{2}(x^2 + y^2)$. Then

$$V'(x, y) = x\left(-x - \frac{x^3}{3} - x \sin y\right) + y\left(-y - \frac{y^3}{3}\right)$$

$$= -x^2 - \frac{x^4}{3} - y^2 - \frac{y^4}{3} - x^2 \sin y.$$

Now $|x^2 \sin y| \leqslant |x^2|$, so that $x^2 + x^2 \sin y \geqslant 0$. Hence

$$V'(x, y) = -\frac{x^4}{3} - y^2 - \frac{y^4}{3} - (x^2 + x^2 \sin y) \leqslant -\frac{x^4}{3} - y^2 - \frac{y^4}{3}.$$

Therefore, V' is negative definite and the origin is asymptotically stable.

In the last example the Lyapunov function was pulled out of a hat. Actually, the problem of finding a Lyapunov function for a particular system is very difficult, especially if there is no way of estimating the total energy of the system. Although a Lyapunov function cannot be found in every case, it is often worthwhile in the case of a system of two first-order equations to try to find one of the form $V(x, y) = x^2 + axy + by^2$. By Theorem 1, such a Lyapunov function will be positive definite if $4b > a^2$, as illustrated by the next example.

Example 7   Consider the system

$$\begin{aligned} x' &= xy^2 + x^2y + x^3, \\ y' &= y^3 - x^3. \end{aligned} \tag{11}$$

Assume that $V(x, y) = x^2 + axy + by^2$ and $4b > a^2$. Then by Theorem 1, V is positive definite and

$$\begin{aligned} V' &= 2x(xy^2 + x^2y + x^3) + ax(y^3 - x^3) \\ &\quad + ay(xy^2 + x^2y + x^3) + 2by(y^3 - x^3). \end{aligned}$$

If we choose $a = 0$ and $b = 1$, then

$$V' = 2x^2y^2 + 2x^3y + 2x^4 + 2y^4 - 2yx^3 = 2(x^2y^2 + x^4 + y^4),$$

which is positive definite. By Theorem 2, the origin is unstable.

EXERCISES 9.4

1. Show that the zero solution of the system

$$x' = xy^2 - \frac{x^3}{2},$$

$$y' = -\frac{y^3}{2} + \frac{yx^2}{5}$$

is asymptotically stable. [*Hint*: Try a Lyapunov

function of the form $V(x, y) = ax^2 + by^2$.]

2. Show that the zero solution of the following system is stable:

$$\begin{aligned} x' &= -6x^2y, \\ y' &= -3y^3 + 6x^3 \end{aligned}$$

3. Consider the undamped pendulum of Example 2 in Section 9.1:

$$\theta'' + \omega^2 \sin \theta = 0, \quad -\pi/2 \le \theta \le \pi/2.$$

Prove by means of an appropriate Lyapunov function that the origin is stable. (*Hint*: Use the result of Example 5.)

4. Consider the system

$$x' = y - xf(x, y),$$
$$y' = -x - yf(x, y),$$

where $f(0, 0) = 0$ and $f(x, y)$ has a convergent power series expansion in a region D around the origin. Show that the zero solution is:

a) stable if $f(x, y) \ge 0$ in some region around $(0, 0)$;

b) asymptotically stable if $f(x, y)$ is positive definite in some region around $(0, 0)$; and

c) unstable if in every region around $(0, 0)$ there are points (x, y) such that $f(x, y) < 0$.

5. Using the results of Exercise 4, examine the stability properties of the zero solutions of the following systems:

a) $x' = y - x(y^3 \sin^2 x),$
   $y' = -x - y(y^3 \sin^2 x);$

b) $x' = y - x(x^4 + y^6),$
   $y' = -x - y(x^4 + y^6);$

c) $x' = y - x(\sin^2 y),$
   $y' = -x - y(\sin^2 y).$

*6. Prove part (iii) of Theorem 2.

*7. Consider the equation

$$x'' + f(x, x') + g(x) = 0. \tag{12}$$

Assume that f and g possess continuous first derivatives, $f(0, 0) = g(0) = 0$, and that $yf(x, y) > 0$ when $y \ne 0$ and $xg(x) > 0$ for $x \ne 0$. After writing Eq. (12) as a system, prove that the origin is stable.

8. Use the result of Exercise 7 to prove the stability of the solutions of the equation

$$x'' + x'^3 + x^5 = 0.$$

(Note that the associated linear system does us no good here since the zero solution of this system is a center.)

*9. Consider the linear system

$$x' = a_{11}x + a_{12}y,$$
$$y' = a_{21}x + a_{22}y, \tag{13}$$

and assume that the zero solution is asymptotically stable (that is, the real parts of the roots of the characteristic equation are negative). Let $(x_1(t), y_1(t))$ and $(x_2(t), y_2(t))$ be the solutions of (13) that satisfy the conditions

$$(x_1(0), y_1(0)) = (1, 0) \quad \text{and} \quad (x_2(0), y_2(0)) = (0, 1).$$

Define the function $V(x, y)$ by

$$V(x, y) = x^2 \int_0^\infty [x_1^2(t) + y_1^2(t)] \, dt + 2xy \int_0^\infty [x_1(t)x_2(t)$$
$$+ \, y_1(t)y_2(t)] \, dt + y^2 \int_0^\infty [x_2^2(t) + y_2^2(t)] \, dt. \tag{14}$$

a) Show that $V(x, y)$ is positive definite.

b) Show that $V'(x, y)$ is negative definite along the orbits of (13).

10. Use the result of Exercise 9 to find a Lyapunov function that could be used to prove the asymptotic stability of the following systems:

a) $x' = -4x - y,$
   $y' = x - 2y;$

b) $x' = -5x - 3y,$
   $y' = 4x + 2y.$

*11. Consider the system

$$x' = a_{11}x + a_{12}y + f(x, y),$$
$$y' = a_{21}x + a_{22}y + g(x, y), \tag{15}$$

where f and g are "small" near the origin in the sense of property (4) in Section 9.3. Assume that the zero solution of the associated linear system is asymptotically stable. Prove that the zero solution of (15) is asymptotically stable. [*Hint*: Prove that there is a region D around $(0, 0)$ such that the function $V(x, y)$ defined in Exercise 9 is a Lyapunov function for (15) and that $V'(x, y) < 0$ in D.]

REVIEW EXERCISES FOR CHAPTER 9

In Exercises 1 through 3, (a) find a related linear equation, (b) find all constant solutions of the nonlinear equation, (c) solve the nonlinear equation, and (d) determine the behavior of the solutions of the nonlinear equation for values of $x(0)$ in the indicated range.

1. $x' = x + x^2$, $\cdot$ $x(0) > 0$

2. $x' = 4x - x^2$, $-\infty < x(0) < \infty$

3. $x' = -x(x^2 - 1)$, $x(0) > 0$

In Exercises 4 through 8, describe the nature of the critical point $(0, 0)$ of each system and sketch the orbits.

4. $x' = -2x - 2y$,
   $y' = -5x + y$

5. $x' = -12x + 7y$,
   $y' = -7x + 2y$

6. $x' = 2x - y$,
   $y' = 5x - 2y$

7. $x' = -2x$,
   $y' = -2y$

8. $x' = 3x + 2y$,
   $y' = -5x + y$

In Exercises 9 and 10, verify that $(0, 0)$ is a critical point and determine the asymptotic behavior of solutions near that point.

9. $x' = 4(\sin x)e^{2y}$,
   $y' = 2xy - 3y$

10. $x' = 3\cos y - 2y - 4e^x + 1 - \sin x$,
    $y' = \tan x + y$

In Exercises 11 through 13, (a) determine the critical points of each nonlinear equation, (b) find the associated linear system for each of these critical points, and (c) determine, if possible, the nature of each critical point.

11. $x' = -x + 2x^3$,
    $y' = 2y + y^3$

12. $x' = -x - x\sin x$,
    $y' = \sin y$

13. $x' = -2x - xy + 2x^2$,
    $y' = 5y + xy - 2y^2$

The Existence and Uniqueness of Solutions

In most of the preceding material in this book, we were seeking techniques for finding solutions to differential equations, assuming the *existence* of *unique* solutions for ordinary differential equations with specified initial conditions. The aim of this chapter is to prove some basic existence and uniqueness theorems for solutions of initial value problems and to show that the solution depends continuously on the initial conditions. In particular, we will prove the existence–uniqueness Theorems 1 in Section 3.1 and 1 in Section 3.11. At this point many readers may ask the following three questions:

1. Why do we need to prove the existence of a solution, particularly if we know that the differential equation arises from a physical problem that has a solution?

2. Why must we worry about uniqueness?

3. Why is continuous dependence on initial conditions important?

To answer the first question, it is important to remember that a differential equation is only a model of a physical problem. It is possible that the differential equation is a very bad model, so bad in fact that it has no solution. Countless hours could be spent using the techniques we have developed looking for a solution that may not even exist. Thus existence theorems are not only of theoretical value in telling us which equations have solutions, but also of value in developing mathematical models of physical problems.

Similarly, uniqueness theorems have both theoretical and practical implications. If we know that a problem has a unique solution, then once we have found one solution, we are done. If the solution is not unique, then we cannot talk about "the" solution but must, instead, worry about *which* solution is being discussed. In practice, if the physical problem has a unique solution, so should any mathematical model of the problem.

Finally, continuous dependence on the initial conditions is very important, since some inaccuracy is always present in practical situations. We need to know that if the initial conditions are slightly changed, the solution of the differential equation will change only slightly. Otherwise, slight inaccuracies could yield very different solutions. This property will be discussed in Exercise 18.

Before continuing with our discussion, we advise the reader that in this chapter we shall use theoretical tools from calculus that have not been widely used earlier in the text. In particular, we shall need the following facts about continuity and convergence of functions. They are discussed in most intermediate and advanced calculus texts:†

A) Let $f(t, x)$ be a continuous function of the two variables t and x and

---

† See, for example, R. C. Buck, *Advanced Calculus*. New York: McGraw-Hill (1956).

let the closed, bounded region D be defined by

$$D = \{(t, x): a \leqslant t \leqslant b, c \leqslant x \leqslant d\},$$

where $a, b, c,$ and d are finite real numbers. Then $f(t, x)$ is bounded for (t, x) in D. That is, there is a number $M > 0$ such that $|f(t, x)| \leqslant M$ for every pair (t, x) in D.

B)   Let $f(x)$ be continuous on the closed interval $a \leqslant x \leqslant b$ and differentiable on the open interval $a < x < b$. Then the *mean value theorem* of differential calculus states that there is a number ξ between a and b $(a < \xi < b)$ such that

$$f(b) - f(a) = f'(\xi)(b - a).$$

This equation can be written as

$$\boxed{\frac{f(b) - f(a)}{b - a} = f'(\xi),}$$

which says, geometrically, that the slope of the tangent to the curve $y = f(x)$ at the point ξ between a and b is equal to the slope of the secant line passing through the points $(a, f(a))$ and $(b, f(b))$ (see Fig. 1).

C)   Let $\{x_n(t)\}$ be a sequence of functions. Then $x_n(t)$ is said to *converge uniformly* to a (limit) function $x(t)$ on the interval $a \leqslant t \leqslant b$ if for every real number $\varepsilon > 0$, there exists an integer $N > 0$ such that whenever $n \geqslant N$, we have

$$|x_n(t) - x(t)| < \varepsilon$$

for every $t, a \leqslant t \leqslant b$.

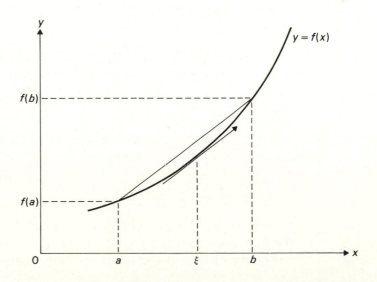

Figure 1

D)   If the functions $\{x_n(t)\}$ of statement (C) are continuous on the interval $a \le t \le b$, then the limit function $x(t)$ is also continuous there. This fact is often stated as "the uniform limit of continuous functions is continuous."

E)   Let $f(t, x)$ be a continuous function in the variable x and suppose that $x_n(t)$ converges to $x(t)$ uniformly as $n \to \infty$. Then

$$\lim_{n \to \infty} f(t, x_n(t)) = f(t, x(t)).$$

F)   Let $f(t)$ be an integrable function on the interval $a \le t \le b$. Then

$$\left| \int_a^b f(t)\, dt \right| \le \int_a^b |f(t)|\, dt,$$

and if $|f(t)| \le M$, then

$$\int_a^b |f(t)|\, dt \le M \int_a^b dt = M(b - a).$$

G)   Let $\{x_n(t)\}$ be a sequence of functions with $|x_n(t)| \le M_n$ for $a \le t \le b$. Then, if $\sum_{n=0}^{\infty} |M_n| < \infty$ (that is, if $\sum_{n=0}^{\infty} M_n$ converges absolutely) then $\sum_{n=0}^{\infty} x_n(t)$ converges uniformly on the interval $a \le t \le b$ to a unique limit function $x(t)$. This is often called the *Weierstrass M-test* for uniform convergence.

H)   Let $\{x_n(t)\}$ converge uniformly to $x(t)$ on the interval $a \le t \le b$ and let $f(t, x)$ be a continuous function of t and x in the region D defined in statement (A). Then

$$\lim_{n \to \infty} \int_a^b f(s, x_n(s))\, ds = \int_a^b \lim_{n \to \infty} f(s, x_n(s))\, ds = \int_a^b f(s, x(s))\, ds.$$

10.1 SUCCESSIVE APPROXIMATIONS: A LOCAL EXISTENCE–UNIQUENESS THEOREM

In this section we shall prove a general theorem about existence and uniqueness of solutions of the first-order initial value problem

$$x'(t) = f(t, x(t)), \quad x(t_0) = x_0, \tag{1}$$

where t_0 and x_0 are real numbers. Equation (1) includes all the first-order equations we have discussed in this book. For example, for the linear nonhomogeneous equation $x' + a(t)x = b(t)$,

$$f(t, x) = -a(t)x + b(t).$$

We shall show that if $f(t, x)$ and $(\partial f/\partial x)(t, x)$ are continuous in some region containing the point (t_0, x_0), then there is an interval (containing t_0) on which a unique solution of Eq. (1) exists. First, we need some preliminary results.

Theorem 1   Let $f(t, x)$ be continuous for all values t and x. Then the initial value problem (1) is equivalent to the integral equation

$$x(t) = x_0 + \int_{t_0}^{t} f(s, x(s))\, ds \tag{2}$$

in the sense that $x(t)$ is a solution of Eq. (1) if and only if $x(t)$ is a solution of Eq. (2).

Proof   If $x(t)$ satisfies Eq. (1), then

$$\int_{t_0}^{t} f(s, x(s))\, ds = \int_{t_0}^{t} x'(s)\, ds = x(s)\Big|_{t_0}^{t} = x(t) - x_0,$$

which shows that $x(t)$ satisfies Eq. (2). Conversely, if $x(t)$ satisfies Eq. (2), then differentiating Eq. (2), we have

$$x'(t) = \frac{d}{dt}\int_{t_0}^{t} f(s, x(s))\, ds = f(t, x(t))$$

and

$$x(t_0) = x_0 + \int_{t_0}^{t_0} f(s, x(s))\, ds = x_0.$$

Hence $x(t)$ also satisfies Eq. (1). ∎

Let D denote the rectangular region in the tx-plane defined by

$$D : a \le t \le b,\ c \le x \le d, \tag{3}$$

where $-\infty < a < b < +\infty$ and $-\infty < c < d < +\infty$. See Fig. 2. We say that the function $f(t, x)$ is *Lipschitz continuous in x over D* if there exists a

Figure 2

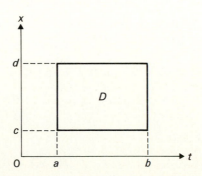

constant $k, 0 < k < \infty$, such that

$$\boxed{|f(t, x_1) - f(t, x_2)| \leq k\, |x_1 - x_2|} \tag{4}$$

whenever (t, x_1) and (t, x_2) belong to D. The constant k is called a *Lipschitz constant*. Clearly, according to Eq. (4), every Lipschitz continuous function is continuous in x for each fixed t. However, *not every continuous function is Lipschitz continuous*.

Example 1 Let $f(t, x) = \sqrt{x}$ on the set $0 \leq t \leq 1$, $0 \leq x \leq 1$. Then $f(t, x)$ is certainly continuous on this region. But

$$|f(t, x) - f(t, 0)| = |\sqrt{x} - 0| = \frac{1}{\sqrt{x}}|x - 0|$$

for all $0 < x < 1$, and $x^{-1/2}$ tends to ∞ as x approaches zero. Thus no finite Lipschitz constant can be found to satisfy Eq. (4).

However, Lipschitz continuity is not a rare occurrence, as shown by the following theorem.

Theorem 2 Let $f((t, x)$ and $(\partial f/\partial x)(t, x)$ be continuous on D. Then $f(t, x)$ is Lipschitz continuous in x over D.

Proof Let (t, x_1) and (t, x_2) be points in D. For fixed t, $(\partial f/\partial x)(t, x)$ is a function of x, and so we may apply the mean value theorem of differential calculus [statement (B)] to obtain

$$|f(t, x_1) - f(t, x_2)| = \left|\frac{\partial f}{\partial x}(t, \xi)\right| |x_1 - x_2|$$

where $x_1 < \xi < x_2$. But since $\partial f/\partial x$ is continuous in D, it is bounded there [according to statement (A)]. Hence there is a constant $k, 0 < k < \infty$, such that

$$\left|\frac{\partial f}{\partial x}(t, x)\right| \leq k$$

for all (t, x) in D. ∎

Example 2 If $f(t, x) = tx^2$ on $0 \leq t \leq 1$, $0 \leq x \leq 1$, then

$$\left|\frac{\partial f}{\partial x}\right| = |2tx| \leq 2,$$

so that

$$|f(t, x_1) - f(t, x_2)| \leq 2\, |x_1 - x_2|.$$

We now define a sequence of functions $\{x_n(t)\}$, called *Picard*† *iterations*, by the successive formulas

$$
\begin{aligned}
x_0(t) &= x_0, \\
x_1(t) &= x_0 + \int_{t_0}^{t} f(s, x_0(s)) \, ds, \\
x_2(t) &= x_0 + \int_{t_0}^{t} f(s, x_1(s)) \, ds, \\
&\;\;\vdots \\
x_n(t) &= x_0 + \int_{t_0}^{t} f(s, x_{n-1}(s)) \, ds.
\end{aligned}
\tag{5}
$$

We will show that under certain conditions the Picard iterations defined by (5) converge uniformly to a solution of Eq. (2). First we illustrate the process of this iteration by a simple example.

Example 3   Consider the initial value problem

$$
x'(t) = x(t), \quad x(0) = 1.
\tag{6}
$$

As we know, Eq. (6) has the unique solution $x(t) = e^t$. In this case, the function $f(t, x)$ in Eq. (1) is given by $f(t, x(t)) = x(t)$, so that the Picard iterations defined by (5) yield successively

$$
\begin{aligned}
x_0(t) &= x_0 = 1, \\
x_1(t) &= 1 + \int_0^t (1) \, ds = 1 + t, \\
x_2(t) &= 1 + \int_0^t (1 + s) \, ds = 1 + t + \frac{t^2}{2}, \\
x_3(t) &= 1 + \int_0^t \left(1 + s + \frac{s^2}{2}\right) ds = 1 + t + \frac{t^2}{2!} + \frac{t^3}{3!},
\end{aligned}
$$

and clearly,

$$
x_n(t) = 1 + t + \frac{t^2}{2!} + \cdots + \frac{t^n}{n!} = \sum_{k=0}^{n} \frac{t^k}{k!}.
$$

Hence

$$
\lim_{n \to \infty} x_n(t) = \sum_{k=0}^{\infty} \frac{t^k}{k!} = e^t
$$

by Formula (14) in Section 5.1.

---

† Emile Picard (1856–1941), one of the most eminent French mathematicians of the past century, made several outstanding contributions to mathematical analysis.

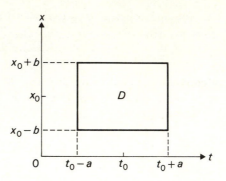

Figure 3

We now state and prove the main result of this chapter.

Theorem 3 *Existence theorem.* Let $f(t, x)$ be Lipschitz continuous in x with the Lipschitz constant k on the region D of all points (t, x) satisfying the inequalities

$$|t - t_0| \leq a, \quad |x - x_0| \leq b.$$

(See Fig. 3.) Then there exists a number $\delta > 0$ with the property that the initial value problem

$$x' = f(t, x), \quad x(t_0) = x_0,$$

has a solution $x = x(t)$ on the interval $|t - t_0| \leq \delta$.

Proof The proof of this theorem is complicated and will be done in several stages. However, the basic idea is simple: We need only justify that the Picard iterations converge uniformly and yield, in the limit, the solution of the integral equation (2).

Since f is continuous on D, it is bounded there [statement (A)] and we may begin by letting M be a finite upper bound for $|f(t, x)|$ on D. We then define

$$\delta = \min \{a, b/M\}. \tag{7}$$

1. We first show that the iterations $\{x_n(t)\}$ are continuous and satisfy the inequality

$$|x_n(t) - x_0| \leq b. \tag{8}$$

Inequality (8) is necessary in order that $f(t, x_n(t))$ be defined for $n = 0, 1, 2, \ldots$. To show the continuity of $x_n(t)$, we first note that $x_0(t) = x_0$ is continuous (a constant function is always continuous). Then

$$x_1(t) = x_0 + \int_{t_0}^{t} f(t, x_0(s)) \, ds.$$

But $f(t, x_0)$ is continuous [since $f(t, x)$ is continuous in t and x], and the integral of a continuous function is continuous. Thus $x_1(t)$ is continuous. In a similar fashion, we can show that

$$x_2(t) = x_1(t) + \int_{t_0}^{t} f(t, x_1(s)) \, ds$$

is continuous and so on for $n = 3, 4, \ldots$.

Obviously the inequality (8) holds when $n = 0$, because $x_0(t) = x_0$. For $n \neq 0$, we use the definition (5) and Eq. (7) to obtain

$$|x_n(t) - x_0| = \left| \int_{t_0}^{t} f(s, x_{n-1}(s)) \, ds \right| \leq \left| \int_{t_0}^{t} |f(s, x_{n-1}(s))| \, ds \right|$$

$$\leq M \left| \int_{t_0}^{t} ds \right| = M \, |t - t_0| \leq M\delta \leq b.$$

These inequalities follow from statement (F). Note that the last inequality helps explain the choice of δ in Eq. (7).

2. Next, we show by induction that

$$|x_n(t) - x_{n-1}(t)| \leq Mk^{n-1} \frac{|t - t_0|^n}{n!} \leq \frac{Mk^{n-1}\delta^n}{n!} . \tag{9}$$

If $n = 1$, we obtain

$$|x_1(t) - x_0(t)| \leq \left| \int_{t_0}^{t} f(s, x_0(s)) \, ds \right| \leq M \left| \int_{t_0}^{t} ds \right|$$

$$= M \, |t - t_0| \leq M\delta.$$

Thus the result is true for $n = 1$.

We assume that the result is true for $n = m$ and prove that it holds for $n = m + 1$. That is, we assume that

$$|x_m(t) - x_{m-1}(t)| \leq \frac{Mk^{m-1} |t - t_0|^m}{m!} \leq \frac{Mk^{m-1}\delta^m}{m!} .$$

Then, since $f(t, x)$ is Lipschitz continuous in x over D,

$$|x_{m+1}(t) - x_m(t)| = \left| \int_{t_0}^{t} f(s, x_m(s)) \, ds - \int_{t_0}^{t} f(s, x_{m-1}(s)) \, ds \right|$$

$$\leq \left| \int_{t_0}^{t} |f(s, x_m(s)) - f(s, x_{m-1}(s))| \, ds \right|$$

$$\leq k \left| \int_{t_0}^{t} |x_m(s) - x_{m-1}(s)| \, ds \right|$$

$$\leq \frac{Mk^m}{m!} \left| \int_{t_0}^{t} (s - t_0)^m \, ds \right|^{\dagger} = \frac{Mk^m |t - t_0|^{m+1}}{(m + 1)!} \leq \frac{Mk^m\delta^{m+1}}{(m + 1)!} ,$$

---

† This inequality follows from the induction assumption that the inequality (9) holds for $n = m$.

which is what we wanted to show.

3. We will now show that $x_n(t)$ converges uniformly to a limit function $x(t)$ on the interval $|t - t_0| \leq \delta$. By statement (D), this will show that $x(t)$ is continuous.

We first note that

$$x_n(t) - x_0(t) = x_n(t) - x_{n-1}(t) + x_{n-1}(t) - x_{n-2}(t) + \cdots + x_1(t) - x_0(t)$$

$$= \sum_{k=0}^{n} [x_m(t) - x_{m-1}(t)]. \tag{10}$$

But by the inequality (9),

$$|x_m(t) - x_{m-1}(t)| \leq \frac{Mk^{m-1}\delta^m}{m!} = \frac{M}{k}\frac{k^m\delta^m}{m!},$$

so that

$$\sum_{m=1}^{\infty} |x_m(t) - x_{m-1}(t)| \leq \frac{M}{k} \sum_{m=1}^{\infty} \frac{(k\delta)^m}{m!} = \frac{M}{k}(e^{k\delta} - 1),$$

by Eq. (14) in Section 5.1 since

$$e^{k\delta} = \sum_{m=0}^{\infty} \frac{(k\delta)^m}{m!} = 1 + \sum_{m=1}^{\infty} \frac{(k\delta)^m}{m!}.$$

By the Weierstrass M-test [statement (G)], we conclude that the series

$$\sum_{m=1}^{\infty} [x_m(t) - x_{m-1}(t)]$$

converges absolutely and uniformly on $|t - t_0| \leq \delta$ to a unique limit function $y(t)$. But

$$y(t) = \lim_{n \to \infty} \sum_{m=1}^{n} [x_m(t) - x_{m-1}(t)]$$

$$= \lim_{n \to \infty} [x_n(t) - x_0(t)] = \lim_{n \to \infty} x_n(t) - x_0(t)$$

or

$$\lim_{n \to \infty} x_n(t) = y(t) + x_0(t).$$

We denote the right-hand side of this equation by $x(t)$. Thus the limit of the Picard iterations $x_n(t)$ exists and the convergence $x_n(t) \to x(t)$ is uniform for all t in the interval $|t - t_0| \leq \delta$.

4. It remains to be shown that $x(t)$ is a solution to Eq. (2) for $|t - t_0| < \delta$. Since $f(t, x)$ is a continuous function of x and $x_n(t) \to x(t)$ as $n \to \infty$, we have, by statement (E),

$$\lim_{n \to \infty} f(t, x_n(t)) = f(t, x(t)).$$

Hence by Eq. (5),

$$x(t) = \lim_{n \to \infty} x_{n+1}(t) = x_0 + \lim_{n \to \infty} \int_{t_0}^{t} f(s, x_n(s)) \, ds$$

$$= x_0 + \int_{t_0}^{t} \lim_{n \to \infty} f(s, x_n(s)) \, ds = x_0 + \int_{t_0}^{t} f(s, x(s)) \, ds.$$

The step in which we interchange the limit and integral is justified by statement (H). Thus $x(t)$ solves Eq. (2) and therefore it solves the initial value problem (1). ∎

It turns out that the solution obtained in Theorem 3 is unique. Before proving this, however, we shall derive a simple version of a very useful result known as *Gronwall's inequality*.

Theorem 4   *Gronwall's inequality.* Let $x(t)$ be a continuous nonnegative function and suppose that

$$x(t) \leq A + B \left| \int_{t_0}^{t} x(s) \, ds \right|, \tag{11}$$

where A and B are positive constants, for all values of t such that $|t - t_0| \leq \delta$. Then

$$\boxed{x(t) \leq A e^{B|t-t_0|}} \tag{12}$$

for all t in the interval $|t - t_0| \leq \delta$.

Proof   We shall prove this result for $t_0 \leq t \leq t_0 + \delta$. The proof for $t_0 - \delta \leq t \leq t_0$ is similar (see Exercise 14). We define

$$y(t) = B \int_{t_0}^{t} x(s) \, ds.$$

Then

$$y'(t) = Bx(t) \leq B \left[A + B \int_{t_0}^{t} x(s) \, ds \right] = AB + By$$

or

$$y'(t) - By(t) \leq AB. \tag{13}$$

We note that

$$\frac{d}{dt} [y(t) e^{-B(t-t_0)}] = e^{-B(t-t_0)} [y'(t) - By(t)].$$

Therefore, multiplying both sides of Eq. (13) by the integrating factor $e^{-B(t-t_0)}$ (which is greater than zero), we have

$$\frac{d}{dt} [y(t) e^{-B(t-t_0)}] \leq AB e^{-B(t-t_0)}.$$

An integration of both sides of the inequality from t_0 to t yields

$$y(s)e^{-B(s-t_0)}\Big|_{t_0}^{t} \leq AB \int_{t_0}^{t} e^{-B(s-t_0)}\,ds = -Ae^{-B(s-t_0)}\Big|_{t_0}^{t}.$$

But $y(t_0) = 0$, so that

$$y(t)e^{-B(t-t_0)} \leq A(1 - e^{-B(t-t_0)}),$$

from which, after multiplying both sides by $e^{B(t-t_0)}$, we obtain

$$y(t) \leq A[e^{B(t-t_0)} - 1].$$

Then by Eq. (11),

$$x(t) \leq A + y(t) \leq Ae^{B(t-t_0)}. \quad \blacksquare$$

Theorem 5   *Uniqueness theorem.* Let the conditions of Theorem 3 (existence theorem) hold. Then $x(t) = \lim_{n\to\infty} x_n(t)$ is the only continuous solution of the initial value problem (1) in $|t - t_0| \leq \delta$.

Proof   Let $x(t)$ and $y(t)$ be two continuous solutions of Eq. (2) in the interval $|t - t_0| \leq \delta$ and suppose that $(t, y(t))$ belongs to the region D for all t in that interval.† Define $v(t) = |x(t) - y(t)|$. Then $v(t) \geq 0$ and $v(t)$ is continuous. Since $f(t, x)$ is Lipschitz continuous in x over D,

$$v(t) = \left\| \left[x_0 + \int_{t_0}^{t} f(s, x(s))\,ds \right] - \left[x_0 + \int_{t_0}^{t} f(s, y(s))\,ds \right] \right\|$$

$$\leq k \left| \int_{t_0}^{t} |x(s) - y(s)|\,ds \right| = k \left| \int_{t_0}^{t} v(s)\,ds \right|$$

$$\leq \varepsilon + k \left| \int_{t_0}^{t} v(s)\,ds \right|$$

for every $\varepsilon > 0$. By Gronwall's inequality, we have

$$v(t) \leq \varepsilon\, e^{k|t-t_0|}.$$

But $\varepsilon > 0$ can be chosen arbitrarily close to zero, so that $v(t) \leq 0$. Since $v(t) \geq 0$, it follows that $v(t) \equiv 0$, implying that $x(t)$ and $y(t)$ are identical. Hence the limit of the Picard iterations is the only continuous solution. $\blacksquare$

Theorem 6   Let $f(t, x)$ and $(\partial f/\partial x)$ be continuous on D. Then there exists a constant $\delta > 0$ such that the Picard iteration $\{x_n(t)\}$ converge to a unique continuous solution of the initial value problem (1) on $|t - t_0| \leq \delta$.

Proof   This theorem follows directly from Theorem 2 and the existence and uniqueness theorems. $\blacksquare$

---

† Note that without this assumption, the function $f(t, y(t))$ may not even be defined at points where $(t, y(t))$ is not in D.

We note that Theorems 3, 5, and 6 are *local* results. By this we mean that unique solutions are guaranteed to exist only "near" the initial point (t_0, x_0).

Example 4   Let

$$x'(t) = x^2(t), \quad x(1) = 2.$$

Without solving this equation, we can show that there is a unique solution in some interval $|t - t_0| = |t - 1| \leqslant \delta$. Let $a = b = 1$. Then $|f(t, x)| = x^2 \leqslant 9 \, (=M)$ for all $|x - x_0| \leqslant 1$, $x_0 = x(1) = 2$. Therefore, $\delta = \min\{a, b/M\} = \frac{1}{9}$, and Theorem 6 guarantees the existence of a unique solution on the interval $|t - 1| \leqslant \frac{1}{9}$. The solution of this initial value problem is easily found by a separation of variables to be $x(t) = 2/(3 - 2t)$. This solution exists so long as $t \neq \frac{3}{2}$. Starting at $t_0 = 1$, we see that the maximum interval of existences is $|t - t_0| < \frac{1}{2}$. Hence the value $\delta = \frac{1}{9}$ is not the best possible.

Example 5   Consider the initial value problem

$$x' = \sqrt{x}, \quad x(0) = 0.$$

As we saw in Example 1, $f(t, x) = \sqrt{x}$ does *not* satisfy a Lipschitz condition in any region containing the point $(0, 0)$. By a separation of variables, it is easy to calculate the solution

$$x(t) = \left(\frac{t}{2}\right)^2.$$

However $y(t) = 0$ is also a solution. Hence without a Lipschitz condition, the solution to an initial value problem (if one exists) may fail to be unique.

The last two examples illustrate the local nature of our existence–uniqueness theorem. We shall show in Section 10.2 that it is possible to derive *global* existence–uniqueness results for certain linear differential equations. That is, we shall show that a unique solution exists for every real number t (see Exercise 17).

EXERCISES 10.1

For each initial value problem of Exercises 1 through 10, determine whether a unique solution can be guaranteed. If so, let $a = b = 1$ if possible, and find the number δ as given by Eq. (7). When possible, solve the equation and find a better value for δ, as in Example 4.

1. $x' = x^3, \quad x(2) = 5$

2. $x' = x^3, \quad x(1) = 2$

3. $x' = \dfrac{x}{t - x}, \quad x(0) = 1$

4. $x' = x^{1/3}, \quad x(1) = 0$

5. $x' = \sin x, \quad x(1) = \pi/2$

6. $x' = \sqrt{x(x - 1)}, \quad x(1) = 2$

7. $x' = \ln |\sin x|, \quad x(\pi/2) = 1$

8. $x' = \sqrt{x(x-1)}, \quad x(2) = 3$

9. $x' = |x|, \quad x(0) = 1$

10. $x' = tx, \quad x(5) = 10$

11. Compute a Lipschitz constant for each of the following functions on the indicated region D:

    a) $f(t, x) = te^{-2x/t}, \quad t > 0, \quad x > 0$

    b) $f(t, x) = \sin tx, \quad |t| \le 1, \quad |x| \le 2$

    c) $f(t, x) = e^{-t^2}x^2 \sin \dfrac{1}{x}, \quad$ all $t, -1 \le x < 1,$

    $x \ne 0$

(Part (c) shows that a Lipschitz constant may exist even when $\partial f/\partial x$ is not bounded in D.)

    d) $f(t, x) = (t^2x^3)^{3/2}, \quad |t| \le 2, \quad |x| \le 3$

12. Consider the initial value problem

$$x' = x^2, \quad x(1) = 3.$$

Show that the Picard iterations converge to the unique solution of this problem.

13. Construct the sequence $\{x_n(t)\}$ of Picard iterations for the initial value problem

$$x' = -x, \quad x(0) = 3,$$

and show that it converges to the unique solution $x(t) = 3e^{-t}$.

14. Prove Gronwall's inequality (Theorem 4) for $t_0 - \delta \le t \le t_0$. [*Hint*: For $t < t_0, y(t) \le 0$.]

15. Let $v(t)$ be a positive function that satisfies the inequality

$$v(t) \le A + \int_{t_0}^{t} r(s)v(s)\, ds, \qquad \textbf{(14)}$$

where $A \ge 0$, $r(t)$ is a continuous, positive function, and $t \ge t_0$. Prove that

$$v(t) \le A \exp\left[\int_{t_0}^{t} r(s)\, ds\right] \qquad \textbf{(15)}$$

for all $t \ge t_0$. What kind of result holds for $t \le t_0$? This is a general form of Gronwall's inequality. [*Hint*: Define $y(t) \equiv \int_{t_0}^{t} r(s)v(s)\, ds$ and show that $y'(t) = r(t)v(t) \le r(t)[A + y(t)]$. Finish the proof by following the steps of the proof of Theorem 4, using the integrating factor $\exp[-\int_{t_0}^{t} r(s)\, ds]$.]

16. Consider the initial value problem

$$x'' = f(t, x), \quad x(0) = x_0, \quad x'(0) = x_1, \qquad \textbf{(16)}$$

where f is defined on the rectangle $D : |t| \le a$, $|x - x_0| \le b$. Prove under appropriate hypotheses that if a solution exists, then it must be unique. [*Hint*: Let $x(t)$ and $y(t)$ be continuous solutions of (16). Verify by differentiation that

$$x(t) = x_0 + x_1 t - \int_0^t (t - s)f(s, x(s))\, ds,$$

$$y(t) = x_0 + x_1 t - \int_0^t (t - s)f(s, y(s))\, ds$$

in some interval $|t| \le \delta, \delta > 0$. Then subtract these two expressions, use an appropriate Lipschitz condition, and apply the Gronwall inequality of Exercise 15.]

17. Consider the first-order linear problem

$$x'(t) = a(t)x + b(t), \quad x(t_0) = x_0, \qquad \textbf{(17)}$$

where $a(t)$ and $b(t)$ are continuous in the interval and $a \le t_0 \le b$.

    a) Using $f(t, x) = a(t)x + b(t)$, show that the Picard iterations $\{x_n(t)\}$ exist and are continuous for all t in the interval $a \le t \le b$.

    b) Show that $f(t, x)$ defined in part (a) is Lipschitz continuous in x over the region D of points (t, x) satisfying the conditions $a \le t \le b, |x| < \infty$.

    *c) Modify the proofs of Theorems 3 and 5 to show that (17) has a unique solution in the *entire* interval $[a, b]$.

    d) Show that if $a(t)$ and $b(t)$ are continuous for all values t, then (17) has a unique solution that is defined for *all* values $-\infty < t < \infty$. (This is a *global* existence–uniqueness theorem.)

18. Consider the initial value problem

$$x' = f(t, x), \quad x(t_0) = x_0. \qquad \textbf{(18)}$$

Show that if $f(t, x)$ satisfies the conditions of Theorem 3, then the solution $x(t) \equiv x(t, x_0)$ depends continuously on the value of x_0. Thus a small change in x_0 produces a small change in the solution over the interval $|t - t_0| \le \delta$. This result is often termed *continuous dependence on initial conditions*. [*Hint*: Define $x_0(t)$ to be the unique solution of (18) and $x_1(t)$ to be the unique solution of

$$x' = f(t, x), \quad x(t_0) = x_1. \qquad \textbf{(19)}$$

Rewrite the initial value problems (18) and (19) as integrals (2) and subtract one from the other to obtain

$$|x_1(t) - x_0(t)|$$

$$\leq |x_1 - x_0| + \left| \int_{t_0}^{t} |f(s, x_1(s)) - f(s, x_0(s))| \, ds \right|.$$

Then apply the Lipschitz condition to show that

$$|x_1(t) - x_0(t)| \leq |x_1 - x_0| + k \left| \int_{t_0}^{t} |x_1(s) - x_0(s)| \, ds \right|.$$

Finally, apply Gronwall's inequality (Theorem 4) to show that

$$|x_1(t) - x_0(t)| \leq |x_1 - x_0| \, e^{k|t - t_0|} \leq |x_1 - x_0| \, e^{k\delta}$$

for $|t - t_0| \leq \delta$, from which the desired result is immediately obtained.]

10.2 SYSTEMS OF LINEAR DIFFERENTIAL EQUATIONS

In this section we shall extend the local results of Section 10.1 in two ways. First, we will show that, with little modification, the existence and uniqueness Theorems 3 and 5 in Section 10.1 are true when $\mathbf{x}(t)$ and $\mathbf{f}(t, \mathbf{x}(t))$ are vectors. Then we will show that *global* existence and uniqueness results can be proved as easy corollaries when the system is linear (see Exercise 17 in Section 10.1).

We consider the initial value system

$$
\begin{aligned}
x_1' &= f_1(t, x_1, x_2, \ldots, x_n), & x_1(t_0) &= x_{10}, \\
x_2' &= f_2(t, x_1, x_2, \ldots, x_n), & x_2(t_0) &= x_{20}, \\
&\;\;\vdots & &\;\;\vdots \\
x_n' &= f_n(t, x_1, x_2, \ldots, x_n), & x_n(t_0) &= x_{n0}.
\end{aligned}
\tag{1}
$$

As in Chapter 8, we write the vectors

$$
\mathbf{x} = \begin{pmatrix} x_1 \\ x_2 \\ \cdot \\ \cdot \\ \cdot \\ x_n \end{pmatrix}, \quad
\mathbf{f}(t, \mathbf{x}) = \begin{pmatrix} f_1(t, x_1, \ldots, x_n) \\ f_2(t, x_1, \ldots, x_n) \\ \cdot \\ \cdot \\ \cdot \\ f_n(t, x_1, \ldots, x_n) \end{pmatrix}, \quad
\mathbf{x}_0 = \begin{pmatrix} x_{10} \\ x_{20} \\ \cdot \\ \cdot \\ \cdot \\ x_{n0} \end{pmatrix}.
$$

Then we may write (1) in the compact form

$$\mathbf{x}' = \mathbf{f}(t, \mathbf{x}), \quad \mathbf{x}(t_0) = \mathbf{x}_0. \tag{2}$$

In order to generalize the results of Section 10.1, it is necessary to generalize the notion of the absolute value of a number to the absolute value or *norm* of a vector $\mathbf{x}$ or matrix A. If $\mathbf{x} = (x_1, x_2)$ is a two-vector, then the distance from (x_1, x_2) to the origin is given by the Pythagorean theorem (see Fig. 4):

$$\|\mathbf{x}\| = \sqrt{(x_1^2 + x_2^2)}. \tag{3}$$

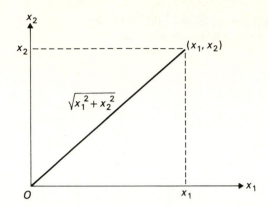

Figure 4

Therefore, it is natural to define the length or *norm* of an n-vector $\mathbf{x} = (x_1, x_2, \ldots, x_n)$, by

$$\|\mathbf{x}\| = \sqrt{(x_1^2 + x_2^2 + \cdots + x_n^2)}. \tag{4}$$

If A is an $n \times n$ matrix, there are several ways to define its norm. For our purposes, the simplest choice for the norm of A is

$$\|A\| = \sum_{i=1}^{n} \sum_{j=1}^{n} |a_{ij}|. \tag{5}$$

That is, the norm of A is the sum of the absolute values of the components of A.

Using Eqs. (4) and (5), we may prove that:

i) $\|\mathbf{x}\| \geq 0$, where the equality holds only if $\mathbf{x}$ is the zero vector. (6)

ii) $\|\alpha \mathbf{x}\| = |\alpha| \|\mathbf{x}\|$ when α is a scalar. (7)

iii) $\|\mathbf{x} + \mathbf{y}\| \leq \|\mathbf{x}\| + \|\mathbf{y}\|$. (8)

Moreover, if A is an $n \times n$ matrix, we can show (see Exercises 1 through 4) that

$$\|A\mathbf{x}\| \leq \|A\| \|\mathbf{x}\|. \tag{9}$$

Now using this notation and a norm $\|\cdot\|$ for every absolute value $|\cdot|$ that appeared in the proofs of Theorems 3 and 5 in Section 10.1, we obtain the existence and uniqueness of a local vector solution $\mathbf{x}(t)$ of the initial value problem (2). The verification of these details is left as an exercise (see Exercise 8). We therefore have the following.

Theorem 1　Let D denote the region [in $(n + 1)$-dimensional space, one dimension for t and n dimensions for the vector $\mathbf{x}$]

$$|t - t_0| \leq a, \quad \|\mathbf{x} - \mathbf{x}_0\| \leq b, \tag{10}$$

and suppose that $\mathbf{f}(t, \mathbf{x})$ satisfies the Lipschitz condition

$$\|\mathbf{f}(t, \mathbf{x}_1) - \mathbf{f}(t, \mathbf{x}_2)\| \leq k \|\mathbf{x}_1 - \mathbf{x}_2\| \tag{11}$$

whenever the pairs $(t, \mathbf{x}_1)$ and $(t, \mathbf{x}_2)$ belong to D, where k is a positive constant. Then there is a constant $\delta > 0$ such that there exists a unique continuous vector solution $\mathbf{x}(t)$ of the system (2) in the interval $|t - t_0| \leq \delta$.

Before leaving this theorem, we should briefly discuss the condition (11). It is easy to see that (11) is implied by the inequalities

$$|f_i(t, x_{11}, \ldots, x_{1n}) - f_i(t, x_{21}, \ldots, x_{2n})| \leq k_i \sum_{j=1}^{n} |x_{1j} - x_{2j}| \tag{12}$$

for $i = 1, \ldots, n$ with $k = n\sqrt{\sum_{i=1}^{n} k_i^2}$. This fact follows from the double inequality

$$\frac{1}{n} \sum_{j=1}^{n} |x_j| \leq \|x\| \leq \sum_{j=1}^{n} |x_j|, \tag{13}$$

which is an immediate consequence of the definition of $\|\mathbf{x}\|$ (see Exercise 5).

Another condition that implies the inequality (11) is

$$|f_i(t, x_{11}, \ldots, x_{1n}) - f_i(t, x_{21}, \ldots, x_{2n})| \leq k_2 \max_j |x_{1j} - x_{2j}| \tag{14}$$

for $i = 1, 2, \ldots, n$. The two inequalities (12) and (14) are useful since it is often very difficult to verify the inequality (11) directly.

Finally, if the partial derivatives $\partial f_i / \partial x_j$, $i, j = 1, 2, \ldots, n$, are continuous in D, then they are bounded on D and conditions (12) and (14) both follow from the mean value theorem of differential calculus (see Exercise 7).

We now turn to the main purpose of this section, which is to show the global existence and uniqueness of solutions of linear systems with continuous coefficients. Consider the system

$$\mathbf{x}' = A(t)\mathbf{x} + \mathbf{f}(t), \quad \mathbf{x}(t_0) = \mathbf{x}_0, \tag{15}$$

where t_0 is a point in the interval $\alpha \leq t \leq \beta$ and $A(t)$ is an $n \times n$ matrix.

Theorem 2　(Theorem 2 of Section 8.2). Let $A(t)$ and $\mathbf{f}(t)$ be a continuous matrix and vector function, respectively, on the interval $\alpha \leq t \leq \beta$. Then there exists a unique vector function $\mathbf{x}(t)$ that is a solution of Eq. (15) on the entire interval $\alpha \leq t \leq \beta$.

Proof   We define the Picard iterations

$$\mathbf{x}_0(t) = \mathbf{x}_0,$$

$$\mathbf{x}_1(t) = \mathbf{x}_0 + \int_{t_0}^{t} [A(s)\mathbf{x}_0(s) + \mathbf{f}(s)]\, ds,$$

$$\vdots$$

(16)

$$\mathbf{x}_{n+1}(t) = \mathbf{x}_0 + \int_{t_0}^{t} [A(s)\mathbf{x}_n(s) + \mathbf{f}(s)]\, ds,$$

$$\vdots$$

Clearly these iterations are continuous on $\alpha \leq t \leq \beta$ for $n = 1, 2, \ldots$. Since $A(t)$ is a continuous matrix function, we have

$$\sup_{\alpha \leq t \leq \beta} \|A(t)\| = \sup_{\alpha \leq t \leq \beta} \sum_{i=1}^{n} \sum_{j=1}^{n} |a_{ij}(t)| = k < \infty.$$

Let

$$M = \sup_{\alpha \leq t \leq \beta} \|A(t)\mathbf{x}_0 + \mathbf{f}(t)\|,$$

which is finite [according to statement (A) of Section 10.1] since $A(t)$ and $\mathbf{f}(t)$ are continuous. Observe that we are unable to define the value δ of Eq. (7) in Section 10.1, since the vector functions $\mathbf{x}(t)$ are *unrestricted*. Thus a slight modification of the proof of Theorem 3 in Section 10.1 is necessary:

i) Note that for any vectors $\mathbf{x}_1$ and $\mathbf{x}_2$ and for $\alpha \leq t \leq \beta$, we have

$$\|[A(t)\mathbf{x}_1 + \mathbf{f}(t)] - [A(t)\mathbf{x}_2 + \mathbf{f}(t)]\| \leq \|A(t)\|\,\|\mathbf{x}_1 - \mathbf{x}_2\| \leq k\,\|\mathbf{x}_1 - \mathbf{x}_2\|.$$

Thus the vector function $A(t)\mathbf{x} + \mathbf{f}$ satisfies a Lipschitz condition for any $\mathbf{x}$ and $\alpha \leq t \leq \beta$.

ii) By induction, we now show that the Picard iterations (16) satisfy the inequality

$$\|\mathbf{x}_n(t) - \mathbf{x}_{n-1}(t)\| \leq Mk^{n-1}\frac{|t - t_0|^n}{n!} \leq Mk^{n-1}\frac{(\beta - \alpha)^n}{n!}. \tag{17}$$

We shall prove the first inequality. The second follows easily. First, if

$n = 1$, then

$$\|\mathbf{x}_1(t) - \mathbf{x}_0(t)\| = \left\| \int_{t_0}^{t} [A(s)\mathbf{x}_0 + \mathbf{f}(s)]\, ds \right\|$$

$$\leqslant \left| \int_{t_0}^{t} \|A(s)\mathbf{x}_0 + \mathbf{f}(s)\|\, ds \right|$$

$$\leqslant M \left| \int_{t_0}^{t} ds \right| = M|t - t_0| \leqslant M(\beta - \alpha).\dagger$$

Assume that the result holds for $n = m$. Then by part (i),

$$\|\mathbf{x}_{m+1}(t) - \mathbf{x}_m(t)\| \leqslant \left| \int_{t_0}^{t} \|[A(s)\mathbf{x}_m(s) + \mathbf{f}(s)] - [A(s)\mathbf{x}_{m-1}(s) + \mathbf{f}(s)]\|\, ds \right|$$

$$\leqslant k \left| \int_{t_0}^{t} \|\mathbf{x}_m(s) - \mathbf{x}_{m-1}(s)\|\, ds \right| \leqslant k \left| \int_{t_0}^{t} Mk^{m-1} \frac{|s - t_0|^m}{m!}\, ds \right|$$

$$= Mk^m \frac{|t - t_0|^{m+1}}{(m + 1)!} \leqslant Mk^m \frac{(\beta - \alpha)^{m+1}}{(m + 1)!},$$

which is the desired result.

The major difference between this proof and the proof of Theorem 3 in Section 10.1 is that, in the linear case, the bound M can be defined independently of x, whereas in Theorem 3 we must restrict x as well as t. This difference enables us to prove the global result that solutions exist and are unique on the entire interval $\alpha \leqslant t \leqslant \beta$.

With the estimate (16) [which is identical to the estimate (9) in Section 10.1] the proof proceeds exactly as those for Theorems 3 and 5 in Section 10.1. Note that Theorems 1 in Section 3.1 and 1 in Section 3.11 are special cases of Theorem 2. ∎

Corollary 3   Let $A(t)$ and $\mathbf{f}(t)$ be continuous on the interval $-\infty < t < \infty$. Then there exists a unique continuous solution $\mathbf{x}(t)$ of (15) defined for *all* t on $-\infty < t < \infty$.

Proof   Suppose $|t_0| \leqslant n$. We define $\mathbf{x}_n(t)$ to be the unique solution of (15) on the interval $|t| \leqslant n$ which is guaranteed by Theorem 2. We observe that $\mathbf{x}_n(t)$ coincides with $\mathbf{x}_{n+k}(t)$ on the interval $|t| \leqslant n$ for $k = 1, 2, 3, \ldots$, since both are solutions of (15) and Theorem 2 requires any solution on $|t| \leqslant n$ to be

---

† The first of these inequalities is called the Cauchy–Schwartz inequality. Its proof may be found in any advanced calculus text. See, for example, R. Buck, *Advanced Calculus*. New York: McGraw-Hill (1956).

unique. Thus the vector function

$$\mathbf{x}(t) = \lim_{n \to \infty} \mathbf{x}_n(t)$$

is defined for all real values t, since $|t| \leq n$ for sufficiently large n. Clearly $\mathbf{x}(t)$ is a solution of (15) on $-\infty < t < \infty$, and such a solution must be unique since it is uniquely defined on each finite interval containing t_0. ∎

EXERCISES 10.2

1. Prove the inequality (6).

2. Prove Eq. (7).

*3. Prove the inequality (8). [*Hint*: (a) First show that the *inner product*

$$\mathbf{x} \cdot \mathbf{y} = x_1 y_1 + x_2 y_2 + \cdots + x_n y_n$$

satisfies the condition $|\mathbf{x} \cdot \mathbf{y}| \leq \|\mathbf{x}\| \|\mathbf{y}\|$, where $\mathbf{x} = (x_1, x_2, \ldots, x_n)$ and $\mathbf{y} = (y_1, y_2, \ldots, y_n)$. (b) Show that $\mathbf{x} \cdot \mathbf{x} = \|\mathbf{x}\|^2$. (c) Apply (b) to $\|\mathbf{x} + \mathbf{y}\|^2$ and use the inequality in (a) to verify (8).]

*4. Prove the inequality (9).

5. Prove the inequality (13).

6. Using the inequality (13), show that the inequalities (11), (12), and (14) are all equivalent.

7. Show that if the partial derivatives $\partial f_i / \partial x_j$ are continuous on the region D defined by (10), then there exists a constant $k_i > 0$ such that the inequality (11) holds for $i = 1, \ldots, n$.

*8. Prove Theorem 1 by carrying out the following steps:

a) Show that the system (2) is equivalent to the integral equation

$$\mathbf{x}(t) = \mathbf{x}_0 + \int_{t_0}^{t} \mathbf{f}(s, \mathbf{x}(s)) \, ds. \qquad \textbf{(18)}$$

b) Define the vector-valued Picard iterates $\{\mathbf{x}_n\}$ as in Eq. (5) in Section 10.1.

c) Prove that

$$M = \sup_{(t, \mathbf{x}) \in D} \|\mathbf{f}(t, \mathbf{x})\|$$

is finite.

d) Show that if $\delta = \min\{a, b/M\}$, then the Picard iterates defined in (b) satisfy the condition $\|\mathbf{x}_n(t) - \mathbf{x}_0\| \leq b$, for $|t - t_0| \leq a$.

e) Show by induction that

$$\|\mathbf{x}_n(t) - \mathbf{x}_{n-1}(t)\| \leq M k^{n-1} \frac{|t - t_0|^n}{n!} \leq M k^{n-1} \frac{\delta^n}{n!}.$$

f) Prove that the series

$$\sum_{m=1}^{\infty} \|\mathbf{x}_m(t) - \mathbf{x}_{m-1}(t)\|$$

converges uniformly for $|t - t_0| < \delta$ and conclude that $\mathbf{x}_n(t)$ converges uniformly to a vector function $\mathbf{x}(t)$ as n tends to ∞.

g) Show that the $\mathbf{x}(t)$ defined in part (f) is a continuous solution to (18) on the interval $|t - t_0| \leq \delta$.

h) Use Gronwall's inequality to show that this solution is unique.

9. Consider the system

$$x_1' = t x_1 x_2 + t^2, \quad x_1(0) = 1,$$
$$x_2' = x_1^2 + x_2^2 + t, \quad x_2(0) = 2.$$

a) Write the system in the form (2).

b) Find a Lipschitz constant for $\mathbf{f}$ in the region

$$D: |t| \leq 1, \quad (x_1 - 1)^2 + (x_2 - 2)^2 \leq 1.$$

c) Find $\delta = \min\{a, b/M\}$ as in Exercise 8.

10. Follow the steps of Exercise 9 for the system

$$x_1' = x_2^2 + 1, \quad x_1(1) = 0,$$
$$x_2' = x_1^2 + t, \quad x_2(1) = 1,$$

in the region $D: |t - 1| \leq 3, \, x_1^2 + (x_2 - 1)^2 \leq 4$.

11. Follow the steps of Exercise 9 for the system

$$x_1' = x_1^2 x_2,$$
$$x_2' = x_3 + t, \quad \mathbf{x}(0) = \mathbf{c},$$
$$x_3' = x_3^2,$$

in the region $D: |t| \leq a, \|\mathbf{x} - \mathbf{c}\| \leq b$.

12. Under the assumption of Theorem 1 consider the systems

$$\mathbf{x}' = \mathbf{f}(t, \mathbf{x}), \quad \mathbf{x}(t_0) = \mathbf{x}_{10},$$
$$\mathbf{x}' = \mathbf{f}(t, \mathbf{x}), \quad \mathbf{x}(t_0) = \mathbf{x}_{20}.$$

Let $\mathbf{x}_1$ and $\mathbf{x}_2$ be solutions of these two systems, respectively. Prove that

$$\|\mathbf{x}_1(t) - \mathbf{x}_2(t)\| \le \|\mathbf{x}_{10} - \mathbf{x}_{20}\| e^{k\delta}.$$

This shows that the solutions of Theorem 1 vary continuously with the initial vector $\mathbf{x}(t_0)$. (*Hint*: See Exercise 18 of Section 10.1.)

***13.** Consider the system

$$\mathbf{x}' = \mathbf{f}(t, \mathbf{x}). \tag{19}$$

Let D denote the region $a \le t \le b$, $\mathbf{x} \in R^n$, and assume that

$$\|\mathbf{f}(t, \mathbf{x}_1) - \mathbf{f}(t, \mathbf{x}_2)\| \le k \|\mathbf{x}_1 - \mathbf{x}_2\|,$$

for any pair of points $(t, \mathbf{x}_1)$ and $(t, \mathbf{x}_2)$ in D. Prove that for any pair $(t_0, \mathbf{x}_0)$ in D there exists a unique solution $\mathbf{x}(t)$ of Eq. (19) defined on the entire interval $a \le t \le b$, which satisfies $\mathbf{x}(t_0) = \mathbf{x}_0$. (*Hint*: Proceed as in the proof of Theorem 2. This is a more general global existence–uniqueness result.)

REVIEW EXERCISES FOR CHAPTER 10

In Exercises 1 through 6, find a Lipschitz constant for the given functions over the given interval(s).

1. $f(x) = \cos x$, $\left[0, \dfrac{\pi}{2}\right]$

2. $f(x) = \dfrac{1}{x^3}$, $[2, 5]$

3. $f(t, x) = \sqrt{t}e^x$, $0 \le t \le 4$, $0 \le x \le 1$

4. $f(t, x) = \dfrac{x^2}{t}$, $t \ge 2$, $1 \le x \le 3$

5. $f(x) = e^{\sqrt{1+x}} \sin x$, $[0, 2]$

6. $f(t, x) = e^{-t^2}x^3 \sin \dfrac{1}{x}$, $t > 0$, $-1 \le x \le 1$, $x \ne 0$

For each initial value problem of Exercises 7 through 12, determine whether a unique solution can be guaranteed. If so, let $a = b = 1$ if possible, and find the number δ as given by Eq. (7) of Section 10.1.

7. $x' = x^4$, $x(1) = 4$

8. $x' = \sqrt{x}$, $x(1) = 3$

9. $x' = \cos x$, $x(0) = \dfrac{\pi}{2}$

10. $x' = \sqrt{x(x + 1)}$, $x(1) = 4$

11. $x' = \tan x$, $x\left(\dfrac{\pi}{4}\right) = 1$

12. $x' = tx^2$, $x(3) = 6$

13. Consider the system

$$x_1' = tx_1 + x_2 + t^3, \quad x_1(0) = 2,$$
$$x_2' = x_1^2 + x_2^2 + t^2, \quad x_2(0) = 3.$$

a) Write the system in the form (2) in Section 10.2.

b) Find a Lipschitz constant for $\mathbf{f}$ in the region $D: |t| \le 1$, $(x_1 - 2)^2 + (x_2 - 3)^2 \le 1$.

c) Find $\delta = \min\{a, b/M\}$ as in Exercise 8 in Section 10.2.

Fourier Series and Boundary Value Problems

11.1 INTRODUCTION

Until now we have considered differential equations whose solutions are determined by initial conditions. In this chapter we shall discuss another equally important way to specify a particular solution of a differential equation, namely, specifying certain values of the function and its derivatives at two or more points. The differential equation together with the given conditions at two or more points is called a *boundary value problem*. (This was defined earlier in Section 1.2.)

In this section we shall present some examples of boundary value problems, together with a discussion of some of the powerful methods that are used to solve them. We shall see how the concepts of eigenvalues and eigenfunctions arise naturally in these situations and discuss the importance of Fourier series techniques in solving nonhomogeneous boundary value problems.

Since a boundary value problem requires that conditions be given at two or more points, we can assume the differential equation involved to be at least of second order, because a first-order equation is usually completely specified by a single condition. (This follows from the existence–uniqueness Theorems 3 and 5 in Section 10.1.)

Example 1   Consider the simple harmonic motion of a mass m attached to a coiled spring with spring constant k. Applying Newton's law of motion and Hooke's law to this situation, we obtained in Section 3.8 [see Eq. (1) there], the differential equation

$$x'' + p^2 x = 0, \quad p^2 = \frac{k}{m},$$ (1)

where $x = x(t)$ denotes the displacement at time t of the mass from its equilibrium position. Suppose the mass is initially ($t = 0$) at its equilibrium position when it is given an unknown initial velocity $v_0 > 0$. How can we guarantee that the mass will again be at its equilibrium position after precisely one second? Obviously, such a mechanism provides a simple, though crude, timepiece. (See Fig. 1.)

Our purpose now is to discover some of the properties of the unknown solution $x(t)$. If the time is measured in seconds, then we have the boundary conditions

$$x(0) = x(1) = 0.$$ (2)

The boundary conditions together with the differential equation (1) specify the boundary value problem we must solve.

We recall from Chapter 3 that to find the general solution of the differential equation (1) we need only solve the characteristic equation

$$\lambda^2 + p^2 = 0.$$

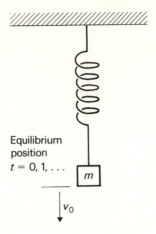

Equilibrium
position
$t = 0, 1, \ldots$

m

v_0

Figure 1

Since the roots of the characteristic equation are $\lambda = \pm ip$, the general solution of Eq. (1) is given by

$$x(t) = A \cos pt + B \sin pt. \tag{3}$$

Setting $t = 0$ in Eq. (3) and using the boundary condition $x(0) = 0$, we observe that $A = 0$, so that the solution must consist only of multiples of $\sin pt$. For the boundary condition $x(1) = 0$ to hold we must also have

$$B \sin p = x(1) = 0.$$

There are two cases to consider: either $B = 0$ or $\sin p = 0$. If $B = 0$, then the solution (3) is constantly zero, which means that the mass remains at its equilibrium position at all times t. This is impossible, since the mass was given an initial velocity $v_0 > 0$. Therefore, $\sin p = 0$, which is possible only if p is a nonzero multiple of π:

$$p = \pm \pi, \pm 2\pi, \pm 3\pi, \ldots .$$

[If $p = 0$, we see that Eq. (3) is again constantly zero.] Thus we have arrived at a surprising conclusion: There are infinitely many solutions of the form

$$x(t) = B \sin (n\pi)t, \tag{4}$$

where n is a nonzero integer, for the boundary value problem (1), (2). Furthermore, the constant B cannot be specified without additional information. Indeed, B depends on v_0 and n, since

$$v_0 = x'(0) = n\pi B$$

or $B = v_0/n\pi$.

Actually, in doing the above calculations, we used one fact that was not part of the boundary value problem (1), (2). This was the assumption, given in the statement of the problem, that $v_0 > 0$. This assumption was used to disallow the *trivial solutions* $x(t) \equiv 0$ for all t of the boundary value problem (1), (2). However, the results we have obtained illustrate one of the basic facts about boundary value problems: *Nontrivial solutions will exist only for certain values of the parameter p.* All such nontrivial solutions (4) are called *eigenfunctions* of the problem, and the corresponding values of p^2 that yield these eigenfunctions are called *eigenvalues* of the problem. Rephrasing our work in this context, we see that

$$x(t) = \left(\frac{v_0}{n\pi}\right) \sin n\pi t \tag{5}$$

is an eigenfunction of this problem corresponding to the eigenvalue

$$\frac{k}{m} = p^2 = (n\pi)^2. \tag{6}$$

It is interesting to discover the physical significance of this solution. Suppose we are given a spring with (fixed) spring constant k. Solving Eq. (6) for m, we obtain the masses

$$m_n = \frac{k}{n^2\pi^2}, \quad n = 1, 2, 3, \ldots, \tag{7}$$

each corresponding to a different value of n. Since k and π are fixed quantities, it is *only* for these masses that a solution of the boundary value problem will exist. For any other choice, no matter what initial velocity is given, the mass will not be back at its equilibrium position after exactly one second. Thus the construction of our clock depends on the selection of one of the masses (7). Furthermore, Eq. (5) indicates that if the mass m_n is chosen, it will be at its equilibrium position n times during the time period $0 < t \le 1$. Since increasing n decreases both the weight m_n and the amplitude $(v_0/n\pi)$ of the oscillations, we arrive at the conclusion that *the lighter the mass, the more rapid the oscillation.* This fact is easy to observe physically.

Example 2   A population is subject to an influenza epidemic. Let $s(t)$ and $i(t)$ be, respectively, the numbers of susceptible and infected individuals at time t. Suppose that the rate of change of the number of susceptible individuals is proportional to the number of infected individuals, whereas the rate of change of the number of infected individuals is proportional to the number of susceptible individuals. (The difference between the change in the numbers of infected and susceptible individuals consists of those who have gained immunity or died.) The epidemic lasts a certain period of time, say two months. [With this assumption, we can set $i(0) = i(2) = 0$.] We wish to discover the number of infected individuals at all time t (in months).

From the hypotheses above, we obtain the system of equations

$$\frac{ds}{dt} = -pi,$$

$$\frac{di}{dt} = qs,$$

(8)

where p and q are unknown positive constants of proportionality. Differentiating the second of the equations in the system (8) with respect to t, and substituting the first equation for ds/dt, we obtain the second-order equation

$$\frac{d^2 i}{dt^2} = q \frac{ds}{dt} = -qpi$$

or

$$i'' + k^2 i = 0, \quad k^2 = pq,$$

(9)

with the boundary conditions

$$i(0) = i(2) = 0.$$

(10)

This boundary value problem is very similar to that of Example 1. We again find the general solution

$$i(t) = A \cos kt + B \sin kt.$$

Setting $t = 0$ and using the first boundary condition, we find that $0 = i(0) = A$. The second boundary condition $t = 2$ implies that

$$B \sin 2k = i(2) = 0.$$

Since we are not interested in the trivial solution $i(t) \equiv 0$, it follows that $B \neq 0$, so that $2k$ must be a nonzero multiple of π. Hence the eigenvalues of this problem are

$$k^2 = \left(\frac{\pi}{2}\right)^2, (\pi)^2, \left(\frac{3\pi}{2}\right)^2, \ldots, \left(\frac{n\pi}{2}\right)^2, \ldots,$$

and the corresponding eigenfunctions $i_k(t)$ are given by

$$i_k(t) = B \sin \frac{n\pi t}{2}, \quad k^2 = \left(\frac{n\pi}{2}\right)^2.$$

(11)

If the number of infected individuals is assumed to be positive during the entire epidemic $0 < t < 2$, then $n = 1$. But if we allow for the possibility of a sequence of several consecutive epidemics, then other values of n could have physical meaning.

The boundary value problems in these two examples will also arise in several different problems in Chapter 12 (see Examples 1 in Section 12.3 and 1 in Section 12.4).

Example 3   We return to Example 1, but assume that the spring-mass system is also subject to a periodic external force $K \sin \omega t$, where K, $\omega > 0$. Using the theory of forced vibrations developed in Section 3.8, we obtain the nonhomogeneous second-order equation

$$m \frac{d^2 x}{dt^2} = -kx + K \sin \omega t.$$

Using the same boundary conditions as before, we are led to the nonhomogeneous boundary value problem

$$x'' + \frac{k}{m} x = \frac{K}{m} \sin \omega t, \quad x(0) = x(1) = 0. \tag{12}$$

There are two cases to consider: either $\omega = n\pi$ for some integer n or $\omega \neq n\pi$ for every integer n.

First, we use the method of undetermined coefficients (Section 3.6) to find a particular solution. We suppose that

$$x(t) = A \sin \omega t + B \cos \omega t. \tag{13}$$

Since $x(0) = 0$, it follows that $B = 0$. Differentiating Eq. (13) twice and substituting into Eq. (12), we have

$$-A\omega^2 \sin \omega t + \frac{k}{m} A \sin \omega t = \frac{K}{m} \sin \omega t.$$

Canceling the $\sin \omega t$ on both sides of this equation and solving for A, we obtain

$$A = \frac{K/m}{(k/m) - \omega^2} = \frac{K}{k - m\omega^2}.$$

CASE 1 $(\omega = n_0 \pi)$ Then

$$x_p(t) = \frac{K}{k - mn_0^2 \pi^2} \sin n_0 \pi t \tag{14}$$

is a particular solution of Eq. (12) provided that

$$m \neq \frac{k}{n_0^2 \pi^2}. \tag{15}$$

From Example 1 we know that the homogeneous boundary value problem

$$x'' + \frac{k}{m} x = 0, \quad x(0) = x(1) = 0, \tag{16}$$

has the eigenfunction

$$x_n(t) = A \sin n\pi t,$$

whenever

$$m = m_n = \frac{k}{n^2\pi^2},$$

and the trivial solution for all other values of m. If $m = m_n$, $n \neq n_0$, then we have the general solution

$$x(t) = A \sin n\pi t + \frac{K}{k - m_n n_0^2 \pi^2} \sin n_0 \pi t$$

$$= A \sin n\pi t + \frac{Kn^2}{k(n^2 - n_0^2)} \sin n_0 \pi t.$$

For all other masses m satisfying Eq. (15), the solution of Eq. (12) is given by Eq. (14). There is no solution if $m = k/n_0^2\pi^2$ (see Section 11.7).

CASE 2 If $\omega \neq n\pi$, we see that the function we have obtained by the method of undetermined coefficients,

$$x_p(t) = \frac{K}{k - m\omega^2} \sin \omega t, \tag{17}$$

does not satisfy the boundary condition $x_p(1) = 0$. Since only linear combinations of periodic functions of the form

$$x_n(t) = \sin n\pi t \tag{18}$$

satisfy the boundary conditions $x(0) = x(1) = 0$, we try to approximate Eq. (17) as closely as possible by a sum of such functions. We shall see in Section 11.3 that the trigonometric series

$$2\pi \sin \omega \sum_{n=1}^{\infty} \frac{(-1)^n n}{\omega^2 - (n\pi)^2} \sin n\pi t, \tag{19}$$

called a *Fourier series*, converges to the function $\sin \omega t$ at all points in $0 \leqslant t < 1$, and to zero at $t = 1$. Making use of this fact, we seek a solution of the form

$$x(t) = 2\pi \sin \omega \sum_{n=1}^{\infty} \frac{(-1)^n n c_n}{\omega^2 - (n\pi)^2} \sin n\pi t. \tag{20}$$

Substituting Eq. (20) into Eq. (12) and using the Fourier series (19), we can easily show that $c_n = K/(k - mn^2\pi^2)$. Using these values in Eq. (20), we obtain the general solution of the boundary value problem (12).

At this point one may wonder whether very many functions can be represented as a Fourier series. The question is significant, since forcing functions can be quite arbitrary. Actually, we shall find that the class of functions that have Fourier series representations includes almost every practical forcing function. Although the Fourier series (19) may appear complicated, we shall discover that it is really quite easy to work with once we have become more familiar with it. We shall see that the nth term in the series is independent of the other terms and behaves essentially like the nth coordinate of a certain vector. This phenomenon, called *orthogonality*, will be one of the central themes of this chapter.

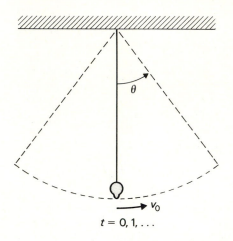

Figure 2

$t = 0, 1, \ldots$

Example 4   Consider the ideal pendulum consisting of a weightless rod of length l supported at one end and attached to a particle of positive weight at the other (Fig. 2). In Exercise 14 of Section 3.8 we found that the angular motion $\theta(t)$ of the pendulum is given by the nonlinear differential equation

$$\frac{d^2\theta}{dt^2} + \frac{g}{l} \sin \theta(t) = 0.$$

Suppose that initially $\theta(0) = 0$ (the rod is vertical) and that we give the pendulum an unknown initial velocity $\theta'(0) = v_0 > 0$ (see Fig. 2). How can we guarantee that the mass will return to its initial position after precisely one second [that is, $\theta(1) = 0$]? The situation, which is essentially that of constructing a pendulum clock, reduces to the solution of the nonlinear boundary value problem

$$\theta'' + \frac{g}{l} \sin \theta = 0, \quad \theta(0) = \theta(1) = 0.$$

In practice, the situation is much more complicated, since it involves damping effects due to friction and a forcing term (such as tension on a spring) to prevent the pendulum from stopping. We shall not investigate nonlinear boundary value problems in this book; instead, we refer the interested reader to more advanced books on the subject.†

Finally, it should be noted that boundary value problems can involve differential equations of order greater than two. For example, in studying the deflection of a beam, one will arrive at the fourth-order boundary value problem‡

$$\frac{d^4 y}{dx^4} = k^2 y,$$

with specified boundary condition $y(0)$, $y'(0)$, $y(L)$, and $y'(L)$, where L is the length of the beam.

EXERCISES 11.1

1. What eigenfunctions and eigenvalues will result in Example 1 if the boundary condition $x(1) = 0$ is replaced by $x(T) = 0$, where T is some fixed constant?

2. Consider the boundary value problem

$$\frac{d^2 x}{dt^2} - kx(t) = 0, \quad x(0) = x(1) = 0,$$

where k is any real number. What are the eigenvalues and eigenfunctions of this problem?

3. Answer Exercise 2 given that the boundary condition $x(1) = 0$ is replaced by $x(T) = 0$ for some fixed constant T.

4. Answer Exercise 2 given that the boundary condition $x(0) = 0$ is replaced by $x(-1) = 0$, all other conditions remaining the same.

5. Find the eigenfunctions and eigenvalues of the boundary value problem

$$x'(t) + k^2 x(t) = 0, \quad x(-T) = x(T) = 0,$$

where T is a fixed constant.

11.2 ORTHOGONAL SETS OF FUNCTIONS AND FOURIER SERIES

Let $f_1(x)$ and $f_2(x)$ be two real-valued functions defined on an interval $a \leq x \leq b$, and suppose that the integral

$$\boxed{(f_1, f_2) = \int_a^b f_1(x) f_2(x)\, dx} \tag{1}$$

exists. We say that the functions f_1 and f_2 are *orthogonal on the interval*

† See for example, P. B. Bailey, L. F. Shampine, and P. E. Waltman, *Nonlinear Two-Point Boundary Value Problems*. New York: Academic Press (1968).

‡ This equation is derived in C. R. Wylie, *Advanced Engineering Mathematics*, p. 323. New York: McGraw-Hill (1966).

$a \leqslant x \leqslant b$ if the integral (1) vanishes; that is, if $(f_1, f_2) = 0$.† A set of real-valued functions $f_1(x)$, $f_2(x)$, $f_3(x)$, ... defined on $a \leqslant x \leqslant b$ is called an *orthogonal set of functions on the interval* $a \leqslant x \leqslant b$, if each integral

$$(f_n, f_m) = \int_a^b f_n(x) f_m(x) \, dx$$

exists and $(f_n, f_m) = 0$ whenever $n \neq m$. The nonnegative square root of the integral

$$(f_n, f_n) = \int_a^b f_n^2(x) \, dx$$

is called the *norm* of the function $f_n(x)$ and is often denoted by $\|f_n\|$ (see Exercise 10):

$$\boxed{\|f_n\| = \sqrt{(f_n, f_n)} = \left[\int_a^b f_n^2(x) \, dx \right]^{1/2}.} \tag{2}$$

An orthogonal set of functions $\{f_n(x)\}$ is called an *orthonormal set of functions on the interval* $a \leqslant x \leqslant b$ if $\|f_n\| = 1$ for all n.‡ Thus, if $\{f_n(x)\}$ is an orthonormal set of functions,

$$(f_n, f_m) = \int_a^b f_n(x) f_m(x) \, dx = \begin{cases} 0 & \text{whenever } n \neq m, \\ 1 & \text{whenever } n = m. \end{cases} \tag{3}$$

Given any orthogonal set of functions $\{f_n(x)\}$ whose norms are nonzero, it is always possible to construct an orthonormal set of functions $\{g_n(x)\}$ by defining

$$g_n(x) = \frac{f_n(x)}{\|f_n\|}, \quad a \leqslant x \leqslant b.$$

---

† For the benefit of those readers familiar with the concept of the orthogonality of vectors in Euclidean n-space, we note that Eq. (1) is a generalization of the usual inner product

$$(\mathbf{f}_1, \mathbf{f}_2) = f_{11}f_{21} + f_{12}f_{22} + \cdots + f_{1n}f_{2n} = \sum_{j=1}^n f_{1j}f_{2j}.$$

Two vectors $\mathbf{f}_1$ and $\mathbf{f}_2$ are orthogonal in Euclidean n-space if $(\mathbf{f}_1, \mathbf{f}_2) = 0$. Also the *norm* of a vector is its Euclidean length

$$\|\mathbf{f}_1\| = \sqrt{(\mathbf{f}_1, \mathbf{f}_1)} = \left(\sum_{j=1}^n f_{1j}^2 \right)^{1/2}.$$

‡ This is equivalent to taking an orthonormal basis in Euclidean n-space, such as the *unit vectors*

$$\mathbf{e}_1 = (1, 0, \ldots, 0), \quad \mathbf{e}_2 = (0, 1, 0, \ldots, 0), \quad \ldots, \quad \mathbf{e}_n = (0, \ldots, 0, 1).$$

Then

$$(g_n, g_m) = \int_a^b \frac{f_n(x) f_m(x)}{\|f_n\| \|f_m\|} \, dx = \frac{1}{\|f_n\| \|f_m\|} (f_n, f_m), \tag{4}$$

which vanishes whenever $m \neq n$ since $\{f_n\}$ is an orthogonal set of functions. If $m = n$, then Eq. (4) yields

$$\|g_n\|^2 = (g_n, g_n)$$

$$= \frac{1}{\|f_n\|^2} (f_n, f_n) = 1,$$

so that $\|g_n\| = 1$ for all n.

Example 1   The functions $f_n(x) = \sin nx$, $n = 1, 2, 3, \ldots$, are an orthogonal set of functions on the interval $-\pi \leq x \leq \pi$. To see this, we use the trigonometric identities

$$\cos(m - n)x = \cos mx \cos nx + \sin mx \sin nx,$$

$$\cos(m + n)x = \cos mx \cos nx - \sin mx \sin nx,$$

which imply (after subtracting and dividing by 2) that

$$\sin nx \sin mx = \tfrac{1}{2}[\cos(m - n)x - \cos(m + n)x].$$

Then

$$(f_n, f_m) = \int_{-\pi}^{\pi} \sin nx \sin mx \, dx$$

$$= \frac{1}{2} \int_{-\pi}^{\pi} [\cos(m - n)x - \cos(m + n)x] \, dx$$

$$= \frac{1}{2} \left[\frac{\sin(m - n)x}{m - n} - \frac{\sin(m + n)x}{m + n} \right] \Big|_{-\pi}^{\pi} = 0, \tag{5}$$

whenever $m \neq n$. If $m = n$, then $\cos(m - n)x = 1$ in the second integral of Eq. (5), so that

$$(f_n, f_n) = \frac{1}{2} \int_{-\pi}^{\pi} (1 - \cos 2nx) \, dx$$

$$= \frac{1}{2} \left(x - \frac{\sin 2nx}{2n} \right) \Big|_{-\pi}^{\pi} = \pi.$$

Hence $\|f_n\| = \sqrt{\pi}$, and we may construct the orthonormal set of functions

$$g_n(x) = \frac{\sin nx}{\sqrt{\pi}}, \quad n = 1, 2, \ldots.$$

Example 2   The functions

$$\frac{1}{\sqrt{2\pi}}, \quad \frac{\cos x}{\sqrt{\pi}}, \quad \frac{\sin x}{\sqrt{\pi}}, \quad \frac{\cos 2x}{\sqrt{\pi}}, \quad \frac{\sin 2x}{\sqrt{\pi}}, \ldots$$

form an orthonormal set of functions on the interval $-\pi \leq x \leq \pi$. We have already demonstrated the orthonormality of the $\sin nx/\sqrt{\pi}$ terms, and clearly

$$\int_{-\pi}^{\pi} \frac{\cos nx \cos mx}{\sqrt{\pi}} \, dx = \frac{1}{2\pi} \int_{-\pi}^{\pi} [\cos (m - n)x + \cos (m + n)x] \, dx = 0$$

whenever $m \neq n$ and equals

$$\frac{1}{2\pi} \int_{-\pi}^{\pi} (1 + \cos 2nx) \, dx = \frac{1}{2\pi} \left(x + \frac{\sin 2nx}{2n} \right) \Big|_{-\pi}^{\pi} = 1$$

if $m = n$. The identities

$$\sin (m + n)x = \sin mx \cos nx + \cos mx \sin nx,$$
$$\sin (m - n)x = \sin mx \cos nx - \cos mx \sin nx$$

imply (after addition and division by 2) that

$$\int_{-\pi}^{\pi} \frac{\sin mx \cos nx}{\sqrt{\pi} \sqrt{\pi}} \, dx = \frac{1}{2\pi} \int_{-\pi}^{\pi} [\sin (m - n)x + \sin (m + n)x] \, dx$$

$$= \frac{-1}{2\pi} \left[\frac{\cos (m - n)x}{m - n} + \frac{\cos (m + n)x}{m + n} \right] \Big|_{-\pi}^{\pi} = 0$$

for all m, n since $\sin (m - n)x = 0$ if $m = n$, and $\cos (-\theta) = \cos \theta$. Finally, the integrals

$$\int_{-\pi}^{\pi} \frac{\sin mx}{\sqrt{\pi}} \frac{1}{\sqrt{2\pi}} \, dx = \frac{-1}{\pi\sqrt{2}} \frac{\cos mx}{m} \Big|_{-\pi}^{\pi} = 0,$$

$$\int_{-\pi}^{\pi} \frac{\cos mx}{\sqrt{\pi}} \frac{1}{\sqrt{2\pi}} \, dx = \frac{1}{\pi\sqrt{2}} \frac{\sin mx}{m} \Big|_{-\pi}^{\pi} = 0,$$

and

$$\int_{-\pi}^{\pi} \left(\frac{1}{\sqrt{2\pi}} \right)^2 \, dx = \frac{1}{2\pi} x \Big|_{-\pi}^{\pi} = 1,$$

complete the verification of the orthonormality.

Orthogonal sets of functions often provide useful series expansions. Let $\{f_n(x)\}$ be an orthogonal set of functions on an interval $a \leq x \leq b$ and suppose that the function $F(x)$ can be represented in terms of the functions

$f_n(x)$ by a convergent series

$$F(x) = \sum_{n=1}^{\infty} c_n f_n(x) = c_1 f_1(x) + c_2 f_2(x) + \cdots. \tag{6}$$

The series (6) is called a *generalized Fourier series* of $F(x)$ and the coefficients $c_1, c_2, \ldots$ are called the *generalized Fourier coefficients of $F(x)$ with respect to the orthogonal set of functions $\{f_n(x)\}$*. It is easy to determine the constants $c_1, c_2, \ldots$ by the following procedure. Fixing m, we multiply both sides of Eq. (6) by $f_m(x)$ and integrate the result over the interval $a \leqslant x \leqslant b$:

$$(F, f_m) = \int_a^b F(x) f_m(x)\, dx = \sum_{n=1}^{\infty} c_n \int_a^b f_n(x) f_m(x)\, dx = \sum_{n=1}^{\infty} c_n (f_n, f_m).$$

Note that we have assumed term-by-term integration to be permissible—an assumption that sometimes is not valid.[†] Since $(f_n, f_m) = 0$ whenever $n \neq m$, we have

$$(F, f_m) = c_m \|f_m\|^2,$$

so that

$$\boxed{c_m = \frac{(F, f_m)}{\|f_m\|^2} = \frac{1}{\|f_m\|^2} \int_a^b F(x) f_m(x)\, dx, \quad m = 1, 2, \ldots.} \tag{7}$$

Example 3   An infinite series of the form

$$\frac{a_0}{2} + \sum_{n=1}^{\infty} [a_n \cos nx + b_n \sin nx], \tag{8}$$

where a_n and b_n are constants, is generally referred to as a *trigonometric* or *Fourier series*. [Note that Eq. (19) in Section 11.1 is a special case of this formula with $a_n = 0$ for all n.]

     If the series (8) converges to a function $F(x)$ on the interval $[-\pi, \pi]$, then it converges for all real x since

$$F(x) = \frac{a_0}{2} + \sum_{n=1}^{\infty} [a_n \cos nx + b_n \sin nx]$$

is a *periodic function of period 2π*:

$$F(x + 2\pi) = F(x) \quad \text{for all } x.$$

This observation is obvious since the functions $\cos nx$ and $\sin nx$ are

---

† Most advanced calculus textbooks contain proofs that term-by-term integration is permissible if the series (6) converges *uniformly* on $a \leqslant x \leqslant b$.

periodic of period 2π. The constants a_n and b_n are called the *Fourier coefficients* of $F(x)$ and are given by the *Euler formulas*:

$$a_n = \frac{1}{\pi} \int_{-\pi}^{\pi} F(x) \cos nx \, dx, \quad b_n = \frac{1}{\pi} \int_{-\pi}^{\pi} F(x) \sin nx \, dx. \qquad \textbf{(9)}$$

These equalities follow from Eq. (7), Eq. (8), and Example 2.

Example 4 Let $P_n(x)$ be the Legendre polynomial of degree n, $n = 0, 1, 2, \ldots$ (see Section 5.5). Then $P_n(x)$ is a solution of Legendre's equation

$$(1 - x^2)y'' - 2xy' + n(n + 1)y = 0$$

in the interval $-1 < x < 1$. Since $P_n(x)$ satisfies the differential equation on this interval, we consider the integral

$$(P_n, P_m) = \int_{-1}^{1} P_n(x)P_m(x) \, dx \qquad \textbf{(10)}$$

and suppose, without loss of generality, that $m < n$. By Rodrigues' formula (9) in Section 5.5,

$$P_n(x) = \frac{1}{2^n n!} \frac{d^n}{dx^n} [(x^2 - 1)^n], \quad n = 0, 1, 2, \ldots,$$

so we may rewrite Eq. (10) as

$$(P_n, P_m) = \frac{1}{2^n n!} \int_{-1}^{1} P_m(x) \frac{d^n}{dx^n} [(x^2 - 1)^n] \, dx. \qquad \textbf{(11)}$$

Integrating Eq. (11) by parts, we have

$$(P_n, P_m) = \frac{P_m(x)}{2^n n!} \frac{d^{n-1}}{dx^{n-1}} [(x^2 - 1)^n] \Big|_{-1}^{1} - \frac{1}{2^n n!} \int_{-1}^{1} P'_m(x) \frac{d^{n-1}}{dx^{n-1}} [(x^2 - 1)^n] \, dx.$$

But $(x^2 - 1)^n = (x - 1)^n(x + 1)^n$, since $x^2 - 1 = (x - 1)(x + 1)$, and $(n - 1)$ repeated differentiations of this function yield a finite sum of terms of the form $(x - 1)^j(x + 1)^{n-j+1}$, with $1 \leq j \leq n$:

$$\frac{d}{dx}(x - 1)^n(x + 1)^n = n(x - 1)^{n-1}(x + 1)^n + n(x - 1)^n(x + 1)^{n-1},$$

$$\frac{d^2}{dx^2}(x - 1)^n(x + 1)^n = n(n - 1)(x - 1)^{n-2}(x + 1)^n + 2n^2(x - 1)^{n-1}(x + 1)^{n-1}$$

$$+ n(n - 1)(x - 1)^n(x + 1)^{n-2},$$

and so on. Clearly, one of the terms $(x - 1)^j$ or $(x + 1)^{n-j+1}$ vanishes at each endpoint of the interval, so that the first term vanishes and

$$(P_n, P_m) = \frac{-1}{2^n n!} \int_{-1}^{1} P'_m(x) \frac{d^{n-1}}{dx^{n-1}} [(x^2 - 1)^n] \, dx.$$

We again integrate by parts and continue doing so until we arrive at the integral

$$(P_n, P_m) = \frac{(-1)^n}{2^n n!} \int_{-1}^{1} P_m^{(n)}(x)(x^2 - 1)^n \, dx. \tag{12}$$

Since $P_m(x)$ is a polynomial of degree m $(<n)$, its nth derivative $P_m^{(n)}$ is zero. Thus $(P_n, P_m) = 0$ whenever $n \neq m$, since one of the subscripts must be smaller than the other.

If $m = n$, then

$$\|P_n\|^2 = (P_n, P_n) = \int_{-1}^{1} P_n^2(x) \, dx = \frac{(-1)^n}{2^n n!} \int_{-1}^{1} P_n^{(n)}(x)(x^2 - 1)^n \, dx$$

by Eq. (12). However, according to Eq. (8) in Section 5.5 the nth-degree term of $P_n(x)$ has the coefficient $(2n)!/2^n (n!)^2$. Thus $P_n^{(n)}(x) = (2n)!2^n n!$ (the other $n!$ term cancels with the term $d^n(x^n)/dx^n = n!$) so that

$$\|P_n\|^2 = \frac{(2n)!}{2^{2n}(n!)^2} \int_{-1}^{1} (1 - x^2)^n \, dx.$$

Setting $x = \sin\theta$ and $dx = \cos\theta \, d\theta$, we obtain

$$\|P_n\|^2 = \frac{(2n)!}{2^{2n}(n!)^2} \int_{-\pi/2}^{\pi/2} \cos^{2n+1}\theta \, d\theta$$

$$= \frac{2(2n)!}{2^{2n}(n!)^2} \int_{0}^{\pi/2} \cos^{2n+1}\theta \, d\theta,$$

since the integrand is symmetric with respect to the y-axis. Finally, by Formula 57 of Appendix 1,

$$\|P_n\|^2 = \frac{2(2n)!}{2^{2n}(n!)^2} \cdot \frac{2^{2n}(n!)^2}{(2n + 1)!} = \frac{2}{2n + 1}. \tag{13}$$

Thus the Legendre polynomials are an orthogonal set of functions, and the polynomials

$$\sqrt{\frac{2n + 1}{2}} \, P_n(x), \quad n = 0, 1, 2, \ldots,$$

are an orthonormal set of functions on the interval $-1 \leq x \leq 1$. An easier proof of this result will be obtained in Example 2 in Section 11.5, after we have developed some additional techniques.

A generalized Fourier series of Legendre polynomials,

$$\sum_{n=0}^{\infty} c_n P_n(x),$$

is called a *Legendre series*. Such series are extremely important for numerical approximations, even when only finitely many coefficients c_n are nonzero, since they provide the "best" *least squares approximation* for any integrable function $F(x)$ on the interval $-1 \leqslant x \leqslant 1$, as we shall shortly see.

Since the Legendre polynomial $P_n(x)$ has degree n, it is possible to express x^n as a linear combination of Legendre polynomials of degree $\leqslant n$. To see this, note that

$$x^0 = 1 = P_0(x), \quad x = P_1(x), \quad x^2 = \tfrac{1}{3}P_0(x) + \tfrac{2}{3}P_2(x), \dots,$$

and if such expressions are known for all powers x^k, $k < n$, then, by Eq. (8) in Section 5.5,

$$\frac{(2n)!x^n}{2^{2n}(n!)^2} = P_n(x) - \sum_{k=1}^{M} \frac{(-1)^k}{2^n k!} \frac{(2n - 2k)!}{(n - k)!(n - 2k)!} x^{n-2k},$$

(M is the greatest integer $\leqslant n/2$) so that x^n can also be expressed as a linear combination of Legendre polynomials of degree $\leqslant n$.

Now suppose we wish to find a polynomial $p(x)$ of degree n that best approximates an integrable function $F(x)$ on the interval $-1 \leqslant x \leqslant 1$, in the *least squares* sense. By this we mean that we want to choose a polynomial $p(x)$ that minimizes the definite integral

$$I = \int_{-1}^{1} [F(x) - p(x)]^2 \, dx.$$

Since $[F(x) - p(x)]^2 \geqslant 0$, this problem amounts to finding the polynomial $p(x)$ that minimizes the area under the curve $y = [F(x) - p(x)]^2$ over the interval $-1 \leqslant x \leqslant 1$.

Using Eq. (7), we calculate the coefficients

$$c_m = \frac{(F, P_m)}{\|P_m\|^2} = \left(\frac{2m + 1}{2}\right) \int_{-1}^{1} F(x)P_m(x) \, dx \tag{14}$$

and define the polynomial

$$p(x) = \sum_{k=0}^{n} c_k P_k(x).$$

Suppose $q(x)$ is any polynomial of degree n. Since every power x^k in $q(x)$ can be expressed as a linear combination of Legendre polynomials of degree $\leq k$, $q(x)$ can also be expressed as a linear combination of Legendre polynomials of degree $\leq n$:

$$q(x) = \sum_{k=0}^{n} b_k P_k(x).$$

(Of course, some of the coefficients b_k might be zero.) Then for this polynomial $q(x)$,

$$I = \int_{-1}^{1} [F(x) - q(x)]^2 \, dx$$

$$= \int_{-1}^{1} F(x)^2 \, dx + \int_{-1}^{1} \left[\sum_{k=0}^{n} b_k P_k(x) \right]^2 dx - 2 \int_{-1}^{1} F(x) \sum_{k=0}^{n} b_k P_k(x) \, dx. \quad \textbf{(15)}$$

The second integral in Eq. (15) can be written as

$$\sum_{k=0}^{n} \sum_{j=0}^{n} b_k b_j \int_{-1}^{1} P_k(x) P_j(x) \, dx = \sum_{k=0}^{n} b_k^2 \|P_k\|^2,$$

since all the terms

$$(P_k, P_j) = \int_{-1}^{1} P_k(x) P_j(x) \, dx = 0$$

if $k \neq j$. Interchanging the finite sum and integral in the last term of Eq. (15), and noting that by Eq. (14)

$$b_k^2 \|P_k\|^2 - 2b_k(F, P_k) = \|P_k\|^2(b_k^2 - 2b_k c_k) = \|P_k\|^2(b_k - c_k)^2 - \|P_k\|^2 c_k^2,$$

we have

$$I = \int_{-1}^{1} F(x)^2 \, dx + \sum_{h=0}^{n} b_k^2 \|P_k\|^2 - 2 \sum_{k=0}^{n} b_k(F, P_k)$$

$$= \int_{-1}^{1} F(x)^2 \, dx + \sum_{k=0}^{n} \frac{2}{2k + 1} (b_k - c_k)^2 - \sum_{k=0}^{n} \frac{2}{2k + 1} c_k^2. \quad \textbf{(16)}$$

Since the c_k terms are fixed [by Eq. (14)] and we have no control over the integral in Eq. (16), we can affect the outcome only by suitably choosing the values b_k. Clearly I is minimized by letting $b_k = c_k$ for $k = 0, 1, \ldots, n$, that is, by choosing $p(x)$ as the minimizing polynomial.

It is often incorrectly assumed by students that the "best" least squares approximation by polynomials of a function $F(x)$ that has a power series expansion is given by the partial sums of that power series. The following example demonstrates this error.

Example 5   Suppose we wish to find the "best" least squares approximation of e^x on

$-1 \leqslant x \leqslant 1$ by a straight line, that is, by a polynomial of degree $\leqslant 1$. Then

$$c_0 = \frac{1}{\|P_0\|^2} (e^x, P_0) = \frac{1}{2} \int_{-1}^{1} e^x \, dx = \frac{e - e^{-1}}{2} = \sinh(1),$$

$$c_1 = \frac{1}{\|P_1\|^2} (e^x, P_1) = \frac{3}{2} \int_{-1}^{1} xe^x \, dx = \frac{3}{2}(x - 1)e^x \bigg|_{-1}^{1} = \frac{3}{e},$$

implying that

$$p(x) = \sinh(1)P_0(x) + \frac{3}{e} P_1(x) = \sinh(1) + \frac{3x}{e}.$$

Clearly $p(x)$ is *not* the first two terms of the Maclaurin expansion of e^x $(= 1 + x + x^2/2 + x^3/3 + \cdots)$.

Some important sets of functions $\{f_n(x)\}$ that occur in applications are not orthogonal, but have the property that for some function $w(x)$ the integral

$$\boxed{(f_n, f_m)_w = \int_a^b w(x)f_n(x)f_m(x) \, dx = 0} \tag{17}$$

whenever $n \neq m$. If this happens, the set $\{f_n(x)\}$ is said to be *orthogonal with respect to the weight function $w(x)$ on the interval $a \leqslant x \leqslant b$*. The *weighted norm* of f_n is defined as

$$\boxed{\|f_n\|_w = \left[\int_a^b w(x)f_n(x)^2 \, dx \right]^{1/2},} \tag{18}$$

and $\{f_n(x)\}$ is said to be *orthonormal with respect to the weight function $w(x)$*, if in addition to being orthogonal with respect to $w(x)$, it satisfies the condition $\|f_n\|_w = 1$ for all n. If $F(x)$ can be represented by a generalized Fourier series

$$F(x) = \sum_{n=0}^{\infty} c_n f_n(x), \tag{19}$$

then the general Fourier coefficients c_k can be determined by multiplying both sides of Eq. (19) by $w(x)f_k(x)$ and integrating over the interval $a \leqslant x \leqslant b$:

$$\int_a^b w(x)F(x)f_x(x) \, dx = \sum_{n=0}^{\infty} c_n \int_a^b w(x)f_n(x)f_k(x) \, dx = c_k \|f_k\|_w^2$$

or

$$\boxed{c_k = \frac{(F, f_k)_w}{\|f_k\|_w^2}.} \tag{20}$$

Example 6   Let $y_n(x)$ be a polynomial solution of *Laguerre's equation,*†

$$(xe^{-x}y')' + ne^{-x}y = 0. \tag{21}$$

[Equation (21) is obtained by multiplying Eq. (18) in Section 5.5 by e^{-x}.] Then y_n is called a *Laguerre polynomial.* Consider the set of Laguerre polynomials $\{y_n(x)\}$, $n = 1, 2, 3, \ldots$, and suppose $m \neq n$. Then we have the equations

$$(xe^{-x}y_n')' + ne^{-x}y_n = 0,$$
$$(xe^{-x}y_m')' + me^{-x}y_m = 0.$$

We multiply the first equation by y_m and the second by $-y_n$ and add them to obtain

$$y_m(xe^{-x}y_n')' - y_n(xe^{-x}y_m')' = e^{-x}(m - n)y_ny_m. \tag{22}$$

Integrating both sides of Eq. (22) on the interval $0 \leqslant x \leqslant \infty$, we have

$$\int_0^\infty [y_m(xe^{-x}y_n')' - y_n(xe^{-x}y_m')'] \, dx = (m - n) \int_0^\infty e^{-x}y_ny_m \, dx. \tag{23}$$

But by the product formula for differentiation,

$$[xe^{-x}(y_my_n' - y_ny_m')]' = (xe^{-x}y_n')'y_m + xe^{-x}y_n'y_m' - (xe^{-x}y_m')'y_n - xe^{-x}y_m'y_n'$$
$$= y_m(xe^{-x}y_n')' - y_n(xe^{-x}y_m')'.$$

Thus Eq. (23) becomes

$$(m - n) \int_0^\infty e^{-x}y_ny_m \, dx = xe^{-x}(y_my_n' - y_ny_m') \Big|_0^\infty = 0, \quad m \neq n,$$

because $f(x) = x(y_my_n' - y_ny_m')$ is a polynomial (since each term is a polynomial) so that the quotient $f(x)/e^x$ tends to zero as $x \to \infty$. This may be verified by applying L'Hôpital's rule as many times as the degree of f to the quotient $f(x)/e^x$:

$$\lim_{x\to\infty} \frac{f(x)}{e^x} = \lim_{x\to\infty} \frac{f'(x)}{e^x} = \cdots = \lim_{x\to\infty} \frac{c}{e^x} = 0.$$

Therefore, the set of functions $\{y_n\}$, $n = 1, 2, \ldots$, is orthogonal with respect to the weight function e^{-x} on $0 \leqslant x < \infty$.

EXERCISES 11.2

In Exercises 1 through 5, show that each given set of functions is orthogonal on the given interval and determine the corresponding orthonormal set.

1. $\{\cos nx\}, \quad n = 0, 1, 2, \ldots; \quad 0 \leqslant x \leqslant 2\pi$

2. $\left\{\sin \dfrac{n\pi x}{T}\right\}, \quad n = 1, 2, 3, \ldots; \quad -T \leqslant x \leqslant T$

3. $\left\{\cos \dfrac{2n\pi x}{T}\right\}, \quad n = 0, 1, 2, \ldots; \quad 0 \leqslant x \leqslant T$

---

† Edmond Laguerre (1834–1886), a French mathematician, made many contributions to geometry and the theory of infinite series.

4. $\{\sin 2nx\}$, $n = 1, 2, 3, \ldots$; $0 \leqslant x \leqslant \pi$

5. $\{\cos 2nx\}$ $n = 0, 1, 2, \ldots$; $0 \leqslant x \leqslant \pi$

6. Represent each of the following polynomials as a linear combination of Legendre polynomials. [*Hint*: Use Eq. (14).]

a) x^4

b) x^5

c) $x^4 - x^3 + 7x^2 - 8x + 2$

d) $x^5 - x + 3$

e) $12x^4 - 8x^2 + 7$

f) $9x^3 - 8x^2 + 7x - 6$

7. Find the first three terms of the Legendre series of the following functions.

a) e^x b) $\sin x$

c) $\cos x$ d) $\sinh x$

e) $\cosh x$ f) $\dfrac{1}{1 + x^2}$

Compare your result with the Maclaurin expansions of the functions.

8. Given that $p(x)$ is a polynomial of degree $n(\geqslant 1)$ and

$$\int_{-1}^{1} x^k p(x)\, dx = 0 \quad \text{for } k = 0, 1, 2, \ldots, n - 1,$$

show that $p(x) = cP_n(x)$ for some constant c.

9. *Hermite polynomials.*† The functions

$$H_0 = 1, \quad H_n(x) = (-1)^n e^{x^2} \frac{d^n}{dx^n} e^{-x^2}, \quad n = 1, 2, 3, \ldots,$$

are called Hermite polynomials (see Exercise 9 of Section 5.5). Prove that:

a) $H_1(x) = 2x$, $H_2(x) = 4x^2 - 2$,

$H_3(x) = 8x^3 - 12x$.

b) The Hermite polynomials satisfy the relation

$$H_{n+1}(x) = 2xH_n(x) - H'_n(x).$$

c) $H_n(x)$ is a solution of *Hermite's equation*

$$y'' - 2xy' + 2ny = 0.$$

d) The set of functions $\{H_n(x)\}$ is orthogonal with respect to the weight function $\exp(-x^2)$ on the interval $-\infty < x < \infty$.

*10. The norm of a function $f(x)$ on an interval $a \leqslant x \leqslant b$ is defined in Eq. (2) by the integral

$$\|f\| = \left(\int_a^b f^2(x)\, dx \right)^{1/2}.$$

This concept is a generalization of the notion of the distance of a point (x, y) in the plane from the origin:

$$d(x, y) = \sqrt{x^2 + y^2}.$$

Assume that f and g are continuous functions on $a \leqslant x \leqslant b$. Prove that the norm satisfies the following three properties:

a) $\|f\| \geqslant 0$, where the equality holds if and only if $f(x) \equiv 0$;

b) $\|af\| = |a| \cdot \|f\|$ for any constant a;

c) $\|f + g\| \leqslant \|f\| + \|g\|$ (triangle inequality).

[*Hint*: (a) Use the fact that if $f(x_0) \neq 0$, then by continuity $f^2(x) \geqslant \varepsilon > 0$ for all x in some interval $x_0 - \delta \leqslant x \leqslant x_0 + \delta$, where $\delta > 0$. (c) Show that for any two real numbers α and β

$$0 \leqslant \|\alpha f - \beta g\|^2 = \alpha^2 \|f\|^2 - 2\alpha\beta(f, g) + \beta^2 \|g\|^2.$$

Then let $\alpha = \|g\|$ and $\beta = \|f\|$, showing that

$$(f, g) \leqslant \|f\| \cdot \|g\|.$$

Finally, use the last inequality to show that

$$\|f + g\|^2 \leqslant (\|f\| + \|g\|)^2.]$$

11.3 FOURIER SERIES ‡

In Section 11.2 we developed some of the basic properties of Fourier series (see Example 3 there), but avoided discussing what kind of functions can be represented by a convergent Fourier series. Actually, the class of functions that can be represented in this fashion is surprisingly large, so large in fact, that it originally aroused a big controversy. The following

---

† Charles Hermite (1822–1901), a French mathematician, was known for his work in number theory.

‡ Named after the French physicist Joseph B. Fourier (1768–1830).

theorem gives sufficient conditions for almost all conceivable practical applications.

Theorem 1   Let $F(x)$ be a periodic function with period $2T$ and such that $F(x)$ and $F'(x)$ are piecewise continuous† on the interval $-T \leqslant x \leqslant T$. Then $F(x)$ has a Fourier series

$$F(x) = \frac{a_0}{2} + \sum_{n=1}^{\infty} \left(a_n \cos \frac{n\pi x}{T} + b_n \sin \frac{n\pi x}{T} \right) \tag{1}$$

whose coefficients are given by the *Euler formulas*

$$a_n = \frac{1}{T} \int_{-T}^{T} F(x) \cos \frac{n\pi x}{T} \, dx, \quad n = 0, 1, 2, \ldots, \tag{2}$$

$$b_n = \frac{1}{T} \int_{-T}^{T} F(x) \sin \frac{n\pi x}{T} \, dx, \quad n = 1, 2, \ldots . \tag{3}$$

The Fourier series (1) converges to $F(x)$ at all points where F is continuous, and to $[F(x + 0) + F(x - 0)]/2$ at all points of jump discontinuity of F.‡

Remarks   Note that $[F(x + 0) + F(x - 0)]/2$ is the average of the right- and left-hand limits at the point x. At any point of continuity both of these values will coincide, so that Eq. (1) converges to $[F(x + 0) + F(x - 0)]/2$ for all x in the interval $-T \leqslant x \leqslant T$.

Although the conditions given in this theorem guarantee the existence and convergence of a Fourier series for the function $F(x)$, they are *not* the most general of such conditions. Moreover, the convergence of a Fourier series to a function $F(x)$ does not imply that F satisfies the conditions given in this theorem. In summary, the conditions given in this theorem are neither necessary nor the most general sufficient conditions. Furthermore, even with these limitations, the proof of the theorem as stated is still too complicated to be presented here.§ Instead, we shall verify the theorem under the additional hypothesis that $F(x)$ has a continuous second derivative.

Proof   Integrating Eq. (2) by parts, we obtain for $n > 0$

$$a_n = \frac{F(x) \sin(n\pi x/T)}{n\pi} \bigg|_{-T}^{T} - \frac{1}{n\pi} \int_{-T}^{T} F'(x) \sin \frac{n\pi x}{T} \, dx.$$

---

† See Section 6.1.
‡ $F(x + 0) = \lim_{h \to 0+} F(x + h)$, $F(x - 0) = \lim_{h \to 0+} F(x - h)$ for $h > 0$.
§ Proofs of this theorem can be found in most advanced calculus or complex variables books. See, for example, W. Kaplan, *Advanced Calculus*, p. 484. Reading, Mass.: Addison-Wesley (1973); or W. R. Derrick, *Introductory Complex Analysis and Applications*, p. 166. New York: Academic Press (1972).

The first term on the right-hand side vanishes, and integrating again by parts, we have

$$a_n = \frac{TF'(x)\cos(n\pi x/T)}{(n\pi)^2}\bigg|_{-T}^{T} - \frac{T}{(n\pi)^2}\int_{-T}^{T} F''(x)\cos\frac{n\pi x}{T}\,dx. \qquad (4)$$

The periodicity of F implies that

$$F'(x + 2T) = \lim_{h\to 0}\frac{F(x + 2T + h) - F(x + 2T)}{h}$$

$$= \lim_{h\to 0}\frac{F(x + h) - F(x)}{h} = F'(x),$$

and since $\cos(-t) = \cos t$, the first term in Eq. (4) is zero. By hypothesis, $F''(x)$ is continuous on $-T \leq x \leq T$, so that it attains its maximum and minimum values on that interval and some positive number M exists such that $|F''(x)| < M$. Hence the inequality $|\cos(n\pi x/T)| \leq 1$ implies that

$$|a_n| \leq \frac{T}{(n\pi)^2}\left|\int_{-T}^{T} F''(x)\cos\frac{n\pi x}{T}\,dx\right| < \frac{TM}{(n\pi)^2}\left|\int_{-T}^{T} dx\right| = \frac{2MT^2}{(n\pi)^2}.$$

A similar inequality also holds for $|b_n|$, so that the series of absolute values of the terms on the right-hand side of Eq. (1) is bounded by the convergent series

$$\frac{|a_0|}{2} + \frac{2MT^2}{\pi^2}\left(1 + 1 + \frac{1}{2^2} + \frac{1}{2^2} + \frac{1}{3^2} + \frac{1}{3^2} + \cdots\right).$$

Thus the Fourier series (1) converges absolutely for all values x. Readers familiar with the notion of uniform convergence will see that the series (1) converges uniformly.[†] Since uniform convergence of a series permits term-by-term integration, the derivation of the Euler formulas (2) and (3), carried out in Example 3 in Section 11.2, can be completely justified. ∎

Although the theory of Fourier series is complicated, the application of these series is very easy. It should be clear from Theorem 1 that Fourier series apply to a much wider class of functions than Taylor series do (even under the assumption we have used in the proof), since discontinuous functions cannot have a Taylor series representation. It is also useful to consider some functions for which Theorem 1 *does not* apply.

Example 1   The functions $F_1(x) = 1/x$ and

$$F_2(x) = (-1)^n, \quad \frac{1}{n+1} < |x| \leq \frac{1}{n}, \quad n = 1, 2, 3, \ldots,$$

[†] Actually, we have shown that the Fourier series (1) converges uniformly according to the Weierstrass M-test discussed on p. 420.

Figure 3

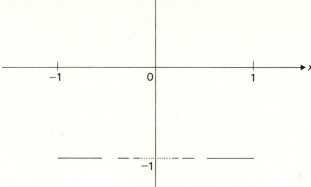

do not satisfy the hypotheses of Theorem 1 in the interval $-1 \le x \le 1$, since neither function is piecewise continuous. The function F_1 has an infinite jump discontinuity at $x = 0$, whereas F_2 has an infinite number of discontinuities in $-1 \le x \le 1$ (see Fig. 3).

Let us now illustrate the procedure involved in obtaining the Fourier series of a function by some examples.

Example 2   Find the Fourier series of the periodic function (see Fig. 4)

$$f(x) = (-1)^n k, \quad n < x < n + 1.$$

Functions of this type occur as off-on controls in mechanical systems.

Figure 4

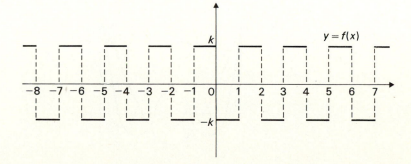

Observe that $f(x)$ has period $2T = 2$, so that by Eq. (2),

$$a_n = \int_{-1}^{1} f(x) \cos n\pi x \, dx = (-k) \int_{-1}^{0} \cos n\pi x \, dx + k \int_{0}^{1} \cos n\pi x \, dx.$$

If $n = 0$, we obtain $a_0 = -k + k = 0$; and if $n \neq 0$, then

$$a_n = \frac{-k}{n\pi} \sin n\pi x \, \Big|_{-1}^{0} + \frac{k}{n\pi} \sin n\pi x \, \Big|_{0}^{1} = 0.$$

Similarly, since $\cos(-t) = \cos t$,

$$b_n = (-k) \int_{-1}^{0} \sin n\pi x \, dx + k \int_{0}^{1} \sin n\pi x \, dx$$

$$= \frac{k}{n\pi} \cos n\pi x \, \Big|_{-1}^{0} - \frac{k}{n\pi} \cos n\pi x \, \Big|_{0}^{1} = \frac{2k}{n\pi} (1 - \cos n\pi),$$

which vanishes for even n and equals $4k/n\pi$ for odd n. Thus

$$f(x) = \frac{4k}{\pi} \left(\sin \pi x + \frac{1}{3} \sin 3\pi x + \frac{1}{5} \sin 5\pi x + \cdots \right). \tag{5}$$

The graphs of $f(x)$ and the first three partial sums of Eq. (5) are shown in Fig. 5.

Figure 5

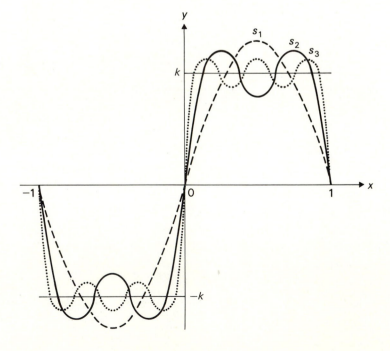

As a bonus for our work above, note that if we set $x = \frac{1}{2}$ in Eq. (5), we obtain the series

$$k = \frac{4k}{\pi}\left(1 - \frac{1}{3} + \frac{1}{5} - \frac{1}{7} + \cdots\right)$$

or

$$\frac{\pi}{4} = 1 - \frac{1}{3} + \frac{1}{5} - \frac{1}{7} + \cdots,$$

since $\sin \pi/2 = 1$, $\sin 3\pi/2 = -1$, and so on. This is a famous result that Leibniz obtained by means of a complicated geometrical construction.

As a final note, observe that the function $f(x)$ in this example satisfies the condition $f(-x) = -f(x)$. Functions having this property are said to be *odd* functions. In particular, observe that all functions of the form $\sin n\pi x$ are odd functions.

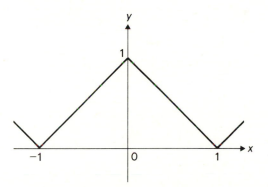

Figure 6

Example 3   Consider the sawtooth function

$$f(x) = \begin{cases} x + 1, & -1 \leqslant x \leqslant 0, \\ -x + 1, & 0 \leqslant x \leqslant 1, \end{cases} \quad f(x + 2) = f(x),$$

shown in Fig. 6. Again $T = 1$ and

$$a_n = \int_{-1}^{0} (x + 1) \cos n\pi x \, dx + \int_{0}^{1} (-x + 1) \cos n\pi x \, dx.$$

If $n = 0$, we have

$$a_0 = \left(\frac{x^2}{2} + x\right)\Big|_{-1}^{0} + \left(x - \frac{x^2}{2}\right)\Big|_{0}^{1} = 1,$$

and integrating by parts for $n \neq 0$, we obtain

$$a_n = \frac{(x+1)}{n\pi} \sin n\pi x \Big|_{-1}^0 - \frac{1}{n\pi} \int_{-1}^0 \sin n\pi x \, dx$$

$$+ \frac{(1-x)}{n\pi} \sin n\pi x \Big|_0^1 + \frac{1}{n\pi} \int_0^1 \sin n\pi x \, dx$$

$$= \frac{1}{(n\pi)^2} \cos n\pi x \Big|_{-1}^0 - \frac{1}{(n\pi)^2} \cos n\pi x \Big|_0^1 = \frac{2}{(n\pi)^2} (1 - \cos n\pi).$$

Therefore, a_n vanishes for even $n \neq 0$ and equals $4/(n\pi)^2$ for odd n. Similarly,

$$b_n = \frac{-(x+1)}{n\pi} \cos n\pi x \Big|_{-1}^0 + \frac{1}{n\pi} \int_{-1}^0 \cos n\pi x \, dx$$

$$+ \frac{(x-1)}{n\pi} \cos n\pi x \Big|_0^1 - \frac{1}{n\pi} \int_0^1 \cos n\pi x \, dx$$

$$= \frac{-1}{n\pi} + \frac{1}{(n\pi)^2} \sin n\pi x \Big|_{-1}^0 + \frac{1}{n\pi} - \frac{1}{(n\pi)^2} \sin n\pi x \Big|_0^1 = 0.$$

Thus

$$f(x) = \frac{1}{2} + \frac{4}{\pi^2} \left(\cos \pi x + \frac{1}{3^2} \cos 3\pi x + \frac{1}{5^2} \cos 5\pi x + \frac{1}{7^2} \cos 7\pi x + \cdots \right). \quad \textbf{(6)}$$

Incidentally, note that if we set $x = 1$, then

$$0 = \frac{1}{2} - \frac{4}{\pi^2} \left(1 + \frac{1}{3^2} + \frac{1}{5^2} + \frac{1}{7^2} + \cdots \right)$$

or

$$\frac{\pi^2}{8} = 1 + \frac{1}{3^2} + \frac{1}{5^2} + \frac{1}{7^2} + \cdots.$$

We observe that the term-by-term derivative of Eq. (6) yields

$$f'(x) = \frac{-4}{\pi} \left(\sin \pi x + \frac{1}{3} \sin 3\pi x + \frac{1}{5} \sin 5\pi x + \cdots \right),$$

which is the same series as Eq. (5) for $k = -1$. An explanation for this fact is found by noting that $f'(x) = (-1)^n(-1)$ for $n < x < n + 1$.

Finally, note that this function satisfies the condition $f(-x) = f(x)$. All such functions are called *even* functions. In particular, $\cos n\pi x$ is an even function for every integer n.

Example 4 Consider the clipped sine wave

$$f(x) = \begin{cases} k \sin Tx, & 0 < x < \pi/T, \\ 0, & -\pi/T < x < 0, \end{cases} \quad f\left(x + \frac{2\pi}{T} \right) = f(x),$$

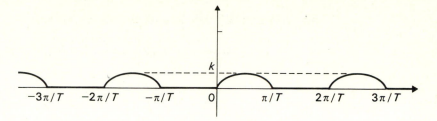

Figure 7

$-3\pi/T \quad -2\pi/T \quad -\pi/T \quad 0 \quad \pi/T \quad 2\pi/T \quad 3\pi/T$

which is obtained by passing a sinusoidal voltage $k \sin Tx$ through a half-wave rectifier (see Fig. 7). Here the period is $2\pi/T$, so that

$$a_n = \frac{T}{\pi} \int_0^{\pi/T} k \sin Tx \cos nTx \, dx, \quad a_0 = \frac{2k}{\pi}.$$

Using the substitution

$$2 \sin Tx \cos nTx = \sin (n + 1)Tx - \sin (n - 1)Tx$$

as in Example 1 in Section 11.2, we have

$$a_n = \frac{kT}{2\pi} \left[\frac{\cos (n - 1)Tx}{(n - 1)T} - \frac{\cos (n + 1)Tx}{(n + 1)T} \right] \Big|_0^{\pi/T}$$

$$= \frac{k}{2\pi} \left[\frac{\cos (n - 1)\pi - 1}{n - 1} - \frac{\cos (n + 1)\pi - 1}{n + 1} \right].$$

When n is odd, $a_n = 0$, and when n is even,

$$a_n = \frac{k}{\pi} \left(\frac{1}{n + 1} - \frac{1}{n - 1} \right) = \frac{-2k}{\pi(n^2 - 1)}.$$

Similarly, for $n \neq 1$,

$$b_n = \frac{T}{\pi} \int_0^{\pi/T} k \sin Tx \sin nTx \, dx$$

$$= \frac{2kT}{\pi} \int_0^{\pi/T} [\cos (n - 1)Tx - \cos (n + 1)Tx] \, dx$$

$$= \frac{2k}{\pi} \left[\frac{\sin (n - 1)Tx}{n - 1} - \frac{\sin (n + 1)Tx}{n + 1} \right] \Big|_0^{\pi/T} = 0;$$

and if $n = 1$, by Formula 18 of Appendix 1,

$$b_1 = \frac{k}{2\pi} (Tx - \sin Tx \cos Tx) \Big|_0^{\pi/T} = \frac{k}{2}.$$

Thus, since only b_1 and the evenly subscripted terms $a_{2n} = -2k/\pi(4n^2 - 1)$ are nonzero,

$$f(x) = \frac{k}{\pi} + \frac{k}{2} \sin Tx - \frac{2k}{\pi} \sum_{n=1}^{\infty} \frac{\cos 2nTx}{4n^2 - 1}. \tag{7}$$

Incidentally, if we set $x = \pi/2T$, then another intriguing identity results:

$$k = \frac{k}{\pi} + \frac{k}{2} - \frac{2k}{\pi} \sum_{n=1}^{\infty} \frac{\cos n\pi}{4n^2 - 1}$$

or

$$\frac{\pi}{2} - 1 = 2\left(\frac{1}{1 \cdot 3} - \frac{1}{3 \cdot 5} + \frac{1}{5 \cdot 7} - \frac{1}{7 \cdot 9} + \cdots\right).$$

Note that in this example the Fourier series (7) contains both sine and cosine terms. Since $f(x)$ is neither even nor odd, Examples 2 and 3 provide the necessary clues for the formulation of the following theorem.

Theorem 2   Let $F(x)$ be a periodic function of period $2T$ that has a Fourier series. If $F(x)$ is an even function, then all the Fourier coefficients b_n are zero, whereas if $F(x)$ is an odd function, then the Fourier coefficients a_n all vanish.

Remark   The Fourier series of an even function,

$$F(x) = \frac{a_0}{2} + \sum_{n=1}^{\infty} a_n \cos \frac{n\pi x}{T}, \qquad (8)$$

is called a *Fourier cosine series*, whereas that of an odd function,

$$F(x) = \sum_{n=1}^{\infty} b_n \sin \frac{n\pi x}{T}, \qquad (9)$$

is said to be a *Fourier sine series*. Observe that Theorem 2 implies that for even and odd functions, we need to calculate only half as many coefficients as are generally required.

Proof   Let $g(x)$ be an odd function and let $x = -t$ so that $dx = -dt$. Then

$$\int_{-T}^{0} g(x)\, dx = -\int_{T}^{0} g(-t)\, dt = \int_{0}^{T} g(-t)\, dt = -\int_{0}^{T} g(t)\, dt,$$

so that we have

$$\int_{-T}^{T} g(x)\, dx = \int_{-T}^{0} g(x)\, dx + \int_{0}^{T} g(x)\, dx = 0.$$

Note now that if we multiply $g(x)$ by an even function $h(x)$, then the product $f(x) = g(x)h(x)$ is again an odd function:

$$f(-x) = g(-x)h(-x) = -g(x)h(x) = -f(x).$$

Now let $F(x)$ be an even function. Since $\sin(n\pi x/T)$ is an odd function,

$$F(x) \sin\left(\frac{n\pi x}{T}\right)$$

is odd and

$$Tb_n = \int_{-T}^{T} F(x) \sin \frac{n\pi x}{T}\, dx = 0,$$

implying that all the coefficients b_n vanish. Similarly, if $F(x)$ is odd, then

$$F(x) \cos \left(\frac{n\pi x}{T} \right)$$

is odd [since $\cos(n\pi x/T)$ is even] and

$$Ta_n = \int_{-T}^{T} F(x) \cos \frac{n\pi x}{T}\, dx = 0. \;\blacksquare$$

EXERCISES 11.3

1. Find the smallest positive period of the functions $\cos 2x$, $\sin \pi x$, $\cos(2\pi nx/T)$, $\sin 2k\pi x$.

2. Show that a constant function is periodic with any period $2T > 0$.

3. Suppose that $f(x)$ has period $2T$. What is the period of $f(ax/b)$?

4. Prove that a convergent infinite series of functions of period T is periodic of period T.

In Exercises 5 through 13, find the Fourier series of each function $f(x)$ of period 2π, where one period is defined, and accurately plot the first three partial sums

$$\frac{a_0}{2} + \sum_{n=1}^{k} (a_n \cos nx + b_n \sin nx), \quad k = 1, 2, 3.$$

5. $f(x) = x, \quad |x| < \pi$

6. $f(x) = \begin{cases} 0, & -\pi < x < 0, \\ 1, & 0 < x < \pi \end{cases}$

7. $f(x) = x^2, \quad |x| < \pi$

8. $f(x) = \begin{cases} 0, & -\pi < x < 0, \\ x, & 0 < x < \pi \end{cases}$

9. $f(x) = |x|, \quad |x| < \pi$

10. $f(x) = \begin{cases} x, & -\pi < x < 0, \\ x - \pi, & 0 < x < \pi \end{cases}$

11. $f(x) = \begin{cases} -1, & -\pi < x < -1, \\ x, & -1 < x < 1, \\ 1, & 1 < x < \pi \end{cases}$

12. $f(x) = \begin{cases} \pi + x, & -\pi < x < 0, \\ \pi - x, & 0 < x < \pi \end{cases}$

13. $f(x) = e^x, \quad |x| < \pi$

In Exercises 14 through 21, find the Fourier series of each function $f(x)$ of period T, where one of the periods is defined.

14. $f(x) = x, \quad |x| < 1, \quad T = 2$

15. $f(x) = x, \quad 0 < x < 2, \quad T = 2$

16. $f(x) = x, \quad 0 < x < 3, \quad T = 3$

17. $f(x) = x^2, \quad |x| < 1, \quad T = 2$

18. $f(x) = x^2, \quad 0 < x < 2, \quad T = 2$

19. $f(x) = \begin{cases} 0, & 0 < x < 1, \\ 1, & 1 < x < 2, \end{cases} \quad T = 2$

20. $f(x) = \begin{cases} 0, & 0 < x < 1, \\ x - 1, & 1 < x < 2, \end{cases} \quad T = 2$

21. $f(x) = \begin{cases} x, & 0 < x < 1, \\ 1, & 1 < x < 2, \end{cases} \quad T = 2$

22. Find the Fourier series of the periodic function of period 2π

$$f(x) = \frac{x^2}{4}, \quad |x| < \pi,$$

and use this series to verify the identities:

$$\frac{\pi^2}{6} = 1 + \frac{1}{2^2} + \frac{1}{3^2} + \frac{1}{4^2} + \frac{1}{5^2} + \cdots,$$

$$\frac{\pi^2}{12} = 1 - \frac{1}{2^2} + \frac{1}{3^2} - \frac{1}{4^2} + \frac{1}{5^2} - \cdots,$$

$$\frac{\pi^2}{8} = 1 + \frac{1}{3^2} + \frac{1}{5^2} + \frac{1}{7^2} + \frac{1}{9^2} + \cdots.$$

11.4 STURM–LIOUVILLE PROBLEMS

Examples 1 and 2 in Section 11.1, as well as several of the homogeneous boundary value problems we shall encounter in Chapter 12, belong to a wide class of problems whose eigenfunctions and eigenvalues have particularly nice properties. We shall develop a small part of the fascinating theory of this class of problems in this and the next two sections.

Consider the differential equation

$$[r(x)y']' + [p(x) + \lambda q(x)]y = 0, \tag{1}$$

where $r(x)$, $r'(x)$, $p(x)$, and $q(x)$ are continuous functions on some interval $a \le x \le b$ and λ is a real parameter. We shall see that many of the differential equations of applied mathematics, such as Legendre's equation and Bessel's equation, can be written in the form (1). Suppose that we impose the boundary conditions

$$
\begin{aligned}
a_1 y(a) - a_2 y'(a) &= 0, \\
b_1 y(b) - b_2 y'(b) &= 0,
\end{aligned}
\tag{2}
$$

at the endpoints of the interval, and require that at least one coefficient in each equation in (2) be nonzero. Equation (1), together with the boundary conditions (2), is known as a *Sturm–Liouville†* *problem.*

Observe, as in Example 1 in Section 11.1, that any Sturm–Liouville problem has the trivial solution $y \equiv 0$. For certain values of the parameter λ, nontrivial solutions of the Sturm–Liouville problem may exist. All such nontrivial solutions are called *eigenfunctions* of the problem, and the corresponding values of λ that yield these solutions are called *eigenvalues* of the problem. In Example 1 in Section 11.1 the eigenvalues of Eq. (1) were given by $\lambda = p^2 = \pi^2, 4\pi^2, 9\pi^2, \ldots, (n\pi)^2, \ldots$ and the eigenfunctions corresponding to the eigenvalue $(n\pi)^2$ ($n \ne 0$) had the form (4) in Section 11.1:

$$x(t) = B \sin n\pi t,$$

where B was any nonzero real number.

As we shall see in the next section, Sturm–Liouville problems have the following four basic properties:

> i) All eigenvalues are real. (This tells us that we need not worry about complex eigenvalues, which may occur for other kinds of boundary value problems. See Exercise 9 in Section 11.5.)

---

† The Swiss mathematician J. C. F. Stürm (1803–1855) made many significant contributions to the theory of differential equations. Joseph Liouville (1809–1882), a French mathematician, was noted for his work in complex analysis.

ii) Corresponding to each eigenvalue there is only one linearly independent† eigenfunction. (This simplifies the task of finding the eigenfunctions.)

iii) There is an infinite number of eigenvalues and eigenfunctions.

iv) The eigenfunctions can be chosen so as to be orthogonal with respect to the weight function $q(x)$. (The last two facts allow us to represent wide classes of functions by generalized Fourier series in terms of the eigenfunctions.)

Example 1 Find the eigenvalues and eigenfunctions of the Sturm–Liouville problem

$$y'' + \lambda y = 0, \qquad y(0) = y'(1) = 0. \tag{3}$$

Setting $r(x) \equiv q(x) \equiv 1$ and $p(x) \equiv 0$, we see that Eq. (3) has the form (1), and letting $a = 0$, $b = 1$, $a_1 = -b_2 = 1$, and $a_2 = b_1 = 0$, we have the right type of boundary conditions. Thus Eq. (3) is a Sturm–Liouville problem.

The roots of the characteristic equation are $\pm\sqrt{-\lambda}$ so that we obtain the general solutions

$$y(x) = \begin{cases} c_1 e^{\sqrt{-\lambda}x} + c_2 e^{-\sqrt{-\lambda}x} & \text{if } \lambda < 0, \\ c_1 + c_2 x & \text{if } \lambda = 0, \\ c_1 \cos\sqrt{\lambda}x + c_2 \sin\sqrt{\lambda}x & \text{if } \lambda > 0. \end{cases}$$

Thus we need to examine three cases:

1. If $\lambda < 0$, then the boundary conditions $y(0) = 0$ and $y'(1) = 0$ yield, after a short computation, the homogeneous system of equations

$$c_1 + c_2 = 0,$$
$$\sqrt{-\lambda}e^{\sqrt{-\lambda}}c_1 - \sqrt{-\lambda}e^{-\sqrt{-\lambda}}c_2 = 0.$$

It is easy to verify that the only solution to this system is $c_1 = c_2 = 0$, which indicates that problem (3) has only trivial solutions if $\lambda < 0$.

2. If $\lambda = 0$, the boundary condition $y(0) = 0$ implies that $c_1 = 0$, and since $y' \equiv c_2$, the second condition forces c_2 to vanish. Again Eq. (3) has only a trivial solution.

3. If $\lambda > 0$, the condition $y(0) = 0$ implies that $c_1 = 0$ so that the solution to the problem must have the form

$$y(x) = c_2 \sin\sqrt{\lambda}x. \tag{4}$$

Differentiating Eq. (4), we have $y'(x) = c_2\sqrt{\lambda}\cos\sqrt{\lambda}x$, and setting $x = 1$, we obtain the equation $c_2\sqrt{\lambda}\cos\sqrt{\lambda} = 0$. Hence in this case we will have nontrivial solutions whenever $\cos\sqrt{\lambda}$ is zero. This occurs whenever the

---
† Any constant multiple of this eigenfunction is also an eigenfunction.

constant $\sqrt{\lambda}$ is one of the numbers

$$\frac{\pi}{2}, \frac{3\pi}{2}, \frac{5\pi}{2}, \frac{7\pi}{2}, \ldots,$$

that is, whenever λ takes on one of the values

$$\frac{\pi^2}{4}, \frac{9\pi^2}{4}, \frac{25\pi^2}{4}, \frac{49\pi^2}{4}, \ldots . \tag{5}$$

The values (5) are the eigenvalues of Eq. (4), and the eigenfunctions corresponding to the eigenvalues $\lambda_k = (2k - 1)^2\pi^2/4$, $k = 1, 2, 3, \ldots$, have the form

$$y_k(x) = A \sin \frac{(2k - 1)\pi x}{2}, \quad A \neq 0.$$

Example 2   Consider the Sturm–Liouville problem

$$(xy')' + \frac{\lambda}{x}y = 0, \quad y(1) = y(e) = 0. \tag{6}$$

If we write $(xy')'$ as $xy'' + y'$ and multiply the differential equation on both sides by x, we obtain the Euler equation considered in Section 3.5. We therefore assume that $y = x^r$ is a solution of Eq. (6) and find, after a short calculation, that

$$(rx^r)' + \lambda x^{r-1} = (r^2 + \lambda)x^{r-1} = 0.$$

Since x does not vanish on $1 \leq x \leq e$, it follows that $r = \pm\sqrt{-\lambda}$. Again we must deal with three cases:

1. If $\lambda < 0$, we have a general solution of the form

$$y(x) = c_1 x^{\sqrt{-\lambda}} + c_2 x^{-\sqrt{-\lambda}}.$$

Using the boundary conditions, we obtain the homogeneous equations

$$c_1 + c_2 = 0,$$
$$e^{\sqrt{-\lambda}}c_1 + e^{-\sqrt{-\lambda}}c_2 = 0.$$

Setting $c_2 = -c_1$ in the second equation, we obtain

$$2c_1 \sinh \sqrt{-\lambda} = c_1(e^{\sqrt{-\lambda}} - e^{-\sqrt{-\lambda}}) = 0,$$

and since $\sinh \sqrt{-\lambda} \neq 0$ if $\lambda \neq 0$, it follows that $c_1 = c_2 = 0$. Thus Eq. (6) has only trivial solutions when $\lambda < 0$.

2. If $\lambda = 0$, Eq. (6) reduces to the equation $(xy')' = 0$. Integrating both sides, we obtain $xy' = c_1$, so that $y' = c_1/x$ and $y(x) = c_1 \ln x + c_2$. The condition $y(1) = 0$ implies that $c_2 = 0$. Then $y(e) = c_1 \ln e = c_1 = 0$. Again we have only trivial solutions.

3. If $\lambda > 0$, we use the identity $e^{i\theta} = \cos\theta + i\sin\theta$ [see Eq. (3) in

Section 3.5] to write

$$y_1(x) = x^{\sqrt{-\lambda}} = (e^{\ln x})^{i\sqrt{\lambda}} = \cos(\sqrt{\lambda}\ln x) + i\sin(\sqrt{\lambda}\ln x),$$
$$y_2(x) = x^{-\sqrt{-\lambda}} = (e^{\ln x})^{-i\sqrt{\lambda}} = \cos(\sqrt{\lambda}\ln x) - i\sin(\sqrt{\lambda}\ln x).$$

Letting $y_1^* = (y_1 + y_2)/2$ and $y_2^* = (y_1 - y_2)/2i$ [see Section 3.5] we may write the general solution of Eq. (6) in the form

$$y(x) = c_1\cos(\sqrt{\lambda}\ln x) + c_2\sin(\sqrt{\lambda}\ln x), \quad \lambda > 0.$$

Setting $x = 1$, we find that the condition $y(1) = 0$ implies that $c_1 = 0$, so that

$$y(x) = c_2\sin(\sqrt{\lambda}\ln x).$$

Finally, setting $x = e$, we have $0 = y(e) = c_2\sin\sqrt{\lambda}$. Therefore Eq. (6) has a nontrivial solution whenever $\sqrt{\lambda} = k\pi$, $k = 1, 2, 3, \ldots$. Thus the numbers $\lambda_k = k^2\pi^2$, $k = 1, 2, 3, \ldots$, are all eigenvalues of Eq. (6), and the eigenfunctions corresponding to λ_k have the form

$$y_k(x) = A\sin(k\pi\ln x).$$

Note that it is not necessary to write this solution in the form $A\sin(k\pi\ln|x|)$ because we are interested only in values of x in the interval $1 \le x \le e$. Thus $x > 0$ and $\ln|x| = \ln x$.

Example 3 Consider the Sturm–Liouville problem

$$y'' + \lambda y = 0, \quad y(0) + y'(0) = 0, \quad y(1) = 0.$$

Then, as in Example 1,

$$y(x) = \begin{cases} c_1 e^{\sqrt{-\lambda}x} + c_2 e^{-\sqrt{-\lambda}x} & \text{if } \lambda < 0, \\ c_1 + c_2 x & \text{if } \lambda = 0, \\ c_1\cos\sqrt{\lambda}x + c_2\sin\sqrt{\lambda}x & \text{if } \lambda > 0. \end{cases}$$

It is easy to verify that the boundary conditions imply that $c_1 = c_2 = 0$ if $\lambda < 0$. If $\lambda = 0$, then we have

$$y(0) = c_1, \quad y'(0) = c_2, \quad y(1) = c_1 + c_2,$$

so that both boundary conditions imply that $c_1 + c_2 = 0$. We therefore obtain the eigenfunctions

$$y_0(x) = c_1(1 - x).$$

If $\lambda > 0$, then

$$y(0) = c_1, \quad y'(0) = \sqrt{\lambda}c_2, \quad y(1) = c_1\cos\sqrt{\lambda} + c_2\sin\sqrt{\lambda}.$$

The boundary conditions imply that

$$c_1 + \sqrt{\lambda}c_2 = 0,$$
$$c_1\cos\sqrt{\lambda} + c_2\sin\sqrt{\lambda} = 0.$$

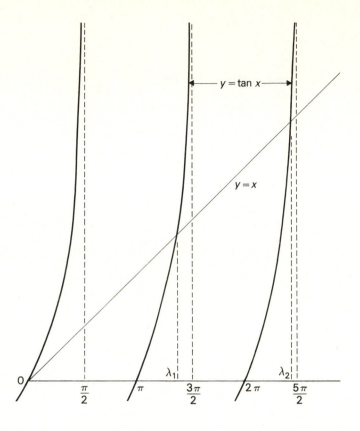

Figure 8

Setting $c_1 = -\sqrt{\lambda}c_2$, we find that the second equation becomes

$$-c_2\sqrt{\lambda}\cos\sqrt{\lambda} + c_2\sin\sqrt{\lambda} = 0$$

or, dividing by $c_2\cos\sqrt{\lambda}$ and simplifying,

$$\tan\sqrt{\lambda} = \sqrt{\lambda}.$$

Unlike the previous examples, there is no explicit way to obtain these eigenvalues. We can easily see that there is an infinite number of real eigenvalues by plotting the curves $y = \tan x$ and $y = x$. The eigenvalues are the squares of the x-values of the points of intersection (see Fig. 8). From Fig. 8 it seems clear that the square roots of the eigenvalues get closer and closer to the vertical asymptotes of $\tan x$. That is,

$$\sqrt{\lambda_n} \approx \left(\frac{2n+1}{2}\right)\pi \quad \text{or} \quad \lambda_n \approx \frac{(2n+1)^2}{4}\pi^2.$$

The eigenfunctions are

$$y_n(x) = A(\sin\sqrt{\lambda_n}x - \sqrt{\lambda_n}\cos\sqrt{\lambda_n}x), \quad n \geq 1, \quad A \neq 0.$$

EXERCISES 11.4

In the following exercises, find the eigenvalues and the corresponding eigenfunctions of the given Sturm–Liouville problems.

1. $y'' + \lambda y = 0, \quad y(0) = y(\pi) = 0$

2. $y'' + \lambda y = 0, \quad y(0) = y'(\pi) = 0$

3. $y'' + \lambda y = 0, \quad y(-\pi/2) = y(\pi/2) = 0$

4. $y'' + \lambda y = 0, \quad y'(0) = y'(\pi) = 0$

5. $(xy')' + \dfrac{\lambda}{x} y = 0, \quad y(1) = y(e^2) = 0$

6. $(x^2 y')' + \lambda y = 0, \quad y(1) = y(e) = 0$

7. $(x^2 y')' + \dfrac{\lambda}{x^2} y = 0, \quad y\left(\dfrac{1}{2}\right) = y(1) = 0$

   [*Hint*: Try $y_1 = \sin(\lambda/x)$.]

8. $\left(\dfrac{1}{2x} y'\right)' - 2x\lambda y = 0, \quad y(0) = y(1) = 0$

11.5 PROPERTIES OF STURM–LIOUVILLE PROBLEMS

In this section we shall investigate the four basic properties of the eigenvalues and eigenfunctions of the Sturm–Liouville problem mentioned in the last section:

$$[r(x)y']' + [p(x) + \lambda q(x)]y = 0, \tag{1}$$

with the boundary conditions

$$a_1 y(a) - a_2 y'(a) = 0, \quad b_1 y(b) - b_2 y'(b) = 0. \tag{2}$$

We begin by showing that the eigenfunctions of this problem are orthogonal with respect to the weight function $q(x)$.

Theorem 1   *Orthogonality theorem.* Let the real-valued functions $r(x)$, $r'(x)$, $p(x)$, and $q(x)$ of Eq. (1) be continuous on the interval $a \le x \le b$, and let $y_m(x)$ and $y_n(x)$ be eigenfunctions corresponding to distinct eigenvalues λ_m and λ_n of the Sturm–Liouville problem (1), (2). Then y_m and y_n are orthogonal with respect to the weight function $q(x)$.

Proof   The functions y_m and y_n satisfy the equations

$$(ry_m')' + (p + \lambda_m q)y_m = 0,$$
$$(ry_n')' + (p + \lambda_n q)y_n = 0.$$

Multiplying the first equation by y_n and the second by $-y_m$ and adding the resulting equations together yields

$$y_n(ry_m')' - y_m(ry_n')' = (\lambda_n - \lambda_m)q y_m y_n.$$

Integrating all terms from a to b and the first two terms by parts, we obtain

$$\left(y_n r y_m'\big|_a^b - \int_a^b ry_m' y_n' \, dx\right) - \left(y_m r y_n'\big|_a^b - \int_a^b ry_n' y_m' \, dx\right) = (\lambda_n - \lambda_m)\int_a^b q y_m y_n \, dx. \tag{3}$$

Canceling the two identical integrals on the left-hand side, we obtain the equation

$$r(b)[y_n(b)y'_m(b) - y_m(b)y'_n(b)] - r(a)[y_n(a)y'_m(a) - y_m(a)y'_n(a)]$$

$$= (\lambda_n - \lambda_m) \int_a^b q y_m y_n \, dx. \quad \textbf{(4)}$$

By hypothesis, at least one of the constants a_1, a_2 in (2) is nonzero [see Eq. (2) in Section 11.4], so that we have either

$$y(a) = \frac{a_2}{a_1} y'(a) \quad \text{or} \quad y'(a) = \frac{a_1}{a_2} y(a). \quad \textbf{(5)}$$

If the first of these equations is permissible, then it is satisfied by both $y_m(a)$ and $y_n(a)$, so the second term in brackets in Eq. (4) becomes

$$y_n(a)y'_m(a) - y_m(a)y'_n(a) = \frac{a_2}{a_1} y'_n(a)y'_m(a) - \frac{a_2}{a_1} y'_m(a)y'_n(a) = 0.$$

Similarly, if the second equation in (5) is permissible, then the second term in brackets will vanish. In the same way, the second boundary condition in (2) causes the first term in brackets in Eq. (4) to vanish. Thus,

$$(\lambda_n - \lambda_m) \int_a^b q y_m y_n \, dx = 0,$$

and since $\lambda_n \neq \lambda_m$, the proof is complete. ∎

Remark   Observe that if $r(a) = 0$, we do not need the first boundary condition in (2) to prove the orthogonality theorem. Similarly, the second boundary condition is not required if $r(b) = 0$. Finally, if $r(a) = r(b)$, we can also obtain the conclusion of the orthogonality theorem by assuming the conditions

$$y(a) = y(b), \quad y'(a) = y'(b) \quad \textbf{(6)}$$

instead of Eq. (2). The proof of this fact is obvious, since the quantities in brackets in Eq. (4) are now identical, so that the left-hand side of Eq. (4) vanishes. Furthermore, *if the functions $r(x)$, $p(x)$, and $q(x)$ are periodic with period $(b - a)$, then any eigenfunction of this problem will also be periodic with period $(b - a)$.* (See Exercise 6).

Example 1   Consider the Sturm–Liouville problem

$$y'' + \lambda y = 0, \quad y(0) = y'(1) = 0.$$

As we saw in Example 1 in Section 11.4, the eigenfunctions of this problem have the form

$$\sin \frac{\pi}{2} x, \quad \sin \frac{3\pi}{2} x, \quad \sin \frac{5\pi}{2} x, \quad \ldots, \quad \sin \frac{(2k-1)}{2} \pi x, \ldots .$$

Theorem 1 implies that these functions are orthogonal, a fact that we established directly in Section 11.2.

Example 2　Using the orthogonality theorem, it is easy to verify that the Legendre polynomials form an orthogonal set of functions. Since $[(1 - x^2)y']' = (1 - x^2)y'' - 2xy'$, we can write Legendre's equation (see Example 4 in Section 11.2) in the Sturm–Liouville form

$$[(1 - x^2)y']' + \lambda y = 0, \quad \lambda = n(n + 1).$$

Since $r(x) = 1 - x^2$ vanishes at $x = \pm 1$, no boundary conditions are needed for the theorem to apply; and since $q(x) \equiv 1$, we immediately have

$$(P_m, P_n) = \int_{-1}^{1} P_m(x)P_n(x)\, dx = 0 \quad \text{if } m \neq n.$$

The endpoints a and b in the orthogonality theorem need not be finite provided the improper integrals in Eq. (3) all exist. We illustrate this situation with the following example.

Example 3　Laguerre's equation (Example 6 in Section 11.2)

$$(xe^{-x}y')' + ne^{-x}y = 0$$

is of the Sturm–Liouville type and $r(x) = xe^{-x}$ vanishes at $x = 0$. By L'Hôpital's rule

$$\lim_{x \to \infty} r(x) = \lim_{x \to \infty} \frac{x}{e^x}$$

$$= \lim_{x \to \infty} \frac{1}{e^x} = 0,$$

so no boundary conditions are required to apply the orthogonality theorem. Thus the Laguerre polynomials $\{y_n(x)\}$ form an orthogonal set of functions with respect to the weight function $q(x) = e^{-x}$:

$$\int_{0}^{\infty} e^{-x}y_m(x)y_n(x)\, dx = 0 \quad \text{if } m \neq n.$$

In every example we have seen so far, the eigenvalues of the given Sturm–Liouville problem are real, not because the examples were carefully chosen, but because the situation holds for every Sturm–Liouville problem. The proof of this fact, stated below, is very similar to the proof of Theorem 1 and is therefore left as an exercise (see Exercise 8).

Theorem 2　The eigenvalues of the Sturm–Liouville problem (1), (2) are all real.

Finally, we have observed that in every example there is an infinite number of eigenvalues, and that corresponding to each eigenvalue there is only one linearly independent eigenfunction. That is, if y_1 and y_2 are two eigenfunctions corresponding to the eigenvalue λ, then there is a constant c such that $y_1 = cy_2$. When the latter condition holds, the eigenvalue is said to be *simple*. These results are summarized in the theorem below, whose proof, however, is beyond the scope of this text.† (The simplicity of the eigenvalues can easily be proved; see Exercise 11.)

Theorem 3 The eigenvalues of the Sturm–Liouville problem (1), (2) are simple. Moreover, there is an infinite number of them, which can be arranged in an increasing order

$$\lambda_1 < \lambda_2 < \lambda_3 < \cdots < \lambda_k < \cdots,$$

where λ_k tends to ∞ as k tends to ∞.

All three theorems of this section will be needed for the solution of nonhomogeneous boundary value problems in Section 11.7.

EXERCISES 11.5

In Exercises 1 through 5, verify the implications of Theorems 1, 2, and 3 for each given Sturm–Liouville problem.

1. $y'' + \lambda y = 0, \quad y(0) = y(\pi) = 0$

2. $y'' + \lambda y = 0, \quad y(0) = y'(\pi) = 0$

3. $y'' + \lambda y = 0, \quad y(-\pi/2) = y(\pi/2) = 0$

4. $(xy')' + (\lambda/x)y = 0, \quad y(1) = y(e^2) = 0$

5. $(x^2y')' + (\lambda/x^2)y = 0, \quad y(\frac{1}{2}) = y(1) = 0$

6. Prove that if $r(x)$, $p(x)$, and $q(x)$ are continuous periodic functions of period $(b - a)$, then all eigenfunctions of the boundary value problem (1), (2) are periodic with period $(b - a)$.

7. a) Show that Hermite's equation (see Exercise 9(c) of Section 11.2) can be written in the form

$$(e^{-x^2}y')' + 2ne^{-x^2}y = 0.$$

   b) Using the orthogonality theorem, prove that the Hermite polynomials are orthogonal with respect to the weight function $\exp(-x^2)$ on $-\infty < x < \infty$.

8. Prove that the eigenvalues of the Sturm–Liouville problem (1), (2) are all real by carrying out the following steps:

   a) Show that if $\lambda = \alpha + i\beta$ is an eigenvalue with the corresponding eigenfunction $y_\lambda(x) = u(x) + iv(x)$, then $\bar{\lambda} = \alpha - i\beta$ is an eigenvalue with the corresponding eigenfunction $\bar{y}_\lambda(x) = u(x) - iv(x)$.

   b) Using the same proof as that of Theorem 1, show that

$$(\lambda - \bar{\lambda}) \int_a^b y_\lambda(x)\bar{y}_\lambda(x)q(x)\,dx = 0.$$

   c) Use the result of part (b) of this exercise and the fact that $y_\lambda\bar{y}_\lambda = u^2 + v^2$ to show that $\beta = 0$.

9. The boundary value problem

$$y'' - \frac{\lambda}{x}y' + \frac{\lambda}{x^2}y = 0, \quad y(1) = y(2) = 0,$$

is not a Sturm–Liouville problem. Show that none of the eigenvalues is real.

10. Consider the boundary value problem

$$y'' + \lambda y = 0, \quad y(-1) = y(1), \quad y'(-1) = y'(1).$$

   a) Explain why it is not a Sturm–Liouville problem.

   b) Calculate the eigenvalues of this problem.

   c) Show that corresponding to each eigenvalue there are two linearly independent eigenfunctions. That is, show that the eigenvalues are not simple.

11. Prove that the eigenvalues of a Sturm–Liouville problem are simple. [*Hint*: Assume that y_1 and y_2 are two eigenfunctions corresponding to the eigenvalue λ. Use the boundary conditions (2) to show that the Wronskian $W(y_1, y_2)(x) = 0$ for $a \leqslant x \leqslant b$.]

---

† See, for example, the excellent book *Methods of Mathematical Physics* by R. Courant and D. Hilbert, Vol. I, Chapter 6. New York: Wiley (1953).

11.6 THE STURM SEPARATION THEOREM AND THE ZEROS OF BESSEL FUNCTIONS (Optional)

In this section we will establish some further properties of the solutions of the second order differential equation

$$[r(x)y']' + [p(x) + \lambda q(x)]y = 0 \tag{1}$$

which, as we saw earlier, arises in a number of physical problems. We begin by analyzing the behavior of the zeros of two solutions of Eq. (1). The procedure we will use is similar to that used in the orthogonality theorem (1) of Section 11.5. *Note that we are not assuming the boundary conditions (2) of Section 11.5 in this section.*

Theorem 1   *Sturm separation theorem.* Let y_1 and y_2 be two linearly independent solutions of Eq. (1) on the interval $a \le x \le b$. Suppose that $r(x) > 0$ for all $a \le x \le b$. Then between any two consecutive zeros of y_1 there will be precisely one zero of y_2.

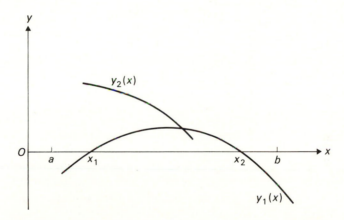

Figure 9

Proof   Since y_1 and y_2 are linearly independent, neither solution is the zero solution. Let x_1 and x_2 be two consecutive zeros of y_1, with $a \le x_1 < x_2 \le b$ (see Fig. 9). We can assume that $y_1(x) > 0$ for $x_1 < x < x_2$, since $-y_1$ is also a solution of Eq. (1) and one of the two functions y_1 and $-y_1$ is positive in this interval. Similarly, we can assume that $y_2(x_1) \ge 0$. Since both y_1 and y_2 satisfy Eq. (1), we have

$$(ry_1')' + (p + \lambda q)y_1 = 0,$$
$$(ry_2')' + (p + \lambda q)y_2 = 0.$$

Multiplying the first of these equations by y_2 and the second by $-y_1$, and adding the resulting equations together, we obtain

$$y_2(ry_1')' - y_1(ry_2')' = 0.$$

Moving the second term to the right-hand side of the equation and integrating both sides from x_1 to x_2, we have

$$\int_{x_1}^{x_2} y_2(ry_1')' \, dx = \int_{x_1}^{x_2} y_1(ry_2')' \, dx. \tag{2}$$

Integrating both sides of Eq. (2) by parts yields the equation

$$y_2(ry_1') \Big|_{x_1}^{x_2} - \int_{x_1}^{x_2} ry_1'y_2' \, dx = y_1(ry_2') \Big|_{x_1}^{x_2} - \int_{x_1}^{x_2} ry_2'y_1' \, dx.$$

Both integrals are the same; so canceling them and gathering all terms involving x_2 on the right-hand side and all terms in x_1 on the left-hand side, we have

$$r(x_1)[y_1(x_1)y_2'(x_1) - y_1'(x_1)y_2(x_1)] = r(x_2)[y_1(x_2)y_2'(x_2) - y_1'(x_2)y_2(x_2)]. \tag{3}$$

Note that the quantities in brackets are the Wronskians of y_1 and y_2 evaluated at the points x_1 and x_2, respectively. Since y_1 and y_2 are linearly independent on $a \leq x \leq b$, the Wronskian $W(x)$ is never zero, by Lemma 1 in Section 3.2. However, by hypothesis, $y_1(x_1) = y_1(x_2) = 0$, so that

$$W(x_1) = -y_1'(x_1)y_2(x_1) \neq 0 \tag{4}$$

and

$$W(x_2) = -y_1'(x_2)y_2(x_2) \neq 0. \tag{5}$$

Recall now that we have assumed $y_2(x_1) \geq 0$. By Eq. (4), we must have $y_2(x_1) > 0$ and $y_1'(x_1) \neq 0$, since $W(x_1) \neq 0$. Since $y_1(x) > 0$ in $x_1 < x < x_2$, we necessarily have $y_1'(x_1) > 0$, and hence $W(x_1) < 0$. Similarly, $y_1'(x_2) < 0$, and since $r(x)$ is always positive on $a \leq x \leq b$, Eq. (3) implies that $W(x_2)$ is negative. Thus, by Eq. (5) and the fact that $y_1'(x_2) < 0$, we have $y_2(x_2) < 0$. Therefore, y_2 changes sign between x_1 and x_2. Since y_2 must be continuous, the intermediate value theorem of calculus implies that y_2 must have a zero between x_1 and x_2.

Finally, we must make sure y_2 has only one zero between x_1 and x_2. If it had more than one zero, we could reverse the roles of y_1 and y_2, and the proof above, applied to y_1, would imply the existence of a zero of y_1 between x_1 and x_2. Since x_1 and x_2 are *consecutive* zeros of y_1, no such zero can exist. Thus y_2 has exactly one zero between x_1 and x_2. ∎

Remark If two solutions of Eq. (1) have a common zero, then they must be linearly dependent, since their Wronskian will vanish at this point.

The Sturm separation theorem indicates that the number of zeros of any two solutions of Eq. (1) on any interval is approximately the same. However, it does not guarantee the existence of *any* zeros. We shall now prove a theorem that compares the number of zeros (that is, the rate of *oscillation*) of solutions of two differential equations

$$[r(x)y']' + p_1(x)y = 0, \tag{6}$$

and

$$[r(x)w']' + p_2(x)w = 0, \tag{7}$$

where r, r', p_1, and p_2 are continuous functions on $a \leqslant x \leqslant b$. The motivation behind this theorem can be seen by examining the solutions $y = \sin x$ and $w = \sin 3x$ of the two equations

$$y'' + y = 0 \quad \text{and} \quad w'' + 9w = 0.$$

The solutions of the second equation ($\sin 3x, \cos 3x$) oscillate more rapidly than those of the first equation ($\sin x, \cos x$). That is, $\sin 3x$ oscillates three times in $[0, 2\pi]$, whereas $\sin x$ oscillates only once. It is reasonable to suspect that whenever p_2 exceeds p_1, there will be an increase in the rate of oscillation.

Theorem 2   *Sturm comparison theorem.* Let $r(x)$ be positive and $y(x)$ and $w(x)$ be solutions of Eqs. (6) and (7), respectively, on the interval $a \leqslant x \leqslant b$. Suppose that x_1 and x_2 are consecutive zeros of y with $a \leqslant x_1 < x_2 \leqslant b$, $p_2(x) \geqslant p_1(x)$ on $x_1 \leqslant x \leqslant x_2$, and that $p_2(x_0) > p_1(x_0)$ for some point $x_1 \leqslant x_0 \leqslant x_2$. Then, if w vanishes at x_1, it will vanish again in the interval $x_1 < x < x_2$. Moreover, in that case, every solution of Eq. (7) will vanish at some point in the interval $x_1 < x < x_2$.

Proof   As in Theorem 1 we can assume $y > 0$ on $x_1 < x < x_2$ and that $y'(x_1) > 0$ and $y'(x_2) < 0$. Multiplying Eq. (6) by $w(x)$ and Eq. (7) by $-y(x)$ and adding the resulting equations together, we obtain

$$w(ry')' - y(rw')' + (p_1 - p_2)yw = 0.$$

Integrating all the terms in this equation from x_1 to x_2 and the first two terms by parts, we have

$$\left(wry' \Big|_{x_1}^{x_2} - \int_{x_1}^{x_2} ry'w' \, dx \right) - \left(yrw' \Big|_{x_1}^{x_2} - \int_{x_1}^{x_2} rw'y' \, dx \right) = \int_{x_1}^{x_2} (p_2 - p_1)yw \, dx.$$

The two integrals on the left-hand side of this equation cancel out, so that gathering like terms yields

$$r(x_2)[w(x_2)y'(x_2) - y(x_2)w'(x_2)] - r(x_1)[w(x_1)y'(x_1) - y(x_1)w'(x_1)]$$

$$= \int_{x_1}^{x_2} (p_2 - p_1)yw \, dx.$$

The second term in brackets is zero since $w(x_1) = y(x_1) = 0$; hence the equation reduces to

$$r(x_2)w(x_2)y'(x_2) = \int_{x_1}^{x_2} (p_2 - p_1)yw \, dx. \tag{8}$$

If $w(x) > 0$ on $x_1 < x < x_2$, then the integrand on the right-hand side of Eq. (8) is nonnegative on $x_1 \leqslant x \leqslant x_2$ and *positive* in some smaller interval containing the point x_0. Hence the right-hand side of Eq. (8) is positive. Since $r(x_2) > 0$ and $y'(x_2) < 0$, it must follow that $w(x_2) < 0$. Since w is continuous, the last conclusion contradicts the assumption that $w > 0$ on $x_1 < x < x_2$. Hence w must vanish in the interval $x_1 < x < x_2$. Finally, if w_1 is another linearly independent solution of Eq. (7), then the Sturm separation theorem 1 implies that w_1 must have a zero between the zeros of w, and therefore in the interval $x_1 < x < x_2$. ∎

Example 1   Let $p(x) < 0$ on the interval $a \leqslant x \leqslant b$ and suppose that the equation

$$y'' + p(x)y = 0 \tag{9}$$

has a nontrivial solution y with zeros at x_1 and x_2, with $a \leqslant x_1 < x_2 \leqslant b$. Since $w = 1$ is a solution of $w'' = 0$, the Sturm comparison theorem 2 implies that w must vanish in $x_1 < x < x_2$. But this is impossible. So every nontrivial solution of Eq. (9) has at most one zero in $a \leqslant x \leqslant b$.

Example 2   Bessel's equation of order p,

$$x^2 y'' + xy' + (x^2 - p^2)y = 0,$$

may be transformed, after an easy calculation, into the equation

$$w'' + \left(1 + \frac{1 - 4p^2}{4x^2}\right)w = 0 \tag{10}$$

by means of the substitution $y = w/\sqrt{x}$, which does not change the zeros. Comparing Eq. (10) with the equation $y'' + y = 0$, the Sturm comparison theorem yields the following results:

1. If $0 \leqslant p < \frac{1}{2}$, then

$$1 + \frac{1 - 4p^2}{4x^2} > 1,$$

so every solution of Eq. (10), and hence of Bessel's equation, will vanish at least once between the zeros of any nontrivial solution of $y'' + y = 0$. But the general solution of $y'' + y = 0$ has the form

$$y = c_1 \cos x + c_2 \sin x = \sqrt{c_1^2 + c_2^2}\, \sin(x + \theta),$$

where $\theta = \tan^{-1}(c_1/c_2)$. Thus every nontrivial solution of $y'' + y = 0$ has zeros separated by an interval of length π. Hence *every solution of Bessel's equation of order p, $0 \leqslant p < \frac{1}{2}$, has at least one zero in every interval of length π, for $x > 0$.*

2. If $p = \frac{1}{2}$, then Eq. (10) reduces to $w'' + w = 0$, with the general solution $w = c_1 \cos x + c_2 \sin x$. Then *every nontrivial solution of Bessel's* *equation of order* $\frac{1}{2}$,

$$y = \frac{w}{\sqrt{x}} = \frac{1}{\sqrt{x}}(c_1 \cos x + c_2 \sin x),$$

has zeros separated by an interval of length π, *for* $x > 0$.

3. If $p > \frac{1}{2}$, then

$$1 + \frac{1 - 4p^2}{4x^2} < 1,$$

so every solution of Bessel's equation can have *at most* one zero in every interval of length π. We leave the proof of the fact that each solution of Bessel's equation of order $p > \frac{1}{2}$ has infinitely many zeros in $x > 0$ as an exercise (see Exercise 8).

Let us now return to the Sturm–Liouville problem (1) with the boundary conditions $y(a) = y(b) = 0$, and ask the following question: *How many eigenvalues does this problem have?* If $q(x)$ is positive on the interval $a \leqslant x \leqslant b$, then a suitably large value of λ will guarantee that $p(x) + \lambda q(x)$ is positive on $a \leqslant x \leqslant b$. Assuming also that $r(x)$ is positive on $a \leqslant x \leqslant b$, we can make the nontrivial solutions of Eq. (1) oscillate as rapidly as we wish by selecting appropriate values for λ. Since it is always possible to pick a solution y_λ of Eq. (1) that vanishes at $x = a$ for each λ, it is reasonable to expect that some number λ_0 exists such that the next zero of y_{λ_0} will occur at $x = b$. Similarly, we can expect to find a λ_k such that $y_{\lambda_k}(b) = 0$ and y_{λ_k} has k zeros between a and b, $k = 1, 2, 3, \ldots$. The above discussion, when made precise, leads to a proof of the existence of an infinite number of eigenvalues for the Sturm–Liouville problem (1), (2) in Section 11.5 (see Theorem 3 there).

EXERCISES 11.6

1. Prove that the substitution $y = w/\sqrt{x}$ will transform Bessel's equation of order p into Eq. (10).

2. Extend Example 1 to equations of the form (6).

3. Use the Sturm separation theorem to show that the functions $f(x) = a \sin x + b \cos x$ and $g(x) = c \sin x + d \cos x$ have alternating zeros whenever $ad - bc \neq 0$.

4. Show that the zeros of the functions $f(x) = \sin \ln x$ and $g(x) = \cos \ln x$ alternate. (*Hint*: Find a differential equation for which f and g are both solutions.)

5. Does the Sturm separation theorem apply to the differential equation $y'' - y = 0$?

6. Which of the equations

$$y'' + (x^2 + 1)y = 0,$$
$$w'' + 2xw = 0$$

has the more rapidly oscillating solution in the interval $1 \leqslant x \leqslant 10$?

7. How many zeros does every solution of

$$y'' + xy = 0$$

have on the interval $0 < x < \infty$?

8. Prove that every solution of Bessel's equation of order $p > \frac{1}{2}$ has infinitely many zeros in the interval $x > 0$.

9. Prove that the distance between successive

zeros of any nontrivial solution of Bessel's equation of order $p \geq 0$ approaches π as x tends to ∞.

*10. Prove that the conclusion of the Sturm comparison theorem will remain valid if the differential equations (6) and (7) are replaced by the equations

$$[r_1(x)y']' + p_1(x)y = 0,$$
$$[r_2(x)w']' + p_2(x)w = 0,$$

with $r_2(x) \leq r_1(x)$ on $a \leq x \leq b$. This result is sometimes called *Picone's theorem*. [*Hint:* Use the identity

$$\left[\frac{y}{w}(r_1y'w - r_2w'y)\right]'$$

$$= (p_2 - p_1)y^2 + (r_1 - r_2)y'^2 + r_2\left(y' - \frac{w'y}{w}\right)^2.\ ]$$

*11. Consider Eq. (6) with $r(x) > 0$ and $p_1(x)$ having continuous derivatives on the interval $a \leq x \leq b$. Suppose that $(rp_1)' \geq 0$. Prove that the absolute values of the relative extremums of every nontrivial solution of Eq. (6) are nonincreasing as x increases. This result, due to *Sonin*, indicates that the solutions are damped as x increases. [*Hint:* Differentiate the function $f(x) = y^2 + (py'^2/q)$ and show that $f' \leq 0$ on $a \leq x \leq b$. Then evaluate f at the points where y' vanishes.]

*12. Let $r(x) > 0$, $r'(x)$ and $p_1(x)$ be continuous on the finite interval $a \leq x \leq b$. Prove that the only solution of Eq. (6) that will vanish infinitely often in this interval is the trivial solution $y = 0$.

11.7 NONHOMOGENEOUS BOUNDARY VALUE PROBLEMS

In Example 3 of Section 11.1 we considered a nonhomogeneous boundary value problem given by Eq. (12). At that time we stated that the solution of Eq. (12) there, for $\omega \neq n\pi$, could be expressed by the Fourier sine series (20). In this section we shall justify that statement and unite the seemingly unrelated concepts of Fourier series and Sturm–Liouville problems. We shall discover that the solutions of certain nonhomogeneous boundary value problems can be obtained as generalized Fourier series in the eigenfunctions of the associated Sturm–Liouville problem.

This method of *eigenfunction expansions* is one of the main techniques used in solving nonhomogeneous boundary value problems. Furthermore, it provides the motivation for the very powerful method of *Green's functions*, developed in Exercises 8 through 12, which is extremely useful for solving such problems.

Suppose that we wish to solve the *nonhomogeneous* differential equation

$$[r(x)w']' + p(x)w = f(x) \tag{1}$$

on $a \leq x \leq b$ with the boundary conditions

$$a_1w(a) - a_2w'(a) = 0, \quad b_1w(b) - b_2w'(b) = 0. \tag{2}$$

We shall consider a different boundary value problem

$$[r(x)y']' + [p(x) + \lambda q(x)]y = 0 \tag{3}$$

with identical boundary conditions

$$a_1y(a) - a_2y'(a) = 0, \quad b_1y(b) - b_2y'(b) = 0, \tag{4}$$

and assume that its eigenvalues and eigenfunctions are known. We are free to choose $q(x)$ in any way we wish; however, the choice is limited, since we must be able to determine the eigenfunctions of (3), (4). Furthermore, different choices of $q(x)$ will yield different sets of eigenfunctions, and some sets may be easier to work with than others. We assume that $r(x)$, $r'(x)$, $p(x)$, and $q(x)$ are continuous and r and q are positive on $a \leqslant x \leqslant b$. By Theorem 3 in Section 11.5 and the orthogonality theorem, we know that the problem (3), (4) has an infinite orthogonal set $\{y_k\}$ of eigenfunctions with respect to the weight function $q(x)$.

The object now is to express the solution $w(x)$ of (1), (2) (if one exists) as a generalized Fourier series [see Eq. (6) of Section 11.2] of the form

$$w(x) = \sum_{n=1}^{\infty} c_n y_n, \tag{5}$$

where the functions y_n are eigenfunctions of (3), (4). Of course, since we are proceeding formally, when the process is complete we shall have to check that our result is indeed a solution. As we saw in Section 11.3, the problem of determining which functions can be represented in this way is not easy. Although the proof is beyond the scope of this book, *any piecewise continuous function $w(x)$ with piecewise continuous derivative $w'(x)$ has a representation* (5) *at all points of continuity, provided that a and b are finite.*† (At points of discontinuity the generalized Fourier series converges to $[w(x + 0) + w(x - 0)]/2$.)

To obtain the formal representation (5), we proceed in a manner similar to the proof of the orthogonality theorem. Multiplying Eq. (1) by y and Eq. (3) by $-w$, we obtain the equation

$$y(rw')' - w(ry')' = fy + \lambda qyw.$$

Integrating both sides from a to b and the left-hand side by parts, we have

$$\left(yrw' \Big|_a^b - \int_a^b rw'y'\, dx \right) - \left(wry' \Big|_a^b - \int_a^b ry'w'\, dx \right) = \int_a^b (fy + \lambda qyw)\, dx.$$

The integrals on the left-hand side cancel out, yielding the equation

$$r(b)[y(b)w'(b) - w(b)y'(b)] - r(a)[y(a)w'(a) - w(a)y'(a)]$$

$$= \int_a^b (fy + \lambda qyw)\, dx. \tag{6}$$

Letting $\lambda = \lambda_k$ and $y = y_k$, we see as in the proof of the orthogonality theorem that the left-hand side of Eq. (6) vanishes. Thus,

$$\lambda_k \int_a^b qwy_k\, dx = -\int_a^b fy_k\, dx,$$

---

† Much more general theorems are known. See, for example, E. A. Coddington and N. Levinson, *Theory of Ordinary Differential Equations*, p. 199. New York: McGraw-Hill (1955).

and since, by Eq. (20) in Section 11.2,

$$c_k = \frac{(w, y_k)_q}{\|y_k\|_q^2} = \frac{\displaystyle\int_a^b qwy_k \, dx}{\displaystyle\int_a^b qy_k^2 \, dx},$$

we finally obtain

$$c_k = -\frac{\displaystyle\int_a^b fy_k \, dx}{\lambda_k \displaystyle\int_a^b qy_k^2 \, dx}. \tag{7}$$

In particular, if the eigenfunctions y_k have been chosen so that they are orthonormal with respect to q, then the denominator in the right-hand side of Eq. (7) reduces to just the eigenvalue λ_k, and we have the representation

$$w(x) = -\sum_{n=1}^{\infty} \left(\lambda_n^{-1}\int_a^b fy_n \, dx\right)y_n(x) \tag{8}$$

for the solution of the boundary value problem (1), (2). We now apply this result to justify the solution (20) of Example 3 in Section 11.1.

Example 1   Suppose that we again consider the forced vibrations of a spring-mass system, with spring constant k, attached to an external periodic force $K \sin \omega t$. For simplicity, we ignore the damping term in Eq. (11) in Section 3.8 and merely consider the nonhomogeneous equation

$$x'' + \frac{k}{m}x = \frac{K}{m}\sin \omega t. \tag{9}$$

We again suppose that the mass is at its equilibrium position initially and when $t = 1$ second, and seek a solution to the nonhomogeneous boundary value problem.

To apply the eigenfunction expansion (8), we consider the Sturm–Liouville problem

$$y'' + (\lambda + 1)\frac{k}{m}y = 0, \quad y(0) = y(1) = 0. \tag{10}$$

The eigenvalues of Eq. (10) are obtained by setting $\sqrt{(\lambda + 1)k/m}$ equal to a multiple of π; hence

$$\lambda_m = \frac{mn^2\pi^2}{k} - 1, \quad n = 1, 2, 3, \ldots .$$

The corresponding eigenfunctions have the form

$$y_n = A \sin n\pi t, \quad n = 1, 2, 3, \ldots,$$

and are orthonormal with respect to $q(x) = k/m$ if $A = \sqrt{2m/k}$. By Eq. (7), the Fourier coefficients c_k are given by

$$c_n = -\sqrt{\frac{2m}{k}} \cdot \frac{K}{m\lambda_n} \int_0^1 \sin \omega t \sin n\pi t \, dt.$$

Using Formula 19 of Appendix 1 and the identity

$$\sin (\omega \pm n\pi)t = \sin \omega t \cos n\pi t \pm \cos \omega t \sin n\pi t,$$

we have

$$c_n = -\sqrt{\frac{2m}{k}} \cdot \frac{K}{2m\lambda_n} \left[\frac{\sin (\omega - n\pi)t}{\omega - n\pi} - \frac{\sin (\omega + n\pi)t}{\omega + n\pi} \right] \Bigg|_0^1$$

$$= -\sqrt{\frac{2m}{k}} \cdot \frac{K}{m\lambda_n} \sin \omega \cos n\pi \frac{n\pi}{\omega^2 - n^2\pi^2}, \quad \omega \neq n\pi.$$

If $\omega = n\pi$, then

$$c_n = -\sqrt{\frac{2m}{k}} \cdot \frac{K}{2m\lambda_n},$$

and all the other Fourier coefficients vanish by the orthogonality of the eigenfunctions. Thus the solution $x(t)$ must be stated for two cases:

1. If $\omega \neq n\pi$, $n = 1, 2, 3, \ldots$, then by Eq. (8) and the identity $\cos n\pi = (-1)^n$,

$$x(t) = -\frac{2K\pi \sin \omega}{k} \sum_{n=1}^{\infty} \frac{(-1)^n n}{\lambda_n(\omega^2 - n^2\pi^2)} \sin n\pi t.$$

It is easy to show that this solution is identical to Eq. (20) in Section 11.1.

2. Suppose that $\omega = n\pi$ for some positive integer n. Then using Eq. (8) and the value of λ_n, we obtain the particular solution

$$x_p(t) = -\frac{K}{k\lambda_n} \sin n\pi t = \frac{K \sin n\pi t}{k - mn^2\pi^2}.$$

This solution is valid provided that the spring constant $k \neq mn^2\pi^2$.

The general solution is now obtained as in Case 1 of Example 3 in Section 11.1. When $k = mn^2\pi^2$, there is *no* solution. Observe that in this case the eigenvalue

$$\lambda_n = \frac{mn^2\pi^2}{k} - 1 = 0.$$

The following result is beyond the scope of this book, but provides the necessary information to decide whether or not there is a solution in the case above.

Theorem 1†   Let one of the eigenvalues λ_k of the problem (3), (4) be zero. Then the nonhomogeneous boundary value problem (1), (2) has a solution if and only if

$$\int_a^b f(t)y_k(t)\, dt = 0.$$

Example 2   Consider the boundary value problem

$$(xw')' + \frac{w}{x} = \frac{1}{x}, \quad w(1) = w(e) = 0. \tag{11}$$

To apply the method of eigenfunction expansion (8), we let $p(x) = q(x) = f(x) = 1/x$ and consider the Sturm–Liouville problem

$$(xy')' + \frac{(1+\lambda)}{x} y = 0, \quad y(1) = y(e) = 0. \tag{12}$$

By Example 2 in Section 11.4, we know that the eigenvalues $\lambda^* = 1 + \lambda$ of Eq. (12) are given by

$$1 + \lambda_k = \lambda_k^* = k^2\pi^2, \quad k = 1, 2, 3, \ldots,$$

so that $\lambda_k = k^2\pi^2 - 1$, and the eigenfunctions are of the form

$$y_k = A \sin(k\pi \ln x).$$

Using the substitution $u = k\pi \ln x$, $du = (k\pi/x)\, dx$, we have

$$\int_1^e \frac{1}{x} \sin^2(k\pi \ln x)\, dx = \frac{1}{k\pi} \int_0^{k\pi} \sin^2 u\, du = \left. \frac{u - \cos u \sin u}{2k\pi} \right|_0^{k\pi} = \frac{1}{2}.$$

Letting $A = \sqrt{2}$, we obtain an orthonormal set of eigenfunctions. By Eq. (7), the coefficients c_k of the generalized Fourier series are given by

$$c_k = -\lambda_k^{-1} \int_1^e \frac{\sqrt{2}}{x} \sin(k\pi \ln x)\, dx = \left. \frac{\sqrt{2}\lambda_k^{-1}}{k\pi} \cos(k\pi \ln x) \right|_1^e$$

$$= \frac{\sqrt{2}(\cos k\pi - 1)}{k\pi\lambda_k} = \begin{cases} 0, & k \text{ even}, \\ \dfrac{-2\sqrt{2}}{k\pi(k^2\pi^2 - 1)}, & k \text{ odd}. \end{cases}$$

---

† See, for example, E. A. Coddington and N. Levinson, *Theory of Ordinary Differential Equations*, p. 294. New York: McGraw-Hill (1955).

Hence the solution of the problem (11) is given by the series

$$w(x) = -4 \sum_{n=0}^{\infty} \frac{\sin\left[(2n + 1)\pi \ln x\right]}{\left[(2n + 1)\pi\right]^3 - \left[(2n + 1)\pi\right]}.$$

A number of further examples of the use of eigenfunction expansions will be found in Chapter 12, where they are used in the solution of certain partial differential equations.

The methods we have presented in this chapter are not the only techniques that can be used to solve boundary value problems. A very powerful procedure, attributed to George Green (1793–1841), involves the representation of the solution of the boundary value problems (1), (2) in the form

$$w(x) = \int_a^b K(x, t)f(t)\, dt. \tag{13}$$

Actually, in light of the eigenfunction expansion (8), a representation of the form (13) is not surprising, for if we use t as the variable of integration and interchange the sum and integral in (8), we will obtain the expression

$$\int_a^b \left(- \sum_{n=1}^{\infty} \frac{y_n(t)y_n(x)}{\lambda_n} \right) f(t)\, dt.$$

Hence the *Green's function $K(x, t)$* may be presumed to equal

$$K(x, t) = - \sum_{n=1}^{\infty} \frac{y_n(t)y_n(x)}{\lambda_n}. \tag{14}$$

All the assumptions we made above can be justified.† Exercises 8 through 12 at the end of this section will indicate another method of obtaining the Green's function $K(x, t)$.

EXERCISES 11.7

In Exercises 1 through 5, use the method of eigenfunction expansions to solve the given nonhomogeneous boundary value problems.

1. $y'' + y = x$, $\quad y(0) = y(\pi) = 0$

2. $y'' + 2y = \cos x$, $\quad y(0) = y(1) = 0$

3. $y'' + 4y = x^2$, $\quad y(0) = y'(1) = 0$

4. $(xy')' + \dfrac{1}{x} y = \ln x$, $\quad y'(1) = y'(e^{2\pi}) = 0$

5. $(xy')' + \dfrac{3}{x} y = \dfrac{1}{x} \sin(\ln x)$, $\quad y(1) = y(2) = 0$

*__6.__ Consider the nonhomogeneous problem

$$y'' + \lambda y = f(x), \quad y(0) = y(1) = 0.$$

Show that if $f(x)$ is continuous, then there is a unique solution to this problem if and only if λ is *not* an eigenvalue of the associated homogeneous equation $y'' + \lambda y = 0$, $y(0) = y(1) = 0$.

---

† See, for example, E. A. Coddington and N. Levinson, *Theory of Ordinary Differential Equations*. New York: McGraw-Hill (1955).

*7. Prove the same claim as in Exercise 6 for the problem

$$y'' + \lambda y = f(x), \quad y(0) = y(1), \quad y'(0) = y'(1).$$

Consider the differential equation

$$(rw')' + qw = 0.$$

It is easy to find a nontrivial solution w_1 of this equation with $w_1(a) = 0$, and a nontrivial solution w_2 with $w_2(b) = 0$. Define the function

$$k(x, t) = \begin{cases} w_1(x)w_2(t), & a < x < t, \\ w_1(t)w_2(x), & t < x < b. \end{cases}$$

8. Ignoring any difficulties at $t = x$, show that

$$\frac{d}{dx}\int_a^b k(x, t)f(t)\, dt = \int_a^b \frac{\partial}{\partial x} k(x, t)f(t)\, dt.$$

9. Show that

$$\frac{d}{dx}\left[r(x)\frac{d}{dx}\int_a^b k(x, t)f(t)\, dt \right].$$

$$= r(x)f(x)W(x) - q(x)\int_a^b k(x, t)f(t)\, dt,$$

where W is the Wronskian of the functions w_1 and w_2.

10. Using the result of Exercise 9, conclude that

$$w_3(x) = \int_a^b k(x, t)f(t)\, dt$$

satisfies the equation

$$[r(x)w_3']' + q(x)w_3 = f(x)r(x)W(x).$$

11. Show that

$$\frac{d}{dx}(r(x)W(x)) = 0,$$

and conclude that $r(x)W(x) = C$, a constant.

12. Prove that

$$w(x) = C^{-1}w_3(x)$$

is a solution of the boundary value problem

$$(r(x)w')' + q(x)w = f(x), \quad w(a) = w(b) = 0.$$

Hence conclude that the Green's function is given by $K(x, t) = C^{-1}k(x, t)$.

13. Using the ideas of Exercises 8 through 12, find the Green's function for the boundary value problem

$$w''(x) - w(x) = f(x), \quad w(0) = w(1) = 0.$$

14. Find the Green's function for the boundary value problem

$$w''(x) + k^2 w(x) = f(x), \quad w(0) = w(a) = 0.$$

*15. Generalize the procedure used in Exercises 8 through 12 to obtain the Green's function for the boundary value problem

$$(rw')' + qw = f, \quad w(0) = w'(1) = 0.$$

Apply the generalized procedure of Exercise 15 to Exercises 16 through 18.

16. $w''(x) = f(x), \quad w(0) = w'(1) = 0$

17. $w''(x) + 4w(x) = f(x), \quad w(0) = w'(1) = 0$

18. $(xw')' = f(x), \quad w(1) = w'(e) = 0$

REVIEW EXERCISES FOR CHAPTER 11

In Exercises 1 through 4, show that the given set of functions is orthogonal on the given interval and determine the corresponding orthonormal set.

1. $\{\sin nx\}, \ n = 1, 2, 3, \ldots; \quad 0 \leq x \leq \pi$

2. $\{\cos n\pi x\}, \ n = 0, 1, 2, \ldots; \quad 0 \leq x \leq 2$

3. $\{\sin 2n\pi x, \cos 2n\pi x\}, \ n = 1, 2, \ldots; \quad 0 \leq x \leq 1$

4. $\{\sin n\pi x\}, \ n = 1, 2, 3, \ldots; \quad 0 \leq x \leq 1$

Expand each of the functions in Exercises 5 through 8 in a Fourier series. Examine each series at all the points of discontinuity.

5. $f(x) = x \sin x, \quad 0 < x < 2\pi$

6. $f(x) = \sqrt{1 - \cos x}, \quad |x| < \pi$

7. $f(x) = |\sin x|, \quad |x| < \pi$

8. $f(x) = \begin{cases} x, & 0 < x < \pi \\ 0, & \pi < x < 2\pi \end{cases}$

Find Fourier sine and cosine series for the functions in Exercises 9 through 12 by extending the given function on the interval $[0, a]$ to an odd or even function on $[-a, a]$.

9. $f(x) = x^2, \quad 0 < x < \pi$

10. $f(x) = e^x, \quad 0 < x < \pi$

11. $f(x) = x, \quad 0 < x < 1$

12. $f(x) = 2 - x, \quad 0 < x < 2$

13. Find a Fourier sine series for $f(x) = x^2 - 2$ in $0 < x < 2$ and use this series to obtain a series for π^3.

In Exercises 14 through 19, find the values or approximate values of the eigenvalues and corresponding eigenfunctions of the given Sturm–Liouville problems.

14. $y'' - \lambda y = 0, \quad y'(0) = y(1) = 0$

15. $y'' + \lambda y = 0, \quad y'(0) = y(\pi) = 0$

16. $y'' - \lambda y = 0, \quad y(0) + y'(0) = 0, \quad y(1) = 0$

17. $y'' + \lambda y = 0, \quad y(0) = 0, \quad y(1) + y'(1) = 0$

18. $y'' + (-9 + \lambda)y = 0, \quad y'(0) = y'(1) = 0$

19. $y'' + (-9 + \lambda)y = 0, \quad y(0) = y(1) + y'(1) = 0$

20. Show that the generalized Laguerre equation

$$xy'' + (a + 1 - x)y' + ny = 0$$

is of Sturm–Liouville type, and determine the weight function for which the resulting polynomials are orthogonal.

21. Show that Chebyshev's equation

$$(1 - x^2)y'' - xy' + n^2 y = 0$$

is of Sturm–Liouville type, and determine the weight function for which the resulting polynomials are orthogonal.

12

Partial Differential
Equations

As was indicated in Section 1.2, a *partial differential equation* is an equation involving a function of two or more variables and some of its partial derivatives. Thus the crucial difference between partial and ordinary differential equations is the number of independent variables involved in the equation.

In this chapter we shall present a brief introduction to partial differential equations. Since the general theory is much too difficult to be presented here, we shall be content merely to examine a few simple examples. Because these examples have a number of important practical applications, even this cursory treatment will be of significant value.

12.1 PRELIMINARIES

In this chapter we shall be concerned only with first- or second-order linear partial differential equations with constant coefficients and in two independent variables; that is, equations of the form

$$a \frac{\partial^2 w}{\partial x^2}(x, y) + 2b \frac{\partial^2 w}{\partial x \, \partial y}(x, y) + c \frac{\partial^2 w}{\partial y^2}(x, y) + k \frac{\partial w}{\partial x}(x, y)$$

$$+ m \frac{\partial w}{\partial y}(x, y) + nw(x, y) = f(x, y), \quad \textbf{(1)}$$

where a, b, c, k, m, and n are constants. (The number 2 in front of the coefficient b will simplify later computations.) Equation (1) is *linear* since it does not involve any nonlinear functions of the dependent variable w and its partial derivatives. That is, Eq. (1) is of first degree in w and its partial derivatives.

If $a = b = c = 0$, we say that Eq. (1) is a *first-order* equation. The first-order equation

$$k \frac{\partial w}{\partial x} + m \frac{\partial w}{\partial y} + nw = f(x, y)$$

with constant coefficients k, m, and n is easy to solve, because the rotation of axes

$$u = x \cos \alpha + y \sin \alpha,$$
$$v = -x \sin \alpha + y \cos \alpha, \quad \textbf{(2)}$$

with $\tan \alpha = m/k$, will transform all such equations into an ordinary differential equation by eliminating the partial derivative with respect to v. We illustrate this technique below.

Example 1   Consider the partial differential equation

$$\frac{\partial w}{\partial x} + \frac{\partial w}{\partial y} - w = 0. \quad \textbf{(3)}$$

Since $k = m = 1$, $\tan \alpha = 1$ and $\alpha = \pi/4$ radians so that $\cos \alpha = \sin \alpha = 1/\sqrt{2}$. Thus, by Eq. (2)

$$u = \frac{x + y}{\sqrt{2}}, \quad v = \frac{-x + y}{\sqrt{2}}, \tag{4}$$

and we have

$$\frac{\partial w}{\partial x} = \frac{\partial w}{\partial u}\frac{\partial u}{\partial x} + \frac{\partial w}{\partial v}\frac{\partial v}{\partial x} = \frac{1}{\sqrt{2}}\left(\frac{\partial w}{\partial u} - \frac{\partial w}{\partial v}\right),$$

$$\frac{\partial w}{\partial y} = \frac{\partial w}{\partial u}\frac{\partial u}{\partial y} + \frac{\partial w}{\partial v}\frac{\partial v}{\partial y} = \frac{1}{\sqrt{2}}\left(\frac{\partial w}{\partial u} + \frac{\partial w}{\partial v}\right). \tag{5}$$

Adding the two equations in (4) together, we solve for y, obtaining $y = (u + v)/\sqrt{2}$. Substituting this value and those of (5) into Eq. (3), we get

$$\sqrt{2}\frac{\partial w}{\partial u} - w = 0. \tag{6}$$

Although Eq. (6) is still a partial differential equation in the independent variables u and v, we treat the variable v as if it were a parameter and solve the first-order linear differential equation

$$\sqrt{2}w' - w = 0, \qquad \text{where} \quad w' = \frac{dw}{du}.$$

Since $(1/w)\, dw = (1/\sqrt{2})\, du$, we get

$$\ln w = \frac{u}{\sqrt{2}} + g(v),$$

where the last term is an arbitrary differentiable function of the parameter v (which will vanish whenever we take its partial derivative with respect to u). Simplifying, we have

$$w = e^{u/\sqrt{2}}g(v).$$

Replacing u and v by the substitutions in (4), we get

$$w = e^{(x+y)/2}g\left(\frac{y - x}{\sqrt{2}}\right). \tag{7}$$

That this is, indeed, a solution of Eq. (3) for any differentiable function g is easily checked by performing the operations indicated in that equation.

Up to now we have stressed the similarity between first-order ordinary and partial differential equations. We shall encounter a substantial difference when we consider initial value problems. The solution of an ordinary differential equation is completely determined by prescribing a value for it at a single point. This is generally not true for partial differential equations. In order to obtain a *unique* solution, it is usually necessary to prescribe values for the solution on an entire *line*. A suitable initial condition is

$$w(x, 0) = w_0(x)$$

for all x, where w_0 is a differentiable function. A solution satisfying this initial condition is then easily obtained by setting $y = 0$ in Eq. (7). For example, suppose we are given the initial condition

$$w(x, 0) = \frac{x}{2} + e^x. \tag{8}$$

Setting $y = 0$ in Eq. (7) and substituting the initial condition for the left-hand side of Eq. (7), we have

$$\frac{x}{2} + e^x = e^{x/2} g\left(\frac{-x}{\sqrt{2}}\right)$$

or

$$g\left(\frac{-x}{\sqrt{2}}\right) = \frac{x}{2} e^{-x/2} + e^{x/2}.$$

Setting $z = -x/\sqrt{2}$ now produces the exact form of the function g:

$$g(z) = \frac{-z}{\sqrt{2}} e^{z/\sqrt{2}} + e^{-z/\sqrt{2}}.$$

Replacing this function for g in Eq. (7) yields

$$w = e^{(x+y)/2}\left[\left(\frac{x - y}{2}\right)e^{(y-x)/2} + e^{(x-y)/2}\right]$$

$$= \left(\frac{x - y}{2}\right)e^y + e^x,$$

which is the solution to the initial value problem that is given by Eqs. (3) and (8).

Returning now to Eq. (1), we assume that at least one of the coefficients a, b, and c is nonzero. If so, Eq. (1) is called a *second-order* equation. The procedure for solving second-order equations is much more complicated than that for first-order equations. Initially, it is convenient to simplify Eq. (1) by another rotation of axes. Using the substitution (2) with $\tan 2\alpha = 2b/(a - c)$, we can eliminate the mixed second partial $\partial^2 w/\partial u \, \partial v$ and obtain an equation of the form

$$A\frac{\partial^2 w}{\partial u^2} + C\frac{\partial^2 w}{\partial v^2} + K\frac{\partial w}{\partial u} + M\frac{\partial w}{\partial v} + nw$$

$$= f(u \cos \alpha - v \sin \alpha, u \sin \alpha + v \cos \alpha) \tag{9}$$

(see Exercise 6), where

$$A = a \cos^2 \alpha + 2b \sin \alpha \cos \alpha + c \sin^2 \alpha,$$
$$C = a \sin^2 \alpha - 2b \sin \alpha \cos \alpha + c \cos^2 \alpha,$$
$$K = k \cos \alpha + m \sin \alpha,$$
$$M = m \cos \alpha - k \sin \alpha.$$

(10)

Define

$$B = (c - a) \sin \alpha \cos \alpha + b(\cos^2 \alpha - \sin^2 \alpha).$$

(11)

Then by the double angle formulas of trigonometry,

$$B = \frac{(c - a)}{2} \sin 2\alpha + b \cos 2\alpha = b \cos 2\alpha \left[\frac{(c - a)}{2b} \tan 2\alpha + 1 \right].$$

Since

$$\tan 2\alpha = \frac{2b}{a - c},$$

it follows that $B = 0$. An easy but messy calculation (see Exercise 7) will show that

$$b^2 - ac = B^2 - AC = -AC.$$

(12)

By analogy with analytic geometry, we call the partial differential equation (9) [or Eq. (1)] an *elliptic* equation if $b^2 - ac < 0$, that is, if A and C have the same sign. If A and C have opposite signs or, equivalently, if $b^2 - ac > 0$, we say that Eq. (9) [or Eq. (1)] is a *hyperbolic* equation. Finally, if $b^2 = ac = 0$, Eq. (9) [or Eq. (1)] is called a *parabolic* equation. In summary, Eq. (1) is called

$$\left. \begin{array}{r} \text{hyperbolic} \\ \text{parabolic} \\ \text{elliptic} \end{array} \right\} \quad \text{if} \quad b^2 - ac \left\{ \begin{array}{l} > 0, \\ = 0, \\ < 0. \end{array} \right.$$

As a final simplification (see Exercises 8 and 9), it is possible by changing the *dependent* variable and the scale to transform Eq. (1) into one of the following four standard forms:

$$\frac{\partial^2 \omega}{\partial u^2} + \frac{\partial^2 \omega}{\partial v^2} + \lambda \omega = F(u, v) \quad \text{(elliptic)},$$

(13)

$$\frac{\partial^2 \omega}{\partial u^2} - \frac{\partial^2 \omega}{\partial v^2} + \lambda \omega = F(u, v) \quad \text{(hyperbolic)},$$

(14)

$$\frac{\partial^2 \omega}{\partial u^2} - \lambda \frac{\partial \omega}{\partial v} = F(u, v) \quad \text{(parabolic)},$$

(15)

$$\frac{\partial^2 \omega}{\partial u^2} + \lambda \omega = F(u, v) \quad \text{(degenerate)}.$$

(16)

The degenerate case may be treated as an ordinary differential equation with parameter v, in a manner very similar to Example 1. For this reason, we shall not consider this case any further. In the next three sections we shall consider an example of each of these equations, showing how each arises in practice and indicating what steps can be taken to obtain a solution.

Example 2   To transform the equation

$$\frac{\partial^2 w}{\partial x^2} + 4\frac{\partial^2 w}{\partial x\, \partial y} + \frac{\partial^2 w}{\partial y^2} + \frac{\partial w}{\partial x} = 0$$

into standard form, observe that $b^2 - ac = 3$, since $a = c = 1$ and $b = 2$, and therefore the equation is hyperbolic. Since $\tan 2\alpha$ is infinite, we have $\alpha = 45° = \pi/4$. Substituting this value into Eq. (10), we obtain

$$3\frac{\partial^2 w}{\partial u^2} - \frac{\partial^2 w}{\partial v^2} + \frac{1}{\sqrt{2}}\frac{\partial w}{\partial u} - \frac{1}{\sqrt{2}}\frac{\partial w}{\partial v} = 0.$$

Setting

$$w = \omega \exp\left[-\frac{\sqrt{2}}{12}(u + 3v)\right]$$

and using Eq. (17) [in the exercises], we find that the last equation reduces to

$$3\frac{\partial^2 \omega}{\partial u^2} - \frac{\partial^2 \omega}{\partial v^2} + \frac{\omega}{12} = 0.$$

Finally, letting $u = \sqrt{3}x$ and $v = y$ yields the equation

$$\frac{\partial^2 \omega}{\partial x^2} - \frac{\partial^2 \omega}{\partial y^2} + \frac{\omega}{12} = 0.$$

EXERCISES 12.1

In Exercises 1 through 4, find the solution $w(x, y)$ for each partial differential equation that satisfies the given condition.

1. $3\dfrac{\partial w}{\partial x} - 4\dfrac{\partial w}{\partial y} + 2w = 7$, $w(x, 0) = e^x$

2. $\dfrac{\partial w}{\partial x} + \dfrac{\partial w}{\partial y} + w = 2$, $w(x, 0) = \sin x$

3. $\dfrac{\partial w}{\partial x} + \dfrac{\partial w}{\partial y} - w = e^x$, $w(x, 0) = 0$

4. $\dfrac{\partial w}{\partial x} - \dfrac{\partial w}{\partial y} + w = y$, $w(x, 0) = x^2$

5. Using the chain rule and the substitution (2), prove that

$$\frac{\partial^2 w}{\partial x^2} = \cos^2 \alpha \frac{\partial^2 w}{\partial u^2} - 2\sin \alpha \cos \alpha \frac{\partial^2 w}{\partial u\, \partial v} + \sin^2 \alpha \frac{\partial^2 w}{\partial v^2},$$

$$\frac{\partial^2 w}{\partial x\, \partial y} = \sin \alpha \cos \alpha \frac{\partial^2 w}{\partial u^2} + (\cos^2 \alpha - \sin^2 \alpha)\frac{\partial^2 w}{\partial u\, \partial v} - \sin \alpha \cos \alpha \frac{\partial^2 w}{\partial v^2},$$

$$\frac{\partial^2 w}{\partial y^2} = \sin^2 \alpha \frac{\partial^2 w}{\partial u^2} + 2\sin \alpha \cos \alpha \frac{\partial^2 w}{\partial u\, \partial v} + \cos^2 \alpha \frac{\partial^2 w}{\partial v^2}$$

6. Substitute the results of Exercise 5 into Eq. (1) to verify Eq. (9), and show that the mixed second partial $\partial^2 w/\partial u\,\partial v$ vanishes if $\tan 2\alpha = 2b/(a - c)$.

7. Obtain Eq. (12) by a direct calculation.

8. Verify that for a suitable choice of α and β the substitution

$$w = e^{\alpha u + \beta v}\,\omega$$

will transform the equation

$$A\frac{\partial^2 w}{\partial u^2} + C\frac{\partial^2 w}{\partial v^2} + K\frac{\partial w}{\partial u} + M\frac{\partial w}{\partial v} + Nw = F$$

into an equation of the form

$$A\frac{\partial^2 \omega}{\partial u^2} + C\frac{\partial^2 \omega}{\partial v^2} + \left(N - \frac{CK^2 + AM^2}{4AC}\right)\omega = G. \tag{17}$$

What can be said about the situation if $C = 0$? Write the equation in one of the forms (15) or (16).

9. Show that the change of scale $u = \sqrt{|A|}\,x,\ v = \sqrt{|C|}\,y$ will transform Eq. (17), with $A,\ C \neq 0$, into one of the standard forms (13), (14).

10. Transform the following equations into standard form:

a) $\ 4\dfrac{\partial^2 w}{\partial x^2} + 3\dfrac{\partial^2 w}{\partial y^2} - w = 0;$

b) $\ \dfrac{\partial^2 w}{\partial x^2} - \dfrac{\partial^2 w}{\partial y^2} + 2\dfrac{\partial w}{\partial x} - 5\dfrac{\partial w}{\partial y} + 7w = 0;$

c) $\ \dfrac{\partial^2 w}{\partial x^2} + 2\dfrac{\partial^2 w}{\partial x\,\partial y} + \dfrac{\partial^2 w}{\partial y^2} + w = 0;$

d) $\ \dfrac{\partial^2 w}{\partial x^2} + 2\dfrac{\partial^2 w}{\partial x\,\partial y} + 4\dfrac{\partial^2 w}{\partial y^2} + 5w = 0.$

12.2 THE VIBRATING STRING

As our first physical application, consider a string that is tightly stretched between two fixed points 0 and L on the x-axis (see Fig. 1). Suppose that the string is pulled back vertically a distance that is very small compared to the length L and released at time $t = 0$, causing it to vibrate. Our problem is to determine the displacement $y(x, t)$ of the point on the string that is x units away from the end 0, at any time t.

To avoid making our equation too complicated, we make two simplifying assumptions:

1. Our "ideal" string has uniform mass m per unit length and offers no resistance to bending.

2. The tension T in the string is so large that the gravitational force on the string may be neglected.

Our procedure will be similar to that of Example 3 in Section 4.1. Consider a small segment of length Δx. By Newton's second law of motion (see Example 4 in Section 2.1), the total force acting on this piece of string

Figure 1

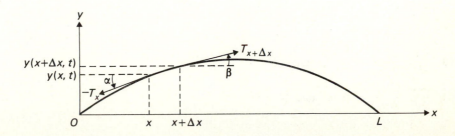

is equal to the mass of the string multiplied by its acceleration:

$$F = ma = (m\,\Delta x)\frac{\partial^2 y}{\partial t^2}. \tag{1}$$

We assumed in this equation that the string is moving only in the xy-plane and that each particle in the string moves only vertically.

Let T_x and $T_{x+\Delta x}$ be the tension vectors at the endpoints of the given segment. These forces are applied tangentially (see Fig. 1) since the string offers no resistance to bending. Since there is no motion in the x-direction, the x-components of the tension vectors must coincide:

$$T_{x+\Delta x}\cos\beta = T_x\cos\alpha \equiv T. \tag{2}$$

Thus T is constant, since x and Δx are arbitrary. Similarly, the difference in the y-components of the tension vectors must equal the total force acting on the string. Then by Eq. (1),

$$T_{x+\Delta x}\sin\beta - T_x\sin\alpha = m\,\Delta x\frac{\partial^2 y}{\partial t^2}. \tag{3}$$

Dividing each term in Eq. (3) by the corresponding term in Eq. (2), we have

$$\frac{T_{x+\Delta x}\sin\beta}{T_{x+\Delta x}\cos\beta} - \frac{T_x\sin\alpha}{T_x\cos\alpha} = \frac{m}{T}\,\Delta x\frac{\partial^2 y}{\partial t^2}$$

or

$$\tan\beta - \tan\alpha = \frac{m}{T}\,\Delta x\frac{\partial^2 y}{\partial t^2}. \tag{4}$$

Since

$$\tan\alpha = \left.\frac{\partial y}{\partial x}\right|_x \quad \text{and} \quad \tan\beta = \left.\frac{\partial y}{\partial x}\right|_{x+\Delta x},$$

we may rewrite Eq. (4) in the form

$$\frac{1}{\Delta x}\left[\left.\frac{\partial y}{\partial x}\right|_{x+\Delta x} - \left.\frac{\partial y}{\partial x}\right|_x\right] = \frac{m}{T}\frac{\partial^2 y}{\partial t^2}.$$

Letting Δx tend to zero, we obtain in the limit the equation

$$\frac{\partial^2 y}{\partial x^2} = \frac{m}{T}\frac{\partial^2 y}{\partial t^2}.$$

Since m/T is positive, it is clear that this is a hyperbolic partial differential equation. The equation, written in the form

$$\boxed{\frac{\partial^2 y}{\partial t^2} = c^2\frac{\partial^2 y}{\partial x^2}, \quad c^2 = \frac{T}{m},} \tag{5}$$

is often called the one-dimensional *wave equation*, where the constant c^2 indicates that the coefficient is positive.

As yet we have not made use of the fact that the string is fixed at its endpoints. We may write these boundary conditions as

$$y(0, t) = y(L, t) = 0, \quad t \geq 0. \tag{6}$$

In addition, we have not taken into account the initial distortion of the string and the fact that it was at rest when released. These initial conditions can be written as

$$y(x, 0) = f(x), \quad 0 \leq x \leq L, \tag{7}$$

$$\left. \frac{\partial y}{\partial t} \right|_{t=0} = 0, \tag{8}$$

where $f(x)$ is a function depicting the original distortion (see Examples 1 and 2), and $(\partial y/\partial t)(x, t)$ is the velocity of the point x units away from the origin at time t.

The direct method we shall use to solve this problem is due to D'Alembert.† Since it is only rarely possible to apply this technique, we shall develop two more applicable methods in the next three sections. We begin by defining the variables

$$u = x + ct, \quad v = x - ct, \tag{9}$$

and transforming the wave equation (5) into one involving variables u and v. By the chain rule, we have

$$\frac{\partial y}{\partial t} = \frac{\partial y}{\partial u}\frac{\partial u}{\partial t} + \frac{\partial y}{\partial v}\frac{\partial v}{\partial t} = c\left(\frac{\partial y}{\partial u} - \frac{\partial y}{\partial v}\right), \tag{10}$$

where we used Eqs. (9) to obtain the partial derivatives $\partial u/\partial t = c = \partial v/\partial t$. Taking the partial derivative with respect to t of Eq. (10), we obtain

$$\frac{\partial^2 y}{\partial t^2} = c\frac{\partial}{\partial t}\left(\frac{\partial y}{\partial u} - \frac{\partial y}{\partial v}\right) = c\left[\frac{\partial}{\partial u}\left(\frac{\partial y}{\partial u} - \frac{\partial y}{\partial v}\right)\frac{\partial u}{\partial t} + \frac{\partial}{\partial v}\left(\frac{\partial y}{\partial u} - \frac{\partial y}{\partial v}\right)\frac{\partial v}{\partial t}\right]$$

$$= c^2\left[\left(\frac{\partial^2 y}{\partial u^2} - \frac{\partial^2 y}{\partial u\,\partial v}\right) - \left(\frac{\partial^2 y}{\partial v\,\partial u} - \frac{\partial^2 y}{\partial v^2}\right)\right].$$

Since the mixed second partials are equal, we finally have

$$\frac{\partial^2 y}{\partial t^2} = c^2\left[\frac{\partial^2 y}{\partial u^2} - 2\frac{\partial^2 y}{\partial u\,\partial v} + \frac{\partial^2 y}{\partial v^2}\right].$$

Similarly, we find that

$$\frac{\partial^2 y}{\partial x^2} = \left[\frac{\partial^2 y}{\partial u^2} + 2\frac{\partial^2 y}{\partial u\,\partial v} + \frac{\partial^2 y}{\partial v^2}\right].$$

---

† The French mathematician J. D'Alembert (1717–1783) is known for his contributions in mechanics.

Substituting these results into Eq. (5) and canceling like terms yield the equation

$$\frac{\partial^2 y}{\partial u \, \partial v} = 0, \tag{11}$$

since $4c^2 \neq 0$. It is now easy to solve Eq. (11) by performing two successive integrations. Integrating with respect to u, we obtain

$$\frac{\partial y}{\partial v} = g'(v), \tag{12}$$

where g' is an unknown function in v. From Eq. (12), it is evident that g' is the partial derivative, with respect to v, of the solution y—which is the reason for using the prime in our notation. Integrating Eq. (12) with respect to v yields

$$y = g(v) + h(u), \tag{13}$$

where h is an unknown function in u. Substituting Eq. (9) into Eq. (13) yields *D'Alembert's solution*

$$y(x, t) = g(x - ct) + h(x + ct) \tag{14}$$

of the wave equation (5).

Since h is arbitrary, if we ignore Eq. (7), we will see that one possible solution of the wave equation is $g(x - ct)$. If we set $t = 0$, then the initial distortion of the string is given by $y(x, 0) = g(x)$. At a fixed time later, its distortion is $y(x, t) = g(x - ct)$. Thus the shape of the string can be obtained from the graph of the function $g(x)$ by moving an interval of length L to the right with velocity c. For this reason, $g(x - ct)$ is called a *traveling wave*. Similarly $h(x + ct)$ is a traveling wave, which moves to the left with velocity c. Hence D'Alembert's solution is a superposition of two traveling waves, one moving to the right, the other to the left, with the same velocity c.

The functions g and h can be determined from the initial conditions. Setting $t = 0$, we find that

$$f(x) = y(x, 0) = g(x) + h(x). \tag{15}$$

Noting that g and h are functions of one variable, we may use the chain rule to differentiate Eq. (14) with respect to t. And setting $t = 0$, we obtain

$$0 = \left.\frac{\partial y}{\partial t}\right|_{t=0} = -cg'(x - ct) + ch'(x + ct)\bigg|_{t=0} = c[h'(x) - g'(x)].$$

From the last equation we know that $h' = g'$, so that

$$h(x) = g(x) + k,$$

where k is a constant. Replacing this function for h in Eq. (15) yields

$f(x) = 2g(x) + k$ or $g = (f - k)/2$. Hence $h = (f + k)/2$, so that the solution of the problem finally becomes

$$y(x, t) = \tfrac{1}{2}[f(x - ct) + f(x + ct)]. \tag{16}$$

Note that since the boundary conditions (6) must be satisfied by Eq. (16), setting $x = 0$ in Eq. (16) will yield

$$0 = \tfrac{1}{2}[f(-ct) + f(ct)]$$

or

$$f(-ct) = -f(ct).$$

Thus $f(x)$ is odd. This result may seem curious, since $f(x)$ has been defined only on the interval $0 \leq x \leq L$. However, it causes no difficulty, since we may extend f to the interval $-L \leq x \leq L$ by defining

$$f(-x) = -f(x) \quad \text{for} \quad -L \leq x \leq 0.$$

This extension is always possible as $f(0) = 0$. Similarly, setting $x = L$ and using the fact that f is odd, we find that

$$f(L + ct) = -f(L - ct)$$
$$= f(ct - L),$$

so that f has period $2L$. Again, it is clear that we can extend $f(x)$ to the entire real line by letting

$$f(x + 2L) = f(x),$$

for all x. This extension of $f(x)$ to the entire real line will seem very reasonable if we return to the notion of traveling waves. It is clear, from Eq. (16), that we must immediately leave the interval $0 \leq x \leq L$ when $t > 0$. Now suppose we move $f(x)$ gradually to the right. Since $y(0, t) = y(L, t) = 0$ for all t, any positive contribution at 0 or L from the traveling wave $f(x - ct)$ must be offset by an equal negative contribution from $f(x + ct)$ [which is obtained by moving $f(x)$ the same distance to the left], and vice versa. In effect, this procedure amounts to a reflection of wave forms at the boundary.

By Theorem 2 in Section 11.3, the function $f(x)$ has a Fourier sine series—a fact we shall refer to in the next section. (The continuity of f is guaranteed by the fact that the string is unbroken. We assume that f' is piecewise continuous, since that is what it will be in most practical situations, such as in the example below.)

Example 1   Suppose that we pluck the string at its center (see Fig. 2) a distance $y(L/2, 0) = y_0$ meters (y_0 is assumed to be small). We can assume that the distortion consists of two straight lines from $(0, 0)$ to $(L/2, y_0)$ and from

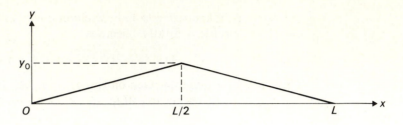

Figure 2

$(L/2, y_0)$ to $(L, 0)$. Hence

$$f(x) = \begin{cases} \dfrac{2y_0}{L}\, x, & 0 \le x \le \dfrac{L}{2}, \\[2ex] \dfrac{2y_0}{L}\,(L - x), & \dfrac{L}{2} \le x \le L, \end{cases}$$

which has the piecewise continuous derivative

$$f'(x) = \begin{cases} \dfrac{2y_0}{L}, & 0 \le x < \dfrac{L}{2}, \\[2ex] \dfrac{-2y_0}{L}, & \dfrac{L}{2} < x \le L. \end{cases}$$

If the string is four meters long, has a mass of 0.08 kilogram, and is subject to a constant tension of two Newtons ($= \text{kg-m/s}^2$), then we obtain the solution

$$y(x, t) = \tfrac{1}{2}[f(x - 10t) + f(x + 10t)],$$

since

$$c^2 = \frac{T}{m} = \frac{2}{0.08/4} = 100\,(\text{m/s})^2.$$

To discover the exact location of a point one meter from the end 0 after exactly one second, we set $x = t = 1$. Then

$$y(1, 1) = \tfrac{1}{2}[f(-9) + f(11)],$$

and since f has period $2L = 8$ and is odd, we get

$$y(1, 1) = \frac{1}{2}[f(-1) + f(3)] = \frac{1}{2}[f(3) - f(1)]$$

$$= \frac{1}{2}\left(\frac{2y_0}{L} - \frac{2y_0}{L}\right) = 0.$$

Example 2   Suppose that $f(x) = y_0 \sin(\pi x/L)$. Then by Eq. (16)

$$y(x, t) = \frac{y_0}{2}\left[\sin\frac{\pi}{L}(x - ct) + \sin\frac{\pi}{L}(x + ct)\right],$$

and by the addition formulas of trigonometry, this reduces to

$$y(x, t) = y_0 \sin \frac{\pi x}{L} \cos \frac{\pi c t}{L}.$$

Thus, if we fix our attention on the point x_0 units from the left, we see that it oscillates with a period $2L/c$ and an amplitude $y_0 \sin (\pi x_0/L)$.

EXERCISES 12.2

In Exercises 1 through 6, use D'Alembert's solution (16) to find the displacement $y(x, t)$ for each given function $f(x)$, point x, and time t. Assume that $c = 5$ and $L = 6$ meters.

1. $f(x) = 0.01 \sin (\pi x/L)$, $x = 2$, $t = 1$
2. $f(x) = 0.1 \sin (\pi x/L)$, $x = 3$, $t = 2$
3. $f(x) = 0.01 \sin (2\pi x/L)$, $x = 3$, $t = 1$
4. $f(x) = 0.1 \sin (2\pi x/L)$, $x = 2$, $t = 2$
5. $f(x) = \begin{cases} 0.1x, & 0 \le x \le 3, x = 2, t = 2 \\ 0.1(6 - x), & 3 \le x \le 6 \end{cases}$
6. $f(x) = \begin{cases} 0.1x, & 0 \le x \le 2 \\ 0.2(3 - x), & 2 \le x \le 4, x = 3, t = 5 \\ 0.1(x - 6), & 4 \le x \le 6 \end{cases}$

7. Assume, instead of the initial conditions (7) and (8), that the string is initially in its equilibrium position, and is set vibrating by each of its points x being given an initial velocity $f'(x)$, where f is a differentiable function. Prove that the solution is given by

$$y(x, t) = \frac{1}{2c} [f(x + ct) - f(x - ct)].$$

Using the result of **Exercise 7**, and setting $c = 5$ and $L = 6$ meters, do Exercises 8 through 11 for the given functions $f'(x)$ and values x and t.

8. $f'(x) = 0.01 \sin (\pi x/L)$, $x = 2$, $t = 3$
9. $f'(x) = 0.1 \sin (2\pi x/L)$, $x = 1$, $t = 1$
10. $f'(x) = 3(6x - x^2)$, $x = 3$, $t = 0.01$ second
11. $f'(x) = 0.1 \sin^2 (\pi x/L)$, $x = 1$, $t = 0.1$ second

12. Suppose that we subject a vibrating string to a damping force that is proportional at each instance to the velocity at each point. Show that the resulting hyperbolic differential equation is of the form

$$\frac{\partial^2 y}{\partial t^2} - k \frac{\partial y}{\partial t} = c^2 \frac{\partial^2 y}{\partial x^2}.$$

12.3 SEPARATION OF VARIABLES

One of the simplest techniques for solving ordinary differential equations consists of separating the variables. Although we now have *two* independent variables, we can nevertheless adapt the technique to all partial differential equations of the forms (13) through (16) in Section 12.1, whenever the function $F(u, v) \equiv 0$. The method is best explained by means of an example.

Suppose that we again consider the problem of the vibrating string given by the wave equation

$$\frac{\partial^2 y}{\partial t^2} = c^2 \frac{\partial^2 y}{\partial x^2}, \quad c^2 = \frac{T}{m}, \tag{1}$$

with boundary conditions

$$y(0, t) = y(L, t) = 0, \quad t \ge 0, \tag{2}$$

and initial conditions

$$y(x, 0) = f(x), \quad \left.\frac{\partial y}{\partial t}\right|_{t=0} = 0, \quad 0 \leqslant x \leqslant L. \tag{3}$$

We begin by seeking a solution of the form

$$y(x, t) = X(x)T(t), \tag{4}$$

where X is a function of x alone, and T is a function involving only the independent variable t. Of course, there is no guarantee that such a solution exists. In fact, as we shall see later, separation is often not possible. Nevertheless, we shall try it out and see if it works. Using primes to denote differentiation, we observe that

$$\frac{\partial^2 y}{\partial t^2} = \frac{\partial^2}{\partial t^2}[XT] = XT'' \quad \text{and} \quad \frac{\partial^2 y}{\partial x^2} = X''T,$$

so that Eq. (1) becomes

$$XT'' = c^2 X''T. \tag{5}$$

It is now possible to separate the variables and write Eq. (5) as

$$\frac{T''}{T} = c^2 \frac{X''}{X}. \tag{6}$$

Initially we had no assurance that it would be possible to separate the variables as we have done. Should such a separation prove impossible, the method would not apply and we would have to turn to other methods of solving the given problem.

Now suppose we fix t and allow x to vary. Since the left-hand side of Eq. (6) is constant, the right-hand side must be constant for all values of x. Consequently, the right-hand side is constant *regardless* of the value of t, and we have

$$\frac{T''}{T} = c^2 \frac{X''}{X} = k,$$

where k is constant. From this set of equalities we obtain two ordinary differential equations

$$T'' - kT = 0, \tag{7}$$

$$X'' - \frac{k}{c^2} X = 0. \tag{8}$$

Thus the problem of solving the partial differential equation (1) has been reduced to solving two ordinary differential equations (7) and (8). The constant k is arbitrary, but its value must be the same for both equations.

Using the characteristic equation (see Chapter 3) $\lambda^2 - k = 0$, we can easily obtain the general solution

$$T(t) = \begin{cases} a_1 e^{\sqrt{k}t} + a_2 e^{-\sqrt{k}t}, & \text{if } k > 0, \\ a_1 t + a_2, & \text{if } k = 0, \\ a_1 \cos \sqrt{-k}t + a_2 \sin \sqrt{-k}t, & \text{if } k < 0. \end{cases}$$

Similarly, we also have the general solution

$$X(x) = \begin{cases} b_1 e^{\sqrt{k}x/c} + b_2 e^{-\sqrt{k}x/c}, & \text{if } k > 0, \\ b_1 x + b_2, & \text{if } k = 0, \\ b_1 \cos \dfrac{\sqrt{-k}x}{c} + b_2 \sin \dfrac{\sqrt{-k}x}{c}, & \text{if } k < 0. \end{cases}$$

Since our solution must satisfy the boundary conditions (2), if a solution of the form (4) exists, we must have the equations

$$X(0)T(t) = X(L)T(t) = 0 \quad \text{for all } t.$$

If $T(t) \equiv 0$, then $y \equiv 0$ and the string is constantly at rest, which is impossible if $f(x) \neq 0$. For $f \neq 0$, T must be nonzero for at least one value of t, which implies that $X(0) = X(L) = 0$. Thus Eq. (8) becomes a Sturm–Liouville problem with these boundary conditions.

Setting $x = 0$ and $x = L$ in the general solution yields, for $k > 0$, the homogeneous system of equations

$$X(0) = b_1 + b_2 = 0,$$
$$X(L) = b_1 e^{\sqrt{k}L/c} + b_2 e^{-\sqrt{k}L/c} = 0.$$

This system has a nonzero solution if and only if the determinant of its coefficients is zero. But

$$\begin{vmatrix} 1 & 1 \\ e^{\sqrt{k}L/c} & e^{-\sqrt{k}L/c} \end{vmatrix} = e^{-\sqrt{k}L/c} - e^{\sqrt{k}L/c} = -2 \sinh \frac{\sqrt{k}L}{c} \neq 0,$$

so that $X(x) \equiv 0$ for $k > 0$. Then $y \equiv 0$, which is impossible if $f(x) \neq 0$. For $k = 0$, the condition $X(0) = 0$ implies that $b_2 = 0$, while $X(L) = 0$ requires that $b_1 = 0$, again leading to the zero solution. So we are left with the remaining possibility that k is negative, and we set $k = -r^2$. This yields the general solution

$$X(x) = b_1 \cos \frac{rx}{c} + b_2 \sin \frac{rx}{c}.$$

Letting $x = 0$ and $x = L$, we have

$$X(0) = b_1 = 0 \quad \text{and} \quad X(L) = b_2 \sin \frac{rL}{c} = 0.$$

To prevent our again having the zero solution, we must choose an r such that rL/c is a positive multiple of π:

$$\frac{rL}{c} = n\pi \quad \text{or} \quad r = \frac{n\pi c}{L}.$$

Thus we obtain an infinite set of solutions

$$X_n(x) = b_2 \sin \frac{n\pi x}{L}, \tag{9}$$

each associated with the choice

$$k = -\frac{n^2 \pi^2 c^2}{L^2}. \tag{10}$$

Hence the corresponding solutions for T are

$$T_n(t) = a_1 \cos \frac{n\pi ct}{L} + a_2 \sin \frac{n\pi ct}{L}.$$

Finally, we obtain an infinite set of solutions

$$y_n(x, t) = X_n(x)T_n(t) = \left(B_n \cos \frac{n\pi ct}{L} + B_n^* \sin \frac{n\pi ct}{L} \right) \sin \frac{n\pi x}{L}, \tag{11}$$

where B_n and B_n^* are constants, that satisfy the partial differential equation (1) and the boundary conditions (2). In the language of Chapter 11, we see that we have found the *eigenvalues* (10) and the corresponding *eigenfunctions* (11) of the boundary value problem (1), (2).

We now try to select a solution that satisfies the initial conditions (3). It is extremely likely that no one solution (11) will satisfy Eqs. (3). However, any finite sum of solutions (11) is again a solution of the boundary value problem (by the *principle of superposition*), so we can try to find a finite linear combination of these solutions that satisfies the initial conditions (3). Generally, even this will fail, so as a last resort we try an infinite series of the solutions (11):

$$y(x, t) = \sum_{n=1}^{\infty} y_n(x, t) = \sum_{n=1}^{\infty} \left(B_n \cos \frac{n\pi ct}{L} + B_n^* \sin \frac{n\pi ct}{L} \right) \sin \frac{n\pi x}{L}. \tag{12}$$

There is no guarantee at this point that such a series will converge, but since its form is very similar to that of the Fourier series (8) in Section 11.2, there is every reason to be optimistic. Furthermore, if Eq. (12) converges and the series obtained by the formal term-by-term partial differentiations $\partial/\partial t$, $\partial^2/\partial t^2$, $\partial/\partial x$, and $\partial^2/\partial x^2$ all converge uniformly, then Eq. (12) will again be a solution of the boundary value problem (1), (2). If, in addition, we can also satisfy the initial conditions (3), then we shall have solved the vibrating string problem.

Setting $t = 0$ in Eq. (12) and using the first of Eqs. (3), we have

$$y(x, 0) = \sum_{n=1}^{\infty} B_n \sin \frac{n\pi x}{L} = f(x). \tag{13}$$

We again assume that $f(x)$ and $f'(x)$ are piecewise continuous (see Section 12.2). The infinite series (13) is a Fourier sine series, which requires that the function $f(x)$ be odd [$f(-x) = -f(x)$], and periodic with period $2L$. As in Section 12.2, it is easy to extend the function $f(x)$, defined on the interval $0 \leqslant x \leqslant L$, in such a way that it is odd and periodic with period $2L$. Since $f(0) = 0$, we let $f(-x) = -f(x)$, on $-L \leqslant x \leqslant 0$ and require that $f(x + 2L) = f(x)$ for all real numbers x. Then the coefficients B_n are given by the Euler formula

$$B_n = \frac{1}{L} \int_{-L}^{L} f(x) \sin \frac{n\pi x}{L} \, dx, \quad n = 1, 2, 3, \dots. \tag{14}$$

Taking the partial derivative of Eq. (12) with respect to t and using the second of the initial conditions (3), we have

$$\frac{\partial y}{\partial t} = \frac{n\pi c}{L} \sum_{n=1}^{\infty} \left(B_n^* \cos \frac{n\pi ct}{L} - B_n \sin \frac{n\pi ct}{L} \right) \sin \frac{n\pi x}{L} \bigg|_{t=0} = 0$$

or

$$\sum_{n=1}^{\infty} B_n^* \sin \frac{n\pi x}{L} = 0.$$

Again we obtain an expression of the form (14) for B_n^*, but this time the function involved is zero. Hence all the coefficients B_n^* vanish. Thus the solution (12) reduces to

$$y(x, t) = \sum_{n=1}^{\infty} B_n \cos \frac{n\pi ct}{L} \sin \frac{n\pi x}{L}, \tag{15}$$

where the coefficients B_n are given by Eq. (14). It is possible to write the series (15) in closed form by using the trigonometric identity

$$2 \sin A \cos B = \sin (A + B) + \sin (A - B).$$

Then

$$y(x, t) = \frac{1}{2} \sum_{n=1}^{\infty} B_n \left[\sin \frac{n\pi}{L} (x + ct) + \sin \frac{n\pi}{L} (x - ct) \right]$$

$$= \frac{1}{2} \left[\sum_{n=1}^{\infty} B_n \sin \frac{n\pi}{L} (x + ct) + \sum_{n=1}^{\infty} B_n \sin \frac{n\pi}{L} (x - ct) \right],$$

and the series can be evaluated by substituting $x + ct$ and $x - ct$, respectively, for the variable x in Eq. (13). Hence

$$y(x, t) = \tfrac{1}{2} [f(x + ct) + f(x - ct)],$$

which is precisely the same result as we obtained directly in Section 12.2.

Example 1   Let a vibrating string have length π and let $c^2 = 1$. Suppose that the initial velocity is zero and the initial distortion is $f(x) = x(\pi - x)$. Instead of using D'Alembert's solution, we shall obtain an expansion of the form (15). We need only calculate the coefficients B_n. Integrating by parts, we obtain

$$
\begin{aligned}
B_n &= \frac{1}{\pi} \int_{-\pi}^{\pi} x(\pi - x) \sin nx \, dx \\
&= \frac{1}{\pi} \left[-x(\pi - x) \frac{\cos nx}{n} \bigg|_{-\pi}^{\pi} + \frac{1}{n} \int_{-\pi}^{\pi} (\pi - 2x) \cos nx \, dx \right] \\
&= \frac{1}{\pi} \left[-\frac{2\pi^2}{n} \cos n\pi + \frac{(\pi - 2x)}{n^2} \sin nx \bigg|_{-\pi}^{\pi} - \frac{2}{n^3} \cos nx \bigg|_{-\pi}^{\pi} \right] \\
&= -\frac{2\pi}{n} \cos n\pi = (-1)^{n+1} \frac{2\pi}{n}.
\end{aligned}
$$

Hence the solution is

$$
y(x, t) = 2\pi[\cos t \sin x - \tfrac{1}{2} \cos 2t \sin 2t + \tfrac{1}{3} \cos 3t \sin 3t - \cdots].
$$

Consider a cylindrical rod composed of a uniform heat-conducting material of length L and radius R (so that the cross-sectional area is $A = \pi R^2$). We assume that heat can enter and leave the rod only through its ends; that is, the lateral surface of the rod is completely insulated. Let x measure the distance along the rod (see Fig. 3) and let $T(x, t)$ denote the absolute temperature at time t at a point x units along the rod (we assume that the temperature is uniform across any cross-sectional area of the rod). Let ρ be the *density* of the rod (mass per unit volume), which is assumed to be constant. The *specific heat* c of the rod is defined to be the amount of heat (Joules, BTUs) that must be supplied to raise the temperature of one unit mass (kilograms, pounds) of the rod by one degree (Celsius, Fahrenheit).

Figure 3

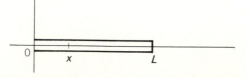

Consider a section of the rod between x and $x + dx$. Since mass = volume $\times$ density, the mass between these two points is $\rho A \, dx$. In order to change the temperature of the rod between these two points from 0 to $T(x, t)$ degrees, we must supply $T(x, t) \cdot c\rho A \cdot dx$ units of heat. Thus between any two points x_0 and x_1, the heat energy contained in the rod at time t is

$$Q(t) = \int_{x_0}^{x_1} T(x, t) c\rho A\, dx. \tag{16}$$

By the law of conservation of energy, if there are no heat sources within the rod, the heat energy in any part of the rod can increase or decrease only because of a lateral flow of heat through the boundaries of that part of the rod. This *heat flux*, written as $Q_F(x, t)$, is the quantity of heat energy per unit time passing through a unit area in the cross section x units from the left-hand end in a positive (rightward) direction. Thus, to find the rate of change of the heat energy between the x_0 and x_1 cross sections, we need only take the difference

$$\frac{dQ}{dt} = AQ_F(x_0, t) - AQ_F(x_1, t), \tag{17}$$

where the first term on the right-hand side is the heat energy flowing in and the second is that flowing out (see Fig. 4).

Figure 4

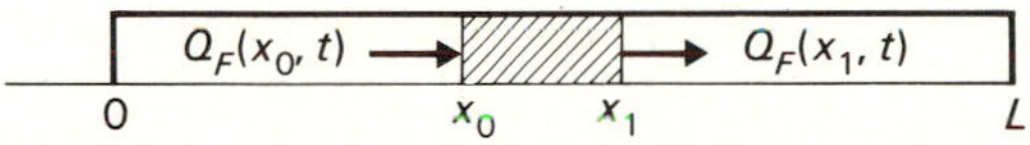

It is an empirical law of physics that the heat flux at any point is proportional to the *temperature gradient* $\partial T(x, t)/\partial x$ at that point. The constant of proportionality is called the *thermal conductivity* of the rod and is denoted by κ. Since heat flows in the direction of decreasing temperature, we have

$$Q_F(x, t) = -\kappa \frac{\partial T}{\partial x}(x, t), \tag{18}$$

where $\kappa > 0$. Since no heat sources are in this part of the rod, we have

$$AQ_F(x_0, t) - AQ_F(x_1, t) = A\left[\kappa \frac{\partial T}{\partial x}(x_1, t) - \kappa \frac{\partial T}{\partial x}(x_0, t)\right]$$
$$= \int_{x_0}^{x_1} \frac{\partial}{\partial x}\left[\kappa \frac{\partial T}{\partial x}(x, t)\right] A\, dx. \tag{19}$$

Substituting the right-hand side of Eq. (19) for the right-hand side of Eq. (17) and differentiating Eq. (12), we have

$$\int_{x_0}^{x_1} \frac{\partial}{\partial x}\left(\kappa \frac{\partial T}{\partial x}\right) A\, dx = \frac{dQ}{dt}$$

$$= \int_{x_0}^{x_1} c\rho \frac{\partial T}{\partial t} A\, dx,$$

or

$$\int_{x_0}^{x_1} \left[c\rho \frac{\partial T}{\partial t} - \frac{\partial}{\partial x} \left(\kappa \frac{\partial T}{\partial x} \right) \right] A \, dx = 0. \tag{20}$$

Equation (20) must hold in any interval $x_0 \le x \le x_1$, so if we assume the functions involved are all continuous, the expression in brackets must vanish. To see this, note that if it were positive (negative) at some point, then by continuity it would be positive (negative) on some interval, in which case Eq. (20) would not hold. Thus, for all x in the interval $[0, L]$

$$c\rho \frac{\partial T}{\partial t} = \frac{\partial}{\partial x} \left(\kappa \frac{\partial T}{\partial x} \right), \tag{21}$$

and if we assume κ is constant,

$$\boxed{\frac{\partial T}{\partial t} = \delta \frac{\partial^2 T}{\partial x^2}} \tag{22}$$

where $\delta = \kappa/c\rho$. Equation (22) is called the *heat (conduction) equation* and is clearly parabolic. The constant δ is positive and measures the *diffusivity* of the material of the rod. To completely specify our problem, we select the case in which the *boundary conditions* are

$$T(0, t) = T(L, t) = 0, \quad t \ge 0, \tag{23}$$

and the *initial condition* is

$$T(x, 0) = f(x), \quad 0 \le x \le L, \tag{24}$$

where f is a given function. In physical terms, we are keeping the ends of the rod at zero temperature and letting $f(x)$ denote the initial temperature at any point x of the rod. It is easy to modify the problem by selecting other, possibly time dependent, boundary conditions (see Exercises 7, 8, and 9).

We begin to solve the heat equation by assuming the existence of a solution to the problem of the form

$$T(x, t) = X(x)\mathcal{T}(t).$$

Substituting this equation into Eq. (22) yields

$$X\mathcal{T}' = \delta X''\mathcal{T}$$

or

$$\frac{\mathcal{T}'}{\delta\mathcal{T}} = \frac{X''}{X}. \tag{25}$$

Since the left-hand side is constant for fixed t and arbitrary x, the right-hand side is a constant, say, k. Thus we again obtain a pair of ordinary differential equations

$$\mathcal{T}' - k\,\delta\mathcal{T} = 0, \tag{26}$$

$$X'' - kX = 0. \tag{27}$$

The boundary conditions (23) may be written as

$$X(0)\mathcal{T}(t) = X(L)\mathcal{T}(t) = 0,$$

implying that $X(0) = X(L) = 0$ unless the rod has zero initial temperature at every point. If we ignore this uninteresting case, we will note that the boundary value problem (27), $X(0) = X(L) = 0$, is almost identical with the boundary value problem for X in the case of the vibrating string, where we discovered that nonzero solutions exist only for negative k. Setting $k = -r^2$, we find that k is an eigenvalue of the problem only if r is a multiple of π/L, and the eigenfunctions corresponding to $-(n\pi/L)^2$ have the form

$$X_n(x) = A \sin\frac{n\pi x}{L}.$$

Using $k = -(n\pi/L)^2$, we find that Eq. (26) yields the general solution

$$\mathcal{T}_n(t) = Be^{-(n\pi/L)^2\delta t}.$$

Hence we consider an infinite series of the form

$$T(x, t) = \sum_{n=1}^{\infty} X_n(x)\mathcal{T}_n(t) = \sum_{n=1}^{\infty} B_n \sin\frac{n\pi x}{L} e^{-(n\pi/L)^2\delta t}. \tag{28}$$

Setting $t = 0$ and making use of the initial condition (24), we have

$$T(x, 0) = \sum_{n=1}^{\infty} B_n \sin\frac{n\pi x}{L} = f(x),$$

so that for Theorem 1 in Section 11.3 to be applicable, f must again be an odd, periodic, piecewise continuous function of period $2L$ with piecewise continuous derivative; the coefficients B_n are given by Eq. (14). Thus, the solution (28) is completely determined and the series must converge, since $T(x, 0)$ converges and the exponential factors are less than 1 for all $t > 0$. Observe that the exponential factors in Eq. (28) will cause $T(x, t)$ to approach zero as t tends to infinity.

Example 2   Suppose that the rod has length π, $\delta = 1$, and initial temperature $f(x) = \sin 2x$. By the orthogonality of the set of functions $\{\sin nx\}$ (see Example 1 in Section 11.2), the coefficients B_n are all zero for $n \neq 2$. For $n = 2$, we have from Eq. (14) and Example 1 in Section 11.2,

$$B_2 = \frac{1}{\pi}\int_{-\pi}^{\pi} \sin^2 2x\, dx = 1.$$

Thus the solution of this problem is given by

$$T(x, t) = (\sin 2x)e^{-4t}.$$

EXERCISES 12.3

In Exercises 1 through 6, find the temperature $T(x, t)$ in an insulated rod π units long whose ends are kept at 0°C, where the initial temperature is given by:

1. $f(x) = x(\pi - x)$

2. $f(x) = x(\pi^2 = x^2)$

3. $f(x) = x^2(\pi - x)$

4. $f(x) = x \cos \dfrac{x}{2}$

5. $f(x) = \begin{cases} x, & 0 \le x \le \pi/2 \\ 0, & \pi/2 < x \le \pi \end{cases}$

6. $f(x) = \begin{cases} 0, & 0 \le x < \pi/3 \\ 1, & \pi/3 \le x < 2\pi/3 \\ 0, & 2\pi/3 \le x \le \pi \end{cases}$

7. Suppose that the ends of the rod are kept at different constant temperatures

$$T(0, t) = T_1, \quad T(L, t) = T_2.$$

Find the temperature at x as t tends to ∞; that is, find the *steady-state* temperature. (*Hint*: The steady-state temperature is *not* time dependent.)

8. Denote the steady-state temperature by $T_s(x)$

and define the *transient* temperature in the rod by

$$T_t(x, t) = T(x, t) - T_s(x).$$

Verify that $T_t(x, t)$ is given by Eq. (28). This shows that we need only superimpose the steady-state temperature on the solution (28) to obtain the solution for nonzero boundary conditions.

9. Suppose that the ends of the rod are kept at the temperatures

$$T(0, t) = T_1 e^{-c^2 \delta t}, \quad T(L, t) = T_2 e^{-c^2 \delta t}.$$

For what initial conditions $f(x)$ can a solution be found by the separation of variables? What happens if cL is a multiple of π?

Find the solutions $y(x, t)$ of the equations in Exercises 10 through 15 by the technique of separation of variables.

10. $\dfrac{\partial^2 y}{\partial x^2} + \dfrac{1}{x^2} \dfrac{\partial^2 y}{\partial t^2} = 0$ **11.** $\dfrac{\partial^2 y}{\partial x\, \partial t} = y$

12. $\dfrac{\partial^2 y}{\partial x^2} + \dfrac{\partial^2 y}{\partial t^2} = 0$ **13.** $\dfrac{\partial^2 y}{\partial x^2} - 2\dfrac{\partial y}{\partial x} = -\dfrac{\partial y}{\partial t}$

14. $\dfrac{\partial^2 y}{\partial t^2} = \dfrac{\partial^2 y}{\partial x^2} + y$ **15.** $\dfrac{\partial^2 y}{\partial t^2} = x^2 \dfrac{\partial^2 y}{\partial x^2}$

12.4 TWO-DIMENSIONAL HEAT FLOW AND LAPLACE'S EQUATION

Consider a rectangular sheet of heat-conducting material of uniform thickness θ, density ρ, specific heat c, and thermal conductivity κ. We may suppose that the set of points (x, y) with $0 \le x \le L$ and $0 \le y \le M$ is a face of the sheet. We assume that the faces of the sheet are insulated and that heat can enter and leave only through the edges of the sheet.

Select any interior point (x, y) on the face and consider a rectangular region $ABCD$ whose corner coordinates are given in Fig. 5. It is reasonable to assume the heat flow in each plane to be identical, so that the flow is two-dimensional. In the discussion below we shall assume that the distances Δx and Δy are very small.

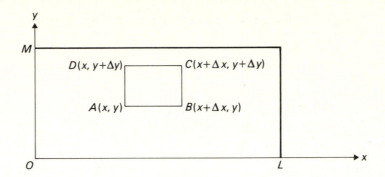

Figure 5

The rate of change of heat energy in the sheet $ABCD$ at any time t is approximately [see Eq. (16) in Section 12.3]

$$c\rho\theta\Delta x\Delta y\frac{\partial T}{\partial t},\tag{1}$$

where $T = T(x, y, t)$ is the temperature at any point (x, y) at time t. Since Δx and Δy are small, we assume that the heat flux along each edge is constant. Then the heat energy passing through $ABCD$ in the vertical direction is

$$\theta\Delta x[Q_F(x, y, t) - Q_F(x, y + \Delta y, t)],\tag{2}$$

where Q_F is the heat flux. In the horizontal direction the heat energy is

$$\theta\Delta y[Q_F(x, y, t) - Q_F(x + \Delta x, y, t)].\tag{3}$$

Using Eq. (18) in Section 12.3 and adding Eq. (2) to Eq. (3), we obtain another approximation of the rate of change of heat energy in the sheet $ABCD$ [see Eq. (17) in Section 12.3]:

$$\kappa\theta\Delta y\left[\frac{\partial T}{\partial x}(x + \Delta x, y, t) - \frac{\partial T}{\partial x}(x, y, t)\right]$$

$$+ \kappa\theta\Delta x\left[\frac{\partial T}{\partial y}(x, y + \Delta y, t) - \frac{\partial T}{\partial y}(x, y, t)\right].\tag{4}$$

Equating Eqs. (4) and (1) and dividing by $\Delta x\Delta y$ yield

$$c\rho\theta\frac{\partial T}{\partial t} = \kappa\theta\frac{\left[\dfrac{\partial T}{\partial x}(x + \Delta x, y, t) - \dfrac{\partial T}{\partial x}(x, y, t)\right]}{\Delta x}$$

$$+ \kappa\theta\frac{\left[\dfrac{\partial T}{\partial y}(x, y + \Delta y, t) - \dfrac{\partial T}{\partial y}(x, y, t)\right]}{\Delta y}.$$

Passing to the limit as Δx and Δy both approach zero, we obtain

$$c\rho\theta\frac{\partial T}{\partial t} = \kappa\theta\left[\frac{\partial^2 T}{\partial x^2} + \frac{\partial^2 T}{\partial y^2}\right],$$

which may be written in the form

$$\boxed{\frac{\partial^2 T}{\partial x^2} + \frac{\partial^2 T}{\partial y^2} = \frac{1}{\delta}\frac{\partial T}{\partial t}\,,} \tag{5}$$

where $\delta = \kappa/c\rho$ is the diffusivity. Equation (5) is called the *two-dimensional heat equation.*

If the edges of the sheet are kept at constant temperatures, and an extremely long time is allowed to pass, then the temperature at any given point will stabilize and remain almost constant for all larger values of t; that is, steady-state conditions will be attained. The temperature T at a point on the sheet will then depend only on its position and not on time. Thus $\partial T/\partial t$ will be zero throughout the sheet, and Eq. (5) becomes

$$\boxed{\frac{\partial^2 T}{\partial x^2} + \frac{\partial^2 T}{\partial y^2} = 0.} \tag{6}$$

This elliptic partial differential equation, commonly referred to as *Laplace's equation,* arises in many other problems of applied mathematics. We shall now present three examples of the solution of Laplace's equation by the method of separation of variables.

Example 1 We begin by studying the steady-state heat flow problem in the rectangular sheet of size $L \times M$ in which Laplace's equation arose. Suppose that the upper horizontal edge is kept at 100°C, while the other three edges are kept at 0°C. We may write these boundary conditions for $T(x, y)$ as follows:

$$T(0, y) = T(L, y) = 0, \quad 0 < y < M, \tag{7}$$

$$T(x, 0) = 0, \quad T(x, M) = 100, \quad 0 < x < L. \tag{8}$$

Since we are seeking the steady-state solution, time will not be a factor in this problem, and therefore no initial condition is needed.

Setting $T(x, y) = X(x)Y(y)$, we find that Eq. (6) becomes

$$X''Y + XY'' = 0,$$

which may be written in separated form as

$$\frac{X''}{X} = -\frac{Y''}{Y}\,. \tag{9}$$

The left-hand side of Eq. (9) is constant for fixed x and arbitrary y. Hence Y''/Y must be constant. Letting k be this constant, we obtain the pair of ordinary differential equations

$$X'' - kX = 0,$$
$$Y'' + kY = 0. \tag{10}$$

From Eq. (7) we have

$$X(0)Y(y) = X(L)Y(y) = 0,$$

and $Y(y) \not\equiv 0$ [since otherwise $T(x, y) \equiv 0$, contradicting the second equation of (8)], so that $X(0) = X(L) = 0$. Thus again we have the same situation that we encountered in Section 12.3, and the eigenvalues are all negative. Setting $k = -r^2$, we find that rL must be a multiple of π in order that we may have a nonzero solution of the boundary value problem for X. Hence $r = n\pi/L$, and the functions

$$X_n(x) = A \sin \frac{n\pi x}{L}, \quad n = 1, 2, 3, \ldots, \tag{11}$$

are the eigenfunctions of the problem. Setting $k = -(n\pi/L)^2$ in the second equation of (10) yields the general solution

$$Y_n(y) = B_1 e^{n\pi y/L} + B_2 e^{-n\pi y/L}.$$

The first condition of (8) implies that $Y(0) = 0$, thus $B_1 = -B_2$, and we can rewrite Y_n as

$$Y_n(y) = B \sinh \frac{n\pi y}{L}. \tag{12}$$

As in Section 12.3, to enlarge the class of possible solutions, we consider an infinite sum of products of the terms (11) and (12):

$$T(x, y) = \sum_{n=1}^{\infty} c_n \sin \frac{n\pi x}{L} \sinh \frac{n\pi y}{L}. \tag{13}$$

Evaluating Eq. (13) at any point (x, M), we obtain by Eqs. (8)

$$100 = \sum_{n=1}^{\infty} \left(c_n \sinh \frac{n\pi M}{L} \right) \sin \frac{n\pi x}{L}, \quad 0 < x < L,$$

which again is a Fourier sine series, requiring that we extend the boundary condition $T(x, M)$ to the interval $-L \leqslant x \leqslant L$ as an odd piecewise continuous periodic function of period $2L$ with a piecewise continuous derivative. Clearly the function

$$f(x) = \begin{cases} 100, & 0 < x < L, \\ -100, & -L < x < 0, \end{cases}$$

with $f(x + 2L) = f(x)$ satisfies these conditions. Hence $c_n \sinh (n\pi M/L)$

must equal the nth Fourier (sine) coefficient of $f(x)$:

$$c_n \sinh \frac{n\pi M}{L} = \frac{1}{L} \int_{-L}^{L} f(x) \sin \frac{n\pi x}{L} \, dx$$

$$= -\frac{100}{L} \int_{-L}^{0} \sin \frac{n\pi x}{L} \, dx + \frac{100}{L} \int_{0}^{L} \sin \frac{n\pi x}{L} \, dx$$

$$= \frac{200}{n\pi}(1 - \cos n\pi) = \frac{200}{n\pi}[1 - (-1)^n].$$

Hence $c_{2k} = 0$, while

$$c_{2k+1} = \frac{400}{\pi(2k+1)\sinh(2k+1)\pi M/L},$$

so that the solution is given by

$$T(x, y) = \frac{400}{\pi}\left[\frac{\sin(\pi x/L)\sinh(\pi y/L)}{\sinh(\pi M/L)} + \frac{\sin(3\pi x/L)\sinh(3\pi y/L)}{3\sinh(3\pi M/L)} + \cdots\right]$$

$$= \frac{400}{\pi} \sum_{n=1}^{\infty} \frac{\sin[(2n-1)\pi x/L]\sinh[(2n-1)\pi y/L]}{(2n-1)\sinh[(2n-1)\pi M/L]}.$$

We may use this formula to compute the steady-state temperature at any point in the rectangle. For example,

$$T\left(\frac{L}{2}, \frac{M}{2}\right) = \frac{400}{\pi} \sum_{n=1}^{\infty} \frac{\sin[(2n-1)\pi/2]\sinh[(2n-1)\pi M/2L]}{(2n-1)\sinh[(2n-1)\pi M/L]}.$$

And since

$$\frac{\sinh(A/2)}{\sinh A} = \frac{e^{A/2} - e^{-A/2}}{e^A - e^{-A}} = \frac{1}{e^{A/2} + e^{-A/2}} = \frac{1}{2\cosh(A/2)},$$

we obtain

$$T\left(\frac{L}{2}, \frac{M}{2}\right) = \frac{200}{\pi}\left[\frac{1}{\cosh(\pi M/2L)} - \frac{1}{3\cosh(3\pi M/2L)} + \frac{1}{5\cosh(5\pi M/2L)} - \cdots\right],$$

which, for given L and M, can be approximated to any desired degree of accuracy.

Example 2   We now consider the steady-state heat flow problem in the disk D of radius 1 centered at the origin. It should be clear from the nature of the situation that the problem will be simplified if we can use polar coordinates (r, θ) instead of rectangular coordinates (x, y). Assume that the boundary of the disk is kept at the temperature

$$T(1, \theta) = f(\theta), \quad 0 \leq \theta \leq 2\pi, \tag{14}$$

where the function $f(\theta)$ is periodic with period 2π and has a continuous derivative. Now we need only write Laplace's equation (6) in polar coordinates. Let us recall the transformation formulas

$$r = \sqrt{x^2 + y^2}, \quad x = r\cos\theta,$$

$$\theta = \tan^{-1}\frac{y}{x}, \quad y = r\sin\theta.$$

By the chain rule, we have

$$\frac{\partial T}{\partial x} = \frac{\partial T}{\partial r}\frac{\partial r}{\partial x} + \frac{\partial T}{\partial \theta}\frac{\partial \theta}{\partial x}$$

$$= \frac{\partial T}{\partial r}\cos\theta - \frac{\partial T}{\partial \theta}\frac{\sin\theta}{r},$$

since

$$\frac{\partial r}{\partial x} = \frac{\partial}{\partial x}\sqrt{x^2 + y^2} = \frac{x}{\sqrt{x^2 + y^2}} = \frac{x}{r} = \cos\theta,$$

and

$$\frac{\partial \theta}{\partial x} = \frac{-y/x^2}{1 + (y/x)^2} = \frac{-y}{r^2} = \frac{-\sin\theta}{r}.$$

Then

$$\frac{\partial^2 T}{\partial x^2} = \frac{\partial}{\partial r}\left(\frac{\partial T}{\partial r}\frac{\partial r}{\partial x} + \frac{\partial T}{\partial \theta}\frac{\partial \theta}{\partial x}\right)\frac{\partial r}{\partial x} + \frac{\partial}{\partial \theta}\left(\frac{\partial T}{\partial r}\frac{\partial r}{\partial x} + \frac{\partial T}{\partial \theta}\frac{\partial \theta}{\partial x}\right)\frac{\partial \theta}{\partial x}$$

$$= \frac{\partial^2 T}{\partial r^2}\cos^2\theta - \frac{\partial^2 T}{\partial r\,\partial\theta}\frac{\sin\theta\cos\theta}{r} + \frac{\partial T}{\partial\theta}\frac{\sin\theta\cos\theta}{r^2}$$

$$- \frac{\partial^2 T}{\partial\theta\,\partial r}\frac{\sin\theta\cos\theta}{r} + \frac{\partial T}{\partial r}\frac{\sin^2\theta}{r} + \frac{\partial^2 T}{\partial\theta^2}\frac{\sin^2\theta}{r^2} + \frac{\partial T}{\partial\theta}\frac{\cos\theta\sin\theta}{r^2}.$$

Similarly,

$$\frac{\partial^2 T}{\partial y^2} = \frac{\partial}{\partial r}\left(\frac{\partial T}{\partial r}\sin\theta + \frac{\partial T}{\partial\theta}\frac{\cos\theta}{r}\right)\frac{\partial r}{\partial y} + \frac{\partial}{\partial\theta}\left(\frac{\partial T}{\partial r}\sin\theta + \frac{\partial T}{\partial\theta}\frac{\cos\theta}{r}\right)\frac{\partial\theta}{\partial y}$$

$$= \frac{\partial^2 T}{\partial r^2}\sin^2\theta + \frac{\partial^2 T}{\partial r\,\partial\theta}\frac{\sin\theta\cos\theta}{r} - \frac{\partial T}{\partial\theta}\frac{\cos\theta\sin\theta}{r^2}$$

$$+ \frac{\partial^2 T}{\partial\theta\,\partial r}\frac{\sin\theta\cos\theta}{r} + \frac{\partial T}{\partial r}\frac{\cos^2\theta}{r} + \frac{\partial^2 T}{\partial\theta^2}\frac{\cos^2\theta}{r^2} - \frac{\partial T}{\partial\theta}\frac{\sin\theta\cos\theta}{r^2}.$$

Adding the two equations, we obtain

$$\boxed{\frac{\partial^2 T}{\partial x^2} + \frac{\partial^2 T}{\partial y^2} = \frac{\partial^2 T}{\partial r^2} + \frac{1}{r^2}\frac{\partial^2 T}{\partial\theta^2} + \frac{1}{r}\frac{\partial T}{\partial r} = 0,}$$

                                                              (15)

which is Laplace's equation in polar coordinates.

Now we let $T(r, \theta) = R(r)\Theta(\theta)$ and transform Eq. (15) into

$$R''\Theta + \frac{1}{r^2} R\Theta'' + \frac{1}{r} R'\Theta = 0$$

or

$$\left(R'' + \frac{1}{r} R'\right)\Theta = -\frac{R}{r^2} \Theta''.$$

Separating the variables, we have

$$\frac{r^2 R'' + rR'}{R} = -\frac{\Theta''}{\Theta} = k,$$

since each side of the first equality is a function of only one variable. Hence we obtain two ordinary differential equations:

$$\Theta'' + k\Theta = 0, \tag{16}$$

and

$$r^2 R'' + rR' - kR = 0. \tag{17}$$

Since $f(\theta) = T(1, \theta) = R(1)\Theta(\theta)$, it is clear that $\Theta(\theta)$ is periodic with period 2π. We assume that f is not identically zero [see Exercise 12 for the case where $f(\theta) \equiv 0$] so that $R(1) \neq 0$. Observe the $\Theta(0) = \Theta(2\pi)$ and $\Theta'(0) = \Theta'(2\pi)$. By the remark following the orthogonality theorem and Exercise 6 of Section 11.5, the boundary value problem in Θ has periodic eigenfunctions of period 2π. Thus the eigenvalues must be $k = n^2$ with the corresponding eigenfunctions

$$\Theta_n(\theta) = A_1 \cos n\theta + A_2 \sin n\theta, \quad n = 0, 1, 2, 3, \dots .$$

Equation (17) is an Euler equation (see Section 3.5) and can be solved by letting $R = r^\lambda$. Letting $k = n^2$, we see that Eq. (17) becomes

$$r^\lambda[\lambda(\lambda - 1) + \lambda - n^2] = r^\lambda(\lambda^2 - n^2) = 0,$$

and the roots of the equation $\lambda^2 - n^2 = 0$ are $\lambda = \pm n$. Hence the general solution of Eq. (17) with $k = n^2$ is

$$R_n(r) = B_1 r^n + B_2 r^{-n}, \quad n = 0, 1, 2, 3, \dots .$$

Since we want R_n to exist for all values in the range $0 \leq r \leq 1$, B_2 must vanish and $R_n(r) = Br^n$, $n = 0, 1, 2, 3, \dots$. Thus we consider the infinite series

$$T(r, \theta) = \frac{A_0}{2} + \sum_{n=1}^{\infty} r^n(A_n \cos n\theta + B_n \sin n\theta), \tag{18}$$

and seek a solution to our problem in this form. To evaluate the constants

A_n, B_n, we note that

$$f(\theta) = T(1, \theta) = \frac{A_0}{2} + \sum_{n=1}^{\infty} A_n \cos n\theta + B_n \sin n\theta. \tag{19}$$

Hence Eq. (19) is the Fourier series of f, and the coefficients A_n and B_n are the Fourier coefficients of f, given by the Euler formulas

$$A_n = \frac{1}{\pi} \int_{-\pi}^{\pi} f(\varphi) \cos n\varphi \, d\varphi, \quad B_n = \frac{1}{\pi} \int_{-\pi}^{\pi} f(\varphi) \sin n\varphi \, d\varphi.$$

Since Eq. (19) converges and $r \leq 1$, the series (18) will also converge. For example, if $f(\theta) = \cos \theta$, then all the coefficients except A_1 will vanish, and $A_1 = 1$. Hence the temperature is given by

$$T(r, \theta) = r \cos \theta$$

at all points in the unit disk.

It is interesting to note what will occur if we replace the coefficients A_n, B_n in Eq. (18) by the Euler formulas and interchange the sums and integrals:

$$T(r, \theta) = \frac{1}{2\pi} \int_{-\pi}^{\pi} f(\varphi) \, d\varphi$$

$$+ \sum_{n=1}^{\infty} r^n \left[\frac{\cos n\theta}{\pi} \int_{-\pi}^{\pi} f(\varphi) \cos n\varphi \, d\varphi + \frac{\sin n\theta}{\pi} \int_{-\pi}^{\pi} f(\varphi) \sin n\varphi \, d\varphi \right]$$

$$= \frac{1}{\pi} \int_{-\pi}^{\pi} f(\varphi) \left[\frac{1}{2} + \sum_{n=1}^{\infty} r^n (\cos n\theta \cos n\varphi + \sin n\theta \sin n\varphi) \right] d\varphi.$$

Since

$$\cos n(\theta - \varphi) = \cos n\theta \cos n\varphi + \sin n\theta \sin n\varphi,$$

we obtain

$$T(r, \theta) = \frac{1}{\pi} \int_{-\pi}^{\pi} f(\varphi) \left[\frac{1}{2} + \sum_{n=1}^{\infty} r^n \cos n(\theta - \varphi) \right] d\varphi.$$

But

$$\cos n(\theta - \varphi) = \frac{e^{in(\theta - \varphi)} + e^{-in(\theta - \varphi)}}{2},$$

so that

$$\sum_{n=1}^{\infty} r^n \cos n(\theta - \varphi) = \frac{1}{2} \sum_{n=1}^{\infty} r^n [e^{in(\theta - \varphi)} + e^{-in(\theta - \varphi)}]$$

$$= \frac{1}{2} \left[\sum_{n=1}^{\infty} [re^{i(\theta - \varphi)}]^n + \sum_{n=1}^{\infty} [re^{-i(\theta - \varphi)}]^n \right].$$

The complex number $e^{it} = \cos t + i \sin t$ can be represented as a vector of length $\sqrt{(\cos t)^2 + (\sin t)^2} = 1$ (see Section 3.5), so that $re^{i(\theta - \varphi)}$ and $re^{i(\varphi - \theta)}$ both have length equal to $r(<1)$. Using the geometric series (6) in Section 5.1, we have

$$\sum_{n=1}^{\infty} r^n \cos n(\theta - \varphi) = \frac{1}{2}\left[\frac{re^{i(\theta - \varphi)}}{1 - re^{i(\theta - \varphi)}} + \frac{re^{-i(\theta - \varphi)}}{1 - re^{-i(\theta - \varphi)}}\right]$$

$$= \frac{1}{2}\left[\frac{r[e^{i(\theta - \varphi)} + e^{-i(\theta - \varphi)}] - 2r^2}{r^2 - r[e^{i(\theta - \varphi)} + e^{-i(\theta - \varphi)}] + 1}\right]$$

$$= \frac{r\cos(\theta - \varphi) - r^2}{r^2 - 2r\cos(\theta - \varphi) + 1}.$$

Thus

$$\frac{1}{2} + \sum_{n=1}^{\infty} r^n \cos n(\theta - \varphi) = \frac{1}{2} + \frac{r\cos(\theta - \varphi) - r^2}{r^2 + 1 - 2r\cos(\theta - \varphi)}$$

$$= \frac{1 - r^2}{2[r^2 + 1 - 2r\cos(\theta - \varphi)]}$$

and

$$T(r, \theta) = \frac{1 - r^2}{2\pi} \int_{-\pi}^{\pi} \frac{f(\varphi)}{r^2 + 1 - 2r\cos(\theta - \varphi)}\, d\varphi. \tag{20}$$

Equation (20) is called the *Poisson integral formula*[†] and is valid for all values $r < 1$ (see Exercise 9). It indicates that the temperature at any interior point (r, θ) of the unit disk may be obtained by integrating the boundary temperatures according to the formula (20). In particular, if $r = 0$, then the temperature at the center of the disk is

$$T(0, \theta) = \frac{1}{2\pi} \int_{-\pi}^{\pi} f(\varphi)\, d\varphi,$$

that is, *the temperature at the center is the integral average of the boundary temperatures*. This fact is often called the *mean value theorem* and holds for all functions that satisfy Laplace's equation on the unit disk $r \leq 1$.

Example 3 In this example we shall consider the three-dimensional Laplace equation

$$\frac{\partial^2 T}{\partial x^2} + \frac{\partial^2 T}{\partial y^2} + \frac{\partial^2 T}{\partial z^2} = 0 \tag{21}$$

associated with the steady-state heat flow problem in a solid.

Suppose the solid is a rectangular cylinder of height π and radius 1

[†] Named in honor of S. D. Poisson (1781–1840), a French mathematician and physicist.

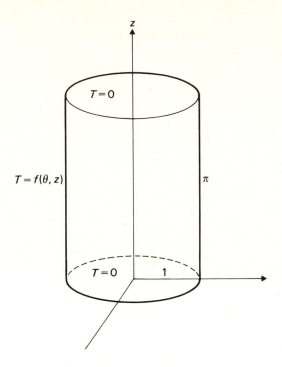

Figure 6

(Fig. 6). Since such a solid is easily described in cylindrical coordinates, it will be convenient to obtain Laplace's equation (21) in terms of the coordinates (r, θ, z), where

$$x = r \cos \theta, \quad y = r \sin \theta, \quad z = z.$$

Obviously, we are simply writing the xy-coordinates in polar form. Thus the calculations we did in Example 2 still apply, and Laplace's equation becomes [from Eq. (15)]

$$\frac{\partial^2 T}{\partial r^2} + \frac{1}{r} \frac{\partial T}{\partial r} + \frac{1}{r^2} \frac{\partial^2 T}{\partial \theta^2} + \frac{\partial^2 T}{\partial z^2} = 0. \tag{22}$$

We now apply the method of separation of variables to the function T and, accordingly, set $T(r, \theta, z) = R(r)\Theta(\theta)Z(z)$ and write Eq. (22) as

$$R''\Theta Z + \frac{1}{r} R'\Theta Z + \frac{1}{r^2} R\Theta''Z + R\Theta Z'' = 0$$

or

$$[(R'' + r^{-1}R')\Theta + r^{-2}R\Theta'']Z = -R\Theta Z''.$$

Separating out the z-variables, we have

$$\frac{R'' + r^{-1}R'}{R} + r^{-2}\frac{\Theta''}{\Theta} = -\frac{Z''}{Z} = k_1,$$

since the left-hand side of the equation is a function of r and θ, whereas the right-hand side is a function of z alone. Thus

$$Z'' + k_1 Z = 0,$$

and

$$\frac{R'' + r^{-1}R'}{R} = k_1 - r^{-2}\frac{\Theta''}{\Theta}.$$

Multiplying both sides of the last equation by r^2, we have

$$\frac{r^2 R'' + rR'}{R} = k_1 r^2 - \frac{\Theta''}{\Theta},$$

or

$$\frac{r^2 R'' + rR'}{R} - k_1 r^2 = -\frac{\Theta''}{\Theta} = k_2,$$

since each side is a function of only one variable. Hence we also obtain the ordinary differential equations

$$\Theta'' + k_2 \Theta = 0$$

and

$$r^2 R'' + rR' - (k_2 + k_1 r^2)R = 0. \qquad \textbf{(23)}$$

If we now assume the boundary conditions

$$T(r, \theta, 0) = T(r, \theta, \pi) = 0, \quad T(1, \theta, z) = f(\theta, z),$$

where f is a continuously differentiable function in θ and z, we can translate the conditions into terms of R, Θ, Z:

$$R(r)\Theta(\theta)Z(0) = R(r)\Theta(\theta)Z(\pi) = 0,$$
$$R(1)\Theta(\theta)Z(z) = f(\theta, z).$$

Since R and Θ are not constantly zero [assuming $f(\theta, z) \not\equiv 0$], it follows that $Z(0) = Z(\pi) = 0$. Also, since f is continuous, it must be periodic with period 2π in θ (since f is the temperature on the surface of the cylinder). Thus $\Theta(\theta)$ is periodic with period 2π, so that $\Theta(0) = \Theta(2\pi)$ and $\Theta'(0) = \Theta'(2\pi)$. Finally, we know that $R(1) \neq 0$ and $R(0)$ is finite. As in Example 2, the eigenvalues of the boundary value problem

$$\Theta'' + k_2\Theta = 0, \quad \Theta(0) = \Theta(2\pi), \quad \Theta'(0) = \Theta'(2\pi),$$

are $k_2 = m^2$, $m = 1, 2, 3, \ldots$, with the corresponding eigenfunctions

$$\Theta_m(\theta) = A_1 \cos m\theta + A_2 \sin m\theta.$$

By the result of Exercise 1 of Section 11.4, the boundary value problem

$$Z'' + k_1 Z = 0, \quad Z(0) = Z(\pi) = 0,$$

has the eigenvalues $k_1 = n^2$, $n = 1, 2, 3, \ldots$, and the corresponding eigenfunctions

$$Z_n(z) = B \sin nz.$$

Setting $k_1 = n^2$ and $k_2 = m^2$ in Eq. (23), we obtain

$$r^2 R'' + rR' - (n^2 r^2 + m^2)R = 0,$$

which may be transformed into Bessel's equation by the substitution $\rho = inr$. To verify this fact, we note that

$$\frac{dR}{d\rho} = \frac{dR}{dr}\frac{dr}{d\rho} = \frac{1}{in} R'(r),$$

and

$$\frac{d^2 R}{d\rho^2} = \frac{d}{d\rho}\left(\frac{1}{in} R'\right) = \frac{1}{(in)^2} R''(r) = -\frac{1}{n^2} R''(r).$$

Substituting these values into the equation, we obtain

$$-n^2 r^2 \frac{d^2 R}{d\rho^2} + inr \frac{dR}{d\rho} - (n^2 r^2 + m^2)R = 0$$

or

$$\rho^2 \frac{d^2 R}{d\rho^2} + \rho \frac{dR}{d\rho} + (\rho^2 - m^2)R = 0. \tag{24}$$

By Theorem 2 in Section 5.4, Eq. (24) has the general solution

$$R(\rho) = C_1 J_m(\rho) + C_2 Y_m(\rho), \quad \rho \neq 0.$$

And since $R(0)$ is finite, the constant $C_2 = 0$, since the Bessel function of the second kind, Y_m, involves a $\ln \rho$ term that approaches $-\infty$ as ρ approaches 0. We are, therefore, led to the double series

$$T(r, \theta, z) = \sum_{m=1}^{\infty} \sum_{n=1}^{\infty} (a_{mn} \cos m\theta + b_{mn} \sin m\theta) \sin nz\, J_m(inr).$$

The coefficients a_{mn} and b_{mn} can be determined by setting $r = 1$ and requiring that

$$f(\theta, z) = \sum_{m=1}^{\infty} \left[\left(\sum_{n=1}^{\infty} a_{mn} J_m(in) \sin nz \right) \cos m\theta \right.$$

$$\left. + \left(\sum_{n=1}^{\infty} b_{mn} J_m(in) \sin nz \right) \sin m\theta \right]. \tag{25}$$

If we define

$$a_m(z) = \sum_{n=1}^{\infty} a_{mn} J_m(in) \sin nz,$$

and   **(26)**

$$b_m(z) = \sum_{n=1}^{\infty} b_{mn} J_m(in) \sin nz,$$

we see that Eq. (25) becomes

$$f(\theta, z) = \sum_{m=1}^{\infty} a_m(z) \cos m\theta + b_m(z) \sin m\theta,$$

which is a Fourier series in θ, where z is an arbitrary parameter. By Euler's formulas, it follows that

$$a_m(z) = \frac{1}{\pi} \int_{-\pi}^{\pi} f(\theta, z) \cos m\theta \, d\theta, \quad b_m(z) = \frac{1}{\pi} \int_{-\pi}^{\pi} f(\theta, z) \sin m\theta \, d\theta.$$

If the functions $a_m(z)$ and $b_m(z)$ can be calculated, we can then use the Fourier sine series (26) in z to calculate the coefficients a_{mn} and b_{mn}:

$$a_{mn} = \frac{2}{\pi J_m(in)} \int_0^{\pi} a_m(z) \sin nz \, dz,$$

$$b_{mn} = \frac{2}{\pi J_m(in)} \int_0^{\pi} b_m(z) \sin nz \, dz.$$

Although the formal procedure delineated above is straightforward, the calculations involved are, to say the least, very tedious. In Exercise 8, the reader will be asked to develop a similar procedure that leads to the use of series of Legendre polynomials in place of Bessel functions.

EXERCISES 12.4

1. A square plate with sides of length L has both faces insulated. The upper horizontal edge is kept at 50°C, while all the other edges are at 0°C. Find the steady-state temperatures at the points $(L/2, L/2)$ and $(L/4, L/4)$.

2. If in Exercise 1 the temperatures along the edge $y = L$ are given by

$$T(x, L) = x(L - x),$$

and all the other conditions remain the same, what is $T(x, y)$?

3. If in Exercise 1 the temperatures along the upper horizontal edge are

$$T(x, L) = 100 \sin(\pi x/L),$$

with all the other conditions remaining unchanged, what is $T(x, y)$?

4. Suppose that the temperature along the edge $y = L$ in Exercise 2 is changed to

$$T(x, L) = x(L^2 - x^2),$$

with all the other conditions remaining the same. Find the temperature at the points $(L/4, L/4)$ and $(L/4, 3L/4)$.

5. Consider the steady-state heat flow problem on the unit disk (see Example 2) and suppose that $f(\theta) = \sin^2 \theta$. Find the temperature at the point $r = \frac{1}{2}, \theta = 0°$ by:

   a) the eigenfunction expansion method,

   b) Poisson's integral formula.

6. Repeat Exercise 5 with $f(\theta) = \sin \theta - \cos \theta$.

7. Repeat Exercise 5 with $f(\theta) = \theta(2\pi - \theta)$.

*8. a) Show that the three-dimensional Laplace equation (21) may be written in spherical coordinates r, θ, φ ($x = r \cos \theta \sin \varphi, y = r \sin \theta \sin \varphi, z = r \cos \varphi$) in the form

$$\frac{\partial^2 T}{\partial r^2} + \frac{2}{r}\frac{\partial T}{\partial r} + \frac{1}{r^2}\frac{\partial^2 T}{\partial \varphi^2} + \frac{\cot \varphi}{r^2}\frac{\partial T}{\partial \varphi}$$

$$+ \frac{1}{r^2 \sin^2 \varphi}\frac{\partial^2 T}{\partial \theta^2} = 0. \quad \textbf{(27)}$$

   b) Separate the variables in Eq. (27) to obtain the ordinary differential equations

$$\Theta'' + k_1\Theta = 0,$$

$$R'' + \left(\frac{2}{r}\right)R' + \left(\frac{k_2}{r^2}\right)R = 0,$$

$$[(\sin \varphi)\Phi']' - \left(\frac{k_2 \sin \varphi + k_1}{\sin \varphi}\right)\Phi = 0.$$

   c) Assume the boundary condition $T(1, \theta, \varphi) = f(\theta, \varphi)$ for a sphere of radius 1, where f is continuously differentiable in θ and φ, and periodic with period 2π in θ. Find the eigenfunctions of the three boundary value problems thus defined. (*Hint*: Use Legendre polynomials.)

   d) Obtain the eigenfunction expansion for $T(r, \theta, \varphi)$.

*9. Justify the steps involved in obtaining Poisson's integral formula (20) from the solution (18) of the steady-state heat equation in the disk $r \leq 1$. [*Hint*: Show that the series (18) converges uniformly in the disk $r \leq r_0 < 1$.]

*10. Generalize Example 2 to obtain the steady-state temperature in a disk of radius R, centered at the origin, and prove that the corresponding Poisson integral formula is

$$T(r, \theta) = \frac{R^2 - r^2}{2\pi}\int_{-\pi}^{\pi}\frac{f(\varphi)\,d\varphi}{R^2 + r^2 - 2rR\cos(\theta - \varphi)},$$
$$r < R,$$

where the continuously differentiable function $f(\varphi)$ describes the boundary temperature in the direction $0 \leq \varphi < 2\pi$.

*11. Let D be any bounded polygon in the xy-plane, and let (x_0, y_0) be a point interior to D. Let u be a real-valued function defined on D that has continuous derivatives of at least order 2.

   a) Show that if u attains its maximal value M at (x_0, y_0), then

$$\left.\frac{\partial^2 u}{\partial x^2} + \frac{\partial^2 u}{\partial y^2}\right|_{(x_0, y_0)} \leq 0.$$

   b) Show that if

$$\frac{\partial^2 u}{\partial x^2} + \frac{\partial^2 u}{\partial y^2} > 0$$

at all interior points of D, then u does not attain its maximal value at any interior point of D.

   c) Suppose that

$$\frac{\partial^2 u}{\partial x^2} + \frac{\partial^2 u}{\partial y^2} \geq 0 \quad \textbf{(28)}$$

at all interior points of D. Show that the function $w(x, y) = u(x, y) + \varepsilon[(x - x_0)^2 + (y - y_0)^2]$ does not attain its maximal value in D at (x_0, y_0), for any value $\varepsilon > 0$.

   d) Conclude that any function satisfying Eq. (28) at all interior points of D must attain its maximal value on the boundary of D. (This is called the *maximum principle*.)

*12. Use the maximum principle obtained in Exercise 11 to show that any function u that satisfies Laplace's equation attains both its maximum and its minimum on the boundary of D. (Physically, this means that in a steady-state heat flow problem, the maximum and minimum temperatures will occur on the boundary of the region.)

12.5 LAPLACE TRANSFORM METHODS FOR PARTIAL DIFFERENTIAL EQUATIONS

The one-dimensional heat equation

$$\frac{\partial T}{\partial t} = \delta \frac{\partial^2 T}{\partial x^2}$$

is sometimes called the *thermal diffusion equation*, since it describes the flow of heat along a uniform rod. The same equation may also be used to describe one-dimensional fluid flow, since we can replace temperature by mass (or concentration) in the considerations of Eq. (22) in Section 12.3. By doing this, we can use the heat equation to study such diverse problems as the dispersal of pollutants in the atmosphere or the flow of a chemical across a membrane. In some cases, the fluid flow is aided (or retarded) by other forces. For example, the motion of a pollutant emitted from a smokestack involves both a mixing (*diffusion*) of the pollutant in the air and the transport (*convection*) of the pollutant by air currents. Thus the change in the concentration T in the interval from x_0 to x_1, due to convection, is

$$v[T(x_0, t) - T(x_1, t)],$$

where v is the velocity of the current. Adding this term to Eq. (19) in Section 12.3, we obtain

$$\frac{dQ}{dt} = \int_{x_0}^{x_1} \frac{\partial}{\partial x}\left(\kappa \frac{\partial T}{\partial x} - vT\right) A \, dx.$$

Differentiating Eq. (16) in Section 12.3, we finally have

$$\boxed{c\rho \frac{\partial T}{\partial t} = \frac{\partial}{\partial x}\left(\kappa \frac{\partial T}{\partial x}\right) - v \frac{\partial T}{\partial x}.}$$

(1)

Equation (1) is generally called the *diffusion equation*. If κ is zero, we call Eq. (1) a *pure convection*; if $v = 0$, a *pure diffusion*.

The method of separation of variables is again very useful in solving diffusion equations. However, in some situations the boundary and initial conditions are such that it is not possible to obtain a solution by this technique. Consider the following example of a pure diffusion.

Example 1   Suppose that κ is constant and $v = 0$ in Eq. (1). Then Eq. (1) reduces to the thermal diffusion equation

$$\frac{\partial T}{\partial t} = \delta \frac{\partial^2 T}{\partial x^2}.$$

(2)

Assume that we are given the initial condition

$$T(x, 0) = 0, \quad 0 \leqslant x < \infty, \tag{3}$$

and the boundary conditions

$$\lim_{x \to +\infty} T(x, t) = \lim_{x \to +\infty} \frac{\partial T}{\partial x}(x, t) = 0, \tag{4}$$

$$T(0, t) = T_0(\neq 0), \quad 0 < t. \tag{5}$$

These conditions could be used to describe the heat flow in an infinitely long rod when a constant source of heat is applied at $x = 0$, or to describe the concentration of a pollutant at varying distances from a smokestack, in the absence of winds, with the stack constantly emitting pollutants, for all time $t > 0$. If we let $T(x, t) = X(x)\mathcal{T}(t)$, we have

$$X\mathcal{T}' = \delta X''\mathcal{T} \quad \text{or} \quad \frac{\mathcal{T}'}{\delta\mathcal{T}} = \frac{X''}{X} = k,$$

from which we obtain the two differential equations

$$\mathcal{T}' = k\,\delta\mathcal{T} \quad \text{and} \quad X'' - \mathcal{T}X = 0. \tag{6}$$

The first differential equation in (6) has the general solution $\mathcal{T}(t) = ce^{k\delta t}$. Using the initial condition (3), we observe that

$$0 = T(x, 0) = X(x)\mathcal{T}(0) = cX(x).$$

Hence either $c = 0$, implying that $\mathcal{T} \equiv 0$, or $X \equiv 0$. In either case $T \equiv 0$, contradicting the second boundary condition (5). Clearly, the method of separation of variables fails for this problem.

It is therefore apparent that other techniques must be developed to treat problems of this type. The effectiveness of Laplace transform methods for ordinary differential equations suggests that they might be useful in this context. The rest of this section will be devoted to a discussion of how transformation techniques may be applied to partial differential equations. It should be noted, however, that the effectiveness of Laplace transforms is subject to several limitations. The equation *must* be linear and should have constant coefficients, and there must be appropriate initial conditions. Even when these conditions are met, there is no guarantee of success; and even if a solution can be obtained, it may be easier to obtain by other methods.

To apply Laplace transforms to a partial differential equation, we must begin by considering the ranges of the independent variables. We shall illustrate the entire procedure as it relates to Example 1. In this problem, the independent variables x and t may both assume all values in the range 0 to ∞. This property is very desirable, since the definition of the Laplace transform of a function requires its integration over this range [see Eq. (1) in Section 6.1]. At this point both variables look promising. We recall, however, that the differentiation property (Theorem 1 in Section 6.2) of Laplace transforms requires an additional initial condition for each order of the derivative involved. In this case, Eq. (2) contains first derivatives in t and second derivatives in x. Since $(\partial T/\partial x)(0, t)$ is not known, there are not enough data for the x variable. Thus we shall treat x as a parameter and consider the Eq. (2) as an ordinary differential equation with t as the only independent variable. Let

$$\mathscr{L}\{T(x, t)\} = \int_0^\infty e^{-st} T(x, t)\, dt.$$

Then $\mathscr{L}\{T\}$ is a function of s and the parameter x. Using the differentiation property (Theorem 1 in Section 6.2) and the initial condition (3), we may transform Eq. (2) into the ordinary differential equation

$$s\mathscr{L}\{T\} - 0 = \mathscr{L}\left\{\frac{\partial T}{\partial t}\right\} = \delta\mathscr{L}\left\{\frac{\partial^2 T}{\partial x^2}\right\} = \delta\frac{\partial}{\partial x^2}\mathscr{L}\{T\}. \tag{7}$$

Note that we have interchanged the operations of taking the Laplace transform and differentiating with respect to x. This exchange may not be valid, but the objection can be ignored if the method succeeds in producing a solution to the problem. Hence it is essential that we verify any result obtained by this method.

It is important now to interpret the boundary conditions (4) and (5) for $\mathscr{L}(T)$ whenever possible. Note that Eq. (5) yields

$$\mathscr{L}\{T\}(0, s) = \int_0^\infty e^{-st} T(0, t)\, dt = \frac{T_0}{s}. \tag{8}$$

Also, after warning that the indicated operations may not always be valid, we obtain

$$\lim_{x \to +\infty} \mathscr{L}\{T\}(x, s) = \lim_{x \to +\infty} \int_0^\infty e^{-st} T(x, t)\, dt$$

$$= \int_0^\infty e^{-st}\left[\lim_{x \to +\infty} T(x, t)\right] dt = 0. \tag{9}$$

Now we treat s as a parameter and x as the independent variable. Setting $z = \mathscr{L}\{T\}$, we may rewrite Eq. (7) as

$$\frac{d^2 z}{dx^2} = \frac{s}{\delta} z, \tag{10}$$

where s is fixed. The characteristic equation for the differential equation (10) has the roots $\pm\sqrt{s/\delta}$, so that z has the general solution

$$z(x) = c_1 e^{\sqrt{s/\delta}\, x} + c_2 e^{-\sqrt{s/\delta}\, x}.$$

Since $s > 0$, the coefficient c_1 must be zero, because the term $e^{\sqrt{s/\delta}\,x}$ tends to infinity as $x \to +\infty$, violating the "identity" (9). Setting $x = 0$, we find that $c_2 = T_0/s$, by Eq. (8), so that we finally have

$$\mathscr{L}\{T\} = z(x) = \frac{T_0}{s}\, e^{-\sqrt{s/\delta}\,x}. \tag{11}$$

Again we treat x as a parameter and seek the inverse Laplace transform of Eq. (11). By Formula 43 of Appendix 2, with $r = x/\sqrt{\delta}$, we see that

$$T(x, t) = T_0\left(1 - \frac{2}{\sqrt{\pi}} \int_0^{x/2\sqrt{\delta t}} e^{-u^2}\, du\right). \tag{12}$$

To check that Eq. (12) is indeed the solution of Example 1, we note from Formula 58 of Appendix 1 that

$$\int_0^\infty e^{-u^2}\, du = \frac{\sqrt{\pi}}{2}. \tag{13}$$

The integral in Eq. (12) equals Eq. (13) if $t \to 0+$ or $x \to +\infty$. Thus Eq. (3) and the first limit of (4) hold. If $x = 0$, we obviously obtain Eq. (5). Differentiating Eq. (12) with respect to x, we have

$$\frac{\partial T}{\partial x} = -\frac{T_0}{\sqrt{\pi\,\delta t}}\, e^{-(x^2/4\delta t)},$$

which vanishes as $x \to +\infty$, and differentiating again, we obtain

$$\delta\frac{\partial^2 T}{\partial x^2} = \frac{T_0 x}{2\sqrt{\pi\delta}}\,\frac{e^{-(x^2/4\delta t)}}{t^{3/2}} = \frac{\partial T}{\partial t}.$$

Thus in this case the Laplace transform method does yield a solution.

Example 2   We shall consider the vibrating string problem of Section 12.2, given by the wave equation

$$\frac{\partial^2 y}{\partial t^2} = c^2\frac{\partial^2 y}{\partial x^2}, \tag{14}$$

with the boundary conditions

$$y(0, t) = y(L, t) = 0 \tag{15}$$

and initial conditions

$$y(x, 0) = f(x), \quad \left.\frac{\partial y}{\partial t}\right|_{(x,0)} = 0. \tag{16}$$

Since $0 \leq x \leq L$, we select t as our independent variable for the Laplace transform. By the differentiation property [see Eq. (4) in Section 6.2], we transform Eq. (14) into

$$s^2 \mathscr{L}\{y\} - sf(x) - 0 = c^2 \frac{\partial^2}{\partial x^2} \mathscr{L}\{y\}.$$

Thus we have the nonhomogeneous second-order ordinary differential equation

$$c^2 Y'' - s^2 Y = -sf(x), \tag{17}$$

where $Y(x) = \mathscr{L}\{y\}$ and s is a parameter. By Eq. (15), we have $Y(0) = Y(L) = 0$. Our problem thus reduces to a nonhomogeneous boundary value problem. It may then be solved by the methods of Chapter 3 or Section 11.6. To simplify matters, we assume that $f(x) = y_0 \sin (\pi x/L)$, so that we can avoid having to use eigenfunction expansions to find the solution Y. A particular solution of Eq. (17) will be of the form

$$Y_{\mathrm{p}} = A \cos \frac{\pi x}{L} + B \sin \frac{\pi x}{L}.$$

Hence

$$-A\left(\frac{c^2 \pi^2}{L^2} + s^2\right)\cos \frac{\pi x}{L} - B\left(\frac{c^2 \pi^2}{L^2} + s^2\right) \sin \frac{\pi x}{L} = -sy_0 \sin \frac{\pi x}{L},$$

implying that $A = 0$ and $B = sy_0/[s^2 + (c^2\pi^2/L^2)]$. Thus the general solution of Eq. (17) is

$$Y = ae^{sx/c} + be^{-sx/c} + \frac{sy_0}{s^2 + (c^2\pi^2/L^2)} \sin \frac{\pi x}{L}. \tag{18}$$

Setting $x = 0$ and $x = L$ in Eq. (18), we obtain the homogeneous simultaneous equations

$$a + b = 0,$$
$$ae^{sL/c} + be^{-xL/c} = 0.$$

Since the determinant of the coefficients on the left-hand side of Eq. (19) is nonzero, $a = b = 0$ and Eq. (18) reduces to

$$\mathscr{L}\{y\} = Y = \frac{sy_0}{s^2 + (c^2\pi^2/L^2)} \sin \frac{\pi x}{L}.$$

Solving for y, we obtain

$$y = y_0 \sin \frac{\pi x}{L} \cos \frac{\pi ct}{L},$$

which agrees with the solution of Example 2 of Section 12.2, which was obtained using d'Alembert's method.

EXERCISES 12.5

In Exercises 1 through 6, obtain the solution of the given boundary and initial condition problem by the method of Laplace transforms. Be sure to verify your solution.

1. $\dfrac{\partial^2 y}{\partial x^2} = 4\dfrac{\partial^2 y}{\partial t^2}, \quad t > 0, \quad x > 0$

$y(x, 0) = 0, \quad \dfrac{\partial y}{\partial t}\bigg|_{(x,0)} = 1, \quad x \geq 0$

$y(0, t) = t, \quad \lim_{x \to \infty} y(x, t)$ is finite

2. $\dfrac{\partial^2 y}{\partial x^2} = 16\dfrac{\partial^2 y}{\partial t^2}, \quad t > 0, \quad x > 0$

$y(x, 0) = 0, \quad \dfrac{\partial y}{\partial t}\bigg|_{(x,0)} = 1, \quad x \geq 0$

$y(0, t) = \sin t, \quad \lim_{x \to \infty} y(x, t)$ is finite

3. $\dfrac{\partial T}{\partial t} = \delta\dfrac{\partial^2 T}{\partial x^2}, \quad t > 0, \quad x > 0$

$T(x, 0) = 0, \quad 0 \leq x < \infty, \quad T(0, t) = 1, \quad t > 0$

$\lim_{x \to \infty} T(x, t) = \lim_{x \to \infty} \dfrac{\partial T}{\partial x}(x, t) = 0, \quad t > 0$

4. $\dfrac{\partial T}{\partial t} = \delta\dfrac{\partial^2 T}{\partial x^2}, \quad t > 0, \quad x > 0$

$T(x, 0) = e^{-x}, \quad x \geq 0, \quad T(0, t) = T_0 (\neq 0),$

$\lim_{x \to \infty} T(x, t) = \lim_{x \to \infty} \dfrac{\partial T}{\partial x}(x, t) = 0, \quad t > 0$

5. $\dfrac{\partial T}{\partial t} = \delta\dfrac{\partial^2 T}{\partial x^2}, \quad t > 0, \quad x > 0$

$T(x, 0) = 0, \quad x \geq 0,$

$T(0, t) = \sin \omega t,$

$\lim_{x \to \infty} T(x, t) = \lim_{x \to \infty} \dfrac{\partial T}{\partial x}(x, t) = 0, \quad t > 0$

6. $\dfrac{\partial T}{\partial t} = \delta\dfrac{\partial^2 T}{\partial x^2} + \mu\dfrac{\partial T}{\partial x}, \quad t > 0, \quad x > 0$

$T(x, 0) = 0, \quad x \geq 0$

$T(0, t) = T_0 (\neq 0), \quad \lim_{x \to \infty} T(x, t)$

$= \lim_{x \to \infty} \dfrac{\partial T}{\partial x}(x, t) = 0, \quad t > 0$

REVIEW EXERCISES FOR CHAPTER 12

In Exercises 1 through 4, find the solution $w(x, y)$ of each partial differential equation that satisfies the given condition.

1. $w_x + w_y - w = e^y, \quad w(x, 0) = x$

2. $w_x + w_y - 2w = 0, \quad w(x, 0) = e^x$

3. $w_x + w_y - w = 1 - x, \quad w(x, 0) = x + 1$

4. $w_x - w_y + w = 0, \quad w(x, 0) = \sin x$

In Exercises 5 through 8, find the temperature in an insulated rod a units long whose ends are kept at 0°C, where the initial temperature is given by:

5. $f(x) = x(a - x)$

6. $f(x) = x^2(a^2 - x^2)$

7. $f(x) = \begin{cases} x, & 0 \leq x \leq a/2, \\ a - x, & a/2 \leq x \leq a \end{cases}$

8. $f(x) = \begin{cases} x^2, & 0 \leq x \leq a/2, \\ 0, & a/2 < x \leq a \end{cases}$

Find solutions of the equations in Exercises 9 through 12 by separation of variables.

9. $\dfrac{\partial^2 y}{\partial x^2} = \dfrac{t^2}{x^2}\dfrac{\partial^2 y}{\partial t^2}$

10. $\dfrac{\partial^2 y}{\partial x^2} + \dfrac{\partial^2 y}{\partial x\,\partial t} = \dfrac{\partial y}{\partial t}$

11. $\dfrac{\partial^2 y}{\partial t^2} = \dfrac{\partial^2 y}{\partial x^2} - y$

12. $\dfrac{\partial^2 y}{\partial x^2} + \dfrac{\partial y}{\partial x} = \dfrac{\partial y}{\partial t}$

13. A tightly stretched string fixed at $x = 0$ and $x = a$ is initially displaced to the position $y(x, 0) = $

$2 \sin^3 (\pi x/a)$. At time $t = 0$, it is released from rest from this position. Find the displacement of any point on the string at any time t.

14. Repeat Exercise 13 if the initial displacement is $y(x, 0) = a^2 x - x^3$.

15. The vibrating string in Exercise 13 is subjected to a damping force that is proportional to the velocity at each point and instant in time.

   a) Find the differential equation that the damped string satisfies.

   b) Solve the equation by separation of variables.

   *c) If the initial displacement is $y(x, 0) = f(x)$, $0 \leqslant x \leqslant a$, express the solution as an infinite series.

16. A rectangular plate is bounded by the lines $x = 0$, $y = 0$, $x = 100$, $y = 50$. Its surfaces are insulated and the termperature along the upper edge is given by $T(x, 50) = x(100 - x)$, while the other edges are kept at 0°C. Find the steady-state temperature.

Appendix

1

Integral Tables

1. $\int u \, dv = uv - \int v \, du$

2. $\int x^n \, dx = \dfrac{x^{n+1}}{n+1} + c, \quad n \neq -1$

3. $\int \dfrac{dx}{x} = \ln |x| + c$

4. $\int e^{ax} \, dx = \dfrac{e^{ax}}{a} + c$

5. $\int \ln x \, dx = x \ln x - x + c$

6. $\int \dfrac{dx}{a^2 + x^2} = \dfrac{1}{a} \tan^{-1} \dfrac{x}{a} + c$

7. $\int \dfrac{dx}{a^2 - x^2} = \dfrac{1}{2a} \ln \left| \dfrac{a+x}{a-x} \right| + c = \dfrac{1}{a} \tanh^{-1} \dfrac{x}{a} + c$

8. $\int \dfrac{dx}{x^2 - a^2} = \dfrac{1}{2a} \ln \left| \dfrac{x-a}{x+a} \right| + c = -\dfrac{1}{a} \coth^{-1} \dfrac{x}{a} + c$

9. $\int \dfrac{dx}{\sqrt{x^2 \pm a^2}} = \ln |x + \sqrt{x^2 \pm a^2}| + c$

10. $\int \dfrac{dx}{\sqrt{a^2 - x^2}} = \sin^{-1} \dfrac{x}{a} + c$

11. $\int \dfrac{x \, dx}{\sqrt{x^2 \pm a^2}} = \sqrt{x^2 \pm a^2} + c$

12. $\int \dfrac{x \, dx}{\sqrt{a^2 - x^2}} = -\sqrt{a^2 - x^2} + c$

13. $\int \sqrt{x^2 \pm a^2} \, dx = \dfrac{x}{2} \sqrt{x^2 \pm a^2} \pm \dfrac{a^2}{2} \ln |x + \sqrt{x^2 \pm a^2}| + c$

14. $\int \sqrt{a^2 - x^2} \, dx = \dfrac{x}{2} \sqrt{a^2 - x^2} + \dfrac{a^2}{2} \sin^{-1} \dfrac{x}{a} + c$

15. $\int \dfrac{\sqrt{x^2 - a^2}}{x} \, dx = \sqrt{x^2 - a^2} - |a| \sec^{-1} \dfrac{x}{a} + c.$

16. $\int \dfrac{\sqrt{a^2 \pm x^2}}{x} \, dx = \sqrt{a^2 \pm x^2} - a \ln \left| \dfrac{a + \sqrt{a^2 \pm x^2}}{x} \right| + c$

17. $\int \sin x \, dx = -\cos x + c$

18. $\int \sin^n x \, dx = -\dfrac{1}{n} \sin^{n-1} x \cos x + \dfrac{n-1}{n} \int \sin^{n-2} x \, dx$

19. $\int \sin mx \sin nx \, dx = \dfrac{\sin(m-n)x}{2(m-n)} - \dfrac{\sin(m+n)x}{2(m+n)} + c, \quad m^2 \neq n^2$

20. $\displaystyle\int \frac{dx}{a + b \sin x} = \frac{2}{\sqrt{a^2 - b^2}} \tan^{-1} \frac{a \tan x/2 + b}{\sqrt{a^2 - b^2}} + c, \quad a^2 > b^2$

21. $\displaystyle\int x^n \sin x \, dx = -x^n \cos x + n \int x^{n-1} \cos x \, dx$

22. $\displaystyle\int \cos x \, dx = \sin x + c$

23. $\displaystyle\int \cos^n x \, dx = \frac{1}{n} \cos^{n-1} x \sin x + \frac{n-1}{n} \int \cos^{n-2} x \, dx$

24. $\displaystyle\int \cos mx \cos nx \, dx = \frac{\sin (m-n)x}{2(m-n)} + \frac{\sin (m+n)x}{2(m+n)} + c, \quad m^2 \neq n^2$

25. $\displaystyle\int \frac{dx}{a + b \cos x} = \frac{2}{\sqrt{a^2 - b^2}} \tan^{-1} \frac{\sqrt{a^2 - b^2} \tan (x/2)}{a + b} + c, \quad a^2 > b^2$

26. $\displaystyle\int x^n \cos x \, dx = x^n \sin x - n \int x^{n-1} \sin x \, dx$

27. $\displaystyle\int \sin mx \cos nx \, dx = \frac{\cos (n-m)x}{2(n-m)} - \frac{\cos (n+m)x}{2(n+m)} + c, \quad m^2 \neq n^2$

28. $\displaystyle\int \sin x \cos x \, dx = \tfrac{1}{2} \sin^2 x + c$

29. $\displaystyle\int \tan x \, dx = -\ln |\cos x| + c$

30. $\displaystyle\int \tan^n x \, dx = \frac{\tan^{n-1} x}{n-1} - \int \tan^{n-2} x \, dx, \quad n \neq 1$

31. $\displaystyle\int \cot x \, dx = \ln |\sin x| + c$

32. $\displaystyle\int \cot^n x \, dx = -\frac{\cot^{n-1} x}{n-1} - \int \cot^{n-2} x \, dx, \quad n \neq 1$

33. $\displaystyle\int \sec x \, dx = \ln |\sec x + \tan x| + c$

34. $\displaystyle\int \sec^2 x \, dx = \tan x + c$

35. $\displaystyle\int \sec^n x \, dx = \frac{1}{n-1} \tan x \sec^{n-2} x + \frac{n-2}{n-1} \int \sec^{n-2} x \, dx$

36. $\displaystyle\int \csc x \, dx = \ln |\csc x - \cot x| + c$

37. $\displaystyle\int \csc^2 x \, dx = -\cot x + c$

38. $\displaystyle\int \csc^n x \, dx = -\frac{1}{n-1} \cot x \csc^{n-2} x + \frac{n-2}{n-1} \int \csc^{n-2} x \, dx$

39. $\displaystyle\int \sin^{-1} \frac{x}{a} \, dx = x \sin^{-1} \frac{x}{a} + \sqrt{a^2 - x^2} + c$

40. $\displaystyle\int \cos^{-1} \frac{x}{a} \, dx = x \cos^{-1} \frac{x}{a} - \sqrt{a^2 - x^2} + c$

41. $\int \tan^{-1} \dfrac{x}{a} \, dx = x \tan^{-1} \dfrac{x}{a} - \dfrac{a}{2} \ln (a^2 + x^2) + c$

42. $\int \cot^{-1} \dfrac{x}{a} \, dx = x \cot^{-1} \dfrac{x}{a} + \dfrac{a}{2} \ln (a^2 + x^2) + c$

43. $\int \sec^{-1} \dfrac{x}{a} \, dx = x \sec^{-1} \dfrac{x}{a} - a \ln |x + \sqrt{x^2 - a^2}| + c$

44. $\int \csc^{-1} \dfrac{x}{a} \, dx = x \csc^{-1} \dfrac{x}{a} + a \ln |x + \sqrt{x^2 - a^2}| + c$

45. $\int x^n \ln (ax) \, dx = \dfrac{x^{n+1}}{n+1} \left[\ln (ax) - \dfrac{1}{n+1} \right] + c, \quad n \neq -1$

46. $\int (\ln x)^n \, dx = x(\ln x)^n - n \int (\ln x)^{n-1} \, dx, \quad n \neq -1$

47. $\int \dfrac{(\ln x)^n}{x} \, dx = \dfrac{(\ln x)^{n+1}}{n+1} + c$

48. $\int \dfrac{dx}{x \ln x} = \ln (\ln x) + c$

49. $\int x^n e^{ax} \, dx = \dfrac{x^n e^{ax}}{a} - \dfrac{n}{a} \int x^{n-1} e^{ax} \, dx$

50. $\int e^{ax} \sin bx \, dx = \dfrac{e^{ax}}{a^2 + b^2} (a \sin bx - b \cos bx) + c$

51. $\int e^{ax} \cos bx \, dx = \dfrac{e^{ax}}{a^2 + b^2} (a \cos bx + b \sin bx) + c$

52. $\int \sinh x \, dx = \cosh x + c$

53. $\int \cosh x \, dx = \sinh x + c$

54. $\int \tanh x \, dx = \ln (\cosh x) + c$

55. $\int_0^\infty x^{n-1} e^{-x} \, dx = \Gamma(n) = (n-1)\Gamma(n-1)$

56. $\int_0^\infty \dfrac{e^{-x}}{\sqrt{x}} \, dx = \Gamma(\tfrac{1}{2}) = \sqrt{\pi}$

57. $\int_0^{\pi/2} \sin^n x \, dx = \int_0^{\pi/2} \cos^n x \, dx = \begin{cases} \dfrac{\pi}{2^{n+1}} \dfrac{n!}{(n/2)!^2}, & n \text{ even} \\[2ex] \dfrac{2^{n-1}[(n-1)/2]!^2}{n!}, & n \text{ odd} \end{cases}$

58. $\int_0^\infty e^{-a^2 x^2} \, dx = \dfrac{1}{2a} \Gamma(\tfrac{1}{2}) = \dfrac{\sqrt{\pi}}{2a}, \quad a > 0$

Appendix

Laplace Transforms

For a more extensive list of Laplace transforms and their inverses see A. Erdelyi, *et. al., Tables of Integral Transforms* (2 vols.), McGraw-Hill, New York, 1954.

$F(s) = \mathcal{L}\{f(t)\}$	$f(t)$
1. $\dfrac{1}{s^r}, \quad r > 0$	$\dfrac{t^{r-1}}{\Gamma(r)}, \quad \Gamma(n+1) = n!$
2. $\dfrac{1}{(s-a)^r}, \quad r > 0$	$\dfrac{t^{r-1}e^{at}}{\Gamma(r)}$
3. $\dfrac{1}{(s-a)(s-b)}, \quad a \neq b$	$\dfrac{e^{at} - e^{bt}}{a-b}$
4. $\dfrac{s}{(s-a)(s-b)}, \quad a \neq b$	$\dfrac{ae^{at} - be^{bt}}{a-b}$
5. $\dfrac{1}{s^2 + k^2}$	$\dfrac{1}{k}\sin kt$
6. $\dfrac{s}{s^2 + k^2}$	$\cos kt$
7. $\dfrac{1}{s^2 - k^2}$	$\dfrac{1}{k}\sinh kt$
8. $\dfrac{s}{s^2 - k^2}$	$\cosh kt$
9. $\dfrac{1}{(s-a)^2 + k^2}$	$\dfrac{1}{k}e^{at}\sin kt$
10. $\dfrac{s-a}{(s-a)^2 + k^2}$	$e^{at}\cos kt$
11. $\dfrac{1}{(s-a)^2 - k^2}$	$\dfrac{1}{k}e^{at}\sinh kt$
12. $\dfrac{s-a}{(s-a)^2 - k^2}$	$e^{at}\cosh kt$
13. $\dfrac{1}{s(s^2 + k^2)}$	$\dfrac{1}{k^2}(1 - \cos kt)$
14. $\dfrac{1}{s^2(s^2 + k^2)}$	$\dfrac{1}{k^3}(kt - \sin kt)$
15. $\dfrac{1}{(s^2 + k^2)^2}$	$\dfrac{1}{2k^3}(\sin kt - kt \cos kt)$
16. $\dfrac{s}{(s^2 + k^2)^2}$	$\dfrac{t}{2k}\sin kt$

$F(s) = \mathscr{L}\{f(t)\}$	$f(t)$
17. $\dfrac{s^2}{(s^2 + k^2)^2}$	$\dfrac{1}{2k}(\sin kt + kt \cos kt)$
18. $\dfrac{1}{(s^2 + a^2)(s^2 + b^2)}, \quad a^2 \neq b^2$	$\dfrac{a \sin bt - b \sin at}{ab(a^2 - b^2)}$
19. $\dfrac{s}{(s^2 + a^2)(s^2 + b^2)}, \quad a^2 \neq b^2$	$\dfrac{\cos bt - \cos at}{a^2 - b^2}$
20. $\dfrac{1}{s^4 - k^4}$	$\dfrac{1}{2k^3}(\sinh kt - \sin kt)$
21. $\dfrac{s}{s^4 - k^4}$	$\dfrac{1}{2k^2}(\cosh kt - \cos kt)$
22. $\dfrac{1}{s^4 + 4k^4}$	$\dfrac{1}{4k^3}(\sin kt \cosh kt - \cos kt \sinh kt)$
23. $\dfrac{s}{s^4 + 4k^4}$	$\dfrac{1}{2k^2}\sin kt \sinh kt$
24. $\sqrt{s - a} - \sqrt{s - b}$	$\dfrac{e^{bt} - e^{at}}{2\sqrt{\pi t^3}}$
25. $\dfrac{s}{(s - a)^{3/2}}$	$\dfrac{e^{at}}{\sqrt{\pi t}}(1 - 2at)$
26. $\dfrac{1}{\sqrt{s + a}\,\sqrt{s + b}}$	$e^{-(a+b)t/2}I_0\left(\dfrac{a - b}{2}t\right)$
27. $\dfrac{(\sqrt{s^2 + k^2} - s)^r}{\sqrt{s^2 + k^2}}, \quad r > -1$	$k^r J_r(kt)$
28. $\dfrac{1}{(s^2 + k^2)^r}, \quad r > 0$	$\dfrac{\sqrt{\pi}}{\Gamma(r)}\left(\dfrac{t}{2k}\right)^{r-1/2} J_{r-1/2}(kt)$
29. $(\sqrt{s^2 + k^2} - s)^r, \quad r > 0$	$\dfrac{rk^r}{t} J_r(kt)$
30. $\dfrac{(s - \sqrt{s^2 - k^2})^r}{\sqrt{s^2 - k^2}}, \quad r > -1$	$k^r I_r(kt)$
31. $\dfrac{1}{(s^2 - k^2)^r}, \quad r > 0$	$\dfrac{\sqrt{\pi}}{\Gamma(r)}\left(\dfrac{t}{2k}\right)^{r-1/2} I_{r-1/2}(kt)$
32. $\dfrac{e^{-k/s}}{s^r}, \quad r > 0$	$\left(\dfrac{t}{k}\right)^{(r-1)/2} J_{r-1}(2\sqrt{kt})$
33. $\dfrac{e^{-k/s}}{\sqrt{s}}$	$\dfrac{1}{\sqrt{\pi t}}\cos 2\sqrt{kt}$

$F(s) = \mathcal{L}\{f(t)\}$	$f(t)$
34. $\dfrac{e^{k/s}}{s^r}, \quad r > 0$	$\left(\dfrac{t}{k}\right)^{(r-1)/2} I_{r-1}(2\sqrt{kt})$
35. $\dfrac{e^{k/s}}{\sqrt{s}}$	$\dfrac{1}{\sqrt{\pi t}} \cosh 2\sqrt{kt}$
36. $-\dfrac{1}{s} \ln s$	$-\ln t - \gamma, \quad \gamma \approx 0.5772$
37. $\ln \dfrac{s-a}{s-b}$	$\dfrac{e^{bt} - e^{at}}{t}$
38. $\ln\left(1 + \dfrac{k^2}{s^2}\right)$	$\dfrac{2}{t}(1 - \cos kt)$
39. $\ln\left(1 - \dfrac{k^2}{s^2}\right)$	$\dfrac{2}{t}(1 - \cosh kt)$
40. $\arctan\left(\dfrac{k}{s}\right)$	$\dfrac{\sin kt}{t}$
41. $\dfrac{1}{s}\arctan\left(\dfrac{k}{s}\right)$	$\text{Si}\,(kt) = \displaystyle\int_0^{kt} \dfrac{\sin u}{u}\,du$
42. $e^{-r\sqrt{s}}, \quad r > 0$	$\dfrac{r}{2\sqrt{\pi t^3}} \exp\left(-\dfrac{r^2}{4t}\right)$
43. $\dfrac{e^{-r\sqrt{s}}}{s}, \quad r \geqslant 0$	$1 - \text{erf}\left(\dfrac{r}{2\sqrt{t}}\right) = 1 - \dfrac{2}{\sqrt{\pi}} \displaystyle\int_0^{r/2\sqrt{t}} e^{-u^2}\,du$
44. $e^{r^2 s^2}(1 - \text{erf}(rs)), \quad r > 0$	$\dfrac{1}{r\sqrt{\pi}} \exp\left(-\dfrac{t^2}{4r^2}\right)$
45. $\dfrac{1}{s} e^{r^2 s^2}(1 - \text{erf}(rs)), \quad r > 0$	$\text{erf}\left(\dfrac{t}{2r}\right)$
46. $\text{erf}\left(\dfrac{r}{\sqrt{s}}\right)$	$\dfrac{1}{\pi t} \sin(2k\sqrt{t})$
47. $e^{rs}(1 - \text{erf}\sqrt{rs}), \quad r > 0$	$\dfrac{\sqrt{r}}{\pi\sqrt{t(t + r)}}$
48. $\dfrac{1}{\sqrt{s}} e^{rs}(1 - \text{erf}\sqrt{rs}), \quad r > 0$	$\dfrac{1}{\sqrt{\pi(t + r)}}$

Appendix 3

Solving Differential Equations with a Programmable Calculator

The following three HP-25 routines are designed to perform the Euler method, improved Euler method, and Runge–Kutta method for a first-order initial value problem. The Euler method and improved Euler method will automatically execute n iterations for specified n, but the Runge–Kutta method performs a single iteration.

Instructions

Suppose we wish to use one of the three methods on the first-order initial value problem

$$y' = f(x, y), \qquad y(x_0) = y_0. \tag{1}$$

1. Move the left switch to ON and the right switch to PRGM.
2. The first few lines of each program, identified by the notation $f(x, y)$, are used for programming the right-hand side of the differential equation. The value of x is stored in register R_0 while the value of y is in R_1. Key in a program for $f(x, y)$ for the

Method	in lines	with last command being*	
Euler method	01–37	GTO	38
Improved Euler method	01–24	GTO	25
Runge–Kutta method	01–17	GTO	18

3. Key in the rest of the program on the lines indicated.
4. Move right switch to RUN.
5. Key $\boxed{f}$ $\boxed{REG}$, $\boxed{f}$ $\boxed{PRGM}$ to clear registers and transfer control to beginning of program.
6. To initialize the program, key the following data

x_0 $\boxed{STO}$ 0

y_0 $\boxed{STO}$ 1, $\boxed{STO}$ 2

$h/2$ $\boxed{STO}$ 3

where h is the step-size of each interval.

7. For the Euler or improved Euler methods, we can automatically do n iterations. For these two methods only, key

n $\boxed{STO}$ 4

---

*Unless last line of $f(x, y)$ program ends on the line just before the one you are going to.

8. Key $\boxed{\text{R/S}}$; the machine calculates and returns the value y_n ($n = 1$ for Runge–Kutta). To find the corresponding x_n, key $\boxed{\text{RCL}}$ 0.

Euler method		Improved Euler method		Runge–Kutta method	
Lines	Key	Lines	Key	Lines	Key
01–37	$f(x, y)$	01–24	$f(x, y)$	01–17	$f(x, y)$
38	RCL 3	25	RCL 3	18	RCL 2
39	2	26	2	19	$x \leftrightharpoons y$
40	×	27	×	20	RCL 3
41	STO + 0	28	×	21	×
42	×	29	STO + 1	22	STO + 4
43	STO + 1	30	RCL 4	23	+
44	1	31	CHS	24	STO 1
45	STO − 4	32	STO 4	25	3
46	RCL 4	33	$g \, x \geqslant 0$	26	RCL 5
47	$g \, x \neq 0$	34	GTO 38	27	$f \, x = y$
48	GTO 01	35	f LAST x	28	GTO 43
49	RCL 1	36	STO + 0	29	1
		37	GTO 01	30	STO + 5
		38	RCL 2	31	$f \, x = y$
		39	STO + 1	32	GTO 40
		40	2	33	RCL 3
		41	STO ÷ 1	34	STO + 0
		42	RCL 1	35	$R \downarrow$
		43	STO 2	36	$f \, x \geqslant y$
		44	1	37	GTO 01
		45	STO − 4	38	f LAST x
		46	RCL 4	39	STO + 1
		47	$g \, x \neq 0$	40	f LAST x
		48	GTO 01	41	STO + 4
		49	RCL 1	42	GTO 01
				43	STO − 5
				44	STO ÷ 4
				45	RCL 4
				46	STO − 4
				47	STO + 2
				48	RCL 2
				49	STO 1

Registers
$R_0 = x$
$R_1 = y$
$R_2 = y$
$R_3 = h/2$
$R_4 = n$ (except RK)
R_5 = used in RK

Appendix

4

Determinants

In many parts of this book we made use of determinants. In this appendix we shall illustrate how determinants arise and discuss their uses.

We begin by considering the system of two linear equations in two unknowns

$$a_{11}x_1 + a_{12}x_2 = b_1,$$
$$a_{21}x_1 + a_{22}x_2 = b_2. \tag{1}$$

For simplicity we assume that the constants a_{11}, a_{12}, a_{21}, and a_{22} are all nonzero (otherwise, the system can be solved directly). To solve the system (1), we multiply the first equation by a_{22} and the second by a_{12} to obtain

$$a_{11}a_{22}x_1 + a_{22}a_{12}x_2 = a_{22}b_1,$$
$$a_{12}a_{21}x_1 + a_{22}a_{12}x_2 = a_{12}b_2. \tag{2}$$

Then subtracting the second equation from the first, we have

$$(a_{11}a_{22} - a_{12}a_{21})x_1 = a_{22}b_1 - a_{12}b_2. \tag{3}$$

Now we define the quantity

$$D = a_{11}a_{22} - a_{12}a_{21}. \tag{4}$$

If $D \neq 0$, then Eq. (3) yields

$$x_1 = \frac{a_{21}b_1 - a_{12}b_2}{D}, \tag{5}$$

and x_2 may be obtained by substituting this value of x_1 into either of the equations of (1). *Thus if $D \neq 0$, the system (1) has a unique solution.*

On the other hand, suppose that $D = 0$. Then $a_{11}a_{22} = a_{12}a_{21}$, and if we subtract the second equation of (2) from the first, we have

$$0 = a_{21}b_1 - a_{12}b_2.$$

Either this equation is true or it is false. If $a_{21}b_1 - a_{12}b_2 \neq 0$, then the system (1) has *no* solution. If $a_{21}b_1 - a_{12}b_2 = 0$, then the second equation of (2) is a multiple of the first and (1) consists essentially of only one equation. Thus we may choose x_1 arbitrarily and calculate the corresponding value of x_2. In this case there are an *infinite* number of solutions. In sum, we have shown that *if $D = 0$, then the system (1) has either no solution or an infinite number of solutions.*

These facts are easily visualized geometrically by noting that (1) consists of the equations of two straight lines. A solution of the system is a point of intersection of the two lines. It is easy to show (see Exercise 5) that $D = 0$ if and only if the slopes of the two lines are the same. If the slopes are different, then $D \neq 0$ and the two lines intersect at a single point, which is the unique solution. If $D = 0$, we either have two parallel lines and no solution, since the lines never intersect, or both equations yield the same line and every point on this line is a solution. This is illustrated in Fig. 1.

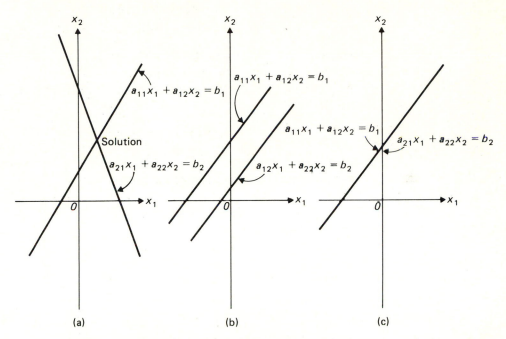

Fig. 1 (a) Unique solution; (b) no solution; (c) infinitely many solutions.

Example 1 Consider the following systems of equations:

i) $2x_1 + 3x_2 = 12,$ ii) $x_1 + 3x_2 = 3,$ iii) $x_1 + 3x_2 = 3,$
$ x_1 + x_2 = 5;$ $ 3x_1 + 9x_2 = 8;$ $ 3x_1 + 9x_2 = 9.$

In system (i), $D = 2 \cdot 1 - 3 \cdot 1 = -1 \neq 0$, so there is a unique solution, which is easily found to be $x_1 = 3$, $x_2 = 2$. In system (ii), $D = 1 \cdot 9 - 3 \cdot 3 = 0$. Multiplying the first equation by 3 and then subtracting the second equation, we obtain the equation $0 = 1$, which is impossible. Thus there is no solution. In (iii), $D = 1 \cdot 9 - 3 \cdot 3 = 0$. But now the second equation is simply three times the first equation. If x_2 is arbitrary, then $x_1 = 3 - 3x_2$, and there are an infinite number of solutions.

Returning again to the system (1), we define the *determinant of the system* as

$$D = a_{11}a_{22} - a_{12}a_{21}. \tag{6}$$

For convenience of notation we denote the determinant by writing the coefficients of the system in a square array:

$$D = \begin{vmatrix} a_{11} & a_{12} \\ a_{21} & a_{22} \end{vmatrix} = a_{11}a_{22} - a_{12}a_{21}. \tag{7}$$

Therefore, a 2 × 2 determinant is the product of the two elements in the upper-left-to-lower-right diagonal minus the product of the other two elements.

We have proved:

Theorem 1 For the 2 × 2 system (1) there is a unique solution if and only if the determinant D is not equal to zero. If $D = 0$, then there is either no solution or an infinite number of solutions.

Let us now consider the general system of n equations in n unknowns:

$$
\begin{aligned}
a_{11}x_1 + a_{12}x_2 + \cdots + a_{1n}x_n &= b_1, \\
a_{21}x_1 + a_{22}x_2 + \cdots + a_{2n}x_n &= b_2, \\
&\ \ \vdots \\
a_{n1}x_1 + a_{n2}x_2 + \cdots + a_{nn}x_n &= b_n,
\end{aligned}
\tag{8}
$$

and define the determinant of such a system. We begin by defining the determinant of a 3 × 3 system:

$$
\begin{aligned}
D &= \begin{vmatrix} a_{11} & a_{12} & a_{13} \\ a_{21} & a_{22} & a_{23} \\ a_{31} & a_{32} & a_{33} \end{vmatrix} \\
&= a_{11}\begin{vmatrix} a_{22} & a_{23} \\ a_{32} & a_{33} \end{vmatrix} - a_{12}\begin{vmatrix} a_{21} & a_{23} \\ a_{31} & a_{33} \end{vmatrix} + a_{13}\begin{vmatrix} a_{21} & a_{22} \\ a_{31} & a_{32} \end{vmatrix}.
\end{aligned}
\tag{9}
$$

Hence to calculate a 3 × 3 determinant, it is necessary to calculate three 2 × 2 determinants.

Example 2

$$\begin{vmatrix} 3 & 5 & 2 \\ 4 & 2 & 3 \\ -1 & 2 & 4 \end{vmatrix} = 3\begin{vmatrix} 2 & 3 \\ 2 & 4 \end{vmatrix} - 5\begin{vmatrix} 4 & 3 \\ -1 & 4 \end{vmatrix} + 2\begin{vmatrix} 4 & 2 \\ -1 & 2 \end{vmatrix}$$

$$= 3 \cdot 2 - 5 \cdot 19 + 2 \cdot 10 = -69.$$

The general definition of the determinant of the $n \times n$ system of equations (8) is simply an extension of this procedure:

$$D = \begin{vmatrix} a_{11} & a_{12} & \cdots & a_{1n} \\ a_{21} & a_{22} & \cdots & a_{2n} \\ \cdot & \cdot & & \cdot \\ \cdot & \cdot & & \cdot \\ \cdot & \cdot & & \cdot \\ a_{n1} & a_{n2} & \cdots & a_{nn} \end{vmatrix}$$

$$= a_{11}A_{11} - a_{12}A_{12} + \cdots + (-1)^{n+1}a_{1n}A_{1n}, \qquad (10)$$

where A_{1j} is the $(n-1) \times (n-1)$ determinant obtained by crossing out the first row and jth column of the original $n \times n$ determinant. Thus an $n \times n$ determinant can be obtained by calculating $n(n-1) \times (n-1)$ determinants. [Note that in the definition (10), the signs alternate.]

Example 3

$$\begin{vmatrix} 1 & 3 & 5 & 2 \\ 0 & -1 & 3 & 4 \\ 2 & 1 & 9 & 6 \\ 3 & 2 & 4 & 8 \end{vmatrix} = 1 \begin{vmatrix} -1 & 3 & 4 \\ 1 & 9 & 6 \\ 2 & 4 & 8 \end{vmatrix} - 3 \begin{vmatrix} 0 & 3 & 4 \\ 2 & 9 & 6 \\ 3 & 4 & 8 \end{vmatrix}$$

$$+ 5 \begin{vmatrix} 0 & -1 & 4 \\ 2 & 1 & 6 \\ 3 & 2 & 8 \end{vmatrix} - 2 \begin{vmatrix} 0 & -1 & 3 \\ 2 & 1 & 9 \\ 3 & 2 & 4 \end{vmatrix}$$

$$= 1(-92) - 3(-70) + 5(2) - 2(-16) = 160.$$

(The values in parentheses are obtained by calculating the four 3×3 determinants.)

It is clear that calculating determinants by this method can be a tedious procedure, especially if $n \geqslant 5$. For this reason, techniques are available for significantly simplifying these calculations. We shall not discuss these methods here, since they can be found in most books on matrix theory.

The reason for considering determinants of systems of n equations in n unknowns is that Theorem 1 also holds for these systems (although this fact will not be proven here).

Theorem 2   For the system (8) there is a unique solution if and only if the determinant D, defined by (10), is not zero. If $D = 0$, then there is either no solution or an infinite number of solutions.

There is a particular case of system (8) which merits special consideration (for example, in checking whether or not solutions to a differential equation are linearly independent). This is the *homogeneous system*

$$
\begin{aligned}
a_{11}x_1 + a_{12}x_2 + \cdots + a_{1n}x_n &= 0, \\
a_{21}x_1 + a_{22}x_2 + \cdots + a_{2n}x_n &= 0, \\
&\ \ \vdots \\
a_{n1}x_1 + a_{n2}x_2 + \cdots + a_{nn}x_n &= 0,
\end{aligned}
\tag{11}
$$

which occurs when all the values b_i, $i = 1, \ldots, n$ in (8) are zero. Clearly, $x_1 = x_2 = \cdots = x_n = 0$ is a solution of (11). Thus for homogeneous systems we have:

Theorem 3   If the determinant $D \neq 0$, the zero solution $x_1 = x_2 = \cdots = x_n = 0$ is the only solution of the homogeneous system (11). If $D = 0$, then there are an infinite number of solutions of (11).

We shall conclude this appendix by introducing a method for obtaining solutions of the system (8). We define the determinants

$$
D_1 = \begin{vmatrix} b_1 & a_{12} & \cdots & a_{1n} \\ b_2 & a_{22} & \cdots & a_{2n} \\ \vdots & \vdots & & \vdots \\ b_n & a_{n2} & \cdots & a_{nn} \end{vmatrix}, \ldots, \quad D_n = \begin{vmatrix} a_{11} & a_{12} & \cdots & a_{1,n-1} & b_1 \\ a_{21} & a_{22} & \cdots & a_{2,n-1} & b_2 \\ \vdots & \vdots & & \vdots & \vdots \\ a_{n1} & a_{n2} & \cdots & a_{n,n-1} & b_n \end{vmatrix},
$$

where

$$
D_k = \begin{vmatrix} a_{11} & a_{12} & \cdots & a_{1,k-1} & b_1 & a_{1,k+1} & \cdots & a_{1n} \\ a_{21} & a_{22} & \cdots & a_{2,k-1} & b_2 & a_{2,k+1} & \cdots & a_{2n} \\ \vdots & \vdots & & \vdots & \vdots & \vdots & & \vdots \\ a_{n1} & a_{n2} & \cdots & a_{n,k-1} & b_k & a_{n,k+1} & \cdots & a_{nn} \end{vmatrix},
\tag{12}
$$

is obtained by replacing the kth column of D by the column

$$
\begin{bmatrix} b_1 \\ b_2 \\ \vdots \\ b_n \end{bmatrix}.
$$

Then we have the following theorem, known as *Cramer's rule*.

Theorem 4 (**Cramer's rule**) Let D and D_k, $k = 1, 2, \ldots, n$, be given as in (10) and (12). If $D \neq 0$, then the unique solution to the system (8) is given by the values

$$x_1 = \frac{D_1}{D}, \qquad x_2 = \frac{D_2}{D}, \qquad \ldots, \qquad x_n = \frac{D_n}{D}. \tag{13}$$

Example 4 Consider the system

$$\begin{aligned}
2x_1 + 4x_2 - x_3 &= -5, \\
-4x_1 + 3x_2 + 5x_3 &= 14, \\
6x_1 - 3x_2 - 2x_3 &= 5.
\end{aligned}$$

We have

$$D = \begin{vmatrix} 2 & 4 & -1 \\ -4 & 3 & 5 \\ 6 & -3 & -2 \end{vmatrix} = 112, \qquad D_1 = \begin{vmatrix} -5 & 4 & -1 \\ 14 & 3 & 5 \\ 5 & -3 & -2 \end{vmatrix} = 224,$$

$$D_2 = \begin{vmatrix} 2 & -5 & -1 \\ -4 & 14 & 5 \\ 6 & 5 & -2 \end{vmatrix} = -112, \qquad D_3 = \begin{vmatrix} 2 & 4 & -5 \\ -4 & 3 & 14 \\ 6 & -3 & 5 \end{vmatrix} = 560.$$

Therefore

$$x_1 = \frac{D_1}{D} = 2, \qquad x_2 = \frac{D_2}{D} = -1, \qquad x_3 = \frac{D_3}{D} = 5.$$

EXERCISES A4

1. For each of the following 2×2 systems, calculate the determinant D. If $D \neq 0$, find the unique solution. If $D = 0$, determine whether there is no solution or an infinite number of solutions.

   a) $2x_1 + 4x_2 = 6$
      $x_1 + x_2 = 3$

   b) $2x_1 + 4x_2 = 6$
      $x_1 + 2x_2 = 5$

   c) $2x_1 + 4x_2 = 6$
      $x_1 + 2x_2 = 3$

   d) $6x_1 - 3x_2 = 3$
      $-2x_1 + x_2 = -1$

   e) $6x_1 - 3x_2 = 3$
      $-2x_1 + x_2 = 1$

   f) $6x_1 - 3x_2 = 3$
      $-2x_1 + 2x_2 = -1$

   c) $\begin{vmatrix} 7 & 2 & 3 \\ 0 & 4 & 1 \\ 0 & 0 & 5 \end{vmatrix}$ d) $\begin{vmatrix} 1 & 0 & 0 \\ 0 & -3 & 0 \\ 0 & 0 & 7 \end{vmatrix}$

   e) $\begin{vmatrix} 1 & 7 & 2 & 3 \\ 3 & 4 & 1 & 6 \\ 2 & 0 & 5 & -1 \\ -1 & 2 & 0 & 4 \end{vmatrix}$ f) $\begin{vmatrix} 2 & -1 & 3 & 5 \\ 0 & 3 & 1 & 6 \\ 0 & 0 & -2 & 4 \\ 0 & 0 & 0 & 5 \end{vmatrix}$

2. Calculate the following determinants.

   a) $\begin{vmatrix} 1 & 2 & 3 \\ 6 & -1 & 4 \\ 2 & 0 & 6 \end{vmatrix}$ b) $\begin{vmatrix} 4 & -1 & 0 \\ 2 & 1 & 7 \\ -2 & 3 & 4 \end{vmatrix}$

   g) $\begin{vmatrix} 1 & 0 & -2 & 3 & 5 \\ 0 & 4 & 2 & 3 & 6 \\ 0 & 0 & 5 & 7 & -8 \\ 0 & 0 & 0 & -1 & 73 \\ 0 & 0 & 0 & 0 & 2 \end{vmatrix}$

3. Determine whether each of the following homogeneous systems has a solution other than the zero solution.

  a) $2x_1 - 3x_2 + 4x_3 = 0$
      $-x_1 + x_2 - 6x_3 = 0$
      $4x_1 - 5x_2 + 16x_3 = 0$

  b) $x_1 + 6x_2 - x_3 = 0$
      $-2x_1 + 7x_2 + x_3 = 0$
      $3x_1 - x_2 + 5x_3 = 0$

4. Solve each of the following systems by Cramer's rule.

  a) $3x_1 - x_2 = 13$
      $-4x_1 + 6x_2 = -8$

b) $2x_1 + 6x_2 + 3x_3 = 9$
    $-3x_1 - 17x_2 - x_3 = 4$
    $4x_1 + 3x_2 + x_3 = -7$

c) $2x_1 \qquad + x_3 = 0$
    $3x_1 - 2x_2 + 2x_3 = -4$
    $4x_1 - 5x_2 \qquad = 3$

d) $x_1 + 2x_2 - x_3 - 4x_4 = 1$
    $-x_1 \qquad + 2x_3 + 6x_4 = 5$
    $-4x_2 - 2x_3 - 8x_4 = -8$
    $3x_1 - 2x_2 \qquad + 5x_4 = 3$

5. Show that the two lines in system (1) have the same slope if and only if the determinant of the system is zero.

Solutions to Odd-Numbered Exercises

CHAPTER 1

Section 1.1

1. a) $y = \dfrac{x^2}{2} + 3x + 2$;   b) $y = \ln\left(\dfrac{x^2 + 5}{6}\right) + 4$;   c) $y = \tan x - x + 1$;

   d) $y = \dfrac{x^4}{12} - \dfrac{9x^2}{2} + 3x + 1$;   e) $y = \cos x - \sin x + 2x + (1 - \pi)$.

3. $v = \sqrt{2g(h_0 - h)}$, where h_0 is the initial height of the object.

5. $x(t) = (v_0 \cos \theta)t + x_0 ; y(t) = -\dfrac{1}{2}gt^2 + (v_0 \sin \theta)t + y_0$

7. 55 min 4 sec   9. 38 min 44 sec   11. 21,822,975

13. 15,815,669   15. 715,718,436

Section 1.2

1. a) First   b) Second;   c) Third;   d) Fifth;
   e) Second;   f) First;   g) Third.

5. $y_1(x) = e^{4x}$, $y_2(x) = e^{-x}$ 7. $\varphi(x) = x$ 11. $\varphi'(1) = 5$, $\varphi''(1) = 22$, $\varphi'''(1) = 140$

Section 1.3

1.

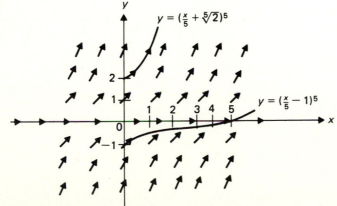

3.

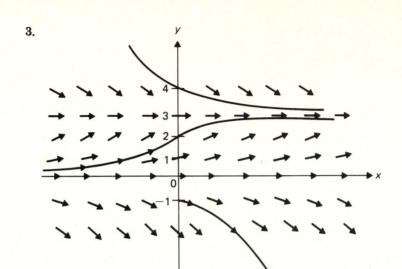

5.

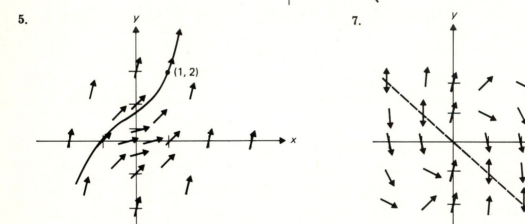

7.

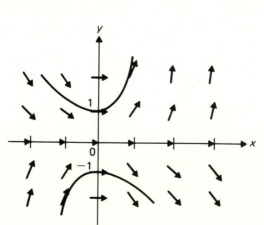

a) It is the constant solution $y = 0$.

b) Their graphs are symmetric with respect to the origin.

CHAPTER 2

Section 2.1

1. $y = \sqrt{e^x + c}$

3. $y = \dfrac{1}{2} \ln(x^2 + 1) + c$

5. $z = \tan\left(\dfrac{r^3}{3} + c\right)$

7. $P = c e^{\sin Q - \cos Q}$

9. $s = e^{(t^3/3) - 2t}$

11. $y = \dfrac{2401}{(1 + x)^3}$

13. $y = c \cos x - 3$

15. $y = \sin(c - \sin^{-1} x)$

17. $y = \dfrac{3x}{4x - 3}$

19. $\dfrac{1}{1 - e^x} = \dfrac{e^t}{1 - e}$

21. $y = \sqrt{2e^x + c}$

23. $y = cx^3 e^{-x}$

25. $3y^2 + 2y^3 = 3x^2 + 5$

27. $y = cx^{-k}$

29. a) $c(t) = \sqrt{\dfrac{\mu}{\lambda}} \left(\dfrac{k e^{2\sqrt{\mu}\,t} - 1}{k e^{2\sqrt{\mu}\,t} + 1} \right)$, where $k = \dfrac{\sqrt{\mu} + c(0)\sqrt{\lambda}}{\sqrt{\mu} - c(0)\sqrt{\lambda}}$;   b) $\sqrt{\dfrac{\mu}{\lambda}}$.

31. $\dfrac{3}{2} (\sqrt{5} - 1)$ hours ≈ 1.85 hours before 11:00 A.M. $\approx$ 9:09 A.M.

33. Revolve $y = kx^4$ about the y-axis to get the cistern's shape.

35. $y = cx + \ln c, \ y = -\ln |x| - 1$ 37. $y = cx - \sqrt{c}, \ 4xy + 1 = 0$

39. $(y - cx)^2 = 1 + c^2, \ x^2 + y^2 = 1$

Section 2.2

1. $x = c e^{2\sqrt{y/x}}$

3. $\ln x + e^{-y/x} = 1$

5. $x = e^{(y - x)/y}$

7. $xy(y - x) = 2$

9. $y + \sqrt{x^2 + y^2} = cx^2$

11. $x + 2y = 2 \tan(2x + c)$

13. $(x + y) + \ln(x + y - 1) = 3x + c$

15. $\tan(x + y) = x + c$

17. $(xy)^{-2} = c - 2x$

19. $-xy = \ln |1 + e^{-1} - x|$

21. $\ln |x + y| = c e^x$

25. $(5x + 2)^2 + 4(5x + 2)(5y + 4) - (5y + 4)^2 = c$

27. $(x + 1)e^{(1 - t)/(1 + x)} = c$

29. $3(x - 2)^2 - 2(x - 2)(y - 3) - (y - 3)^2 = c$

31. $x e^{tx} = ct$, by setting $v = tx$

Section 2.3

1. $x = c e^{3t}$

3. $x = 2e^t - 1$

5. $x = y^y(1 + c e^{-y})$

7. $y = x^4 + 3x^3$

9. $x = c e^{2t} + \dfrac{t^3 e^{2t}}{3}$

11. $s = \left(c + \dfrac{u^2}{2}\right) e^{-u} + 1$

13. $x = e^{-y}(c + y)$

15. a) $\dfrac{1}{k} \ln 2$;   b) $\dfrac{2 \ln 2}{k}$.

17. $3 \ln 10 \approx 6.9$ yr

19. $e^{2x} = y^2(x^2 + c)$

21. $x^3 = 3 \sin t + \dfrac{9 \cos t}{t} - \dfrac{18 \sin t}{t^2} - \dfrac{18 \cos t}{t^3} + \dfrac{c}{t^3}$

23. $y^2 = x^2(c - 2 \ln|x|)$

Section 2.4

1. $x^2 y + y = c$

3. $x^4 y^3 + \ln\left|\dfrac{x}{y}\right| = e^3 - 1$

5. $x^2 - 2y \sin x = \dfrac{\pi^2}{4} - 2$

7. $e^{xy} + 4xy^3 - y^2 + 3 = 0$

9. $x^2 y + xe^y = c$

11. $\tan^{-1} \dfrac{y}{x} + \ln\left|\dfrac{x}{y}\right| = c$

13. $2x + \ln(x^2 + y^2) = c$ and $x^2 + y^2 = 0$

15. $x^2 \ln|x| - y = cx^2$ and $x = 0$

17. $y^2(x^2 + y^2 + 2) = c$

19. $x^2 y = c$

Section 2.5

1. $I = \dfrac{6}{5}(1 - e^{-10t})$

3. $I = 2(1 - e^{-25t})$

5. $I = \dfrac{1}{20}(e^t - e^{-t})$

7. $Q = \dfrac{1}{680}\left[3 \sin 60t + 5 \cos 60t - 5e^{-100t}\right]$

9. $Q = \dfrac{1}{100}(1 + 99e^{-100t})$

11. $I(0.1) = \dfrac{e^{-10}}{100} + \dfrac{600\,\pi\,(1 - e^{-10})}{(100)^2 + (120\,\pi)^2}$

13. $Q(60) = \dfrac{1}{2000}\left[1 - e^{-10^5(600\,+\,3600)}\right]$

15. $I(t) = \dfrac{E_0 C}{1 + (\omega RC)^2}\left[RC\omega^2 \cos \omega t - \omega \sin \omega t + \dfrac{1}{RC}\,e^{-t/RC}\right]$;

$Q(t) = \dfrac{E_0 C}{1 + (\omega RC)^2}\left[(\cos \omega t - e^{-t/RC}) + \omega RC \sin \omega t\right]$.

17. $I_{\text{transient}}(0) = \dfrac{E_0}{R[1 + (\omega RC)^2]} \approx \dfrac{E_0}{R}$ for very small R

19. $I(t) = \begin{cases} \dfrac{3}{50}(1 - e^{-50t}), & 0 \leqslant t \leqslant 10 \\[2ex] \left[\dfrac{e^{500}}{(70)^2} - \dfrac{3}{50}\right]e^{-50t} + \dfrac{7}{100} - \dfrac{e^{10-t}}{98}, & t \geqslant 10 \end{cases}$

Section 2.6

3. $y = \dfrac{x}{2}\left[\left(\dfrac{x}{b}\right)^{v/w} - \left(\dfrac{b}{x}\right)^{v/w}\right]$

5. Yes, at $(0, -bv/w)$

7. $r = e^{\theta/\sqrt{3}}$; $r = 3e^{(\theta - \pi)/\sqrt{3}}$

9. a units

Section 2.7

1. 2000-year-old wood has $\left(\dfrac{1}{2}\right)^{20/57} \approx 0.784$ the C^{14}-concentration of freshly cut wood.

3. $I(t) = \dfrac{1+N}{1+Ne^{-k(1+N)t}}$

5. $t = 25 \ln 2 \approx 17.3$ min

7. $47\dfrac{43}{91}$ g/liter

9. $P(t) = 400 - \dfrac{4}{\pi} - \dfrac{t}{6} - \dfrac{4}{\pi} \sin \dfrac{\pi}{12}\,(t-6)$

11. $x(t) = \dfrac{A}{k}\,(1-e^{-kt}) + x(0)e^{-kt} + \dfrac{B}{k^2+\omega^2}\cdot\left[k\sin\omega t + \omega(e^{-kt} - \cos\omega t)\right]$

Review Exercises for Chapter 2

1. $y = \dfrac{1}{1-\ln|x|}$

3. $y = \sin(\ln|x| + c)$

5. $y = \dfrac{2}{c-x^2}$

7. $y = \sqrt{2\sin x}$

9. $y = cx + \dfrac{1}{c}$ and $y = 2\sqrt{x}$

11. $y = e^{(x^2-1)/2}$

13. $y = ce^{-\cos x} - 1$

15. $y = \dfrac{x+c}{\sqrt{1+x^2}}$

17. $y = x^2\,(1+\ln|x|)$

19. $y = \begin{cases} ce^{x^2/2} - 1, & x \leqslant 0, \\[2mm] (c-1)e^{x^2/2}, & x > 0. \end{cases}$

21. $x^2 - 2xy - 2y^2 + 2 = 0$

23. $2\sqrt{xy+1} = x + c$

25. $y^{-1} = 1 - x + ce^{-x}$

27. $xy + c = e^y \tan x$

29. $\dfrac{y}{x^3} + \dfrac{3}{x} + \dfrac{x}{y^2} = c$

31. If $I =$ the amount of light incident on a layer of thickness Δx, then $\Delta I = -kI\Delta x$ or $I' = -kI$. Thus, $I(x) = I(0)e^{-kx}$.

33. $x = \dfrac{n^2kt}{nkt+1}$

35. $x = \begin{cases} \dfrac{1}{1001}\,(1-e^{-1001t/10^9}), & 0 \leqslant t \leqslant 3600 \\[4mm] \dfrac{1-e^{-0.0036036}}{1001e^{-0.0036}}\,e^{-t/10^6}, & t \geqslant 3600 \end{cases}$

37. $x = \dfrac{1}{100}\,(1 - e^{-t/192})$

39. c) $y' + \sqrt{1+(y')^2} = e^{wx/T_H}$; d) $y = \dfrac{T_H}{2w}\,(e^{wx/T_H} - 2 + e^{-wx/T_H})$

41. b) $y = e^{-\int f(x)dx}\,[c + \int g(x)e^{\int f(x)dx}\,dx]$

43. b) $y = c_1 e^{-2x} + c_2 e^{-3x}$

45. $y = (c_1 + c_2 x)e^{-ax}$

47. $I = I(0) - L^{-1}\cos t$, so the current is $90°$ out of phase with the voltage if $I(0) = 0$.

CHAPTER 3

Section 3.1

1. Linear, homogeneous, variable coefficients   3. Nonlinear
5. Linear, nonhomogeneous, constant coefficients
7. Linear, nonhomogeneous, variable coefficients
9. Linear, homogeneous, constant coefficients
11. 3   13. 3   15. $y = c_1 + c_2 x$
17. $y = c_1 + c_2 x^2$
19. Note that $y_1(x_0) = y_1{}'(x_0) = 0$ for some x_0 in the interval $[\alpha, \beta]$. By Theorem 1 there is a unique solution satisfying the differential equation and both conditions. Obviously $y \equiv 0$ satisfies the equation and the two conditions. Thus $y_1 \equiv 0$.
21. If $c_1 y_1 + c_2 y_2 + c_3 y_3 \equiv 0$, then we also must have
$$c_1 y_1{}' + c_2 y_2{}' + c_3 y_3{}' \equiv 0,$$
$$c_1 y_1{}'' + c_2 y_2{}'' + c_3 y_3{}'' \equiv 0.$$
In order for all three of these identities to hold at x_0, it must be that $c_1 = c_2 = c_3 = 0$.

Section 3.2

1. b) $a(x) = -1/x$ is not defined at $x = 0$.   3. $y_3 = 2y_1 - \dfrac{1}{2} y_2$

5. Let y_1 be the given solution and let y_2 be some other solution. Then $W(y_1, y_2)(0) = 0$, implying that y_1 and y_2 are linearly dependent.

7. b) $-2/x$ 11. $y = -\dfrac{3}{2} \cos x - \dfrac{5}{2} \sin x + \dfrac{5}{2} e^x$

Section 3.3

1. $y_2(x) = xe^x$ 3. $y_2(x) = \dfrac{3x^2 - 1}{4} \ln \left| \dfrac{1+x}{1-x} \right| - \dfrac{3x}{2}$

5. $y_2(x) = \dfrac{1}{x^2}$ 7. $y_2(x) = 2x - 1$

9. $y_2(x) = \cos(x^2)$ 11. $y_2(x) = (\cos x)/\sqrt{x}$

13. a) $y_1(v')'' + (3y_1{}' + ay_1)(v')' + (3y_1{}'' + 2ay_1{}' + by_1)v' = 0$;

c) $v' = \dfrac{W(y_1, y_2)}{y_1{}^2} \displaystyle\int \dfrac{y_1 e^{-\int a(x)dx}}{W^2(y_1, y_2)} \, dx$

Section 3.4

1. $y = c_1 e^{2x} + c_2 e^{-2x}$ 3. $y = c_1 e^x + c_2 e^{2x}$ 5. $x = \left(1 + \dfrac{9}{2} t\right) e^{-5t/2}$

7. $x = -\dfrac{1}{5} (e^{3t} + 4e^{-2t})$ 9. $y = c_1 + c_2 e^{5x}$

11. $y = (c_1 + c_2 x)e^{-\pi x}$ 13. $z = c_1 e^{-5x} + c_2 e^{3x}$ 15. $y = (1 + 2x)e^{4x}$

17. $y = c_1 e^{\sqrt{2}x} + c_2 e^{-\sqrt{2}x}$ 19. $y = e^{\sqrt{5}x} + 2e^{-\sqrt{5}x}$

21. b) $y = c_1 e^{\lambda_1 x} + c_2 e^{\lambda_2 x} + c_3 e^{\lambda_3 x}$;

    c) $y = c_1 e^{\lambda_1 x} + (c_2 + c_3 x)e^{\lambda_2 x}$;

    d) $y = (c_1 + c_2 x + c_3 x^2)e^{\lambda_1 x}$.

23. $y = (1 + x)e^x$ 25. $y = 1 + e^{3x} + e^{-3x}$

27. $y = c_1 + c_2 x + c_3 x^2 + c_4 x^3$ 29. $y = c_1 e^x + c_2 e^{-x} + c_3 e^{2x} + c_4 e^{-2x}$

31. $y = 1 - x + e^{2x} - e^{-2x}$ 35. $y = \dfrac{e^x - 2e^{-x}}{e^x + 2e^{-x}}$

37. $y = 1 + (c + x)^{-1}$ 39. $y = \dfrac{2ce^{3x} - 1}{ce^{3x} + 1}$

Section 3.5

1. $y = e^{-x}(c_1 \cos x + c_2 \sin x)$

3. $x = e^{-t/2}\left(c_1 \cos \dfrac{3\sqrt{3}}{2}t + c_2 \sin \dfrac{3\sqrt{3}}{2}t\right)$

5. $x = -\dfrac{3}{2}\cos 2\theta + \sin 2\theta$ 7. $y = \sin \dfrac{x}{2} + 2 \cos \dfrac{x}{2}$

9. $y = e^{-x}(c_1 \cos 2x + c_2 \sin 2x)$ 11. $y = e^{-x}(\sin x - \cos x)$

13. $y = c_1 e^x + c_2 \cos x + c_3 \sin x$

15. $y = c_1 e^{3x} + e^{-3x/2}\left(c_2 \cos \dfrac{3\sqrt{3}x}{2} + c_3 \sin \dfrac{3\sqrt{3}x}{2}\right)$

17. $y = c_1 x + c_2 x^{-1}$ 19. $y = x(c_1 \cos(\ln|x|) + c_2 \sin(\ln|x|))$

21. $y = x^{3/2} - x^{1/2}$ 23. $y = c_1 x + c_2 x^3$

25. $y = \dfrac{1}{x^2}(c_1 \cos(\ln|x|) + c_2 \sin(\ln|x|))$

27. $y = c_1 x^3 + c_2 x^{-4}$ 29. $y = c_1 x + c_2 x^2 + c_3 x^{-1}$

Section 3.6

1. $y = c_1 \sin 2x + c_2 \cos 2x + \sin x$ 3. $y = c_1 e^x + c_2 e^{2x} + 3e^{3x}$

5. $y = e^x(c_1 + c_2 x - 2x^2)$ 7. $y = 3e^{5x} - 10e^{2x} + 10x + 7$

9. $y = c_1 + c_2 e^{-x} + \dfrac{x^4}{4} - \dfrac{4}{3}x^3 + 4x^2 - 8x$

11. $y = e^{2x}(c_1 \cos x + c_2 \sin x) + xe^{2x}\sin x$

13. $y = e^{-3x}(c_1 + c_2 x + 5x^2)$

15. $y = c_1 e^{3x} + c_2 e^{-x} + \dfrac{20}{27} - \dfrac{7}{9}x + \dfrac{1}{3}x^2 - \dfrac{1}{4}e^x$

17. $y = (c_1 + c_2 x)e^{-2x} + \left(\dfrac{1}{9}x - \dfrac{2}{27}\right)e^x + \dfrac{3}{25}\sin x - \dfrac{4}{25}\cos x$

Section 3.7

1. $y = c_1 + c_2 e^x - \ln|\cos x|$

3. $y = c_1 \cos 2x + c_2 \sin 2x + \frac{1}{2}x \sin 2x + \frac{1}{4} \cos 2x \ln|\cos 2x|$

5. $y = e^x [c_1 + c_2 x - \ln|1 - x|]$　　　　**7.** $y = c_1 e^x + c_2 e^{-x} + e^x \ln|x|$

9. $y = e^{2x} [c_1 + c_2 x + (x + 1) \ln|x + 1|]$

11. $y = c_1 x^{-5} + c_2 x^{-1} + \frac{1}{12} x$　　　　**13.** $y = c_1 x^2 + c_2 x^{-1} - \frac{1}{2} \ln|x| + \frac{1}{4}$

15. $y_p = -\frac{1}{2} - \frac{x}{2} \ln|x| + \left(\frac{x}{2} - \frac{1}{2x}\right) \ln|x + 1|$

19. $y_p = e^{-x} \int e^{-x} \sec x \, dx + e^{-2x} [(\cos x - \sin x) \ln|\sec x| - x(\cos x + \sin x)]$

Section 3.8

1. a) $x = \cos 10\, t;$　　　　　　　　**b)** $x = (1 + 10t)e^{-10t};$

c) $x = \cos 10t + \frac{1}{2000} \sin 10t - \frac{t}{200} \cos 10t;$

d) $x = \frac{2001}{2000}(1 + 10t)e^{-10t} - \frac{1}{2000} \cos 10t.$

3. a) $x = 5 \sin(t + \alpha),\ \tan \alpha = 3/4;$

b) $x = \left(\frac{3\sqrt{5} + 11}{2}\right)e^{[(1 - \sqrt{5})t/2]} - \left(\frac{3\sqrt{5} + 5}{2}\right)e^{[(-1 - \sqrt{5})t/2]};$

c) $x = 3 \cos t + \frac{81}{20} \sin t - \frac{t}{20} \cos t;$

d) $x = \frac{1}{100}[(555 + 151\sqrt{5})e^{(1 - \sqrt{5})t/2}$
$\qquad\qquad - (255 + 149\sqrt{5})\ e^{(-1 - \sqrt{5})t/2} - 2\sqrt{5} \cos t].$

5. a) $x = \frac{3}{5} \sin 5t;$　　　　　　　　**b)** $x = e^{-4t} \sin 3t;$

c) $x = \frac{9}{16} \sin 5t + \frac{1}{16} \sin 3t;$

d) $x = \frac{1}{104}[e^{-4t}(106 \sin 3t + 3 \cos 3t) - 3 \cos 3t + 2 \sin 3t]$

7. $\pm \frac{\sqrt{g}}{50}$ m/s

9. $\frac{2\pi}{\sqrt{5\pi g}}$ s; $x = \left(\frac{1}{5\pi} - 1\right) \cos \sqrt{5\pi g}\, t$ m

11. $k = \frac{100\pi^2 + 1}{160}$ N/m $=$ kg/s^2

13. $x = \frac{25}{19{,}408}\left[\frac{1213}{11} e^{-2t} - \frac{400}{11} e^{-19.6t} + 88 \sin 2t - 108 \cos 2t\right]$

15. $\frac{7\sqrt{5}}{10\pi} Hz = \frac{42\sqrt{5}}{\pi} \approx 29.89$ ticks/min

Section 3.9

1. $I(t) = 6(e^{-5t} - e^{-20t}); \; Q(t) = \frac{1}{10}(9 - 12e^{-5t} + 3e^{-20t}).$

3. $I_{\text{steady state}} = \cos t + 2 \sin t$

5. $I_{\text{steady state}} = \frac{1}{13}(70 \sin 10t - 90 \cos 10t)$

7. $I_{\text{transient}} = e^{-t}(c_1 \cos t + c_2 \sin t)$

9. $I_{\text{transient}} = c_1 e^{-2t} + c_2 e^{-5t}$

11. $I_{\text{transient}} = e^{-t}(c_1 \cos 7t + c_2 \sin 7t)$

13. $I_{\text{transient}} = \dfrac{e^{-600t}}{2320}[297 \sin 800t - 96 \cos 800t];$

$I_{\text{steady state}} = \dfrac{1}{580}[24 \cos 600t - 27 \sin 600t]$

15. $Q = \begin{cases} c_1 \cos \dfrac{t}{\sqrt{LC}} + c_2 \sin \dfrac{t}{\sqrt{LC}} + (CE_0 + LC\omega^2) \sin \omega t, & \omega \neq \dfrac{1}{\sqrt{LC}}, \\[4mm] \left(c_1 - \dfrac{E_0 t}{2\omega L}\right) \cos \omega t + c_2 \sin \omega t, & \omega = \dfrac{1}{\sqrt{LC}}. \end{cases}$

17. b) $\omega = \dfrac{\sqrt{(4L/C) - R^2}}{2L}$

19. b) No ω produces resonance.

Section 3.10

1. $x = c_1 e^{-t} + c_2 e^{4t},$

$y = -c_1 e^{-t} + \frac{3}{2} c_2 e^{4t}$

3. $x = c_1 e^{-3t} + c_2(1 - t)e^{-3t},$

$y = -c_1 e^{-3t} + c_2 t e^{-3t}$

5. $x = c_1 e^{10t} + c_2 t e^{10t},$

$y = -(2c_1 + c_2)e^{10t} - 2c_2 t e^{10t}$

7. $x = -\frac{1}{4}(t^2 + 9t + 3) + c_1 - 3c_2 e^{2t},$

$y = \frac{1}{4}(t^2 + 7t) - c_1 + c_2 e^{2t}$

9. $x = e^{4t}(17c_1 \cos 2t + 17c_2 \sin 2t),$

$y = e^{4t}[(8c_1 - 2c_2) \cos 2t + (8c_2 + 2c_1) \sin 2t]$

11. $x_1' = x_2,$

$x_2' = -3x_1 - 2x_2$

13. $x_1' = x_2,$

$x_2' = x_3,$

$x_3' = x_1^3 - x_2^2 + x_3 + t$

15. $x_1' = x_2,$
$\quad x_2' = x_3,$
$\quad x_3' = x_1^4 x_2 - x_1 x_3 + \sin t$

17. $x_1' = x_2,$
$\quad x_2' = x_3,$
$\quad x_3' = x_1 - 4x_2 + 3x_3$

19. a) $x_1 = c_1 e^t,$
$\quad\quad x_2 = c_2 e^t;$
$\quad\quad c_1, c_2$ constant.

21. $x_1 = 4c_1 e^{-2t} + 3c_2 e^{-t},$
$\quad\quad x_2 = -5c_1 e^{-2t} - 4c_2 e^{-t} + c_3 e^{2t},$
$\quad\quad x_3 = -7c_1 e^{-2t} - 2c_2 e^{-t} - c_3 e^{2t}$

23. $x' = \dfrac{-3x}{100 + t} + \dfrac{2y}{100 - t},$

$\quad y' = \dfrac{3x}{100 + t} - \dfrac{4y}{100 - t}$

25. $y_{max} = \dfrac{500}{\sqrt{3}} \, [(2 + \sqrt{3})^{(1 - \sqrt{3})/2} - (2 + \sqrt{3})^{(-1 - \sqrt{3})/2}]$ lb,

$\quad t_{max} = \dfrac{25}{\sqrt{3}} \, \ln (2 + \sqrt{3})$ min.

27. $m_1 x_1^{(4)} + \left[k_1 + k_2 \left(1 + \dfrac{m_1}{m_2} \right) \right] x_1'' + \dfrac{k_2}{m_2} \, (2k_2 + k_1) x_1 = 0;$

$\quad x_1 = c_1 \cos \sqrt{6}t + c_2 \sin \sqrt{6}t + c_3 \sin 2t + c_4 \cos 2t;$

$\quad x_2 = \dfrac{c_1}{2} \cos \sqrt{6}t + \dfrac{c_2}{2} \sin \sqrt{6}t + c_3 \sin 2t + c_4 \cos 2t.$

29. 780.9 counts per minute

Section 3.11

1. b) $W = e^{-6t};$
$\quad$ c) $\{ c_1 e^{-3t} + c_2 (1 - t)e^{-3t}, -c_1 e^{-3t} + c_2 t e^{-3t} \}.$

Section 3.12

1. $\{ e^t, e^t \}, \{ 3e^{-t}, 5e^{-t} \}$

3. $\{ e^t \cos t, e^t (2 \cos t - \sin t) \}, \{ e^t \sin t, e^t (2 \sin t + \cos t) \}$

5. $\{ e^{-3t}, -e^{-3t} \}, \{ (t - 1)e^{-3t}, -te^{-3t} \}$ 7. $\{ 3, 4 \}, \{ e^{-2t}, 2e^{-2t} \}$

11. $\left\{ -\dfrac{1}{4}(t^2 + 9t + 3), \dfrac{1}{4}(t^2 + 7t) \right\}$ 13. $\{ \sin t - \cos t, 2 \sin t - \cos t \}$

15. a) $x' = -0.134x + 0.02y,$
$\quad\quad y' = 0.036x - 0.02y;$
$\quad$ b) $\{ 10c_1 e^{-0.14t} + c_2 e^{-0.014t}, -3c_1 e^{-0.14t} + 6c_2 e^{-0.014t} \}$

Section 3.13

1. $\left\{1 - 1.025e^{-0.05}, 1 - 1.05e^{-0.05}\right\}$

3. $\left\{100(k_1 e^{\lambda_1 t} + k_2 e^{\lambda_2 t}) + 1, -8(k_1\lambda_1 e^{\lambda_1 t} + k_2\lambda_2 e^{\lambda_2 t}) + 1\right\}$

where $\left.\begin{matrix} k_1 \\ k_2 \end{matrix}\right\} = \dfrac{\mp 3\sqrt{2} - 4}{800}$, $\left.\begin{matrix} \lambda_1 \\ \lambda_2 \end{matrix}\right\} = -50 \pm 25\sqrt{2}$

5. The general solution $\left\{I_L, I_R\right\} = \left\{I_L, I_R\right\}_h + \left\{I_L, I_R\right\}_p$ is given by

$$\left\{I_L, I_R\right\}_p = \left\{A \sin \omega t + B \cos \omega t, C \sin \omega t + D \cos \omega t\right\},$$

where $\omega = 60\pi$, $\Delta = \omega^2 + 2500$, $A = (2500/\Delta)^2$, $B = -25\omega(\omega^2 + 7500)/\Delta^2$, $C = -2500(\omega^2 - 2500)/\Delta^2$, $D = -250{,}000\omega/\Delta^2$, and

a) $\left\{I_L, I_R\right\}_h = \left\{\dfrac{e^{-50t}}{2}\left[k_1 + k_2\left(t + \dfrac{1}{25}\right)\right], \ e^{-50t}\left[k_1 + k_2\left(t + \dfrac{1}{25}\right)\right]\right\}$

b) $\left\{I_L, I_R\right\}_h = \left\{e^{-50t}[k_1 \cos 50\sqrt{3}t + k_2 \sin 50\sqrt{3}t],\right.$
$\left. e^{-50t}[k_3 \cos 50\sqrt{3}t + k_4 \sin 50\sqrt{3}t]\right\}$

c) $\left\{I_L, I_R\right\}_h = \left\{e^{-50t}(k_1 e^{25\sqrt{2}t} + k_2 e^{-25\sqrt{2}t}),\right.$
$\left. e^{-50t}[(2 - \sqrt{2})k_1 e^{25\sqrt{2}t} + (2 + \sqrt{2})k_2 e^{-25\sqrt{2}t}]\right\}$

7. $I_1 = \dfrac{1}{20}(8 \sin t - 6 \cos t + 5e^{-t} + e^{-3t})$;

$I_2 = \dfrac{1}{20}(2 \sin t - 4 \cos t + 5e^{-t} - e^{-3t})$

Section 3.14

1. $\lim_{I_* \to 0} S(\infty) = 0$, so everyone gets the disease

5. $\lim_{I_* \to 0} T = \infty$, so susceptibles continue to become infective; for all time

Review Exercises for Chapter 3

1. $y_2 = \cos 2x$

3. $y_2 = x^{-2}$

5. $y_2 = -2 + x \ln\left|\dfrac{1 + x}{1 - x}\right|$

7. $y = 13e^{4x} - 10e^{5x}$

9. $y = \dfrac{2}{\sqrt{7}} e^{(3/2)x} \sin \dfrac{\sqrt{7}}{2} x$

11. $y = (c_1 + c_2 x)e^{-x/2}$

13. $y = e^x(c_1 \cos \sqrt{6}x + c_2 \sin \sqrt{6}x)$

15. $y = c_1 e^x + c_2 e^{2x} + c_3 e^{3x}$

17. $y = -3e^x + x^2 + 4x + 5$

19. $y = c_1 e^x + c_2 x e^x + \dfrac{e^x}{x}$

21. $y = (c_1 + c_2 \ln|x|)x^{-2}$

23. $x_1' = x_2$,
$x_2' = x_3$,
$x_3' = 6x_3 - 2x_2 + 5x_1$

25. $x_1' = x_2$,
$x_2' = x_3$,
$x_3' = (\ln|t| - x_1 x_3)/x_2$

27. $x = c_1 e^{5t} + c_2 e^{-t}$,

$y = 2c_1 e^{5t} - c_2 e^{-t}$

29. $x = e^{2t}(c_1 \cos 3t + c_2 \sin 3t)$,

$y = \dfrac{e^{2t}}{2}((3c_2 - c_1)\cos 3t - (c_2 + 3c_1)\sin 3t)$

31. $x = c_1 e^{-t} + 3e^{-2t}$,

$y = (c_2 - 2c_1 t)e^{-t} + 12e^{-2t}$

CHAPTER 4

Section 4.1

1. Linear, nonhomogeneous, constant coefficients

3. Nonlinear

5. Linear, homogeneous, constant coefficients

7. Nonlinear

9. Linear, nonhomogeneous, constant coefficients

11. (a) Yes;　　(b) yes;　　(c) no;　　(d) no.

15. (a) $g_{n+1} = (1.04)g_n$;　　(b) $g_2 \approx 5.41$, $g_4 \approx 5.84$.

23. Integrate by parts

$$\int_0^\infty t^{n-1}e^{-t}\,dt = -e^{-t}t^{n-1}\Big|_0^\infty + (n-1)\int_0^\infty t^{n-2}e^{-t}dt$$

and note that $\lim\limits_{t \to \infty} t^{n-1}e^{-t} = 0$ by L'Hôpital's rule.

25. Assuming a_n and b_n are nonzero for all n, if $y_k = y_{k+1} = 0$, then $y_{k+2} = -a_k y_{k+1} - b_k y_k = 0$ and $y_{k-1} = (-y_{k+1} - a_{k-1}y_k)/b_{k-1} = 0$.

Section 4.2

1. $y_n = y_0 + 2\left(1 - \dfrac{1}{2^n}\right)$

3. $y_n = (-1)^n y_0$

5. $y_n = n + 1$

7. $y_n = \dfrac{5^{n+1} - 1}{2}$

9. $y_n = e^{-n^2 + n}\left(y_0 + \dfrac{e^n - 1}{e - 1}\right)$

11. $P_n = \dfrac{2}{3} + \dfrac{1}{3}\left(-\dfrac{1}{2}\right)^n$

13. $P_n = P_0/n!$

17. a) $(n + 8)x_{n+2} + 2x_{n+1} - x_n = 0$;

b) $2 \cdot 3^n(3^{n+1} - 2)x_{n+2} - 2(3^n - 1)x_{n+1} + x_n = 0$

Section 4.3

1. 1.8171 **3.** 0.5671 **5.** 1.1656

7. $x_{n+1} = \dfrac{x_{n-1}\,F(x_n) - x_n F(x_{n-1})}{F(x_n) - F(x_{n-1})}$

Section 4.4

1. $C_n = -2^n$

3. $C_n = 1$ $\left(\text{since } \sin\left[(n+1)\dfrac{\pi}{2}\right] = \cos\dfrac{n\pi}{2} \text{ and}\right.$

$\left.\cos\left[(n+1)\dfrac{\pi}{2}\right] = -\sin\dfrac{n\pi}{2}\right)$

5. $C_n = 12^n$

Section 4.5

1. $y_n = n$

3. $y_n = \displaystyle\sum_{k=0}^{n-1} \dfrac{(-1)^{k-1}}{(k+1)!}$

5. $y_n = 2^n$

7. $y_n = n! \displaystyle\sum_{k=0}^{n-1} \dfrac{(-1)^k}{k+1}$

Section 4.6

1. $y_n = c_1 4^n + c_2(-1)^n$

3. $y_n = \left(\dfrac{1}{3}\right)^{n-1} - \left(\dfrac{1}{2}\right)^{n-1}$

5. $y_n = c_1(-1)^n + c_2 n(-1)^n$

7. $y_n = \left(\dfrac{1}{3}\right)^n (c_1 + nc_2)$

9. $y_n = c_1\left(\dfrac{1+\sqrt{41}}{20}\right)^n + c_2\left(\dfrac{1-\sqrt{41}}{20}\right)^n$

11. $P_n = \dfrac{\sqrt{5}}{2}\left[\left(\dfrac{1+1/\sqrt{5}}{2}\right)^n - \left(\dfrac{1-1/\sqrt{5}}{2}\right)^n\right];\; P_{11} = 0.088$

13. $P_n = 1000(1.6^n + 1.4^n)$

15. $y_n = c_1 + c_2 2^n + c_3 3^n$

17. $y_n = c_1 + c_2 n + c_3(-2)^n$

19. $y_n = c_1 + c_2 n + c_3 n^2$

Section 4.7

1. $y_n = c_1 \cos\dfrac{n\pi}{4} + c_2 \sin\dfrac{n\pi}{4}$

3. $y_n = 2^{3n/2}\left(c_1 \cos\dfrac{n\pi}{2} + c_2 \sin\dfrac{n\pi}{2}\right)$

9. $y_n = \dfrac{x_n}{x_{n+1}} + 1$, where $x_n = c_1\left(\dfrac{1}{\sqrt{2}}\right)^n + c_2\left(-\dfrac{1}{\sqrt{2}}\right)^n$

11. $y_n = \dfrac{x_n}{x_{n+1}} + \dfrac{3}{4}$, where $x_n = c_1\left(\dfrac{-2}{3}\right)^n + c_2\left(\dfrac{-4}{3}\right)^n$

13. $y_n = c_1 2^n + c_2 \cos \dfrac{n\pi}{2} + c_3 \sin \dfrac{n\pi}{2}$

15. $y_n = c_1 + c_2 \cos \dfrac{n\pi}{2} + c_3 \sin \dfrac{n\pi}{2}$

17. $y_n = c_1(-6)^n + 2^n \left(c_2 \cos \dfrac{n\pi}{3} + c_3 \sin \dfrac{n\pi}{3} \right)$

Section 4.8

1. $y_n = \dfrac{1}{6} \cdot 5^{n+1}$

3. $y_n = 2^n \left(\dfrac{n^3}{24} - \dfrac{n^2}{8} \right)$

5. $y_n = \dfrac{1}{4} \sin \dfrac{n\pi}{2}$

11. $y_n = n \cdot 2^{n-1} + \dfrac{2^{2-n}}{3} + c_1 + c_2 2^n$

13. $y_n = \dfrac{\sin n + \sin (n-2)}{2(1 + \cos 2)} + c_1 \cos \dfrac{n\pi}{2} + c_2 \sin \dfrac{n\pi}{2}$

15. $y_n = c_1(-1)^n + 3^{n/2} \left(c_2 \cos \dfrac{n\pi}{6} + c_3 \sin \dfrac{n\pi}{6} \right) + \dfrac{5}{26} \cos \dfrac{n\pi}{2} - \dfrac{1}{26} \sin \dfrac{n\pi}{2}$

17. $y_n = -6 - 2n - n^2 + \left(\dfrac{3}{2} \right)^{n/2} [c_1 \cos n\theta + c_2 \sin n\theta]$, where $\tan \theta = \sqrt{5}$

Section 4.9

1. \$9 to have a better than even chance; Player B will *never* have better than a 55% chance to win all of A's money no matter how much he starts with.

3. $P_{n+3} + \dfrac{p}{q} P_{n+2} - \dfrac{1}{q} P_{n+1} + \dfrac{r}{q} P_n = 0$, $P_0 = 0$, $P_{2N} = P_{2N+1} = 1$

5. The general solution is $P_n = c_1 + c_2(-1 + \sqrt{2})^n + c_3(-1 - \sqrt{2})^n$ and use $P_0 = 0$, $P_{2N} = P_{2N+1} = 1$ to evaluate c_1, c_2, c_3.

7. a) $P_n = \dfrac{3n + (-2)^{n-2N} - (-2)^{-2N}}{6N + 1 - (-2)^{-2N}}$; no; $P_{10} \approx \dfrac{30}{61}$

b) $P_n = \dfrac{3n + (-2)^{n-30} - (-2)^{-30}}{91 - (-2)^{-30}}$; $P_{10} \approx \dfrac{30}{91}$

Review Exercises for Chapter 4

1. $y_n = y_0 + n$

3. $y_n = 3^n y_0 + (1 + 3 + 3^2 + \cdots + 3^{n-1})2 = 3^n y_0 + 3^n - 1$

5. $y_n = n! \left(y_0 + \displaystyle\sum_{k=0}^{n-1} \dfrac{1}{(k+1)!} \right)$

7. $y_n = 2^n \cdot 5 + 2$

9. 1.3702

11. $y_n = c_1 + c_2 \left(\dfrac{5}{3} \right)^n$

13. $y_n = \left(-\dfrac{3}{2} \right)^n (c_1 + nc_2)$

15. $y_n = c_1 \cos \dfrac{n\pi}{3} + c_2 \sin \dfrac{n\pi}{3}$

17. $z_n = \dfrac{1}{42} 4^{n+1} = \dfrac{2}{21} 4^n$

19. $z_n = \dfrac{3^n}{16}$

21. $x_n = c_1 + c_2 3^n$, $y_n = -c_1 + c_2 3^n$

23. $x_n = c_1 2^n + c_2(-3)^n$, $y_n = 4c_1 2^n - c_2(-3)^n$

25. $x_n = n2^{n+1}$, $y_n = (1 - 2n)2^n$

27. $x_n = \dfrac{5}{4} - \dfrac{1}{4} 3^n + \dfrac{n}{2}$, $y_n = \dfrac{1}{4}(3^n - 1) + \dfrac{n}{2}$

29.
$$x_{n+1} = 2.4 \min(x_n, y_n) + x_n - 300{,}000,$$
$$y_{n+1} = 1.6 \min(x_n, y_n) + y_n - 200{,}000$$

so that

$$x_{n+1} = \frac{3}{2}(y_0 - 125{,}000)(2.6)^{n+1} + \left(x_0 + \frac{3}{2}(y_0 - 125{,}000)\right),$$
$$y_{n+1} = (2.6)^{n+1}(y_0 - 125{,}000) + 125{,}000.$$

Extinction occurs if $y_0 < 125{,}000$.

CHAPTER 5

Section 5.1

11. $R = 1$ **13.** $R = 0$ **15.** $R = 1/4$

Section 5.2

1. $y = e^x + x + 1$

3. $y = c_0 \cos x + (c_1 - 1)\sin x + x$

5. $y = c_0(1 + x \tan^{-1}x) + c_1 x$

7. $y = xe^x$

9. $y = 1 - 2x^2$

11. $y = x + \sin x$

13. $y = \dfrac{1}{1 - x}$

15. $y = e^{x^2} - \dfrac{x}{4}$

17. $y = c_0 \displaystyle\sum_{n=0}^{\infty} \frac{1 \cdot 4 \cdot \cdots \cdot (3n - 2)}{(3n)!} x^{3n} + c_1 \sum_{n=1}^{\infty} \frac{2 \cdot 5 \cdot \cdots \cdot (3n - 1)}{(3n + 1)!} x^{3n+1}$

19. $y = 1 + \dfrac{(x - 1)^2}{2!} + \dfrac{(x - 1)^3}{3!} + \dfrac{(x - 1)^4}{4!} + \dfrac{4(x - 1)^5}{5!} + \cdots$

21. a) No; (b) no.

Section 5.3

1. $y_0 = c_0 \cos \sqrt{x} + c_1 \sin \sqrt{x}$

3. $y = c_0 \dfrac{\sinh x}{x^3} + c_1 \dfrac{\cosh x}{x^3}$

5. $y = c_0 \dfrac{\sin x^2}{x^2} + c_1 \dfrac{\cos x^2}{x^2}$

7. $y = c_0 x + \dfrac{c_1}{x^2}$

9. $y = c_0 \dfrac{\sin x}{x} + c_1 \dfrac{\cos x}{x}$

11. $y = c_0 e^x + c_1 e^x \ln|x|$

13. $y = c_0 \sqrt{x}e^x + c_1 \sqrt{x}e^x \ln|x|$

15. $y = \dfrac{c_0}{1 - x} + c_1 \dfrac{\ln|x|}{1 - x}$

17. $y = (c_0 + c_1 \ln|x|)\left(1 + \frac{x^2}{2^2} + \frac{x^4}{(2\cdot4)^2} + \cdots\right) - c_1\left(\frac{x^2}{4} + \frac{3x^4}{8\cdot16} + \cdots\right)$

19. $y = c_0\sqrt{x}\left(1 - \frac{7}{6}x + \frac{21}{40}x^2 + \cdots\right) + c_1(1 - 3x + 2x^2 + \cdots)$

21. $y = c_0 x + c_1\left(x\ln|x| + \sum_{n=1}^{\infty}\frac{(-1)^n}{n!n}x^{n+1}\right)$

25. b) $y_2 = xe^{-1/x}$

Section 5.4

1. $\left(\frac{384}{x^4} - \frac{72}{x^2} + 1\right)J_1(x) - \left(\frac{192}{x^3} - \frac{12}{x}\right)J_0(x)$

13. Use Eq. (24).

15. Set $z = \sqrt{x}$, then $y = AJ_p(\sqrt{x}) + BY_p(\sqrt{x})$.

17. Set $y = xu$, then $y = x[AJ_1(x) + BY_1(x)]$.

19. Set $y = ux^{-k}$, then $y = x^{-k}(AJ_k(x) + BY_k(x))$.

21. Set $y = \sqrt{x}u$, $z = kx^3/3$, then $y = \sqrt{x}(AJ_{1/6}(kx^3/3) + BY_{1/6}(kx^3/3))$.

Section 5.5

1. $P_5 = \dfrac{63x^5 - 70x^3 + 15x}{8}$, $P_6 = \dfrac{231x^6 - 315x^4 + 105x^2 - 5}{16}$,

$P_7 = \dfrac{429x^7 - 693x^5 + 315x^3 - 35x}{16}$,

$P_8 = \dfrac{429(15x^8 - 28x^6) + 630(11x^4 - 2x^2) + 35}{128}$

9. $H_0(x) = 1$, $H_1(x) = 2x$, $H_2(x) = 4x^2 - 2$, $H_3 = 8x^3 - 12x$, $H_4(x) = 16x^4 - 48x^2 + 12$

Review Exercises for Chapter 5

1. (a) Converge; (b) converge; (c) converge if $x < 1$; (d) diverge.

7. $y = x^2 + e^x$

9. $y = x(\sin x + 1)$

11. $y = e^{-x^2}$

13. $y = c_0 e^x + c_1\sqrt{x}$

15. $y = \dfrac{c_0}{x} + \dfrac{c_1}{1-x}$

17. $y = c_1\dfrac{e^{x/2}}{\sqrt{x}} + c_2 x\left(1 + \sum_{n=1}^{\infty}\dfrac{x^n}{5\cdot7\cdot\cdots\cdot(2n+3)}\right)$

23. $y = c_0 xJ_0(x) + c_1 xY_0(x)$

25. $y = P_n(\cos x)$

CHAPTER 6

Section 6.1

1. $\dfrac{5}{s^2} + \dfrac{2}{s}$, $s > 0$

3. $\dfrac{18}{s^3} - \dfrac{7}{s}$, $s > 0$

5. $\dfrac{2}{s^3} + \dfrac{8}{s^2} - \dfrac{16}{s}$, $s > 0$

7. $\dfrac{3}{4s^4} + \dfrac{1}{2s^3} + \dfrac{1}{2s^2} + \dfrac{1}{s}$, $s > 0$

9. $\dfrac{a}{s^2} + \dfrac{b}{s}$, $s > 0$

11. $\dfrac{e^2}{s - 5}$, $s > 5$

13. $\dfrac{1}{s - 1/2}$, $s > 1/2$

15. $\dfrac{e^{-1/2}}{s + 1}$, $s > -1$

17. $\dfrac{3}{s^2 + 9}$, $s > 0$

19. $\dfrac{s}{s^2 + 49}$, $s > 0$

21. $\dfrac{5 \cos 2}{s^2 + 25} + \dfrac{s \sin 2}{s^2 + 25}$, $s > 0$

23. $\dfrac{s \cos b}{s^2 + a^2} - \dfrac{a \sin b}{s^2 + a^2}$, $s > 0$

25. $\dfrac{s}{s^2 - \frac{1}{4}}$, $s > \frac{1}{2}$

27. $\dfrac{s \cosh 2}{s^2 - 25} - \dfrac{5 \sinh 2}{s^2 - 25}$, $s > 5$

29. $\dfrac{a \cosh b}{s^2 - a^2} + \dfrac{s \sinh b}{s^2 - a^2}$, $s > |a|$

31. $\dfrac{1}{(s - 1)^2}$, $s > 1$

33. $\dfrac{6}{(s + 1)^4} - \dfrac{1}{s + 1}$, $s > -1$

35. $\dfrac{1}{(s - 1)^2 + 1}$, $s > 1$

37. $\dfrac{s - 4}{(s - 4)^2 + 4}$, $s > 4$

39. $\dfrac{s + 2}{(s + 1)^2 + 1}$, $s > -1$

43. $9t^2 + 7$

45. $\cos t + \sin t$

47. $\cosh \sqrt{2}t - \sqrt{2} \sinh \sqrt{2}t$

49. te^t

51. $\dfrac{3}{\sqrt{5}} e^{-2t} \sin \sqrt{5}t$

53. $2e^{-t} \cos \sqrt{7}t - \dfrac{3}{\sqrt{7}} e^{-t} \sin \sqrt{7}t$

55. $ce^{-at} \cos \sqrt{b - a^2}t + \dfrac{d - ac}{\sqrt{b - a^2}} e^{-at} \sin \sqrt{b - a^2}t$

63. $\dfrac{2abs}{(s^2 - (a + b)^2)(s^2 - (a - b)^2)}$

65. $\dfrac{s(s^2 + b^2 - a^2)}{(s^2 + a^2 + b^2)^2 - 4a^2 s^2}$

67. $\dfrac{a(s^2 - a^2 - b^2)}{(s^2 + a^2 + b^2)^2 - 4a^2 s^2}$

71. $\dfrac{6}{(s + 1)^4}$

73. $\dfrac{2s^3 - 54s}{(s^3 + 9)^3}$

75. $\dfrac{(s - a)^2 - b^2}{[(s - a)^2 + b^2]^2}$

77. $\dfrac{3[(s + 1)^2 + 1]}{[(s + 1)^2 - 1]^2}$

Section 6.2

1. $\cos t$

3. $A \cosh at + \dfrac{B}{a} \sinh at$

5. $e^{-t}(\cos 2t + \sin 2t)$

7. $\dfrac{1}{3} - e^{t} + \dfrac{5}{3}\, e^{3t}$

9. $-\dfrac{t}{9} + \dfrac{23}{27}\, e^{3t} + \dfrac{4}{27}\, e^{-3t}$

11. e^{-t}

13. $\sinh t$

15. $\left(1 + \dfrac{t}{2k}\right) \sin kt$

17. $\left(a + \dfrac{1}{2a^2}\right) \sin at + \left(a - \dfrac{t}{2a}\right) \cos at$

19. $\dfrac{5}{4}\cosh t - \dfrac{1}{4}\left(\cos t + t \sin t\right)$

21. $\dfrac{s^2 + 2a^2}{s(s^2 + 4a^2)}$

23. $\dfrac{2a(3s^2 - a^2)}{(s^2 + a^2)^3}$

25. $\dfrac{8 + 6s^2}{s^2(s^2 + 4)^2}$

27. $\dfrac{2a^2(4a^2 + 3s^2)}{s^2(s^2 + 4a^2)^2}$

29. $\dfrac{32(3s^4 + 24s^2 + 128)}{s^3(s^2 + 16)^3}$

33. $\dfrac{\pi}{2} - \tan^{-1} s = \tan^{-1}(1/s)$

35. $\dfrac{\pi}{2} - \tan^{-1}(s/3) = \tan^{-1}(3/s)$

37. $\tan^{-1} k/s$

39. $\dfrac{1}{2} \ln \dfrac{s^2 - a^2}{s^2}$

41. $\dfrac{1}{2s} \ln \dfrac{s^2 + a^2}{s^2}$

43. $\dfrac{e^{s^2/4}}{s}\left(1 - \operatorname{erf}\left(\dfrac{s}{2}\right)\right)$

45. $\dfrac{2}{t}\left(1 - \cos at\right)$

47. $\dfrac{\sin t}{t}$

49. a) $Y'' + s^2 Y = 1;$

b) $Y(s) = c_0 \left(1 - \dfrac{s^4}{4 \cdot 3} + \dfrac{s^8}{8 \cdot 7 \cdot 4 \cdot 3} - \cdots\right)$

$\qquad + c_1 \left(s - \dfrac{s^5}{5 \cdot 4} + \dfrac{s^9}{9 \cdot 8 \cdot 5 \cdot 4} - \cdots\right)$

$\qquad + \dfrac{1}{2}\left(s^2 - \dfrac{s^6}{6 \cdot 5} + \dfrac{s^{10}}{10 \cdot 9 \cdot 6 \cdot 5} - \cdots\right).$

51. $I(t) = \dfrac{1}{676}\left[e^{-5t}(-12 - 65t) + 5 \sin t + 12 \cos t\right]$

53. $I(t) = \dfrac{1}{125}\left[e^{-5t}(30 - 250t) - 30 \cos 10t + 40 \sin 10t\right]$

Section 6.3

9. $\dfrac{b}{s(e^{as} + 1)}$

11. $\dfrac{b(1 - e^{-as})}{s(1 + e^{-2as})}$

13. $\dfrac{1 - e^{-as}}{s^2(1 + e^{-2as})}$

15. $\dfrac{(1 - e^{-as})^2}{s^2(1 + e^{-2as})}$

17. $\dfrac{s(1 - e^{-3\pi s/2})}{s^2 + 1}$

19. $f(t) = \cos(t - 3\pi)H(t - 3\pi) = \begin{cases} 0, & t < 3\pi \\ \cos t, & t > 3\pi \end{cases}$

21. $f(t) = t - (t - 2)H(t - 2) = \begin{cases} t, & t < 2 \\ 2, & t > 2 \end{cases}$

23. $f(t) = \sinh(t - 2)H(t - 2) = \begin{cases} 0, & t < 2 \\ \sinh(t - 2), & t > 2 \end{cases}$

25. $f(t) = 2H(t - 10) + 2H(t - 1) - 2,$

$$\mathcal{L}\{f(t)\} = \frac{2}{5}(e^{-10s} + e^{-s} - 1)$$

Section 6.4

1. $I(t) = \dfrac{10}{\sqrt{6}}\, e^{-20(t-30)} \sin\sqrt{600}\,(t - 30)H(t - 30)$

3. $I(t) = 1 - \cos 4t + H(t - 5)[\cos 4(t - 5) - 1]$

5. $I(t) = 1 - \cos\sqrt{10}t - H(t - 2)[1 - \cos\sqrt{10}(t - 2)]$
$\qquad + 2H(t - 4)[1 - \cos\sqrt{10}(t - 4)]$

7. a) $x(t) = \dfrac{t}{2} - \dfrac{\sin 2t}{4} - \dfrac{1}{4}H\!\left(t - \dfrac{\pi}{2}\right)[2t - \pi - \sin(2t - \pi)];$

$\quad$ b) $x(t) = \dfrac{t}{2} - \dfrac{\sin 2t}{4} + \cos 2t - \dfrac{1}{4}H\!\left(t - \dfrac{\pi}{2}\right)[2t - \pi - \sin(2t - \pi)]$

Section 6.5

1. $\dfrac{3!}{s^4(s^2 + 1)}$

3. $\dfrac{3!5!}{s^{10}}$

5. $\dfrac{19!}{s^{20}(s - 17)}$

7. $\dfrac{at - \sin at}{a^2}$

9. $\dfrac{1}{a^2}(1 - \cos at)$

11. $\dfrac{1}{2}(t - 3)^2 H(t - 3)$

13. $e^{-t}(1 - t)^2$

15. $y = \dfrac{e^{-2t}}{9}(1 - \cos 3t) - \dfrac{e^{-2(t-\pi)}}{9}(1 - \cos 3(t - \pi))H(t - \pi)$

Section 6.6

1. $x = \cosh t, \ y = \sinh t$

3. $x = e^{3t}(2\cos 3t + 2\sin 3t); \ y = e^{3t}(-2\cos 3t + 4\sin 3t)$

5. $x = \dfrac{3}{2} \cos t + \dfrac{1}{2} \sin t + \dfrac{7}{2} e^t - 5e^{-t} - 4t,$

$y = \cos t + \dfrac{7}{2} e^t - \dfrac{5}{2} e^{-t} - 1 - 3t$

7. $x = \dfrac{e^{3t}}{4(13)^3} (6887 \cos 2t + 2637 \sin 2t) + \dfrac{e^t}{4} - \dfrac{5t^2}{13} - \dfrac{34t}{(13)^2} - \dfrac{74}{(13)^3},$

$y = \dfrac{e^{3t}}{4(13)^3} (-9524 \cos 2t + 4250 \sin 2t) + \dfrac{4}{13} t^2 + \dfrac{48t}{(13)^2} + \dfrac{184}{(13)^3}$

9. $x = \cos t; \; y = -\cos t - \sin t$

11. $x = \cos t - \sin t; \; y \equiv 1; \; z = \sin t + \cos t$

Review Exercises for Chapter 6

1. $\dfrac{3}{s^2} - \dfrac{2}{s}$ **3.** $\dfrac{1}{e(s-2)}$

5. $\dfrac{1}{(s+1)^2}$ **7.** $\dfrac{3 \cosh 4 - s(\sinh 4)}{s^2 - 9}$

9. $\dfrac{(s-1)^2 - 1}{[(s-1)^2 + 1]^2}$ **11.** $\dfrac{s^2 + 2}{s(s^2 + 4)}$

13. $\dfrac{2s(s^2 - 12)}{(s^2 + 4)^3}$ **15.** e^{-3s}

17. $\dfrac{1 + se^{-2\pi s}}{s^2 + 1}$ **19.** -14

21. te^{2t} **23.** $e^{-2t} \sin t$

25. $2e^{2t} - e^t$ **27.** $-2e^{-t} - 5te^{-t} + 2 \cos t + 4 \sin t$

29. $\dfrac{2}{t} (1 - \cos 2t)$

31. $\cos t - \cos \left(t - \dfrac{\pi}{2}\right) H\left(t - \dfrac{\pi}{2}\right) = \begin{cases} \cos t, & t < \dfrac{\pi}{2} \\[2mm] \cos t - \sin t, & t > \dfrac{\pi}{2} \end{cases}$

33. $y = \cos t + 3 \sin t$ **35.** $y = 5e^{2t} - 3e^{3t}$

37. $y = \dfrac{e^{2t}}{9} (3t - 4) + \dfrac{4}{3} e^t - \dfrac{8}{9} e^{-t}$ **39.** $H(t - 3)e^{3 - t} (1 - \cos(t - 3))$

41. $y = e^{2t}(1 - t) + (t - 1)e^{2(t - 1)} H(t - 1)$

43. $\dfrac{4! \, 7!}{s^{13}}$

45. a) $\displaystyle\int_0^t \sin(t - u)u^2 \, du = t^2 + 2 \cos t - 2;$

b) $\displaystyle\int_0^t \dfrac{1}{2} \sin 2u \, du = \dfrac{1}{4}(1 - \cos 2t)$

47. $x = 4e^t - 2$; $y = 2e^t - 1$

49. $x = \dfrac{6}{5} e^{-4t} - \dfrac{1}{5} e^t$; $y = \dfrac{9}{5} e^{-4t} + \dfrac{1}{5} e^t$

CHAPTER 7

Section 7.1

1. $y = 2e^x - x - 1$, $y(1) = 2(e-1) \approx 3.44$;

    (a) $y_E = 2.98$; (b) $y_{IE} = 3.14$; (c) $y_{RK} = 3.44$.

3. $y^2 + 2xy - x^2 = 1$, $y(1) = \sqrt{3} - 1 \approx 0.73$

    (a) $y_E = 0.71$; (b) $y_{IE} = 0.73$; (c) $y_{RK} = 0.73$.

5. $y + \sqrt{y^2 + 1} = e^{(x^2-1)/2}$, $y(3) = (e^4 - e^{-4})/2 \approx 27.29$;

    (a) $y_E = 8.31$; (b) $y_{IE} = 21.67$; (c) $y_{RK} = 27.03$.

7. $y = (x^3 + x^{-2})^{-1/2}$, $y(2) = 2/\sqrt{33} \approx 0.35$;

    (a) $y_E = 0.34$; (b) $y_{IE} = 0.35$; (c) $y_{RK} = 0.35$.

9. $y = 2e^{e^{x}-1}$, $y(2) = 2e^{e^2-1} \approx 1190.59$;

    (a) $y_E = 156.45$; (b) $y_{IE} = 781.56$; (c) $y_{RK} = 1164.76$.

11. a) $y_1 = 1.02$, $y_2 = 1.04$, $y_3 = 1.07$, $y_4 = 1.09$, $y_5 = 1.12$;

    b) $y_1 = 1.02$, $y_2 = 1.04$, $y_3 = 1.07$, $y_4 = 1.10$, $y_5 = 1.12$.

13. a) $y_1 = 0.34$, $y_2 = 0.56$, $y_3 = 0.76$, $y_4 = 0.98$, $y_5 = 1.34$;

    b) $y_1 = 0.38$, $y_2 = 0.61$, $y_3 = 0.78$, $y_4 = 0.98$, $y_5 = 1.35$.

15. a) $y_1 = 1.28$, $y_2 = 1.65$, $y_3 = 1.46$, $y_4 = 1.09$, $y_5 = 0.87$, $y_6 = 0.79$,
       $y_7 = 0.93$, $y_8 = 0.95$;

    b) $y_1 = 1.33$, $y_2 = 1.91$, $y_3 = 1.61$, $y_4 = 1.16$, $y_5 = 0.92$, $y_6 = 0.79$,
       $y_7 = 0.54$, $y_8 = 0.77$.

17. a) $y_1 = 1.10$, $y_2 = 1.22$, $y_3 = 1.35$, $y_4 = 1.48$, $y_5 = 1.63$, $y_6 = 1.79$,
       $y_7 = 1.97$, $y_8 = 2.16$, $y_9 = 2.37$, $y_{10} = 2.60$;

    b) $y_1 = 1.11$, $y_2 = 1.22$, $y_3 = 1.35$, $y_4 = 1.48$, $y_5 = 1.63$, $y_6 = 1.79$,
       $y_7 = 1.97$, $y_8 = 2.16$, $y_9 = 2.37$, $y_{10} = 2.60$.

19. a) $y_1 = 1.60$, $y_2 = 1.27$, $y_3 = 1.00$, $y_4 = 0.80$, $y_5 = 0.64$;

    b) $y_1 = 1.59$, $y_2 = 1.26$, $y_3 = 1.00$, $y_4 = 0.79$, $y_5 = 0.64$.

21. No method will provide a correct answer since the solution to the differential equation is the hyperbola $x^2 - 2xy - y^2 = 4$, which is not defined if $x = 1$.

23. The solution to the differential equation is $y = [x^2(2 - x^2)]^{-1/2}$, which is not defined at $x = 3$.

Section 7.2

1. (a) $|e_n| \leqslant 0.859h$; (b) $h = 0.1, |e_n| \leqslant 0.086$; $h = 0.2, |e_n| \leqslant 0.172$.

3. $|e_n| \leqslant 6.06h$; (a) $1{,}212{,}000$; (b) $12{,}120{,}000$.

Section 7.3

1. $a = \frac{1}{4}$, $b = 0$, $c = \frac{3}{4}$, $d = 0$ **3.** $n = p = \frac{2}{3}$

5. Because the determinant of the resulting 4×4 system is zero. There are an infinite number of solutions; no.

Section 7.4

1. $y = 2e^x - x - 1$, $y(1) = 2(e - 1) \approx 3.43656$;

   (a) $y = 3.43761$; (b) $y = 3.43022$.

3. $y^2 + 2xy - x^2 = 1$, $y(1) = \sqrt{3} - 1 \approx 0.73205$;

   (a) $y = 0.74146$; (b) $y = 0.74566$.

5. $y + \sqrt{y^2 + 1} = e^{(x^2-1)/2}$, $y(3) = (e^4 - e^{-4})/2 \approx 27.28992$;

   (a) $y = 26.19221$; (b) $y = 26.55498$.

7. $y = (x^3 + x^{-2})^{-1/2}$, $y(2) = 2/\sqrt{33} \approx 0.34816$;

   (a) $y = 0.34840$; (b) $y = 0.34465$.

9. $y = 2e^{e^x - 1}$, $y(2) = 2e^{e^2 - 1} \approx 1190.58883$;

   (a) $y = 1082.39224$; (b) $y = 1086.87818$.

Section 7.6

1. Exact solution: $x = e^{3t}(\cos 3t - \sin 3t)$, $y = e^{3t}(2 \cos 3t + \sin 3t)$,
   $x(1) = -22.719$, $y(1) = -36.935$

(a) $x = -17.43$,	(b) $x = -30.09$,	(c) $x = -19.17$,
$y = 7.76$	$y = -31.31$	$y = 4.67$

3. Exact solution: $x = (2/5)(e^{4t} - e^{-t})$, $y = (1/5)(3e^{4t} + 2e^{-t})$, $x(1) = 21.692$,
   $y(1) = 32.906$

(a) $x = 7.43$,	(b) $x = 16.98$,	(c) $x = 21.54$,
$y = 11.47$	$y = 25.84$	$y = 32.68$

5. Exact solution: $x = (1/27)(16e^{3t} + 9t^2 + 6t + 11)$,
   $y = (1/27)(16e^{3t} - 18t^2 - 21t - 16)$, $x(1) = 12.866$, $y(1) = 9.866$

(a) $x = 7.13$,	(b) $x = 11.58$,	(c) $x = 12.84$,
$y = 4.43$	$y = 8.61$	$y = 9.84$

7. Exact solution: $x = (33/8)(e^{2t} - 1) - (1/4)(t^2 + 9t)$,
   $y = (1/8)(27 - 11e^{2t}) + (1/4)(t^2 + 7t)$, $x(1) = 23.855$, $y(1) = -4.785$

(a) $x = 15.61$,	(b) $x = 22.67$,	(c) $x = 23.85$,
$y = -2.07$	$y = -4.39$	$y = -4.78$

9. $y(1) = 1.10$

11. Maximum satisfies $y(x) = \sqrt{2(y'(0) - x)}$. Exact solution can be obtained by transforming the Riccati equation $y' + y^2/2 = y'(0) - x$ and using Example 4 of Section 5.4.

Review Exercises for Chapter 7

1. $y^2 = 2(e^x + 1)$, $y(3) = \sqrt{2(e^3 + 1)} \approx 6.4939$;
   (a) $y_{IE} = 6.56$; (b) $y_{RK} = 6.4942$.

3. $y = x + \sqrt{1 + x^2}$, $y(3) = 3 + \sqrt{10} \approx 6.1623$;
   (a) $y_{IE} = 5.96$; (b) $y_{RK} = 6.1605$.

5. $y^{-2} = (2x - 1 + 3e^{-2x})/2$, $y(3) = 0.6320$;
   (a) $y_{IE} = 0.6356$; (b) $y_{RK} = 0.6329$.

7. The exact solution is $y^2(y + 1) = x^2$ with $y(6) = 3$. If we start at the initial condition on the graph of the solution curve and move to the right, we note that the branch does not continue to $x = 6$.

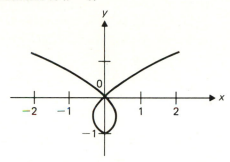

9. Solution $y = \tan x$ becomes infinite at $x = \pi/2$, so no numerical method will yield $y(2)$.

11. $y = \cos(\ln|x|) + \sin(\ln|x|)$, $y(2) = \cos(\ln 2) + \sin(\ln 2) \approx 1.4082$;
    (a) $y_E = 1.42163$; (b) $y_{RK} = 1.18$; (c) $y_{PC} = 1.39531$.

13. $x = \left(\dfrac{2 - \sqrt{2}}{4} \right) e^{(3 + \sqrt{8})t} + \left(\dfrac{2 + \sqrt{2}}{4} \right) e^{(3 - \sqrt{8})t}$,

    $y = \dfrac{\sqrt{2}}{4} e^{(3 + \sqrt{8})t} - \dfrac{\sqrt{2}}{4} e^{(3 - \sqrt{8})t}$,

    $x(2) \approx 16912.88$, $y(2) \approx 40827.91$.
    (a) $x_E = 333.57$, (b) $x_{RK} = 15783.45$, (c) $x_{PC} = 5090.404$,
      $y_E = 801.94$; $y_{RK} = 38101.20$; $y_{PC} = 12285.920$.

CHAPTER 8

Section 8.1

1. $\mathbf{x}'(t) = A\mathbf{x}(t)$; $A = \begin{pmatrix} 2 & 3 \\ 4 & -6 \end{pmatrix}$

3. $\mathbf{x}'(t) = A(t)\mathbf{x}(t) + \mathbf{f}(t)$; $A(t) = \begin{pmatrix} 0 & 1 & 0 \\ 0 & 0 & 1 \\ 1 & 4t & -2 \end{pmatrix}$; $\mathbf{f}(t) = \begin{pmatrix} 0 \\ 0 \\ \sin t \end{pmatrix}$

5. $\mathbf{x}'(t) = A(t)\mathbf{x}(t) + \mathbf{f}(t)$; $A(t) = \begin{pmatrix} 2t & -3t^2 & \sin t \\ 2 & 0 & -4 \\ 0 & 17 & 4t \end{pmatrix}$; $\mathbf{f}(t) = \begin{pmatrix} 0 \\ -\sin t \\ e^t \end{pmatrix}$

17. a) $\mathbf{x}'(t) = (1,\, \cos t)$; $\int \mathbf{x}(t)\, dt = \left(\dfrac{t^2}{2},\, -\cos t \right)$

b) $\mathbf{y}'(t) = \begin{pmatrix} e^t \\ -\sin t \\ \sec^2 t \end{pmatrix}$; $\int \mathbf{y}(t)\, dt = \begin{pmatrix} e^t \\ \sin t \\ -\ln|\cos t| \end{pmatrix}$

c) $A'(t) = \begin{pmatrix} \dfrac{1}{2\sqrt{t}} & 2t \\ 2e^{2t} & 2\cos 2t \end{pmatrix}$; $\int A(t)\, dt = \begin{pmatrix} \dfrac{2}{3} t^{3/2} & \dfrac{t^3}{3} \\ \dfrac{e^{2t}}{2} & \dfrac{-\cos 2t}{2} \end{pmatrix}$

d) $B'(t) = \begin{pmatrix} \dfrac{1}{t} & e^t(\sin t + \cos t) & e^t(-\sin t + \cos t) \\ \dfrac{5}{2} t^{3/2} & \sin t & -\cos t \\ -\dfrac{1}{t^2} & e^{t^2}(1 + 2t^2) & e^{t^3}(2t + 3t^4) \end{pmatrix}$;

$\int B(t)\, dt = \begin{pmatrix} t\ln|t| - t & \dfrac{1}{2} e^t(\sin t - \cos t) & \dfrac{1}{2} e^t(\sin t + \cos t) \\ \dfrac{2}{7} t^{7/2} & -\sin t & \cos t \\ \ln|t| & \dfrac{e^{t^2}}{2} & \dfrac{e^{t^3}}{3} \end{pmatrix}$

Section 8.2

1. Fundamental   **3.** Fundamental   **5.** Not fundamental

7. $C = \begin{pmatrix} 1 & -2 \\ -1 & 1 \end{pmatrix}$ **9.** $C = \begin{pmatrix} 1 & -1 & 1 \\ 0 & 1 & 1 \\ 1 & 0 & 0 \end{pmatrix}$

13. $\Psi(t) = e^{6t} \begin{pmatrix} \cos 2t - \sin t & \dfrac{1}{2}\sin t \\ -4\sin t & \cos 2t + \sin 2t \end{pmatrix}$

15. $\Psi(t) = \dfrac{1}{6} \begin{pmatrix} -e^{-t} + 9e^t - 2e^{2t} & -2e^{-t} + 2e^{2t} & 7e^{-t} - 9e^t + 2e^{2t} \\ 6e^t - 6e^{2t} & 6e^{2t} & -6e^t + 6e^{2t} \\ -e^{-t} + 3e^t - 2e^{2t} & -2e^{-t} + 2e^{2t} & 7e^{-t} - 3e^t + 2e^{2t} \end{pmatrix}$

17. a) $e^t \begin{pmatrix} 1 - 2t \\ 2 - 2t \end{pmatrix}$ **b)** $e^t \begin{pmatrix} -10t - 2 \\ -10t + 3 \end{pmatrix}$

c) $e^{t-1} \begin{pmatrix} 2 - 2t \\ 3 - 2t \end{pmatrix}$ **d)** $e^{t+1} \begin{pmatrix} 4 + 2t \\ 3 + 2t \end{pmatrix}$

e) $e^{t-3} \begin{pmatrix} 3 \\ 3 \end{pmatrix}$ **f)** $e^{t-a} \begin{pmatrix} 2(c - b)(a - t) + b \\ 2(c - b)(a - t) + c \end{pmatrix}$

19. a) $\mathbf{x}' = A(t)\mathbf{x}$, where $A(t) = \begin{pmatrix} 0 & 1 \\ -b(t) & -a(t) \end{pmatrix}$

21. $\varphi_2(t) = e^{t^2} \int e^{-t^2} \, dt$

Section 8.3

1. $-4, 3$: $E_{-4} = \text{span}\left\{ \begin{pmatrix} 1 \\ 1 \end{pmatrix} \right\}$; $E_3 = \text{span}\left\{ \begin{pmatrix} 2 \\ -5 \end{pmatrix} \right\}$

3. $i, -i$: $E_i = \text{span}\left\{ \begin{pmatrix} 2+i \\ 5 \end{pmatrix} \right\}$; $E_{-i} = \text{span}\left\{ \begin{pmatrix} 2-i \\ 5 \end{pmatrix} \right\}$

5. $-3, -3$; $E_{-3} = \text{span}\left\{ \begin{pmatrix} 1 \\ 0 \end{pmatrix} \right\}$

7. $0, 1, 3$; $E_0 = \text{span}\left\{ \begin{pmatrix} 1 \\ 1 \\ 1 \end{pmatrix} \right\}$; $E_1 = \text{span}\left\{ \begin{pmatrix} -1 \\ 0 \\ 1 \end{pmatrix} \right\}$;

$E_3 = \text{span}\left\{ \begin{pmatrix} 1 \\ -2 \\ 1 \end{pmatrix} \right\}$

9. $1, 1, 10$; $E_1 = \text{span}\left\{ \begin{pmatrix} 1 \\ 0 \\ -2 \end{pmatrix}, \begin{pmatrix} 0 \\ 1 \\ -2 \end{pmatrix} \right\}$; $E_{10} = \text{span}\left\{ \begin{pmatrix} 2 \\ 2 \\ 1 \end{pmatrix} \right\}$

11. $1, 1, 1$; $E_1 = \text{span}\left\{ \begin{pmatrix} 1 \\ 1 \\ 1 \end{pmatrix} \right\}$

13. $-1, i, -i$; $E_{-1} = \text{span}\left\{ \begin{pmatrix} 0 \\ -1 \\ 1 \end{pmatrix} \right\}$; $E_i = \text{span}\left\{ \begin{pmatrix} 1+i \\ 1 \\ 1 \end{pmatrix} \right\}$;

$E_{-i} = \text{span}\left\{ \begin{pmatrix} 1-i \\ 1 \\ 1 \end{pmatrix} \right\}$

15. $1, 2, 2$; $E_1 = \text{span}\left\{ \begin{pmatrix} 4 \\ 1 \\ -3 \end{pmatrix} \right\}$; $E_2 = \text{span}\left\{ \begin{pmatrix} 3 \\ 1 \\ -2 \end{pmatrix} \right\}$

17. $-1, -1, -1$; $E_{-1} = \text{span}\left\{ \begin{pmatrix} 3 \\ -6 \\ 2 \end{pmatrix} \right\}$

19. $2, 2, 4, 6$; $E_2 = \text{span}\left\{ \begin{pmatrix} -1 \\ 1 \\ 0 \\ 1 \end{pmatrix}, \begin{pmatrix} 0 \\ 0 \\ 1 \\ 0 \end{pmatrix} \right\}$;

$E_4 = \text{span}\left\{ \begin{pmatrix} 1 \\ 1 \\ 1 \\ -1 \end{pmatrix} \right\}$; $E_6 = \text{span}\left\{ \begin{pmatrix} 1 \\ 1 \\ -1 \\ 1 \end{pmatrix} \right\}$

21. $a, a, a, a;\ E_a = \text{span}\left\{\begin{pmatrix}1\\0\\0\\0\end{pmatrix}, \begin{pmatrix}0\\0\\1\\0\end{pmatrix}, \begin{pmatrix}0\\0\\0\\1\end{pmatrix}\right\}$

23. $a, a, a, a;\ E_a = \text{span}\left\{\begin{pmatrix}1\\0\\0\\0\end{pmatrix}\right\}$

25. $\begin{pmatrix}e^t & 3e^{-t}\\ e^t & 5e^{-t}\end{pmatrix}$

27. $\begin{pmatrix}1 & e^{4t}\\ 2 & -2e^{4t}\end{pmatrix}$

29. $\begin{pmatrix}e^t \cos t & e^t \sin t\\ e^t(2\cos t - \sin t) & e^t(2\sin t + \cos t)\end{pmatrix}$

31. $\begin{pmatrix}e^{-t} & 3e^t & e^{2t}\\ 0 & 2e^t & 3e^{2t}\\ e^{-t} & e^t & e^{2t}\end{pmatrix}$

45. $E_1 = \text{span}\left\{\begin{pmatrix}1\\0\\0\\0\end{pmatrix}, \begin{pmatrix}0\\1\\0\\0\end{pmatrix}, \begin{pmatrix}0\\0\\1\\0\end{pmatrix}, \begin{pmatrix}0\\0\\0\\1\end{pmatrix}\right\},$ $E_2 = \text{span}\left\{\begin{pmatrix}1\\0\\0\\0\end{pmatrix}, \begin{pmatrix}0\\0\\1\\0\end{pmatrix}, \begin{pmatrix}0\\0\\0\\1\end{pmatrix}\right\},$

$E_3 = \text{span}\left\{\begin{pmatrix}1\\0\\0\\0\end{pmatrix}, \begin{pmatrix}0\\0\\0\\1\end{pmatrix}\right\},$ $E_4 = \text{span}\left\{\begin{pmatrix}1\\0\\0\\0\end{pmatrix}\right\}$

Section 8.4

1. a) $p(\lambda) = \lambda^2 + \lambda - 12 = 0;$ c) $A^{-1} = \dfrac{1}{12}\begin{pmatrix}-1 & -2\\ -5 & 2\end{pmatrix}.$

3. a) $p(\lambda) = -\lambda^3 + 4\lambda^2 - 3\lambda = 0;$ c) A^{-1} does not exist.

5. a) $p(\lambda) = -\lambda^3 + 3\lambda^2 - 3\lambda + 1 = 0;$ c) $A^{-1} = \begin{pmatrix}3 & -3 & 1\\ 1 & 0 & 0\\ 0 & 1 & 0\end{pmatrix}.$

7. a) $p(\lambda) = -\lambda^3 + 6\lambda^2 + 18\lambda + 9 = 0;$ c) $A^{-1} = \dfrac{1}{9}\begin{pmatrix}-27 & 18 & -9\\ -6 & 3 & 0\\ 19 & -11 & 6\end{pmatrix}.$

9. a) $p(\lambda) = (a - \lambda)^4 = 0;$ c) $A^{-1} = \begin{pmatrix}1/a & -b/a^2 & cb/a^3 & -bcd/a^4\\ 0 & 1/a & -c/a^2 & cd/a^3\\ 0 & 0 & 1/a & -d/a^2\\ 0 & 0 & 0 & 1/a\end{pmatrix}.$

Section 8.5

1. $\dfrac{1}{7}\begin{pmatrix}5e^{-4t} + 2e^{3t} & 2e^{-4t} - 2e^{3t}\\ 5e^{-4t} - 5e^{3t} & 2e^{-4t} + 5e^{3t}\end{pmatrix}$ 3. $\begin{pmatrix}2\sin t + \cos t & -\sin t\\ 5\sin t & -2\sin t + \cos t\end{pmatrix}$

5. $e^{-t}\begin{pmatrix} 1+4t & -2t \\ 8t & -4t+1 \end{pmatrix}$

7. $e^{-t}\begin{pmatrix} 3/4 + t \\ 1 + 2t \end{pmatrix}$

9. $e^{-t}\begin{pmatrix} 2-2t \\ 5-4t \end{pmatrix}$

11. $\dfrac{1}{6}\begin{pmatrix} 2+3e^t+e^{3t} & 2-2e^{3t} & 2-3e^t+e^{3t} \\ 2-2e^{3t} & 2+4e^{3t} & 2-2e^{3t} \\ 2-3e^t+e^{3t} & 2-2e^{3t} & 2+3e^t+e^{3t} \end{pmatrix}$

13. $\begin{pmatrix} 4e^t-3e^{2t}+6te^{2t} & -12e^t+12e^{2t}-6te^{2t} & 6te^{2t} \\ e^t-e^{2t}+2te^{2t} & -3e^t+4e^{2t}-2te^{2t} & 2te^{2t} \\ -3e^t+3e^{2t}-4te^{2t} & 9e^t-9e^{2t}+4te^{2t} & -4te^{2t}+e^{2t} \end{pmatrix}$

15. $\dfrac{1}{9}\begin{pmatrix} 5e^t+4e^{10t} & -4e^t+4e^{10t} & -2e^t+2e^{10t} \\ -4e^t+4e^{10t} & 5e^t+4e^{10t} & -2e^t+2e^{10t} \\ -2e^t+2e^{10t} & -2e^t+2e^{10t} & 8e^t+e^{10t} \end{pmatrix}$

17. $\dfrac{1}{2}\begin{pmatrix} e^{2t}+e^{6t} & -e^{2t}+e^{4t} & 0 & -e^{4t}+e^{6t} \\ -e^{2t}+e^{6t} & e^{2t}+e^{4t} & 0 & -e^{4t}+e^{6t} \\ e^{2t}-e^{6t} & -e^{2t}+e^{4t} & 2e^{2t} & 2e^{2t}-e^{4t}-e^{6t} \\ -e^{2t}+e^{6t} & e^{2t}-e^{4t} & 0 & e^{4t}+e^{6t} \end{pmatrix}$

19. $\dfrac{1}{6}\begin{pmatrix} 4+2e^{3t} \\ 4-4e^{3t} \\ 4+2e^{3t} \end{pmatrix}$

21. $\begin{pmatrix} -4e^t+3e^{2t}+6te^{2t} \\ -e^t+e^{2t}+2te^{2t} \\ 3e^t-e^{2t}-4te^{2t} \end{pmatrix}$

Section 8.6

1. $\varphi_p(t)=\begin{pmatrix} \dfrac{e^{2t}}{3} \\ \dfrac{e^t}{2}-\dfrac{2}{3}e^{2t} \end{pmatrix}$

3. $\varphi(t)=\begin{pmatrix} -t\cos t \\ -t\sin t-2t\cos t+\cos t+\sin t \end{pmatrix}$

5. $\varphi(t)=\begin{pmatrix} -\dfrac{3}{2}e^{-t}+\dfrac{7}{4}e^t+\dfrac{3}{2}te^t+\dfrac{1}{3}te^{2t}-\dfrac{1}{9}e^{2t}-\dfrac{1}{8}e^{3t} \\ 2e^t+te^t+te^{2t}+\dfrac{1}{2}e^{3t} \\ -\dfrac{3}{2}e^{-t}+\dfrac{3}{4}e^t+\dfrac{1}{2}te^t-\dfrac{1}{9}e^{2t}+\dfrac{1}{3}te^{2t}+\dfrac{3}{8}e^{3t} \end{pmatrix}$

7. $\varphi_p(t)=\begin{pmatrix} t \\ t^2 \\ t^4 \end{pmatrix}$

9. $\varphi_p(t)=\begin{pmatrix} -5\sin t \ln|\csc t+\cot t| \\ 1-(2\sin t-\cos t)\ln|\csc t+\cot t| \end{pmatrix}$

11. $\Phi(t)=\begin{pmatrix} 1/t & \ln t/t \\ -1/t^2 & (1-\ln t)/t^2 \end{pmatrix}$

Section 8.7

1. $\mathbf{x}(t) = -\dfrac{1}{5}\begin{pmatrix} 12 + 11i \\ 6 + 2i \end{pmatrix} e^{it}$

3. $\mathbf{x}(t) = -\dfrac{1}{754}\begin{pmatrix} 353 + 205i \\ -197 - 595i \end{pmatrix} e^{-5it}$

9. a) Let $x_1 = x$, $x_2 = x'$, then $\begin{pmatrix} x_1 \\ x_2 \end{pmatrix}' = \begin{pmatrix} 0 & 1 \\ -\lambda/m & 0 \end{pmatrix}\begin{pmatrix} x_1 \\ x_2 \end{pmatrix} + \begin{pmatrix} 0 \\ k/m \end{pmatrix} e^{i\omega t}.$

   b) $\mathbf{x}(t) = \dfrac{k}{\lambda - \omega^2 m}\begin{pmatrix} 1 \\ i\omega \end{pmatrix} e^{i\omega t};$

   c) $\Psi(t) = \begin{pmatrix} \cos\sqrt{\lambda/m}\,t & \sqrt{\lambda/m}\,\sin\sqrt{\lambda/m}\,t \\ -\sqrt{\lambda/m}\,\sin\sqrt{\lambda/m}\,t & \cos\sqrt{\lambda/m}\,t \end{pmatrix}.$ Resonance.

Review Exercises for Chapter 8

1. $\begin{pmatrix} x_1 \\ x_2 \end{pmatrix}' = \begin{pmatrix} 3 & -4 \\ -2 & 7 \end{pmatrix}\begin{pmatrix} x_1 \\ x_2 \end{pmatrix}$

3. $\begin{pmatrix} x_1 \\ x_2 \end{pmatrix}' = \begin{pmatrix} 1 & 1 \\ -3 & 2 \end{pmatrix}\begin{pmatrix} x_1 \\ x_2 \end{pmatrix} + \begin{pmatrix} e^t \\ e^{2t} \end{pmatrix}$

5. a) $\dfrac{1}{5}\begin{pmatrix} -2e^t + 12e^{6t} \\ 3e^t + 12e^{6t} \end{pmatrix};$

   b) $\dfrac{1}{5}\begin{pmatrix} -2e^t - 3e^{6t} \\ 3e^t - 3e^{6t} \end{pmatrix};$

   c) $\begin{pmatrix} 0 \\ 0 \end{pmatrix};$

   d) $\dfrac{1}{5}\begin{pmatrix} 18e^t + 17e^{6t} \\ -27e^t + 17e^{6t} \end{pmatrix};$

   e) $\dfrac{1}{5}\begin{pmatrix} 2(a - b)e^t + (3a + 2b)e^{6t} \\ -3(a - b)e^t + (3a + 2b)e^{6t} \end{pmatrix}.$

7. $2, 2;\ E_2 = \text{span}\left\{\begin{pmatrix} 1 \\ 0 \end{pmatrix}\right\}$

9. $1, -1, 2;\ E_1 = \text{span}\left\{\begin{pmatrix} 1 \\ 0 \\ -1 \end{pmatrix}\right\};\ E_{-1} = \text{span}\left\{\begin{pmatrix} -1 \\ 2 \\ -7 \end{pmatrix}\right\};\ E_2 = \text{span}\left\{\begin{pmatrix} 1 \\ -1 \\ -1 \end{pmatrix}\right\}$

11. $-2, -2, -2;\ E_{-2} = \text{span}\left\{\begin{pmatrix} 1 \\ 0 \\ 0 \end{pmatrix}\right\}$

13. $e^{At} = e^{2t}\begin{pmatrix} \dfrac{1}{3}\sin 3t + \cos 3t & -\dfrac{5}{3}\sin 3t \\ \dfrac{2}{3}\sin 3t & -\dfrac{1}{3}\sin 3t + \cos 3t \end{pmatrix}$

15. $e^{At} = e^{-2t}\begin{pmatrix} 1 - 2t & 4t \\ -t & 1 + 2t \end{pmatrix}$

17. $e^{At} = e^t\begin{pmatrix} 1 - 2t - \dfrac{15}{2}t^2 & 2t + \dfrac{5t^2}{2} & t + \dfrac{3t^2}{2} \\ -7t - \dfrac{17t^2}{2} & 1 + 3t + \dfrac{t^2}{2} & 2t + \dfrac{t^2}{2} \\ -5t - 8t^2 & 3t + t^2 & 1 + t + t^2 \end{pmatrix}$

19. $e^{At} = \dfrac{e^{-t}}{2}\begin{pmatrix} 0 & 0 & 0 \\ 0 & 1 & -1 \\ 0 & -1 & 1 \end{pmatrix} + \dfrac{\cos t}{2}\begin{pmatrix} 2 & 0 & 0 \\ 0 & 1 & 1 \\ 0 & 1 & 1 \end{pmatrix} + \dfrac{\sin t}{2}\begin{pmatrix} 2 & 2 & 2 \\ -2 & -1 & -1 \\ -2 & -1 & -1 \end{pmatrix}$

21. $e^{At} = \begin{pmatrix} \frac{1}{2} & -\frac{1}{2} & 0 \\ -\frac{1}{2} & \frac{1}{2} & 0 \\ 0 & 0 & 0 \end{pmatrix} + e^{-3t}\begin{pmatrix} 0 & 0 & 0 \\ 0 & 0 & 0 \\ 0 & 0 & 1 \end{pmatrix} + e^{4t}\begin{pmatrix} \frac{1}{2} & \frac{1}{2} & 0 \\ \frac{1}{2} & \frac{1}{2} & 0 \\ 0 & 0 & 0 \end{pmatrix}$

23. $e^{At} = e^{-6t}\begin{pmatrix} 0 & 0 & 0 & 0 \\ 0 & 0 & 0 & 0 \\ 0 & 0 & 1 & 0 \\ 0 & 0 & 0 & 1 \end{pmatrix}\begin{pmatrix} 1+9t & t & 0 & 0 \\ 0 & 1+9t & 0 & 0 \\ 0 & 0 & 1 & t \\ 0 & 0 & 0 & 1 \end{pmatrix}$

$\qquad + e^{3t}\begin{pmatrix} 1 & 1 & 0 & 0 \\ 1 & 1 & 0 & 0 \\ 0 & 0 & 0 & 0 \\ 0 & 0 & 0 & 0 \end{pmatrix}\begin{pmatrix} 1 & t & 0 & 0 \\ 0 & 1 & 0 & 0 \\ 0 & 0 & 1-9t & t \\ 0 & 0 & 0 & 1-9t \end{pmatrix}$

25. $\frac{1}{3}\begin{pmatrix} 2e^{2t}+e^{5t} & e^{2t}-e^{5t} \\ 2e^{2t}-2e^{5t} & e^{2t}+2e^{5t} \end{pmatrix}$

27. $e^{-2t}\begin{pmatrix} -5t^2+t+1 & \frac{5t^2}{2}-18t & \frac{-5t^2}{2}-7t \\ -3t^2+t & \frac{3t^2}{2}-11t+1 & \frac{-3t^2}{2}-4t \\ 7t^2-t & \frac{-7t^2}{2}+25t & \frac{7t^2}{2}+10t+1 \end{pmatrix}$

29. $e^{2t}\begin{pmatrix} 3\cos 2t + \frac{19}{8}\sin 2t + \frac{1}{4}t \\ -6\sin 2t + \frac{19}{4}\cos 2t - \frac{11}{4} \end{pmatrix}$

CHAPTER 9
Section 9.1

1. (a) $x' = x$; (b) $x = 0, x = 1$; (c) $x(t) = \dfrac{x(0)e^t}{x(0)e^t + 1 - x(0)}$.

3. (a) $x' = 2x$; (b) $x = 0, x = -\dfrac{2}{3}$; (c) $x(t) = \dfrac{2x(0)e^{2t}}{2 + 3x(0)(1 - e^{2t})}$.

5. (a) $x' = 2x$; (b) $x = 0, x = 1, x = 2$;

(c) $\dfrac{x^2 - 2x}{(x-1)^2} = ce^{2t}$ where $c = \dfrac{x(0)^2 - 2x(0)}{(x(0)-1)^2}$.

7. a) The orbits are the circles $x^2 + y^2 = a^2 + b^2$.

9. The orbits are $x = \exp\left[\dfrac{1}{2}(\ln^2 y - 2t_0 \ln y)\right]$.

Section 9.2

1. Saddle point

3. Unstable focus

5. Stable focus

7. Unstable focus

15. a) $x = c_1, y = c_1 + c_2 e^t$;

c) (c, c) is a critical point for any real number c.

Section 9.3

1. $(0, 0)$ is a saddle point (unstable).   3. $(0, 0)$ is unstable.

5. $(0, 0)$ is an unstable node.

7. $(0, 0)$ is the only critical point and is an unstable node or focus.

9. $(0, 0)$ is an unstable node or focus, $\left(0, \frac{1}{3}\right)$ and $(1, 0)$ are saddle points and $\left(\frac{8}{7}, \frac{1}{7}\right)$ is a stable focus.

11. $(0, 0)$, $(3, -9)$ and $(-2, -4)$ are saddle points; $(1, -1)$ is a stable focus and $(-1, -1)$ is an unstable focus.

13. $(0, 0)$ is the only critical point and is a stable focus.

Section 9.4

1. Let $V(x, y) = x^2 + 2y^2$.   3. Let $V(x, y) = \frac{y^2}{2} + \omega^2(1 - \cos x)$.

5. (a) Unstable;   (b) Asymptotically stable;   (c) Stable.

7. Let $V(x, y) = \frac{y^2}{2} + \int_0^x g(x)\, dx$.

Review Exercises for Chapter 9

1. (a) $x' = x$;   (b) $x \equiv 0$, $x \equiv -1$;

   (c) $x(t) = [(x(0)^{-1} + 1)e^{-t} - 1]^{-1}$;

   (d) Solutions become infinite as $t \to \ln \dfrac{x(0) + 1}{x(0)}$.

3. (a) $x' = x$;   (b) $x \equiv 0$, $x \equiv 1$, $x \equiv -1$;

   (c) $x(t) = \sqrt{\dfrac{1}{1 - ke^t}}$ where $k = \dfrac{x^2(0) - 1}{x^2(0)}$;

   (d) Solutions become infinite as $t \to \ln \dfrac{x^2(0)}{x^2(0) - 1}$.

5. Stable node   7. Stable node (star-shaped)

9. $(0, 0)$ is a saddle point (unstable).

11. $(0, 0)$ is a saddle point; $\left(\dfrac{1}{\sqrt{2}}, 0\right)$ and $\left(-\dfrac{1}{\sqrt{2}}, 0\right)$ are unstable (star-shaped) nodes.

13. $(0, 0)$ is a saddle point; $(3, 4)$ is a saddle point; $(0, 5/2)$ is a stable node; $(1, 0)$ is an unstable node.

CHAPTER 10

Section 10.1

1. Yes; $\delta = \dfrac{1}{216}$ $\left(\text{better: } \delta = \dfrac{1}{50}\right)$

3. Yes, but $a = b = 1$ is not possible. You need $a + b < 1$. If $a = b = \frac{1}{3}$, then $\delta = \frac{1}{4}$.

5. Yes; $\delta = 1$

7. Yes, but you need $b < 1$. If $b = \frac{1}{2}$, then $\delta = 1$.

9. Yes; $\delta = \frac{1}{2}$ (better: $\delta = +\infty$; there is a unique solution defined for $-\infty < t < \infty$).

11. (a) $k = 1$;   (b) $k = 1$;

    (c) $k = 3$ $\left(\text{a smaller constant is } \sup_{|x| \leqslant 1} \left| 2x \sin \frac{1}{x} - \cos \frac{1}{x} \right| \right)$;

    (d) $972 \sqrt{3} \approx 1683$.

13. $x_n(t) = 3 \sum_{k=0}^{n} \frac{(t-3)^k}{k!}$

Section 10.2

9. (a) $\begin{pmatrix} x_1 \\ x_2 \end{pmatrix}' = \begin{pmatrix} tx_1 x_2 + t^2 \\ x_1^2 + x_2^2 + t \end{pmatrix}$; $x(0) = \begin{pmatrix} 1 \\ 2 \end{pmatrix}$

    (b) $k = 10$;   (c) $\delta = \frac{1}{7\sqrt{5}} \approx 0.064$.

11. (a) $\begin{pmatrix} x_1 \\ x_2 \\ x_3 \end{pmatrix}' = \begin{pmatrix} x_1^2 x_2 \\ x_3 + t \\ x_3^2 \end{pmatrix}$; $x(0) = c$;

    (b) $k \leqslant \max_{\substack{1 \leqslant i \leqslant 3 \\ (t, x) \& D}} \left| \frac{\partial f}{\partial x_i} \right| \leqslant \max \{1 + a, 2(b + |c|)^2\}$;

    (c) $\delta = \min \left\{ a, \frac{b}{M} \right\}$ where $M \leqslant ((b + |c|)^6 + (b + |c| + a)^2 + (b + |c|)^4)$.

Review Exercises for Chapter 10

1. $k = 1$ 3. $k = 2$ 5. $k = \frac{3}{2} e^{\sqrt{3}} \approx 8.48$

7. Yes; $\delta = \frac{1}{625}$ 9. Yes; $\delta = 1$

11. Yes; $\delta = \frac{1}{|\tan 2|} \approx 0.458$

13. (a) $\begin{pmatrix} x_1 \\ x_2 \end{pmatrix}' = \begin{pmatrix} tx_1 + x_2 + t^3 \\ x_1^2 + x_2^2 + t^2 \end{pmatrix}$, $x(0) = \begin{pmatrix} 2 \\ 3 \end{pmatrix}$;

    (b) $k = 14$;

    (c) Choosing $a = b = 1$, $\delta = \frac{1}{\sqrt{64 + 2500}} \approx 0.01975$.

CHAPTER 11
Section 11.1

1. Eigenvalues: $\left(\dfrac{n\pi}{T}\right)^2$, eigenfunctions: $A \sin \dfrac{n\pi t}{T}$, $n = 1, 2, 3, \ldots$

3. Eigenvalues: $-\left(\dfrac{n\pi}{T}\right)^2$, eigenfunctions: $A \sin \dfrac{n\pi t}{T}$, $n = 1, 2, 3, \ldots$

5. Eigenvalues: $\left(\dfrac{n\pi}{2T}\right)^2$, eigenfunctions: $A \sin \dfrac{n\pi(t + T)}{2T}$, $n = 1, 2, 3, \ldots$

Section 11.2

1. $\dfrac{1}{\sqrt{2\pi}}, \dfrac{\cos x}{\sqrt{\pi}}, \dfrac{\cos 2x}{\sqrt{\pi}}, \ldots$ 3. $\dfrac{1}{\sqrt{T}}, \sqrt{\dfrac{2}{T}} \cos \dfrac{\pi x}{T}, \sqrt{\dfrac{2}{T}} \cos \dfrac{2\pi x}{T}, \ldots$

5. $\sqrt{\dfrac{1}{\pi}}, \sqrt{\dfrac{2}{\pi}} \cos 2x, \sqrt{\dfrac{2}{\pi}} \cos 4x, \ldots$

7. a) $\sinh (1)P_0(x) + \dfrac{3}{e} P_1(x) + \dfrac{5}{2}\left(e - \dfrac{7}{e}\right) P_2(x)$

   b) $3 \sin (1)P_1(x) + 15 \sin (1)P_2(x)$

   c) $\sin (1)P_0(x) + [15 \cos (1) - 10 \sin (1)]P_2(x)$

   d) $3[\cosh (1) - \sinh (1)]P_1(x)$

   e) $\sinh (1)P_0(x) + [20 \sinh (1) - 15 \cosh (1)]P_2(x)$

   f) $\dfrac{\pi}{4} P_0(x) - \dfrac{5}{2}(3 - \pi)P_2(x)$

Section 11.3

1. $\pi, 2, T/n, 1/k$ 3. $2bT/a$

5. $2\left(\sin x - \dfrac{1}{2} \sin 2x + \dfrac{1}{3} \sin 3x - \dfrac{1}{4} \sin 4x + \cdots\right)$

7. $\dfrac{\pi^2}{3} - 4\left(\cos x - \dfrac{1}{4} \cos 2x + \dfrac{1}{9} \cos 3x - \dfrac{1}{16} \cos 4x + \cdots\right)$

9. $\dfrac{\pi}{2} - \dfrac{4}{\pi}\left[\cos x + \dfrac{1}{3^2} \cos 3x + \dfrac{1}{5^2} \cos 5x + \cdots\right]$

11. $\dfrac{2}{\pi}\left[(1 + \sin (\pi - 1)) \sin x - \dfrac{1}{2}\left(1 + \dfrac{1}{2} \sin 2(\pi - 1)\right) \sin 2x\right.$

   $\left. + \dfrac{1}{3}\left(1 + \dfrac{1}{3} \sin 3(\pi - 1)\right) \sin 3x - \cdots\right]$

13. $\dfrac{\sinh \pi}{\pi}\left[1 + 2 \displaystyle\sum_{n=1}^{\infty} \dfrac{(-1)^n}{1 + n^2} \cos nx - 2 \displaystyle\sum_{n=1}^{\infty} \dfrac{n(-1)^n}{1 + n^2} \sin nx\right]$

15. $1 - \dfrac{2}{\pi} \displaystyle\sum_{n=1}^{\infty} \dfrac{\sin n\pi x}{n}$ 17. $\dfrac{1}{3} + \dfrac{4}{\pi^2} \displaystyle\sum_{n=1}^{\infty} \dfrac{(-1)^n}{n^2} \cos n\pi x$

19. $\frac{1}{2} - \frac{2}{\pi} \left(\sin \pi x + \frac{1}{3} \sin 3\pi x + \frac{1}{5} \sin 5\pi x + \cdots \right)$

21. $\frac{3}{4} - \frac{1}{\pi} \sum_{n=1}^{\infty} \frac{1}{n} \sin n\pi x - \frac{2}{\pi^2} \left(\cos \pi x + \frac{1}{3^2} \cos 3\pi x + \frac{1}{5^2} \cos 5\pi x + \cdots \right)$

Section 11.4

1. $\lambda_k = k^2,\, y_k = A \sin kx,\, k = 1, 2, 3, \ldots$

3. $\lambda_k = k^2,\, y_k = A \sin k\left(x + \frac{\pi}{2} \right),\, k = 1, 2, 3, \ldots$

5. $\lambda_k = \frac{k^2 \pi^2}{4},\, y_k = A \sin \left(\frac{k\pi \ln x}{2} \right),\, k = 1, 2, 3, \ldots$

7. $\lambda_k = k^2 \pi^2,\, y_k = A \sin \frac{k\pi}{x},\, k = 1, 2, 3, \ldots$

Section 11.5

1. $\lambda_k = k^2$ are real and simple, $y_k = A \sin kx,\, k = 1, 2, 3, \ldots,$ are orthogonal.

3. $\lambda_k = k^2$ are real and simple, $y_k = A \sin k\left(x + \frac{\pi}{2} \right),\, k = 1, 2, 3, \ldots,$ are orthogonal.

5. $\lambda_k = k^2 \pi^2$ are real and simple, $y_k = A \sin \frac{k\pi}{x},\, k = 1, 2, 3, \ldots,$ are orthogonal with respect to $1/x^2$ on $1/2 \leqslant x \leqslant 1$.

9. $\lambda \neq 1$, since $y = Ax + Bx \ln x$ cannot satisfy the boundary condition. Use Eq. (11) of Section 3.5 with $\lambda = \lambda_1 + i\lambda_2$. Then $\lambda_1 = 1$ and $\lambda_2 = \pm \frac{2k\pi}{\ln 2},\, k = 1, 2, 3, \ldots$.

Section 11.6

5. Yes, trivially   **7.** Infinitely many

Section 11.7

1. $\displaystyle \sum_{k=1}^{\infty} \frac{2(-1)^k}{k(k^2 - 1)} \sin kx$

3. $\displaystyle 4 \sum_{k=1}^{\infty} \frac{\left[1 + (-1)^k \left(\frac{2k-1}{2} \pi \right) \right]}{\left(\frac{2k-1}{2} \pi \right)^3 \left[\left(\frac{2k-1}{4} \pi \right)^2 - 1 \right]} \sin \left(\frac{2k-1}{2} \right) \pi x$

5. $\displaystyle 2(\ln 2)^2 \sin (\ln 2)\pi \sum_{k=1}^{\infty} \frac{(-1)^k k}{[3(\ln 2)^2 - (k\pi)^2][(\ln 2)^2 - (k\pi)^2]} \sin \left(\frac{k\pi}{\ln 2} \ln x \right)$

13. $K(x, t) = \begin{cases} -\dfrac{\sinh(1-t)\sinh x}{\sinh(1)}, & x < t, \\[3mm] -\dfrac{\sinh(1-x)\sinh t}{\sinh(1)}, & t < x \end{cases}$

17. $K(x, t) = \begin{cases} -\dfrac{\sin 2x \cos 2(1-t)}{2\cos 2}, & x < t, \\[3mm] -\dfrac{\cos 2(1-x)\sin 2t}{2\cos 2}, & t < x \end{cases}$

Review Exercises for Chapter 11

1. $\left\{ \sqrt{\dfrac{2}{\pi}} \sin nx \right\}$ **3.** $\left\{ \sqrt{2} \sin 2n\pi x, \ \sqrt{2} \cos 2n\pi x \right\}$

5. $-1 + \pi \sin x - \dfrac{1}{2} \cos x + 2 \displaystyle\sum_{n=2}^{\infty} \dfrac{\cos nx}{n^2 - 1}$

7. $\dfrac{2}{\pi} \left[1 - 2 \displaystyle\sum_{n=1}^{\infty} \dfrac{\cos 2nx}{4n^2 - 1} \right]$

9. $2\pi \displaystyle\sum_{n=1}^{\infty} \left\{ \left(\dfrac{1}{2n-1} - \dfrac{4}{(2n-1)^{2n-1}\,\pi^2} \right) \sin(2n-1)x - \dfrac{1}{2^n} \sin 2nx \right\};$

$\dfrac{\pi^2}{3} + 4 \displaystyle\sum_{n=1}^{\infty} \dfrac{(-1)}{n^2} \cos nx$

11. $\dfrac{2}{\pi} \displaystyle\sum_{n=1}^{\infty} \dfrac{(-1)^{n-1}}{n} \sin n\pi x; \ \dfrac{-4}{\pi^2} \displaystyle\sum_{n=1}^{\infty} \dfrac{1}{(2n-1)^2} \cos(2n-1)\pi x$

13. $\dfrac{-32}{\pi^3} \left(\sin \dfrac{\pi x}{2} + \dfrac{\pi^2}{8} \sin \dfrac{2\pi x}{2} + \dfrac{1}{3^3} \sin \dfrac{3\pi x}{2} + \dfrac{\pi^2}{16} \sin \dfrac{4\pi x}{2} + \cdots \right);$

$\pi^3 = 32 \left(1 - \dfrac{1}{3^3} + \dfrac{1}{5^3} - \dfrac{1}{7^3} + \cdots \right)$

15. $\lambda_n = \dfrac{(2n-1)^2}{4}, \ y_n(x) = \cos \dfrac{(2n-1)x}{2}, \ n = 1, 2, 3, \ldots$

17. $y_n(x) = \sin \sqrt{\lambda_n}\, x$, where λ_n are the roots of $\tan k = -k$.

For large n, $\sqrt{\lambda_n} \approx \dfrac{(2n-1)\pi}{2}$.

19. Same as Exercise 17.

21. Multiply by the weight function $q(x) = 1/\sqrt{1 - x^2}$ to get

$$(\sqrt{1 - x^2}\, y')' + \frac{n^2}{\sqrt{1 - x^2}}\, y = 0.$$

Since $r(x) = \sqrt{1 - x^2}$ vanishes at ± 1, no boundary conditions are needed for the orthogonality theorem to apply. The Chebyshev polynomials are orthogonal with respect to the weight function $q(x)$ over the interval $[-1, 1]$.

CHAPTER 12
Section 12.1

1. $W(x, y) = \dfrac{7}{2} + e^{x + (5/4)y} - \dfrac{7}{2} e^{y/2}$ **3.** $W(x, y) = ye^x$

Section 12.2

1. -0.0075 m   **3.** 0.0 m

5. 0.1 m   **9.** $-\dfrac{0.045}{\pi}$ m

11. $\dfrac{0.03}{\pi}\left[\dfrac{\pi}{6} - \dfrac{1}{4}\right]$ m

Section 12.3

1. $T(x, t) = \dfrac{4}{\pi} \displaystyle\sum_{n=1}^{\infty} \dfrac{[1 - (-1)^n]}{n^3}\,(\sin nx)e^{-n^2 \delta t}$

3. $T(x, t) = 4 \displaystyle\sum_{n=1}^{\infty} \left(\dfrac{2(-1)^{n+1} - 1}{n^3}\right)(\sin nx)e^{-n^2 \delta t}$

5. $T(x, t) = \dfrac{2}{\pi} \displaystyle\sum_{n=1}^{\infty} \dfrac{1}{n^2}\left[\sin \dfrac{n\pi}{2} - \dfrac{n\pi}{2}\cos\left(\dfrac{n\pi}{2}\right)\right](\sin nx)e^{-n^2 \delta t}$

7. $[(L - x)T_1 + xT_2]/L$

9. $f(x) = \dfrac{c_0^2}{T_1}\cos cx + c_0 c_2 \sin cx$, where $c_2 = c_0(1 - \cos cL)/T \sin cL$. If cL is a multiple of π, then c_2 is arbitrary.

11. $y(x, t) = e^{kx + (t/k)}$ **13.** $y(x, t) = e^{x - kt}(c_1 e^{\sqrt{1 + k}x} + c_2 e^{-\sqrt{1 + k}x})$

15. $y(x, t) = \sqrt{x}(c_1 e^{\sqrt{k}t} + c_2 e^{-\sqrt{k}t})(b_1 x^{\sqrt{1 + 4k}/2} + b_2 x^{-\sqrt{1 + 4k}/2})$

Section 12.4

1. $T(x, y) = \dfrac{100}{\pi} \displaystyle\sum_{n=1}^{\infty} \left(\dfrac{1-(-1)^n}{n \sinh n\pi} \right) \sin \dfrac{n\pi x}{L} \sinh \dfrac{n\pi y}{L}$, where we evaluate at $\left(\dfrac{L}{2}, \dfrac{L}{2} \right)$

and $\left(\dfrac{L}{4}, \dfrac{L}{4} \right)$.

3. $T(x, y) = \dfrac{100}{\sinh \pi} \sin \dfrac{\pi x}{L} \sinh \dfrac{\pi y}{L}$

5. a) $A_0 = 1$, $A_2 = -\dfrac{1}{2}$, all other coefficients are zero, so that

$T(r, \theta) = \dfrac{1}{2}(1 - r^2 \cos 2\theta)$. Hence $T\left(\dfrac{1}{2}, 0 \right) = \dfrac{3}{8}^{\circ}$.

b) $T\left(\dfrac{1}{2}, 0 \right) = \dfrac{3}{8\pi} \displaystyle\int_{-\pi}^{\pi} \dfrac{\sin^2 \varphi}{5/4 - \cos \varphi}\, d\varphi = \dfrac{3}{8}^{\circ}$. This last equality can be proved

using the calculus of residues.

7. a) $T(r, \theta) = -\dfrac{\pi^2}{3} - 4 \displaystyle\sum_{n=1}^{\infty} (-r)^n \left(\dfrac{\cos n\theta}{n^2} + \dfrac{\pi \sin n\theta}{n} \right)$

b) $T(r, \theta) = \dfrac{1-r^2}{2\pi} \displaystyle\int_{-\pi}^{\pi} \dfrac{\varphi(2\pi - \varphi)\, d\varphi}{r^2 + 1 - 2r \cos (\theta - \varphi)}$

Section 12.5

1. $y(x, t) = t$ 3. $T(x, t) = 1 - \text{erf} \left(\dfrac{x}{2\sqrt{\delta t}} \right)$

5. $T(x, t) = \displaystyle\int_{0}^{t} \sin \omega (t - u)\, \dfrac{x}{2\sqrt{\pi \delta u^3}}\, e^{-x^2/4\delta u}\, du$

Review Exercises for Chapter 12

1. $w(x, y) = xe^y$ 3. $w(x, y) = x + e^y$

5. $T(x, t) = \dfrac{4a^2}{\pi^3} \displaystyle\sum_{n=1}^{\infty} \dfrac{[1-(-1)^n]}{n^3} \sin \dfrac{n\pi x}{a} e^{-(n\pi/a)^2\, \delta t}$

7. $T(x, t) = \dfrac{4a}{\pi^2} \displaystyle\sum_{n=0}^{\infty} \dfrac{(-1)^n}{(2n+1)^2} \sin \dfrac{(2n+1)\pi x}{a} e^{-[(2n+1)\pi/a]^2 \delta t}$

9. $y = X(x)T(t)$ where the general solutions to X and T are

$$X(x) = \begin{cases} c_1 x^{\lambda_1} + c_2 x^{\lambda_2}, & k > -\frac{1}{4} \\ c_1 \sqrt{x} + c_2 \sqrt{x} \ln x, & k = -\frac{1}{4} \\ \sqrt{x}\,[c_1 \cos(\ln|x|^{\beta}) + c_2 \sin(\ln|x|^{\beta})], & k < -\frac{1}{4}, \end{cases}$$

$$T(t) = \begin{cases} b_1 t^{\lambda_1} + b_2 t^{\lambda_2}, & k > -\frac{1}{4} \\ b_1 \sqrt{t} + b_2 \sqrt{t} \ln t, & k = -\frac{1}{4} \\ \sqrt{t}\,[b_1 \cos(\ln|t|^{\beta}) + b_2 \sin(\ln|t|^{\beta})], & k < -\frac{1}{4}, \end{cases}$$

where $\left.\begin{matrix} \lambda_1 \\ \lambda_2 \end{matrix}\right\} = \dfrac{1 \pm \sqrt{1+4k}}{2}$, respectively, and $\beta = \dfrac{\sqrt{-(1+4k)}}{2}$.

11. $y = X(x)T(t)$ where the general solutions to X and T are

$$X(x) = \begin{cases} c_1 e^{\sqrt{k+1}\,x} + c_2 e^{-\sqrt{k+1}\,x}, & k > -1 \\ c_1 + c_2 x, & k = -1 \\ c_1 \cos\sqrt{-(k+1)}\,x + c_2 \sin\sqrt{-(k+1)}\,x, & k < -1, \end{cases}$$

$$T(t) = \begin{cases} b_1 e^{\sqrt{k}\,t} + b_2 e^{-\sqrt{k}\,t}, & k > 0 \\ b_1 + b_2 t, & k = 0 \\ b_1 \cos\sqrt{-k}\,t + b_2 \sin\sqrt{-k}\,t, & k < 0. \end{cases}$$

13. $y(x, t) = \dfrac{1}{2}\left(3 \sin\dfrac{\pi x}{a} \cos\dfrac{c\pi t}{a} - \sin\dfrac{3\pi x}{a} \cos\dfrac{3c\pi t}{a}\right)$

15. a) $\dfrac{\partial^2 y}{\partial t^2} = c^2 \dfrac{\partial^2 y}{\partial x^2} - 2b\dfrac{\partial y}{\partial t}$, where b is a constant of proportionality;

b) $y(x, t) = \dfrac{e^{-bt}}{4}\left[3\left(\cos k_1 t + \dfrac{b}{k_1}\sin k_1 t\right)\sin\dfrac{\pi x}{a}\right.$

$$\left. - \left(\cos k_3 t + \dfrac{b}{k_3}\sin k_3 t\right)\sin\dfrac{3\pi x}{a}\right];$$

c) $y(x, t) = e^{-bt}\displaystyle\sum_{n=1}^{\infty} A_n\left(\cos k_n t + \dfrac{b}{k_n}\sin k_n t\right)\sin\dfrac{n\pi x}{a}$,

where $\qquad k_n = \sqrt{n^2\pi^2 c^2 - b^2 a^2}/a$

and $\qquad A_n = \dfrac{2}{a}\displaystyle\int_0^a f(x)\sin\dfrac{n\pi x}{a}\,dx.$

APPENDIX 4

1. (a) $D = -2$; $x_1 = 3$, $x_2 = 0$; \qquad (b) $D = 0$; no solutions;

(c) $D = 0$; infinite number of solutions of the form $x_1 = c$, $x_2 = \dfrac{3-c}{2}$, where c is a constant;

(d) $D = 0$; infinite number of solutions of the form $x_1 = c$, $x_2 = 2c - 1$;

(e) $D = 0$; no solutions;   (f) $D = 6$; $x_1 = \dfrac{1}{2}$, $x_2 = 0$.

3. (a) Yes;   (b) No

Index

Abel's formula, 65, 319
Acceleration, 2
Adams–Bashforth formula, 295
Adjoint of a matrix, 344
Algebraic multiplicities, 331
Amplitude, 91
Analytic function, 179
Associated linear system, 398
Associated matrix equation, 322
Asymptotic stability, 377
Autonomous system, 377

Bernoulli, J., 206
Bernoulli's equation, 35, 145
Bessel, F. W., 214
Bessel equation, 72, 200, 202
Bessel function, 72, 188, 206
  first kind, 208
  generating function, 216
  integrals of, 213
  modified, 216
  order 0, 72, 188
  order $\frac{1}{2}$, 200
  order 1, 203
  oscillation, 480
  zeros, 480
Bessel series, 188
Binomial series, 182
Binomial theorem, 182
Birth rate, 5
Black box, 247
Block diagram, 51
Boundary value problems, 10
  nonhomogeneous, 482
  numerical solution of, 305

Capacitance, 42
Casoratian, 152
Cayley–Hamilton theorem, 344
Center, 393
Characteristic equation, 72, 117,
      158, 330
  polynomial, 330
  of a system, 330
Chebyshev's equation, 224
Clairaut's equation, 23, 147
Closed system, 51
Coefficient, Fourier, 451
Comparison theorem, Sturm, 479
Compartmental analysis, 51
Complex number, 76
Constant coefficients, 62
Continuous dependence on initial
      conditions, 430
Convection, 526
Convergence
  of an improper integral, 226
  radius of, 177
  quadratic, 151
  of series, 176
  uniform, 181, 419
Convolution, 265
Cramer's rule, A–18
Critical point, 382
Cross-derivative test, 37
Curves of pursuit, 46

d'Alembert, J., 499
  solution of wave equation, 500
Damped vibration, 93
Damping factor, 94

Damping force, 93
Damping ratio, 96
Dead space, 138
Death rate, 5
Density, 508
Determinant, A–14
Difference equation, 138–173
  Clairaut, 147
  linear, 141–147
  order of, 139
  Ricatti, 146
  system of, 172
Differential equation, 2
  constant coefficients, 62
  direction field of, 13
  exact, 37
  homogeneous, 61
  linear, 30, 60
  nonhomogeneous, 61
  order of, 10
  ordinary, 9
  ordinary point of, 191
  partial, 9
  singular point of, 191
    irregular, 192
    regular, 192
  singular solution of, 24
  solution of, 10
  system of, 103
Diffusion equation, 526
  pure, 526
Diffusivity, 510
Dirac delta function, 254
Direction field, 13
Discontinuity, jump, 229

Discrete harmonic motion, 163
Discretization error, 282
Divergence, 177, 226

Ecosystem, 7
Eigenfunction, 468
    expansion, 482
Eigenspace, 332
Eigenvalue, 329
Eigenvector, 329
Electric circuit, 42, 100, 125
Electromotive force, 42
Elliptic equation, 495
Energy
    kinetic, 407
    potential, 407
Epidemic, 129
Error
    analysis, 287–291
    discretization, 282
    round-off, 282
Euler constant, 210
Euler equation, 79, 205
Euler formula, 76
    for Fourier coefficients, 452
Euler's method, 280
    improved, 283
    for systems, 301
Even functions, 464
Exact differential, 37
Exact equation, 37
Existence–uniqueness theorems,
    10, 60, 424–428
Exponential decay, 4, 31
Exponential growth, 4, 31
Exponents of a differential
        equation, 193

Feedback, 105
Fibonacci numbers, 160
Focus
    stable, 392
    unstable, 392
Force
    damping, 93
    electromotive, 42
    gravitational, 2
    sinusoidal, 97

Forced vibrations, 95
Forcing vector, 366
Fourier, J., 458
Fourier series, 451, 458
    coefficients, 451
    cosine, 466
    generalized, 451
    sine, 466
    theorem, 459
Free fall, 21
Free vibration, 95
Frequency, natural, 92
Frequency ratio, 96
Frobenius, method of, 192
Fundamental matrix solution,
    318
Fundamental set of solutions,
    316

Games and quality control, 168–
    172
Gamma function, 207
Gaussian elimination, 308
Gauss's hypergeometric equation,
    224
General solution, 19, 64, 113
Geometric series, 177
Global asymptotic stability, 385
Golden ratio, 160
Gravitational acceleration, 2
Green, G., 487
Green's function, 482, 487
Gronwall's inequality, 427
Growth rate, 5

Half-life, 9
Harmonic motion, 78, 92, 163
Heat conductivity, 509
Heat equation, 510, 514
Heat flux, 509
Heaviside function, 251
Hermite, Charles, 458
Hermite equation, 223, 458
Hermite function, 223
    orthogonality, 458
Hermite polynomials, 223, 458
Heun's formula, 294
Homogeneous equation, 61, 72,
    142

Homogeneous systems, 115
Hooke's law, 91
Hyperbolic equation, 495
Hypergeometric series, 224

Improper integral, 226
    convergence of, 226
    divergence of, 226
Improved Euler's method, 283
Indicial equation, 193
Inductance, 42
Infectives, 129
Initial value problem, 10
Integral equation, Volterra, 269
Integrating factor, 32
Interval of convergence, 177
Intravenous feeding, 34
Inverse Laplace transform, 227
Irregular singular point, 192

Jump discontinuity, 229

Kernel, 336
Kinetic energy, 407
Kirchhoff's current law, 125
Kirchhoff's voltage law, 42, 125
Kutta-Simpson $\frac{3}{8}$ rule, 293

Lagrange, J. L., 57, 87
Lagrange's method, 87
Laguerre, E., 223, 457
Laguerre equation, 223
Laguerre polynomials, 223, 457
Lambert, J. H., 56
Laplace equation, 514
Laplace transforms, 226–277
    of convolution integrals, 266
    differentiation property, 237
    first shifting property, 234
    inverse, 227
    linearity property, 231, 237
    periodicity property, 256
    second shifting property, 252
    for systems, 270–275
    uniqueness, 230
Law of mass action, 57
Law of reflection, 25
Least-squares approximation, 454

Legendre, A. M., 216
Legendre equation, 71, 216
Legendre function, 216
Legendre polynomials, 221
    generating function, 221
    orthogonality, 453
    Rodrigues's formula, 219
Legendre series, 454
Limit cycle, 406
Linear combination, 62, 113, 152
Linear differential equation, 30,
    60, 109
Linear system, 103
Linearly dependent, 62, 113
Linearly independent, 62, 113,
    152, 316
Liouville, J., 468
Lipschitz constant, 422
Lipschitz continuous function,
    422
Logistic equation, 5, 20
Logistic growth, 5
Lotka–Volterra equation, 378,
    399
Lyapunov, A. M., 407
Lyapunov function, 409

Maclaurin series, 181
Method of determinants, 117
Method of elimination, 106
Method of Frobenius, 192
Method of Newton, 147
Method of separation of vari-
    ables, 18
Milne's predictor-corrector
    method, 297
Motion, Newton's second law of,
    21, 92

Natural frequency, 92, 368
Natural vibration, 95
Negative definite function, 408
Negative semidefinite function,
    408
Newton's method, 147
Node
    proper, 389
    stable, 386
    star-shaped, 389

Nonautonomous system, 377
Nonhomogeneous boundary
    value problem, 482
Nonhomogeneous equation, 61,
    142
Nonhomogeneous system, 133,
    358
Norm, 432
    matrix, 432
    weighted, 456
Numerical instability, 300

Odd function, 464
Ohm's law, 42
Open system, 51
Orbit, 378
Order, 10
Ordinary differential equation,
    see Differential equation
Ordinary point, 191
Orthogonal function, 448
    weighted, 456
Orthogonality, 447
    Hermite polynomials, 476
    Laguerre polynomials, 475
    Legendre polynomials, 453
    theorem, 473
Orthonormal functions, 448
    weighted, 456

Parabolic equation, 495
Pareto, V., 23
Pareto's law, 23
Partial differential equation, 492
    degenerate, 495
    elliptic, 495
    first order, 492
    hyperbolic, 495
    linear, 492
    parabolic, 495
    second-order, 494
Partial sum, 176
Pendulum, 374, 403, 446
Perturbation, 374, 399
Phase angle, 96
Phase plane, 378
Phase shift, 368
Picard, E., 423

Picard iterations, 423
Picone's theorem, 482
Planck, B. M., 272
Point, critical, 382
    asymptotically stable, 383
    equilibrium, 382
    ordinary, 191
    singular, 191
    spiral, 392
    stable, 383
Poisson, S. D., 520
Poisson integral formula, 520
Polar coordinates, 76
Polar form, 77
Polynomials
    Hermite, 476
    Laguerre, 223
    Legendre, 218
Positive definite function, 408
Potential energy, 407
Power series, 176
    center of, 176
    interval of convergence, 177
    method, 183
    radius of convergence, 177
Predator-prey equations, 7
Predictor-corrector formulas,
    294–298
    for systems, 302
Principal matrix solution, 319
Principle of superposition, 69,
    80, 155, 365, 506
Propagation of error, 298
Pure imaginary number, 76

Quadratic convergence, 151
Quadrature formulas, 294

Radius of convergence, 177
Ratio test, 179
Recursion formula, 186
Regula falsi, 152
Regular singular point, 192
Remainder term, 176
Resistance, 42
Resonance, 98, 368
Retarded fall, 21
Riccati equation, 75, 146

Rodrigues, O., 219
Root test, 177
Round-off error, 282
Row operations, 308
Runge–Kutta method, 284, 291–294
   for systems, 303

Saddle point, 389
Separation of variables, method of, 18, 503
Separation theorem, Sturm, 477
Series
   Bessel, 188
   Binomial, 182
   Fourier cosine, 466
      sine, 466
   Frobenius, 192
   geometric, 177
   Legendre, 454
   Maclaurin, 180
   power, 176
   Taylor, 179
Shifting theorem
   first, 234
   second, 252
Shooting method, 305
Simple harmonic motion, 92
Simpson's rule, 294
Singular point, 191
   irregular, 192
   regular, 192
Solution, matrix, 318
Solution of a differential equation, 10

Solution of a system of differential equations, 112, 318
Sonin's theorem, 482
Specific heat, 508
Specific infection rate, 55
Spiral point, 392
Spring constant, 91
Stable critical point, 383
   node, 386
Sturm, J. C. F., 468
   comparison theorem, 479
   separation theorem, 471
Sturm–Liouville problem, 468
Substitution technique, 24
Successive approximations, 423
Superposition, principle, 69, 155
Susceptibles, 129
System, 103–127
   autonomous, 377
   characteristic equation of, 117
   closed, 51
   example of, 7
   linear homogeneous, 115
   linear nonhomogeneous, 115
   numerical solution of, 301
   open, 51

Taylor series, 179
Taylor's formula, 179
Terminal velocity, 22
Thermal diffusion equation, 526
Torricelli, E., 23
Torricelli's law, 23
Tractrix, 46
Transfer function, 247

Transform
   inverse Laplace, 227
   Laplace, 226
Trapezoidal rule, 283
Trigonometric series, 451

Undetermined coefficients, 81, 167
Uniform convergence, 181
Unit impulse function, 251
Unstable critical point, 383

Van der Pol, equation, 406
Variation of constants, 87, 164
   for linear systems, 124, 359
Variation of parameters, 87
Vector
   forcing, 366
   function, 309
   input, 366
   output, 366
   solution, 314
Vibrating string, 497–503
Vibration
   damped, 93
   forced, 95
   free, 95
   natural, 95
Volterra, V., 268
Volterra integral equation, 269

Wave equation, 499
   traveling, 500
Weierstrass M-test, 420
Weight function, 456
Wronskian, 65
   of a system, 113, 319